P9-CMC-668

BETHANY
COLLEGE
LIBRARY

DISCARD

Communication in International Politics

Communication
in International Politics

EDITED BY *Richard L. Merritt*

UNIVERSITY OF ILLINOIS PRESS

Urbana, Chicago, London

© 1972 by The Board of Trustees of the University of Illinois
Manufactured in the United States of America
Library of Congress Catalog Card No. 75–165042
ISBN 0–252–00210–5

For HAROLD D. LASSWELL,

who pioneered this and

other intellectual paths

327.1
C 737

CONTENTS

one
Transmission of Values across National Boundaries, 3
Richard L. Merritt

two
Transfer of Meaning across National Boundaries, 33
Davis B. Bobrow

part I People to People

three
Effects of International Student Exchange, 65
Richard L. Merritt

four
The Impact of a Foreign Culture: South Koreans in America, 95
Rita M. Kelly and *Lorand B. Szalay*

five
Education of Foreign Nationals in the Soviet Union, 120
Edward A. Raymond

six
American Views of Soviet-American Exchanges of Persons, 146
Frederick C. Barghoorn and *Ellen Mickiewicz*

seven
The Problem-Solving Workshop in Conflict Resolution, 168
Herbert C. Kelman

part II People at Home and Events Abroad

eight
The American Press and Indochina, 1950–56, 207
Susan Welch

nine
Public Opinion and Foreign Affairs:
The Mediating Influence of Educational Level, 232
Alvin Richman

ten
Events, Mass Opinion, and Elite Attitudes, 252
Sophia Peterson

eleven
Consistency in Foreign Policy Views, 272
Robert Jervis

part III   Influencing Foreign Cultures

twelve
International Transfer of the Ombudsman, 295
Larry B. Hill

thirteen
Madison Avenue Imperialism, 318
Herbert I. Schiller

fourteen
Nuclear Desalting in the Middle East, 339
Paul D. Wolfowitz

fifteen
Germans and American Denazification, 361
Anna J. Merritt

part IV   Government to Government

sixteen
Old Boys, Alumni, and Consensus at ECLA Meetings, 387
John R. Mathiason

seventeen
The National Boundary in Politics and Economics, 405
Hans O. Schmitt

eighteen
Political Aspects of Exchange-Rate Systems, 423
Anthony Lanyi

Contributors, 447

Index, 451

PREFACE

THE field of international political communication has enjoyed immense growth in the last half-century. The intellectual ferment attending this growth has brought with it a wealth of new studies, analytic techniques, and verified propositions. Characteristically, it has also engendered a diffusion of approaches, concerns, and definitions. In reading through the literature of the field, it nonetheless seemed to me that there were some central elements in this patchwork quilt that deserved closer attention.

The opportunity to pursue this notion came when Karl W. Deutsch, 1969–70 President of the American Political Science Association, appointed me as Program Chairman for the Association's Sixty-Sixth Annual Meeting, held on September 8–12, 1970, in Los Angeles. One of the twenty-seven sets of panels comprising the Annual Meeting was devoted exclusively to the field of international political communication. In it I sought to bring together some of the more productive scholars to present and discuss research within a rather broad framework (spelled out in the first chapter of this volume). In all, there were five panels, under the guidance of Harry G. Gelber, John D. Montgomery, Charles E. Osgood, Irene Tinker, and myself; panelists not represented in this volume were Ton DeVos, Charles T. Goodsell, Robert J. Lieber, Hamid Mowlana, and Bryant Wedge.

The experiment seemed sufficiently successful to justify the publication of the papers, after revisions to take into account the comments of chairmen and panelists. This volume, then, represents the fruits of this effort. Its production was made possible by Judith L. Graham, who performed the tedious task of footnote-checking; Linda Church, who typed the manuscript; Wanda Morrison and Lorraine F. Selander, who prepared it; Ann Lowry Weir, who edited it; and Anna J. Merritt, who indexed it. The Institute of Communications Research at the University of Illinois, directed by James W. Carey, provided both financial assistance and technical facilities. To both the Los Angeles participants and the Urbana production staff, I would like to express my appreciation. I would also like to thank Ithiel de Sola Pool and Harold D. Lasswell for their perceptive comments on the final manuscript.

It is perhaps in the nature of symposia that they do not tie together as neatly as their organizers hope. This necessitated some reorganization of the papers as originally presented in order to maximize the continuity of the finished volume. The original organizational scheme is presented in the first chapter; it continues to be the organizational focus of my own thinking. This volume, however, proceeds along more traditional lines. After preliminary discussions by myself and Davis Bobrow of the field of international political communication, the volume proceeds from the particular to the general: Part I deals with interpersonal communication; Part II with the interaction between individuals and the overseas environment; Part III with efforts by governmental and nongovernmental actors to influence foreign cultures in this overseas environment; and Part IV with intergovernmental communication. In Chapter 1 I have tried to clarify the interface between the two organizational frameworks, and to suggest research that needs to be done to fill in the gaps. The result is by no means a comprehensive and integrated approach to international political communication. I am nonetheless hopeful that the volume will lead us in this direction.

RICHARD L. MERRITT

Urbana, Illinois
June, 1971

Communication in International Politics

one

Transmission of Values across National Boundaries

Richard L. Merritt

IN one sense the study of international political communication dates back at least to the days when Plato discussed the morality of propaganda and Aristotle wrote about relations among Greek city-states. Yet in another sense it is an emergent field of study. Only within the last dozen years have scholars turned from their often parochial concerns with propaganda, migration, foreign student exchange, trade and exchange rates, and even cultural anthropology to focus upon a more general field of international political communication. As yet no integrated theory explains or purports to explain cause and effect, or relates specific propositions to general phenomena. A major reason for this is simply the wide diversity of types of political communication on the international level, no less than a certain amount of disagreement about what constitutes the subject matter of international political communication as a field of study.

This chapter sets forth a broad framework for the analysis of international political communication—one that can serve as a basis for integrating the plethora of relevant studies already completed and research currently under way in this field of study, one that in fact served as the basis for organizing the symposium presented in this volume. Two points must be stressed at the outset. First, it is not a theory of international political communication, although it will hopefully provide a framework that will encourage theory-building. Second, even as a framework it is far from finished. Further work in the area will doubtless point to those aspects that need more or less modification. In this sense the chapter and the volume as a whole comprise a view of the state of the field as it presently is.

THE CONTENT OF COMMUNICATION

Among analysts of international political communication there is general acceptance of Harold D. Lasswell's deservedly famous formulation of the communication process:[1]

> Who
> Says What
> In Which Channel
> To Whom
> With What Effect?

In Lasswell's view, *control* analysis studies the "who" or source and transmitter in the communication process, *content* analysis the "what" (as well as the process of encoding and decoding the messages), *media* analysis the channels, *audience* analysis the "whom" or receptors and recipients, and *effect* analysis the impact of that that is communicated, both upon the audience and, through processes of feedback, upon the original communicator.

Crucial to an understanding of the communication process is the "what" that people communicate. At a technical level, to use Ithiel de Sola Pool's broad definition, communication is "any transmission of signs, signals, or symbols between persons."[2] Yet, as Pool goes on to point out, the merely mechanical transmission of these elements is insufficient if the recipients are unable to decode them in any meaningful way. More properly, then, "meaning" in its semantic aspect becomes our focus of attention.[3] Thus Davis Bobrow writes that "social communication" concerns "the transfer of meaning between persons and groups," suggesting that the transfer, if effective, generates a similarity of the referents associated by the receiver with those associated by the originator relevant to the set of messages transmitted.[4] Both views underline the cognitive aspects of meaning

---

1   Harold D. Lasswell, "The Structure and Function of Communication in Society," in *The Communication of Ideas*, ed. Lyman Bryson (New York: Harper, 1948), p. 37.

2   Ithiel de Sola Pool, "Communication, Political: Introduction," in *International Encyclopedia of the Social Sciences*, ed. David L. Sills (New York: Macmillan and The Free Press, 1968), vol. 3, p. 90.

3   Cf. Charles W. Morris, *Signs, Language and Behavior* (Englewood Cliffs, N. J.: Prentice-Hall, 1946); and Charles E. Osgood, George J. Suci, and Percy H. Tannenbaum, *The Measurement of Meaning* (Urbana: University of Illinois Press, 1957).

4   Davis B. Bobrow, "Transfer of Meaning across National Boundaries," in this volume, p. 57.

while, to be sure, also recognizing the importance of their noncognitive aspects. Both, by implication at least, suggest that the messages transmitted can affect the perceptions and dispositions or values of the actors. And both properly direct our attention to the study of the capacity, range, scope, fidelity, efficiency, and other attributes of the communication system, as well as the type and distribution of the signs, signals, and symbols used.

Such approaches focus upon fairly direct forms of the primary communicative processes of society—those that Edward Sapir has termed language and gesture "in its widest sense."[5] (To the extent that people respond to implicit commands, these approaches also include the third of Sapir's four primary communicative processes: the "imitation of overt behavior.") These semantic aspects are of extreme importance. The phrase "I love brownies," for instance, can mean vastly different things to a hungry little boy, a dirty old man, a white miscegenationist, the denizen of a drug culture, and a railroader. This is a problem in the transmission and manipulation of signs. Equally important are the performance characteristics of a communication system in getting the message from the sender to the recipient. And clearly both have important policy implications for the design of communication systems and the transmission of messages.

Transactions and the Ecology of International Communication

But there are other, more indirect forms of communication that should also interest analysts of international political communication. Suppose, for example, that merchants in country *I* exchange goods with merchants in country *J*. Such a transaction, of course, presumes some fairly direct forms of communication at the outset: channels for striking the bargain, credit and exchange facilities, ships or some other carrier, and, above all, a common notion of the obligations entailed in such commercial transactions. Such communication is not of moment here. More to the point is that the transaction may have secondary effects. It can generate:

1. *Identification statements.* Other citizens profiting from the transaction may identify themselves with the tradesmen who arranged it; or citizens may identify themselves with a larger (trading) community that includes both countries *I* and *J*.

5 Edward Sapir, "Communication," in *Encyclopedia of the Social Sciences,* ed. Edwin R. Seligman (New York: Macmillan, 1931), vol. 4, p. 78.

2. *Expectation statements.* The merchants and others in countries *I* and *J* who profited from the transaction may expect the continuation of future trade of this sort.

3. *Demand statements (preference).* First, the merchants of the two countries may not only expect but also desire the continuation of future transactions. Second, they may express preferences about the behavior of their countrymen: "Since our trade with country *J* is profitable," the merchants of country *I* may say (and vice versa), "it behooves us to treat its citizens respectfully, to develop greater facility in its language so as to ease future negotiations, and, more generally, to encourage among our citizens a more positive image of country *J*." Third, they may request that their governments make arrangements to facilitate future transactions (through most-favored-nation agreements, for instance).

4. *Demand statements (volitional).* Trade can create dependency relationships. Thus some Latin American countries continued to purchase locomotives from the United Kingdom long after rolling stock had become cheaper in the United States, simply because in the early years of railroading they had adopted the standard British track gauge. Similarly, the leaders of a country whose merchants have a single market for their produce, such as the Cuban relationship to the United States before 1960, will think twice before adopting policies that would alienate the market country. In effect, such dependency relationships create strong political demands upon governments.[6]

Tradesmen and others may develop an elaborate symbolic web both to support their own perspectives (or pattern of identifications, expectations, and demands), and to justify governmental actions that, by strengthening the political relationship between countries *I* and *J*, improve the climate for trade still further. Indeed, if some current notions about processes of unification are accurate, then increased transactions between the two countries could even guide them ultimately toward political integration.

The point is not that these consequences necessarily follow the initiation of the commercial transaction. Rather, by means of the fourth of Sapir's primary communicative processes, "social suggestion," the transaction can change the ecology within which value and

6   The delineation of identification, expectation, and demand statements stems from Harold D. Lasswell and Abraham Kaplan, *Power and Society: A Framework for Political Inquiry* (New Haven and London: Yale University Press, 1950), pp. 12, 17, 21.

perceptual structures exist.[7] If it may be said that Pool and Bobrow stress the transfer of language and symbolisms as techniques to facilitate these primary communicative processes (again to adopt the distinctions made by Sapir), then flows of trade, mail, and other transactions as a technique create the "physical conditions for the communicative act." They provide a stimulus to other, more direct forms of communication. And, in this sense, they fit into Colin Cherry's definition of communication as "the relationship set up by the transmission of stimuli and the evocation of responses."[8]

Transactions as Information

Such transactions are also germane to Karl Deutsch's concept of communication.[9] He adopts the viewpoint of communication engineering that it "transfers information," defined nontechnically as "a patterned relationship between events." "Information has physical, 'material' reality," he adds; "without exception, it is carried by matter-energy processes." Now, at first glance, this is similar to and possibly even narrower than the viewpoint expressed by Pool, Bobrow, and others. A strict interpretation would have communication analysts focusing upon state descriptions of clustering bits on a magnetic tape, sound waves, patterns of light and dark in photographs, and the like. Such studies could be extremely valuable in measuring aspects of communication systems. A broader interpretation suggests that a question of primary importance for Deutsch as well as Pool and Bobrow is whether or not the originator and recipient of a message see a common meaning in it. Indeed, when Deutsch turns to the implications of his cybernetic framework for research in social communication, he proposes by way of example that "we can measure the 'integration' of individuals in a people by their ability to receive and transmit information on wide ranges of different topics with relatively little delay or loss of relevant detail."[10]

Viewed somewhat differently, however, Deutsch's analysis provides us with a means for bringing together the apparently contradictory approaches sketched above. Trade transactions are directly related to his concept of information. In noting, with Deutsch, that communication engineering transfers patterned relationships among

7   Sapir, "Communication," p. 79.
8   Colin Cherry, *On Human Communication: A Review, a Survey and a Criticism* (Cambridge and New York: M.I.T. Press and John Wiley and Sons, 1957; New York: Science Editions, 1961), p. 7. Italics omitted.
9   Karl W. Deutsch, *The Nerves of Government: Models of Political Communication and Control* (New York: The Free Press, 1962, 1966), pp. 82–84.
10   Deutsch, *The Nerves of Government*, p. 150.

events rather than the events themselves, we must ask whether a transaction—for example, the shipment of a quantity of goods from country *I* to country *J*—is an event in this sense. As far as *Webster's Seventh New Collegiate Dictionary* is concerned, the answer is "yes."[11] The fact that the crates stacked up in the hold of a ship are in transit is an "occurrence," just as each of the crates is an "entity of observed physical reality." But, then, the act of transferring information as well as the "physical, 'material' reality" of the information itself are "events" in this dictionary sense. What interests us in the transmission of information is not its "event" characteristics but rather the fact that its patterned relationships can convey meaning. Similarly, for present purposes, it is neither the act of shipment nor the crates themselves that are important in examining a trade transaction. More important is the fact that the "physical, 'material' reality" of the crates constitutes a pattern of relationships (analogous to magnetic bits on a tape) that conveys meaning about something. Now, what is that "something"?

Communication as the Transmission of Values

Such transactions—the transmission of messages (signs, signals, symbols) as well as goods—convey values.[12] There are, of course, many ways of viewing values. The framework that I find most helpful is that proposed by Harold Lasswell and Abraham Kaplan in their analysis of *Power and Society.* They discuss, on the one hand, *welfare values,* "those whose possession to a certain degree is a necessary condition for the maintenance of the physical activity of the person" or other actor. These are:

1. Well-being: "the health and safety of the organism";
2. Wealth: "income: services of goods and persons accruing to the individual in any way whatever";
3. Skill: "proficiency in any practice whatever, whether in arts or crafts, trade or profession";
4. Enlightenment: "knowledge, insight, and information concerning personal and cultural relations."

A second set comprises *deference values,* "those that consist in being

11 *Webster's Seventh New Collegiate Dictionary* (Springfield, Mass.: G. and C. Merriam, 1963), p. 287. The second lexical definition that follows refers to relativity theory, but it is germane here, too.

12 Lasswell and Kaplan, *Power and Society,* pp. 55–56. "A value is a desired event—a goal event. That *X* values *Y* means that *X* acts so as to bring about the consummation of *Y*" (ibid., p. 16).

taken into consideration (in the acts of others and of the self)." They include:

5. Power: participation in making decisions entailing severe sanctions;
6. Respect: "the value of status, of honor, recognition, prestige, the 'glory' or 'reputation' which Hobbes classes with gain and safety as one of the three fundamental human motivations";
7. Recititude: "the moral values—virtue, goodness, righteousness, and so on";
8. Affection: "includes the values of love and friendship."

Although here is not the place for a detailed discussion of the value configuration offered by Lasswell and Kaplan, we should note briefly that deference values are more highly competitive than welfare values in most social arenas, that values are distributed unequally in any social system, and that they tend toward "agglutination" (that is, an actor with more of values *A* and *B* is also likely to have more of values *C* and *D*). Central to the approach is the "maximization" postulate: actors in a system seek to maximize the likelihood that they will attain their (scope) values as economically as possible.

Assuming a high degree of communicative effectiveness—the relatively noise-free transmission of messages from the source to the recipient—the messages comprise information that redistributes values between source and recipient. The primary value affected is enlightenment: the recipient may learn something that he did not know before. This, of course, may have secondary effects—for example, on his wealth if the message comprises the news that his rich uncle died leaving him a fortune, or on his skill if the message tells him how to do something that he could not do before. But the transmission of signs, signals, and symbols may also affect values other than enlightenment. The fact that the communicator is a prestigious or powerful person may enhance the respect or power that the recipient enjoys in his own circle. A threatening signal may endanger the recipient's well-being (physical or psychological). The mere act of transmitting a message may increase the originator's communicative skills (or even, for those of us who are chronically poor correspondents, our sense of virtue or rectitude!).

In similar fashion transactions entailing commodities redistribute values among actors in a communication system. The most obvious case is the transfer of currency (or bank drafts, which are claims upon currency) that affects the wealth of senders and recipients alike. Shipments of foodstuff can improve the well-being of the recipients and, depending on the motives and financial arrangements involved, the wealth or perhaps rectitude and respect positions of the shippers. Changes in the flow of mail among residents of different countries may have the cumulative effect of altering the social distance among the populations as a whole and hence levels of mutual affection. Such transactions can also have secondary effects. Sending tractors to Indian villages may lead the recipients to develop their farming and mechanical skills, besides, conceivably, their wealth; but shipping winter coats to Saharan populations (or tanks equipped with snow shovels to Egypt) may endanger the respect status accorded the donor.

THE POLITICAL ASPECTS OF INTERNATIONAL COMMUNICATION

A serious problem with this broadened view of communication as the transmission of values is its very broadness. It sees the world as a large organization or system through which communication flows at all levels. At the very least this view smacks of disciplinary imperialism. Yet it is true both that communication is at the very heart of all forms of human interaction, and that any communication at any point in the network affects, however trivially, every subsequent outcome in the organization as a whole. More to the point, such a formulation requires us to impose severe limits upon the scope of our research and analysis. It is not often practicable to study the whole of human communicative behavior. Hence we focus upon manageable areas, such as those aspects of communication that are both politically and internationally relevant. This enables us to make useful distinctions among various types of communicative behavior: the function of communication varies with the organizational complexity of the actors, for instance, and, given comparable levels of complexity, with characteristics of the political system of which the actors are a part. The danger of such specialization, however, is that we may begin to ignore the basic communality of all types of communicative behavior.

Political Communication

Political communication implies those transactions that affect the distribution of power in a human action system. A system, in brief, is a set of elements (actors) connected by regular patterns of interaction (processes), and distinguishable from its environment or other similar systems by more or less definable boundaries. The political process in such a system deals with the control of human behavior through a combination of enforcement and voluntary compliance. It is thus a "who-whom" relationship, to use Lenin's phrase, based on probabilities: the probability that A can change the behavior of B to a given extent with respect to given realms of action. This control relationship embodies the value of power, in the sense defined earlier.

Although power relationships are at the core of politics, it is clear that other values affect them and hence are also germane to the study of politics. To the extent that they are acting consciously, actors seek to utilize their resources (base values, in the Lasswellian sense) to achieve their goals (scope values) in accordance with the maximization postulate. A millionaire may use his wealth to attain a position in which he has relatively more power in a system. Or a movie actor enjoying popular prestige for his acting talents may parlay this affection, respect, and skill into a gubernatorial position from which he can exercise power over a large number of people. The fact of interlocking value relationships is what makes the study of politics as complicated as it is fascinating: the analyst, facing a vast array of transactions, must sort out and focus upon those that are more, rather than less, likely to affect the distribution of power in an arena.

There are no absolute criteria of relevance for separating political from nonpolitical events. At either end of the continuum, to be sure, the probabilities of relevance are fairly clearcut. A meeting between Soviet and American leaders will doubtless have political implications. By the same token it is highly doubtful that two lovers exchanging affection will influence national elections. If one of the two is a presidential candidate, then the general proposition may not hold true; but to take account of the deviant case is not to suggest that political scientists must study all affection relationships. Similarly, an individual's effort to amass wealth usually goes unnoticed until he, say, contributes substantial amounts to the campaign coffers of a particular congressional candidate, or bribes local officials to secure tax rulings that enable him to amass even more wealth. It is thus difficult to make a priori specifications. Any form of communication transaction that significantly affects the power position of one actor relative to others in a system is a political communication. But the definition of significance, at least until we can operationalize our variables better than we have in the past, rests upon the perspicacity and judgment of the analyst.

International Communication

International communication in turn implies a situation that, although true, is not the whole truth: that the chief organizing unit in the world today is the nation-state. The world actually abounds in other actors. With respect to the value of power, they range from the United Nations, with its claim to universality, through regional defense pacts (NATO, Warsaw Treaty Organization), national governments, state governments, and city governments all the way to the individual acting in his political capacity (for example, as a voter or politician). Among actors concerned primarily with the value of enlightenment there are the Nobel Prize Committee and UNESCO, national academies of science, universities, and individual scholars. And similar ranges of actors exist for each of the other six values mentioned earlier. Potentially and in fact, all these actors can initiate politically relevant action in the world arena.

The boundaries of national actors nonetheless remain paramount in our thinking about "international" politics. This is more than a matter of mere convenience. Above the level of the family (or sometimes the extended family) throughout most of the world, the all-purpose political unit commanding the major portion of people's attention and allegiance is the nation-state. It has not always been this way. Indeed, there were times when ruling houses were more central to populations than were nations and the notion of a nation-state. Nor do I mean to suggest that the current preeminence of the nation-state should or always will be the case. Rather, for the present at least, it is the nation-state that acts as the bottleneck through which the world's power is distributed. Supranational actors live by the suffrance and donations of nation-states, just as subnational actors such as individuals and corporations ultimately rely upon national laws, national defense forces, and, should they get into trouble abroad, national diplomatic agents.

In this view, international communication comprises those transactions taking place either across national boundaries or else within a national actor but affecting the ecology within which international transactions take place. This definition includes such diverse events as diplomatic negotiations, trade or inflationary trends that affect a nation-state's balance of payments, a newspaper campaign to arouse a population against an alleged foreign enemy, shifts in the flow of migrants, and even military occupation.

Clearly such a view opens yet another Pandora's box. The continuum from communication that is outspokenly international to that which is insignificant for international politics is a long one; the gray area between the extremes is particularly large. The probability is slight that processes for distributing power internationally will grind when two neighbors discuss last year's elections or a husband at the breakfast table asks his wife for the butter. In most cases the ramifications of such communication doubtless remain on the interpersonal level. In some cases, however, they flow over to other levels of the larger system. What seems to be merely a breakfast table conversation can become important if the husband happens to be a king who gets unhappy when he does not get "some butter for the Royal slice of bread" and carries his misery into the day's subsequent round of conferences and other activities. This fact creates the potential analytic problem that every single act of human communication in some way affects international outcomes. Again, at this stage anyway, it is the analyst's discretion that ultimately separates the trivial from the internationally important.

The forest of communication transactions relevant to international politics is thus a large one. The analyst runs several risks. Efforts to encompass the whole field may peter out in meaningless generalities. The temptation arises to restrict the scope of the field artificially— for example, by defining political communication as solely that emanating from governmental bodies—and thereby to disregard or fail to see other communicative behavior redistributing power internationally. Concentration upon particular aspects, such as the exchange of students, may lead to a loss of perspective on the field as a whole and hence to a distortion of the relevance of the particular aspects. Avoiding such risks requires that we pay more attention to the boundary conditions of international political communication. That is, how can we begin to specify more precisely the circumstances in which affection or other value relationships impinge upon the international political arena? A beginning might be the classification of various types of such transactions.

TYPES OF INTERNATIONAL POLITICAL COMMUNICATORS

The communication process as a transaction affecting value distributions implies several discrete stages. Earlier these were characterized in terms of two communicants—the "who" and "whom" in the transaction. The communicant initiating the transaction, however, actually encompasses both a source (or value-explicator) and an effector (or output-transducer). The *source* is the repository of values. It holds values, orders them in terms of some set of priorities, and explicates them so as to increase the probability of their maximization. The *effector* is the agent that transmits and/or guides transactions aimed at maximizing these values. We may similarly differentiate between the receptor (or input-transducer) and recipient. The *receptor* is the agent completing the transaction, whereas the *recipient* holds (and explicates) the values affected by the transaction. Our primary concern is with the source and recipient of a particular transaction rather than the agents (effector-receptor, transmitter-receiver) acting as transducers.

Broadly speaking, social behavior comprises interactions among individuals, organized groups, and the larger societies in which they live. In this sense the sources and recipients of communication transactions comprise the personality, the group consciousness, and the culture, respectively. The traditional study of communication has indeed focused upon these value configurations at various system levels (besides, of course, problems of coding, transmission, and meaning) and the interactions among them. This division of actor types has much to recommend it. Our interest in *political* communication nonetheless suggests the usefulness of paying special attention to those actors (sources and recipients) concerned with the distribution of power; and our interest in transactions across national boundaries suggests the singular importance of the nation-state's political organ.

Hence our initial concern must be with *governmental actors*. Even though we sometimes simplify our discourse by speaking of a nation-state or its government as a single communicator (for example, "France proposed yesterday . . ."), we know that governments comprise more or less separate branches, the spokesmen of which not only communicate with each other but also with the outside world. Within the American government the President sends and receives envoys, the Senate must consent to treaties before they become effective, Congress makes appropriations for defense and foreign aid, Supreme Court justices tour foreign countries, customs officers determine whether a modern sculpture is a duty-free work of art or dutiable iron scrap, the Central Intelligence Agency gathers information and performs other tasks, and so forth. Sometimes the individual voices of governments initiate partially contradictory transactions. This may be due to a lack of coordination within a government, or to conscious policy aimed at transmitting different values to different targets. At other times the imaginary situation of a single governmental communicator comes close to reality. When the various governmental actors in a nation-state are prepared to implement a policy enunciated by the head of state (or some other authoritative deputy, such as the foreign minister), we speak of a national policy.

Second, there is a wide range of *nongovernmental actors* with varying levels of organizational complexity. Some are business corporations, such as the United Fruit Company or General Motors, pursuing predominantly the scope value of wealth. Others include charitable associations such as CARE or the American Red Cross, missionary societies, foundations interested in promoting research or student exchange, and trade unions. Still another type comprises existential organizations, formed by people with a common national heritage, language, race, or ethnic background. Finally, there are individuals, acting not as representatives or employees of some other actor but in their individual capacities as travelers, letter-writers, migrants, attitude-holders, and even deranged assassins. At first glance there seems to be little justification for treating this great variety of actors as a single type. Such gigantic corporations as General Motors, with an annual turnover greater than the gross national product of all but a dozen nation-states, are closer in some regards to miniature governments than to the Federation of German Expellees, the Baptist Missionary Society, or the Italian tourist in France. All, however, share two important characteristics in common.

For one thing, the predominant scope value they pursue in the international political arena is something other than power. The ostensible purpose of a missionary society is not to take over governmental structures but to convert, in the words of Bret Harte, "the heathen Chinee"—that is, to change the distribution of rectitude in the world. To the extent that even corporations try to control the behavior of foreign governments and citizens, the ultimate purpose is to amass more wealth for their owners, managers, or stockholders. For our concern, then, the central purpose of these actors is peripheral to the secondary effects that their behavior has in politics.

For another thing, each of these actors is subject to the political demands of the nation-state. (Note that this formulation ignores the role of nongovernmental actors in setting the demands of their governments. It is possible, for instance, that Orthodox Jews in Israel or corporations in America may seek to bend governmental processes as a means of achieving their own goals.) Governments enact the rules controlling less or more significant aspects of their behavior. Such rules can prevent citizens from leaving the country or restrict the amount of money that they may take with them, limit or foster the export of goods and investment capital, and even offer military support to domestic corporations or citizens residing abroad. Except to the extent that governments accountable to their citizens enact such rules, these nongovernmental actors are not subject to external controls from within their own country.

A third type of communicator, sadly neglected in many studies of international political communication, consists of *cultures*. The culture of a country or other group comprises the sum total of its artifacts and perspectives. This means, on the one hand, its institutions, language, tools, accumulated knowledge, and other regularized procedures for doing things, and, on the other hand, the identification, expectation, and demand statements of its members. How can a culture be a communicator in international politics? We are actually quite used to the notion that a culture can be the more or less passive recipient of influences from abroad. The whole idea of military occupation, missionary activities, and even foreign economic assistance rests upon the probabilities that foreign intervention can produce cultural change.

What is more problematic is to imagine a culture in the active role of communicator. A culture *is* simply there, we frequently say; it does not *do* anything. It is a *source* of communications. When Ruth Benedict studied Japanese culture during World War II on behalf of the American government, for instance, she sought to discern patterns in a large mass of artifacts and perspectives.[13] To be sure, the culture itself did not directly transmit anything to her. Her act of deriving something from the culture nevertheless amounted to an indirect or passive transmission. Similarly, when a foreign student comes to our shores, he comes into contact with an alien culture, part of which he takes back to his homeland as he departs. To the extent that his subsequent behavior reflects "American ways of life," we can say that American culture influenced him. In this sense a culture "transmits" its content through mediators. That is, it takes some individual or corporate actor to see or assimilate its patterns and to introduce them in his own setting. Even an underlying malaise producing a student demonstration cannot have any influence among student groups abroad until journalists or other mediators spread the news.

In another sense, although their usual role is as sources or passive communicators, there are circumstances in which cultures come directly into contact with each other. Thus, until the late nineteenth century fixed its division between France and Italy, and the twentieth century produced national communication systems, the Piedmont

---

13   Ruth Benedict, *The Chrysanthemum and the Sword: Patterns of Japanese Culture* (Boston: Houghton Mifflin, 1946).

was an area where two separate cultures met and mixed. Other such borderlands have produced conflict within the last century: Alsace and Lorraine, the Alto Adige (or South Tyrol), the marshlands on the Ussuri River. The amorphousness of such situations, however, has led students of international political communication to shy away from them.

SOME DIRECTIONS OF RESEARCH

The delineation of three types of potential communicators in the international political arena—governmental actors (G), nongovernmental actors (N), and cultures (C)—suggests two major areas of research that require both further work and substantial synthesization. One of these focuses on the process by which actor types make decisions affecting their international transactions. The second seeks to generate case studies and establish general propositions about each of the nine predominant types of communication flows among these actors (Figure 1). Clearly this volume can concentrate upon only a

Figure 1. Types of International Political Communication Flows

Source	Recipients		
	Governmental actors	Nongovernmental actors	Cultures
Governmental actors	$G_I G_J$	$G_I N_J$	$G_I C_J$
Nongovernmental actors	$N_I G_J$	$N_I N_J$	$N_I C_J$
Cultures	$C_I G_J$	$C_I N_J$	$C_I C_J$

few of these processes and flows. Since the volume's organization does not follow the above format precisely, it may be useful at this point to outline those areas with which it deals and those that must be left for later treatment.

International Images and Decision-Making

A major concern of social scientists in the last decade and a half has been the process by which actors arrive at decisions. Most studies have centered on either specific cases or else specific levels of actors; some few on the effect of organizational complexity on decision-making processes.[14] For studies of international political communi-

14   For excellent summaries of this literature, see James A. Robinson and Richard C. Snyder, "Decision-Making in International Politics," in *International Be-*

cation, the role of national boundaries is particularly important in setting the framework within which actors make decisions. Typically, communication boundaries are conterminous with national boundaries. That is, the volume and rate of transactions within a nation-state are vastly greater than those across national boundaries. The consequence is that much of our information about events outside our country is filtered through mediating agents such as the press or governmental spokesmen, compounding the effects of psychological processes on the formation and change of images about the outside world.

How people base their behavior upon images, and what differentiates national decision-makers from other actors and the general public in this regard, become important questions. After reviewing theoretic developments in the study of international political communication, Davis Bobrow ("Transfer of Meaning across National Boundaries") examines three models that social scientists have used to explain such processes: a broad range of social-psychological approaches using the notion of mediated stimulus-response; balance theory derived from Fritz Heider, Theodore Newcomb, and others; and cybernetics, stemming particularly from Norbert Wiener and Karl Deutsch. Each has only limited use for explaining the phenomena that interest us in international politics. Bobrow goes on to propose the development of "models not of international relations but of structures and processes which result in different degrees of something, such as violence, equity, arms procurement, or adaptation." This should aim toward the construction of a formal theory about the transfer of meaning. Only in this way, he concludes, can we turn the field of international poltical communication from an art into a science akin to engineering.

Several chapters (Part II) of the volume deal directly with the mediating effects of events and institutions upon the formation of actors' perceptions of international politics. Susan Welch ("The American Press and Indochina, 1950–56") finds that, on critical issues, the mass media are heavily reliant upon governmental opinion-makers. She examines the coverage of the Indochina conflict between 1950 and 1956 in four major daily newspapers published in the United States. Their news reports and editorial positions alike, she

havior: A Social-Psychological Approach, ed. Herbert C. Kelman (New York: Holt, Rinehart and Winston, 1965), pp. 435–63; James A. Robinson and R. Roger Majak, "The Theory of Decision-Making," in *Contemporary Political Analysis*, ed. James C. Charlesworth (New York: The Free Press, 1967), pp. 175–88; and James N. Rosenau, "The Premises and Promises of Decision-Making Analysis," ibid., pp. 189–211.

finds, were almost totally dependent upon news sources within the American government. Not only did they rely upon official initiatives —entertaining visiting diplomats, announcing increases in aid, conferring with cabinet officials, and the like—in determining the extent of their coverage, but they also accepted completely the cognitive framework of the Indochinese situation proposed by Administration spokesmen. This reliance did not prepare the American people for the shock they received in later years when more independent reporters in Vietnam began sending back articles sharply at odds with the official view.

Alvin Richman ("Public Opinion and Foreign Affairs: The Mediating Influence of Educational Level") focuses on changing American images of the Soviet Union and expectations of war between 1943 and 1965, as revealed in survey data. The more educated are both more attentive to and knowledgeable about foreign affairs— although clearly this assertion does not imply a causal relationship. It is for this reason, no doubt, that the short-run attitudes of the more-educated tend to fluctuate somewhat more than those of the less-educated. For the two dozen years as a whole, there are no significant differences among groups with varying degrees of education in their overall pattern of swinging moods. It would seem that common exposure to "opinion-makers" and the mass media yields a congruence of attitudes that mitigates the effects associated with higher levels of education.

Sophia Peterson ("Events, Mass Opinion, and Elite Attitudes") raises in a more direct manner the question of how events influence images. On the one hand, survey and content-analytic data from the United States show a high degree of correlation between mass and elite attitudes on foreign policy issues. On the other hand, there is no significant relationship between mass opinion and conflictual events occurring between the United States and the Soviet Union, and only a weak positive relationship between the events and elite opinion. The timing of attitude changes in the decade between 1955 and 1964 reveals that elite attitudes serve as a cue for mass opinion rather than the other way around. Events influence elites, whose subsequent interpretations are passed along by local opinion leaders to the masses.

Robert Jervis ("Consistency in Foreign Policy Views") deals specifically with the relevance of notions of cognitive balance for studies in decision-making. Attempts to apply such theories to perceptions of and beliefs about states' intention have often been misleading because of a failure to distinguish between kinds of attitudinal consistency that can be explained by a person's rational analysis and those that cannot be so explained. Jervis argues that certain kinds of consistency are necessarily involved in any attempt to understand phenomena. Neither in constructing scientific theories nor in developing images of other actors do facts "speak for themselves." All stages of the identification and analysis of bits of information are influenced by the person's basic perspectives, a fact that imposes a certain consistency on his images and behavior. The transference of this process from the personal to the group level may well serve to increase the constraints working toward consistency.

These conceptual analyses and empirical studies are far from a complete treatment of the formation of international images and their influence in the decision-making of actors at various levels. Their concerns are the traditional ones of students of international politics: foreign policy decision-making. These are important concerns, to be sure. What will be needed in the future, however, are additional studies of international imagery and decision-making in such nongovernmental actors as corporations, missionary societies, and existential groups. Then, too, we need systematic analyses of how particular images and modes of doing things become entrenched in the political culture of a nation-state.

Governmental Actors as Communicators

Interaction between the governmental agencies of two countries (G_IG_J) is the core subject matter of most approaches to international politics. The instrumentalities include:

- bargaining and diplomacy: personal contacts, envoys and other representatives, conferences, summitry;
- trade agreements between governments, exchange-rate manipulation, economic assistance for weapons purchases or to cover balance of payments deficits;
- military intervention, ranging from threats to use force to the shelling of ports, punitive raids, outright invasion;
- subversion aimed at getting I's personnel into decision-making roles in J;
- international laws and norms;
- espionage as a form of extractive communication.

Similarly, we are familiar with the sorts of communication problems that such transactions entail. Not the least important of these deal with the codes used by those doing the actual communicating: the need for translation compounds the normal semantic issues in verbal communication; simultaneous interpretation at international conferences assumes great importance; nonverbal communication such as the use of prominent solutions (the selection of a river as the boundary between two territories) and behavioral cues (signals aimed at deescalating a conflict, or the selection of persons with well-known points of view as representatives) runs the risk of misinterpretation. Then, too, the long list of studies detailing behavioral outcomes in international politics ranges from Machiavelli's *The Prince* to current inductive efforts resting upon empirical investigations and the compilation of data about the occurrence of events.

Indeed, so numerous are such studies that this volume could not begin to do justice to them.[15] Hence the decision to focus in on just a few of the less-known aspects of intergovernmental communications among students of politics, namely, those dealing with economic relationships (Part IV). John R. Mathiason ("Old Boys, Alumni, and Consensus at ECLA Meetings") reports the results of his investigation into a highly significant proposition about contact nets among governmental representatives at intergovernmental conferences aimed at enhancing regional integration: the more common experience in a situation, the greater the likelihood of substantive agreement (in the form of increased interaction or increased understanding). Mathiason compares those conferences of the United Nations Economic Commission for Latin America, where there are relatively large numbers of individuals with previous personal contacts at other ECLA conferences, with those with small numbers of "old boys." It turns out that the former in fact produce more agreements—but they are facilitative ones generating new conferences, rather than substantive resolutions and agreements actively furthering Latin American integration.

Hans Schmitt ("The National Boundary in Politics and Economics") proceeds from the observation that state boundaries do not always coincide with those of a nation or an economy. Each boundary is affected by its own set of principles as well as by interactions among them. But the degree to which they are not congruent also produces stress for the populations living within them. The economic community is bounded by a common currency, the political significance of which lies in the fact that a disciplined surrender of command over its own resource base is required of each locality if the larger economic community is to have unchallenged purchasing power over the territory as a whole. Shifts in the distribution of resources— caused perhaps by portfolio investment attracted by technical prog-

15 See, for example, K. J. Holsti, *International Politics: A Framework for Analysis* (Englewood Cliffs, N. J.: Prentice-Hall, 1967).

ress—can extend economic boundaries in ways that produce conflicts among political authorities. This in turn has wider implications for areas contemplating political integration.

Anthony Lanyi ("Political Aspects of Exchange-Rate Systems") demonstrates how economic and political analysis can combine to deal with problems of international monetary reform. The specific issue is whether the present "adjustable peg" system of regulating foreign exchange markets should be replaced by another plan, the most politically acceptable of which is the "crawling peg." If the latter system would produce a payoff matrix in which devaluation or upward revaluation of the exchange rate becomes a superior alternative to merely financing (without eliminating) a payments imbalance, then a more smoothly working adjustment mechanism will result. Interestingly enough, this conclusion is independent of whether or not the new system would facilitate explicit international cooperation. The conclusion also points up the distinction between two kinds of international political issues: the underlying strategic considerations of policy, and the methods of communication and implementation used to reach international agreement.

A second type of governmental communication aims at foreign nongovernmental actors (G_1N_J). The twentieth century has seen a growth of the concept of "relevant audience" for governmental communicators. Woodrow Wilson, for instance, tried to appeal to whole European populations over the heads of their leaders to garner support for the League of Nations; in the 1930s Joseph Goebbels developed fairly refined techniques for propagandizing masses; even today spokesmen for the U.S. government praise "public diplomacy," by which they mean the cultivation of public opinion in other countries. Governments also appeal to special interest groups in foreign countries. Thus Adolf Hitler laid claim to Germans everywhere and supported German ethnic minorities trying to take over governments in such countries as Czechoslovakia. Fearful that all people of Japanese ancestry in the state would remain loyal to the Imperial Japanese government at the outset of World War II, and hence fearful of the possibility of sabotage and a "fifth column," Californians interned the Japanese-Americans in relocation centers for the duration of the war. Other examples abound: through the Comintern (Communist International) the Soviet government sought to exercise control over Communist parties elsewhere during the 1930s; the Israeli government has upon occasion sought to mobilize world Jewry in its behalf; the government of the People's Republic of Vietnam has wooed some student and other dissidents in the United States during the late 1960s and 1970s. Finally, governments may control the behavior of foreign firms through such devices as import quotas, contracts, monopolies, taxation, and expropriation; they regulate private individuals through immigration quotas, visas, and rewards such as prizes.

The only paper in this volume dealing primarily with transactions from governments to nongovernmental actors is by Edward Raymond ("Education of Foreign Nationals in the Soviet Union"). An empirical study of political communication through leadership training, but also one with clear policy implications, this chapter uses data derived from questionnaires sent to U.S. Foreign Service posts in developing countries, as well as more standard sources. Traditionally, Soviet schools aimed at training foreigners already committed to the Communist cause. In the war years they indoctrinated German prisoners of war who would return to their home country to assist in building the German Democratic Republic. Since 1961, however, Soviet leaders have supplemented their international party schools and trade union programs with relatively free student exchange programs aimed at developing countries. As these students return home and move gradually into leading positions in their countries, we may expect some reorientation in the basic political positions of those countries.

Much more, particularly of a synthetic nature, needs to be done with respect to this type of communication flow. There are ample studies, for instance, on the transmission of enlightenment: propaganda techniques, government-controlled news agencies, the use of public relations firms, and even, to cite an extreme case, brainwashing. The same is true about the transmission of skill (technical assistance programs), wealth (sales of government securities, bringing wealth to the selling government and ultimately, through interest payments, to the purchasers), well-being (shipments of surplus wheat, on the one hand, but the use of strategic bombing on the other), and other values. They need to be brought together into a common framework that can begin to differentiate between the primary and secondary effects of this type of value transmission.

Third, governments occasionally try to change aspects of a foreign country's culture (G_iC_j). In contrast to efforts described above to influence specific policies of foreign governments or specific attitudes of foreign nongovernmental actors, this type of communication aims at resetting a foreign culture's agenda. Thus governmental information programs, foreign economic assistance, imperialism, and military occupation all (at least in part) seek changes in the predispositions

of the affected populations. The extent to which they are successful
is a matter of degree, and it may not be noticeable until after a lapse
of several years. To substitute a whole new set of value orientations
for those existing in a culture would require complete control over
the internal communication media in a country, as well as an extensive ability to reward and penalize individual actors.

The bulk of Part III of this volume deals with some important but
lesser-known aspects of foreign intervention to induce changes in
political culture. Larry Hill ("International Transfer of the Ombudsman") focuses upon the spread of political institutions from one political culture to the next. In this case, however, there is no pressure
from the government of country *I* to impose a pattern upon country
J; rather, citizens of the latter country have seen the merits of a particular pattern in country *I*, and want their own country to adopt it.
The ombudsman in Swedish politics acts as a spokesman for private
citizens who feel treated unjustly by governmental institutions. The
effectiveness of this office has turned it into a model for other countries, including New Zealand, Australia, the United Kingdom, and
other Scandinavian countries. This chapter examines the problems
and consequences of trying to change the politics of a country by the
introduction of political roles from abroad.

Paul Wolfowitz ("Nuclear Desalting in the Middle East") explores the transfer of technology, usually from developed to developing nations, as a process of communication. His research stressed the
fact that, first, just as a message can have several, sometimes conflicting, interpretations, so a technology introduced into a new environment can have a range of consequences and applications, some
of which are very different from those intended by the transmitting
nation. In the Middle East, technologies for desalting sea water can
also affect the spread of nuclear weapons in the area. Second, the case
emphasizes the importance of governmental actors as mediators in
communication between other actors. In this case the political interests of the Middle Eastern governments ultimately determine the way
in which the new technology will be received. But the government
of the country transmitting the technology, in encoding the "message," can affect the way in which it will be received by means of the
control mechanisms it chooses to impose, the incentives and subsidies it provides, and the choice of the particular kind of technology
itself. For example, the choice between nuclear and fossil fuel technologies may determine the ultimate consequences of the development of sea-water desalting in the Middle East.

Anna Merritt ("Germans and American Denazification") discusses one of the most elaborate and systematic attempts to change the political culture of an entire country. This study of the effects of the American program of denazification in postwar Germany rests upon an intensive analysis of public opinion data gathered by offices of the American Military Government. It demonstrates how initial German receptivity to the program changed as overall American policy in the emerging Cold War began to stress anti-Communism in the place of denazification. Most particularly, modifications that worked to the advantage of persons who had held responsible positions under Nazism produced an aura of cynicism that damaged the perceived sincerity of the American program. In retrospect it is doubtful that this aspect of the postwar Allied "democratization" of Germany produced any lasting, positive effect.

Nongovernmental Actors as Communicators

The very diffuseness of nongovernmental actors communicating within the international system makes it a rich area for study. Corporations like the United Fruit Company sometimes exert a direct influence upon the governments of countries within which they operate (N_iG_j). Indeed, a favorite theme of Communist potboilers used to be how private American firms control the politics of even the advanced industrialized countries of Western Europe. Occasionally immigrants, such as Adolf Hitler in Germany, have risen to positions of power in their new homes; or foreigners gain the ears of rulers, as did T. E. Lawrence and Sir John Bagot Glubb in the Arab world. Individual merchants and weapons dealers have sometimes cost rulers their thrones by withholding credit and deliveries at crucial times. Interestingly enough, however, there have been no significant attempts to integrate the wealth of memoirs, case studies, and other material bearing upon this type of international political communication. Alas, this volume makes no further contribution.

There is more to report by way of politically relevant interactions among nongovernmental actors (N_iN_j), although, again, this volume contains no studies directly related to this type of international communication. Nowadays interpersonal interactions seldom spill over into the political realm; when they do, they are usually subordinate to political considerations. This was not always the case. For centuries the monarchs of Europe saw transnational familial relationships as a means of controlling the politics of other states. We think typically of the Bourbons, Habsburgs, and Bonapartes in this connection, but the British Hannoverians were also practitioners. Thus, in writing about the state funeral of Edward VII in 1910,

Barbara Tuchman pointed out that the English monarch was frequently called the "Uncle of Europe":

> He was the uncle not only of Kaiser Wilhelm [of Germany] but also, through his wife's sister, the Dowager Empress Marie of Russia, of Czar Nicholas II. His own niece Alix was the Czarina; his daughter Maud was Queen of Norway; another niece, Ena, was Queen of Spain; a third niece, Marie, was soon to be Queen of Rumania. The Danish family of his wife, besides occupying the throne of Denmark, had mothered the Czar of Russia and supplied kings to Greece and Norway. Other relatives, the progeny at various removes of Queen Victoria's nine sons and daughters, were scattered in abundance throughout the courts of Europe.[16]

Such interfamilial ties, it may be added, failed to prevent the outbreak of war a mere four years later. Cross-national friendships, as Mathiason points out, may be no more productive of substantial progress in improving international relations.

Economists have directed considerable attention to international interaction among business concerns. Strictly commercial transactions fall into the realm of international trade; more recently studies have examined the nature of international cartels and conglomerates. Unfortunately, however, their political aspects remain an underdeveloped field of study, despite some interesting work in recent years by Marxist-oriented economists.[17] Another trend focuses upon the political effects of the gross flow of such transactions as trade, migration, and student exchange.[18] It begins with the formulation of a "null model": given the absence of any intervening variable, trade can be expected to be distributed randomly among a set of countries in accord with each country's propensities to export and import. To the extent that actual trade patterns deviate from expected trade patterns, a special relationship (in a statistical sense) exists that may say something about the level of political integration among the countries concerned.

Nongovernmental actors affect foreign cultures (N_iC_j) in gener-

16   Barbara W. Tuchman, *The Guns of August* (New York: Macmillan, 1962), p. 4.

17   See, for example, Herbert I. Schiller, *Mass Communications and American Empire* (New York: Augustus M. Kelley, 1969).

18   I. Richard Savage and Karl W. Deutsch, "A Statistical Model of the Gross Analysis of Transaction Flows," *Econometrica* 28, no. 3 (July 1960): 551–72; Hayward R. Alker, Jr., and Donald J. Puchala, "Trends in Economic Partnership in the North Atlantic Area, 1928–1963," in *Quantitative International Politics: Insights and Evidence*, ed. J. David Singer (New York: The Free Press, 1968), pp. 287–316.

ally the same ways as do governmental actors. Firms frequently influence the behavior patterns in their host countries. Thus primary producers like the United Fruit Company can set occupational and foreign trade patterns for an entire country, often creating dependency relationships that are difficult to break. Manufacturers can generate and satisfy markets. And more recently such service industries as advertising and public relations agencies have played a role.

Herbert Schiller ("Madison Avenue Imperialism") examines the international aspect of such tertiary industries. American manufacturers, in their search for markets, have used an ever-growing arsenal of weapons to improve their international positions: advertising agencies that sell American products (and, since advertising rests mainly upon the mass media, a consequence is usually a rapid commercialization of these media), public relations firms that "sell" the image of the firm rather than its products (thereby giving it local prestige that may facilitate its takeover of local firms), opinion polling and market research organizations that create information and reinforce tendencies toward consumption, and business consulting firms and stock brokerage offices. One effect, Schiller argues, besides extending the influence of American firms, is that national communication systems lose control over the character and content of the messages streaming into their culture.

Then, too, noncommercial and even individual actors have penetrated alien cultures. Missionary groups, representatives of the Red Cross and other charitable associations, teachers, and men like Albert Schweitzer have gone into developing countries seeking to improve educational standards, health, social organization, and the level of skill held by the local inhabitants. Alternatively, individuals from one country—George Washington, Mahatma Gandhi, Patrice Lumumba, Gamal Abdal Nasser—have served as models of behavior in countries that they never visited. Little is known about such communication, except anecdotally. We know even less on a systematic basis about the secondary effects of such transactions: improved health standards, for instance, may increase life expectancy within a population, and hence produce food shortages. Nor do we know very much about the circumstances in which the appearance of alien actors will produce reactive rather than receptive responses in a culture. Actors enjoying high status because of existing cultural patterns may well resist changes that would either eliminate their roles (witch doctors) or else reduce their relative status. But there are other circumstances in which an entire population will take arms against the "stranger at the gates," to use Kipling's phrase, since they see his mere presence as a threat to their culture's existence. Finally, a crucial question is the diffusion rate of innovation in both reactive and receptive cultures.

Cultures as Communicators

Since the flow of transactions from cultures to governmental actors (C_IG_J), as suggested earlier, is nonintentional, scholars frequently acting in behalf of governmental agencies have devised means of extracting certain types of information from cultural patterns. The culture of country I transmits messages to J's government, to be sure —but only because agencies within J's government feel that aspects of I's culture are important for their own policy-making, and are willing to go out and search for that information. Thus the State Department and other agencies of the American government have sponsored cultural-anthropological studies of "national character" in such countries as Japan and the Soviet Union, public opinion polls among the populations of various countries, and, on the assumption that the press "represents" the political culture of a country, analyses of that country's elite and mass journals. The intent of J's investigations is ostensibly unobtrusive. In practice, however, it turns out that some in country I may perceive such studies to be intrusive (and perhaps counterrevolutionary).[19] The irony is that, though we know a great deal about techniques for evaluating foreign cultures and have a great deal of information about varieties of such cultures, we really have little idea of how governments make use of it, if at all.

Another topic with which researchers have dealt extensively is the impact of a culture upon nongovernmental actors (C_IN_J). This is particularly true with respect to student exchange programs. Numerous surveys of foreign students attending American universities, for example, have documented such findings as "The greater the similarity between countries I and J, the greater is the likelihood that a student from country J studying in host country I will have a positive attitude toward country I's social system," or "The greater the amount of interaction between the student from country J and nationals of host country I, the greater will be his knowledge of the social system of country I." Still other studies have surveyed the per-

19   See, for example, Irving Louis Horowitz, ed., *The Rise and Fall of Project Camelot: Studies in the Relationship between Social Science and Practical Politics* (Cambridge: M.I.T. Press, 1967).

spectives of returning travelers, attempting to determine the impact that exposure to a foreign culture has had upon them.[20] And the scientific literature contains a vast array of measures of the extent to which a dominant culture has assimilated its ethnic or immigrant minorities.[21]

Part I of this volume deals primarily with the effects that a foreign culture has upon individuals who come into contact with it. Richard Merritt ("Effects of International Student Exchange") presents an extensive review of the literature in this area, as well as numerous propositions about the effects of international student exchanges. Of particular concern here are the current research gaps and the types of research needed to fill them.

Rita Kelley and Lorand Szalay ("The Impact of a Foreign Culture: South Koreans in America") present an empirical study using the Associative Group Analysis technique. It investigates the extent to which politically relevant concepts and beliefs of South Koreans who have studied in the United States for an average of two and one-half years show greater similarity to American students than to a comparable group of South Korean students who never left their homeland. The findings challenge the most important assumptions underlying private and public sponsorship of such exchanges of persons: that foreign contacts increase the likelihood of accurate, nonstereotyped perceptions, and that foreign contacts lead to a convergence of images and attitudes. It is among the first studies of student exchange to utilize control groups in the home country in measuring the impact of a foreign educational experience.

Frederick Barghoorn and Ellen Mickiewicz ("American Views of Soviet-American Exchanges of Persons") conducted an extensive survey in 1966–67 of American scholars, scientists, businessmen, government officials, and others who had visited the Soviet Union under various exchange programs. The chapter focuses upon the variables that seem to explain differences in experiences and perceptions. For example, members of all categories found exchanges professionally useful, such as by "turning abstractions into realities," but, to a statistically significant degree, natural scientists reported greater success than others in making and continuing close contacts

20   See, for example, Ithiel de Sola Pool, "Effects of Cross-National Contact on National and International Images," in *International Behavior*, ed. Kelman, pp. 104–29.

21   A recent summary of some of the issues is in Michael Parenti, "Ethnic Politics and the Persistence of Ethnic Identification," *The American Political Science Review* 61, no. 3(September 1967): 717–26.

with their Soviet colleagues. The authors conclude with a discussion of the implications of these findings for American educational exchange policies.

Herbert Kelman ("The Problem-Solving Workshop in Conflict Resolution") explores some experimental approaches to interpersonal communication. His review of recent "action research" programs, which bring together representatives of conflicting countries as a means to develop and test ways to manage and resolve international conflicts, leads him to the conclusion that such workshops have indeed been effective in changing the perceptions and attitudes of individuals. However, international conflict clearly is not merely a matter of misperception to be rectified by improved communication. Thus workshop approaches, rather than being a substitute for the usual political and diplomatic procedures, are a potentially useful addition to them or preparation for them. Their usefulness depends on our ability to specify the points in foreign policy decision-making and international politics at which the attitudes and perceptions of certain individuals make a difference, and to develop procedures specifically suited to the occasion for which they are introduced.

Finally, as noted earlier, contacts between discontiguous cultures ($C_I C_J$) seldom exist without mediators. Returning from a foreign country with tales of strange and wondrous things, the traveler can sometimes influence the culture of his homeland. And even stay-at-homes such as Franz Kafka, Karl May, Giacomo Puccini, and Bertolt Brecht could produce works of art about countries and peoples they had never seen—works that could subsequently condition their own countrymen's views about these faraway lands. Strangely enough, however, the study of this impact has been left to historians and literary scholars. To date, communication researchers have not ventured much beyond surveys of attitude change experienced by travelers overseas. What the secondary effects of such experiences are in the traveler's own culture is less defined. Alternatively, of course, media of mass communication can serve this mediating function. News about student demonstrations in Berkeley and elsewhere clearly contributed to the outburst of anomic demonstrations at universities in other countries, but how much this news contributed is not known. Research in this area has focused more upon the effects of messages upon individuals rather than upon their culture as a whole.

Geographers and others have examined the more direct effects of intercultural contacts. One such phenomenon is the borderland—an area lying between two well-established cultures. In centuries gone by, the wanderer could move along the Mediterranean seacoast from Sicily to southern Spain, communicating easily with the people in one village if he fully understood the language of the last village he visited; and yet the ship voyager from Sicily would find it difficult to talk with the residents of southern Spain if he bypassed this long series of marginal changes. One of the most sharply delineated borderlands was the Piedmont, a province with a fairly common culture that was split between France and Italy. Even the political division did not entirely reduce the cultural mix of the area, although the imposition of effective governmental systems in the late nineteenth century helped to do so—as did, to a much more significant degree, the introduction in the twentieth century of French and Italian national communication systems, particularly television. Other borderlands saw the emergence of a culture in which one group dominated over the other. Examples include the Germans and Czechs in Bohemia until 1945, and the Anglos and Chicanos in the American Southwest even today. Still other borderlands, such as the territories on both sides of the Indian-Chinese border, remain subjects of dispute.

There is also an emerging literature on more autonomous processes of interaction between countries. What role, for instance, does cultural similarity play in relations between *I* and *J*? We are inclined to respond immediately that cultural similarity and mutual friendliness go hand in hand. Yet a glance at the history and present condition of diplomacy in Western Europe, no less than a review of relations among the states comprising the Communist bloc, might lead us to think otherwise. Similarly, what is the importance of distance? As the 1930s were drawing to a close, George Kingsley Zipf postulated that interaction between two groups increased directly according to the product of their populations and inversely to the distance separating them. Subsequent research has indicated that there may be something valid in a modified version of this "gravitational" proposition.[22]

22   See George Kingsley Zipf, *Human Behavior and the Principle of Least Effort: An Introduction to Human Ecology* (Reading, Mass.: Addison-Wesley, 1949); Karl W. Deutsch and Walter Isard, "A Note on a Generalized Concept of Effective Distance," *Behavioral Science* 6, no. 4 (October 1961): 308–11; Richard L. Merritt, "Distance and Interaction among Political Communities," in *General Systems: Yearbook of the Society for General Systems Research, IX*, ed. Ludwig von Bertalanffy and Anatol Rapoport (Ann Arbor: Society for General Systems Research, 1964), pp. 255–63; and Rudolph J. Rummel, "A Social Field Theory of Foreign Conflict Behavior," in Peace Research Society (International), *Papers, IV: Cracow Conference, 1965* (Philadelphia: Peace Research Society, 1966), pp. 131–50.

But, as in the case of numerous areas discussed above, more research and, particularly at this juncture, synthesis and integration of existing research results are required to move us beyond the level of vague notions and isolated empirical findings. Being a relatively new scientific discipline, the study of international political communication has a long way to go. What is encouraging is that progress in this direction is presently being made. We need not ignore the immense problems confronting the discipline to express hope about its future.[23]

23   I am grateful to Davis B. Bobrow, Ton DeVos, Harold D. Lasswell, and Charles E. Osgood for helpful comments on this chapter; and to the Institute of Communications Research at the University of Illinois, James W. Carey, Director, for its support of this research.

two

Transfer of Meaning
across National Boundaries

Davis B. Bobrow

WHY aren't the scientific and engineering contributions of international political communication accelerating? What different orientation seems likely to improve this situation?

The first section of the paper reviews how international political communication emerged as a response to historical events—a response resulting in an accumulation of technically and normatively uncoordinated activities. The second section examines the usefulness and limitations of three frameworks (mediated stimulus-response, cognitive balance, and cybernetics) borrowed from other fields. We find these frameworks inherently inappropriate organizing devices for international political communication. The final section suggests that we view our problem as social communication in the narrow sense of transferring meaning, and that we try to build formal theory that deals with that phenomenon.

SOURCES OF A TOPIC

In retrospect, much of international political communications analysis resulted from three phenomena of the twentieth century: (1) fundamental notions about the behavior of persons and groups that stressed the explanatory inadequacy of explicit, public rules (for example, written law) and formal structures; (2) radical changes in the forms of international competition and conflict—actual or imminent; (3) massive changes in the state of media technology. International political communication was and is heavily affected by these origins. The heterogeneity and historical quality of these influences inherently and severely limits the extent to which coherent theory can emerge. Moreover, the timely (and indeed socially urgent) nature of the influences tilted the work toward applied analyses that, although producing informed advice, were relatively unlikely to yield engineering technology.

Fundamental Social Science Notions

Analysts of international political communication took their orientation from a few perspectives about persons and groups. These perspectives may seem trite in the 1970s, but when initially stated, they carried the excitement of intuitively compelling challenges to widely shared assumptions. These fundamental notions are:

Persons select actions and form judgments not only to accomplish some public purpose but also to satisfy certain private (and perhaps not even conscious) needs.[1]

Persons form judgments and select actions primarily on the basis of the *subjective* images of reality provided by their own cognitions, emotions, and memories, not primarily on the basis of some *objective* external reality.[2]

Language provides a limiting structure within which persons notice, categorize, and interpret extrapersonal phenomena. As languages differ, so do treatments of these phenomena.[3]

Culture also provides a limiting structure. Thus differences between cultures lead to variation in the cognition and evaluation of extrapersonal phenomena.[4]

Organizational behavior is a product of *informal* flows of information and influence and cannot be adequately understood or altered on the basis of the organization's *formal* structure or charter.[5]

I have purposely used words like "perspective" because these notions were *meta*theories, not theories or engineering models. They

1   Harold D. Lasswell, *Psychopathology and Politics* (Chicago: University of Chicago Press, 1930).

2   George Herbert Mead, *Mind, Self and Society*, ed. Charles W. Morris (Chicago: University of Chicago Press, 1934).

3   Benjamin L. Whorf, *Language, Thought and Reality: Selected Writings*, ed. John B. Carroll (Cambridge: Technology Press of the Massachusetts Institute of Technology; New York: John Wiley and Sons, 1956).

4   Ruth Benedict, *Patterns of Culture* (Boston: Houghton Mifflin, 1934).

5   Chester I. Barnard, *The Functions of the Executive* (Cambridge: Harvard University Press, 1938); Elton Mayo, *The Human Problems of an Industrial Civilization* (New York: Macmillan, 1933).

basically said to the researcher: "If you want to understand what people are doing, you should acquire the following classes of information." They did not provide him with a deductive apparatus—that is, with a set of axioms from which he could derive noncontradictory consequences testable across time. The lack of specified connections between the elements under study also limited the application of these perspectives. To amplify, *engineering seeks to establish the ensemble of entities and relationships that will most efficiently meet specified performance conditions for a given range of situations.* Accordingly, in the first instance engineers are concerned with the importance of particular variables for other variables in the group (a sensitivity-analysis question). They do not stop there, however, but go on to establish conditions to be met by design. Metatheories may promote some answers to such sensitivity questions. For example, if I accept a metatheory stating that men can only attribute intentions to an actor to the extent that they believe it conceivable that the actor has those intentions, then certain sensitivity conclusions follow. Should X assume that Y has only hostile intent toward him, then he will not treat and respond to friendly actions by Y as signs of good will. Such metatheories make a contribution to engineering, but they do not suggest ensembles of necessary and sufficient conditions for producing specified behavioral outcomes.

These metatheories have frequently given rise to descriptive, historical studies. For example, the idea that persons screen external stimuli through mental content made men ask what the content was for actors of interest.[6] The metatheory about cultural differences led to efforts at drawing profiles of politically important cultures.[7] These painstaking and creative endeavors were certainly in the directions suggested by the metatheory involved. Yet their reliance on that metatheory predetermined the results; they could only be descriptions and sensitive interpretations of particular historical situations. Results like these were helpful for applied purposes, but their helpful-

6 For example, see Hadley Cantril, *The Politics of Despair* (New York: Basic Books, 1958); Lloyd A. Free, *Six Allies and a Neutral: A Study of the International Outlooks of Political Leaders in the United States, Britain, France, West Germany, Italy, Japan, and India* (Glencoe, Ill.: The Free Press, 1959); Hans Speier, *German Rearmament and Atomic War: The Views of German Military and Political Leaders* (Evanston, Ill.: Row, Peterson, 1957).

7 For review and bibliography, see Margaret Mead, "The Study of National Character," in *The Policy Sciences: Recent Developments in Scope and Method*, ed. Daniel Lerner and Harold D. Lasswell (Stanford: Stanford University Press, 1951), pp. 70–85; Alex Inkeles and Daniel J. Levinson, "National Character," in *The Handbook of Social Psychology*, ed. Gardner Lindzey and Elliot Aronson, 2d ed. (Reading, Mass.: Addison-Wesley, 1969), vol. 4, pp. 418–506.

ness resembled that of a skilled and thoughtful observer more than that of an engineer. No intellectual foundation existed for the cumulative development of theory.

In sum, the metatheories were neither trivial nor unfruitful. The investigations employing them were limited, not in methodological terms, but in terms of conceptual and relational equipment. By proceeding as if metatheories had the potential of more powerful conceptual schemes, international communications researchers tended to become historians and social interpreters.

One other limitation of the orienting perspectives should be noted. Each dealt primarily with a single type of actor (the individual, culture group, linguistic community, large organization), frequently treating it in isolation from the rest of the international system. Of course, international relations involves *all* these units of analysis.[8] The orienting perspectives did not encourage work *across* levels; they led to work on a particular isolated unit.

International Competition and Conflict

Because their orientations did not suggest situations for attention, social scientists were prone to choose socially salient cases. As different historical situations became socially salient, few conceptual constraints prevented social scientists from modifying their current research and switching to these. International conflict and competition are major environmental characteristics which social scientists have studied since World War I. The influence of these led analysts (1) to recognize and analyze many transmitter-receiver sets of actors involved in international relations; (2) to develop quantitative instruments for collecting and reducing data from media content; (3) to provide policy advice consisting primarily of descriptive information and sensitive interpretation. These influences also diverted attention from theory development and induced the use of historical relevance to international affairs as a criterion for the allocation of intellectual resources.

Before World War I international political communication was viewed as a two-way flow of messages between personally or diplomatically linked national elites.[9] That war revealed two aspects of mass populations important to war and peace. First, the outcomes

8   J. David Singer, "The Level-of-Analysis Problem in International Relations," *World Politics* 14, no. 1 (October 1961): 77–92.
9   Harold Nicolson, *Diplomacy*, 3rd ed. (London: Oxford University Press, 1963).

rested heavily upon the preferences and morale of civilian soldiers, the civilian populations of combatant nations, and attentive publics in potential ally or enemy countries. A one-way flow of influence from the elite of one country to the publics of another became an instrument of war.[10] The ability to reach a foreign population, to deny that channel to a hostile power, or to swamp its contents with more persuasive communications to a national public became a significant dimension of national security capability.[11] The social scientists' major role was to point out and describe these phenomena. Second, elite-to-elite communication's failure to avoid war and the revelation of secret treaties led to prescriptions that a fair peace required a flow of influence from publics in many countries to belligerent elites. The rectitude of world public opinion was assumed. Most work on communication from world public opinion took the form of normative prescription and political essays.[12]

The rise of totalitarian movements after World War I gave additional importance to manipulative communication across national lines. Two asymmetries between democratic and totalitarian systems made it seem particularly threatening to liberals. The first asymmetry was the relative ease with which totalitarian governments could communicate to publics in democratic societies, contrasted with the limited access of democratic governments to populations of totalitarian societies. The second was the ability of totalitarian regimes to mobilize emotion through the media, using appeals that democratic leadership found repugnant. Then, too, democratic governments and liberal social scientists knew that foreign political movements communicated with revolutionary groups in their own societies, providing them with symbols for mobilizing mass support. Thus the historical situation stimulated several types of analysis: (1) description of the symbols being used to manipulate foreign publics;[13]

10 Harold D. Lasswell, *Propaganda Technique in the World War* (New York: Alfred A. Knopf, 1927).

11 For example, see Robert T. Holt and Robert W. van de Velde, *Strategic Psychological Operations and American Foreign Policy* (Chicago: University of Chicago Press, 1960); Ernst Kris and Hans Speier, *German Radio Propaganda: Report on Home Broadcasts during the War* (New York: Oxford University Press, 1944); Alex Inkeles, *Public Opinion in Soviet Russia: A Study in Mass Persuasion* (Cambridge: Harvard University Press, 1958); Frederick T. C. Yu, *Mass Persuasion in Communist China* (New York: Praeger, 1964).

12 It was in partial response to this view that Walter Lippmann wrote *Public Opinion* (New York: Harcourt, Brace, 1922) and *The Phantom Public* (New York: Harcourt, Brace, 1925).

13 For example, Harold D. Lasswell and Dorothy Blumenstock, *World Revolutionary Propaganda: A Chicago Study* (New York: Alfred A. Knopf, 1939).

(2) demonstration of common design in the communications from foreign governments and from their associates in a target country;[14] (3) clarification of the manipulative strategy being used by the hostile foreign leadership;[15] and (4) reconstructions of the network used to transmit directives to domestic revolutionary groups from a foreign source.[16] The first two types required techniques to extract and summarize the messages; the third suggested hypotheses about propaganda effectiveness.

Given the experience of World War I and subsequent emphasis by Axis leaders (through such salient acts as terror bombing and verbal messages to weaken the will of foreign publics to oppose Germany), American and other Allied leaders felt it important to know more about the foreign-policy perceptions and preferences of their own publics. They needed information about direction and rates of change. The applied need was for data collection techniques to provide descriptions of mass opinion that were both accurate and comparable over time. Survey interviewing and panels of participant observers turned mass-to-elite communication within a nation from the peaceful constraint envisioned after World War I into an indicator of national war potential akin to production indicators.[17]

The types of international communication work noted above continued during World War II as social scientists analyzed psychological warfare and war information programs.[18] The work went beyond

14   For example, see Harold D. Lasswell, "Detection: Propaganda Detection and the Courts," in *Language of Politics: Studies in Quantitative Semantics*, ed. Harold D. Lasswell, Nathan Leites, et al. (New York: G. W. Stewart, 1949); Bernard Berelson and Sebastian de Grazia, "Detecting Collaboration in Propaganda," *Public Opinion Quarterly* 11, no. 2 (Spring 1947): 244–53.

15   For example, Leonard W. Doob, "Goebbels' Principles of Propaganda," *Public Opinion Quarterly* 14, no. 3 (Summer 1950): 419–42; John C. Clews, *Communist Propaganda Techniques* (New York: Praeger, 1964); Frederick C. Barghoorn, *The Soviet Cultural Offensive: The Role of Cultural Diplomacy in Soviet Foreign Policy* (Princeton: Princeton University Press, 1960); Frederick C. Barghoorn, *Soviet Foreign Propaganda* (Princeton: Princeton University Press, 1964).

16   For example, see two papers by Barton Whaley, *Guerrilla Communications* (Cambridge: Center for International Studies, Massachusetts Institute of Technology, Paper C/67–4, March 1967) and *Soviet Clandestine Communication Nets* (Cambridge: Center for International Studies, Massachusetts Institute of Technology, Paper C/67–10, September 1969).

17   For example, see Hadley A. Cantril, *Gauging Public Opinion* (Princeton: Princeton University Press, 1944); Charles Madge and Tom Harrisson, *Britain by Mass-Observation* (Hammondsworth, England: Penguin Books, 1939); Elizabeth A. Herzog, "Pending Perfection: A Qualitative Compliment to Quantitative Methods," *International Journal of Opinion and Attitude Research* 1, no. 3 (September 1947): 31–48.

18   For example, see Daniel Lerner, *Sykewar: Psychological Warfare against Germany, D-Day to VE-Day* (New York: G. W. Stewart, 1949); Daniel Lerner,

description, but it did so primarily through case knowledge and trial-and-error prescription. The result was maxims without specified scope conditions (for example, the "cry wolf" phenomenon).

A greater departure from World War I activities saw the use of communications less as means of persuasion than as sources of intelligence. Communications from a foreign elite to its own population enabled analysts to infer current information about the intentions and capabilities of foreign regimes and to monitor long-run changes in their priorities and expectations.[19] Although the work was largely descriptive, it was interpretive, suggesting actions toward policy goals. But the suggestions were less the product of a formal analytic set of procedures than of a private synthesis.

The presence of nuclear weapons after World War II, and the need to prevent their use, stimulated analysts to enlarge their views of communication processes and purposes. First, attention returned to publics as a constraint on elite belligerency, but in a more complex form than after World War I.[20] Communication between publics in different nations seemed to be a basis for creating public opinion that international differences could be resolved short of war, and for creating empathy through exposure of one set of nationals to another. Social scientists examined exchanges and foreign travel to determine their effectiveness, primarily by comparing before-and-after descriptions.[21]

Second, it was recognized that, since they were not unitary actors, communication between national elites required greater differentiation than previous studies had provided. The bureaucratic complex between the receipt or transmission of messages on the one hand and national leaders on the other required attention. Concrete situ-

ed., *Propaganda in War and Crisis* (Materials for American Policy; New York: G. W. Stewart, 1951); William E. Daugherty and Morris Janowitz, compilers, *A Psychological Warfare Casebook* (Baltimore: Johns Hopkins University Press, 1958).

19 For example, see Alexander L. George, *Propaganda Analysis: A Study of Inferences Made from Nazi Propaganda in World War II* (Evanston, Ill.: Row, Peterson, 1959); Lasswell, Leites, et al., *Language of Politics*.

20 For example, see Hadley Cantril, ed., *Tensions That Cause Wars: Common Statement and Individual Papers Brought Together by UNESCO* (Urbana: University of Illinois Press, 1950); William Buchanan and Hadley Cantril, *How Nations See Each Other: A Study in Public Opinion* (Urbana: University of Illinois Press, 1953).

21 For example, see Ithiel de Sola Pool, "Effects of Cross-National Contact on National and International Images," in *International Behavior: A Social-Psychological Analysis*, ed. Herbert C. Kelman (New York: Holt, Rinehart and Winston, 1965), pp. 104–20; Anita L. Mishler, "Personal Contact in International Exchanges," ibid., pp. 548–64.

ations such as the attack on Pearl Harbor (in which the bureaucratic system had failed spectacularly to transmit strategic warning) helped stimulate this recognition. It also reflected a concern with command and control—that is, insuring that national security policy implementors did only what they were told to do and did that without fail. Social science called attention to these problems, engaged in cautionary examinations of historical cases of failure,[22] and, in the activities of human-performance and human-engineering psychologists, contributed to the design of technological palliatives.

Finally, renewed importance was attached to improving communication between national elites. This was stimulated partly by the view that nuclear weapons delivery times were too short to enable publics to intervene and security issues too complex for publics to understand. And it rested partly on the view that, since the costs of nuclear war would outweigh the gains, nuclear weapons established a common interest among competitive governments to avoid such wars. Finally, it also rested on the implicit assumption that nuclear weapons made the possibility of international conflict sufficiently salient that signals from a foreign elite would be prime determinants of policy.

Three approaches were taken to the flows of signals between national elites about questions of war and peace, yet each was concerned with negotiation and bargaining. The first applied metatheories to the behavior of particular actors, with the informative but historically confining types of results noted earlier.[23] The other two drew on the higher-level abstractions used in other areas of social science. Economics and game theory provided various models of utility and choice, suggesting that the main applied communications problem was to convey what cell in a utility matrix was germane to a particular situation.[24] However, the communications elements were

22   For example, see Roberta Wohlstetter, *Pearl Harbor: Warning and Decision* (Stanford: Stanford University Press, 1962); Barton Whaley, *Operation Barbarossa* (Cambridge: Center for International Studies, Massachusetts Institute of Technology, 1969); Johan Jörgen Holst, "Surprise, Signals and Reaction: The Attack on Norway, April 9, 1970—Some Observations," *Cooperation and Conflict* 1, no. 1 (1966): 31–45.

23   For example, see Davis B. Bobrow, "Chinese Communist Response to Alternative U.S. Continental Defense Postures," in *Weapons Systems Decisions: Political and Psychological Perspectives on Continental Defense*, ed. Davis B. Bobrow (New York: Praeger, 1969), pp. 151–213; Bryant Wedge and Cyril Muromcew, "Psychological Factors: Soviet Disarmament Negotiation," *The Journal of Conflict Resolution* 9, no. 1 (March 1965): 18–36.

24   For example, see Thomas C. Schelling, *The Strategy of Conflict* (Cambridge: Harvard University Press, 1960); Thomas C. Schelling, *Arms and Influence* (New Haven: Yale University Press, 1966).

often treated in a manner not derived from the models of utility and choice being used. Without constraints from theory or models, a rich set of plausible conjectures often resulted. The conjectures were not always compatible, nor did their support or disconfirmation have any clear implication for the value of the utility or choice model. As engineering prescription, the reliability of much of this work seems an artifact of the initial model, rather than the application of that model to international communication.

Psychology contributed a set of concepts which were not historically limited and which had prima facie relevance to some of the phenomena involved in deterrence, arms control, and disarmament.[25] The concepts (such as threat, reinforcement, and trust) were elaborated enough to be used experimentally. Even so, the contribution was primarily one of isolated hypotheses and not one of theory or models. Their deductive potential was limited accordingly. It was not clear how to apply the concepts to the simultaneous treatment of many variables that engineering involves. Attempts to increase the isomorphism with international situations took the form of enriching the experimental situation.[26] However, the enriched experiments have been intended primarily to answer sensitivity rather than design questions, as we distinguished these earlier.

The streams of work we have just been discussing involve de facto alteration of the scope of signals. Although the psychological warfare work had recognized both actions and words as signals, the overwhelming emphasis was on media content (words and visual images). The new definition of "international communication" became "all behaviors by one actor of which another actor could be aware." Given the concern with military matters, particular attention was focused on the procurement, deployment, and use of military capabilities.

Changes in Media Technology

The third group of influences on international political communications research came from changes in media technology and the

---

25 For a good sampling of these contributions, see Kelman, ed., *International Behavior*; Dean G. Pruitt and Richard C. Snyder, eds., *Theory and Research on the Causes of War* (Englewood Cliffs, N.J.: Prentice-Hall, 1969); Roger Fisher, ed., *International Conflict and Behavioral Science: The Craigville Papers* (New York: Basic Books, 1964).

26 For a state-of-the-art overview, see Harold Guetzkow, "Some Correspondences between Simulations and 'Realities' in International Relations," in *New Approaches to International Relations*, ed. Morton A. Kaplan (New York: St. Martin's Press, 1968), pp. 202–69.

resultant social science activities. Although not initially or primarily concerned with such issues, the concepts, topics, hypotheses, and instruments for collecting data came to have applications for international affairs. With the joint stimuli of radio, film, and mass literacy, social scientists began talking about the phenomena of mass communication. They evolved such concepts as audience, source, channel, exposure, appeal, impact, and target.[27]

These concepts were not limited to any particular media technology or historical situation. Their primary value, however, was taxonomic in that they grouped descriptive information; they were devoid of deductive implication.

The categories made possible and were refined by exploratory inquiries about relationships between media and people.[28] These efforts tried primarily to learn about the direct receivers of media transmissions. Who exposed themselves to what communications? Why? In addition to historical descriptions of media-audience relationships in particular populations at particular times, two more generalized products resulted. One was a technology for collecting and analyzing data useful for (1) directly querying a mass population (survey interviewing), and (2) reducing many responses from many persons to a few patterns.[29] This technology and its descriptive questions could readily be applied to the audience for communications about international affairs.[30] The second benefit of the initial descriptive work was increased awareness of the enhanced media's implications.

27   Particularly helpful anthologies for the evolution are Bernard Berelson and Morris Janowitz, eds., *Reader in Public Opinion and Communication*, 2nd ed. (New York: The Free Press, 1966); Wilbur Schramm, *Mass Communication* (Urbana: University of Illinois Press, 1949); Wilbur Schramm, *Communications in Modern Society: Fifteen Studies of Mass Media* (Urbana: University of Illinois Press, 1948).

28   For example, see Paul F. Lazarsfeld, *Radio and the Printed Page: An Introduction to the Study of Radio and Its Role in the Communication of Ideas* (New York: Duell, Sloan, and Pearce, 1940); Paul F. Lazarsfeld and Frank Stanton, *Radio Research, 1941* (New York: Duell, Sloan, and Pearce, 1941); Paul F. Lazarsfeld and Frank Stanton, *Radio Research, 1942–43* (New York: Essential Books, distributed by Duell, Sloan, and Pearce, 1944); Paul F. Lazarsfeld and Frank Stanton, eds., *Communication Research, 1948–49* (New York: Harper, 1949); Douglas Waples, *People and Print: Social Aspects of Reading in the Depression* (Chicago: University of Chicago Press, 1938).

29   Two volumes with numerous examples from communications research (and some from elsewhere) are Paul F. Lazarsfeld and Morris Rosenberg, eds., *The Language of Social Research: A Reader in the Methodology of Social Research* (Glencoe, Ill.: The Free Press, 1955); Samuel A. Stouffer et al., gen. eds., *Studies in Social Psychology in World War II*, vol. 4: *Measurement and Prediction*, by Samuel A. Stouffer (Princeton: Princeton University Press, for Special Committee of the Social Science Research Council, 1950).

30   For a summary of findings, see Alfred O. Hero, *Mass Media and World Affairs* (Boston: World Peace Foundation, 1959).

These included its ability to show general norms and models of behavior, to induce changes in specific audience attributes, and to
change the terms of interaction between the audience and distant
events and persons.[31]

If it was true that the media both formed and mirrored collective
norms and behavior, then aggregate summaries of media content
seemed useful for determining (1) the nature of major socialization
influences, (2) the relative importance of different issues, values, and
actors, and (3) assemblies of traits that an audience would view as
related. If it was true that exposure to common media content had
these effects, then it became equivalent to membership in a common
culture, such as "mass culture." The transfer of these research perspectives to international political communication took the forms of
(1) descriptive summaries, either of media content about some
general aspects of foreign affairs directed toward a domestic population, or of the content of foreign media;[32] (2) studies treating a
population with shared exposure to media as a potential unit of analysis in international relations, to be distinguished from geogra-
phically bounded units;[33] and (3) the generation of models or
near-models relating media exposure to change in pre-industrial
societies.[34] Most work was of the first kind and involved long periods
of social monitoring to locate empirical patterns. The second and
third approaches, related to attempts to import theory, are discussed in the next section.

Most attention was focused on media's role in inducing specific
behaviors in the mass audience. The behaviors usually involved in-

31 For example, see Rudolf Arnheim, "The World of the Daytime Serial," in
Radio Research, 1942–43, ed. Lazarsfeld and Stanton, pp. 34–85; Leo Lowenthal,
"Biographies in Popular Magazines," ibid., pp. 507–48; Louis Wirth, "Consensus and
Mass Communication," *American Sociological Review* 13, no. 1 (February 1948):
1–15; Martha Wolfenstein and Nathan Leites, *Movies: A Psychological Study* (Glen-
coe, Ill.: The Free Press, 1950); Herta Herzog, "What Do We Really Know about
Day-Time Serial Listeners?" in *Radio Research, 1942–43*, ed. Lazarsfeld and Stan-
ton, pp. 3–33.
32 Ithiel de Sola Pool, with the collaboration of Harold D. Lasswell et al.,
The Prestige Press: A Comparative Study of Political Symbols (Cambridge: M.I.T.
Press [1951–52], 1970).
33 For example, see Karl W. Deutsch, *Nationalism and Social Communication:
An Inquiry into the Foundations of Nationality* (Cambridge: Technology Press of
the Massachusetts Institute of Technology; New York: John Wiley and Sons, 1953);
Karl W. Deutsch et al., *Political Community and the North Atlantic Area: International Organization in the Light of Historical Experience* (Princeton: Princeton
University Press, 1957).
34 For example, see Daniel Lerner, *The Passing of Traditional Society: Modernizing the Middle East* (Glencoe, Ill.: The Free Press, 1958); Lucian W. Pye, ed.,
Communications and Political Development (Princeton: Princeton University Press,
1963).

dividual allocations of resources (money, votes, time). The questions included the nature of and relationships between media exposure in a physical sense, characteristics of audiences prior to their exposure to media, relevant interpersonal communications, and changes in the behavior of receivers.[35] These questions were suitable for experimental and quasi-experimental treatment. They were generalized, not emphasizing the importance of particular individuals or groups or even situations. Research produced some generalized relational statements about communication networks and changes in attitudes: abstention in response to cross-pressure, the sleeper effect, the two-step flow of influence, the gatekeeper.[36] Since they lacked historical specificity, these statements could be (and were) applied to the international mass persuasion cases mentioned previously. There was also much support for this research as a means of achieving particular goals in the real world, such as sales of a product or majorities for a candidate. The transfer to international communication came through analysis of the market for specific foreign policies, or even for information about international affairs, and attempts to influence the behavior of consumers in that market.[37] Although advanced relative to the other work we have been discussing, the relational statements were not unified by theory, nor were generalized modeling

35 For example, see Stouffer et al., gen. eds., *Studies in Social Psychology in World War II*, vol. 3: C. I. Hovland and F. D. Sheffield, *Experiments on Mass Communication* (Princeton: Princeton University Press for Special Committee of the Social Science Research Council, 1950); Paul F. Lazarsfeld, Bernard Berelson, and Hazel Gaudet, *The People's Choice: How the Voter Makes up His Mind in a Presidential Campaign* (New York: Duell, Sloan, and Pearce, 1944); Elihu Katz and Paul F. Lazarsfeld, *Personal Influence: The Part Played by People in the Flow of Mass Communications* (Glencoe, Ill.: The Free Press, 1955); and for a summary of the early work, Joseph T. Klapper, *The Effects of Mass Communication* (Glencoe, Ill.: The Free Press, 1960).

36 Many of the findings are summarized in terms of implications for international communication by Irving L. Janis and M. Brewster Smith, "Effect of Education and Persuasion on National and International Images," in *International Behavior*, ed. Kelman, pp. 188–235. On the gatekeeper concept, see Kurt Lewin, "Group Decision and Social Change," in *Readings in Social Psychology*, eds. Eleanor E. Maccoby, Theodore M. Newcomb, and Eugene L. Hartley (New York: Henry Holt, 1958), pp. 197–211.

37 For example, see William A. Scott and Stephen B. Withey, *The United States and the United Nations: The Public View, 1945–1955* (New York: Manhattan Publishing, 1958); Shirley A. Star and Helen MacGill Hughes, "Report on an Educational Campaign: The Cincinnati Plan for the United Nations," *American Journal of Sociology* 55, no. 4 (January 1950): 389–400; Herbert H. Hyman and Paul B. Sheatsley, "Some Reasons Why Information Campaigns Fail," *Public Opinion Quarterly* 11, no. 3 (Fall 1947): 412–23; Kenneth P. Adler and Davis Bobrow, "Interest and Influence in Foreign Affairs," *Public Opinion Quarterly* 20, no. 1 (Spring 1956): 89–101; Gabriel A. Almond, *The Appeals of Communism* (Princeton: Princeton University Press, 1954).

procedures to be used in a variety of campaigns successfully produced.

Finally, researchers knew electronic media changed the relationships of persons to distant events and individuals. The latter acquired greater immediacy and impact; they lost context and increased in importance; insufficient time had elapsed for intervening events to clarify their significance.[38] When applied internationally, a number of effects seemed important: decreases in reliance on field officials for information, increases in the volume of information transmitted, and decreases in the time between receipt of messages and response to them. However, these observations were not pursued systematically.

Against this background, it is not surprising that no unifying intellectual structure emerged to characterize international political communication. Chapter headings from a major text illustrate the residues composing the field:[39]

Introduction: Communication as a Tool of Foreign Policy

Part One: The Flow and Effects of Communications

The International Network
Impact of Communications on the Individual
Communication and Organization
The Political Role of Communication in Democracies
Communication in Communist States
Communication in Developing Nations

Part Two: The Use of Communications to Advance Policy

The Structure of International Communication Programs
Communist International Communication
Foreign Information and Cultural Activities of the United States
Focusing Official American Communication Programs
Role of the U.S. Government in International Communication

Appendix: Channels for International Communication

Shared faith in the importance of factors not studied by traditional analysts and practitioners of international relations were all that connected members of the field. This bond and the salience of con-

---

38 For example, see Hadley Cantril, Hazel Gaudet, and Herta Herzog, *The Invasion from Mars: A Study in the Psychology of Panic* (Princeton: Princeton University Press, 1940); Kurt Lang and Gladys Engel Lang, "The Unique Perspective of Television and Its Effect: A Pilot Study," *American Sociological Review* 18, no. 1 (February 1953): 3–12.

39 W. Phillips Davison, *International Political Communication* (New York: Published for the Council on Foreign Relations by Frederick A. Praeger, 1965).

temporary events led them to master historically unique descriptions and offer policy suggestions as soon as possible. We would not expect such influences and habits to help develop theory or engineering models. Indeed, with the exceptions of media exposure and audience persuasion, relatively little conceptual development took place.[40]

PARADIGMS

In contrast, three other recent streams of effort in the field attempt to use what hopefully is a powerful theory to treat the relations between nations in a cumulative manner: mediated stimulus-response, cognitive balance, and cybernetics. None of the paradigms was formulated with international relations in mind. Our concern is with their inherent possibilities for the study of international relations.

Mediated Stimulus-Response

The mediated stimulus-response paradigm was borrowed from psychology. In its simplest form, it posits that the response of a receiver to a signal is a function not only of the signal itself but also of the previous attributes of the receiver. These attributes affect the definition of the behavior of others (stimulus) and of the self (response). As transferred to international relations by Robert C. North and his associates, the paradigm took the now familiar form shown in Figure 1.[41] The mediated stimulus-response paradigm is a metatheory, not a theory. Accordingly, its contribution can only be sensitizing and taxonomic.

The paradigm directs analysts to take into account three classes of variables: (1) the behavior of the actor, (2) the actor's perception of the behavior of others, (3) the actor's perception of his own behavior. Interaction can be adequately described and understood, and sequences predicted, only on the basis of all three kinds of informa-

---

40 A notable engineering step has been taken by John Francis Kramer in his *A Computer Simulation of Audience Exposure in a Mass Media System* (Cambridge: Center for International Studies, Massachusetts Institute of Technology, Paper C/69–11, July 1969). For a general description of the model's applications, see Ithiel de Sola Pool, *Final Report of the Research Program on Problems of International Communication and Security* (Cambridge: Center for International Studies, Massachusetts Institute of Technology, Paper C/69–26, September 1969). On the simulation itself, see John C. Klensin and John D. Nagle, *Mass Media Simulation Program Users' Manual* (Cambridge: Center for International Studies, Massachusetts Institute of Technology, Paper C/69–3, April 1969).

41 Ole R. Holsti, Robert C. North, and Richard A. Brody, "Perception and Action in the 1914 Crisis," in *Quantitative International Politics: Insights and Evidence*, ed. J. David Singer (New York: The Free Press, 1968), p. 133.

tion. The paradigm encompasses both classes of variables suggested by the metatheories discussed earlier, which focused primarily upon the attributes of actors and their actions. It seems to bring together

Figure 1. A Mediated Stimulus-Response Paradigm

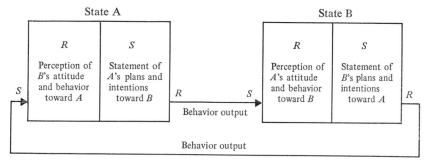

for international relations the *acts* with which traditional analysis have dealt and the *characteristics of the actors*—whether heads of state, national populations, or departments of government—which behavioral science contends are important. However, the paradigm simply asserts the *existence* of a chronological relationship among these considerations. It has no propositions or derived consequences about the *nature* of those relationships. No relational possibility is excluded; none is given priority. International relations analysts are left to search historically for such relationships. The inductive scholarship which results can be and often has been empirically precise, stating conclusions in ahistorical terms.[42] For subsequent work, however, it can only contribute hypotheses confirmed in a particular case(s) (the typicality of which is unknown) and techniques for testing them in additional cases. The applied usefulness of the paradigm is limited to describing, rather than predicting, the behavior of particular actors in particular situations. These descriptions may reveal unrecognized traits of the actors under examination or resolve long-standing disagreements about them through evidence. Such descriptions have cautionary value for statecraft: for example, demonstrating the role of misperception as a factor in the outbreak of World War I serves to alert the prudent statesman to difficulties in

42 For examples, see ibid.; Ole R. Holsti, "The 1914 Case," *American Political Science Review* 59, no. 2 (June 1965): 365–78; Ole R. Holsti, "Perceptions of Time, Perceptions of Alternatives, and Patterns of Communication as Factors in Crisis Decision-Making," in Peace Research Society (International), *Papers*, vol. 3, 1965 (Chicago Conference, 1964), ed. Walter Isard and Julian Wolpert, pp. 79–120; Dina A. Zinnes, "The Expression and Perception of Hostility in Prewar Crisis: 1914," in *Quantitative International Politics*, ed. Singer, pp. 85–122.

avoiding escalation. But the paradigm is still not equivalent to a model that, when supplied with situationally specific parameter values, predicts behavioral outcomes.

Cognitive Balance

Analysts have also borrowed the paradigm of cognitive balance from psychologists. Although a number of different formulations of balance exist, two are particularly relevant here: Fritz Heider's seminal formulation of a theory of personal decision-making, and Theodore M. Newcomb's theory of interpersonal influence.[43]

The Heider formulation consists of two types of entities (persons and objects) and two types of relations between them (sentiments and unit formations). The unit-formation relationship seems to include all non-sentimental relations, such as "making," "owning," "voting for," and "working with." All relations are studied from the viewpoint of a fixed person (p). From this perspective, a cognitive system of entities and relations may or may not be in balance. Balance exists when, from the point of view of p, the sets of relationships are either all positive or an even number is negative. The theory proposes that (1) if there is imbalance, then there is a tendency to achieve balance by changing signs or the set of related elements; (2) persisting imbalance gives rise to internal tensions; (3) with the exception of certain unit relations, there is an inherent tendency toward transitive sentiment relations (if a likes b, and b likes c, then a will like c).

Newcomb's formulation differs in several important respects. First, it consists of two persons (A and B) who send communications to and receive them from each other about something (X). It is less a theory of personal decision-making than of interpersonal influence. The relations between A, B, and X are not p-centered; that is, they can be viewed from the perspective of A or B or, more important, from that of an observer concerned with the behavior of the A-B-X system. The relationships between the entities are both affective and cognitive. The affective relationships between A and B are called attraction; and between A or B and X, attitudes. As in Heider's view, balance exists when the number of negatively signed relations is zero

43   See Fritz Heider, "Attitudes and Cognitive Organization," *Journal of Psychology* 21, no. 1 (1946): 107–12; Fritz Heider, *The Psychology of Interpersonal Relations* (New York: John Wiley and Sons, 1958); Theodore M. Newcomb, "An Approach to the Study of Communicative Acts," *Psychological Review* 60, no. 6 (November 1953): 393–404. I rely heavily on the lucid discussion by Joseph Berger et al., *Types of Formalization in Small-Group Research* (Boston: Houghton Mifflin, 1962).

or even. Like Heider, Newcomb posits that imbalanced states of the system are stressful and that there will be a tendency to seek balanced states. In his case, this will take the form of communication from *A* to *B* or vice versa to achieve similar orientations toward *X*.

These brief summaries purposely omit limiting conditions implicit or explicit in the two formulations; we shall return shortly to these conditions and their implications for the transfer of the theories to our field of interest. Before that, it seems useful to note how the theories have been used in the study of international political communication. Two types of uses should be distinguished. First, analysts have sought to demonstrate the presence of the central phenomenon in international relations—the strain toward balance. This approach involves describing the state of some historical triadic system(s) and monitoring it over time to show that one or several of the following occurred: (1) changes were made toward a balanced state; (2) despite information warranting change away from balance, the status quo of balance was preserved; (3) change in a balanced system involved not a change to an imbalanced state, but a more comprehensive set of changes to achieve a different though still balanced system; and (4) persistence of imbalance was characterized by more stress among participants than in a balanced situation.[44] The analysts' strategy rested on the view that, once the presence of the central phenomenon was established, they could use the deductive apparatus of balance formulations, not only for the instances examined but also as a general theory of elite decision-making and processes entailing influence in international relations. The second approach begins by assuming that balance mechanisms operate in major areas of international relations and communication. It offers a critique of current policy and prescriptions for future policy within the perspective of a strain toward balance.[45]

Whatever their benefits, the uses made of the Heider and Newcomb formulations (as well as of their kin, such as cognitive con-

44 For examples, see Ole R. Holsti, "Cognitive Dynamics and Images of the Enemy," in *Enemies in Politics*, ed. David J. Finlay, Ole R. Holsti, and Richard R. Fagan (Chicago: Rand-McNally, 1967), pp. 25–96; P. Terrence Hopmann and Barry B. Hughes, "Attitudinal and Behavioral Measures of Cohesion and Integration in International Political Coalitions," paper prepared for the annual meeting of the Midwest Political Science Association, Chicago, April 30–May 2, 1970; and, as a general caution against assuming the cross-cultural applicability of the balance family of theories, Paul Hiniker, *Chinese Attitudinal Reactions to Forced Compliance* (Cambridge: Center for International Studies, Massachusetts Institute of Technology, Paper C/65–18, May 1965).

45 For examples, see Charles E. Osgood, *An Alternative to War or Surrender* (Urbana: University of Illinois Press, 1962); Ralph K. White, *Nobody Wanted War: Misperception in Vietnam and Other Wars* (Garden City, N.Y.: Doubleday, 1968).

sistency and dissonance) in the study of international relations have not attended to the scope conditions of the theories. Because of the scope conditions, however, the theories have no implications for certain classes of international communications phenomena.

1.1 The theories do not apply when the logic of the unit relations in a system precludes two parties from having the same relationship to a third entity (object or person). Examples include relationships involving possession, scarce commodities, or role differentiation. Such situations fall outside the scope of the theory, because the dominant tendency may be toward imbalanced rather than balanced states of the system. Obviously, many international phenomena—sovereignty, competition for shares of a limited export market, military superiority, and others—entail such excluded unit relationships.

1.2 The theory does not apply in the absence of a complete cycle, nor does it generate completion as a necessary consequence.[46] To illustrate, the state of relations may resemble the figure below. The theory does not imply that, from the point of view

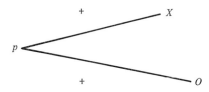

of p, any relations will develop between O and X. Should such a connection in fact develop, the theory would say that, unless it is positive, the system will be in a state of imbalance. Applied to international relations, this limitation requires that we not assume completion. For example, if we know that a particular government views two given foreign regimes as its friends, we should not assume that the transitivity rule of balance theory will bring the first government to view the two foreign regimes as friends of each other. That may happen, but the prediction does not derive from balance theory. The presence of completion is an empirical question about the perceptions of the actor under examination.

Although I have stated these scope conditions in language more akin to that of Heider, they are equally applicable to Newcomb's

46   Dorwin Cartwright and Frank Harary, "Structural Balance: A Generalization of Heider's Theory," *Psychological Review* 63, no. 5 (September 1956): 277–93.

formulation. Accordingly, the latter's propositions about a strain toward symmetry resulting in particular patterns of communication are not appropriate deductive hypotheses for the situations noted above. Newcomb recognizes these limits. He also makes two assumptions about communications as a process for achieving symmetry that further limit the applicability of his theory to international relations.

    2.1 Communicative acts are intentionally initiated. That is, party *A* deliberately sends specific signals to party *B*. These make up the universe of signals to *B* for which *A* is the source.

    2.2 All communications from *A* to *B* are attended to by *B*, although *B* may interpret them in a distorted manner.

As we know, these conditions are not met by many international communication situations. That is no reflection on the theory. It nonetheless implies that international phenomena must meet certain conditions before we apply the theory to them.

The scope conditions also have implications for the engineering use of balance theories. Problems of territorial control, resource competition, and dominant-subordinate relations are among the most urgent for international communication. Yet these are often excluded by the first condition (1.1). Even when unit relations are within the scope of balance formulations, the last two conditions (2.1 and 2.2) are frequently not met. Communicators in international relations sometimes discover that a message intended for one party reaches an unintended audience. Many messages (either within a nation or crossnationally) are not received, let alone attended to, by decision-makers.

If the scope conditions are met, two areas of ambiguity still limit the engineering value of balance concepts.[47] A person or group can handle a strain toward balance in several ways. For particular international situations and with particular policy goals, we are not indifferent about which alternative is chosen. Except for general notions of tolerance of imbalance, the work to date on balance does not provide relational statements enabling the analyst to predict how imbalance is handled or to distinguish factors that determine the adaptation selected. Defining the system is an equally important and unresolved problem for engineering uses of balance concepts. The rules of balance begin with a system characterized by a degree of balance or imbalance, symmetry or asymmetry. The initial charac-

---

47 I have elaborated the implications of these points for defense policy analysis in "Cognitive Interaction in Strategic Choice," paper prepared for the Conference on Prospects and Problems in the Psychology of Knowledge: On Cognitive Interaction, Philadelphia, April 19–21, 1965.

terization must be of the total system (the full set of entities cyclically related to each other) in which the actor(s) under examination is involved. That is, we need much more information than simply that the system meets the second scope condition (at least one cycle, as stated in 1.2). Of course, an analyst can arbitrarily select the entities that interest him; he may even be able to arrive at and find support for inferences consistent with the principles of balance. The work will have little implication for engineering, however, unless his definition of the system accurately represents the system in which the actor makes decisions and communicates.

Cybernetics

The cybernetic paradigm treats adjustment or adaptive relationships between decision-making entities (physical or biological) and their environments.[48] The central mechanism of the paradigm is feedback —that is, the adjustment of subsequent behavior in light of the discrepancy between the consequences of previous behavior and a desired goal. The quality of feedback determines the effectiveness of the system in achieving goals or performance standards and, ultimately, its survival. Proponents of the paradigm contend that it provides a coherent framework for building theories of and powerful engineering models for communication and control in all organized systems. If correct, it follows that the paradigm can contribute to work on the international system and its subsystems. Given the nature of the paradigm, the theory and models incorporate international communication in its political (control) aspects.

The paradigm states that an organized system must have at least three classes of connected elements: receptors, decision centers, and effectors. Receptors receive signals from the environment and transmit signals about it to decision centers. Decision centers receive signals from receptors, retrieve information about the past from memory and elsewhere, and apply to it a decision rule embodying a goal. Comparison of remembered information with the most recent information establishes direction or rate of change of positions relative to the goal. After the comparison, decision centers select a behavioral alternative and transmit signals to effectors to implement it. Effectors, by engaging in a behavior, signal the environment. These

48   Norbert Wiener, *Cybernetics, or Control and Communication in the Animal and the Machine* (Cambridge: Technology Press of the Massachusetts Institute of Technology, 1948); Norbert Wiener, *The Human Use of Human Beings*, 2nd ed. rev. (Garden City, N.Y.: Doubleday, 1954); John Voevodsky, *Behavioral Cybernetics* (mimeographed, 1970).

elements all may vary in capacity to receive and send signals, as may the channels or circuits that connect them. An organized system may also have a fourth class of elements that receive signals (not about the environment, but about the system) and transmit these to decision centers.

The system constrains the operation of the feedback mechanism, but its adequacy or effectiveness for adjustment and adaptation is a function of the system's properties relative to an environment. In particular, the extent, rate, and patterning or nonrandomness of change in relevant portions of the environment determine the quantity and speed at which an organized system must be able to receive and handle information.

As developed outside the social sciences, cybernetics has produced a number of important formalized propositions for predicting the quality of system adaptation and for designing adaptive systems. These contributions have extended to the adaptation of two organized systems to each other. The theory and models nonetheless seem limited to situations that meet the following scope conditions: (1) the behaviors or actions involved are repetitive and variable over time; (2) the distance of the system from its goal is affected by the behavior of the system; (3) the goal must include or depend on the presence of some environmental characteristic. Not all situations customarily included in international communication or international relations meet these conditions.

One use which analysts of international relations have made of cybernetics clearly respects these scope conditions: work using feedback equations to deal with the interaction of arms procurement and defense budgeting. The results are impressive. The equations have yielded accurate predictions about the (amplifying) nature and magnitudes of interactive processes among the European powers before World War I.[49] Other work has shown that different elements in a cybernetic system have at least some appropriate analogues in national defense budgeting and arms procurement. Differences in the attributes of elements have analagous consequences. For example, alternative military goals are similar to servo-mechanisms with predictable implications for amplifying or damping a particular proc-

49 Voevodsky, *Behavioral Cybernetics*, Ch. 8; Jeffrey S. Milstein and William Charles Mitchell, "Computer Simulation of International Processes: The Vietnam War and the Pre–World War I Naval Race," in Peace Research Society (International), *Papers*, vol. 12, 1969 (Cambridge Conference, 1968), ed. Walter Isard and Julian Wolpert, pp. 117–36; Richard P. Lagerstrom, *An Anticipated Gap: Mathematical Model of International Dynamics* (Stanford: Institute of Political Studies, Stanford University, ditto, February 8, 1968).

ess.[50] The results suggest that the paradigm can help us design a foreign policy system that tends, for example, to damp feedback.

The cybernetic paradigm has also been treated as the framework for a general theory of international relations. In doing so, John Burton emphasizes the desirable social consequences that will follow if the cybernetic paradigm replaces more traditional international frameworks.[51] He is not concerned with the formalized intellectual apparatus that makes "feedback" more than a metaphor. Whether world affairs will turn toward peace and mutual respect when statesmen accept the paradigm seems to me an open question. Derivation of hypotheses from the theory is more logically constrained. The theory does not imply which behaviors—for example, violent or pacific acts—will be chosen when feedback is excellent (or poor). Rather, the theory implies how the relationship between a previous and a current choice of action varies with the quality of feedback. Cybernetics is no more a model for peaceful than for aggressive purposes.

The final use of the cybernetic paradigm concerning us here is that of Karl Deutsch.[52] His concern is not with the demonstration of particular propositions or even with all of international relations. Instead, he offers a steering or adaptive perspective on both a science and engineering of politics based on cybernetic concepts. He formulates numerous concepts, relational hypotheses, requirements for data, and maxims for politicians relevant to international relations. The perspective is exciting, even though the extent to which the analogue retains or generates the power of the original theory remains to be seen. Acceptance of a general perspective on politics as communication and control clearly implies that we work toward theories and models of politics and not solely toward those of international relations.

This brief discussion of the cybernetic paradigm suggests two points. First, the road to theory about and models for treating important phenomena in international relations may lie in treating them as instances of processes and structure found in *all* social universes.

50   P. E. Chase, "Feedback Control Theory and Arms Races," in *General Systems: Yearbook of the Society for General Systems Research*, vol. 14, 1969, ed. Ludwig von Bertalanffy, Anatol Rapoport, and Richard L. Meier (Ann Arbor: Society for General Systems Research, 1969), pp. 137–49.

51   John W. Burton, *International Relations: A General Theory* (New York: Cambridge University Press, 1965).

52   Karl W. Deutsch, *The Nerves of Government: Models of Political Communication and Control* (New York: The Free Press, 1963). For a less optimistic view of the utility of analogue models, see David Willer, *Scientific Sociology: Theory and Method* (Englewood Cliffs, N.J.: Prentice-Hall, 1967).

Second, feedback is not equivalent to communication. The central concern of cybernetic theories and models is adaptive in the sense of aiding a system better to achieve its goals. Adaptation requires communication, but the reverse is not the case. Accordingly, we still must determine some central focus for a theory and engineering of communication between persons and groups in international relations.

A CHANGING ORIENTATION

The previous sections suggest that treating international political communication as a theoretic or engineering subject is not very helpful. This section discusses some fundamental reasons for the noted lack of coherence and proposes, in extremely preliminary form, a different orientation. That orientation consists of attempting to develop highly generalized theories and models of meaning transfer between persons and groups.

We have found that the topics pursued under the rubric of international political communication have little commonality. Any attempt to relate them in terms of concepts, theories, measures, or social purposes is tenuous at best. If one tries to relate particular topics to research pursued elsewhere in the social sciences, the resemblances and connections often are greater. When statistical analysis reveals such a situation (that is, for example, when intraclass variance exceeds interclass variance), we often conclude that our class categories are more misleading than helpful.

International relations is not itself an appropriate universe for a theory or theories, nor is it a system unit that lends itself to an engineering model or models. We have found it hard to move from a historical level to a higher level of generalization in international relations because it is difficult to find concepts that are not equally applicable in other social universes. One sign of our difficulty is the way we keep using "international" as a prefix to the concepts in which we are interested. We should move more rapidly toward treating phenomena that cross national lines as instances of phenomena that occur in several types of social units. Accordingly, alliances become coalitions; negotiations between nations become bargaining; foreign policy choices become decision-making. The problems with international relations as a systems unit for engineering have been discussed less often. Engineering models are intended to predict differences in actual end states on some particular variable(s). Accordingly, *we need models not of international relations but of structures and processes which result in different degrees of some-*

thing, such as violence, equity, arms procurement, or adaptation. These models inform engineers in their efforts to design vehicles to reach goals or performance standards. One engineers a spacecraft, but not the solar system. This is not to say that the engineer can afford to be ignorant of the environment in which the vehicle is intended to operate. However, knowledge of the environment is an input to, rather than the principal intended result of, engineering activity. Accordingly, fields of social engineering should be distinguished by dependent variable (conceptualized ahistorically) and perhaps by type of program (our vehicles), but not principally by the universe in which they are intended to operate. This argument does not contend that theory and engineering are irrelevant to international relations. Rather, it implies that it is unrewarding to develop a theory or engineering of international relations. It also suggests that the heterogeneity found in analyzing international communications may have resulted from de facto recognition of this situation. Progress may have been achieved in particular cases because international relations was not treated as a separate theoretical domain or engineering system.

We found no less variety in what was thought to be involved in communication. This reflects concern with aspects of human behavior that clearly are neither disjoint nor congruent. We may distinguish between a particular subject, theory, or model in its own right on the one hand and, on the other, subjects, theories, and models that incorporate all or part of the former. For example, theories and models of persuasion clearly involve communication, as do theories of adaptation, conflict resolution, and many others. But, we unduly complicate the pursuit of a theory or the construction of models of communication if we include all the variables from related subjects. We are constantly tempted to do so if we have no conceptualizations of communication apart from those treating it as only a piece of a larger intellectual structure. Similarly, unless we develop a conceptualization of social communication as between persons and groups, we are vulnerable to diversions of another kind as well. I have in mind conceptualizations from other areas of science (such as statistical communication theory and information theory)[53] that, be-

53   The classic presentation of communication theory of that type is Claude E. Shannon and Warren Weaver, *The Mathematical Theory of Communication* (Urbana: University of Illinois Press, 1964). For analysis of its limited relevance to social communication, see Colin Cherry, *On Human Communication: A Review, a Survey, and a Criticism* (Cambridge: Technology Press of the Massachusetts Institute of Technology, 1957).

cause of terminological similarity, may seem to deal with our problem. Although we should benefit from these developments, we should benefit selectively. We cannot be selective unless our conceptualization of social communication provides grounds on which to pick and choose.[54]

Let us define *social communication as the transfer of meaning between persons and groups.* Theories and models of social communication deal with conditions determining the degree of meaning transfer or distortion. By meaning, I refer to the semantic or signification aspect of messages—that is, to the set of associations that the symbols in a message suggest. Of course, this theoretic definition does not provide an operational definition. That is best done with reference to the historical situation being studied. Operational definitions are necessarily historical. Theoretical definitions are necessarily *not* historical. I suspect that one reason "meaning" has seemed such a difficult concept for communications analysts is that we have not made that distinction. Transfer refers to the extent that, for any set of messages, the referents associated by the receiver are similar to those associated by the originator. For any system that ostensibly transfers meaning, we seek to determine and affect the statistical probability of different degrees of similarity. Theories and models of social communication are valuable if they increase our ability to do so. Before elaborating upon the above formulation, it seems useful to explain what we are *not* doing by pursuing it.

First, we are not pursuing an analogy to communication and information theory as these originated in electrical engineering. Two major differences merit mention. The units in systems for transferring meaning are, as developed below, social and not technological; their key attributes are social and not mechanical characteristics. More fundamentally, transferring meaning is not the same as transmitting information. Information in electrical engineering theories is equivalent to the reduction of uncertainty. Transfer of meaning probably is not even linearly related to the extent of a message's uncertainty reduction. For example, John Foster Dulles was highly likely to receive the aggressive meaning of certain Soviet actions, although he was not uncertain about the Soviets having aggressive intentions.[55]

---

54 For selective interpretation and adaptation, see Wendell R. Garner, *Uncertainty and Structure as Psychological Concepts* (New York: John Wiley and Sons, 1962); and Charles A. McClelland, "Access to Berlin: The Quantity and Variety of Events, 1948–1963," in *Quantitative International Politics*, ed. Singer, pp. 159–86.

55 Holsti, "Cognitive Dynamics and Images of the Enemy."

If we distinguish transfer of meaning from information, we will become more alert to important relationships between the two phenomena. Two propositions illustrate this point:

3.1 The extent to which meaning is transferred tends to become a bimodal distribution when receiving persons and groups are very certain or very uncertain about what the meaning of messages from some source will be. Similarity will be very high or very low.

3.2 The distribution tends to be unimodal (even normal) when receivers are moderately certain in advance of the message.

Second, our rather bloodless formulation does not concern the literal referents attached by any party in the system, except as they bear on the technical problem of measuring degree of similarity. It does not predict the probability of successful transfer of any specific item of meaning, no matter how socially important. If a theory develops within the formulation, it will have no inherent implication for the behavioral consequences of different structures or processes for transfer, except as they involve the distribution of meaning. Yet these restrictions do not make knowledge of social communication any less important. To the extent that theories or models with different purposes must take into account transfer of meaning, they will benefit by borrowing from work on social communication.

The study of systems for transferring meaning can be approached parsimoniously and ahistorically. The structure of the system can be fairly simple; propositions can be stated, with derived consequences applicable to situations in international relations and other social universes. Following are some illustrative notions about the elements of transfer of meaning systems and propositions about their relations. They do not constitute an integrated theory, a set of "new" ideas, or a body of empirically confirmed relationships. I include them to indicate how we might begin to think about social communication if we would develop more rewarding theories and models.

Systems for transferring meaning are composed of:

1. Originating units (O) that can vary in number, social group membership, status position in the group, and in range, rate, and volume capacity for the dispatch of meaning;

2. Receiving units (R) that can vary in number, social group membership, status position in the group, and in range, rate, and volume capacity for receipt of meaning;

3. Channels (C) that can vary in number and in range, rate, and volume capacity for the flow of meaning;

4. Intermediate nodes (N) that can vary in number, social group

membership, status position in the group, and in range, rate, and volume capacity for the receipt and dispatch of meaning.

Systems for transferring meaning exist when at least one channel connects at least one originating with at least one receiving unit. I speak of receivers and not targets to indicate that a theory of the transfer of meaning should *not* stipulate that the receiver is the party selected by the originator before dispatching the message. The attribute variables are self-evident, with the possible exception of "range." Range capacity refers to the diversity of meaning that a component of the system can handle. Hence, the attributes enable the analyst to compare each element of the system with every other on several characteristics.

Propositions about meaning transfer should be expressed at the same level of generalization as those that follow, but with a more precise statement of the relationship. Many of the illustrative propositions are familiar to analysts of international political communication, but they have not been stated or pursued ahistorically.

4.1 Distortion increases as a function of the sum of the difference in social group membership between O and R. For example, we would expect less transfer of meaning between an American Catholic and a Vietnamese Buddhist than between an American Catholic and a Vietnamese Catholic.

4.2 Distortion increases with the differences of status between O and R in the groups of which they are both members.

Taken together, propositions 4.1 and 4.2 allow the transfer of meaning to be no more probable between levels in a group than between similar levels in two groups.

4.3 In systems with intermediate nodes, distortion increases as a function of the sum of differences in group membership between each linked pair of nodes through which a message flows. The sum includes the difference between O and N_i and between N_j and R. A similar proposition can be formulated for differences in status.

To illustrate the importance of refining the relational term, let us consider an alternative formulation in which distortion is a function of the mean difference in group membership. The engineering implications of the alternative are formidable. If it holds, then the effect of an outlying node may well get averaged out and cause little distortion.

5.1 Distortion is related to the excess of the capacity of the originator over that of any other set of elements in the transferral system. This bottleneck proposition simplifies analysis considerably and suggests the applicability of forms of network analysis to work on systems for transferring meaning.[56]

5.2 The probability of successfully transferring meaning to some receiver is a function of the ratio of receivers to originators.

5.3 The probability of successfully transferring meaning to any one receiver is a function of the ratio of originators to receivers.

The final group of propositions deals with overloads in systems for transferring meaning. To say that overload occurs is to say that distortion occurs. What determines the point at which overload occurs—that is, the point at which an additional input degrades the handling of all inputs? Overload can afflict receiving units, intermediate nodes, and channels in our system, although the propositions offered here involve only the first two of these. To simplify matters, I assume that the attributes describing the capacity of the entities are constant for any transferral period.

6.1 The probability of distortion increases with: the sum of the volume per unit time of meaning carried by input channels; *or* the mean volume per unit time carried by the input channels; *or* the maximum volume per unit time carried by any one input channel.

6.2 The probability of distortion increases with: the sum of the standard deviations of the range of meaning carried by input channels; *or* the mean standard deviation of the range carried by input channels; *or* the largest standard deviation for the range carried by any one channel.

The alternative formulations indicated by *or* statements reflect uncertainty about the elasticity and interdependence of resources for receiving messages. It also seems reasonable to suggest that there are important effects of the interaction among range, rate and volume capacities, and loads.

6.3 The probability of distortion increases multiplicatively as a function of a relationship between volume per unit time and the standard deviation of the range. Homogeneity of meaning would lessen the burden for a given volume; heterogeneity would increase it.

Difference in group membership and status position may affect the

56 For introductory discussions, see Frank Harary, Robert Z. Norman, and Dorwin Cartwright, *Structural Models: An Introduction to the Theory of Directed Graphs* (New York: John Wiley and Sons, 1965), pp. 362–91; and Howard Frank and Ivan T. Frisch, "Network Analysis," *Scientific American* 223, no. 1 (July 1970): 94–103.

closeness of a system for transferring meaning to an overloaded state even before originators can dispatch any messages. The line of reasoning here is that the amount of difference indicates membership in other systems for transferring meaning that themselves place burdens on receiving units and intermediate nodes. Accordingly, propositions 6.1 through 6.3 would apply only when differences in group membership or status position are held constant.

Finally, the distorting effects of overload may not affect equally the transfer of all items of meaning. We may want to entertain propositions that posit differentiated effects, such as:

6.4 As overload increases, distortion increasingly affects items near or at the central tendency of the range of meanings sent previously in the transfer period. Overload may be the enemy of the exceptional more than of the routine.

As we develop knowledge about meaning-transfer systems, we should be able to use it to treat appropriate phenomena in many social domains—including international relations. The treatment will not deal directly with much of international relations, but because the transfer of meaning is involved in treating international relations from many other perspectives (theoretical and social), advances in a science and engineering of social communication should have broad second-order effects.

part 1

People to People

three

Effects of International Student Exchange

Richard L. Merritt

A common form of international communication today is the flow of students from one country to another. At one level it is a mechanism for person-to-person interaction across national boundaries: the individual student has an opportunity to broaden his own horizons, to learn things that he might not be able to at home, to test his own abilities to withstand the trials and enticements of life in a foreign culture; and, by the same token, his mere presence in a foreign culture may have an impact upon those whom he encounters there. At another level the foreign student acts as a mediator between two societies, providing myriad possibilities for the two-way transferrence of the values, images, and techniques that comprise the content of cultures.

International student exchange is far from a new phenomenon. Not only does it date back to the earliest of the medieval universities but also, one suspects in the absence of reliable data, the flow nowadays is no greater proportionate to the total number of students than it was in bygone generations and centuries. What gives exchange programs an aura of importance previously unknown is a recognition (or at least the belief) that they facilitate the implementation of a nation-state's foreign policy. Governments, private foundations, and universities seeking public support for such programs argue eloquently that they will produce a mutual understanding conducive to friendship and peace. The argument is plausible. It is one that, for various reasons, we would like to believe. But is it true?

The naïve version of the argument asserts that the foreign student who comes to our shores to pursue his education will go away with a warm feeling toward the United States, Americans, and the American way of life. He will learn to appreciate our forms of democracy and our foreign policies. This appreciation in turn will help him to institute democratic reforms in his homeland and, when he moves into a decision-making position, to assume a pro-American posture in foreign affairs. There are, to be sure, some classic instances where this expectation has become a reality. By and large, however, as I shall discuss at greater length later, available data do not support a simple correlation between student exchange and mutual friendliness.[1] And it sometimes even turns out that individual students merely achieve an understanding of why they hate America and everything it stands for!

More sophisticated is the idea that the type of understanding produced by international student exchange programs yields, not necessarily a positive affection toward the host country, but more significantly a realization of the differentiated nature of its society. The visitor to America may learn that there are "middle Americans," radical lawyers, racial bigots, civil libertarians, little old ladies in white tennis shoes running about trying to do good, student conservatives, and a wide variety of other types of citizens; he may learn that national leaders and national policies enjoy varying amounts of support from different groups; and, more generally, he may learn that life in the United States is a far more complicated set of relationships than his local newspapers describe. A differentiated image may be better than a rosy picture. The student, after his return home, may be better equipped to consider intelligently American ideas and policies.

Still a third justification for student exchange programs stresses international interdependence. "Both students and professional scholars are increasing their residence abroad," Robert C. Angell has noted, "and are on the whole being drawn more closely to their counterparts in other countries."[2] This argument is akin to the functional approach to integration on the supranational level: limited areas of intense cooperation, if successful and mutually rewarding to those engaged in them, will spill over (or, more properly speaking, will create a climate of interaction encouraging their spillover) into

1   For some data, see Richard L. Merritt, "Foreign Contacts and Attitude Change: Educational Exchange," in *Interkulturelle Kommunikation zwischen Industrieländern und Entwicklungsländern,* ed. Gerhard Maletzke (Berlin: Deutsches Institut für Entwicklungspolitik, 1967), pp. 311–55, esp. pp. 315–20; the latter part of the present chapter is a revision of portions of this paper.
2   Robert C. Angell, *Peace on the March: Transnational Participation* (New York: Van Nostrand Reinhold Company, 1970), pp. 56–57.

other spheres of life. Concrete ties of mutual interest and experience among scholars and among the future leaders of a set of countries—so runs the argument—encourage them to pressure their national decision-makers to adopt accommodating policies that contribute ultimately to peace.

Widening the area of international cooperation of course is not the sole reason for developing student exchange programs. In many cases purely nationalistic or commercial considerations may be far more important: political trade-offs among governments, the search for prestige for national universities, a means for using up soft currencies blocked by foreign exchange restrictions, the recruitment or training of political agents, providing rewards for services previously rendered, recruiting grounds for private industry in the host country, training foreign technicians to use equipment manufactured by the host country (thereby seeking to create a consumer demand for such equipment after these technicians return home), political subversion of the host country, tapping the intellectual resources of exchange scholars, and even using the foreign students as a source of cheap labor. It is interesting to note that few studies of international student exchange focus upon such noncooperative motivations.

Indeed, given the length of time that governments have actively fostered exchange programs and the relatively large amount of money devoted to this purpose, it is remarkable how little information we have to evaluate their overall effectiveness in achieving the cooperative objectives. This is not to say that we have no data on foreign students. To the contrary, as this chapter makes clear, we have an abundance of such data. The point is, rather, that crucial types of information are missing and may require large-scale research efforts to gather. The remainder of this chapter summarizes part of what we already know and suggests where some of the more important gaps are.

THE IMPACT OF EDUCATION ABROAD

In considering the impact of education abroad, it is easiest to view "the foreign student" as a genre. Obviously, however, there is no such thing as "*the* foreign student." Data and conclusions about students studying abroad vary according to their individual characteristics: age, length of stay abroad, marital status, knowledge of the language of the host country, race, cultural affinity to the host country, differences between the level of living enjoyed by the student at home and that he can afford in the host country, intelligence, adaptability, motivation. Any comprehensive study of foreign students must consider the impact of each of these variables. But in this brief chapter, dealing more in aggregate than in individual statistics, I shall frequently (if reluctantly) glide over these important distinctions; where I do, the reader must note the probability of variance.

Who Goes Abroad to Study?

How can we characterize the foreign student? How does he differ from his fellows who are unable or do not want to study abroad? Is he ceteris paribus brighter (as indicated by academic achievement) than the rest? Or is it that the way to foreign study is eased by his intention to concentrate on a field that his government considers particularly important? Or is it simply a function of economics—the wealthier families being better able than the poorer to send their children abroad to school? Or, finally, is there no set of manifest characteristics that distinguish him, leaving us to assume that motivation or other personality factors are paramount?

As far as I know, no study to date has focused in any concentrated manner on this type of question. What is required is information about the distribution of such characteristics as age, personality variables, academic standing, and financial status among three samples of students: those who are not interested in studying abroad; those who would like to do so but who, for whatever reason, do not in fact study abroad; and those who *do* go abroad to pursue their formal education. Ideally, sample surveys of students would provide such information.[3] Second best, and far from ideal, would be comparison of surveys of those who do go abroad with surveys of students in general from the same country. Available information and intuition nonetheless suggest:

> 1.1. There are substantial differences between students who do and students who do not go abroad to carry on their formal studies.

That is, foreign students are not simply a random sample of their stay-at-home counterparts—and still less, of course, is either group representative of the national population of which they are a part.

---

3   Not even the massive survey in the spring of 1961 by the National Opinion Research Center (NORC) of 33,982 American college seniors contained questions on their intent to pursue graduate study abroad; responses to questions on attitudes toward the embryonic Peace Corps have not yet been published. See James A. Davis, *Great Aspirations: The Graduate School Plans of America's College Seniors* (Chicago: Aldine, 1964).

But what is likely to lead a young person to consider foreign studies? We have little direct evidence about the magnitude and direction of the differences between the small fraction who go abroad and the large majority for whom foreign study is not the right cup of tea.[4] A survey in the mid-1950s among students who had and had not participated in the Sweet Briar Junior Year Abroad program in France revealed insignificant differences in their sex, economic status, or the degree to which their parents had previously traveled in foreign lands; but, and this is a point that I shall pick up later, 54 per cent of the participants had majored in modern foreign languages and literature, whereas only nine per cent of the control sample of nonparticipants had done so.[5] We may hypothesize:

    1.2. A major determinant in the student's decision to study abroad is his academic field of concentration.

This suggests that, at least in the American university situation, foreign study programs may aim particularly at students of language and literature. More crucial, therefore, is a previous question: What is it that draws students to the study of language and literature rather than to some other field? This question of how interests develop brings us to a fairly obvious but important point:

    1.3. Personality variables are more important than social background characteristics in determining who does or does not go abroad to study.

It would be helpful to know more about both the personality characteristics of foreign students and the patterns of socialization that helped to shape these traits.

Variations in personality have important consequences for the effects of any experiences that foreign students go through. A comparison of foreign students with other nationals of comparable background who did not go abroad to study but who, because of business, personal, or other reasons, spent an equivalent time in the host country would reveal that:

    1.4. Students who go abroad to study experience an impact on

4 Complete figures on the number of Americans studying abroad doubtless do not exist. The Institute of International Education, *Open Doors 1970: Report on International Exchange* (New York: Institute of International Education, September, 1970), p. 16, reports 25,117 such students in 1968–69—or roughly one-third of 1 percent of the total number of college and university students in the United States that year.

5 C. Robert Pace, *The Junior Year in France: An Evaluation of the University of Delaware–Sweet Briar College Program* (Syracuse: Syracuse University Press, 1959), pp. 15–16.

their perspectives by the host country significantly different from that experienced by students and others who go abroad but not to study.

The proposition, if verified, would imply that the foreign student, after returning to his home country, would communicate a set of perspectives (particularly in their attitude toward the host country) that would not correspond to those enjoyed by equally experienced persons who did not happen to study formally in the host country. At this point we can say nothing about the direction of the differences— that is, for example, whether the returned student has a more positive or negative image of the country he visited than the returning nonstudents. A corollary proposition about the impact of the students themselves is:

1.5. Changes in perspectives of nationals of host country *I* after experiencing contact with students from country *J* differ from those deriving from contacts with nonstudents from country *J*.

This is merely a formal way of saying that residents of the host country who make up their minds about certain countries on the basis of experience with students from those countries may very well construct inaccurate images. Not only are these foreign students whom they meet nonrepresentative of their countrymen in general, but they are not even representative of their fellow students in the country from which they come.

Why Do they Go Abroad to Study?

Looking at their fields of concentration enables us to answer a preliminary question about why students go abroad to study. We saw earlier that about six times as many participants in the Sweet Briar Junior Year Abroad program studied languages and literature as did nonparticipants. More generally, roughly one-sixth of all American students are in the humanities, but well over one-third (37%) of those who go abroad study in this area.[6] A similar proportion (17%) of West German university students major in the humanities and linguistics at home, but 40 percent of those studying in the United States major in this area; 16 percent study medicine in German universities, but only 3 percent of those who come to America do so; 10 percent study law in Germany, 2 percent in America.[7]

6   Institute of International Education, *Open Doors 1970*, p. 16.
7   Ibid., pp. 30–31; and Statistisches Bundesamt, *Statistisches Jahrbuch für die Bundesrepublik Deutschland, 1970* (Stuttgart and Mainz: Verlag W. Kohlhammer, August, 1970), p. 78. A similar type of crude indicator might be a comparison of students who ultimately do or do not go abroad for any reason whatsoever.

The stress on the humanities is not so strong among students from less-developed countries. Of the African, Middle Eastern, Far Eastern, and Latin American students at U.S. colleges and universities in 1969–70, half (50%) were in the sciences (physical and life science, engineering, and medicine) and only 30 percent in the humanities and social sciences together (17 and 13 percent, respectively). For Europeans the figures were nearly reversed: 34 percent in the sciences and 47 percent in the humanities and social sciences.[8] Similarly, among foreign students holding German Academic Exchange Service (DAAD) scholarships in 1969, 56 percent of the Europeans but only 18 percent of the Africans and 21 percent of the Asians were in the arts, humanities, and social sciences; only 36 percent of the Europeans but 76 per cent of the Africans and 64 per cent of the Asians were in medicine or the natural or technical sciences.[9] Hence we may hypothesize:

   2.1. Students from developed, industrialized societies tend to go to other industrialized societies to study the humanities and social sciences; those from less-developed countries tend to study the natural, physical, and technical sciences in industrialized countries.

The flow of students from advanced to less-advanced societies is too slight for any accurate delineation of trends. Again, however, we would suspect that they would concentrate on the arts, languages and literature, and the social sciences.

But to say what people study once they get there is to skirt the basic question of why students go to a foreign country in the first place. What goals do they hope to attain? Doubtless numerous conscious and less clearly recognized factors play a role here. These may range from the desire to further their education by gaining new enlightenment or skills, to the wish to add to their prestige among peer groups at home, to enjoy at least temporarily a higher standard of living, to pass the time in an amusing way, or even to escape an uncomfortable situation at home. Judging from published research, discerning the true motivation for foreign study is no less difficult than trying to figure out why a young person goes to college at all.

Perhaps we can approach the question of motivation less directly. Why do students go to a particular country to study? The most obvious answer—and that probably included on the application forms of

---

8   Institute of International Education, *Open Doors 1970*, pp. 30–35; the percentages ignore those who did not respond to the IIE questionnaire (6 percent of the Europeans, 4 percent of the others).
9   Statistisches Bundesamt, *Statistisches Jahrbuch, 1970*, p. 83.

most students who would study abroad—is that they perceive the universities of that particular country as offering them the best training in their field of interest. Closer examination nonetheless reveals that achievement-oriented rationality couched in terms of professional interests or careers does not seem to play *the* major role in a student's decision to study in a given country.[10] Noncareer grounds such as simple wanderlust or accidental circumstance appear to be more important. Consider, for example, data from two concurrent surveys of African students in the United States, one set from self-administered questionnaires and the other from interviews (Table 1). In the latter set of responses the strong element of achievement-oriented rationality dropped by almost half, and the noncareer responses emerged strikingly, both visually and in the sense of statistical significance (using a difference of proportions test).

Table 1. Reasons Given by African Students for Studying in the United States

	Questionnaire	Personal interview
Education (training) best in the United States	43%	26%
Sent here (had no choice)	19	25
Interested in observing and establishing ties with America and Americans	10	19
Friend influenced decision	6	21
Other	8	8
No answer	14	1
Total	100%	100%
	N=999	N=208

SOURCE: James M. Davis, Russell G. Hanson, and Duane R. Burnor, *IIE Survey of the African Student: His Achievements and His Problems* (New York: Institute of International Education, November 1961), p. 12.

Similarly, the reasons offered by students from developing countries for attending West German universities are remarkably varied, but with achievement-oriented rationality the largest single category (Table 2). It is particularly prominent if we ignore responses of students from the single industrialized state in the list, Norway. Responses of students from five of the seven less-developed countries listed nonetheless cluster around different response categories. To

10   Similar principles of selection seem to govern the choice of university; see Ralph L. Beals and Norman D. Humphrey, *No Frontier to Learning: The Mexican Student in the United States* (Minneapolis: University of Minnesota Press, 1957), pp. 39–40. Jeanne Gullahorn and John T. Gullahorn, "American Students Abroad: Professional versus Personal Development," *Annals of the American Academy of Political and Social Science* 368 (November 1966): 43–59, find that professional and personal development tend to be alternative outcomes of study abroad for students but complementary outcomes for lecturers, researchers, and exchange teachers.

Table 2. A. Motives of Foreign Students for Studying in the German Federal Republic, by Nationality, 1960

Nationality	Reputation of German Science	German Industry Building in Homeland	Admission Easier	Limited Possibility to Study in Homeland	Examination Easier	Not Admitted in Other Countries	Received Scholarship	Did Not Like Other Countries	For Political Reasons	Study Cheapest	Purely Accidental	Influenced by Relatives or Friends
Egypt	28	—	7	6	—	—	1	6	48	10	6	13
India	37	3	12	5	2	2	14	2	6	11	3	25
Indonesia	28	—	6	4	4	2	25	—	28	8	2	9
Iran	24	—	8	5	8	—	—	—	28	37	2	37
Jordan	44	—	7	4	6	4	4	2	24	19	4	6
Ghana	14	—	14	9	9	—	45	—	35	5	5	9
Nigeria	54	—	19	—	—	—	8	4	8	4	12	15
Norway	22	—	6	66	—	—	3	—	—	12	3	3
Other*	—	—	1	1	—	—	—	—	1	1	1	2
Total	31	1	9	10	3	1	10	2	23	15	4	17

B. Adjusted Motives of Foreign Students for Studying in the German Federal Republic, by Nationality, 1960

Nationality	Reputation of German Science	(German Industry / Admission / Limited Possibility / Examination / Not Admitted)	Received Scholarship	For Political Reasons	Study Cheapest	Purely Accidental	Influenced by Relatives or Friends
Egypt	—	52	1	32	3	—	12
India	5	63	14	1	2	—	15
Indonesia	—	41	25	26	2	—	6
Iran	2	49	—	7	10	—	32
Jordan	4	59	4	24	4	—	5
Ghana	—	41	45	—	5	—	9
Nigeria	—	81	8	—	—	—	11
Norway	—	94	3	—	3	—	—
Other*	—	3	—	—	1	—	2
Total	1	58	10	14	4	—	13

* In absolute figures

SOURCE: Prodosh Aich, *Farbige unter Weißen* (Cologne and Berlin: Kiepenheuer & Witsch, 1962), pp. 51–52. See the text for the means used to adjust the data.

check the firmness of the respondents' replies, the investigator asked a subsequent series of apparently unrelated questions, using the answers to them to "correct" the initial responses. The adjusted data (also shown in Table 2) indicate that well over half the foreign students surveyed went to West German universities for reasons that were extremely practical. They went, not necessarily because West German universities offered them the best training, but rather because these universities offered the students the best opportunity to get the training required for admission to their preferred careers:

2.2. Students interested in studying abroad seek to maximize any or several of a variety of values, some of them perhaps dimly perceived.

2.3. For students from less-developed countries, the opportunity provided by the institutions of the more-developed countries to gain skills needed to enter a career are more important than the quality of those institutions.

It may be that the findings propositionalized in 2.3 cover up a spurious correlation, since neither study breaks down the responses according to the respondents' field of study. It may be, for example, that engineering students from modern countries are just as opportunity-minded as their colleagues from the less-developed countries.

If this career-oriented rationality—the search for opportunity rather than quality—is typical of foreign students from underdeveloped countries as a whole, then we are left with a series of new questions. One of these was asked in the previous section: To what extent do foreign students differ from their colleagues who never left home as far as achievement-oriented vs. career-oriented rationality is concerned? Others refer to policies for industrialized states that play host to students from developing countries. How can the universities of, let us say, West Germany or the United States best accommodate the career-oriented foreign student? Are the curricula and overall formats used for national students appropriate for this purpose? Alternatively, would it be advantageous to institute selection procedures geared more to achievement-oriented students? Although on the face of it this might seem to be desirable, such a course of action might have unwanted outcomes. For one thing, achievement-oriented students seem more likely than others to want to remain in the industrialized country permanently. In contrast to the marginal increment in trained manpower that this would mean for the developed state, increasing the "brain drain" would be a serious blow to the underdeveloped countries from which these students come. For another thing, it might very well be that career-oriented students who return to their homelands provide the developed state the best avenue to influence in the developing countries.

So far we have concentrated on the positive side of the question, Why do they go abroad to study? There is a negative side, too: Why don't they stay home to complete their studies? What is important here are the loads on and capabilities of national education systems in the developing countries. To what extent can they accommodate students in various fields of study and at different levels? Is there a relationship between the capacities of national education systems and the outward flow of students to foreign countries? These questions will be touched upon in our later discussion of structural changes in the cross-national flow of students.

What Do They Do While Studying Abroad?

This question, fairly well researched as far as foreign students in the United States are concerned,[11] does not need to be discussed at length here. Underlying much of this research has been the assumption that the foreign student's behavior influences the formation and change of his attitudes. To date, however, information on behavior has stemmed either from self-administered questionnaires or from interviews in which the foreign student is asked to reconstruct his behavioral patterns. To be sure, the points on which data of this sort

11   Among the more important references are: W. Reginald Wheeler, Henry H. King, and Alexander B. Davidson, eds., *The Foreign Student in America* (New York: Association Press, 1925); Sverre Lysgaard, "Adjustment in a Foreign Society: Norwegian Fulbright Grantees Visiting the United States," *International Social Science Bulletin* 7, no. 1 (1955): 45–51; John Useem and Ruth Hill Useem, *The Western-Educated Man in India: A Study of His Social Roles and Influence* (New York: Dryden Press, 1955); Jeanne Watson and Ronald Lippitt, *Learning across Cultures: A Study of Germans Visiting America* (Ann Arbor: University of Michigan Press, 1955); Cora Du Bois, *Foreign Students and Higher Education in the United States* (Washington: American Council on Education, 1956); Richard D. Lambert and Marvin Bressler, *Indian Students on an American Campus* (Minneapolis: University of Minnesota Press, 1956); Franklin D. Scott, *The American Experience of Swedish Students: Retrospect and Aftermath* (Minneapolis: University of Minnesota Press, 1956); Beals and Humphrey, *No Frontier to Learning*; John W. Bennett, Herbert Passin, and Robert K. McKnight, *In Search of Identity: The Japanese Overseas Scholar in America and Japan* (Minneapolis: University of Minnesota Press, 1958); George V. Coelho, *Changing Images of America: A Study of Indian Students' Perceptions* (Glencoe, Ill.: The Free Press, 1958); Richard T. Morris, *The Two-Way Mirror: National Status in Foreign Students' Adjustment* (Minneapolis: University of Minnesota Press, 1960); James M. Davis, Russell G. Hanson, and Duane R. Burnor, *IIE Survey of the African Student: His Achievements and His Problems* (New York: Institute of International Education, November, 1961); William H. Sewell and Oluf M. Davidsen, *Scandinavian Students on an American Campus* (Minneapolis: University of Minnesota Press, 1961); Claire Selltiz, June R. Christ, Joan Havel, and Stuart W. Cook, *Attitudes and Social Relations of Foreign Students in the United States* (Minneapolis: University of Minnesota Press, 1963).

have been gathered are rich: academic achievement, housing and dining arrangements, variety as well as frequency and intimacy of interaction with Americans, nationality and race of friends, proportion of time spent with Americans, discrimination and other problems encountered, participation in orientation programs, variety of roles in which they have seen Americans, leisure activities, and extent of travel in America.

It is nonetheless questionable how reliable some of these data are. We have no really good indication of the influence that personality structure has upon the responses of foreign students to questionnaires of this sort. As Selltiz and his associates have written, "some persons may tend to give expansive or optimistic or favorable answers to all questions, and thus to report that they have made close friends and that they like various aspects of American life, while others, describing not very different relationships and reactions, may not call their associates close friends and may be more restrained in their statements of liking."[12] Then, too, it seems possible that a respondent's recollection of his behavior, particularly his interaction with foreign nationals, may be colored strongly by his evaluations. The desire to reduce cognitive dissonance may produce distortion, whether conscious or unconscious.

What is needed is a means of independently checking the validity of responses about behavior. One method, suggested by Selltiz and his associates, would involve the use of sociometric techniques to get independent assessments: the roommates and friends or acquaintances of the foreign student included in the survey would be asked about such things as the foreign student's interaction with Americans.[13] Second, research on time budgets of foreign students would serve to clarify ambiguities about relationships between behavior and perspectives. What I have in mind here is either the "yesterday interview"—getting detailed information on how the respondent spent the previous day[14]—or the distribution of "diaries" that require the respondent to keep hourly records for a week of his conversation

12   Selltiz et al., *Attitudes and Social Relations*, p. 276. See also my earlier discussion of the reasons given by foreign students for wanting to study in a particular country.

13   Ibid., p. 212; for an example of the possibilities of such research, see Robert H. Schaffer and Leo R. Dowling, *Foreign Students and Their American Student Friends* (Cooperative Research Project No. 5-0806; Bloomington: Indiana University, 1966; mimeographed).

14   See Alexander Szalai, "Differential Evaluation of Time Budgets for Comparative Purposes," in *Comparing Nations: The Use of Quantitative Data in Cross-National Research*, ed. Richard L. Merritt and Stein Rokkan (New Haven and London: Yale University Press, 1966), pp. 239–58.

partners, eating and study habits, and time spent in other activities.[15] A distinct advantage of time-budget studies, in addition to the short time intervals over which the respondent must recall his activities, is that they can be administered independently of surveys asking about the perspectives of foreign students. In this way evaluative cues that might bias recollection of information would be reduced to a minimum. At some later point, then, after information about behavior has been gathered, the researcher could inquire about overall time use and perspectives. It must be added, however, that the most effective use of time-budget studies would be in the context either of time budgets of national students pursuing similar courses of study or of the foreign student's use of time in a comparable situation at home.

Another, and more obvious, research point should be noted here. To date relatively few large-scale studies have looked at students from underdeveloped countries studying in industrialized states other than the United States.[16] It is also true that little work has been done on students from industrialized states who have studied in less-developed countries. A complete analysis of cross-national contact and attitude change would have to examine the effects of both these processes.

HOW DO THEY CHANGE THEIR PERSPECTIVES WHILE STUDYING ABROAD?

When exploring how foreign students changed their moods and perspectives, many observers have seen a pattern resembling a U-shaped curve.[17] The first stage is one of mild euphoria, doubtless the result

15 American market researchers have used this technique to good effect in studying audience patterns for mass media; Klaus Liepelt and Wolfgang Hartenstein of the Institut für angewandte Sozialwissenschaft in Bad Godesberg have used it for political research.

16 Notable exceptions are K. H. Pfeffer, *Foreign Training for Pakistanis: A Study of Pakistanis Returned from Training in Germany* (Lahore: Social Sciences Research Centre, University of the Punjab, 1961); Prodosh Aich, *Farbige unter Weißen* (Cologne and Berlin: Kiepenheuer & Witsch, 1962); Jean-Pierre N'Diaye, *Enquête sur les étudiants noirs en France* (Paris: Éditions Réalités Africaines, 1962); Amar Kumar Singh, *Indian Students in Britain: A Survey of Their Adjustment and Attitudes* (Bombay: Asia Publishing House, 1963); Ingrid Eide Galtung, "The Impact of Study Abroad: A Three-by-Three-Nation Study of Cross-Cultural Contact," *Journal of Peace Research* 2, no. 3 (1965): 258–276; and Genevieve Dupeux, "Étudiants étrangers au travail," *Revue de psychologie des peuples* 23, no. 3 (September 1968): 276–87. See also Loan Eng Tjioe, *Asiaten über Deutsche: Kulturkonflikte Ostasiatischer Studentinnen in der Bundesrepublik* (Frankfurt, 1971).

17 See Lysgaard, "Adjustment in a Foreign Society"; Coelho, *Changing Images of America*; Morris, *The Two-Way Mirror*; Sewell and Davidsen, *Scandinavian Students*; Selltiz et al., *Attitudes and Social Relations*. For a summary, see Otto Kline-

both of predispositions about the host country and of the warm welcome accorded the visitor.[18] This usually gives way after a few weeks to what has come to be called "culture shock," with its attendant distaste for the host country, its nationals, and anyone having anything to do with it. At this point the student is often counting the days until he can return home honorably. If he remains in the host country long enough, however, he generally adapts to life there and gains an enhanced appreciation of the country. How long the transitional period lasts is an unresolved question; Selltiz and his associates, in summarizing relevant literature on this point, suggest that it may not end until the eighteenth month of the student's sojourn[19]—a suggestion that is fraught with implications in a world in which exchange students frequently do not remain in their host country for more than a year. We might, then, hypothesize:

3.1. Normally, the period spent by the student from country J in country I comprises three phases: (a) a high degree of warm generalized feelings or mood; (b) an increasingly and indiscriminately negative mood; and (c) a growing positive mood that increases with the length of time spent in country I.

3.2. The foreign student displaces his general mood in the form of attitudes toward host country I and its population.

There are several possible explanations for the position posited in proposition 3.1. First, a self-elimination process leads the strongly discontented to go back to their native lands; second, with a longer period to study and understand the host country, the foreign student learns to cope with its culture even if he never fully adopts it as his own; and, third, the student who remains in the host country over a long period of time may be contemplating permanent residence, and hence be adapting himself either consciously or unconsciously to its culture. If, however, the student is anticipating his return to the homeland with dread, his mood may become increasingly depressed as he reaches the end of his stay in the host country:[20]

3.3. Foreign students dreading their return to home country J ex-

---

berg, "Research in the Field of International Exchanges in Education, Science and Culture," *Social Sciences Information* 4, no. 4 (December 1965): 97–138, esp. pp. 105–7.

18   At the same time it is not difficult to think of instances where the student went into culture shock just after or even before he stepped off the boat; see Singh, *Indian Students in Britain*, pp. 52–54, for some pathetic, if perversely amusing, cases in point.

19   Selltiz et al., *Attitudes and Social Relations*, p. 245.

20   Tamar Becker, "Patterns of Attitudinal Changes among Foreign Students," *The American Journal of Sociology* 73, no. 4 (January 1968): 431–42.

perience a fourth phase in the U-curve: an increasingly depressed mood as his day of departure from host country *I*
approaches.

He may be facing unemployment or some touchy personal situation
at home, or else he may be reluctant to leave his newfound friends
and environment; what he may be anticipating at home will be discussed in a later section of this chapter.

The above discussion moved from a concern with basic perspectives and moods to reporting data about attitude change. The reason
for this is that most studies have failed to deal adequately with values
as well as with surface attitudes and beliefs.[21] This unbalanced focus
is all the more remarkable when we read in the autobiographies of
African or Asian leaders how important their own educational experience abroad was in forming and reshaping their values. The research gap is understandable. It is difficult enough to define values,
even though most social scientists agree upon their importance for
both individuals and societies, and still more difficult to design research projects that can tell us much about values and value change;
then, too, the programmatic nature of many previous studies, designed to improve the situation of the foreign student or to improve
the host country's image in his eyes, has militated against basic
research on values. Though understandable, it is nonetheless a situation that deserves rectification.

In What Ways Do Their Perspectives Change?

This is not the place for a thoroughgoing propositional analysis of
research done on attitude change among foreign students in the
United States.[22] It would nonetheless be worthwhile to summarize in
propositional form some of the major findings of these many studies.

    4.1. The greater the similarity between countries *I* and *J*, the
        greater is the likelihood that a student from country *J* study-
        ing in host country *I* will have a positive attitude toward
        country *I*'s social system.

In short, social distance and positive attitudes toward the host country
by foreign students are negatively correlated.[23] The term "social

21 See, however, Beals and Humphrey, *No Frontier to Learning,* and some of
the other studies cited in n. 9 above. Nonsystematic studies quite frequently focus
on values and value change due to culture contact.

22 The best sumary is in Selltiz et al., *Attitudes and Social Relations,* pp.
242–97.

23 Angell, *Peace on the March,* p. 47, notes that, "other things being equal,
transnational participation between members of two societies at the same level of
development is more likely to make for accommodation among nations than that

system" in this proposition is intended to include patterns on both the individual level (interpersonal and familial relationships) as well as the societal level (social structure, government).

> 4.2. The more favorable the student perceives the attitudes of nationals of host country *I* to be toward his home country *J*, the more positive will be his attitudes toward country *I*.

Foreign students at American universities evidently feel their own status to be bound inextricably to that of their native land. If Americans seem to the foreign student to look positively upon his homeland, he himself gains status in his own eyes, and he is likely to respond positively in his attitudes toward the United States. If, however, he feels that Americans are unduly harsh in evaluating his homeland, he feels his own status bruised and is likely to reciprocate by viewing the United States in a negative light. A corollary to proposition 4.2 is:[24]

> 4.3. Positive attitudes toward host country *I* vary inversely with the intensity of racial, ethnic, or other prejudice perceived by the foreign student to be directed toward him by residents of country *I*.

In parts of the United States, of course, as well as in West Germany, the United Kingdom, and other Western countries, racial discrimination against foreign students has proved to be a continuing problem. Even when there is no overt discrimination foreign students of particular nationalities tend to band together.[25]

> 4.4. The better the student from country *J* adjusts to the social system of host country *I*, the greater will be the degree of improvement in his attitudes over his predispositions toward country *I*.

The student from abroad who finds that he can fit into the American university system without overwhelming difficulties is more likely

between members of a developed and an underdeveloped society." See also Prodosh Aich, "Soziale Determinanten der politischen Einstellung der afrikanischen und asiatischen Studenten in deutschsprachigen Ländern," *Kölner Zeitschrift für Soziologie und Sozialpsychologie* 18, no. 2 (1966): 482–515, for some important modifications of this principle; and Galtung, "The Impact of Study Abroad," p. 268–71.

24   Aich, *Farbige unter Weißen*; Aich, "Soziale Determinanten"; Henri Tajfel and John L. Dawson, eds., *Disappointed Guests: Essays by African, Asian, and West Indian Students* (London and New York: Oxford University Press, 1965); Henri Tajfel, "I pregiudizi di colore in Gran Bretagna: l'esperienza degli studenti d'Africa, d'Asia e delle Indie Occidentali," *Rivista di sociologia* 4, no. 9 (January–April 1966): 53–82.

25   Ingrid Galtung, "The Impact of Study Abroad," pp. 271–72, finds that this tendency has little effect on outcomes, but Geneviève Dupeux, "Étudiants étrangers au travail," suggests that the creation of nationality groups negatively affects their own self-esteem.

than his less comfortable colleagues to revise upward his preconceived estimate of life in the United States.[26]

4.5. The greater the amount of interaction between the student from country *J* and nationals of host country *I*, the greater will be his knowledge of the social system of country *I*.

What is suggested here is that the foreign student who enjoys a large number of intimate contacts with Americans is more likely than others to have a richer and more accurate set of beliefs about the United States. How he evaluates these beliefs, however, is a different matter.[27]

4.6. The greater the amount of interaction between the student from country *J* and nationals of host country *I*, the more likely it is that he will have a positive attitude toward lower level characteristics of country *I*'s social system.

As Selltiz and his associates have written, "students who have more extensive interaction with Americans tend to see personal relations in the United States as being closer than do those who interact less with them, and to be more approving of such aspects of American life as friendship and family patterns and the characteristics of Americans as individuals."[28]

4.7. Interaction between the student from country *J* and nationals from host country *I* is unrelated to his attitudes toward higher-level characteristics of country *I*'s social system.

Again to quote Selltiz and his associates, the "extent of interaction with Americans seems to have no effect at all on beliefs or feelings about broader social patterns (e.g., the treatment of Negroes or the extent of freedom of speech) or about American foreign policy."[29]

---

26   The type of university visited by foreign students seems to affect their ability to adjust satisfactorily; see Henry A. Selby and Clyde M. Woods, "Foreign Students at a High-Pressure University," *Sociology of Education* 39, no. 2 (Spring 1966): 138–54. Ingrid Galtung, "The Impact of Study Abroad," pp. 266–68, finds that training at home in cultural pluralism and ideologies that foster cultural pluralism facilitate the foreign student's adjustment.

27   The findings on the extent to which foreign students adopt the value and belief patterns of the host country is still open to question and needs further research. See J. K. Bhatnager, "The Values and Attitudes of Some Indian and British Students," *Race* 9, no. 1 (July 1967): 27–35; Rita M. Kelly and Lorand B. Szalay, "The Impact of a Foreign Culture: South Koreans in America," chapter 4 in this volume.

28   Selltiz et al., *Attitudes and Social Relations*, p. 274.

29   Ibid., p. 275; Aich, "Soziale Determinanten," by way of contrast, finds that satisfaction with their leisure activities and social contacts correlates positively with the foreign students' attitudes toward the West. Another point of interest, not covered in this chapter, is the foreign student's impact upon the residents of the host country whom he encounters; see Schaffer and Dowling, *Foreign Students and Their American Student Friends*; Steven E. Deutsch, "The Impact of Cross-Cultural Relations on the Campus," *Sociology and Social Research* 53, no. 2 (January 1969): 137–46.

4.8. The greater the likelihood that the student from country *J*
has a close friend among the nationals of host country *I*, the
greater will be the likelihood that he has a positive attitude
toward country *I*'s social system.

This proposition seems intuitively sound, for it gets around the possibility that high rates of interaction were accompanied uniformly
by high rates of frustration on the part of the foreign student. During
his stay in America, he had made at least one close friend among his
American colleagues, and this fact alone made it more likely that he
would go home with a favorable image of America.

This brief list of propositions, however far from comprehensive,
points to several implications for policy-makers and scholars concerned with foreign contacts and attitudes. First of all, a measure of
social distance among countries would predict the direction and degree of changing attitudes of foreign students toward their host
countries. This underlines and brings into focus a point that should
be quite obvious: host countries and institutions, if they want to enhance the likelihood that foreign students will return home with
favorable images of their hosts, should make special efforts to accommodate students from countries which are high on the scale of
social distance from the host country. And, of course, this admittedly
differential treatment is most important during the student's period
of adjustment to his new life. This does not necessarily mean that
an elaborate orientation program is what is needed. Selltiz and his
associates even found that "a summer orientation program designed
to facilitate adjustment to American academic and community life
seemed to have little effect."[30] Individual attention to foreign students
seems to produce better adjustment rates.

Second, the personality of the foreign student is an important
factor. This again suggests the possibility that officials of host countries, particularly those in the industrialized West, might want to
review their selection procedures. In this regard data on the adjustment potential of career-oriented vs. achievement-oriented foreign
students would be of value in considering policy alternatives. The
importance of personality also raises the question of whether or not
the availability and quality of counseling for foreign students are adequate. (And here we may ask whether other foreign students or
professional counselors can best socialize the new foreign student
into the life of the host country.)

Above all it is clear that simple exposure to life in the industri-

30   Selltiz et al., *Attitudes and Social Relations*, p. 259.

alized state is not sufficient to give foreign students, who are also potential leaders in their emerging nations, a positive image of all aspects of the host country. Policies on student exchange that rest on this premise are likely to lead to frustrating outcomes—outcomes that in turn may jeopardize the formulation of sound student exchange policies.

What Is the Ultimate Impact of Their Study Abroad?

When the foreign student returns to his native shores, what does he carry with him? Which aspects of the foreign experience are forgotten, which put into the forefront of his thought? To what degree is there conflict between his new ways of viewing things and people and the more traditional outlooks of those to whom he is returning, and what difference does it make if there is conflict? In the process of readjustment to his native land, how important is the length of time spent abroad? What changes in perspectives take place as the years pass, leaving the foreign experiences ever further behind him?

When we try to assess the ultimate impact on perspectives of education abroad, the data with which we must work are especially spotty, as well as partially contradictory. The questions asked above have not been answered with any degree of comprehensiveness. Moreover, the findings of individual studies have not been integrated into a systematic analysis of influences on the patterns of post-return behavior. Some of the most revealing information is anecdotal in character. In fact, we would probably gain our greatest insights into this topic by content analyzing the mass of novels on the theme "return of the native" written by Indians, Nigerians, and other natives of emerging nations.[31]

One point of particular concern is the returned student's changing attitudes toward the host country. Some investigators report that such attitudes improve, as the rush of daily events pushes the petty irritations of life in the host country out of his mind and replaces them with the realities of living in his own country.[32] Another study found that returnees became increasingly critical of their former host country as they slowly readopted the attitudes held by their nontraveling peers.[33] Still others have argued that subsequent attitude

31 In this regard, however, the self-reinforcing effect of novelists reading each other's novels might reduce the scientific validity of such a content analysis. See the forthcoming paper by Jane E. Mohraz, "Western Education and the West African Writer."

32 Selltiz et al., *Attitudes and Social Relations*, pp. 279–80.

33 O. W. Riegel, "Residual Effects of Exchange of Persons," *Public Opinion Quarterly* 17, no. 3 (Fall 1953): 319–27.

change is a function of the length of time spent in the host country: a study of the development of an international point of view among Germans studying in the United States concluded that "the most productive stay . . . may be one just long enough to challenge old assumptions and suggest new ones but not long enough to permit the new ideas to jell, so that the re-thinking and re-evaluation may be carried out in the setting where the results are to be applied."[34]

The nature of the home environment seems to be particularly important for students returning to underdeveloped countries. How the returnee is received, especially by his peers, what the experience of education abroad turns out to mean in terms of his job aspirations, and what the climate of opinion is toward the host country all affect the returnee's own perspectives. Then, too, the situation of the returnee may be adversely affected if he appears to have acquired foreign outlooks and ways of doing things. "The immature," write John and Ruth Useem, "acquire foreign standards which they use as their models in India"[35]—foreign standards that jar the sensibilities not only of the envious but also of those who see positive value in keeping processes of modernization within a framework of Indian tradition. To date, however, despite the careful and insightful research of the Useems and others, no one has sought to sort out the differential impact of the environment upon returnees; and, until someone does, it is perhaps fitting that anecdotes, novels, and autobiographical sketches remain among our best sources of information.

Some students, of course, do not return home, but remain to live and work in the host country. They, together with trained scientists and other professionals who emigrate, constitute what has come to be called the "brain drain."[36]

A SPECIAL PROBLEM IN STUDENT EXCHANGE: THE "BRAIN DRAIN"

An increasing problem for underdeveloped and for some highly industrialized countries is the rate at which trained professionals, scientific manpower, and students emigrate or remain abroad after

34　The quotation is from Selltiz et al., *Attitudes and Social Relations*, p. 281, referring to Watson and Lippitt, *Learning Across Cultures*.

35　Useem and Useem, *The Western-Educated Man in India*, p. 94. See also Scott, *The American Experience of Swedish Students*, pp, 89–96; Pfeffer, *Foreign Training for Pakistanis*; and Dieter Fröhlich and Burkhard Schade, "Zur Frage der Rückanpassung von Studenten aus Entwicklungsländern," *Kölner Zeitschrift für Soziologie und Sozialpsychologie* 18, no. 2 (1966): 271–99.

36　I am indebted to Derek J. de Solla Price of Yale University for opening my eyes about and giving me data on this problem; responsibility for the interpretations is, of course, my own.

they have gone for a short visit. It has led some responsible leaders both in the United States and abroad to question the value of exchange programs, and it has led some countries to take elaborate precautions to insure that students who go abroad to study or scholars who go overseas to teach or perform research do in fact return to the home country.

Only recently have scholars begun to inquire into the nature of this "brain drain." Some of the problems on which they have focused attention are quantitative: What is the absolute and relative magnitude of the flow of scholarly migrants? What are the differential magnitudes for various fields of study? One of the more promising, if also laborious, efforts in this regard is currently being undertaken by Stevan Dedijer of the University of Lund, who is constructing a matrix showing the flow of such migrants between all pairs of countries.[37] Another interesting facet of the "brain drain" problem is the net balance of migration. In what circumstances is there likely to be a donor-recipient relationship? How great must this imbalance be before it causes structural dislocations in the countries involved? What impact does a balanced flow at either high or low levels have on the individual countries and the various professions affected?

Looked at from the point of view of the individual, the key question is one of motivation: Why does the student or scholar want to migrate to a new country or to establish permanent residence in a country in which he is a guest? The quick and easy answer to this question is "economic opportunity"—the chance to enjoy a better standard of living. If British scientists who migrated to Canada and the United States may serve as an example, however, this quick and easy response is also dead wrong. As James A. Wilson pointed out of British scientists who emigrated, only "a *minority* . . . invoked either the 'better-opportunities-for-research' type of explanation (about 33 per cent), or the 'better-standard-of-living' type of explanation (27 per cent) in support of their own case."[38] Rather, adapting one of Wilson's conclusions to propositional form, we may assert:

> 5.1. Students and scholars from industrialized country K who migrate to industrialized country I do so because of their feeling that their talents will be more extensively utilized,

37 Such a matrix, when completed, will also be useful for studies of interaction through transaction flow analysis.

38 James A. Wilson, "The Depletion of National Resources of Human Talent in the United Kingdom: A Special Aspect of Migration to North America, 1952–1964" (Ph.D. dissertation, Queen's University, Belfast, 1964), second page of unpaginated summary; see p. 391 for the data.

applied, and intensively challenged in the adopted country. Going back to an earlier distinction, it would seem that the British scientists who migrated were more achievement-oriented than career-oriented. On the basis of this it seems fair to generalize:

5.2. Achievement-oriented students and scholars are more likely than career-oriented students and scholars to migrate to industrialized country *I* that can more extensively utilize, apply, and intensively challenge their talents.

To the extent that student exchange programs encourage the flow of achievement-oriented students to foreign lands, they may also be encouraging an increased "brain drain" away from their home countries.

Economic opportunities doubtless play a greater role in the decisions of students and scholars in emerging nations who are contemplating emigration. Only rarely do such people receive incomes commensurate to what they would get in an American university; and even if they did, their standard of living would not be so high as that of their American colleagues. Economic considerations, however, are not sufficient to explain the high rates of migration. More important seems to be an absence of any real opportunity in their native lands to fill roles in which they were interested and for which they were educated.

5.3. Students and scholars from underdeveloped country *J* who migrate to industrialized country *I* do so for two primary reasons: because they feel that their talents will be more extensively utilized, applied, and intensively challenged in country *I*; and because of their desire to improve their economic status.

John and Ruth Useem point to a pattern in India that seems to be typical of many emerging nations. In their survey of students sponsored by the central and state governments, they found that 55 percent "were not employed in the work for which they were sent for training."[39] They add that, in some instances, "additional persons were being sent for training in fields where the previously trained were still unemployed or were employed outside their field of specialization." In the mid-1960s less than 5 percent of Korean university students had jobs waiting for them when they graduated, and only one-third of the 1965 graduates had found employment by early 1966.[40] Is it any wonder, then, that of almost 8,000 Korean students

39   Useem and Useem, *The Western-Educated Man in India*, p. 125; see n. 35 above.
40   Emerson Chapin, "Korean Jobs Few, Graduates Many: 1,200 of 23,000 Finishing Studies Have Found Work," *New York Times*, February 27, 1966, p. 8.

who came to the United States in the first two postwar decades, only about 800 subsequently returned to their homeland?[41]

Turning to policy aspects of the "brain drain," there are two main categories of problems. First, how can the developing country retain the students, scholars, and other scientific manpower that it needs to continue its development? Is a contractual obligation to return sufficient? If proposition 5.3 is valid, what would it cost the government of the developing country to retain potential emigrants? Should the government even try to retain those whom it cannot accommodate immediately? What seems to be lacking in many an underdeveloped country, and particularly in those that need it most, as Dedijer has pointed out, is a policy on science,[42] a policy that can use rational calculations of costs and goals to guide educational development. A second set of problems is faced by the industrialized countries: In what circumstances may a host country feel itself justified in persuading a visiting student or scholar to remain as a permanent resident? When and how should it encourage the visiting scholar to return to his native land to participate in its development? For the United States, with its newly relaxed immigration policies, problems such as these may become acute in the near future.[43]

STRUCTURAL CHANGES IN STUDENT EXCHANGE

Although the discussion to this point has concentrated on the static elements of student exchange, it is clear that its dynamic elements are equally important. Some of these are fairly obvious. The changing magnitude of the cross-national flow of students, for instance, has caught the attention of statesmen and educators alike. UNESCO

41 As reported by Gregory Henderson in an unpublished paper, "Foreign Students: Exchange or Immigration?" 2,411 were still listed in 1966 by the Institute of International Education as students, leaving a residual group of about 4,800 non-returnees. The problem remains acute for Asian students; see Man Singh Das, Donald E. Allen, and F. Gene Acuff, "Brain Drain and Students from Less Developed and Developing Countries," (unpublished paper presented at the Seventh World Congress of the International Sociological Association, Varna, Bulgaria, September 14–19, 1970).

42 Stevan Dedijer, "Underdeveloped Science in Underdeveloped Countries," *Minerva* 2, no. 1 (Autumn 1963): 61–81.

43 The United States is not alone. In the mid-1960s, for example, Paris contained nearly 3,000 Vietnamese students who refused to go home despite pressure from Saigon; and, according to the Vietnamese consul general, "There are more Vietnamese doctors in France than there are in Vietnam." Of the French position the journalist wrote: "The French want Vietnamese students here. It is a form of insurance, so that if the students ever do return, France will not have lost her influence among the educated in Vietnam" (Gloria Emerson, "Vietnamese Trained in Paris Refuse to Go Home," *New York Times*, March 13, 1966, p. 2).

statistics reveal that the estimated total of exchange students increased by 9.3 percent per year from 1950–51 to 1966–67, reaching a total of over 375,000 in the latter year. The number of foreign students in the United States alone jumped from 16,000 in 1947 to 34,000 in 1955 and to 135,000 in 1969–70. A second dramatic change has been in the national composition of foreign students. Looking again at young people who come to the United States to study, the percentage share of Africans rose from 3 percent in 1948–49 to 4 percent in 1959–60 and 6 percent ten years later, the share of Middle and Near Eastern students from 8 to 11 percent over the same period, and the share of Asians from 24 to 36 percent, whereas the share of Europeans actually dropped from 16 to 14 percent. For the world as a whole in 1960, over 62 percent of the exchange students in the United States for whom we have data came from countries in which the per capita income was less than $500 annually.[44] When we examine educational contacts between industrialized and modernizing countries, paying particular attention to the future of such patterns, we must take into account still a third transformation: structural changes in the pattern of student exchange.

With modernization comes diversification. This is true in the economic sphere, where modernizing nations are building roads and communication networks, steel mills, cement factories, and even national airlines. It is true in the personal sphere, as people learn the magic of empathy no less than the sweet and bitter tastes of urbanization, industrialization, political mobilization, and social mobility. It is true in the realm of politics, where new ideas and an enhanced sense of national importance in a multipolar world permeate the atmosphere. And, in the area of higher education, modernizing nations generally seek to create a system that can accommodate the need of the state for educated leaders and (eventually if not immediately) to provide competent nationals with channels for upward social mobility.[45]

6.1. The goal of educational policy in a modernizing state is to

44   Data in this paragraph on exchange students are from UNESCO, *Study Abroad, 1970–1972* (Paris: UNESCO, 1969), p. 17; Institute of International Education, *Education for One World* (New York: Institute of International Education, 1949), pp. 10–14; *Open Doors 1954–55* (New York: Institute of International Education, 1955), p. 6; and *Open Doors 1970*, pp. 7–8. Data on gross national product per capita are for 1963–68; see United Nations, Statistical Office, Department of Economic and Social Affairs, *Yearbook of National Account Statistics 1969* (New York: United Nations, 1970), vol. 2, pp. 3–8. A comparable figure for a decade earlier was 55 percent from countries with less than $300 per capita GNP.

45   See Frederick Harbison and Charles A. Myers, *Education, Manpower, and*

create a university system that enables the state to be self-sufficient in the production of trained manpower.

The goal of complete educational diversification is rarely, if ever, attained. Even modern industrial states differ as to the capabilities of their national education systems in various fields of study; not all of them can handle the load of potential students. But most are sufficiently developed and diversified that they can give adequate training to most of the best qualified students in most areas of study.

The question of levels of training is problematic. At this point it might be useful to differentiate between two types of study, whether at home or abroad. One type encompasses students trying to attain their major professional degrees: B.A. for the public administrator or elementary school teacher, LL.B. for the lawyer, B.S. for the civil engineer, Ph.D. for the nuclear physicist or university professor, M.D. for the doctor. The second type is interim or postgraduate study, and may include such diverse forms as a junior year abroad, evening school, a Fulbright or Rotary International scholarship for a year in a foreign university, brush-up courses, and short-term training seminars. However important this interim or postgraduate training is for admission to or advancement in some occupations or professions, it is designed to supplement rather than to supplant the major professional degree.

    6.2. Students who do not intend to migrate prefer ceteris paribus to get their major professional degree at a national university. In an industrialized state with a diversified educational system, like the United States, in which it is possible for a qualified student to obtain a major professional degree in almost any field, the need to go outside the country to study is slight.[46] Indeed, the American who nowadays goes abroad to get his major professional degree may be disadvantaged because of it when he returns home. That the same

Economic Growth: Strategies of Human Resource Development (New York: McGraw-Hill, 1964); and Stewart Fraser, ed., *Governmental Policy and International Education* (New York: John Wiley & Sons, 1965).

46 This pattern seems to obtain for students in subnational areas of the United States as well. The more the student is looking at the local area as his source of future professional rewards, the more likely it is that he will go to a university in the area. A glance at charts showing the distribution by state of residence of freshmen entering four major colleges in 1964 also suggests complementary patterns of localization: 52 percent of Yale freshmen were from the New England and Mid-Atlantic states; 64 percent at Northwestern were from North-Central states; 61 percent of Duke freshmen were from the South; and 87 percent of the first-year students at Pomona College came from the West Coast and the Rocky Mountains. I am indebted to R. Inslee Clark, Jr., formerly dean of admissions of Yale, for these data, but would absolve him of any blame for my interpretation of them.

proposition holds true for developing countries is suggested by the changing background characteristics of elites, who appear ever more likely to eschew the prospect of being identified as "Western" if this will be interpreted to mean "counternationalistic" by their reference groups.[47]

    6.3. The student who gets his major professional degree abroad when comparable opportunities are available at a national university will suffer relative deprivation from his reference groups after his return.

This may take the form of job discrimination, whether from envious or xenophobic employers or from the rational calculation of the prospective employer that a local university graduate would be more familiar with and have a greater range of contacts in the local area than would someone who has spent years abroad studying. Or it may take the form of distrust from peer groups, who may be particularly sensitive about status relationships or who, like some of the Burmese studied by Lucian Pye,[48] may view extensive contacts with the former colonial masters as tantamount to a betrayal of the new nation and its people.

Some of the clearest evidence supporting propositions 6.1–6.3 has been presented by Eri Yagi Shizume and Derek de Solla Price. They traced the educational background of three generations of Japanese physicists, from the period immediately after the opening of Japan to the West in the mid-nineteenth century until the 1930s. Price reports:

> . . . The first step was the importation of foreign science teachers from the United States and Great Britain, and the export of young Japanese students to foreign universities for advanced training. The shock wave of Western science hit the country abruptly and caused Japan's population of physicists to rise from 1 to 15 in only six years [Figure 1]. By 1880, the shock wave had begun to die away, at first rapidly as the foreigners went home, then more slowly as foreign-trained students and teachers retired and died, so that this wave finished by 1918. But in 1880, when the imported curve was at its maximum, a new wave was rising rapidly; this was the first generation of Japanese students trained by the aforementioned foreigners and their disciples.
>
> The first generation of students was a small group; there were 10

47   See, for example, Marshall R. Singer, *The Emerging Elite: A Study of Political Leadership in Ceylon* (Cambridge: M.I.T. Press, 1964); and Frederick W. Frey, *The Turkish Political Elite* (Cambridge: M.I.T. Press, 1965).

48   Lucian W. Pye, *Politics, Personality, and Nation Building: Burma's Search for Identity* (New Haven: Yale University Press, 1962), pp. 231–43 et passim.

in 1880, and their numbers never rose above 22, reaching a stable balance between training and mortality. Later, around World War I, they begin to decline noticeably in number, the last dying in 1928.

The second generation of students, those who were now being

Figure 1. Number of Trained Physicists in Japan as a Function of Date

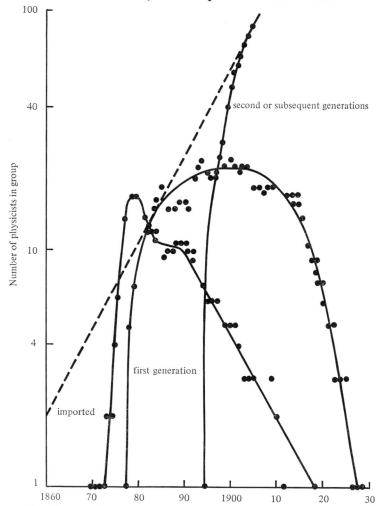

NOTES: The "imported" curve counts Europeans and those trained in Europe. The next curve gives the numbers of their students. The third curve gives the number of Japanese students trained at home by Japanese teachers—this number grows as if it started from the original shock wave and grew exponentially to the present day, but only after a waiting period of about 15 years while the first generation was prepared.
SOURCE: Derek J. de Solla Price, *Little Science, Big Science* (New York and London: Columbia University Press, 1963), p. 99, from data prepared by Eri Yagi Shizume, Yale University.

trained by Japanese in Japan, began in 1894 and rose to 60 graduates by 1900. Shortly thereafter growth settled down to the familiar exponential pattern, doubling every 10 years. This growth, continued without serious break or disturbance, led to the state of physics in Japan through the last war.[49]

The process of modernization of education includes a nationalization of the training staff. Hence an appropriate indicator of the level of modernization that a nation has attained, at least in the field of education, may be the percentage of the teaching staff who received their own training in the country from nationals—that is, in the terms of Price and Shizume, the proportion of "second generation" scholars.

What is true of education for a major professional degree, however, need not hold true for short-term training. Indeed, we may hypothesize:

> 6.4. Regardless of whether or not comparable opportunities are available at a national university, interim or postgraduate study abroad is considered in a favorable light.

It is at this point that we might expect to encounter the clichés about travel or study abroad being broadening—provided, of course, that the person who does so does not bring back "foreign ways." The norm in many professions is that a person's upward career pattern should include a stop in a foreign country for educational purposes, however loosely or strictly they may be defined. And, as suggested earlier, the sojourn ideally should be "just long enough to challenge old assumptions and suggest new ones but not long enough to permit the new ideas to jell, so that the re-thinking and re-evaluation may be carried out in the setting where the results are to be applied."[50] In brief, short-term training abroad most often carries with it considerable prestige in the home country, some career advantages, and few of the disadvantages that accrue to those who stay abroad long enough to get their major professional degrees.

If all these propositions are valid, and if we may assume that modernization brings with it a diversified, "nationalized," and self-sufficient university system, then it follows that:

> 6.5. With increasing modernization, students from modernizing country *J* going to industrialized country *I* to study are in-

49   Derek J. de Solla Price, *Little Science, Big Science* (New York: Columbia University Press, 1963), pp. 98–100. Price adds: "We have neglected the crucial point that the greatest difficulty of all was to decide the language of instruction. Not until the second generation could it possibly be in their native tongue, and then not before new vocabularies and new dictionaries had been compiled."

50   See n. 34 above.

creasingly likely to be seeking short-term training rather than major professional degrees.

The test of this proposition could be carried out in two different ways. First, we could examine the actual flows over time of students from modernizing countries, to see what changing proportion of them seeks major professional degrees. Second, using gross data analysis techniques, we could correlate for as many states as possible the level of modernization with the proportion of students abroad seeking major professional degrees. Either approach would require more data than have been put together in any single source, but a simple test using the latter approach and currently available information supports the proposition.[51] To this should be added the fact suggested in proposition 2.1 that, with increasing modernization, students from a modernizing country going to an industrialized country are increasingly likely to be studying the humanities and social sciences rather than the physical, natural, and applied sciences.

The total picture suggests that increasing modernization in the world today is changing the structure of cross-national student exchange patterns. Depending upon the degree to which current and future efforts to modernize are successful, we may expect significant changes in the type of student that will be going to the United States and other industrialized countries to pursue his studies. He will have been trained in a competent manner at a national university. His expected sojourn will be relatively brief. He is more likely than are present-day exchange students to be studying the liberal arts rather than the sciences. He is more likely than are present-day exchange students to be viewing his home country as the ultimate source of professional rewards. And yet by no means does this lead necessarily to greater parochialism. To the contrary, given other trends in the academic profession, most particularly the increased geographic mobility on an international scale of students and scholars alike, it is more probable that this exchange student of a few years hence will share a set of fairly cosmopolitan professional perspectives with his colleagues at home and abroad.

51 The test correlated levels of modernization (as indicated by gross national product per capita in the late 1950s) and the proportion of students abroad seeking major professional degrees (as indicated by the number of undergraduate vs. graduate or "special" students at American colleges and universities); the Spearman rank correlation coefficient $r_s = .23$ which, although not very strong, is significant at better than the .05 level of probability. Data were from Bruce M. Russett and Hayward R. Alker, Jr., Karl W. Deutsch, and Harold D. Lasswell, et al., *World Handbook of Political and Social Indicators* (New Haven: Yale University Press, 1964), pp. 155–57; and Institute of International Education, *Open Doors 1965*, pp. 16–21, 28–33.

If and when these changes occur, the universities of industrialized states will no longer serve merely as places to train inadequately prepared students from underdeveloped countries in the basics of their chosen professions, with the transmission of culture and skills flowing in only one direction; rather, they will act as centers of genuine interchange between the less- and the more-developed nations of the world.

four

The Impact of a Foreign Culture: South Koreans in America

Rita M. Kelly and Lorand B. Szalay

SINCE World War II the United States has very actively encouraged the educational and cultural exchange of persons between itself and other countries.[1] Beginning with the Fulbright Act of 1946 and the Smith-Mundt Act of 1948, the United States has spent millions of dollars on these exchanges. In the 1950s the appropriations for these two programs usually ranged between $20–30 million annually.[2] By 1962, although the U.S. government's financial support was still substantial, it accounted for less than 10 percent of foreign students coming to this country.[3] The increase in international communications, the sharp rise in new nations, and the desire of these peoples of old cultures to have their youth trained in a technologically advanced society accounted for most of the sharp increase in the number of foreign students.[4] While there were only 2,673 foreign students enrolled in 1904, and about 10,000 in 1946, there were close to 90,000 in 1965–66, and nearly 135,000 in 1969–70.[5]

1   The data utilized in this study were collected under a contract between American Institutes for Research (AIR) and the Department of the Army. The authors express their gratitude to the Army for the use of the data in this independent study and to AIR for its support in this endeavor. The views expressed here are those of the authors. The authors wish to express their gratitude to Won T. Moon for his extensive and valuable comments.
2   U.S. Congress, Senate Committee on Appropriations, *Appropriations for the Departments of State, Justice, the Judiciary and Related Agencies, 1958 Hearings,* before a subcommittee of the Committee on Appropriations, Senate, on H. R. 6871, 85th Cong., 1st sess., 1957.
3   George V. Coelho, "Introduction: Impacts of Studying Abroad," *The Journal of Social Issues* 18, no. 1 (January 1962): 4.
4   Ibid.
5   Kenneth W. Thompson, "American Education and the Developing Areas,"

Though the reasons for the increase in foreign students are complex, the major basis of public and private support for educational exchanges is the belief that they will improve international communication and understanding. As Westin points out, "It has become a tenet of American national policy and of social science literature on cross-cultural images that the greater the flow of visitors between nations (and the flow of information and personal contacts that are expected to follow visitor exchanges), the greater the likelihood of accurate, nonstereotyped perceptions of each other's country."[6] Additionally there is the assumption that the foreign students who come to the United States to study will not only understand American policies better than their compatriots back home, but also that they will become more like American students in their beliefs as a result of their experiences here. Flack reflects this opinion when he states that ". . . international exchange can be viewed as contributing to international social changes, to an integration of varying patterns of human cultures."[7]

Although great optimism about the mutually beneficial effects of exchanges of persons pervades the halls of academia, Congress, and diplomacy, not all evaluators find this optimism well-founded. As early as 1953 Riegel found that though Belgian exchangees tended to remain more friendly in outlook to America than their fellow compatriots, they did not appear to be more inclined to support U.S. national policies and behavior.[8] They also expressed a greater desire to emigrate from Belgium, usually to the United States, than other Belgians.[9] Cormack notes that this problem of balancing the Americanization of foreign students with the need for stability in their self- and national identity still remains in the 1970s.[10]

Recent assessments by nonwhites of being a foreign student in the

Annals of the American Academy of Political and Social Science 366 (July 1966): 19. See also William Benton, "Education as an Instrument of American Foreign Policy," ibid., p. 35; Institute of International Education, *Open Doors*, 1969–70 ed. (Washington: Institute of International Education, 1969–70).

6   Alan F. Westin, in editorial comments to excerpt from Bryant Wedge's "Why Visitors Don't Always 'See' America," in *Views of America*, ed. Alan F. Westin et al. (New York: Harcourt, Brace, and World, 1966), p. 327.

7   Michael J. Flack, "An Attempt at Perspective," *International, Educational, and Cultural Exchange* 5, no. 2 (Fall 1969): 3.

8   O. W. Riegel, "Residual Effects of Exchange of Persons," *Public Opinion Quarterly* 17, no. 3 (Fall 1953): 319–27.

9   Ibid., p. 322.

10   Margaret L. Cormack, "International Educational Exchange: Visas to What?" *International, Educational and Cultural Exchange* 5, no. 2 (Fall 1969): 56–57.

West also challenge optimistic assumptions about student exchanges. In Great Britain an essay contest requesting views of university students from Africa, Asia, and the West Indies resulted in seventy-three commentaries. Generally, the darker the color of the student, the less complimentary he was about Great Britain (and the United States) and his experience with his host country.[11] Selltiz and Cook also challenged the assumption that the exchange experience inclines individuals to have more favorable attitudes of their host country.[12] Other studies, however, have found that foreign students became more positive toward the United States while simultaneously desiring to return to their homeland.[13]

The assumptions, policies, and problems associated with the exchange of persons obviously raise important questions needing investigation. As Thompson notes, "The fact is that the thorough-going studies and fundamental inquiries on which to base conclusions [regarding a proper appraisal of the exchange programs] are lacking. There is need for 'a Conant study' of international student exchange. We have impressions, but little hard data on the effects of mass student exchange programs."[14]

ASSOCIATIVE GROUP ANALYSIS OF FOREIGN STUDENT VIEWS

The purpose of this chapter is to assess empirically the impact which being a student in an alien culture has on attitudes and beliefs. Using the Associative Group Analysis (AGA) method, it explores whether selected concepts about social systems and interaction held by South Koreans who have studied for two and one-half years in the United States show greater similarity to American students than to a comparable group of students who never left South Korea. The focus is twofold. First, how do the meanings of visiting students relate to those of comparable students in the United States and in Korea—that is, how similar or different are these groups in respect to their interpretation and evaluation of selected concepts? Second,

11   Henri Tajfel and John L. Dawson, eds., *Disappointed Guests: Essays by African, Asian, and West Indian Students* (New York: Oxford University Press, under the auspices of the Institute of Race Relations, London, 1965), pp. vii, 158.
12   Claire Selltiz and Stuart W. Cook, "Factors Influencing Attitudes of Foreign Students toward the Host Country," *Journal of Social Issues* 18, no. 1 (January 1962): 7–24.
13   See, for example, Joseph Veroff, "African Students in the United States," *Journal of Social Issues* 19, no. 3 (July 1963): 48–60.
14   Thompson, "American Education and the Developing Areas," p. 19.

what are those specific components of meaning on which the foreign environment has had an effect?

The subjects for the analysis comprise three different student groups of fifty people each.[15] The American student group is a random sample of recruits reporting to four major U.S. Army basic training centers. They represent all geographical areas in the United States, have had at least one year of college, and are all males, aged eighteen to twenty-three. The Korean group that never left Korea is a random sample of students who had just reported to the Nonsan central military recruit training center in South Korea. All again have had at least one year of college and are males, aged eighteen to twenty-three. The South Korean group who had spent on the average two and one-half years in the United States consisted of twenty-five males and twenty-five females, aged eighteen to thirty, who were studying between 1964 and 1966 at various universities in the Washington, D. C., area. The latter will be called the *visitors*, the former *South Korean students* or simply the students in Korea. The Americans will be called either the Americans or the U.S. group. It must be noted that variations between the two Korean groups in interpretations and evaluations of concepts based on sex or sophistication in educational training cannot be empirically accounted for with these subjects.[16]

Nine concepts are used to assess whether or not the experience of studying in the United States tends to change the interpretations and evaluations of South Koreans. The first four are systemic concepts: COMMUNISM, SOCIALISM, CAPITALISM, and DEMOCRACY; the next

15   The data stem from studies developing and testing the Associative Group Analysis method as an instrument for analyzing cultures and measuring meanings, not with the specific intent of evaluating the impact of the U.S. environment on foreign students. The data on Korean students studying in the United States come from a 1966 study measuring intercultural differences; the data on the other students were collected in 1968 in the context of measuring intrasocietal, interstrata differences. Therefore, perfectly matched comparability among the groups discussed does not exist.

16   For more information on these and other variables as well as assessments of their possible impact on foreign students, see the following sources: R. K. Goldsen, E. A. Suchman, and R. M. Williams, "Factors Associated with the Development of Cross-Cultural Social Interaction," *Journal of Social Issues* 12, no. 2 (April 1956): 26–32; R. T. Morris, "National Status and Attitudes of Foreign Students," ibid., pp. 20–25; C. Selltiz, A. L. Hopsen, and S. W. Cook, "The Effects of Situational Factors on Personal Interaction between Foreign Students and Americans," ibid., pp. 33–44; Steven E. Deutsch and George Y. M. Won, "Some Factors in the Adjustment of Foreign Nationals in the United States," *Journal of Social Issues* 19, no. 3 (July 1963): 115–22. Additional articles of interest can be found in the complete issue of *Journal of Social Issues* 18, no. 1 (January 1962).

four deal with social interactions: SOCIAL, EQUALITY, COOPERATION, and PROGRESS. In addition, we examine the concept UNITED STATES. These words were given to each of the three student groups as stimuli for free verbal associations.

Associative Group Analysis (AGA) examines psychological meanings of concepts as revealed by the responses given to each of the selected stimulus words during one minute of free verbal association.[17] The meanings studied are not those found in dictionaries, representing products of linguistic convention or categories defined by logic. They are, rather, subjective, personal reactions determined by a person's present state and past experiences. The neurophysiology of this meaning reaction is largely unknown, but in terms of the presently accepted theories,[18] this psychological meaning reaction is a composite including both denotative and connotative or, by a slightly different terminology, both cognitive and affective meaning components. The psychological meaning of "drug," for example, is a personal reaction that reflects what a particular person thinks as well as how he feels about this concept and issues relating to it. While no dictionaries show the full meanings that Christian Scientists, drug addicts, and pharmacists have for "drug," recognition of their different meanings, and of their different cognitive organizations, is

17   The AGA method was developed by Lorand B. Szalay in order to provide a methodology for analyzing difficulties in intercultural communication. For more detailed information on the method, see Lorand B. Szalay and Jack E. Brent, "The Analysis of Cultural Meanings through Free Verbal Associations," *Journal of Social Psychology* 72, pt. 2 (August 1967): 161–87; Lorand B. Szalay, "Use of Word Associations in Foreign Area Study," in American Psychological Association, *Proceedings of the Seventy-fifth Annual Convention* (Reading, Mass.: Addison-Wesley, 1967), pp. 373–74; Lorand B. Szalay and Charles Windle, "Relative Influence of Linguistic versus Cultural Factors on Free Verbal Associations," *Psychological Reports* 22, no. 1 (February 1968): 43–51; Lorand B. Szalay, Charles Windle, and Dale A. Lysne, "Attitude Measurement by Free Verbal Associations," *Journal of Social Psychology* 82, pt. 1 (October 1970): 43–55.

Experimental psychology, especially in the classical learning experiments, has focused heavily in the past on the use of free verbal associations as mechanical connections established by the common occurrence, contiguity of objects or events. Recently increasing attention is paid by psychologists to the fact that verbal associations reflect people's subjective meanings and personal evaluations: James Deese, "On the Structure of Associative Meaning," *Psychological Review* 69, no. 3 (May 1962): 161–75; Julius Laffal and Sheldon Feldman, "The Structure of Single Word and Continuous Word Associations," *Journal of Verbal Learning and Verbal Behavior* 1, no. 1 (February 1962): 54–61; Howard R. Rollio, *The Structure Basis of Word Association Behavior* (The Hague: Mouton, 1966). Associative Group Analysis represents an extension and application of the theory of the meaning mediated association process.

18   Charles E. Osgood, "Meaning Cannot Be r_m?" *Journal of Verbal Learning and Verbal Behavior* 5, no. 4 (August 1966): 402–7.

needed to understand their different behavior. The AGA procedures permit inferences about those psychological meanings based on free verbal associations produced by selected samples.

Response lists—consisting of scores for the responses weighted according to their rank order of emission—constitute the primary data used for the present analysis. The three measures used in the present analysis are the following.

1. *Correlational measures of intergroup associative affinity.* To measure in broad terms the extent of the agreement in the meaning of concepts, the response lists of the three separate groups were correlated using the Pearsonian *r* coefficient of correlation. The higher the positive correlation, the greater the agreement between the groups and the more likely it is that communication difficulties will be small. Conversely, the lower the correlation or the more negative the correlation, the greater the disagreement and the greater the probability of communication problems.

2. *Dominance scores.* This measure shows the importance of a particular concept as a theme within a particular group or culture. Do the visiting Korean students assign the same relative importance to the selected concepts as do the students back in Korea, or have they become more like American students in the amount of emphasis they put on these concepts? The number of responses expressed in the weighted shared response score (the "dominance" score) given by a group of persons for a particular stimulus word is a well-known measure of relative "meaningfulness."[19] Greater meaningfulness implies that a word is more frequently used and that it has greater subjective importance. A previous study indicates that this total score varies greatly across different words and cultures, providing a sensitive measure of the subjective importance of concepts studied.[20]

3. *A content analysis of each particular group's response list.* To determine in which specific aspects the particular concepts differed for the visiting Korean students compared to the South Koreans at home and the American students, each concept's meanings were analyzed in terms of its main components. A panel of judges representing both cultures placed the response words to each stimulus into content categories. Among six judges the average interjudge reliability across categories of (the Pearsonian) *r* was .7. This procedure permits meaningful inferences and generalizations to be made about

19   C. E. Noble, "An Analysis of Meaning," *Psychological Review* 54, no. 6 (November 1952): 421–30.

20   Lorand B. Szalay and Jack E. Brent, *Cultural Meanings and Values: A Method of Empirical Assessment* (Washington: Special Operations Research Office, American University, 1965).

whether or not, where, and how the meaning components overlap as it reveals the relative size, content, and priority of the various meaning components for each concept analyzed.

CONCEPTS ABOUT SOCIAL SYSTEMS

As White and Wedge note, the concepts of DEMOCRACY, CAPITAL-ISM, SOCIALISM, and COMMUNISM are particularly prone to different interpretations by people of different social backgrounds.[21] Since these concepts symbolize prevalent choices of socioeconomic politi-cal systems in the world today and are related to East-West conflicts, it is pertinent to inquire whether being a foreign student in the United States tends to alter the interpretation and evaluation of these concepts.

The visiting Koreans tend to have slightly higher positive cor-relations with the American students than do the Koreans at home on three of the four concepts (Table 1). Only on DEMOCRACY do the Korean students show greater agreement with the American students than the visiting Koreans do.

Table 1. Correlational Measures of Intergroup Associative Affinity for the Four System Concepts

Concepts	Korean visiting students and U.S. students		Korean students and U.S. students		Korean visiting students and Korean students	
	(N)	r	(N)	r	(N)	r
Communism	(88)	.528	(84)	.470	(91)	.467
Socialism	(57)	.424	(62)	.366	(50)	.754
Capitalism	(61)	.619	(71)	.469	(64)	.648
Democracy	(67)	.580	(58)	.607	(61)	.842
(Average)		(.538)		(.478)		(.678)

N = number of response pairs
r = Pearson coefficient of correlation; all coefficients in this table are statisti-cally significant at the .01 level, as indicated by a *t*-test.

A comparison of the relative size of the correlations within each of the three groupings indicates that the visitors and the American students agree least on the meaning of SOCIALISM and most on the meaning of CAPITALISM. The Koreans at home also agree least on SOCIALISM, but agree most with the U.S. students on the meaning of DEMOCRACY. Looking at the two Korean student groups themselves it

21 Bryant M. Wedge, *Visitors to the United States and How They See Us* (Princeton, N.J.: Van Nostrand, 1965), pp. xi, 168; Ralph K. White, " 'Socialism' and 'Capitalism': An International Misunderstanding," *Foreign Affairs* 44, no. 2 (January 1966): 216–28.

is evident that they agree most on the meaning of DEMOCRACY and least on the meaning of COMMUNISM. On the basis of these correlations it appears that the visiting students became more like the American students in their interpretation and evaluation of COMMUNISM, CAPITALISM, and to a lesser extent SOCIALISM. They became less like the Americans in their reaction to the concept DEMOCRACY.

Table 2. Dominance Scores of the Four System Concepts

Concepts	U.S. students	Korean students	Korean visiting students
Communism	964	1,011	915
Socialism	763	563	485
Democracy	916	820	949
Capitalism	886	898	780

The dominance scores (Table 2) provide further evidence of differences among the three groups. The American students place the greatest subjective importance on COMMUNISM and the least on SOCIALISM, as do the Koreans at home. The visiting Koreans, however, show greatest concern for DEMOCRACY, then COMMUNISM, CAPITALISM, and SOCIALISM. These dominance scores indicate that the Koreans' concern for DEMOCRACY may have become greater and their concern for COMMUNISM less salient during their visit to the United States. It is evident from the very low dominance scores for SOCIALISM that this concept is of relatively small concern for all three of the groups.

Though the above broad measures suggest changes in the interpretation of these concepts on the part of the visiting students, it must be noted that the agreement between both of the Korean groups and the American students on all of the concepts is relatively high. It thus seems that a substantial amount of agreement among South Korean and American students exists on these four concepts, regardless of exposure to the American environment as a foreign student. Such a finding is reasonable given the long time period the two countries have been allies.

The specific aspects in which the three groups agree or disagree in their interpretation and evaluation of these system concepts appear in a content analysis of the main components of meaning.

Communism

The following are ten meaning components for COMMUNISM: (1) Democracy, Freedom; (2) No freedom, Oppression; (3) General negative feelings; (4) Fight, Kill, Eliminate; (5) Korean War; (6) Nations; (7) Leaders; (8) Government, Dictatorship; (9) Ideology; and (10) Miscellaneous. The category "Nations" received the greatest emphasis from all three groups. The nations referred to by the American group are the Soviet Union, China, and Vietnam. Both the Korean groups show concern for Communist nations near South Korea: the USSR, North Korea, China, and the Vietcong. That North Korea and the USSR are mentioned as prime examples of Communist nations is reasonable in terms of the history of Korea. It is nonetheless interesting that these responses outweigh emphasis on Korea's neighbor, China.

The only other category where all three groups had similar large responses was "Leaders" (22 percent for the Americans, 15 percent for the students in Korea, and 18 percent for the visitors). The Americans gave Karl Marx their greatest attention, followed by Lenin, Stalin, and Khrushchev. The Koreans also displayed some historical associations (Marx, Lenin, Stalin) but devoted even greater attention to contemporary political leaders like Mao Tse-tung and the North Korean leader, Kim Il-song.

In addition to the "Nations" and "Leaders" categories, the Korean visitors have roughly the same response scores as their fellow students back home in the "Democracy, Freedom" and "Korean War" categories. These components arouse little interest among American students. The four categories in which substantial changes are found between the visiting Korean students and their compatriots at home lie in the more abstract, ideological realm. For example, the meaning component "Ideology" is almost twice the size for visiting students as it is for the Korean group at home (10 and 5 percent, respectively). The size of the component for the American group, however, is much higher still (24 percent).

The visitors also seem to have reduced their negative attitude toward COMMUNISM after being in the United States for a period of time. A substantial portion (39%) of responses by the Korean group at home stressed three negative categories: "No freedom," "Negative feelings in general," and "Fight, Kill, Eliminate." For the visitors, however, only 22 percent of their references were in these categories; only 12 percent of the American responses were. It thus seems that the South Korean visiting students became closer to the Americans in that the theoretical-ideological aspects of COMMUNISM came to assume more importance than earlier and the more concrete negative features of COMMUNISM, and the desire to eliminate it, became less important. That they still react more negatively than the

Americans toward this concept, however, is illustrated by the "Government, Dictatorship" category. Whereas over four-fifths of the American score here is due to the *descriptive* responses "government," "politics," "political," "party," and "state," over four-fifths of the Korean visitors' score comprises the *evaluative* words "dictatorship" and "imperialism."[22]

Socialism

As was mentioned earlier, of the four systemic concepts examined, SOCIALISM is the least salient within the belief systems of all three groups. The two Korean groups show some ambiguity and contradictions in their interpretation and evaluation of SOCIALISM; the Americans are more consistent and negative in their responses.

The analyses produced thirteen main meaning components here: (1) Democracy, Equality; (2) Negative feelings; (3) Communism; (4) Capitalism; (5) Economics; (6) Communist and non-Communist nations; (7) Ideologues, Communist leaders; (8) Government, Politics, Nation; (9) Programs, Issues; (10) Ideas, Beliefs; (11) Interpersonal relations; (12) People, Way of life; and (13) Miscellaneous. There are four response categories on which the Americans have especially high scores: "Government, Politics, Nation" (16%), "Communist and non-Communist nations" (23%), "Communism" (13%), and "Programs, Issues" (12%). The first category's items indicate a strong inclination to perceive SOCIALISM as a political system characterized by centralized political power and governmental control. The category "Communism" suggests a relatively close identification of SOCIALISM with Communism, but the specific responses in the categories "Ideologues, Communist leaders" (Marx, Lenin, Norman Thomas) and "Communist and non-Communist nations" suggest a differentiation between these two concepts of social systems. The positive evaluations are too few to form a separate category; hence, they are in the "Miscellaneous" category.

The ambiguous reaction of the Koreans to SOCIALISM appears to stem from their simultaneous association of the concept with democracy, equality, and social progress on the one hand and with Com-

22   This high association of *dictatorship* to COMMUNISM is not surprising, given that the South Korean government often uses these two words synonymously. In April, 1968, for example, such was the case in a nationwide public opinion poll. See Republic of Korea, Kongbobu (Ministry of Public Information), *Pan'gong Sich'aek-o Taehan Chon'guk Kukmin Yoron Chosa Kyolgwa* (A Nationwide Public Poll with Regard to Anti-Communist Measures) (Seoul: Ministry of Public Information, 1968), esp. p. 234.

munism on the other. Both the Korean and the visiting students have a substantially greater proportion of their responses in the "Democracy, Equality" category (15 and 19 percent, respectively) than do the American students (only 3 percent). On the other side of the coin the two Korean groups associate SOCIALISM with "Communism" even more than the American students do. Whereas 22 percent of the visiting students' responses and 18 percent of the Korean responses are in the "Communism" category, only 13 percent of the American responses are.

South Koreans seem to reconcile these positive and negative associations with SOCIALISM by maintaining the denotations of the concept at rather vague and abstract levels. To illustrate, although they associate SOCIALISM with Communism very strongly in general terms, the more specific association with known socialist nations is much lower. Whereas 23 percent of the American responses refer to specific nations, only 14 and 11 percent, respectively, of the visiting and Korean students' responses do. This less concrete aspect of the Koreans' associations is further evidenced by the fact that the two Korean groups associate SOCIALISM more often with "Ideas and Beliefs" than do the American students.

Of the four categories discussed so far (roughly two-thirds of the total visiting group's response scores), the visiting students score proportionately higher than their compatriots in Korea. Apparently the abstract and theoretical features of SOCIALISM have assumed greater importance as a result of the American experience. The fact that none of the responses of the visitors are in the "Negative feelings," "Programs, Issues," and "Interpersonal relations" categories provides further support for this suggestion.

Capitalism

The main meaning components for CAPITALISM number twelve: (1) Free enterprise, Profit, Competition; (2) Democracy and freedom; (3) The Economy, Business; (4) Money; (5) Government, Dictatorship; (6) Own and other nations; (7) Nation, Country, Society; (8) Communism and socialism; (9) Rich and poor; (10) Good; (11) Bad; and (12) Miscellaneous. In only two categories does it seem that the visitors become more like the Americans in their responses. The Korean students at home associate CAPITALISM with "Democracy and freedom" about twice as often (10%) as either the visiting (4%) or the American students (6%). The visiting students are also more like American students in that they counter-pose CAPITALISM to "Communism and socialism" as frequently as the latter do (13 and 12 percent, respectively). The Korean students in Korea, however, have only 6 percent of their responses in this category. Other than these instances, the Korean perception of CAPTIALISM appears unaltered by experience in the United States.

A large part of the meaning of CAPITALISM for both Korean groups is negative. About 14 percent of the responses of both groups as-sociate sharp differences between the rich and poor with CAPITALISM; whereas 3 percent of both Korean groups associate "bad" things with this concept, no American students do. Conversely, although 4 per-cent of the U.S. response evaluates CAPITALISM directly as "good," no visiting Korean student does, and only about 1 percent of the Korean students at home hold this view. Obviously, CAPITALISM has less positive connotations for the Korean than the American students.

The different cultural evaluations of CAPITALISM undoubtedly re-flect the different empirical referents of the concept. The Koreans tend to avoid responses describing or defining the term. Rather, they denote the concept by example. Both the visiting and the Korean students associate CAPITALISM with "Own and other nations" more than the American students do (21, 18, and 12 percent, respectively). The Korean students associate CAPITALISM with Korea; the visiting students do not, but show an increased association with the United States. The U.S. group refers exclusively to their own country and to the West (12%). Thirty percent of the American students' re-sponses are in the descriptive "Free enterprise, Profit, Competition" category. Less than 9 percent of either of the Korean groups' re-sponses fall here. Moreover, the specific responses of the Koreans do not mention free enterprise, but rather profit and competition.

Democracy

The eleven meaning components for DEMOCRACY reveal substantial cultural variations in interpretation. These were: (1) Freedom and Liberty; (2) Rights, Ideals, Equality; (3) Own country and specific nations; (4) Nations: Alliance, Cooperation; (5) Elections, Elected office; (6) Doctrines, -Isms; (7) People: Participation, Cooper-ation; (8) Constitution, Republic; (9) Belief, Faith; (10) Good; and (11) Miscellaneous. The most important component of mean-ing for the visiting students is the "Doctrine,-Isms" category (19%). This component is not quite so large for the Koreans at home (13%) and is very low (2%) for the American group. On the basis of these data, we conjecture that student experience in the United States raised the saliency of the ideological aspects of DEMOCRACY for the visiting Korean students.

All three groups associate DEMOCRACY substantially with "Freedom and Liberty" (U.S., 22 percent; visiting Koreans, 16 percent; and the Koreans at home, 17 percent). Both the Korean groups (18 percent for each) seem to feel that "Rights and Ideals"—especially equality and peace—represent an essential core of DEMOCRACY. The American group, however, does not link these ideas to DEMOCRACY as much (7%). Both Korean groups stress equality much more than does the U.S. group. Given the fact that "democratic theory stresses the doctrine of the equality of all men,"[23] this relatively low attention to equality by the Americans is interesting.

The U.S. group has close to half of its responses on DEMOCRACY in two categories—references to the United States, that is, the "Own country and specific nations" category (20%) and in the "Elections, Elected office" category (28%). It is in these two categories that a substantial discrepancy between the visitors and the students who never left Korea is observable. The visiting students have a much lower proportion of their responses in the "Own country and specific nations" category than do their colleagues in Korea (14 and 24 percent, respectively). The visiting Koreans refer less to their own country, but no more to the United States as nations exemplifying democracy. They nonetheless have a substantially larger proportion of their responses in the "Elections" category (11%) compared to the students at home in Korea (4%). The experience of being a student in the United States thus seemed to alter to some extent the views of the visiting students: their own country, Korea, became a less characteristic representative of democracy, while the technical, procedural aspects of the democratic process and the doctrinal aspects of the democratic system were enhanced in importance.

CONCEPTS OF SOCIAL INTERACTION

Prior studies of the acculturation of foreign students[24] suggest that visiting students might be less like Americans in areas referring to close social interaction than in areas of international concern. Re-

---

23   Robert K. Carr, Marver H. Bernstein, and Walter F. Murphy, *American Democracy*, 5th ed. (New York: Holt, Rinehart, and Winston, 1968), p. 25.
24   John T. Gullahorn and Jeanne E. Gullahorn, "An Extension of the U-Curve Hypothesis," *Journal of Social Issues* 19, no. 3 (July 1963): 33–47; see also the references in n. 16 above.

gardless of political views, each visiting student must adjust personally to the American environment. Gullahorn and Gullahorn point out:

> Essentially, the acculturation process may be interpreted as a cycle of adult socialization occuring under conditions where previous socialization offers varying degrees of facilitation and interference in the new learning context. As a consequence of previous socialization sojourners learn value orientations which provide a framework for evaluating behavior in role interactions. The result is that when two members of a particular social system are interacting each can anticipate the other's responses with sufficient accuracy so that his behavior is likely to elicit the results he desires. This complementarity of role expectations generally becomes disturbed when an individual moves from one social system to another where differing value orientations and normative expectations are characteristic.[25]

The complementarity of role expectations not only becomes disturbed, but the difficulties in accommodating to the new role expectations are also numerous. Schild writes,

> The learning is complicated to the extent that to someone in the position of the stranger the norms and role performances are less "visible" than they are to members of the host society. Thus, he is not always aware of the range of permissible deviations from the declared official norms of the society and he may try to live up to the strict letter of these norms—he overconforms.[26]

South Koreans seem to encounter such difficulties when they go to the United States. There is very little agreement between either of the Korean student groups and the Americans on any of the four social interaction concepts tested (Table 3). In only one instance does a statistically significant correlation between a Korean group and the American group occur—and that is a negative correlation on the word SOCIAL. Both the visitors and the Koreans at home agree most with Americans, but not at a statistically significant level, on the meaning of COOPERATION.

There are nonetheless indications that the visiting Koreans have altered their perceptions in some areas. For example, the differences in the numerical values of the correlations point to the possibility that the visiting Koreans did become somewhat less distant from the American students during their stay. Generally speaking, their nega-

25   Ibid., p. 34.
26   Erling O. Schild, "The Foreign Student, as Stranger, Learning the Norms of the Host Culture," *Journal of Social Issues* 18, no. 1 (January 1962): 41.

tive correlations are lower and the one positive correlation (in CO-OPERATION) is slightly higher than the Koreans at home. These correlational measures of intergroup associative affinity still in no

Table 3. Correlational Measures of Intergroup Associative Affinity for Social Interaction Concepts

Concepts	Korean visiting students and U.S. students (N)		Korean students and U.S. students (N)		Korean visiting students and Korean students (N)	
	(N)	r	(N)	r	(N)	r
Social	(85)	−.203	(94)	−.360*	(73)	.110
Equality	(67)	−.089	(74)	−.058	(63)	.483*
Cooperation	(65)	.142	(80)	.129	(66)	.515*
Progress	(73)	−.035	(73)	−.135	(77)	.805*
(Average)		(−.046)		(−.106)		(.478)

N = number of response pairs
r = the Pearson coefficient of correlation
* = statistically significant at the .01 level, as indicated by a *t*-test

way indicate that Korean foreign students in the United States became similar in any noteworthy way to the Americans in their interpretation of these social interaction concepts.

The dominance measures for these four concepts (Table 4) show a marked variation among the three groups. For the American students SOCIAL is of greatest subjective importance, with PROGRESS being the least. For the Korean students in Korea COOPERATION is

Table 4. Dominance Scores for the Social Interaction Concepts

Concepts	U.S. students	Korean students	Korean visiting students
Social	837	660	551
Equality	777	780	634
Cooperation	804	803	545
Progress	746	783	849

the concept receiving the greatest emphasis and SOCIAL receives the least. The Korean visitors in the United States also place the least stress on SOCIAL, but place the greatest subjective importance upon PROGRESS. Although these dominance scores do not indicate that the visiting students became like the American students, they do suggest that the concept PROGRESS assumed greater saliency among the Korean foreign students as a result of their stay in the United States.

Social

The concept SOCIAL produced eleven meaning components: (1) Morality, Justice; (2) Position, Status, Class; (3) People, Social beings; (4) Group, Community, Nation; (5) Friendly, Sociable; (6) Security, Welfare, Economics; (7) Problems, Phenomena; (8) Studies, Science, Education; (9) Political, -Isms; (10) Party, Dance; and (11) Miscellaneous. The Americans give one-third (32%) of their responses in the "Party, Dance" category. The visitors have only 2 percent of their responses here; the students in Korea have none. Obviously, the meaning of SOCIAL does not include parties and dancing in the Korean culture.

The Koreans associate the word SOCIAL rather with political and broad public concerns. This tendency is very evident in the "Morality, Justice" category. Here the visitors give 21 percent of their responses, the students in Korea 23 percent, while the Americans have only 5 percent. Similarly, in the "Political, -Isms" category the visitors have 12 percent of their responses, the students in Korea 4 percent, and the Americans only 1 percent. Manifestations of the same tendency are also seen in the "Problems, Phenomena" and the "Position, Status, Class" categories.

Although the sharp variation of interpretation of SOCIAL certainly stems in part from the traditional prohibition of free association between the sexes in Korea, a substantial portion also stems from the difference in defined and expected roles of students in the two countries. As Shils notes: "In advanced countries, students are not regarded as ex officio intellectuals; in underdeveloped countries, they are."[27] As Kim states:

> One of the most conspicuous characteristics of today's Korean college student can be said to be his deep concern for current political problems. He is confident that he is the elite of his country and that he is not to concern himself with his studies alone delegating political and social matters to the older generation only.[28]

Kim further sees the Korean students as especially sensitive about matters of morality and social justice,[29] as is reflected in our data here.

The great stress placed by the two Korean groups on "Position, Status, Class" (17 percent for the visitors, 23 percent for the Koreans) compared to the Americans (8%) reveals further the dif-

27   Edward Shils, "The Intellectuals in the Political Development of the New States," in *Political Change in Underdeveloped Countries: Nationalism and Communism*, ed. John H. Kautsky (New York: John Wiley and Sons, 1962), pp. 203–4.

28   T'ae-gil Kim, "The Changing Morals of Korean Students," *Korea Journal* 6, no. 3 (1966): 11. See also Gregory Henderson, *Korea: The Politics of the Vortex* (Cambridge: Harvard University Press, 1968), p. 201: "Probably nowhere else in the world is there so ancient and continuous a tradition of student demonstration, memorializing, and active participation in national politics as in Korea."

29   Kim, "The Changing Morals of Korean Students," p. 12.

ferences existing between the two countries in terms of structural social features. Numerous writers have commented on the sharp class dichotomy that divides the Korean society and impedes social interaction.[30] The variability in the amount of social cleavage and social mobility between the American and the Korean societies is reflected in the variation of the responses in this category given by the two different cultural groups.

It is of some interest that the response in the category of "Friendly, Sociable" is half as large for the visitors (4%) as it is for either the Korean students at home (9%) or the U.S. students (9%). The students in Korea emphasize more the humanistic-societal aspects of interaction, not friendliness or sociability as the Americans do. The visiting Koreans, however, respond with *popularity* and *sociability*, as do the Americans.

Equality

An analysis of the thirteen components derived for EQUALITY reveals that this concept's meaning varies substantially from the Korean to the American context. These components are: (1) Democracy, Human rights, Law; (2) Economic, Occupational standing; (3) Same, Equal, Alike; (4) Civil rights, Race; (5) Man-woman relationship; (6) People, Everyone; (7) Society, Class, Nation; (8) Countries; (9) Negative reactions; (10) Good, Fair, Peaceful; (11) Respect, Love; (12) Political references; and (13) Miscellaneous. Although all three student groups place the greatest emphasis upon "Democracy, Human rights, Law" in their associations with EQUALITY, both the visiting Koreans (41%) and the Koreans at home (32%) place a much higher emphasis on this type of response than the Americans do (25%). The next greatest meaning component of EQUALITY for the Americans (23%) consists of references to "Civil rights, Race"—quite understandable considering the decade of the 1960s. The Koreans have almost no responses in this category.

In another specific area of human rights, the Koreans show relatively substantial concern with the "Man-woman relationship." The visitors have 9 percent of their responses in this category, the Korean students at home 8 percent. The American students, in spite of the recent women's liberation movement, the pill, and concern with abortion, have only 1 percent of the meaning of EQUALITY in this category. It may well be that in the United States the ideological,

---

30   See, for example, Cornelius Osgood, *The Koreans and Their Culture* (New York: Ronald Press, 1951), p. 333.

legal, and political aspects of equality of the sexes is considered to be accepted. In Korea this is a relatively new concept. The old Confucian tradition saw the most important relationship in the family between the father and the son, and relegated women to a relatively low position in the family and in the society. Only after World War II and particularly after the Korean War has the notion of sexual equality come to assume significant importance as a political, ideological, and emotional concern in Korea.[31]

Other areas of relative uniformity between the two Korean groups and nonconformity with American group are in the "Society, Class, Nation" and the "Political references" categories. A small but substantial part of the Korean responses are in these two categories, whereas no American responses are in either. It would seem that the Americans do not associate EQUALITY with politics so much as with law and a more philosophical aspect of human rights.

The concept of EQUALITY for the visitors appears thus to be relatively similar to that of their compatriots back home. It should be noted, however, that whereas the Korean students at home gave 5 percent of their responses to the word EQUALITY in the "Economic, Occupational standing" category, none of the American students and few visitors did. In addition, the Korean students at home gave only 1 percent of their responses to the category "Same, Equal, Alike," but the American students gave 18 percent and the visiting students 10 percent. The strictly definitional element of EQUALITY appears to have assumed more significance for the Korean students who have been in the United States.

In the category "Good, Fair, Peaceful," the visiting students score 18 percent, the Korean student group back home 7 percent, and the U.S. group 11 percent. The visiting student group shows similarities with the Americans by introducing the idea of "fairness."

Cooperation

The meaning of COOPERATION is also quite different for the Korean and the American students. The ten main meaning components here are: (1) Help, Aid, Assistance; (2) Solidarity, Unity, Togetherness; (3) Working together, Cooperative behavior; (4) Family, Friends,

---

31   See Yim Seong-hi, "Changing Patterns in the Family Structure," and Lee Hoe-yong, "Modernization of the Family Structure in an Urban Setting—with Special Reference to Marriage Relations," in *Aspects of Social Change in Korea*, ed. C. I. Kim and Ch'angboh Chee (Kalamazoo: Korea Research and Publications, 1969), pp. 32–43 and 44–69.

People; (5) Organization, Group; (6) Nation and international relations; (7) Goals, Accomplishments, Desiderata; (8) Personality characteristics and positive evaluations; (9) Mind, Spirit; and (10) Miscellaneous. The largest component of meaning for both of the Korean student groups is "Family, Friends, People" (visitors, 22 percent; students in Korea, 18 percent), whereas it is only 8 percent for the American students. This is not surprising, given the historical background and cultural traditions of Korea. It is nonetheless surprising that this particular aspect of COOPERATION is not reduced for the Koreans in the United States, given their two and one-half years away from their close friends and families.

The second-largest category for both Korean groups and also a relatively large category for the Americans was the general one of "Working together, Cooperative behavior." Close to one-fifth of the responses for all three groups are in this category. All three groups show general agreement in the amount of meaning COOPERATION has in terms of "Organization, Groups."

The only area of responses to COOPERATION in which the visiting students show a strongly noticeable variation from their compatriots back home and a greater similarity to the American group is in the category "Goals, Accomplishments, Desiderata." Six percent of both visitor and the American response scores fall in this category, while 15 percent of those of students back home do.

In all other categories the Korean students show a great similarity to each other and substantial contrast to the Americans. For example, in the "Help, Aid, Assistance" category, U.S. students have 25 percent of their responses, the visitors 14 percent, and the students in Korea 10 percent. Although the visitors seem closer to the Americans in this category, they are closer still to their compatriots at home. Both Korean groups also show less attention to the "Solidarity, Unity, Togetherness" category and to the "Personality characteristics and positive evaluations" category than do the Americans.

In summary, one can say that for the Koreans, both the visitors and those at home, COOPERATION is closely associated to the "ingroup" of the extended family and friends and to positive affective situations, that is, to love, respect, and close personal relationships. For the Americans, by way of contrast, the processes of cooperation, the togetherness and actual working out of things, are more important. The responses in the "Nation and international relations" category indicate that the two Korean groups additionally have a greater concern for international cooperation than the U.S. students.

Progress

The eleven meaning components for PROGRESS are: (1) Advancement, Improvement; (2) Development; (3) Economy, Industry; (4) Achievement, Success; (5) Science, Innovation; (6) Education; (7) Life, Man; (8) Goal, Hope; (9) Antonyms; (10) Society, Nation; and (11) Miscellaneous. PROGRESS for American students means primarily "Advancement, Improvement" (48%). Next in importance are "Economy, Industry" (18%), "Goal, Hope" (10%), and "Science, Innovation" (8%). Thus 84 percent of their responses associate PROGRESS with a technological, goal-oriented, constantly improving, materialistic future.

The two Korean groups also show substantial interest in "Advancement, Improvement" (visitors, 23 percent; Koreans at home, 16 percent), but pay almost as much attention to "Development" (21 and 19 percent, respectively). The Americans have no responses at all in this category. Both Korean groups also pay much less attention to the "Economy, Industry" aspect of PROGRESS (8 percent for both Korean groups, 18 percent for the American group). The two Korean groups are much less concerned about the relation of "Science, Innovation" to PROGRESS, but much more concerned than the American group with the connection of "Education" and "Life, Man" to PROGRESS. The Koreans also associate PROGRESS with their total "Society, Nation" (visitors, 9 percent; Koreans, 12 percent) more than the Americans do (1%).

These data, in addition to pointing out the large discrepancy between the U.S. students and the Korean students in their interpretation and evaluation of PROGRESS, also reveal interesting insights. The scores of both Korean groups in the "Economy, Industry" category are less than one might expect (both 8 percent) given the general notion that economic development has been accepted as a pervasive, central value in underdeveloped countries because of its critical importance for all types of social change.[32] There can be no doubt of the stress that Koreans place upon development itself and on their total nation as a collectivity in the context of PROGRESS. Apparently they consider the politically organized national collec-

32   For statements of this general view, see Wilbert E. Moore, *Social Change* (Englewood Cliffs, N.J.: Prentice-Hall, 1963), p. 11; Max F. Millikan and Donald L. M. Blackmer, eds., *The Emerging Nations: Their Growth and United States Policy* (Boston: Little, Brown, 1961), p. 44; Paul E. Sigmund, ed., *The Ideologies of the Developing Nations* (New York: Praeger, 1963), p. 11.

tive more vital to their progress than the economy and industry.[33]

The fact that the students in Korea have the highest percentage of responses of the three groups in the "Education" category (9 percent, compared to the visitors' 6 percent, and the Americans' 3 percent) is noteworthy. Being a student in a foreign country, particularly in one recognized as being advanced and progressive, suggests that the individual would view a strong relationship between PROGRESS— his own, if not his country's—and education. Yet this meaning component of PROGRESS decreased. The low proportion of the Americans' responses here is also surprising. It suggests either that U.S. students take for granted the connection between their formal education and their personal and national progress, or that the relationship is not a matter of great concern.

UNITED STATES

The national image projected by one's own country has intrigued numerous researchers. Conjectures and stereotypes of the "national character" of the Americans, Russians, and Koreans abound. Shortly after the founding of the United Nations UNESCO sponsored a project attempting to assess "the conceptions which the people of one nation entertain of their own and of other nations."[34]

The Americans are particularly noted for their worries about their self-image and the image of their country as a whole. Dean Acheson described this concern as follows:

> An American is apt to stare like Narcissus at his image in the pool of what he believes to be world opinion, until he pines away; or else, he makes himself over into the image he would like to see, only to have his shrewder self tell him that he looks a fool. . .
> . . . We are setups for the caricatures of the Ugly American, of the stupid diplomat, the contemptuous, grasping, wily foreigner taking our money. . . .[35]

33   The great stress on the national political collectivity by the Koreans would be expected from previous studies. See Sung-Chick Hong, "Values of Korean College Students," *Journal of Asiatic Studies* 6, no. 1 (May 1963): 73 (Table 15). See also a similar survey based on military and civilian groups: Sung-Chick Hong, "Political Diagnosis of Korean Society: A Survey of Military and Civilian Values," *Asian Survey* 7, no. 5 (May 1967): 336 (Table 4).

34   One report resulting from this UNESCO endeavor was William Buchanan's and Hadley Cantril's work, *How Nations See Each Other: A Study in Public Opinion* (Urbana: University of Illinois Press, 1953).

35   Dean Acheson, "The American Image Will Take Care of Itself," *The New York Times Magazine*, February 28, 1965, pp. 24–25, 95, passim.

It is partly because of the desire to improve the image of the United States that educational and other types of cultural exchanges are encouraged. As Spiller states: "A cultural foreign policy is always and inevitably directed toward correcting or at least ameliorating the attitudes of other nations, so that the national self-image and the opinions of other nations may be brought into closer agreement."[36]

The experience of being a foreign student in America seems in fact to influence visiting Koreans' associations with the stimulus word UNITED STATES. The main meaning components derived here are: (1) Country, Nation, Inhabitants; (2) Political organization, Government; (3) Freedom, Democracy; (4) Leaders, Famous men; (5) People; (6) Economic characteristics, Development; (7) Outstanding qualities, Physical characteristics; (8) Technology; (9) War, Military; (10) Geographic locations; (11) Historic, Symbolic references; and (12) Miscellaneous. The Americans overwhelmingly associate UNITED STATES with "Country, Nation, Inhabitants" (30%), "Outstanding qualities, Physical characteristics" (15%), "Political organization, Government" (16%), and "Freedom, Democracy" (13%). A large proportion of the U.S. students also associates its country's name with "War, Military" (13%). By contrast, only 1 percent of the visiting students associate UNITED STATES with "War, Military" items; 8 percent of the Koreans at home do. The visitors devote most of their responses to the "Outstanding qualities, Physical characteristics" (30%) and the "Economic characteristics, Development" (28%) of the United States. UNITED STATES is also closely associated with "Freedom, Democracy" (16%) by the visitors. Thus these three generally positive categories account for 74 percent of the responses of the visiting students. Korean students who have never been to America place a much smaller proportion (45%) of their responses in these three categories.

In the "Outstanding qualities, Physical characteristics" category the students in Korea respond with such terms as big, wide, peaceful, tall, nose, big nose, strength, white, black and white, racial problem. While the visitors also see the United States as big and strong, with racial problems, the saliency of the American nose decreases. The visitors additionally associate beautiful, good and best, kind, progressive, capitalistic, and powerful. A few were less kind. Imperialism and selfish were also mentioned as outstanding qualities of UNITED STATES by some visiting Korean students.

36   Robert E. Spiller, "American Studies Abroad: Cultural and Foreign Policy," *Annals of the American Academy of Political and Social Science* 366 (July 1966): 4.

In the "Economic characteristics, Development" category the Koreans at home associate assistance and help much more often than the visitors do. The latter devote great attention to car, highway, machine, development, and to rich and wealthy.

It seems from these data that the Korean students in Korea are less certain than the visitors in their responses, dividing them among many more meaning components. They additionally seem to be more concrete in empirical terms and to have less tendency to evaluate the United States either positively or negatively. For example, 6 percent of the Korean students' responses refer to the United States' "Geographical locations," and another 14 percent refer to "Leaders, Famous men," both very specific categories. The American students have no responses in either of these categories. The visiting students' responses are negligible. The Americans and the visitors also have absolutely no responses in the "Technology" category, whereas the students in Korea associate science, airplane, artificial satellite, atomic bomb, and advanced with UNITED STATES. In the "Historic, Symbolic references" category the visitors have only hippies as a response, the Americans mention flag, and the Koreans at home refer to White House, Yankees, and cowboy.

These differences between the visiting Korean students and those at home provide support for the finding reported by Selltiz and Cook that the characteristics attributed to another country by peoples who have never been to that country are generally subject to the official actions and interpretations of those people's government.[37] Seemingly, individuals who have not visited the foreign country in question do not feel that they have sufficient data to make a valid judgment. Hence, their perceptions are prone to vary with changes in the international situation. It should be noted, however, that some Koreans at home responded to UNITED STATES with a longing to visit and study in the country, thus indicating that they would like to have the opportunity to eliminate this handicap. The visitors also associate studying abroad and travel with UNITED STATES. The Americans have only a small response referring to foreign travel.

THE IMPACT OF ENVIRONMENT UPON FOREIGN STUDENTS

In view of the narrow scope of the analysis (nine words) and the heterogeneous composition of the sample groups, the data provide

37 Selltiz and Cook, "Factors Influencing Attitudes of Foreign Students toward the Host Country," p. 13; see also Buchanan and Cantril, *How Nations See Each Other.*

insights into rather than firm conclusions about the diverse psychological dimensions of environmental influences upon visiting Korean students. The Associative Group Analysis method revealed that, while there are specific instances of visitors moving closer to the American students, there are also numerable instances in which they became less like the Americans than their fellow students back home. The correlational measures of similarity indicate that sharp overall changes in the meaning of these concepts did not occur as a result of study abroad.

The analysis of the four systemic concepts—COMMUNISM, SOCIALISM, CAPITALISM, and DEMOCRACY—showed very substantial agreement in meaning between the Koreans and the Americans regardless of whether the Koreans had been students in the United States or not. But there is very little cross-cultural agreement between the Koreans and the Americans regarding the meaning of the four social interaction concepts—SOCIAL, EQUALITY, COOPERATION, and PROGRESS. There is, in addition, very little overall agreement among the three groups in the interpretation and evaluation of the concept UNITED STATES.

In sum, the findings of this analysis of visiting South Koreans indicate that the two central assumptions underlying the American encouragement of exchanges of persons (see page 96 above) need substantial refining. A closer analysis of actual effects is needed. These effects are obviously complex and multidimensional. Paradoxical changes are observable whereby the visitors become not only less like their counterparts in the old, but also less like those in their new environment.

All this suggests that, although the experience of studying in the United States can alter meanings, this alteration need not and probably will not take the form of becoming essentially like Americans. Individuals studying in or experiencing a foreign environment appear to form a new conceptual framework, combining into that framework some elements of the host country's meanings, but to a large extent retaining and/or adapting the original meanings brought from their own culture.

These findings suggest the hypothesis that student exchanges may be leading to a new "subculture" that not only provides a partial bridge between native and host cultures, but also may introduce new dimensions in the political arena. Two questions of importance for international communication and politics are raised. (1) Is the subculture phenomenon found in this study the typical result of most student exchanges? (2) To what extent are these cultural groups similar to each other? That is, are Japanese, African, and Latin American students who study in the United States forming similar concepts as a result of their experience here? If so, is this process leading to a new third world political force? The natural logic of the latter question raises a fascinating additional one: To what extent are foreign students studying in the Soviet Union similar in their conceptual development to foreign students studying in the United States? Hopefully, analytic techniques such as the Associative Group Analysis method will aid researchers in the search for answers to these questions.

five

Education of Foreign Nationals in the Soviet Union

Edward A. Raymond

OF all the forms of political communication, education of the future elites of foreign countries within one's own country is certainly one of the most direct. It has also proved to be one of the most effective. Traditionally, the Soviet approach to this technique has been the recruitment of "hard-core" Communists from abroad and their rigorous indoctrination in the USSR. Results were spectacular, especially in countries adjoining the Soviet Union after World War II. Expansion of Western international student exchange programs since 1946 may have been influenced by the Soviet success. The United States alone now makes a far larger exchange effort than the Soviet Union (121,000 American academic exchanges compared with 21,000 Soviet exchanges in 1968). Other non-Communist countries swell the Western total to many times the total for the Communist world.[1] Particularly as former colonial countries have attained their independence, the Western approach has begun to pay off—a low-key approach that left the foreign student free to observe, inquire, and establish his own values. The Soviets did not abandon their high-pressure training of cadre (party leaders), Young Communists, and trade union leaders from abroad, but they have expanded greatly upon this by introducing relatively free academic and technical exchanges of their own. They concentrate on the developing countries

1 Institute of International Education, *Open Doors, 1969* (New York: Institute of International Education, 1969), p. 7; U.S. Department of State, *Educational and Cultural Exchanges between Communist and Noncommunist Countries in 1968* (Unclassified Research Memorandum RSE-25, May 7, 1969), p. 12.

of Africa, Asia, and Latin America. The emphasis is technical, and there is a minimum of political indoctrination. To date, few graduates from the non-Party programs appear to have been politically active after their return to their native lands.

POLITICAL SCHOOLS FOR FOREIGNERS

Political schools have traditionally dominated the Soviet program for educating foreigners. In the period of the Third Communist International (1919–43), the four largest and most influential cadre schools in the USSR were the Lenin International School, to provide theoretical and practical training to selected Party members from abroad; the Sun Yat-sen University and Communist University for Toilers of the East, for Asian students; and the Communist University for Nationalities of the West, for students from Eastern Europe and the Middle East. The success of this program is measured by the number of high posts that graduates and faculty members from these and related institutions in the Soviet Union have attained (Table 1).

Table 1. Highest Posts of Former Students of Comintern-Period Schools

	Head of government	Chief of state	Ministers of War or Interior	Head of Party	Central Party Committee
Austria	—	—	1	1	1
Bulgaria	2 (Chervenkov, Dimitrov)	—	2	—	6
China, People's Republic of	—	—	—	2	16
China, Republic of	—	—	1	—	—
Czechoslovakia	1 (Gottwald)	—	2	—	3
Finland	—	—	2	3	6
German Democratic Republic	1 (Ulbricht)	1 (Pieck)	—	1	5
Hungary	2 (Gerö, Nagy)	—	1	1	7
North Korea	1 (Kim Il-sung)	1 (Ch'oe Yung-kon)	1	1	3
Outer Mongolia	1 (Choy Balsan)	—	—	—	—
Poland	1 (Gomulka)	1 (Bierut)	1	1	1
Rumania	—	—	—	1	4
North Viet Nam	1 (Ho Chi Minh)	—	—	—	1
Yugoslavia	1 (Tito)	—	—	—	4
Other states	—	—	—	26	52
Total leaders*	11	3	11	37	109
Total countries**	9	3	8	24	24

* Showing only one post per leader. Priority to government over party positions.
** Excluding six provisional and five revolutionary governments.

The Comintern Schools

The spectacular revolutionary success of a handful of Bolsheviks in Russia dazzled their leaders, who openly called their overthrow of the moderate Kerensky regime "the first stage of a world revolution." The Third Communist International (Comintern) was set up in Moscow as the headquarters of that revolution.[2] The Red Army went to the support of the Communist movement in Poland. By 1924, however, the year that Lenin died, Communist uprisings in Germany, Hungary, and Finland and disorders in Italy and Austria had been crushed. The prospects of an imminent Communist takeover of the world had faded. It was obvious that it would take much time and much organization. To the executive committee of the Comintern, it seemed clear that the success of Communism in Russia, and its failure in Europe, vindicated Russian Bolshevik theory and practice. Communists in other countries must learn from and copy them. Schools of political warfare seemed to be necessary.[3]

Training professional revolutionaries in political schools was no new idea to the Communists. Before World War I, Lenin himself had lectured in a school for revolutionaries at Longjumeau, near Paris. Maxim Gorky, celebrated Communist writer, taught in another on the peaceful island of Capri, near Naples. These two schools were set up by Russian exiles after the failure of the 1905 revolution. Another was established later at Bologna, in northern Italy. At all three, instructors included the most prominent Communist leaders abroad, and from all three came cadres which took a leading role in the Bolshevik Revolution of November, 1917.[4]

An ex-member of the Comintern executive committee, who joined it in 1924, summarized the reasons for setting up the international party schools in Moscow, rather than in various centers abroad:

> A number of leaders of the different parties thought [the schools] should be organized in countries where the Communist Party was legal, if necessary subsidised by the Comintern Executive. The strongest argument against this proposal was that the communist parties in Europe, with the exception of Germany and France, were either illegal, as in Poland, Bulgaria, Italy, or insignificant in num-

2 Helmut Gruber, comp., *International Communism in the Era of Lenin: A Documentary History* (Ithaca: Cornell University Press, 1967), pp. 503–5.
3 Guenther Nollau, *International Communism and World Revolution: History and Methods* (New York: Praeger, 1961), p. 171.
4 Stephan T. Possony, *A Century of Conflict: Communist Techniques of World Revolution* (Chicago: Henry Regnery, 1953), p. 118.

bers, as in England, Belgium or the Scandinavian countries. And in any case, neither in the Comintern nor in the parties did they believe in the durability of "bourgeois legality."

They thought the communist cadres should not be at the mercy of arbitrary capitalist governments. There was another reason, too, for choosing Moscow. There was a shortage of instructors everywhere else, while in Moscow the Executive would be there to take charge. The Russian communists were deeply and honestly convinced that "real Marxists" capable of giving "the foreign comrades" an understanding of revolutionary theory and practice, were to be found only among the Russian bolsheviks. Also, having the Schools in Moscow made it easier to organise and finance them. It wasn't always easy in the twenties to get the necessary sums of money transferred abroad in foreign currency. And the final argument advanced was that by staying a year or more in Moscow the students would not only imbibe theoretical knowledge, but also get a practical insight into Soviet affairs and the methods of work which Soviet communists used.[5]

Formal announcement of a comprehensive system of political schools appeared in a resolution of the Fifth Congress of the Comintern, June–July, 1924. Actually, of course, schooling of foreign Communists in the Soviet Union had started with the indoctrination of German and Austrian POWs in World War I, and continued with courses for foreigners in Leningrad and an institution for Chinese students in Moscow as early as 1921. The 1924 Congress called for a more systematic approach. The new drive "to broaden and deepen the propaganda of the theory of Marxism-Leninism" envisioned three levels of schools for foreign Communists: training in the Soviet Union of the leaders of foreign parties; central national leadership schools, legal or illegal, wherever conditions in foreign countries would permit; and more elementary courses for the rank-and-file at the local level.[6] The concept was essentially one of throwing a stone into a still pond: the rings on the water would spread out from the point where the stone struck. Moscow-trained leaders would carry the word to the national schools, and from there it would pass to the communities.

The Lenin International School in Moscow is deservedly the most famous of the Comintern schools of the interwar period, although it was only one in a system of schools that rose and fell and overlapped

5 Walter Laqueur, ed., "Friendship University—The Early Version," *Survey* 34, no. 7 (July–September 1961): 19.

6 Edward H. Carr, *Socialism in One Country: 1924–1926* (London: Macmillan, 1964), p. 1018.

their jurisdictions and shared faculties with truly Byzantine complexity. It was organized directly under the Comintern itself. It seems clear that both the OGPU (Secret Police) and Red Army took a hand in the instruction, and could have been able to call on the services of graduates. It would be a mistake, however, to consider the Lenin School primarily a school for spies. Its true role was to train world Communist leaders—the privileged, trusted class of Comintern representatives that served to bind all Communist parties to the will of Joseph Stalin in the prewar period.

Organization and recruitment for the school took nearly two years. In August, 1925, it was announced that, owing to unavoidable delays in "the selection of suitable teachers and the preparation of study materials, the opening of the courses had had to be postponed. Instruction eventually began in October, 1926."[7] Students were organized in sections by language, rather than by nationality. British, Americans, Canadians, and Indians went into the English section; most of the Scandinavians could speak German and went into the German section; Czechs, Poles, and Finns who could speak Russian went into a Russian section. By 1932, when enrollment had reached a peak of close to one thousand, there were ten sections, of which the Chinese, German, and Spanish were the largest. A separate Finnish section with about 40 students was the smallest.[8] By this time there were two other cadre schools for Chinese, and their inclusion in the Lenin School as well reflects the "eastern orientation" that followed the defeat of Communist hopes in Germany. It also emphasizes the fact that the Comintern schools were only partially arranged on a geographic basis; there was a vertical separation by quality as well. The large numbers of German Communists at the school may reflect their availability in Moscow after failure of their armed uprisings at home. At the time, Spain was not Communist, but the size of the Spanish contingent at the Lenin School is an indication that Moscow intended to make it so.[9] In 1926, when the school opened, the Communist Party of the United States (CPUSA) sent a small contingent of ten students to Moscow (not all to the Lenin school). The following year twenty were sent, and after that, forty to fifty per year.[10]

In principle, the School admitted students who had proved them-

7   Ibid., pp. 1018–19.
8   Arvo Tuomimen, *Kremls Klockor* (Helsinki: Tammi, 1956), p. 322.
9   Ruth Fischer, *Stalin and German Communism: A Study in the Origins of the State Party* (Cambridge: Harvard University Press, 1948), p. 509.
10   Benjamin Gitlow, *The Whole of Their Lives: Communism in America, a Personal History and Intimate Portrayal of Its Leaders* (Boston: Western Islands, 1948), p. 246.

selves in their national parties. The national parties made the selections, subject to security review by the OGPU in Moscow. Actually, the caliber and qualifications of students varied widely from one country to another. Comments Theodore Draper of students from the United States: "These students, generally of district or section organizer caliber, were chosen as much for their dispensability as for their ability. A top leader could not afford to spend so much time in Moscow. He preferred to send those of his lieutenants who could be spared."[11]

The importance that the Soviets attached to the Comintern schools is obvious from the fact that top party and government figures lectured to the foreign students. Joseph Stalin did so himself on a number of occasions. Leon Trotsky appeared as a lecturer before his banishment in December, 1927. Marshals Tukachevsky and Budyenny spoke on military tactics, and Vyacheslav Molotov, commissar of foreign affairs, lectured on tasks of the Comintern. All of the heads of the Comintern spoke regularly: Nikolai Bukharin (1926–29); Dimitri Manuilski (1929–35), and Georgi Dimitrov (1935–38). So did the heads of the national sections of the Comintern and key members of its secretariat, including such well-known names as Tito, Pieck, Ulbricht, Browder, Gottwald, Juusinen, Togliatti, Thorez, Florin, and Carr. The permanent instructional staff was highly trained and competent, and some members who survived the Stalin purges and World War II have become Communist figures of consequence.[12]

The school occupied three locations during various stages of its development. The first building, opposite the British embassy, was described as "the best living quarters in Moscow."[13] About 1932, the school moved to the present site of Moscow University, on the Lenin Hills, overlooking the city from the south. In 1936, the school was virtually shut down because of the Spanish Civil War. Students were expected to volunteer to fight in the Republican Army. There was another move, back to the other side of the city.[14] There were also

---

11   Theodore Draper, *American Communism and Soviet Russia: The Formative Period* (New York: Viking Press, 1960), p. 169.

12   Nollau, *International Communism and World Revolution*, p. 171; Possony, *A Century of Conflict*, p. 171; John Hladun, "They Taught Me Treason," *Maclean's Magazine*, October 15, 1947, p. 73; U.S. Congress, Senate Committee on the Judiciary, *Hearings* before the Subcommittee to Investigate the Administration of the Internal Security Act and Other Internal Security Laws of the Committee on the Judiciary, Senate, on S. 1689, 86th Cong., 1st sess., 1959. Testimony of Joseph Zack Kornfeder, June 17–19, 1959, pt. 2, pp. 114–17.

13   Gitlow, *The Whole of Their Lives*, p. 242.

14   Tuomimen, *Kremls Klockor*, p. 325.

facilities in the outskirts of the city for military instruction, including exercises in street fighting and guerrilla warfare.[15]

There were two kinds of courses at the school: a short course of nine months' to a year's duration, and a long course of two or three years. As the school grew older, the courses grew longer. Students assigned to short courses were expected to return to the regional, or at most the national, level of their native parties. They studied in their own languages, using materials translated for them or imported from their countries of origin. Long-course students were considered capable of reaching the national level in their own parties, or, if exceptionally able, of entering the international corps of Comintern agents. These learned Russian, and used it in their course work. For both sets of students, a pattern of intensive indoctrination was developed which has spread to national and regional Communist schools throughout the world.[16] Meyer describes it well when he says:

> The fundamental principles [on which the moulding of a Communist is based are] eradication of every vestige of non-Communist beliefs and their replacement by the Marxist-Leninist ideology; the psychological transformation of the person into the Communist person; emphasis upon unity of theory and practice; the utilization of pressure, intellectual and psychological, as the decisive tool of training, and, in climax, the inculcation of a final and absolute loyalty to the Party as the necessary and sacred agent and executor of History.[17]

The Lenin International School was no liberal arts university. It existed to mold revolutionaries. It taught in the broad fields of ideology, agitation, propaganda, and military techniques, with about equal emphasis on each of the four. The subjects were taught simultaneously throughout the academic year. Methods of instruction were thorough. The school day was from eight to four, five days a week, usually with half a day devoted to a single subject. Each "brigade" of seventeen or eighteen students had a regular instructor in each subject. A fixed amount of time would be allocated for reading source material, as well as for preliminary discussion in subgroups of four or five students. Instructors would be available for individual consultation on difficult points. The class would then meet as a

15   Hladun, "They Taught Me Treason," p. 78; Gitlow, *The Whole of Their Lives*, p. 247.
16   Leonard Patterson, interview with Eugene Methvin, Jamaica, N.Y., October 8, 1964. Unpublished manuscript, p. 6.
17   Frank S. Meyer, *The Moulding of Communists: The Training of the Communist Cadre* (New York: Harcourt, Brace, 1961), pp. 161–62.

whole, and one of its members would give a critique, followed by a question-and-answer period or written quiz. Years before the Harvard Graduate School of Business Administration had popularized the "case method" of instruction in the United States, the Lenin School based its instruction on this concept. Leonard Patterson, a black American who attended the Lenin School in 1929, writes:

> We'd study specific examples, analyze them, criticize the mistakes, make new proposals—how the mistakes could be corrected. For example, we took the Canton Commune, the uprising in Canton, China in 1927, and analyzed why it was a failure—because the Party had not prepared the broad masses, they did not reach the "highest political level," etc. Then we studied the general strike of Rosa Luxemburg in Germany. She raised the slogan of the general strike, but she had never done anything to properly prepare for it. No, they're not gonna make that mistake here in the United States. They raise the question of civil rights for Negroes, and they organize mass protest movements to make sure that generates steam—they're already preparing for it. What they did was not to teach you what to do in this or that situation, but to give you procedures on how to decide what to do. And when the opportunity arises, you would know how to take advantage of it.[18]

Most of the students who attended the Lenin School traveled on false passports, under assumed names, and reached the Soviet Union via indirect routes. While there, they lived and studied under cover names. A permanent OGPU staff was assigned to the school. It operated in the background, leaving a "Special Section" of the school to handle such routine matters as collecting passports, issuing identification cards, and the like. The OGPU formed a net of informers from faculty and students. Means, a professor of philosophy on the faculty, was also a police agent. Americans who kept a check on discontented fellow students included Steve Nelson (later an atomic spy for the Soviets in the United States), Morris Childs (born Chilevsky), Beatrice Siskind (who later engaged in industrial espionage for the USSR in the American Midwest), and Mrs. Earl Browder, whose husband was later secretary of the CPUSA and then was actively connected with the OGPU. He visited the school from time to time, took part in some of its discussion sessions, and kept an eye on its discipline. Some of these police agents and informers used to affect a critical attitude of their own, in order to trap students. The mildest form of punishment for even a slight deviation from the Party

18 Patterson, interview with Eugene Methvin, pp. 5–7.

line of the moment was public exposure. This would be followed by an abject confession in the presence of the other students of the section. In more serious cases, students, faculty, and eventually even Kirsonova, the directress, disappeared.[19]

It may be considered surprising that this grim side of Soviet indoctrination, including its constant harping upon the supremacy of Soviet interests and the poisoned atmosphere of surveillance, suspicion, and deadly menace at the school itself, did not cause more defections once the students returned to their native lands. The fact is that the school was remarkably successful. Its very rigors created a sense of belonging to an elite. The system, with all its hardships, effectively changed men and women into dedicated activists, questioning nothing they were told and largely devoid of personal feelings.

A number of other Comintern schools operated along similar lines. The Communist University for National Minorities of the West (KUNMZ) was named for the founder of the Polish Communist Party, Jan Marchievski, and had a branch in Leningrad. It started as a school for minority groups within the Soviet Union but added more and more foreigners as time went on.[20] In principle, it was of lesser caliber than the Lenin School but, in practice, some of its instructors and students were just as capable.[21] By 1925, the Soviets had lost faith in immediate revolutionary victory in Europe and were turning their attention to wars of national liberation in Asia. Making common cause with the Kuomintang Party in China, they set up a school for training elite political cadres, the Communist University for Peoples of the East (KUNV). They named it for Sun Yat-sen, founder of the Kuomintang.[22] As of 1945, 57 percent of the Central Committee of the Chinese Communist Party had been trained in the KUNV or, to a lesser extent, in other Comintern schools in the USSR.[23] Most non-Chinese Asiatics received political training in the Soviet Union at another institution, the Stalin Communist University for Toilers of the East (KUTV). This institution, like its counterpart for Western students, the KUNMZ, was originally set up for internal

19   U.S. Congress, House Special Committee on Un-American Activities, *Investigation of Un-American Propaganda Activities in the United States, Hearings* before a Special Committee on Un-American Activities, House of Representatives, on H.R. 282, 76th Cong., 1st sess., 1939. Testimony of William O. Nowell, July 11, 1939, pp. 7024–25; Hladun, "They Taught Me Treason," p. 78; Nollau, *International Communism and World Revolution*, p. 172; Tuomimen, *Kremls Klocker*, p. 24.

20   John H. Hodgson, *Communism in Finland: A History and Interpretation* (Princeton: Princeton University Press, 1967), p. 149.

21   Laqueur, "Friendship University," p. 22.

22   Ibid., p. 20.

23   Robert C. North, *Kuomintang and Chinese Communist Elites* (Stanford: Stanford University Press, 1952), p. 172.

minorities. Later, its international division became entirely separate. The KUTV proved to be the largest of the Comintern cadre schools, and the longest lived.[24] Probably its greatest contribution to the extension of Communism was the training it gave to an Indochinese expatriate who reached Moscow from Paris in 1923, under the name of Nguyen Ai-quoc. Later he changed it to Ho Chi Minh. He is said to have made remarkable progress in Russian at the university (he already knew French well and some English and Chinese), and to have aided less-gifted foreign students with the language. He also lectured at the university on colonial subjects. At the KUTV, he formed his first revolutionary group of fellow students from his native Annam. All this must have been crowded into two years, since in 1925 the Comintern sent him to China, which was to be his base of operations until World War II.[25] Comintern Executive Committee member M. N. Roy, the founder of KUTV, established the Indian Communist Party in 1921; Kazama, a KUTV graduate, organized the Japanese Communist Party in 1931; and the founders of the Korean, Philippine, and Indonesian Communist Parties also received their political training in the KUTV.[26]

On occasion, the Comintern arranged to have foreign students attend the Frunze Military Academy (which was the command and staff college of the Red Army) or the International Agrarian Institute. Several of the highest-ranking Communist generals in the Chinese Civil War were Frunze graduates, as have been the Ministers of Defense in most Eastern European countries since World War II. Agrarian Institute graduates have included Premier Imre Nagy of Hungary and economic ministers in East Germany and Bulgaria.[27]

By the autumn of 1941, when Hitler's armies were at the gates of Moscow, the Comintern was evacuated to Ufa, in the Urals. A new international school was established in a small village some forty miles away. It was a political leadership school, but for security reasons it was named the Technical School for Agricultural Economy No. 101. Started in August, 1942, its first one-year course was inter-

24   Malcolm D. Kennedy, *A History of Communism in East Asia* (New York: Praeger, 1957), p. 124.
25   Jean Lacouture, *Ho Chi-minh: A Political Biography* (New York: Random House, 1968), p. 42.
26   Kennedy, *A History of Communism in East Asia*, p. 510; Xenia Joukoff Eudin and Robert C. North, *Soviet Russia and the East, 1920–1927: A Documentary Survey* (Stanford: Stanford University Press, 1957), p. 87.
27   U.S. Congress, House Committee on Foreign Affairs, Subcommittee No. 5, *National and International Movements: Strategy and Tactics of World Communism, Five Hundred Leading Communists*, H. Doc. 707, 80th Cong., 2nd sess., 1948, pp. 14, 18–21, 59, 65.

rupted by the dissolution of the Comintern in May, 1943. Primarily, the school served the children of Comintern personnel; there were also a few older Communists in the student body. Probably the best-known of these was Heinz Hoffmann, later a Lieutenant General and Deputy Minister of Defense in the German Democratic Republic.[28]

Higher Party School

Apex of the cadre training system within the USSR is the Higher Party School in Moscow, which is directly subordinate to the Central Committee of the Communist Party of the Soviet Union (CPSU).[29] Especially in the early 1920s, before the Comintern schools for foreign cadre were in full operation, some foreigners attained the Party school (then designated the Sverdlovsk University).[30] In the period before World War II, this was exceptional. With the dissolution of the Comintern, however, the Higher Party School has assumed the position formerly occupied by the Lenin International School.

According to available testimony, trusted foreign Communists were assigned to the Higher Party School in some numbers before or just after the end of World War II. These included a few students— all Communists of long standing—from the Central Antifa (Anti-fascist) School for POWs, located near Moscow. Some instructors lectured at the Party School and the Antifa School as well. These included Wilhelm Pieck, later president of the German Democratic Republic.[31]

A top Canadian Communist, Tom Buck, has testified that there is now a separate Higher Party School for Foreigners outside Moscow, with a capacity twice as great as that of the original Lenin School (that is, close to one thousand students).[32] Separation of the foreigners could have been done to provide secrecy, to protect students whose roles would be covert upon their return home, or to

28 Wolfgang Leonhard, *Child of the Revolution* (Chicago: Henry Regnery, 1958), pp. 195–96, 205–7, 220.
29 "Vysshaya Partinaya Shkola Pri Tsk VKB(b)" (The Higher Party School of the CC-CPSU), *Bol'shaya Soyyetskaya Entsiklopedia* (Great Soviet Encyclopedia) (Moscow: State Scientific Publishing House, 1959), vol. 9, p. 507.
30 Robert Conquest, *The Politics of Ideas in the U.S.S.R.* (New York: Praeger, 1967), p. 111.
31 Alfred Burmeister, *Dissolution and Aftermath of the Comintern: Experiences and Observations, 1937–1947* (New York: Research Program on the USSR, 1955), p. 11.
32 Hladun, "They Taught Me Treason," p. 74; U.S. Congress, House Committee on Un-American Activities, *Hearings Relating to H.R. 352, H.R. 1617, H.R. 5368, H.R. 8320, H.R. 8757, H.R. 10036, H.R. 10037, H.R. 10077, and H.R. 11718, providing for the Creation of a Freedom Commission and Freedom Academy*, 88th Cong., 2nd sess., February 18–May 20, 1964, p. 1191.

shelter Afro-Asian students from racial incidents, such as those that
have occurred at state universities in the Soviet Union. Another reason may have been the necessity to gear down instruction to students
whose command of Russian, even after a preliminary year's instruction, is incomplete.

Since 1956–57, the period of regular instruction at the Higher
Party School has been two years.[33] A 1963 resolution, apparently not
altered materially since, established curricula for Party training institutions. Writes Barghoorn:

> All programs include such basic political subjects as history of
> the CPSU, [Marxist-Leninist philosophy], political economy, and
> the history of the international "labor and national-liberation move-
> ment," as well as history of the USSR and "party and Soviet con-
> struction." In addition, all require a wide range of technical and
> specialized as well as "practical" subjects. . . .
> Admission to the Moscow Higher Party School is open to persons
> not more than forty years of age. . . . Passage of "state examinations"
> in four subjects (party history, dialectical and historical materialism,
> political economy, and either agricultural or industrial economics)
> is required for graduation from the party schools. In the journalism
> programs an examination in that subject is substituted for the one
> in economics.
> The range of textbooks and other reading material for the political
> courses is now much wider than it was during the Stalin era . . .
> [although] the basic theme of all this literature remains the Lenin-
> Stalin thesis of a struggle between "socialism" and "capitalism."[34]

While military subjects seem to have been eliminated from this
curriculum, in other respects it resembles closely that of the Lenin
International School. Whether the Higher Party School for Foreigners proves as influential as its predecessor, only time will tell.

Higher Komsomol School

In a recent address, Rector N. V. Trushchenko of the elite Higher
Komsomol School, attached to the Komsomol Central Committee,
omitted any mention of foreign students.[35] Nevertheless, it seems that
this institution has graduated several hundred per year since approximately 1960.

33 Bruno Kalnins, *Der Sowjetische Propagandastaat* (Stockholm: Tidens For-
lag, 1956), p. 48.
34 Frederick C. Barghoorn, *Politics in the USSR* (Boston: Little, Brown,
1966), p. 136–37, 139.
35 *Komsomolskaya Pravda,* May 30, 1970.

For ambitious Soviet young people, from their mid-teens to their mid-twenties, the CPSU provides the Lenin Communist Youth League (Komsomol). It serves as a training ground for Party membership and as a social instrument to further Party interests. Its 1961 yearbook, *Outlines of Komsomol History*, reported a drive to intensify relations between the Komsomol and youth organizations abroad, including those of the non-Communist countries. In 1960, five times as many young people were induced to visit the USSR as in 1958, and 100 foreign countries were represented, including all the countries of Latin America. According to the yearbook, "Soviet youth is developing ties with the young men and women of the capitalist countries, united in the Communist and democratic union of youth with all young people and their organizations, regardless of their political tendencies in the interests of the fight for peace and a better future for the young generation."[36]

To this end, surely the "progressive" (that is, Communist or pro-Communist) elements among foreign young people can expect an opportunity for political training and development at the Higher Komsomol School parallel to that provided to Communist party officials at the Higher Party Schools and to Communist trade unionists at the Central Trade Union School.

Central Trade Union School

Thousands of foreigners from non-Communist countries go to the Soviet Union, not for formal education, but for training in taking over and running trade unions. The All-Union Central Council of Trade Unions grants scholarships to students from developing countries for this purpose. Foreign students either study in the Central Trade Union School established in Moscow in 1949, or possibly in a separate international division. Courses last about nine months, with training in Russian and in Marxist ideology in addition to the teaching of trade union history, organization, and tactics.[37] For students from developing countries, great emphasis is placed on questions of "colonialism," and the role of the trade unions in the "continuing struggle" for national independence.[38]

36 Vsesoyuzniy Leninskiy Kommunisticheskiy Soyuz Molodezhi, *Leninskiy Komsomol: Ocherki po Istorii* (Moscow: Molodaya Gvardiya, 1961), pp. 681–82.

37 Isaac Deutscher, *Soviet Trade Unions: Their Place in Soviet Labour Policy* (London: Royal Institute of International Affairs, 1950), p. 147.

38 Robert Bass and Elizabeth Bass, "Eastern Europe," in *Africa and the Communist World*, ed. Zbigniew K. Brzezinski (Stanford: Published for the Hoover Institution on War, Revolution, and Peace by Stanford University Press, 1963), p. 107.

In 1968, one thousand Nigerians received Trade Union scholarships, and Africans seem to enjoy priority at the school.[39]

INDOCTRINATION OF PRISONERS OF WAR

Indoctrination of Soviet-held military prisoners in World War I and World War II was a relatively short-term program in each instance, but it affected larger numbers than all other forms of education of foreigners combined. In World War I, according to the Swedish Red Cross, 167,000 Germans and 2,100,000 Austro-Hungarians surrendered to the Russian armies of the tsar and the Kerensky government and were prisoners of the Bolsheviks. In World War II there were between three and four million Germans in Soviet prison camps prior to the Nazi capitulation in the West. There were also hundreds of thousands from Hitler's satellites, chiefly Hungarians, Rumanians, Italians, and Finns. An estimated 800,000 Japanese were transferred from mainland China to Siberia in August, 1945.[40]

At first glance, it might seem that men who had fought the Russians and then had to endure a harsh captivity were unlikely to become converts to the Soviet cause. Surprisingly, they joined the Bolsheviks in a tide in World War I, and even in World War II substantial numbers were won over.

The humiliating peace treaty of Brest-Litovsk was announced on March 3, 1918. Through the Bureau of War Prisoners, attached to the Soviet Commissariat of Foreign Affairs, emissaries were dispatched to visit all prison camps in Russia and Siberia to encourage the formation of socialist organizations.[41] The Central Committee of the Russian Communist Party (Bolshevik) formed foreign sections of the Party that also carried on work among POWs. "In Moscow alone," writes Wheeler-Bennett, "ten thousand German and Austrian prisoners were organized along Bolshevik lines and began an active propaganda among their countrymen."[42] According to the Soviet *Znamya Truda*, revolutionary propaganda among war prisoners assumed large proportions. In addition to sending agitators into the

39   Author's correspondence with U.S. officials in Nigeria, Ruanda, and Malaysia.

40   Elsa Brandstrom, *Among Prisoners of War in Russia and Siberia* (London: Hutchinson, 1930), p. 34; David J. Dallin and Boris I. Nikolaevski, *Forced Labor in Soviet Russia* (New Haven: Yale University Press, 1947), pp. 277–81.

41   John W. Wheeler-Bennett, *Brest-Litovsk: The Forgotten Peace, March 1918* (New York: William W. Morrow, 1939), p. 94.

42   E. D. Stasova and K. T. Novogorodseva, "Iz Perepisky Mart-Dekabr 1918g" (Selected Correspondence, March–December, 1918), *Voprosi Istorii* (Problems of History) October, 1956, p. 100; Wheeler-Bennett, *The Forgotten Peace*, p. 94.

POW camps, the Communists printed pamphlets and leaflets and formed a committee in Moscow to organize international legions of the Red Army.[43] The Central Committee of War Prisoners estimated that the number of POWs in the ranks of the Red Army was at least 50,000. These fought on all the internal fronts in Russia and formed some of the earliest strength of the Red Army.[44] Walter Krivitsky, a former high Soviet intelligence official, has spoken of schools set up in the first few months of the Bolshevik Revolution under the Foreign Liaison Section of the Red Army to teach POWs the arts of revolutionary war, including propaganda: "Brief training courses were given to German and Austrian war prisoners in the hope that these 'cadres' would use their knowledge on the barricades of Berlin and Vienna. Later, these courses became organized institutions."[45] POWs who returned to Germany helped spread defeatism before the collapse of the imperial government. They also assisted the Spartacus League and the German Communist Party in their attempts to overthrow the postwar Ebert regime. The first Spartacus revolt in Berlin was at Christmas, 1918. In 1919, Soldiers' and Workers' Republics were proclaimed in Bavaria, the Ruhr, and a number of northern and central German cities. Disorders continued sporadically through the sanguinary Hamburg Insurrection of 1923.[46] After the German revolts were put down, relatively few ex-POWs remained in the hard core of the German Communist Party, and eventually Hitler's Gestapo eliminated most of these.

Russian-trained POWs also had an impact in other countries. A group of Hungarian POWs had spectacular if short-lived success on their return to Hungary. Their leader was the fanatical Bela Kun, who declared Hungary a Soviet Republic in March, 1919. One of his revolutionary brigade leaders and a commissar in his government was his fellow-POW, Matyas Rakosi. Rakosi was the first Communist leader of Hungary after World War II.[47] An Austrian POW officer who joined the Red Army in 1917 was Grigori Stern. He became a celebrated Soviet general and adviser to Mao Tse-tung after World

43   *Znamya Truda*, April 17, 1918, p. 3. Quoted in James Bunyan, comp., *Intervention, Civil War and Communism in Russia, April–December 1918: Documents and Materials* (Baltimore: The Johns Hopkins Press, 1936), p. 95.

44   Max von Hoffmann, *The War of Lost Opportunities* (London: Kegan Paul, Trench, Trubner and Company, 1924), p. 236.

45   Walter G. Krivitsky, *In Stalin's Secret Service: An Exposé of Russia's Secret Policies by the Former Chief of the Soviet Intelligence in Western Europe* (New York: Harper and Brothers, 1939), p. 57.

46   Georg von Rauch, *A History of Soviet Russia* (New York: Praeger, 1957), p. 362.

47   Hugh Seton-Watson, *The East European Revolution* (New York: Praeger, 1951), p. 39.

War II.[48] A young Austro-Hungarian POW was Josip Broz, later known as Tito. He spent six highly adventurous years in Russia, returning to his native Yugoslavia in 1920 after serving in the Red Guard and marrying a Russian wife.[49]

Soviet efforts to indoctrinate POWs held in the USSR during and after World War II obtained more lasting results. For the most part, the men returned to Soviet-dominated homelands, and a large percentage went directly into government jobs. The enlisted men became administrative workers, police, or the nuclei for the new armies. Many of their officers and senior noncommissioned officers received responsible posts in national, state, and local governments. Japanese POWs contributed importantly to the postwar rebirth and growth of the Japanese Communist Party.

A feature of World War II on the eastern front was the success of "national liberation" movements, led by émigrés from Germany and its satellites residing in the Soviet Union at the outset of the war and manned by proseletysed POWs. Best-known of these was the National Committee "Free Germany," and its offshoot, the League of German Officers. In addition to these, states the official Soviet history of the war,

> An active program was carried out by antifascist organizations of emigrants from countries occupied by German-Fascist invaders (for example, the Union of Polish Patriots, the Organization of Czech Democrats . . .). Established on the initiative of Communists and other political activists, these organizations unified the patriotic forces of the emigrants for armed warfare against the German-Fascist invaders. Many emigrants fought in the ranks of the First Polish Army, [and in] Czechoslovak and Rumanian organizations and units.[50]

The League of German Officers largely engaged in front-line propaganda, though it assisted in recruitment for the Antifa schools. It contained many of the top Stalingrad generals, and eventually Marshal von Paulus, Stalingrad commander. It occupied a comfortable estate at Lyunovo, not far from Moscow.[51] The National Committee "Free Germany" operated the Antifa school system. This extended to many of the POW camps, but its hub, where instructors

48 Ypsilon, *Pattern for World Revolution* (Chicago: Ziff-Davis, 1947), p. 421.
49 Fitzroy Maclean, *Tito: The Man Who Defied Hitler and Stalin* (New York: Ballantyne Books, 1957), p. 16.
50 USSR Ministry of Defense, *History of the Great Patriotic War* (Moscow: Voyenizdat, 1964), vol. 6, p. 120.
51 Bodo von Scheurig, *Verrat hinter Stacheldraht* (Treason behind Barbed Wire) (Munich: Deutscher Taschenbuch Verlag, 1965), p. 33.

for camp schools were trained, was established in the winter of 1941–42 at Krasnogorsk, about ninety minutes' drive northwest of Moscow. The site was a large prison-camp complex that had held German and Austro-Hungarian prisoners in World War I.[52] An effort was made to give the POW students good physical treatment. For the most part, instructors were civilian émigrés, though qualified POWs replaced them in time. Students were all volunteers, certified as Communist sympathizers by the political commissars of the POW camps from which they were recruited. In each course, lasting from four to six months, there were about 200 Germans. Émigré organizations from the other Nazi satellite countries also staffed additional sections, with a combined enrollment of about 200, for Austrians, Italians, and Rumanians. The students were about equally divided between officers and enlisted men. Subjects paralleled those in the Comintern political schools, stressing Communism, imperialism, and history of the labor movement, and including Party tactics. In self-criticism periods, each student gave a public account of his life, confessing attitudes contrary to the Party line. Listeners joined in the criticism. Nearly all the students were reporting on their fellows to the secret police. Upon graduation, each student took an oath to fight Hitler to the death. Most graduates then went out to camp schools, where there were full-time courses for "activists" as well as lectures and meetings for other POWs.[53]

At the end of World War II, the Soviet Union placed some 150 German émigrés into top political positions in its occupation zone in Germany. These men subsequently led the Communist-dominated Socialist Unity Party (a 1946 fusion in East Germany of the Communist and Social Democratic parties) and, after 1949, the government of the German Democratic Republic (GDR). Initial use of indoctrinated POWs, by way of contrast, was highly selective. Most were left in the USSR for several years to work in camps. A number of the general officers from Lyunovo received high police posts, however, including Vincenz Müller, who later became the GDR's top general.

ACADEMIC INSTRUCTION FOR FOREIGNERS

In the post–World War II Stalin era, there was little development of cultural relations between the non-Communist world and the USSR.

52   Jesco von Puttkamer, *Irrtum und Schuld* (Error and Guilt) (Neuwied and Berlin: Michael Verlag, 1948), p. 27.
53   Ibid., p. 30–37; Heinrich von Einsiedel, *I Joined the Russians: A Captured German Flier's Diary of the Communist Temptation* (New Haven: Yale University Press, 1953), pp. 97–101.

Territorial expansion of the Soviet Union itself during World War II and the acquisition of East European satellites led to heavy pressure on the available institutions of higher learning. There would have been few places available for foreign students even if the Cold War climate of the time had not discouraged educational exchanges. With Stalin's death in March, 1953, and the gradual emergence of peaceful coexistence, foreign cultural relations gained more support.

A serious educational and training program for foreign students was introduced in 1955. Frederick C. Barghoorn has termed it, "for long-term impact, probably the most significant aspect of the exchange-of-person effort."[54] At its inception, the program included between four and five hundred non-Communist students. By 1958, the number had grown to 1,000 and by 1960 to 1,757—a fourfold increase in four years.[55] Growth continued in the early 1960s, until by 1965 over 10,000 from non-Communist countries were numbered among approximately 21,000 foreign students in the Soviet Union.[56] This set a plateau which has been maintained in recent years, as succeeding inputs started to be offset by graduates returning to their countries after four, five, or six years of study, and as Soviet-sponsored educational and training facilities in the developing countries themselves began to function.[57] About 12,000 non-Communists were studying in the USSR in 1967–68. Over half (6,080) came from Africa. The next-largest contingent came from the Near East and South Asia (3,565) followed by Latin America (1,500), the Far East (635), Western Europe (200), and the United States (30). There were also about 700 technical trainees, particularly from the United Arab Republic and India, undergoing training for work on Soviet aid projects in their countries.[58]

About two-thirds of these students study in state universities and technical institutes on the same basis as Soviet students. The remainder attend the Patrice Lumumba People's Friendship University in Moscow, set up especially for students from Africa, Asia, and Latin America. The Soviet Union has notified the United Nations that ten state universities and fifty-seven specialized institutes are open to

54 Frederick C. Barghoorn, *Soviet Foreign Propaganda* (Princeton: Princeton University Press, 1964), p. 273.
55 George A. Modelski, *The Communist International System* (Princeton: Center of International Studies, Woodrow Wilson School of Public and International Affairs, Princeton University, 1961), p. 38.
56 United Nations Educational, Scientific, and Cultural Organization (UNESCO), *Study Abroad, 1968–1970* (Paris: UNESCO, 1968), p. 10.
57 U.S. Department of State, *Education and Cultural Exchanges*, 1968, p. ii.
58 Ibid., pp. 12, 21; Institute of International Education, *Open Doors, 1969*, p. 59.

foreign students. Six of these universities and three of the institutes, like Friendship University, offer preparatory courses for foreigners in separate faculties. These are designed to give foreigners a good working knowledge of the Russian language. In addition, students from developing countries who lack other academic qualifications required for study at Soviet institutions receive courses and lectures in the preparatory faculties in subjects pertinent to their fields. Courses at preparatory faculties are usually for one year, but they may be extended to two or even three if the student has a severe lack of secondary education and comes from a country that is deemed politically strategic.[59]

In the years up to 1960, an influx of foreigners from Africa, Asia, and Latin America into Soviet universities and institutes posed many problems other than the simple barrier of language. It was difficult for the Soviets, first of all, to find professors and texts with sufficient focus on the special problems of students from these cultures, environments, and economies. The foreigners brought difficulties with regard to their diet, their health, and their tendency to band together and defy authority. There were a number of ugly cases of racial prejudice and violence.[60] Andrew Amar of Uganda, who quit Moscow University voluntarily, has complained of organized efforts of the Komsomol to prevent Russians, and especially Russian girls, from maintaining friendships with African students.[61] Mohamed Nur Samantar of Somalia spent twenty-five days in a hospital after being beaten by Soviet young men, evidently for dancing with a Russian girl.[62] In Kiev, two policemen watched a crowd of Soviet students beat up an African on a main street, then arrested the partly conscious victim for disturbing the peace. African students then staged a demonstration in front of the main academic building.[63] Asare Addo, a medical student from Ghana engaged to a Russian girl, was found dead in the snow some ten miles from Moscow. Soviet authorities refused to report on the incident; a student demonstration in front of the Ghanian embassy proved futile, and next day the Africans staged a protest march on the Kremlin—the first in forty years —with banners reading "Stop Killing Africans" and "Moscow a

59   U.S. Department of State, *Education and Cultural Exchanges*, 1968, p. 13.
60   "Moscow, Trouble in Paradise," *New Statesman*, December 27, 1963, p. 931.
61   Andrew R. Amar, *A Student in Moscow* (London: Ampersand, n.d.), pp. 34–35.
62   Charles McCarry, "African Students Who Quit the Soviet Union," *AFL–CIO American Federationist*, January, 1963, pp. 20–21.
63   "Moscow, Trouble in Paradise," p. 931.

Second Alabama."[64] A Ghanian student was found stabbed to death in Baku. African students followed this incident with a week-long sit-in at a railroad station, near the point where the body was found. Though they suffered from hunger and cold, they finally obtained their return by special aircraft to their native Kenya.[65] It was clear that something would have to be done to avoid such incidents.

Premier Nikita S. Khrushchev was speaking at Gadjah University in Indonesia in February, 1960, when he announced the establishment of a separate "People's Friendship University" for students from developing countries. This marked a departure from the previous practice of admitting foreign students to state universities and institutes, and their preparatory courses.[66] Rather surprisingly, on March 24, 1961, *Izvestiya* reported that some foreign students had been dissatisfied with regular Soviet institutions for such reasons as racial discrimination, poor accommodations, controls, restrictions and surveillance, and academic obstacles. The advantages and disadvantages to the Soviet Union in spending millions of rubles on the new university—a unique international experiment—must have been extremely hard to balance.

The advantages of a separate institution of higher learning for foreigners, from the Soviet point of view, start with the age-old Russian preoccupation with security. First, a separate institution minimizes contacts between foreigners and Soviet citizens. Second, it is easier for a separate institution to provide specialized instruction to foreigners. Third, political indoctrination can be adapted to foreigners in a separate institution. Indoctrination is in a low key, but it is present, from the readings in elementary Russian language instruction through to optional courses in Marxist ideology available to medical students.[67] Finally, the hothouse atmosphere of Lumumba University enables the Soviet Union to protect the *amour-propre* of its sometimes sensitive visitors, and to give them the feeling of being honored guests. These considerations won out.

Disadvantages of a separate institution in the USSR start with the cost, which would be materially lower if instruction were offered in

64 "Africans in Russia: Le Rouge et le Noir," *The Economist*, December 21, 1963, p. 247.

65 N. Ayangira, "Africans Don't Go to Russia to Be Brainwashed," *New York Times Magazine*, May 16, 1965, p. 52.

66 Seymour M. Rosen, *The Peoples' Friendship University in the U.S.S.R.* (Washington: Department of Health, Education, and Welfare, Office of Education, 1962), p. 4.

67 Ram Desai, "Lumumba University in Moscow," *University Review* (S.U.N.Y.) 1, no. 2 (Summer 1968): 18; Amar, *A Student in Moscow*, p. 38.

the visitors' own countries. Further, the very existence of a separate university, even though some Soviet students attend it as well, implies a hint of racial bias. A final disadvantage of segregation of foreigners is found in the caliber of students. Political considerations affect the national quotas and, in some cases, political pull and graft have been involved when overseas Communist parties or their auxiliary organizations select the students. As a result, many students who have attended Friendship University have had a weak educational background, and a number of countries have been reluctant to honor the University's degrees. At least insofar as technical degrees are concerned, this reluctance is on the decline.[68]

Selection and Recruitment of Students

It is clear that one of the purposes in establishing Lumumba University was to free the USSR from its earlier dependence upon foreign governments in the selection of students. In Khrushchev's dedication remarks at the new University he said:

> Many students from all countries of the world now study in our country, but the majority of these students have been sent by government organs. Of course, these organs are unable to meet all requests. Therefore, many talented young people coming from poor families are deprived of the possibility of realizing their wish to study in the Soviet Union. We propose that the new university train both those who are sent by government organs and those who express their personal wish to study.[69]

This objective has not been met in full. Most countries that send students to the USSR still insist on selecting the candidates themselves. U.S. officials stationed in forty-two developing countries, most of which have cultural exchange agreements with the Soviet Union, provided substantive answers to the author's queries on Soviet student recruitment. Of these, twenty-six indicated that their countries of residence nominated candidates.

Non-Communist countries with intergovernmental agreements for the exchange of students and for cultural, technical, and scientific cooperation are in force between the USSR and Afghanistan, Burma, Ceylon, Denmark, Finland, France, Federal Republic of Germany, Guinea, India, Indonesia, Iraq, Italy, Lebanon, Nepal, Norway, Spain, Sudan, Sweden, United Arab Republic, and United States.

68   Desai, "Lumumba University in Moscow," p. 18.
69   Rosen, "The Peoples' Friendship University," p. 4.

There is also a cultural agreement between the Soviet Union and Yugoslavia. Students applying for scholarships in the USSR under the terms of these agreements usually apply to the Ministry of Education in their own country. A qualified student from any other developing country in Africa, Asia, or Latin America may apply, providing that his Minister of Education will process the request.[70]

In countries that make their own selections, it is not always the Ministry of Education or its equivalent that performs this function. The U.S. State Department, through its Board of Foreign Scholarships, merely ratifies the selection made for many years by an interuniversity committee, and made since January, 1970, by the International Research and Exchanges Board.[71] The British Council (equivalent to the U.S. Information Agency) processes fellowships available to postgraduate students in the United Kingdom. The French Centre National de la Recherche Scientifique selects candidates for scientific research fellowships under the terms of a Franco-Soviet agreement.[72] In El Salvador, the National University makes the selection. In the small West African country of Chad, as in Ghana, there is a special scholarship office in the Ministry of Plans and Cooperation. The Central African Republic attaches such importance to the selections that it entrusts them to the Council of Ministers itself. In the Somali Republic, in the horn of Africa, deputies in the National Assembly select candidates on their own (usually on the recommendation of the Soviet-financed Benedir secondary school).[73] When Oginga Odinga, opponent of Jomo Kenyatta in Kenya, was vice-president and Home Secretary, he was reported to nominate candidates himself.[74]

Three of the countries, according to the responding American officials, go to the other extreme and leave the selection of academic candidates to the Soviet embassies in their capitals. Kenya is now one of these, and the others are Jordan and Malaysia.

Where political conditions permit, the Soviet Union has made an effort to bypass foreign governments in recruiting students from abroad. One channel of direct recruiting is the United Nations program for students from non–self-governing and trust territories, Southwest Africa (Namibia), and Territories under Portuguese Administration. Recruits under this program can make scholarship

70 UNESCO, *Study Abroad, 1968–1970*, p. 433.
71 Robert F. Byrnes, "American Scholars in Russia Soon Learn about the K.G.B.," *New York Times Magazine*, November 16, 1969, p. 104.
72 UNESCO, *Study Abroad, 1968–1970*, pp. 433–34.
73 Author's correspondence with U.S. officials in these countries.
74 Victor Lasky, *The Ugly Russian* (New York: Trident Press, 1965), p. 85.

applications directly to the Ministry of Higher and Secondary Education or to the Admissions Committee of the Patrice Lumumba Friendship University in Moscow.[75] The Soviet Women's Committee in Moscow makes scholarships available directly to women from African countries for study or training in the USSR.[76] Even Soviet religious bodies offer scholarships on the basis of direct recruitment. The Ethiopian Coptic Church in Abyssinia and church bodies in several other African countries receive scholarships to theological seminaries in the Soviet Union.[77]

Soviet "front" organizations supplement official scholarships abroad or, in the absence of intergovernmental exchange agreements, substitute for them. Scholarships are offered through the International Union of Students (with headquarters in Prague) to undergraduate and graduate students from any country outside the USSR. Selection of candidates is by the Union with the approval of the Soviet Government. Approximately 100 scholarships are available to young people from developing countries for undergraduate study in the USSR upon application through national youth organizations to the International Union of Students or the World Federation of Democratic Youth.[78] The International Organization of Journalists is active in recruiting students from Latin America.

There is also clandestine recruitment. In the considerable number of countries that do not recognize the Soviet Union and ban national Communist parties, recruitment of students for study in the USSR is carried on by covert Communist movements. Additionally, there is illegal recruitment in countries that attempt to make their own selections. "In Africa," wrote McCarry in 1963, "a smooth working underground railroad conveys candidates from their homes to Moscow without benefit of travel documents. West Africans have merely to make their way to Ghana or Guinea, where Soviet diplomats await them with airplane tickets. For East Africans, the process is more complicated. Mostly they cross over the Uganda border to Juba, Sudan, a sort of staging area for Communist students. From there they go to Khartoum and then to Cairo, where they are supposed to be met by Soviet agents."[79]

Another aspect of Soviet recruiting is pirating, or the recruitment

75   UNESCO, *Study Abroad, 1968–1970*, pp. 432–33.
76   Ibid.
77   U.S. Department of State, *Educational and Cultural Exchanges between Communist and Noncommunist Countries in 1967* (Unclassified Research Memorandum RSB 65, May 13, 1968), p. 16.
78   UNESCO, *Study Abroad, 1968–1970*, p. 433.
79   McCarry, "African Students Who Quit the Soviet Union," p. 19.

of students already studying in Western countries. This is particularly prevalent among Africans and Asians in the United States and in Europe, where the students may have encountered racial or social prejudice, or difficulty in keeping up with the program of studies or in making ends meet financially. American and European Communists seek out such prospective dissidents and try to intensify their discouragement, disillusionment, and resentment toward the West. Once recruited for study in the USSR, these transfer students are particularly valuable in indoctrinating their fellow students in the evils of capitalistic society. Such students, like those who leave their country illegally, usually lack proper passports and visas, and hence are particularly vulnerable to Soviet pressure.[80]

Influence of Graduates in Developing Countries

A survey of U.S. officials in forty-two less-developed countries reveals considerable consensus on the question of what influence the graduates of Soviet universities have after returning to their home countries. To be sure, the greatest proliferation of cultural agreements between the Soviet Union and developing countries did not come until 1963, and the bulk of students sent there from many countries are still studying in the USSR. Nor have the few years that have passed since Lumumba University graduated its first class in 1965 given its alumni, in particular, much time to prove themselves at home.

Generally, the returning students have concentrated upon practicing their specialty rather than engaging in political activism. As a group, students from Mohammedan countries have shown considerable resistance to ideological assaults on their faith. Be they Moroccans, Somalis, or Yemeni, they remain proud Moslems. Iraqui, Syrian, and Sudanese appear to have been the strongest collaborators with Communism, but whether from conviction or expediency, it is hard to tell. In South Yemen, several returnees are lawyers, one is a municipal judge in Aden, and another is an official of the Ministry of Interior, which controls the police. In the United Arab Republic, Soviet-trained Egyptians staff the Russian section of the Alson Language School, which sends graduates into most Egyptian economic and cultural organizations.

In another group of countries, where Communist parties are outlawed, graduates must be extremely circumspect or stay out of their native countries entirely. Ghana (since 1966), Saudi Arabia, and

80   Amar, *A Student in Moscow*, p. 8.

Senegal are typical of areas where ex-Soviet students tend to stay underground or remain out of the country. Malawi is a militantly anti-Communist country, and the handful of Malawians who studied in Communist countries prior to Malawi's independence in 1964 have been excluded from employment except in menial jobs and have been treated as outcasts when they returned to their villages.

In Africa south of the Sahara, former exchange students sometimes complain about the harsh Russian climate they have endured and the politico-ideological impositions encountered in undergraduate studies, but the program has had measurable success. Returning Soviet trainees are in responsible positions in various areas of teaching and the professions, including social and developmental work, journalism, and law.

Senegal and Guinea are examples of countries in which the government is the principal employer and gives employment to returnees. Senegal has outlawed the Communist-led Parti Africain d'Indépendence, but nonetheless it gives professional employment to returnees whom the PAI had selected for their Soviet training. Guinea, a country with close Communist ties, has lost about half its technical and administrative personnel since Sekou Touré took power in 1958, and about 500 Guinean students studying in the United States, France, and other European countries have refused to return home. Guinean students in the Soviet Union and other Communist countries usually have returned, but they have found it difficult to apply what they have learned to the administrative and technical procedures of their native land, still based upon the French pattern. Other non-African examples of governments that are the principal or sole employers of returned students are Afghanistan, Burma, and Nepal. Here the graduates, like most other citizens, are circumspect in the expression of political views.

Governmental pressure is not the only reason for the relatively low political profile of returnees. Many of these went to the USSR with a weak secondary education, or because they were indifferent students and could not qualify for education in the West. There is a tendency for such students to get through their courses in Moscow, return to their countries, and slip happily into their old niches in the social structure. A number of Chadians, Costa Ricans, and Hondurans have been cited as conforming to this pattern, and showing no interest in revolution.

With time, however, Soviet programs for educating students from less-developed countries may well bring rich political dividends to the USSR and contribute to the spectacular success that its schools have already enjoyed in furthering the spread of Communism. Graduates of political schools have attained leading positions in foreign Communist parties, have served in the forefront of Communist revolutions, and have ruled Communist countries. Political training continues for party cadres, party youth, and trade union leaders from abroad. Additionally, the Soviets have paid the West the sincerest kind of compliment—imitation. They have offered academic and scientific training to non-Communist students, with only a mild amount of indoctrination involved. There are long-term benefits to be gained from the gratitude of these students, few of whom could have received a comparable education elsewhere.

six

American Views of Soviet-American Exchanges of Persons

Frederick C. Barghoorn and Ellen Mickiewicz

PERSON-TO-PERSON communication among members of such politically competitive and ideologically estranged societies as the Soviet Union and America is at best fraught with tensions and hazards. This chapter explores the experiences and perceptions of American participants in Soviet-American exchanges of persons. It reports the essential findings of a survey conducted in 1966–67 among scholars, scientists, and others who had recently visited the USSR. The communication and perceptual patterns that emerged resulted from highly purposive, face-to-face encounters between an extraordinarily qualified, knowledgeable collection of Americans and the Soviet citizens with whom they interacted, mostly while the Americans were lecturing, doing research, traveling, or studying in the USSR, but also in contacts with Soviet visitors to the United States.

SURVEYING AMERICAN VISITORS TO THE SOVIET UNION

In brief, we sent open-ended questionnaires to 650 individuals who had had extensive contacts with Soviet culture. Of these, 179 returned completed questionnaires, most of which were full responses and many of which were voluminous essays. A postcard questionnaire was subsequently sent to nonrespondents, of whom 293 responded. The questions themselves, preceded by biographical inquiries, sought to ascertain the results and quality of experience involved in American-Soviet scholarly and scientific exchanges of persons.

The Sample

The original questionnaires were sent to several categories of knowledgeable individuals: (1) every twentieth member (1966 membership list) of the American Association for the Advancement of Slavic Studies, using a coin-flipping technique of randomization; (2) all Americans who had, up to August 31, 1967, participated in the exchange between the American Council of Learned Societies or the National Academy of Sciences on the one hand and, on the other, the USSR Academy of Sciences; (3) all professors of the faculties of eleven American universities offering graduate programs in Soviet and Eastern European Studies; and (4) members of the Editorial Board and Advisory Committee of the *Slavic Review*. We also sent it to a number of individuals, such as some U.S. government officials concerned with Soviet affairs and some recent Yale undergraduates and graduates, whom we had reason to believe would be well-informed respondents.

The rate of return was about what can be expected from mail interviews: a total of 179 persons, or about two in seven of those to whom we sent questionnaires, returned them. The reasons for this were several. First, of course, there are the normal limitations of mail interviews. Face-to-face interviews would doubtless have achieved better results, at least in terms of the number of respondents. Second, some persons apparently refrained from filling out our questionnaire on the ground that systematic investigation of this delicate sphere of human relations constituted an objectionable, "political" intrusion into an area that should be shielded from even the most discreet form of inquiry. Some of the reticence we encountered may also be due to hypercaution, disapproval of survey research methods, antipathy to what may have looked like a "Cold War" project, or even, despite our explicit assurances to the contrary, that in our written or other reports we might attribute specific responses to specific individuals. Probably more important was a third factor: the length of the time required to fill out the questionnaire properly. A brief, follow-up postcard questionnaire that we used to probe the failure of many to fill out the original questionnaire led us to conclude that pressure of time, combined with reluctance to speculate on the part of recipients who had not been in the USSR, seemed to explain most of the lack of response.

Respondents vs. Nonrespondents

The postcard questionnaire, returned by 293 of the nonrespondents to the original questionnaire, enabled us to gauge the representativeness of the respondents. We found that the following variables were of no statistical significance in telling us who was likely not to return the original questionnaire: age, sex, place of birth, occupation, citizenship, and country of higher education. Those variables that did seem to be statistically significant in affecting the response rate are shown in Table 1. Those who spent most of their time dealing with Soviet affairs and who were most fluent in Russian tended not to return the questionnaire. Those who had visited the USSR, whose highest academic degree was the doctorate, and who were part of the

Table 1. Characteristics of Respondents and Nonrespondents

Time Spent on Soviet Affairs $\times^2 p < .001$

Questionnaire	Most		About Half		Some		Little or None	
Returned	57	43%	24	92%	59	84%	31	70%
Did not return	77	57%	2	8%	11	16%	13	30%
	134	100%	26	100%	70	100%	44	100%

Visited USSR $\times^2 p < .001$

Questionnaire	Yes		No	
Returned	150	39%	21	18%
Did not return	231	61%	99	82%
	381	100%	120	100%

Highest Academic Degree $\times^2 p < .001$

Questionnaire	B.A.		M.A.		Ph.D.		Other	
Returned	6	25%	19	20%	140	42%	9	45%
Did not return	18	75%	77	80%	194	58%	11	55%
	24	100%	96	100%	334	100%	20	100%

Command of Russian $\times^2 p < .001$

Questionnaire	Fluent		Less Than Fluent		No Competence	
Returned	98	42%	37	69%	39	85%
Did not return	137	58%	17	31%	7	15%
	235	100%	54	100%	46	100%

Sample $\times^2 p < .001$

Questionnaire	In Elite Sample		Not in Elite Sample	
Returned	25	33%	151	27%
Did not return	51	67%	418	73%
	76	100%	569	100%

"elite" faculty sample tended to return the questionnaire with a frequency greater than average. And satisfaction with their experience in the USSR seemed to make no difference as far as the number of recipients returning the long questionnaires was concerned.

Turning to the respondents as a whole, they were an extraordinarily knowledgeable, distinguished, sophisticated, perceptive, and articulate group. Although most of them were highly trained scholars and specialists, they varied widely in a number of significant respects. Eighty percent held Ph.D. degrees, and 10 percent of the remainder had master's degrees. Most were in three roughly equal categories: forty-one natural scientists, fifty-five specialists in the humanities, and fifty-six social scientists. Fourteen of the forty-one scientists who filled out the questionnaire were members of the National Acad-

Table 1A. Professional Interests of Respondents and Nonrespondents

A. Questionnaire	Social Scientists		Natural Scientists		Humanities		Government		Other	
Returned	56	30%	41	40%	55	26%	5	22%	19	30%
Did not return	130	70%	61	60%	156	74%	18	78%	44	70%
	186	100%	102	100%	211	100%	23	100%	63	100%

B. Postcard	Social Scientists		Natural Scientists		Humanities		Government		Other	
Returned	122	66%	78	76%	150	71%	14	61%	36	57%
Did not return	64	34%	24	24%	61	29%	9	39%	27	43%
	186	100%	102	100%	211	100%	23	100%	63	100%

Table 1B. Postcard Replies of Those Who Returned Long Questionnaire and of Those Who Did Not Return Long Questionnaire

Characterization of Experience in USSR

Questionnaire	Very satisfactory		Satisfactory		Fair		Un-satisfactory		Very Un-satisfactory		Other	
Returned	48	44%	37	36%	9	33%	3	75%	1	20%	8	27%
Did not return	61	56%	65	64%	18	66%	1	25%	4	80%	22	63%
	109	100%	102	100%	27	100%	4	100%	5	100%	30	100%

Reasons for Not Returning Questionnaire, by Professional Interest

	Social scientists		Natural scientists		Humanities		Other	
Pressure of time or Never fill out questionnaires	23	27%	22	58%	37	35%	12	38%
Never visited USSR	23	27%	—	——	35	33%	13	41%
Questions too long and detailed	5	6%	6	16%	—	——	1	3%
Other	34	40%	10	26%	33	32%	6	18%
	85	100%	38	100%	105	100%	32	100%

emy of Sciences. One was a Nobel laureate. Among those outside the natural sciences, a group including both specialists on Soviet affairs as well as leading social scientists with an intelligent layman's concern and curiosity about the USSR, not a few ranked at or close to the top of their respective professional pecking orders. For example, our respondents included a world-renowned sociologist and two of the leaders in the "scientific" analysis of public opinion. All but twenty-one of those outside the natural sciences had experience in the USSR, some several times and some for periods of a year or more.

They varied considerably in other regards, most notably age and contact with the Soviet Union. In terms of age, thirteen of our subjects were under thirty, thirty-five were in their thirties, sixty-seven in their forties, forty-two in their fifties, and eighteen were aged sixty or older. The overwhelming majority were born in the United States. Twelve were born in what is now the USSR; and most of the others originated in Western or Eastern Europe. About a third of our respondents reported that they spent "most of their time" working on Soviet affairs, and about a sixth spent "one half of their time" in this field. Another third spent "some time" and the remaining sixth reported that they devoted "little or no time" to the professional analysis of Soviet developments. Well over half (56%) of the sample judged themselves "fluent" in the Russian language. Another 21 percent reported that they had some Russian but were less than fluent.

There are of course some important gaps in the overall distribution of the respondents. It would have been desirable, for instance, to cast a much wider net, in terms of both the numbers and categories of respondents. Very few were writers; none were artists, bluecollar workers, or farmers; only fourteen were women, only a handful were businessmen, and relatively few were officials. We are nonetheless inclined to agree with those respondents who appeared to think that only a few categories of exchangees (such as those to which they belonged) had the experience and other qualifications to render useful judgments. The one great exception to this generalization is doubtless diplomats specializing in Soviet affairs; in this case we felt that any polling procedure would return a very low, if any, response. It is nonetheless gratifying that some present or former officials were willing to fill out the questionnaire.

The Questionnaire

The bulk of the questionnaire comprised a set of eleven open-ended questions, such as, "To what extent do you think that contacts with

Soviet citizens or experiences in the Soviet Union affect the Americans involved?" and "What, in your opinion, are the objectives pursued by the USSR in exchanges?" Our feeling was that the expert, high-status, highly individualistic, and self-confident respondents we were dealing with would have been irritated and bored by a conventional type of questionnaire. Although some respondents as well as nonrespondents were critical of this open-endedness and what they saw as the ambiguity of some questions, we feel that by and large our strategy paid off. Our respondents evidently wanted to "sound off," freely and at length, in their own fashion, on the subjects that they considered important. Not infrequently did they volunteer information not necessarily required by the questions.

The use of open-ended questions permitted us to avoid premature closure on the items of interest to us, and to maintain as open and exploratory a posture as possible. To be sure, we operated on the basis of certain assumptions and hypotheses which were based on expert knowledge of and our own experience in exchanges (and which seem for the most part to have been well confirmed by the data generated). We thought that highly competent, experienced scholars and scientists, with extensive experience in the USSR or with expertise based on years of specialized research, would testify that American-Soviet exchanges were of great value—both in personal, professional terms, and in terms of the "national interest" of the United States. Our findings overwhelmingly confirmed the correctness of this hypothesis, as well as of our associated belief that an expert sample would find much to criticize in the role in exchanges played by the political authorities of the United States and the Soviet Union.

Second, we hypothesized that American natural scientists, social scientists, and scholars in the humanities would be guided by the values of the "open society" in evaluating their experience in the Soviet Union and the impact of the Soviet political system upon face-to-face communication. We suspected that the respondents would have been shocked by the evidence that came to their attention of the prevention and frustration by Soviet political authorities (especially the political police) of the kinds, levels, and scope of freedom of information and expression that American scholars, scientists, and professionals tend to regard as normal and appropriate. This hypothesis, too, stood up well under the test of the experiential evidence.

Third, we felt that members of some groups (such as natural scientists and mathematicians) operating in relatively nonideological fields would find it easier than, say, political scientists or economists to establish or maintain fruitful personal contacts with Soviet colleagues. Again the findings were positive.

Another of our views, confirmed by the data, was that our respondents would consider that "serious," scholarly, and scientific exchanges and travel such as they had undertaken were infinitely more useful in every respect than, for example, ordinary tourist travel or junkets by "delegations" of politicians, businessmen, and other groups.

Somewhat surprising, however, was the finding that our respondents attributed relatively little significance to the background and training of the exchangees. The ideological orientation of the exchanges or the preliminary "briefing" of participants, they felt, did little to determine the outcome of the exchanges. The respondents attributed practically no significance to the state of Soviet-American political relations at the time the exchange occurred.

THE RESPONSE TO THE EXCHANGE EXPERIENCE

Concern for Self and Others

Purposive travelers though they were, many of our respondents found contact with Russians an exciting, sometimes shocking experience. Both the "expressive" component of their reports, and the quantitative distillation thereof, confirm this evaluation. Although the questionnaire did not ask whether or not exchanges were in general a "good thing," the sample with one or two exceptions volunteered the opinion that they were beneficial and significant. Forty to 50 percent, depending on the subsets involved, expressed the view that exchanges had "great" impact on American and Soviet participants, respectively. Asked whether the impact of exchange experience was greater or less on Soviet than on American participants, the replies of a somewhat smaller number were about even. It is extremely interesting —as can be seen from Tables 2, 3, and 4—that there were no statistically significant differences among respondents in their answers to these questions.

A very wide range of individual opinions and classes or types of opinions was offered regarding the "human relations" aspects of exchanges. Thus about twenty-five classes of answers could be categorized as indications that participants found in exchanges personal, emotional, philosophic, or even aesthetic content. In an almost bewildering variety of ways, 116 participants reported that Soviet people were human beings, "without horns or tails." One man actually reported having told his wife this after his first encounter with

Table 2. Degree of Impact on Americans

Professional Interest

	Social Scientists		Natural Scientists		Humanities	
Great impact	23	43%	21	51%	29	60%
Little or no impact	31	57%	20	49%	19	40%
	54	100%	41	100%	48	100%

Time Spent on Soviet Affairs

	Most or About Half Time		Some or Little or No Time	
Great impact	40	51%	42	51%
Little or no impact	38	49%	41	49%
	78	100%	83	100%

Command of Russian

	Fluent in Russian		Less Than Fluent or No Russian	
Great impact	43	46%	41	59%
Little or no impact	50	54%	29	41%
	93	100%	70	100%

Table 3. Impact of Exchange on Soviet Citizens

Professional Interest

	Social Scientists		Natural Scientists		Humanities	
Great impact	20	43%	19	53%	24	51%
Some, little, or no impact	26	57%	17	47%	23	49%
	46	100%	36	100%	47	100%

Time Spent on Soviet Affairs

	Most and About Half Time		Some or Little or No Time	
Great impact	38	51%	35	48%
Some, little, or no impact	36	49%	38	52%
	74	100%	73	100%

Command of Russian

	Fluent in Russian		Less Than Fluent or No Russian	
Great impact	42	47%	33	55%
Some, little, or no impact	48	53%	27	45%
	90	100%	60	100%

Age

	Under 50		50 and Over	
Great impact	48	49%	27	51%
Some, little, or no impact	50	51%	26	49%
	98	100%	53	100%

Table 4. Effect of Exchange on Soviet Citizens

Professional Interest

	Social Scientists		Natural Scientists		Humanities	
Greater than on Americans	14	74%	8	47%	8	44%
Similar to or less than on Americans	5	26%	9	53%	10	56%
	19	100%	17	100%	18	100%

Time Spent on Soviet Affairs

	Most or About Half Time		Some, Little, or No Time	
Greater than on Americans	20	65%	14	47%
Similar to or less than on Americans	11	35%	16	53%
	31	100%	30	100%

Command of Russian

	Fluent in Russian		Less Than Fluent or No Russian	
Greater than on Americans	23	64%	13	48%
Similar to or less than on Americans	13	36%	14	52%
	36	100%	27	100%

a visiting Soviet delegation. A distinguished biologist wrote that "intellectual community and sympathy turn into affection in case after case; maybe the cause is the wonderful qualities of Russians as Russians, but surely one factor is the shock of revelation of community against a larger background of estrangement."

If many of our respondents were happy to report that they shared values with Soviet colleagues, many—often the same individuals—struck somber notes of apprehension and anxiety regarding what they had experienced or observed. As one former U.S. government employee pointed out, it can be a "shattering" experience for Americans to witness Soviet friends "being accosted for interrogation." A literary scholar observed that an American who gets acquainted with Soviet citizens at "a deeper level than the usual superficial contacts" soon "finds himself so involved in their personal confidences . . . that he is obliged to take on some of the caution, the reticence, the vagueness of the Soviet citizens himself—simply in order to avoid becoming a menace" to them.

Professional Benefits of Exchanges

It is not easy to summarize the varied and often vague evaluations offered by exchangees regarding the professional value of their experience. Sixty-six respondents volunteered that exchanges had affected their work, however, and only five said they had not. Not very surprisingly, but perhaps a trifle paradoxically, the data tend to indicate that the more knowledgeable an exchangee is about a "nonpolitical" discipline, such as mathematics, the better position he is in to avail himself of whatever professional advantages he thinks may be offered by comparing notes with Soviet colleagues, if indeed he thinks the enterprise has value at all (Tables 5 and 6). A kind of

Table 5. Exchangee's Ease in Establishing Close Contacts

Professional Interest

A. Fisher's exact test: probability of these frequencies under H_o = .003797

	Social Scientists		Natural Scientists	
No difficulty	3	23%	10	83%
Difficulty	10	77%	2	17%
	13	100%	12	100%

B.

	Social Scientists		Humanities	
No difficulty	3	23%	4	33%
Difficulty	10	77%	8	67%
	13	100%	12	100%

Time Spent on Soviet Affairs

Fisher's exact test: probabilities of these frequencies under H_o = .00183

	Most or About Half Time		Some, Little, or No Time	
No difficulty	3	14%	11	65%
Difficulty	18	86%	6	35%
	21	100%	17	100%

Command of Russian

	Fluent in Russian		Less Than Fluent or No Russian	
No difficulty	7	37%	8	40%
Difficulty	12	63%	12	60%
	19	100%	20	100%

complement to this tentative finding is that the more knowledge, skills, and background of a "socio-political" character are possessed by a participant, the greater his difficulties are likely to be in establishing or continuing professionally useful or relevant relations with Soviet counterparts. Of course, it is precisely in ideologically sensitive fields such as political science, economics, law, philosophy, etc., that the potential benefits of exchanges are greatest.

Table 6. Continuation of Contacts after Exchanges

Professional Interest

A. $\times^2$ p $<$ .05	Social Scientists		Natural Scientists	
Definitely continued	6	33%	16	64%
Slightly or not continued	12	67%	9	36%
	18	100%	25	100%

B.	Social Scientists		Humanities	
Definitely continued	6	33%	15	58%
Slightly or not continued	12	67%	11	42%
	18	100%	26	100%

Time Spent on Soviet Affairs

$\times^2$ p $<$ .05	Most or About Half Time		Some, Little, or No Time	
Definitely continued	13	39%	28	62%
Slightly or not continued	20	61%	17	38%
	33	100%	45	100%

Command of Russian

	Fluent		Not Fluent or No Russian	
Definitely continued	21	48%	22	61%
Slightly or not continued	23	52%	14	39%
	44	100%	36	100%

Age

	Under 50		50 and Over	
Definitely continued	26	52%	16	53%
Slightly or not continued	24	48%	14	47%
	50	100%	30	100%

It should be noted that scholars and experts in both "hard" and "soft" fields reported many direct or indirect benefits of exchanges. It should also be pointed out, however, that members of both groups expressed the view that by no means the full potential was realizable under prevailing conditions.

Natural scientists appeared to think that there were only a few areas in which American scientists could learn much from the Russians. Several nonetheless said that they had benefited significantly, in terms of acquaintance with new ideas or data, from their Russian visits. One metallurgist reported that he had undertaken three major research projects as a direct result of his visits to the USSR. A mathematician reported that he had been saved a year's work because of a chance remark made by a Soviet colleague. A vertebrate paleontologist wrote, "Sharing knowledge has led to progress." By way of contrast, a number of scientists and mathematicians pointed to numerous obstacles to full scientific cooperation, such as poor living and working conditions in the USSR, and the frustration by the Soviet authorities of the desire of able young Soviet scientists to study or travel in America.

Historians and social scientists were much more conscious of barriers to communication interposed by political and ideological factors than were the natural scientists. They nevertheless felt that experience in Russia could be enormously valuable and even indispensable—partly just because it made potential specialists aware of the total pattern of which these barriers were a feature. A very strong statement of this position was made by a distinguished legal scholar who wrote that experience in "socialist" countries was "so important that I feel that what is written by those who have not been in socialist countries constitutes nothing more than interesting hypotheses for examination by others who can make the 'field' trips to the East." A young political scientist touched on an important benefit when he reported that, as a result of his contact with scholars at a research institute, he became fully aware for the first time of the differences in point of view among Soviet scholars working on the same subjects.

THE PERCEPTION OF SOVIET VIEWS

Effects on Soviet Political Attitudes and Behavior

Data we received seem to justify a qualifiedly affirmative answer to the question of whether or not exchanges significantly affect the attitudes or behavior of those Soviet citizens with whom the exchangees came in contact. We must be cautious because only a minority of respondents volunteered relevant opinions, and some of these were skeptical or negative. The strong statements of some of our respondents, however, in the context of the Kremlin's well-known reluctance to relax controls over contacts between Soviet citizens and Americans (or indeed foreigners generally, whether from "bourgeois" or "socialist" societies) indicate that contacts with Americans and with the "West" in general can have a significant political impact. While this impact might be "subversive" from the point of view of the Soviet authorities, or perhaps of the more conservative elements among them, it could also be regarded as wholesome insofar as it might trigger a constructive, competitive Soviet response. Twenty-seven respondents, or 15 percent of those commenting on this point, expressed the view that exchanges did affect the value and behavior patterns of Soviet youths. A representative statement was that of a young political scientist with extensive experience in Russia who wrote, "In my judgment, a very large part of the culture of Soviet urban youth is the product of contact with the West," and he added, "the role of the West in catalyzing latent dissent is, I believe, quite widespread." Twelve respondents reported that, for Soviet citizens, contacts created a threat of disturbing inner conflicts. Several pointed to the deep impression made on Soviet people by the freedom of Americans to travel all over the world. Fourteen asserted that Soviets were favorably impressed by the personal security enjoyed by Americans, and ten reported that exchanges stimulated, among Russians, the desire to visit foreign countries. In this connection, a former graduate exchange student wrote that the group of Soviet students whom he saw regularly "began to raise questions" regarding such matters as the difficulty of foreign travel and the requirement that citizens carry internal passports.

A number of exchangees referred to the powerful impact on Russians of information derived from contacts with foreigners. This information sometimes led in the opinion of some to erosion of the CPSU's authority by casting doubt on such matters as the validity of the official Soviet picture of world affairs. For example, a zoologist reported that "after our acquaintanceship one politically active person became convinced that it would be more democratic to have more than one choice in elections and suggested this at a local meeting." There was talk of the profound effect of books made available to Soviet students by their foreign friends, including a young philosopher's statement that the entire philosophical outlook of one Soviet citizen was changed "from orthodox Marxism to a devotion to the ideas of Erich Fromm" as a result of conversations and reading of Western literature acquired from American exchangees.

Five sources volunteered the observation that Soviets who had been to the West could always be distinguished—by their receptivity to new ideas, and so forth—from those who had not.

For want of space no attempt will be made to deal with the extensive evidence of the impact of Western concepts and methods in the natural and social sciences, except to note that thirty-eight respondents referred to specific changes in history and the social sciences resulting wholly or partly from exchanges.

Lest the impression be created of unanimity regarding the positive impact—from the Western liberal-democratic point of view—of exchanges, we close this section with mention of the thoughtful, balanced essay written by a sociologist. He expressed the opinion that "Soviet citizens whose business it is to deal officially with Americans" had "developed their own viewpoints and attitudes about what makes Americans tick, a series of stereotypes or clichés as valid, probably, as the Americans' conception of the inner gears of Soviet people." He expressed the view that continued contacts might accentuate differences rather than similarities of outlook. Also, some sources pointed out that as Soviet students grew older their sense of the risks of exposure to "bourgeois" thinking grew stronger. On balance, however, our respondents tended to stress the role of exchanges as catalysts of dissent, as sources of alternatives to established models, and as a factor helping to strengthen the hand of "progressive" Soviet intellectuals and scientists vis-à-vis the political authorities.

Exchanges, American-Soviet Relations, and World Peace

One hundred and thirty-six respondents said that they perceived connections between exchanges and Soviet-American relations; one denied such a link. For the most part, there was little specificity in these statements. Ten believed that they strengthened confidence in the possibility of coexistence. A number expressed the opinion that they fostered, in both countries, increased tolerance of the social and political system of the other. A strongly conservative respondent wrote, "Insofar as Soviet citizens have learnt about the capabilities of the United States, their attitudes have been changed—probably in favor of 'peaceful coexistence.'" Four sources, including two political scientists expert in arms control matters and a physicist, indicated that exchanges had contributed significantly to mutual understanding in the arms control field.

Perceived Attitudes of Soviet Social-Political Groups Toward Exchanges

Seventy-five persons answered a question asking for a ranked list of Soviet "social, occupational or professional groups" most or least favorable to exchanges. Almost all reported that all Soviet individuals or groups with whom they had had personal contact favored exchanges, but on the basis of inference or general knowledge some thought that certain elements, such as party executives or the KGB (security police), were hostile to all but a minimal, formalistic type of exchange. Social scientists, exchangees fluent in Russian, and those who devoted a large proportion of their working time to Soviet affairs were significantly more likely than others to be aware of Soviet forces opposed to "intimate communication" (Table 7). A

Table 7. Perceptions of Soviet Groups Opposing Exchange

Do you know of any groups in the USSR who oppose more intimate communication?

Professional Interest

A. $\times^2 p < .01$		Social Scientists		Natural Scientists	
Yes		21	60%	5	19%
No		14	40%	21	81%
		35	100%	26	100%
B.		Social Scientists		Humanities	
Yes		21	60%	24	65%
No		14	40%	13	35%
		35	100%	37	100%

Time Spent on Soviet Affairs

$\times^2 p < .01$		Most or About Half Time		Some, Little, or No Time	
Yes		41	66%	17	34%
No		21	34%	33	66%
		62	100%	50	100%

Command of Russian

$\times^2 p < .01$		Fluent in Russian		Less Than Fluent in Russian	
Yes		46	64%	15	35%
No		26	36%	28	65%
		72	100%	43	100%

Age

		Under 50		50 and Over	
Yes		48	58%	13	41%
No		35	42%	19	59%
		83	100%	32	100%

handful of respondents indicated that some members of certain Soviet occupational categories, such as artists and scientists, regarded support by them for the exchange program as a way of contributing to the liberalization of Soviet intellectual life (Table 8). A few averred that Soviet experts attempted to utilize exchanges as a way of persuading the authorities that they needed additional funds for research programs, lest they lag behind their American competitors.

Table 8A. Soviet Groups Perceived as Favoring Exchanges
(Placed in first or second place in rank order of "most favorable")

	Soviet Groups								
Occupation	Natural scientists		Writers and artists		Intellectuals		University students		Engineers
Social scientists	13	25%	15	35%	13	42%	7	58%	2	22%
Natural scientists	23	43	4	9	1	3	1	8	4	44
Humanities	12	23	18	42	12	39	2	17	1	12
Other	5	9	6	14	5	16	2	17	2	22
Total	53	100%	43	100%	31	100%	12	100%	9	100%

Table 8B. Soviet Groups Perceived as Opposing Exchanges
(Placed in first or second place in rank order of "most opposing")

	Soviet Groups										
Occupation	Party executives, ideologists, and activists		KGB (Secret Police)		Workers and peasants		Govt. and/or diplomatic officials		Leadership propaganda and youth orgs.		Military
Social scientists	17	37%	9	56%	6	40%	4	27%	3	50%	2	40%
Natural scientists	4	15	2	13	2	13	7	47	—		—
Humanities	18	39	4	25	4	27	2	13	1	17	2	40
Other	7	9	1	6	3	20	2	13	2	33	1	20
Total	46	100%	16	100%	15	100%	15	100%	6	100%	5	100%

EXCHANGEE ATTRIBUTES AND THE VARIABILITY OF EXCHANGE EXPERIENCES

Of some twenty factors volunteered in answer to a question asking for a ranked listing of six factors which might influence the outcome of exchanges (individual personality, language, ideological preconceptions, briefing or instructions issued to participants, professional competence, or field of interest), the overwhelming majority listed as first or second individual personality or professional competence— the latter being variously described in terms of "role," "status," "professional reputation," and so forth. To a somewhat surprising degree, language, ideology, and briefing were played down. Regarding ideology, in particular, there seemed to be considerable confusion. Some who gave a low weighting to this factor assumed that, since the Soviets would in any case be "Marxists," any overt calling of attention to it should be avoided. Some interesting interpretive essays on various of these factors were offered. For example, a social psychologist wrote that "the role in which one visits (foreign service officer, reporter, scholar, tourist, etc.) so specifies what one sees and does, how one is treated, how he himself acts, etc., that, in my mind it is the single most important factor affecting one's judgment. Hence the danger in relying primarily on one group as sources on the Soviet world (e.g., the Embassy, the press, etc.)."

A sociologist stressed the significance of "integrity"—which he defined as "personal and professional honesty, and an ability to stick by one's guns . . . to appear to the Soviets as sure, competent and articulate." Only two respondents volunteered "political climate," or the state of Soviet-American relations at the time of the exchange, as an important factor affecting the outcome of exchanges. Vietnam, the German problem, or other specific foreign policy questions were mentioned occasionally in connection with this question or at other points in the questionnaire.

Comparative Advantages of Different Categories of Exchange

The fact that most members of the sample were university professors may have biased them in favor of academic exchanges. At any rate, the category "exchange of graduate students, post-doctoral students, and established professionals" that emerged in the coding process from a listing of six types beginning with "long-term graduate student exchanges" was put in first or second rank by 101 respondents—far ahead of any other. Strong plugs were made, however, for other types of exchange. For example, American Friends Service Committee seminars, performances by the Yale Russian Chorus, official U.S. traveling exhibitions, and other categories were singled out for special praise—the exhibitions by five respondents. Fourteen thought that exchanges of businessmen and political leaders could be very useful, but twenty-three depreciated such exchanges. Ten of our respondents heaped scorn on ordinary tourist travel: some noted that most tourists, not knowing Russian and usually having little knowledge of Soviet conditions, often fell easy prey to propaganda. One, however, regarded it as the most important type of exchange.

A good many respondents argued strongly, and in some cases at length, that all kinds of contacts were valuable and that all should be expanded. Fifty persons, sometimes in strong terms, expressed a preference for close, personal, face-to-face unrestricted contacts and working relationships with Russians in contrast to organized group or "delegation" contacts. As one of them put it, the only worthwhile contacts were "*à deux*."

BARRIERS TO COMMUNICATION AND THE FEASIBILITY OF REDUCING THEM

Running through much of the testimony of our respondents was the strong clear message that, although face-to-face contact between Americans and Russians is often mutually rewarding and is highly desirable, it is nevertheless an unnecessarily difficult and frustrating process. Table 9 indicates, albeit schematically and feebly, the wide distribution of complaints among our three main categories of respon-

Table 9A. Does the Respondent Have Complaints Concerning the Conduct of Exchanges?

	Professional Interest		
	Social Scientists	Natural Scientists	Humanities
Yes	44	31	40
No	—	6	—

Table 9B. Significant Improvement Would Require Fundamental Changes in the Soviet System

	Professional Interest		
	Social Scientists	Natural Scientists	Humanities
Yes, it would	10	1	9
No, it would not	1	1	—

dents regarding the exchange process as they had experienced it. Rather inconclusively, the same table points to a belief, very much more salient among social scientists, historians, and literary scholars than among natural scientists, that significant improvements in exchange experience and results would require fundamental changes in the Soviet political system, particularly in relations between political authorities and the citizenry. Sixty-three respondents, or more than one-third of the entire sample, mentioned "fear" on the part of Soviet citizens in the presence of foreigners as a factor obstructing normal communication. Quite a few spelled out in detail, supported by specific illustrations, precisely what they meant. One source wrote that this kind of fear was "not surface scare but up-from-the-crib caution and keep your nose clean."

Against this background, criticisms were voiced of Soviet exchange strategy in general and of many of its particular aspects, such as travel and itinerary restrictions, failure to supply statistical information to economists, and failure to admit historians to archives.

There was wide agreement that Soviet policy was in the USSR's "national interest" (Table 10), but one senior political scientist who

Table 10. Is the Soviet Exchange Policy in USSR's National Interest?

	Professional Interest					
	Social Scientists		Natural Scientists		Humanities	
Yes	38	75%	23	74%	32	82%
No	13	25%	8	26%	7	18%
	51	100%	31	100%	39	100%

	Time Spent on Soviet Affairs			
	Most or About Half Time		Some, Little, or No Time	
Yes	54	75%	54	79%
No	18	25%	14	21%
	72	100%	68	100%

	Command of Russian			
	Fluent in Russian		Less Than Fluent or No Russian	
Yes	67	81%	42	72%
No	16	19%	16	28%
	83	100%	58	100%

	Age			
	Under 50		50 and Over	
Yes	75	77%	34	77%
No	22	23%	10	23%
	97	100%	44	100%

set forth his views very systematically pointed out that it was not a policy of "the greatest good for the greatest number." Much of the comment on it could be summed up by a single expression—shrewd in the short run, perhaps self-defeating in the long run. Table 11 amplifies this view in its breakdown of imputed Soviet exchange objectives.

There was much criticism, often in highly emotional language, of the role in obstructing or even crippling communication of what the questionnaire referred to as (Soviet) "political officers"—labeled by some exchangees as "informers," "thugs," or "police agents," or in such Russian terms as *nyanki* (nursemaids, or nannies) and *nadsmotrshchiki* (overseers). Again, social science and humanities spe-

Table 11. Objectives Pursued by the USSR in Exchange of Persons

Frequency of Responses

Objectives	Social scientists	Natural scientists	Humanities	Government	Other	Total Responses*
1. Acquisition of technical, scientific, and industrial skills	43	26	36	4	15	124
2. Gaining of respect, influence, good will, and prestige	31	11	19	3	15	79
3. Espionage or recruitment of agents	10	6	9	4	3	32
4. Acquisition of first-hand knowledge of US	13	13	7	–	3	36
5. Acquisition of hard currency	8	2	4	2	6	22
6. Implementation of strategy of detente	8	2	7	–	2	19
7. Improvement in training of diplomats and other professionals	4	–	7	–	4	15
8. Improvement of regime's standing among Soviet intellectuals	7	2	4	–	1	14
9. Proof USSR is not afraid of foreign contacts	5	2	4	–	2	13
10. Fostering of mutual understanding	4	2	3	–	2	11
11. Gratification of Soviet self/system by displaying achievements abroad	3	2	2	–	3	10
12. Rewarding talent and achievement	2	1	1	–	2	6

* The number of responses exceeds the total number of questionnaires returned, because many respondents volunteered more than one "objective pursued."

cialists tended to perceive it significantly more frequently than did natural scientists (Table 12).

What could be done to render exchanges more useful? Drastically condensing respondents' comments and proposals—which were in some cases specific and extensive—we should say, first, that many (especially among the scientists) were reasonably content with established routines. Those who were strongly critical tended to think that more vigorous efforts by individual Americans to prepare themselves

Table 12. Do Political Officers Interfere with Communication?

Professional Interest

A. (Fisher's exact test: probability of these frequencies under H_o = .06009)	Social Scientists		Natural Scientists	
Yes, they do	26	90%	12	67%
Neutral, or No, they do not	3	10%	6	33%
	29	100%	18	100%

B.	Social Scientists		Humanities	
Yes, they do	26	90%	21	95%
Neutral, or No, they do not	3	10%	1	5%
	29	100%	22	100%

Time Spent on Soviet Affairs

	Most or About Half Time		Some, Little, or No Time	
Yes, they do	39	91%	33	80%
Neutral, or No, they do not	4	9%	8	20%
	43	100%	41	100%

Command of Russian

	Fluent in Russian		Less Than Fluent or No Russian	
Yes, they do	43	90%	31	82%
Neutral, or No, they do not	5	10%	7	18%
	48	100%	38	100%

Age

	Under 50		50 and Over	
Yes, they do	42	79%	27	82%
Neutral, or No, they do not	11	21%	6	18%
	53	100%	33	100%

better, linguistically and in terms of knowledge both about their own culture and the history, philosophy, and administrative practices of the USSR, might be very helpful. Many also felt that private American organizations and especially the U.S. government should bargain hard—should, as one scholar put it, "insist on a strict *quid pro quo* in terms of enhancement of real personal contact in return for measures USSR wants," while discouraging "casual American tourism" in Russia. Also typical, however, was an epidemiologist's recommendation to treat Soviet exchange participants in America "gently and with natural dignity." Actually, the "hard" and "soft" lines recommended, directed as they were to different aspects of a single process, did not seem incompatible. Finally, with regard to substantial changes in official Soviet exchange policy: beyond firmness in protesting violations of agreements, a sophisticated application of a *quid pro quo* policy, and some interesting organizational suggestions (for example, one man thought that the United States should set up a structure similar to the British Council), responses tended to be tinged with skepticism or in some cases with exasperation. Thus, one sociologist suggested that we "must be joking" in asking what the Soviet government might do "to make exchanges more pleasant, profitable and useful to Americans"—while a historian with extensive experience in Russia suggested: "Abolish the KGB!"

In conclusion, it should be said that the kinds and styles of communication described have not, so far as evidence available to us indicates, changed significantly. Moreover, there is no reason to believe that they will be altered in the next few years, barring the unlikely contingencies of catastrophe or a sudden and fundamental liberalization of Soviet political life.[1]

1   This study received generous financial aid from the Stimson Fund of Yale University. We thank the administrators of this Fund, and also Hazel O'Donnell, secretary of the Russian and East European Studies Council, Yale University, for secretarial assistance.

We are grateful to the late Hadley Cantril, and to Chester I. Bliss, Hayward R. Alker, Jr., Richard L. Merritt, Charles L. Taylor, and Bruce M. Russett for advice and suggestions regarding the questionnaire and suggestions on problems of statistical interpretation. We owe special thanks to Urie Bronfenbrenner for suggesting that we send a follow-up postcard questionnaire to obtain data that would help us to interpret the rate of return from our basic questionnaire. Analysis of responses to the postcard indicated that failure to fill out the long questionnaire was associated mainly with factors of time and lack of experience in Russia—not to respondents' attitudes.

For assistance in connection with coding and statistical matters we also express our appreciation to John Sibley, Paul Mason, and Peter Moody, and also to Carol Thomas, Kwailing Chen, and Stewart Thomas of the staff of the Computer Institute for Social Science Research, Michigan State University, and its director, Charles F. Wrigley. Assistance in coder reliability checking was provided by E. Ann Kelley and David Klingman.

seven

The Problem-Solving Workshop
in Conflict Resolution

Herbert C. Kelman

THE idea that face-to-face communication among parties in conflict, in a context other than diplomatic negotiations, may contribute to conflict management and resolution is certainly not new. The American Friends Service Committee, in particular, has pioneered in such endeavors. In the last few years we have seen some exciting new experiments in this type of international communication, based on concepts and techniques from the behavioral sciences. Notable among these are the exercises in "controlled communication" of John Burton and his associates at the Centre for the Analysis of Conflict at University College, London,[1] and the Fermeda Workshop, organized by Leonard Doob and his associates at Yale University.[2] Both approaches are designed to bring together representatives of nations or national (ethnic) communities involved in an active conflict, for face-to-face communication in a relatively isolated setting, free from governmental and diplomatic protocol. Discussions, following a relatively unstructured agenda, take place under the guidance of social scientists who are knowledgeable both about group process and about conflict theory. The talks are designed to produce changes in the participants' perceptions and attitudes and thus to facilitate creative problem-solving.

This chapter summarizes the Burton and Doob approaches and then compares, evaluates, and attempts to integrate them.[3] The ge-

1 See John W. Burton, *Conflict and Communication: The Use of Controlled Communication in International Relations* (London: Macmillan, 1969).
2 See Leonard W. Doob, ed., *Resolving Conflict in Africa: The Fermeda Workshop* (New Haven: Yale University Press, 1970).
3 This chapter is a product of a research program on social influence and

neric term "problem-solving workshop"[4] is used to refer to both approaches, since it emphasizes the fact that these approaches utilize "workshop" techniques, but that their orientation is toward problem-solving rather than sensitivity training or personal growth as such.

The workshop approach (and psychological analysis more generally) is often greeted with skepticism; indeed, I share some of that skepticism myself. Before turning to the work of Burton and Doob, therefore, let me clarify some assumptions that I bring to this analysis—and with which, I believe, Burton and Doob generally concur.

(1) I do not assume that most international conflicts are simply products of misunderstanding and misperception that can be cleared up through improved communication.[5] Real conflicts of interest or competing definitions of national interest are often at the center of such disputes. In such cases, improved understanding may demonstrate more clearly that the goals of the conflicting parties are indeed incompatible. Communication may still be useful, in that it may reveal more precisely to each party what the costs of pursuing various alternative policies are likely to be. Nevertheless, more accurate perception would clearly not alter the realities of the underlying conflict.

Moreover, even where there is misperception, face-to-face communication can directly affect only the perceptions and attitudes of the participating individuals. International conflicts, however, usually involve not only individual misperceptions, but also institutionalized ones—that is, misperceptions that are built into and perpetuated through the decision-making apparatus. Vested interests and organizational commitments become attached to a given perception of a conflict situation at various levels in the decision-making bureaucracy, making it difficult for changed perceptions to penetrate.

Clearly, then, problem-solving workshops are not meant as panaceas or as total solutions. They are merely inputs into a more complex resolution process. They are not alternatives to diplomatic and political negotiations, but supplementary or preparatory to them. Burton argues that his procedures of controlled communication are potentially significant and central inputs into conflict resolution; yet

---

commitment to social systems, supported by U.S. Public Health Service Research Grant Number MH–17669–02 from the National Institutes of Mental Health.

4   Richard E. Walton, "A Problem-Solving Workshop on Border Conflicts in Eastern Africa," *Journal of Applied Behavioral Science* 6, no. 4 (October–December 1970): 453–89.

5   I have discussed some of these issues in the introductory and concluding chapters of *International Behavior: A Social-Psychological Analysis*, ed. Herbert C. Kelman (New York: Holt, 1965); and in "The Role of the Individual in International Relations: Some Conceptual and Methodological Considerations," *Journal of International Affairs* 24, no. 1 (1970): 1–17.

he too speaks of these procedures as preparing the ground for negotiation and as establishing the preconditions of agreement—not as
substituting for negotiation.

(2) The problem-solving workshops discussed here are not to be
equated with T-groups or sensitivity training as usually defined.
They do use some of the techniques and approaches derived from
T-group experience. The Fermeda Workshop utilized fairly standard
T-groups during its first phase, although in retrospect its organizers
are inclined to view this decision as a mistake. In any event, the main
task of these workshops is not to increase personal sensitivity, or
even interpersonal trust and understanding of the other side; nor is
there any assumption that international conflict can be redefined and
resolved at an interpersonal level. Workshops are designed to promote trust and openness in communication. However, these are seen
not as ends in themselves, but as means toward the development of
an atmosphere in which creative problem-solving becomes possible.
Unlike the standard T-group, the problem-solving workshop is oriented toward carrying out a concrete task and achieving a usable
product.

THE BURTON EXERCISES IN
CONTROLLED COMMUNICATION

John Burton's book[6] and other papers on controlled communication
draw on experiences gained in two workshops, one involving an international conflict and the other an intercommunal conflict. I was
on the panel of social scientists in the second exercise, and I base my
impressions of the approach on that experience. It differed in several
ways from the first exercise and from further ones that Burton and
his associates are currently planning—both because of different circumstances and because the technique itself is still evolving—but it
illustrates Burton's general orientation.

The exercise dealt with the conflict between the Greek and Turkish communities in Cyprus. It was held in the fall of 1966, in a university setting in London. It lasted a week. The participants included
two representatives of the Greek community and two of the Turkish
community. They were selected by the top decision-makers in their
respective communities, but they participated essentially as private
citizens rather than as official representatives. The exercise was presented to them basically as an academic project, which would meet

6 Burton, *Conflict and Communication.*

the interests of the sponsoring organization in the analysis of concrete conflict situations. At the same time, the organizers indicated that the communication between the two parties might also contribute to resolution of their conflict. The exercise's potential relevance to conflict resolution was clearly understood on all sides, but the organizers made no promises—nor did the parties, in agreeing to participate, commit themselves to anything other than a contribution to an academic enterprise.

In addition to the four Cypriots, a panel of six social scientists (one of whom served as chairman) participated in the discussions. Meetings were held each morning and afternoon during the week (and continued informally during lunch and tea). The discussions were relatively unstructured and designed to encourage participants to share their definitions of the conflict, their perceptions of their own and others' goals and actions, and their assessments of the costs and benefits of alternative conflict resolutions. The chairman and the panel tried to move the discussion away from mutual accusations and legalistic attempts to assign blame and toward a behavioral analysis of the conflict's causes, escalation, and perpetuation, as well as toward efforts to explore possible solutions.

The discussions can be roughly divided into three phases. In the first, the conflicting parties presented their respective views of the conflict; the social scientists generally intervened only to ask questions of detail, which sometimes helped sharpen and clarify an issue or lay the groundwork for subsequent analysis. During the second phase, the social scientists presented various models of conflict. The discussion following each focused first on the origins and processes of conflict in general, and then on the specific conflict at hand. Applicability of the various models to the Cyprus situation was explored, largely by the parties themselves. The social scientists intervened to inform and elaborate, and to propose tentative interpretations of the conflict in terms of the models presented. The social scientists used conflict theory and other theoretical concepts as a psychotherapist might use personality theory: they provided general models for analyzing conflict and then encouraged the parties to confront possible implications of these models for their situation. Where relevant, they drew on these models to raise questions about the two parties' differing perceptions of the same situation.

During the third phase, the parties considered various approaches to resolving the conflict. The social scientists contributed to this phase in two ways: by bringing in relevant experiences from the resolution of other international or intercommunal conflicts, especially through the development of patterns of functional cooperation; and by systematically attempting to explain why solutions that seemed very reasonable to one party caused anxiety and rejection in the other. The social scientists did not themselves propose solutions, nor did they convey the expectation that an agreed-upon solution was to be found. The assumption was that solutions would eventually have to be achieved through formal channels of negotiation, but that new insights about the conflict and new ideas for its resolution emerging from the workshop would be communicated to the relevant decision-makers and might thus influence the negotiation process.

The outcome of the workshop is difficult to assess. The parties seem to have communicated to each other some new and potentially important facts about their respective goals and intentions. Some new insights about the origins and escalation of the conflict have apparently been developed. Certainly by the end of the sessions the parties were able to communicate with each other more freely and within a shared frame of reference. Moreover, there is no doubt that the new information and insights acquired by the participants were transmitted to the top leaders of their own groups, because of the relationship of the participants to the decision-making process. We can only speculate, however, about the extent to which and the way in which these entered into subsequent negotiations. At the time of the exercise, the two parties had not been in official communication with each other for some time. Shortly after the exercise, communication between them was resumed. It is quite likely that the exercise played some role in this development, though we cannot be certain. At the very least, it may have provided a mechanism for the two sides to test each other out in a noncommittal fashion and an opportunity to learn whether resumption of negotiations would be fruitful.

THE FERMEDA WORKSHOP

The Fermeda Workshop was named after a hotel in the mountains of South Tyrol, where the Yale team of Leonard W. Doob, William J. Foltz, and Robert B. Stevens organized a workshop focusing on the border disputes in the horn of Africa between Somalia and its two neighbors, Ethiopia and Kenya. I did not witness this workshop firsthand. My information is based on various written accounts[7] and on

7   Leonard W. Doob, William J. Foltz, and Robert B. Stevens, "The Fermeda Workshop: A Different Approach to Border Conflicts in Eastern Africa," *Journal of Psychology* 73, no. 2 (November 1969): 249–66; Doob, *Resolving Conflict in Africa*; Walton, "Problem-Solving Workshop."

personal communications with several of the participants, particularly with Leonard Doob and Richard Walton. In this connection, I also benefited from a working conference sponsored by the United Nations Institute for Training and Research in May, 1970, in which experiences from both the Fermeda Workshop and the controlled communication exercises were presented, discussed, and evaluated in detail.[8]

The African participants in the Fermeda Workshop included six Somalis, six Ethiopians, and six Kenyans. The Ethiopian and Kenyan participants all held academic posts; the participants from Somalia—which had no university—were professionals or civil servants working in areas unrelated to foreign policy. Plans for the workshop were cleared with the three governments, but the participants were selected by the organizers and came as private individuals, rather than as official representatives. Participants from the same country did not constitute a team and, as far as is known, did not even communicate with each other in anticipation of the workshop. They were told that the workshop would follow the format of sensitivity-training groups, and that some innovative solutions to the countries' border problems were hoped for. They knew this was a highly exploratory effort, which might or might not yield significant results. In addition to the African participants and the three Yale organizers, the workshop included four American specialists in sensitivity training and related techniques, who came in the roles of "trainers" or "process consultants."

The workshop lasted two weeks, with a two-day break in the middle. From the beginning, the participants were broken up into two T-groups, each including three Somalis, three Kenyans, three Ethiopians, two trainers, and one or two of the organizers. During the first few days, the groups, which met intensively, followed standard T-group procedures, aimed at developing self-awareness and open communication among the participants. The trainers did not structure or lead the discussions, but functioned as observers and interpreters of group process. During this period, there were also several meetings of the total group in which theoretical notions about leadership styles and about cooperative and competitive strategies were presented by the trainers and illustrated through simulation exercises. These sessions were designed both to improve the working processes within the T-groups and to provide concepts that could be drawn upon in later discussions of the border disputes.

8 See "Social Psychological Techniques and the Peaceful Settlement of International Disputes," *UNITAR Research Reports*, no. 1 (1970).

During these first few days, the meetings did not deal at all with the substantive issues relating to the border disputes. They focused on individual and group development instead. During the second phase, the workshop turned specifically to the border disputes. First, participants met in their three separate national groups; each group was asked to list its own grievances and the grievances of the other two national groups, as they perceived them, and to present these lists to the total group. The procedure did not work too well, since two of the groups failed to engage in the requested role reversal. In general, the total group seemed to make little progress at this point, and the participants' planning committee (which had since been formed) decided to revert to the original T-groups to work out concrete solutions. The general assembly was used during this phase for presentation and practice of brainstorming techniques and for reports of the activities of the individual T-groups.

Within each of the two T-groups, proposals were developed that all group members, regardless of their national affiliations, were willing to endorse. These proposals were then brought to the general assembly with the aim of achieving a joint solution. However, this particular effort did not succeed, apparently because the trust developed in the T-groups did not carry over to the larger group. National differences came to the fore; participants who had agreed to a solution hammered out in their individual T-group sometimes reverted to rigid defenses of their national position; in some cases, participants from one T-group accused fellow nationals from the other group of betraying their national cause by subscribing to a detrimental proposal. The workshop closed without being able to meet the staff's original goal of developing a joint proposal supported by the total group.

Though the workshop did not arrive at a joint proposal, it did have some positive outcomes. Within the T-groups, trust and an openness of communication developed. These yielded, in each group, a proposal for resolving the conflict that was generally supported by all group members. In response to a questionnaire, the participants indicated (on the whole) that they had acquired new knowledge about the cultures and problems of the other countries, that they had gained a better understanding of the other countries' views of the disputes, and that they were somewhat more open now to alternative solutions. Participants did not feel that the workshop yielded many innovative ideas for solving the border disputes. About a year after the workshop, Doob carried out follow-up interviews with thirteen of the eighteen African participants to gain some impressions of the

impact the workshop had on them and on their respective countries.[9]
On the whole, their reactions to the experience (and in some cases
to the workshop techniques) were positive: they felt close to the
other participants, regardless of nationality, and eager to remain in
touch with them, and they showed an understanding of the intense
emotional meanings that their respective positions had for each of
the parties. On the other hand, their own attitudes on the best ways
to resolve the conflict were not appreciably affected. News of the
workshop reached important officials in each of the three countries,
although most of the participants did not make extensive efforts to
communicate their experiences.

THE TWO APPROACHES COMPARED

In comparing the two approaches—and particularly in noting the
differences between them—we must keep in mind that neither one
represents a "closed system," a set of established and tightly defined
procedures. Both are seen by their inventors as exploratory, as requiring further refinement, and as open to change, extension, and
recombination. In this spirit, differences between the two approaches
do not necessarily reflect incompatible views, but rather different
starting-points and experiences. There is every reason to suppose
that the two approaches can borrow from each other and be combined in various ways, and to treat them as two variants of a more
general model, each applicable to a special set of circumstances.

The two approaches have several important features in common:

(1) *Setting.* In both approaches, workshops are held in settings
isolated from political and diplomatic environments. The Fermeda
Workshop was held in a physically isolated setting; the London exercise was held in an academic setting, removed from the pressures and
publicity that typically surround official negotiations. The isolation
is partly to reduce distraction and permit participants to concentrate
intensively on the task. More important, it allows participants to
explore issues while free of constant preoccupation with the public
statements they must issue and the impressions they will be making
on their various constituencies.

(2) *Sponsorship.* Both types of workshops are sponsored by academic organizations, independent of governmental or intergovernmental agencies. The governments concerned were informed and

9   Leonard W. Doob, "The Impact of the Fermeda Workshop on the Conflicts
in the Horn of Africa," *International Journal of Group Tensions* 1, no. 1 (1971):
91–101.

consulted and, in fact, gave their approval of the workshops, but the workshops had no official status whatsoever. The sponsors' legitimacy depended entirely on their status as scholars and people of good will, whose interest in the exercise derived from their research concerns and their desire to make a constructive contribution to the resolution of a violent conflict. The organization of the Fermeda Workshop was greatly aided, however, by the backing of the United Nations Institute for Training and Research.

(3) *Participants.* Although the two approaches differed significantly in the criteria for selecting participants, both sets of participants had two characteristics in common. On the one hand, they were prestigious members of their respective communities, who at least potentially (in the London workshop quite clearly and, indeed, by the nature of their selection) had access to their top decision-makers. On the other hand, they participated in the sessions as private citizens who spoke only for themselves. Even the participants in the London workshop, who were almost certainly briefed by their respective administrations, did not come as official, instructed delegates.

(4) *Interpersonal atmosphere.* In both workshops the discussions and the environments were designed to create an informal atmosphere in which participants would be free to express their views openly and to get to know and respect each other as individuals. The atmosphere fostered mutual trust, a sense of shared values, and commitment to a common task, cutting across national or ethnic divisions.

(5) *Discussion format.* Central to both workshops was the opportunity for direct, face-to-face communication among the conflicting parties. The agenda for discussion was relatively unstructured. The initiative for introducing issues—or for following up on inputs from the third parties—was largely left to the participants themselves. Third parties refrained from imposing their definitions of the situation and their interpretations of actions and events on the participants; rather, they encouraged participants to speak for themselves—to describe their own motives and perceptions, express their own hopes and fears. In particular, both workshops were committed to the idea that solutions must emerge from the group discussions, rather than be imposed from the outside.

(6) *Role of third parties.* Both workshops were under the general guidance of third parties, defined in terms of their professional skills and knowledge as theoretical or applied behavioral scientists rather than in terms of some official capacity as mediators. Though they

participated in the proceedings, their primary task was to provide tools that the participants could utilize in their discussions and analyses, to offer relevant information and suggest interpretations, and to facilitate the group process in other ways. In short, they played a role similar to that of the psychotherapist. And like psychotherapists, they tried to maintain analytical rather than evaluative attitudes toward the participants' pronouncements.

These common features of the two approaches are essentially designed to achieve two ends. First and foremost, they are designed to give participants the freedom, opportunity, and impetus to move away from a rigid reiteration of official positions and from efforts to justify their own sides and score points against the other side, and, instead, to absorb new information, explore new ideas, revise their perceptions, reassess their attitudes, and engage in a process of creative problem-solving. The isolated setting, the academic sponsorship, the participants' nonrepresentative roles, the informal atmosphere, the development of trust, the encouragement of self-expression and of an analytical orientation, and the inputs and attitudes of the social scientists all are geared to facilitating these processes.

Second, some common features of both approaches are designed to enhance the probability that the new information and ideas, the changed perceptions and attitudes, and the innovative proposals for solutions generated by the workshop will be fed into the policy process. The selection of potentially influential participants, the coordination with their governments, and a format that allows the definition of the issues and the development of solutions to emerge out of group discussions, rather than being externally imposed (thus discouraging analyses and solutions that go considerably beyond what the decision-makers are prepared to entertain), are geared to achieving this end. Both approaches, it seems to me (as I shall elaborate later), are more effectively designed to produce changes in participants than to feed such changes into the policy process—although the balance between these two ends is one respect in which the two approaches differ from each other.

Let me turn to some of the differences between the two approaches. In terms of the six categories used to describe common features of the two approaches, several distinctions can be drawn. (1) The Fermeda Workshop, held in a physically isolated setting, placed greater emphasis on the creation of a "cultural island" and on the psychological insulation of workshop participants. (2) The London workshop was sponsored by a research center concerned with international relations theory, diplomacy, and the analysis of conflict, representing a research project within that center's ongoing program; the Fermeda Workshop was sponsored by social scientists interested in African studies and staffed by specialists in group process, representing an experimental application of the human-relations training laboratory to conflict resolution. (3) Participants in the London exercise were considerably closer to foreign policy decision-making and came as a team; those in the Fermeda Workshop were more removed from the foreign policy process and came as individuals, thus manifesting greater diversity and division within each national contingent. (4) The Fermeda Workshop placed more deliberate emphasis on creating an interpersonal atmosphere marked by emotional involvement, group solidarity, and mutual trust, and in forging cross-national bonds within the working group. (5) To facilitate discussion of the substantive issues of the conflict, the London workshop made greater use of theoretical models of conflict and of illustrative cases, while the Fermeda Workshop focused more extensively on the ongoing group process and interpersonal behavior; in discussion of the substantive issues themselves, the Fermeda Workshop made more deliberate efforts than the London workshop to hammer out an agreed-upon proposal for resolving the conflict. (6) In the London workshop, the social scientists made more theoretical inputs, both in their own presentations and in their interventions, and they were generally more active in the course of the discussion itself; in the Fermeda Workshop, they provided more feedback on the basis of their observations of group process and were more active in programming the workshop activities—in setting the tasks to which the participants were to devote themselves.

These differences in detail reflect certain underlying differences between the two approaches, both in their conception of the enterprise as such and in their definition of the workshop task. They differ in their views of the workshop's relationship to the larger process of conflict resolution, and in their views of precisely what ought to be happening within the workshop itself. My formulation of these differences may be overly sharp, but it should be helpful in pointing up the unique contributions of each approach.

How do the two approaches differ, first, in their conceptions of the enterprise? As I have indicated before, both are concerned with creating an atmosphere in which change—in the form of revised perceptions and attitudes and innovative solutions—can take place, in the hope that this change can be fed into the political processes of conflict resolution. However, the two approaches differ, it seems to me, in their conceptions of precisely where the workshop fits into these political processes and what it is intended to accomplish.

In Burton's conception, the workshop is much more closely linked to national and international political processes. The concept of controlled communication flows out of a theoretical orientation toward international relations, containing such propositions as these: that "international conflict is a spill-over from internal or communal strife";[10] that "the starting point in analysis and resolution of conflict is at the systems level of highest transactions";[11] that "conflict occurs as a result of ineffective communication, and that its resolution, therefore, must involve processes by which communication can be made to be effective";[12] and that "since the resolution of conflict depends upon effective communication, it can come only from the parties themselves. Processes are required that alter perceptions, and promote the points of view of the parties, and not of third parties."[13] In Burton's view, then, procedures like those of controlled communication represent crucial steps in the conflict resolution process.

In keeping with this conception, Burton's workshops are closely coordinated with the relevant decision-makers. The participants must be individuals who are fully aware of the positions of these decision-makers. Though they need not be officials themselves (and do not come to the workshop in any official capacity), they are nominated by the top decision-makers and are in touch with them both before and after the workshop. Burton himself, both before and after conducting a workshop, tries to establish and maintain contact with the relevant governmental and intergovernmental agencies. In the first project conducted by the London Centre, the meetings themselves extended over a period of several months: after an initial week of intensive discussions, the group reconvened under the Centre's auspices whenever the parties felt that a session would be useful. In principle, then, controlled communication is not a one-shot exercise, but can be tied into a continuing process of conflict resolution at various points in time. Of course, such coordination of workshops with ongoing political processes is greatly facilitated when the sponsoring organization is specifically devoted to research on international conflict.

The Fermeda Workshop was further removed from the political process. Though the organizers communicated with the governments

10   Burton, *Conflict and Communication*, p. 17.
11   Ibid., p. 19.
12   Ibid., p. 49.
13   Ibid., p. 55.

concerned, their purpose was to inform the governments and get their approval, rather than to coordinate directly with decision-making bodies. Though the participants were potentially influential members of their societies, they were selected by the organizers and could not be viewed as even unofficial representatives of their respective governments. Both Burton and Doob took pains to hold the workshop itself in a setting isolated from the pressures of political and diplomatic environments, but Doob placed greater emphasis on separating the total enterprise from the political process.

In Doob's conception, as I understand it, a workshop can contribute to conflict resolution by creating certain products that can then be fed into the political process. In other words, the workshop itself is not directly linked to national decision-making or diplomatic efforts at conflict resolution, but its products may well be relevant to these activities. The workshop's potential products are of two kinds: they may take the form of attitude changes in influential persons, which would be reflected over time in the inputs these individuals make into their national policy debates; and they may be documents, setting forth possible solutions that would not have emerged as readily from the usual political procedures.

The difference between Burton's and Doob's conceptions of the enterprise thus has some clear implications for what the workshop is intended to accomplish. For Doob, it is a more self-contained enterprise, standing or falling on the immediate products that emerge from it. There is, therefore, more emphasis on the personal learning of the participants—on whether they come away from the workshop with demonstrably greater knowledge and insight. There is also more emphasis on producing an agreed-upon solution, in the form of a document that can serve as an input to the policy debate. For Burton, too, it is important to produce changes in the participants and to promote problem-solving; however, these effects are viewed as steps in the conflict-resolution process more than as ends in themselves. There is less emphasis on the personal learning of the participants, except insofar as it influences the new information and insights that they can feed into the policy process. Similarly, there is less emphasis on the production of agreed-upon documents within the workshop itself. The presumption is that the actual working out of solutions must happen elsewhere; the workshop will have made its contribution if it has brought some new possibilities for solutions to the attention of the relevant decision-makers.

If we look at the two ends of the enterprise that are central to both approaches—creating an atmosphere in which change can take place, and feeding new information and insights into the policy process—we can probably say, at the risk of some oversimplification, that Doob's conception places relatively more emphasis on creating the conditions for *change*, while Burton's places relatively more emphasis on creating the conditions for *transfer*. In selecting independent participants, in insulating the workshop on a "cultural island," in breaking up the national groupings, in encouraging group solidarity and emotional involvement, and in emphasizing group process and personal learning, the Fermeda Workshop made it more probable that participants would experience changes, but by the same token it made the transfer of such changes once the participants returned to their home settings—and particularly the penetration of the changes into the policy process—less likely. On the other hand, the London exercise, by working more closely with the decision-making agencies, by selecting participants more directly tied to the decision-making process, by maintaining the national teams as the basic unit and avoiding divisions within it, and by keeping the discussions more fully at an intellectual and substantive level, took less advantage of the workshop's potential for producing changes, but increased the probability that any changes that did occur would be transferred to the policy process.

Given these somewhat distinct conceptions of the enterprise, how does each approach define the task of the workshop itself? What are the means by which the workshop brings about the desired changes, and what roles do the participants and the social scientists have to enact if these changes are to take place?

Both approaches are designed to create the conditions for effective problem-solving. To this end, participants must learn to communicate with each other in new ways, to revise perceptions distorted by a long history of conflict, and—in Burton's words—to see "the conflict as a problem to be solved and not as a contest to be won."[14] In relation to each other, they must move from the roles of antagonists engaged in a zero-sum game, in which neither party dares to yield a point, to the role of collaborators searching for a positive-sum solution to a common problem. The social scientists' role is to facilitate this movement. The two approaches diverge in emphasis in their views of how this movement comes about.

In Burton's approach, the primary mediating process is the behavioral analysis of conflict. The workshop is designed to draw the participants into this process of conflict analysis along with the panel of social scientists. Anthony de Reuck, a member of the Centre for

14   Ibid., p. 157.

the Analysis of Conflict, has distinguished three roles that participants may play in a workshop: combatant representative, conflict analyst, and cooperative representative. He points out:

> An essential part of the controlled communication technique is to divest the parties of their roles and inhibitions as combatant representatives, and to offer them alternative roles, first as conflict analysts and later as cooperative representatives. In their roles as combatant representatives, the parties' reference groups are their governments and people at home. In their analytical roles, each party's reference group is that physically present around the conference table. At first, no doubt, it comprises only the academic panel, but as the meeting proceeds, I believe it could be shown to expand to include also the opponent party.[15]

The role of conflict analyst, fostered by the definition of the situation, gradually guides participants into that of cooperative representative. It also remains as an alternative when the cooperative process becomes too difficult or threatening: participants can retreat into the more intellectual role of general conflict-analyst.

The role of conflict analyst is readily available insofar as the workshop is presented—as was the case in the London workshop—as a research project. The research context, more generally, can facilitate entry into communication and broaden the content of what is communicated. Thus, when research serves as the context of the encounter, it becomes possible to bring together conflicting parties who until now refused to communicate, because to do so would have meant to yield a political point or to take unacceptable risks. The research context permits communication with minimum commitment and minimum risk. Similarly, within the situation, the research context allows participants to discuss issues and entertain ideas that they would have to avoid if they were speaking "for the record." Having agreed to collaborate in an ongoing research program, to which their conflict is relevant as a case in point, they can graciously defer to the wishes of the "professors" and pursue certain lines of discussion that would otherwise have met with objection. The combination of research with conflict resolution thus creates an ambiguity that may greatly help to move the process along. As Burton points out:

15   Anthony de Reuck, "Controlled Communication: Rationale and Dynamics," paper prepared for UNITAR Workshop on Social Psychological Aspects of Peaceful Settlement, New Paltz, N.Y., May 15–17, 1970.

> The ambiguity of the role of representatives—whether they are acting as official representatives in expressing viewpoints, or whether as honorary academics participating in an exercise designed to examine conflict—is itself an asset. It provides a reason for exploration even on matters on which official policy has been firmly stated, it makes possible a working relationship between the participants as persons, and it removes any implications of official commitments. Traditional means of peaceful settlement require commitment: this procedure depends for its success on the absence of any commitment, and the establishment of relationships that do not require it.[16]

In short, the research context can surmount some of the barriers to communication that characterize the relationship of conflicting parties—provided, of course, that the sponsors of the workshop are genuinely interested in conflict research and not just using it as a device to bring the parties together. At the same time, the research context makes the role of conflict analyst particularly natural. After all, conflict analysis is the substance of the research in which the participants have agreed to help out. They are acting as informants, providing data for the social science panel, and gradually entering into the process of analysis itself. Thus the research context creates not only a general readiness to engage in communication, but a natural occasion for the specific process that Burton considers to be a crucial step in conflict resolution. Furthermore, insofar as both parties are working with the social science panel in a research effort, they can more readily come to regard each other as collaborators in a common enterprise.

In line with Burton's definition of the workshop task, the primary role of the social scientists is "to inject into discussion new information, not about the dispute in question, but about conflict, its origins and processes drawn from theoretical analyses and empirical studies."[17] Later in the workshop, when solutions are under discussion, the social scientists also contribute information designed to extend the range of integrative mechanisms and possibilities for functional cooperation that the participants can consider. The social science panel, and particularly the discussion chairman, are by no means oblivious to the group process. They try to encourage movement away from the role of combatant representative and toward the role of conflict analyst and increasingly toward that of cooperative

16 Burton, *Conflict and Communication*, p. 43.
17 Ibid., p. 157.

representative. But the key professional input of the social scientists is at the level of theory and empirical findings.

In the Fermeda model, the primary mediating process is sensitization of participants to their own interpersonal behavior and to group process. The workshop essentially offers training in the skills of effective communication through the use of the "laboratory approach to learning." The training is designed to enhance participants' awareness of ways in which their own emotional commitments and the nature of group interaction may hinder effective communication and problem-solving, and to increase their ability to overcome these obstacles. The trainers convey the process of analyzing the ongoing interaction through demonstration, exposition, and the use of special exercises, and they draw the participants into active involvement in this process. As one of the trainers at Fermeda describes it, "The basic feature of this approach is that participants learn through analysis of, and generalizations from, their own experience and that of others with whom they interact. Laboratory participants, in different words, must first participate (interact, behave); then they are encouraged to reflect upon the meaning and impact of that behavior in relation to both themselves and others."[18] To adapt de Reuck's terminology, in the Fermeda model the participants move from the role of combatant representative to that of cooperative representative through adopting the role of process analyst—a role calling for self-conscious attention to what is happening in the group and what each participant is contributing to that process, and thus mediating change from self-defeating to more constructive modes of interaction.

Adoption of the process-analyst role is facilitated by definition of the workshop as essentially a learning experience—a training laboratory. In this context, participants are more prepared to go along with procedures (such as the T-group) that have no obvious connection to the substantive issues with which they are concerned, and to accept exercises (such as simulation and brainstorming) that might otherwise strike them as overly artificial. (Even so, some of the participants in Fermeda apparently resented procedures that had no clear and immediate relationship to the objective that had brought them to the workshop.) Furthermore, the context of a training laboratory—like the context of a research project in the London exercise—permits communication with relatively little commitment and risk. In this playful, protective, and insulated environment, the in-

18   Thomas E. Wickes, "The African Context and the Schedule," in Doob, *Resolving Conflict in Africa*, p. 26.

dividual is moved to pursue and express ideas that would be unacceptable in other settings, and he feels free to do so without worrying that he will be held accountable for it. In the Fermeda T-groups, participants felt free to consider and support positions that deviated from the normative positions of their own national groups. It is interesting, however, that when the two T-groups came together in the general assembly and participants were exposed to fellow nationals, with whom they had not shared the common T-group experience, they tended to revert to a nationalistic stance. The learning context, which had served to reduce inhibitions, was overwhelmed by the real-life context provided by the presence of "outsiders" (particularly from one's own national group) and by the approaching end of the workshop and anticipated return home. As long as the learning context is maintained, however, the freedom to explore with a minimal sense of risk can greatly facilitate creative problem-solving.

Other important features of the training laboratory situation can help to push the problem-solving process forward. The development of a sense of solidarity, an openness of communication, and warm personal bonds within the learning group not only contributes to the learning process; it also constitutes an important element of the problem-solving that this learning process is designed to facilitate. A cohesive group can more readily approach the conflict to be resolved as a joint task for the conflicting parties, to be tackled in a collaborative spirit. Similarly, the deliberate utilization of the here and now as a source of insights, through observation and analysis of ongoing interaction, facilitates both the learning process and the conflict-resolution process itself. The T-group, according to a Fermeda trainer, "replicates in microcosm the dynamics of the real system without acting it out. It focuses on an examination of its own process, analyzing and learning from what is happening right here and now. It provides an instrument to 'see' problems or divisions between people more clearly because they are projected and illustrated in the group and to accelerate the search for solutions that personal and shared identification with problems stimulates."[19] Insofar as participants can draw on the here and now in analyzing the conflict, they can partly overcome constraints imposed on the problem-solving process by formulations of the conflict that are rooted in historical arguments and the public positions of their respective governments.

In line with the Fermeda Workshop's definition of its task, the

19 Charles K. Ferguson, "Appraisal by a Trainer," in Doob, *Resolving Conflict in Africa*, p. 133.

primary role of the social scientists is to encourage the development of sensitivity to group process and effective communication patterns among the participants. As the group turns to direct efforts at problem-solving, the social scientists' role is to facilitate the process —to help the group identify snags when the process seems to break down and to develop strategies that would keep it moving. In both the training and the problem-solving phases (which need not be temporally separated), they help the group observe and analyze the interaction in which members are currently engaged. As in Burton's exercises, the social scientists may inject relevant theoretical considerations or empirical information, but their major inputs in the Fermeda model consist of observations and interpretations of the ongoing group process.

The differences between Burton's and Doob's approaches are mostly differences in emphasis. Despite their different origins, both approaches are built on a surprisingly similar set of insights about the use of "clinical" procedures to promote change and collaborative problem-solving among conflicting parties, and about the potential contributions of these procedures to conflict resolution at the political level. Both are concerned with producing change, and with its feedback to national and international decision-making; to facilitate change, both use inputs from conflict theory and from group-process analysis. They differ essentially in their ways of maximizing the unique strengths of the workshop approach and of minimizing its limitations.

In the following sections, I consider some of these strengths and limitations of the workshop approach. In each case, I try to show how insights from both Burton's and Doob's experiences might be combined to utilize the workshop most effectively. My general assumption is that workshops, though rooted in the same basic principles, may vary along a number of dimensions—such as the degree of emphasis on personal probing or theoretical analysis, the proximity of participants to the decision-making process, or the specific attributes of third parties present. The Burton and Doob experiments occupy different positions on some of these dimensions and thus represent different combinations of the possible features by which a workshop might be defined—different cells, as it were, in a multi-dimensional matrix of workshop types. Various other combinations should be possible, each best suited to a particular set of circumstances. Further conceptualization and experimentation in this area can help us specify the circumstances in which a workshop is likely to be useful and, if so, the combination of techniques most likely to be effective, given the nature of the particular conflict, the occasion for convening a workshop, and the relationship of both the organizers and the participants to the various decision-making units.

UNIQUE STRENGTHS OF THE WORKSHOP APPROACH

In the most general terms, the unique strength of the workshop approach is that it allows certain processes of communication that are almost impossible to achieve in the settings (particularly the more public and formal ones) where conflicting parties usually interact. The workshop facilitates such interactions, first, by providing a novel *context* for communication and, second, by using a unique set of *techniques* and third-party inputs to guide the communication process.

In many conflict situations, the very fact that communication is taking place may be seen, by one or both sides, as a concession— because it suggests that the other side may have a valid claim, or even because it constitutes recognition of the other side's existence as a legitimate entity. Communication may also be avoided because it represents unacceptable risks: decision-makers may be afraid that their willingness to talk would be taken as a sign of weakness, or that talks would reduce the pressure on the opponent, or that they would inevitably lead to compromises which would weaken the regime's domestic and international standing, or that they would end in failure with a resulting loss in credibility and prestige. Conflicting parties may, therefore, refuse to communicate at all, or at least to engage in meaningful communication. Once such a pattern has been established, public commitments and private fears make it difficult for the parties to break out of it—even when they have come to feel that something might be gained from communication. In this type of situation the workshop may be particularly helpful by providing a context in which parties can enter into discussion with minimum commitment and risk. If the outcome of the workshop seems promising, decision-makers can continue discussions through more formal channels; if it yields nothing useful, they can ignore it without feeling discredited; if, for some reason, it blows up, they can easily disown it, since it was merely an academic exercise to which they had no formal commitment.

These considerations suggest one criterion for determining whether mounting of a workshop is indicated. When there is some desire for communication among the conflicting parties but the official channels for communication are unavailable, or their use entails unacceptable risks at this point, a workshop may provide the needed alternative mechanism. It may allow decision-makers to transmit and receive information otherwise unobtainable, and to see whether officially acknowledged initiation or resumption of communication is likely to have more positive than negative consequences. In the limiting case, a workshop may serve as dress rehearsal for more formal negotiations.

For the individual participants, the workshop also offers an opportunity to communicate with minimum commitment and risk. This fact has a bearing not only on their willingness to participate, but also on the type of communication they are prepared to engage in. I have already indicated how the context of both Burton's and Doob's workshops enhances the participants' freedom to entertain and express ideas that they would be inclined to eschew in settings marked by greater public accountability. The usual norms against deviating from the position of one's own side, so pervasive in a conflict situation, are relaxed in the workshop context. More than that, an opposing set of norms, calling for uninhibited exploration of all possibilities, is generated in this setting. In Burton's workshop it derives from the requirements of the research for careful analysis of all dimensions and ramifications of the conflict; in Doob's, from the requirements of the laboratory method for open and honest communication. Having committed themselves to the enterprise, the participants feel a sense of obligation to abide by its norms.

To provide a novel context, it seems to me, the workshop must be held under the auspices of some institution independent of the political process which can bring an overarching set of norms to bear on the proceedings. In other words, there needs to be some institutionalized basis for the norms governing the workshop, if the participants are to regard them (while they are in the situation) as binding and as superseding their national norms. A workshop held under the auspices of a body such as the United Nations Security Council, for example, might not provide the necessary novel context, since it does not claim a set of norms independent of those of the member-states.[20] An agency more nearly transnational in character—set up to perform a function that cuts across (rather than coordinates) national interests—would be more suitable. Burton's and Doob's experiences suggest that such a transnational institution for conflict resolution might be most effective if it included research and training as part of its mission.

20   Burton discusses other limitations of the Security Council as a possible institutional base for conflict resolution. See his *Conflict and Communication*, p. 235.

For both the London and the Fermeda workshops, the institutional base was the university. They provided the novel normative context of a research project in one case and of a training laboratory in the other. The research project seems to me to present a very useful context, particularly when the participants are relatively senior and high in status, and when the workshop requires the cooperation of decision-making agencies. Both the decision-makers who are asked to approve or support the enterprise and the participants themselves can usually understand and accept a research-linked workshop without difficulty, and they can readily justify their cooperation with such an effort. It is quite evident why students of conflict would want to meet with representatives of conflicting parties in a face-to-face encounter, and why the parties themselves would be prepared to support such a scholarly enterprise and to regard it as a source of potentially useful findings. Another virtue of the research context is that it offers the workshop participants the roles of expert informant and research collaborator—roles that are inherently rewarding and in keeping with their status. Finally, the research context allows a continuing relationship between the sponsors and the conflicting parties, and a resumption of the workshop if the need and opportunity arise: the natural life of the research project coincides with the natural life of the conflict.

The training-laboratory context strikes me as somewhat less powerful on all of these counts. Doob and his associates themselves seem to have concluded that the rationale and value of workshops within this context are not always manifest to governments and participants, and that the role of trainee is resented by some participants as insulting and out of keeping with their status. The training-laboratory context is also less amenable to a continuing relationship, since repeated workshops presumably offer diminishing returns from a training point of view. Finally, this context is more vulnerable to failure: a workshop that produces little learning and problem-solving can be assimilated in a research context, since (regardless of outcome) it provides grist for the research mill, but it may be quite demoralizing to both participants and staff in a training context. Nevertheless, there are occasions on which the training laboratory context may be highly appropriate and productive. Thus, a workshop might be organized specifically to serve an educational purpose —involving as its participants, for example, groups of students representing conflicting parties or diplomats seeking to gain insight into the nature of conflict and the techniques of its resolution. Furthermore, it must be kept in mind that training, in some fashion, is at least a *component* of all workshops. Thus even in the Burton model participants must gradually learn the language and the attitudes required for the role of conflict analyst, and the hope is that this learning will generalize to their post-workshop behavior.

The context of the workshop, as we have seen, helps overcome some of the barriers to communication that are so prevalent in conflict situations. The relative lack of commitment gives participants the *freedom* to talk more openly and honestly, and the norms of the setting create an *expectation* that they will do so. The fact that the parties have come together for a task defined, essentially, by a third party, makes it possible and necessary for them to abandon, to some degree, their competitive stance toward each other and to adopt a more trusting and collaborative one. To capitalize on this favorable context for communication, the workshop approach utilizes a set of techniques and interventions to guide the communication process. Some of these are more pronounced in Burton's approach; others, in Doob's.

Interactions between conflicting parties are usually highly repetitive and stereotyped. Alternative versions of the historical record are recited, old accusations and justifications are rehearsed, and fine legalistic points about rights and wrongs are debated. The workshop approach is designed to cut through this type of argumentation and to set a more constructive communication process into motion. The social scientists contribute to this end by setting the stage for a different communication process, by keeping the process moving and preventing a reversion to less-productive exchanges, and by injecting ideas, observations, and information on which new learning and insight can be built.

In setting the stage, the social scientists communicate the ground rules that are to govern the proceedings. In both word and action, they try to make clear that discussions will be mostly unstructured, that the basic raw material for analysis and problem-solving will have to emerge from the participants, and that the norms of the situation call for honest communication of perceptions and motives and for free exploration of a wide range of ideas. Through the attitudes they convey in their own interventions, they try to create a task-oriented, collaborative atmosphere, and an analytical, nonevaluative approach to the conflict. Stage-setting is mostly done at the beginning, but it has to continue throughout the proceedings. The social scientists must periodically remind the group of the ground rules. Furthermore, they must reinforce the norms and the atmosphere they have tried to convey whenever the opportunity arises—by the

kinds of questions they ask, by their reactions to what the participants say and do, and by the way they handle participants' efforts
to induce them to assume leadership, to take sides, or to make authoritative pronouncements.

To keep the discussions moving in constructive directions, the
social scientist injects observations about the ongoing group process
whenever the group seems to have reached an impasse. He may simply point out that the discussions have stalled or that the participants
have reverted to the standard pattern of argumentation among conflicting parties. He may describe what has been happening in the
group, thus bringing to the members' attention some of the interactions that may have failed to register on them, but leaving up to
them the interpretation of these events. At times, he may himself
offer possible interpretations of the dynamics of the group process
that seem to be impeding progress. Such interpretations, in my view,
ought to be relatively infrequent. Moreover, they must be presented
in the form of tentative hypotheses, recognizing that they may be
wrong or (even if they are perfectly accurate) that the group may
not be quite ready for them. (These considerations are similar to
those governing a psychotherapist's tentative allusions to his patient's unconscious defenses in interpreting his resistances to the
therapeutic work.) Finally, such interpretations in a problem-
solving workshop must be at the level of group process, rather than
personality dynamics.

Group process observations are useful, not only in keeping the
discussions moving in constructive directions, but also in transmitting
to the participants a potentially effective tool for problem-solving.
Participants are encouraged to engage in process analysis themselves
and thus to acquire a more analytic stance concerning their own and
other members' interactions in the group. The ability to step aside
and observe the ongoing interaction process is particularly valuable
in the resolution of intergroup conflicts, which by their very nature
inhibit effective communication and problem-solving.

The purpose of initiating and facilitating new patterns of communication in the workshop is to provide opportunities for the emergence of ideas, observations, and information on which new learning
and insight can be built. It is such new learnings and insights that
make it possible, and sometimes necessary, for participants to reassess their attitudes and reformulate the issues in ways more conducive to problem-solving. Some of the new information is injected
directly into the discussion by the social science panel. Much of the
information is specifically introduced by participants, or emerges

from their discussions, or is generated by their interactions; but the social scientists contribute to the process by helping to elicit the information, by encouraging the participants to focus on it, and by suggesting some of its implications.

One can distinguish at least three sources of new information in the workshop situation from which potentially new learnings and insights may emerge:

(1) In the course of the discussions, participants may acquire new information about the perceptions and intentions of the other side. The relatively private and relaxed setting may induce them to express sentiments that have not previously been acknowledged in public statements. Such information is bound to be useful, by adding depth to one's understanding of the other side's position, but there is also some danger in overemphasizing the significance of this information: the public positions of a government may be better indicators and predictors of policy than the private sentiments of individuals, even if these individuals are high officials (particularly since public pronouncements set constraints on future action). The workshop setting not only encourages the transmission of such new information, but also increases the probability that others will be receptive to it, to the extent that a degree of openness and mutual trust has developed. The social scientists contribute to the transmission and reception of this type of information by creating an atmosphere in which there is greater openness to new information and setting a task around which trust can be built. Moreover, when new information is introduced, the social scientists can call attention to it and make it a focus for discussion. They can encourage the participants to confront the information, making sure that it is neither avoided nor distorted and that its implications are duly drawn.

(2) The workshop can introduce the participants to a new conceptual framework for the analysis of conflict, a set of theoretical propositions, and a body of empirical findings, all of which may be applicable to their own situations. In the London workshop, such information was provided fairly systematically by the panel of social scientists, who then drew the participants into discussion of the theoretical models and their implications for various conflicts. The participants thus acquired some new insights into the nature of conflict, as well as a common language and frame of reference for analyzing specific conflict situations. The learning process may be aided, as in the Fermeda Workshop, by the introduction of games and simulations when such procedures might help illustrate and give experiential meaning to a theoretical proposition. In any event, the

application of the new concepts and analytical tools to their own situations must be left largely to the participants themselves. The social scientists can encourage the participants to make such efforts; they can ask leading questions, engage in gentle probings, and suggest tentative hypotheses to explain the nature and course of the conflict. But, in the final analysis, the application must be made *by the participants* if it is to have major impact on the resolution process. The timing of interpretations is also crucial, even if they are presented in tentative fashion. Again, one can take a leaf from the psychotherapist's book: an experienced therapist does not offer an interpretation unless he feels confident that the patient is ready for it.

(3) As the participants interact with each other and with the third parties in the course of the workshop, they may be illustrating—here and now—some of the underlying dynamics of the conflict between the communities they represent. Their behavior in the group may reflect the nature of the relationship between their communities and the self-perpetuating pattern of interaction that they have adopted. For example, in the course of the London workshop, I developed (but was unable to explore) the hypothesis that some of the interactions of the Greek-Cypriot and Turkish-Cypriot participants, with each other and with the social science panel, could be understood in terms of their statuses as members of the majority and minority populations respectively. The exploration of such hypotheses, based on ongoing interactions, can be a source of profound insight, since the participants can see the conflict in operation. They can observe its concrete manifestations in the very situation in which they are still actively involved and almost at the very moment that the interaction occurs. This type of experience has much in common with the "corrective emotional experiences" that many psychotherapists see as the heart of the therapeutic process.[21] In the context of psychotherapy, "the essence of a corrective emotional experience is the fact that the patient's examination of his attitudes and behavior patterns occurs simultaneously with their actual manifestation at a real-life level of emotional intensity. He examines his attitudes and behavior while he is still experiencing the relevant feelings, which makes this more than a mere intellectual exercise."[22] Like the psychotherapist, the social scientist in a workshop can facilitate such insights by calling attention to ongoing interactions that might illuminate

21 Franz Alexander and Thomas M. French, *Psychoanalytic Therapy* (New York: Ronald Press, 1946), pp. 66–68.
22 Herbert C. Kelman, "The Role of the Group in the Induction of Therapeutic Change," *International Journal of Group Psychotherapy* 13, no. 4 (October 1963): 415.

the relationship between the conflicting parties, and by helping participants explore their implications. Again, of course, his interventions must be tentative and sensitively timed.

In sum, I have described three major types of new information and insight that the workshop can provide and that can facilitate attitude change and problem-solving: direct information about the perceptions and sentiments of the other side, theoretical concepts for conflict analysis with potential applicability to the specific conflict under discussion, and analysis of ongoing interactions that might reflect the relationships between the conflicting parties. The first was common to both the London and the Fermeda experiences, the second was more prominent in London, and the third in Fermeda.

The combination of Burton's systematic use of theoretical inputs with Doob's greater emphasis on analysis of group process and on emotional learning would, in my view, maximize the workshop's potential for producing change. Process analysis can promote change, not only by facilitating movement in the group, but also by utilizing the ongoing interactions as a source of new insights. However, problem-solving workshops in conflict resolution ought not to be equated with sensitivity training in the usual sense of that term. Though they encourage interpersonal trust and personal learning among the participants in order to achieve their goals, their purpose is not to promote personal growth or strong in-group feelings. Their purpose is to facilitate creative problem-solving in a specific conflict situation. It is essential that this task-orientation and problem-solving emphasis be reflected in the organization of the workshop and all of its components. In line with this view, I would agree with the tentative conclusion of Doob and his associates that it would be inadvisable, in future workshops, to separate "training" from work on the substantive issues.[23] The substantive issues ought to be the focus of attention throughout, with group process observations, as well as special laboratory devices (simulations, role reversals, brainstorming, or the setting of operational goals or subgoals), brought in whenever they become relevant and the participants seem ready for them.

23 The first few days of the Fermeda Workshop were devoted to T-groups in order to prepare participants for subsequent collaborative efforts to find solutions to their border disputes. The organizers concluded that "the sharp temporal distinction . . . between training in behalf of developing self-awareness and, more especially, communication skills on the one hand and the discussion of the substantive issues may have been a mistake and ought, therefore, to be blurred in the future. . . . It would . . . perhaps be better to begin a workshop with the substantive issue as the thesis and to let personal probing creep in slowly but inevitably as the antithesis." See Doob, *Resolving Conflict in Africa*, p. 122.

LIMITATIONS OF THE WORKSHOP APPROACH

The ultimate goal of a problem-solving workshop is to feed the changes and solutions it has generated into the policy process. As I have already pointed out, however, it is more effectively designed to *produce* changes in its participants and to generate innovative solutions than it is to *transfer* these products to the policy process. Much of the workshop's strength derives from its separation from the policy process. It is held under independent auspices, in a setting removed from decision-making agencies, with participants acting as relatively uncommitted individuals, and according to ground rules that encourage the transcendence of official positions. All of these features, by removing some of the usual barriers to change, make its occurrence more probable, but by the same token they make its transfer more difficult.

The problem of transfer actually involves two interrelated questions. First, if an individual changes in the workshop setting—that is, if he reassesses his attitudes and accepts a new approach to resolving the conflict—what is the likelihood that he will maintain these new attitudes and formulations once he returns to his home setting? Second, assuming he does—or to the extent that he does—maintain these changes, what is the likelihood that he will be able to bring his new attitudes and formulations effectively to bear on the policy process?

The first question is common to all types of workshops, ranging from those primarily oriented toward individual change to those oriented toward organizational problem-solving. It refers to what has been called the "reentry" problem. The workshop takes the individual into a different world, frees him from the usual pressures and constraints that bind him to a limited perspective, and thus allows him to reexamine his assumptions and to develop new ways of looking at things. But once he leaves this more open and protective environment and returns to the real world, there is a great danger of backsliding. The old pressures will come into play, and the dominant frame of reference will begin to reassert itself. Moreover, the individual may find that the new ideas he expresses are met with hostility and that the proposals he puts forth are systematically shot down. Of course, the severity of the reentry problem varies as a function of many factors. But I think it can be fairly said that, given an influence attempt that removes an individual or a small group from their usual environments, any feature that enhances the probability for change almost invariably compounds the problem of reentry.

Workshops involving conflicting nations or communities may well present serious reentry problems, because here the issue of group loyalty is particularly salient. An individual who returns with a less militant view of the conflict may find himself treated as one who has been coopted by the other side, who has betrayed his own group, or who has inadequately defended its position. These pressures may make it difficult for him to express and ultimately to maintain his new attitudes.

The ease of maintaining changes produced in the workshop depends partly on the nature of the setting and the experiences it provided for the participants. The more different the setting and experiences are from those in which the participants habitually find themselves, the greater the likelihood that the workshop will present novel inputs, break up old thought-patterns, and produce change. These same conditions make the probability of transfer less likely, however. New attitudes may be closely associated with the unique stimuli of the workshop setting and fail to generalize to the home environment's radically different stimuli. Furthermore, a setting so different that it removes all reminders of home fails to prepare the individual for the reactions his new attitudes are likely to elicit upon his return. By keeping reminders of the home setting to a minimum, the workshop may reduce resistance to change, but at the same time fail to build immunity against the pressures to which the new attitudes will later be exposed.

These considerations must enter into the decision of how much the workshop should insulate its participants from family, work, and political distractions. As Walton points out, comparative insulation "allows for a deeper immersion in the mental and emotional processes of the workshop and permits the development of a 'cultural island,' which in turn encourages participants to challenge cherished assumptions, break old thought processes, and modify attitudes." But it also has its disadvantages:

> Because the attitudes, views, and products generated by the workshop must eventually be persuasive also to countrymen who have not attended the workshop, it is possible for the cultural island effect to be too complete, if it leads to proposed solutions which will later be dismissed out-of-hand back home as unrealistic or idealistic. Similarly, some would consider the cultural island too complete if upon returning home a participant expresses conciliatory atti-

tudes which are so deviant from the national norms that he loses credibility.[24]

Thus changes are more likely to take place in a cultural island, but more difficult to maintain once the individual returns to the mainland. Another workshop feature that is relevant in this connection is the extent to which participants are functioning as members of a national team or as individuals. If they function in teams, they are more likely to stick to the official positions of their respective groups longer. If they function as individuals, variations in point of view within each national group can emerge more quickly and a wider range of ideas thus becomes available for discussion and problem-solving. Also, participants can learn more quickly that the other side is not monolithic, and they can come to appreciate some of the diversity in its views. Thus change may occur more readily in workshops where national contingents are not treated as units.[25] At the same time, however, such a procedure may make transfer of new attitudes more difficult. Positions developed without having to achieve consensus within the national contingent may be more vulnerable to attack and rejection by fellow nationals once participants return home. In fact, this possibility became apparent at the Fermeda Workshop even before the participants left; changes achieved in the intimacy of the T-groups did not quite survive "reentry" into the general assembly.

The ease of maintaining changes produced in the workshop depends not only on the conditions of the workshop itself, but also on the nature of the setting and experiences to which the participants return. If they come back to fairly conservative settings that are committed (ideologically or organizationally) to the official group position, then the changes they underwent are less likely to maintain themselves. Thus, for example, changes are more likely to be maintained among participants who return to an academic setting, since diversity in views on national issues is more readily accepted there.

24 Walton, "Problem-Solving Workshop," pp. 482–83.
25 Walton argues that when participants (as in the Fermeda Workshop) come as individuals rather than in national teams, and when the representatives from the same national group do not know each other or have not previously worked together, it would be best—even when trying to maximize change—to meet with each national contingent separately before bringing members together in a multinational grouping. Such a procedure would help develop trust within each national group and make it easier for it to "tolerate and indeed encourage differences in viewpoints among its members" ("Problem-Solving Workshop," p. 479), thus "improving the quality of the deliberations . . . and the likelihood that the community would converge on some areas of substantive agreement" (p. 486).

On the other hand, participants returning to government agencies, which are committed to a particular way of formulating the conflict, may find their new attitudes and formulations ignored or rejected. As they continue to work under these pressures and within the built-in framework of assumptions, they are more likely to revert to the official position on the conflict.

The question of participants' organizational background leads us directly to the second problem involved in the transfer of changes generated by a workshop: what is the likelihood that participants will be able to bring their new attitudes and formulations (assuming these have been maintained) to bear on the policy process? Since the workshop is, by its nature, removed from the policy process, the problem of feeding its products back into that process must inevitably arise. The ease of achieving such feedback depends largely on the participants' characteristics and their relationships to the policy process.

In general, it stands to reason that if the decision-makers are involved in the plans for the workshop, if the workshop organizers consult with them both before and after, and if the participants themselves are close to the center of decision-making and are at least informally acting as representatives of the decision-makers, then the opportunity for feedback will be greater. There is probably less *change* in this case than in a workshop where the participants act purely as private citizens. The closer the participants are to decision-making agencies, the more likely they are to be constrained by official positions and decision-makers' expectations, and the less likely they are to be open to change. Whatever changes *do* occur, however— whatever new learnings and insights the participants acquire—will come to the attention of the decision-makers much more readily in this case. Thus it would again appear that there is a reciprocal relationship between change and transfer: the closer the participants are to the center of decision-making, the less open they are to change, but the more capable they are to feed whatever changes they do experience into the policy process.

On closer examination, it seems to me that the picture is considerably more complicated than the one I have drawn so far. Whether or not participants closest to the locus of decision-making are most likely to inject their changes into the policy process may well depend on the nature of the changes in question, as well as on the precise relationship of the participants to the decision-making units. For example, if change takes the form of some new learning about the intentions of the other side, then the proposition no doubt holds. Say a workshop participant concludes from the discussions that the other side may be willing (despite previous public pronouncements) to entertain certain new lines of negotiation; he would be in a much more favorable position to carry this information to the decision-makers and to persuade them to act on it if he is close to the decision-making unit and has in fact been sent to the workshop by that unit (presumably to obtain just this kind of information). On the other hand, if the change he experienced is more fundamental—if he comes away from the workshop convinced that the whole policy pursued by his government is inappropriate, and committed to a thorough reformulation of the issues and the possibilities for solution—then his proximity to the locus of decision-making may make little difference. It may not enhance his ability to inject his new insights into the policy process and may, in fact, reduce it, depending on the exact nature of his relationship to the decision-making bureaucracy.

In conceptualizing this problem, I start with the assumption that the workshop approach can change *individual* perceptions, attitudes, and formulations of problems and solutions. Thus workshop techniques can be most useful when directed at those points in the decision-making process at which individual perceptions and formulations of the conflict become relevant and important. It can be argued that diplomats and foreign-policy officials do *not* represent such points in the process. They are relatively unlikely to act as individuals, bringing their own attitudes and perceptions to bear on their official role performance. They tend to act within a highly institutionalized conceptual framework; the assumptions of that framework are built into the routine operations of the decision-making apparatus and are constantly reinforced by the interactions of its various units. Perceptions and attitudes certainly enter into the role performance of diplomats and foreign-policy officials, but they are most likely to be the shared and frozen perceptions and attitudes that pervade the decision-making bodies. Diplomats and officials are usually not in a position to reexamine them or to call for their reexamination. Thus, it is not too likely that (acting within their roles) these individuals would effectively use changes gained through a workshop experience.

On the other hand, the situation might be quite different for legislators or their staff assistants, or for the leaders or executives of various powerful pressure groups. These are individuals whose task in the foreign-policy process is to formulate and define issues in keeping with the interests (at least as they interpret these) of the constituencies they represent. Though they can generally be counted on to support the administration's foreign policy, they are not necessarily bound by the perspectives of the decision-making units and are relatively free to promote changes in direction or emphasis of existing policy. If they revise their perceptions and attitudes, their own inputs into the policy process may well be affected. These inputs, in turn, while not determining policy, may influence it considerably. I would hypothesize that individuals in these kinds of roles might be best able to make effective use of changes resulting from a workshop experience, because it is their business (unlike that of the diplomat or foreign-policy official) to bring their own perceptions and attitudes to bear on the policy process.

Thus my analysis tentatively suggests that the ideal participants in a workshop (even if its goal is to have maximal impact on the policy process) are not necessarily those closest to the locus of decision-making. Such individuals may not only be less likely to experience substantial changes in attitude, when compared to individuals more remote from the locus of decision-making, but they may also be less able to inject the changes they do experience into the policy process. Perhaps the ideal candidates for workshops are individuals at some intermediate distance from the decision-making apparatus. They must be influential members of their societies, preferably with an active interest in foreign-policy issues, but—if our criterion is their ability to feed the products of the workshop into the policy process— it may be better if their role is to influence and evaluate foreign policy, rather than to make it or carry it out.

There is, of course, more than one type of workshop and more than one model of the "ideal participant." Perhaps, if my argument is correct, individuals at such intermediate positions in the foreign-policy process as legislators or lobbyists may be the most "natural" candidates for workshop participation, but there are sure to be occasions when a very different type of participant—closer to the policy process or farther removed from it—would be highly appropriate. Selection of appropriate participants depends on the purpose of a particular workshop and on its place in the larger context of efforts at conflict resolution. The proper matching of participants and occasions is one of the major issues for further conceptualization and experimentation.

CONCLUSION

The pioneering work of Burton and Doob has demonstrated the feasibility and suggested the potential usefulness of problem-solving workshops as inputs to international conflict resolution. Their experiments have pointed to the unique strengths and limitations of this approach, and they have revealed some of the dimensions along which workshops may vary. There is now a need for further experimentation, along with theoretically based efforts to specify just where the workshop approach can fit into the conduct of international relations and thus contribute to processes of conflict resolution. Such efforts, in turn, require a conceptualization of international politics in terms of the entire range of interactions that culminate in official state behavior.

I have argued that the workshop approach can have significant impact at those points in the policy process at which individual perceptions and attitudes play a determining role. To assess the potential of the approach, therefore, we must look beyond the points at which the final, official foreign-policy steps are taken—in other words, beyond the foreign-policy bureaucracy and the diplomatic corps—since at these points individual perceptions and attitudes are unlikely to play a major part (except perhaps in influencing style and detail of policy execution). Instead, we must take a more total view of the international political process and its ramifications. It involves multiple actors—individual and collective, official and unofficial—all of whom influence foreign policy and the shape of international relations. Within this larger process, there are many points at which individual perceptions and attitudes may have major impact, both on short-term decisions and on long-term trends. The analytical task required now is identification of these points and specification of the types of individuals who are located at them and of the nature of their contributions to the policy process. Such an analysis would provide a systematic basis for determining the occasions on which problem-solving workshops may produce useful inputs to conflict resolution and for selecting the participants appropriate to a given occasion.

The occasions on which a workshop may contribute to conflict resolution vary widely. The relevance of workshops is perhaps most apparent in situations where conflict has reached violent proportions, but communication between the conflicting parties has never been initiated, or has broken down, or has reached an impasse, with each side frozen into a position totally unacceptable to the other side. Typically, in such situations, the decision-making units on each side are boxed in by a set of images of the other side, assumptions about the nature of the conflict, commitments to a national posture, and real or imagined constraints that prevent them from breaking out of their conceptual prisons and exploring new alternatives. New ideas and insights are desperately needed to cut into these self-perpetuating processes, and problem-solving workshops may be uniquely able to provide these. On such occasions, it seems to me, the most appropriate participants would be (as I suggested before) individuals at an intermediate distance from the foreign-policy apparatus, who are politically powerful and widely respected and whose loyalty to the national cause is beyond question, but who are not themselves completely caught up in the existing policy framework.

Other occasions for workshops may be tied much more specifically and closely to the process of diplomatic negotiations. There are moments in the interaction between conflicting parties when a workshop might be precisely the mechanism needed to facilitate negotiations—to bridge a specific gap between the position at which the parties find themselves and the one they know they want to reach. For example, a workshop may provide a context for exploring (with minimum risk) whether there is a basis for resuming broken-down negotiations; or for running a "dress rehearsal" before making a final commitment to formal negotiations; or for discussing certain new proposals in a relatively noncommittal fashion, away from the limelight in which official negotiations may be simultaneously proceeding; or, finally, for working out certain technical details of an agreement, which can be handled more effectively in a problem-solving format than in a diplomatic one. Participants in workshops of this type would most likely be diplomats, foreign-policy officials or advisers, or technical experts, depending on the specific occasion for the workshop.

At the other end of the continuum are workshops that are primarily educational. Such workshops may be occasioned by a specific conflict. They may bring together influential members of the two conflicting nations or communities, such as leaders of civic associations, journalists, intellectuals, business or labor leaders—or perhaps future influentials, such as students. The purpose might be modest and entirely long-range: to develop new ways of conceptualizing the conflict among elite segments of the populations, in the hope that these would eventually contribute to changes in public opinion and thus help create an atmosphere for alternative policies. Needless to say, such a workshop would probably contribute little to averting an imminent crisis. Educational workshops may also be organized independently of any specific conflict, to sensitize the participants to the nature of conflict and provide insights into its resolution. Diplomats or students of international relations in particular might benefit from such exercises.

The occasion for the workshop should help determine not only the types of participants selected, but also the mix of individuals composing the group. Various possibilities for composing the national groups and the total group suggest themselves, calling for experimentation and conceptual clarification. Depending on the purpose of the workshop, the national contingents may be selected to be homogeneous or they may be deliberately composed to represent different segments within each nation. In selecting the parties, an interesting possibility, particularly (though not exclusively) germane to general educational workshops, would be to include participants representing several pairs of conflicting nations or communities. Such a format would permit comparisons, would bring in a range of empirical inputs, and would allow participants to develop insights and to sharpen their conceptual tools through analysis of conflicts other than their own.

The criteria for selecting the parties in any given conflict situation are by no means self-evident, since the definition of the parties is itself often a matter of controversy. In selecting the Greek-Cypriot and Turkish-Cypriot communities—rather than Greece and Turkey —as the parties for the London workshop, the organizers took a position on the nature of the conflict. So did the organizers of the Fermeda Workshop in selecting Somalia, Ethiopia, and Kenya— the three nation-states—as the parties, rather than the Somali people and neighboring ethnic groups. The definition of the parties is even more controversial in conflicts in which one party is reluctant to recognize the other as a legitimate entity. Workshop organizers cannot avoid deciding how the parties are to be defined and thus indirectly taking a position in the controversy, but in making this decision it is important to analyze the relevance of different sets of parties to the workshop's particular purpose.

A workshop may be a way of establishing communication between parties unwilling or unable to communicate through official channels. However, if one party has refused to communicate, as a matter of policy, because of an unwillingness to recognize the other as a legitimate entity, then it may be equally reluctant to participate in a workshop. Communication, even in the context of an unofficial workshop, may represent too great a concession, particularly if the other party has *favored* a policy of communication. Thus, the organization of a workshop—creating the conditions under which both parties could participate without feeling that they are compromising their positions—is a complex problem in its own right, requiring some experimentation. To overcome some of the barriers to initiating a workshop, it may be useful to think of it in stages. In some situations, it may be necessary to start with separate workshops for the national groups, paving the way for joint meetings. Such preparatory workshops may also confront divisions within the national groups and select the teams to represent them at the joint workshop. It may also be useful, by the same token, to experiment with separate follow-up workshops for each national group, preferably augmented by other participants from the same society.

One final set of issues requiring further conceptual and experimental analysis concerns the role of the social scientists in the problem-solving workshop. I have discussed their possible inputs to the proceedings in some detail. It would be useful to specify which of these inputs are most appropriate on what occasions. It is also important to keep in mind that these inputs are never mere scientific statements or process observations, devoid of value presuppositions. The organizers bring to the situation their own definitions of the nature of the conflict, their own assumptions about the possibilities for resolution, and their own preferences for the directions resolution should take. It would be well to make these explicit for themselves and for the participants.

part **II**

People at Home
and Events Abroad

eight

The American Press
and Indochina, 1950-56

Susan Welch

THE press is an important source of foreign policy news for opinion leaders and decision-makers within a political system, as well as for the public at large. Since most people, including many in decision-making positions, never come into direct contact with the foreign events that are the basis for policy-making, they must rely upon communications media for information about the particular issue and even the more generalized frame of reference within which it is being discussed. This fact may be crucial for policy-making. Once the framework of ideology and the context of large issues by which a particular situation is to be viewed are established, policy alternatives are automatically narrowed, if not necessarily preordained.

This chapter surveys a segment of the American press during a series of related foreign policy decisions made by the United States about Indochina in the seven-year period from 1950 to 1956. This period covers the beginning of American aid to the French in Indochina, the increasingly losing struggle on the part of the French in that area, the settlement at Geneva, and the establishment of an American policy of firm support for the Vietnamese government of Ngo Dinh Diem in the south. More specifically, the chapter examines (1) the quantity and content of the press coverage of the American role in Indochina, (2) how and why the press defined the situation as it did, and (3) some possible implications of the behavior of the press for rational foreign policy decision-making.[1]

---

1 This paper, then, virtually ignores an equally important link in the chain of communications: the impact made by the press on those who read it. (See n. 3.)

THE PRESS AND INDOCHINA: THE DATA

Sampling American Press Views

The study concentrated on the *New York Times* and, more selectively, three other newspapers providing some degree of geographic and ideological distribution. It analyzed each issue of the *Times* from January, 1950, through December, 1956. For selected intervals during this period, three other major metropolitan newspapers— *Chicago Tribune, Washington Post,* and *San Francisco Chronicle*— were examined in detail. The time periods analyzed were those in which important events affecting the relations of the United States with Indochina took place:

May	1–15, 1950	Big Three foreign ministers meeting; aid promised to Indochina
September	1–30, 1951	Visit to United States of General Jean de Lattre (commander of the French forces in Vietnam) to appeal for more aid
June	1–15, 1952	Visit to the United States of French Overseas Minister Jean Le Tourneau to appeal for more aid
March	20–31, 1953	Visit to the United States of French Premier Réné Mayer to discuss a variety of matters, including Indochina; visit to Indochina of General Mark Clark
July	20–30, 1953	Senate slash in foreign aid for Indochina
September	1–10, 1953	Major policy statement on Indochina by John Foster Dulles
January	1–10, 1954	Eisenhower's State of the Union address
March	10–15, 1954	Situation in Indochina worsening; preparations for Geneva Conference
April	1–10, 1954	Consultations by Eisenhower with military and congressional leaders over appropriate Indochina strategies
May	10–15, 1954	Deadlock at Geneva; policy statement by Dulles
June	10–15, 1954	Continued Geneva deadlock

July	20–30, 1954	Geneva settlement
October	25–30, 1954	Eisenhower letter to Ngo Dinh Diem pledging support and asking for reforms
December	25–30, 1954	Diem's government on verge of collapse
January	16–30, 1955	Diem continues to have difficulties with opposition
May	1–15, 1955	Attempts to overthrow Diem; Franco-American agreement on Indochina
January	1–15, 1956	Dulles's "brinksmanship" article

The frequency of articles, editorials, and signed columns that dealt with the role, or the potential role, of United States involvement in Indochina, whether military, economic, diplomatic, or otherwise, was tallied, as were their locations within the papers. The survey also recorded information about the tone and content of each item. That is, was the item a news story, "backgrounder," signed column, or editorial? Was it phrased in anti-Communist vs. Communist, colonial vs. anticolonial, isolationist vs. nonisolationist rhetoric?[2]

Quantity of Coverage

To create an issue, the press must cover the situation. In the case of Indochina, there was relatively little coverage in the *Times* during the first three years of American involvement there—that is, from 1950 to 1952. Coverage was substantial in 1953, reached a peak in 1954, and then dropped off sharply so that, by 1956, coverage had declined to the pre-1950 level (Table 1). Only in 1954 did coverage average more than one item per day; and only from 1953 through 1955 was there more than one item every three days. Distribution within each year fluctuated greatly.

Given the virtually unchallenged preeminence of the *Times* in the extent of its coverage, it is reasonable to assume that this was the maximum coverage given the Indochinese situation by any newspaper in this time period. Indeed, in the overwhelming majority of the specific intervals examined (fourteen of seventeen), the *Times*

2 Because of the limited quantity and nonrandomness of the selection of data, the findings cannot be generalized with statistical precision. The conclusions of this chapter were based not only on the data presented below, however, but also on a review of other kinds of communication data relevant to this topic: periodicals, religious and other interest group literature, and other contemporary coverage of the 1954 Indochina crisis. See Susan Welch, "Groups and Public Policy: The Case of Indochina, 1950–1956" (Ph.D. dissertation, University of Illinois, 1970).

Table 1. The Frequency of *New York Times* Articles on Indochina*

Year	Daily Average	Total
1948	0.02	7
1949	0.01	2
1950	0.31	109
1951	0.16	52
1952	0.23	72
1953	0.35	126
1954	2.32	808
1955	0.52	185
1956	0.12	38
1957	0.10	35
1958	0.02	7

* Includes only those items relating the Indochinese struggle to the United States.

did show greater coverage than the others, both with regard to total stories and editorial coverage (Table 2). In two cases the *Post* led in coverage, in one the *Tribune*. On the whole, the papers tended to rank the newsworthiness of the Indochina story in certain periods about the same.[3] For example, three of the four papers had the

Table 2. Items on Indochina per Day, in Four Newspapers during Selected Periods

	New York Times	Washington Post	San Francisco Chronicle	Chicago Tribune
May 1–15, 1950	.56	.31	.19	.38
September 1–30, 1951	.23	.13	.19	.06
June 1–15, 1952	.38	.06	.13	.00
March 20–31, 1953	.92	.17	.50	.75
July 20–30, 1953	.64	.09	.00	.18
September 1–10, 1953	.55	.18	.18	.18
January 1–10, 1954	.18	.36	.18	.09
March 10–15, 1954	1.17	.50	.67	.83
April 1–10, 1954	2.37	1.73	1.54	1.09
May 10–15, 1954	3.00	2.33	2.17	.83
June 10–15, 1954	2.00	2.17	.50	1.17
July 20–31, 1954	1.27	1.45	1.73	1.09
October 25–30, 1954	.12	.00	.17	.17
December 25–30, 1954	.67	.33	.00	.00
January 16–30, 1955	.63	.19	.06	.06
May 1–15, 1955	1.38	.81	.94	.69
January 1–15, 1956	.56	.18	.13	.13

3   The rank order correlation for the four papers on the extent of coverage is $r = .68$, with 1.0 being perfect agreement and 0.0 maximum nonagreement. It might be noted here that the increase in news coverage from 1950–54 paralleled a growth in the public awareness of the Indochina issue: whereas in 1952 only 57 percent of the public claimed to have heard of the Indochina war, by February, 1954, 74 percent and by May of that year 82 percent made that claim. Such data suggest, although they do not prove, the impact on public awareness of increased press coverage of the war.

heaviest coverage of the story in May, 1954, and the *Tribune* had the fourth-heaviest coverage in that period, with the heaviest coverage in the June, 1954, period.

Kinds of Coverage

The kind of coverage given a story is at least as important as the frequency with which a story appears. A very careful reader might catch a two-inch story on page 27 announcing the arrival of an American aid mission to Indochina, but a far greater percentage is likely to see it if it is displayed prominently on the first page or if it is the subject of an editorial. "News" stories are likely to be based on official sources and handouts, and to reflect official points of view. Editorials or articles by such columnists as Walter Lippmann might rely on these official sources for basic information, but they are more likely to reflect other viewpoints than those of the administration.

The percentage of total items devoted to editorials decreased from 20 percent in 1950–52 to 17 percent in 1953–54 and 13 percent in the post-Geneva period (Table 3). The *Times* consistently had the

Table 3. Editorials as Percentage of Total Items in Selected Periods

	New York Times	Washington Post	San Francisco Chronicle	Chicago Tribune
1950–52	22.3%	20.0%	20.0%	12.5%
1953–mid 1954	20.4	16.3	16.7	13.7
Post-Geneva	16.7	14.3	5.2	6.7
Total	19.3%	16.2%	13.9%	12.2%

greatest percentage of editorials, the *Tribune* the least. In addition, three newspapers had columnists active in covering the Indochina question: Joseph and Stewart Alsop as well as Walter Lippmann in the *Washington Post*; Anne O'Hare McCormick, C. L. Sulzberger, and Hanson Baldwin in the *New York Times*; and Royce Brier and Drew Pearson in the *San Francisco Chronicle*. Only the *Chicago Tribune* had no columnists presenting their views on this issue. By contrast, in terms of "hard news" (that is, coverage of events taking place within the past few days or notice of events to come, such as projected trips or conferences, in which news analysis or review of background events play a minor role), the *Tribune* was the leader (85.1%), followed by the *Chronicle* (76.1%), the *Times* (69.9%), and the *Post* (54.6%). The *Post*, then, was the paper most frequently displaying editorials and signed editorial columns.

The Indochina story received the maximum front-page coverage in about the same periods that it received maximum total coverage: in April, May, and July, 1954, and May, 1955 (Table 4). In June,

Table 4. Front Page Stories per Day in Selected Periods

	New York Times	Washington Post	San Francisco Chronicle	Chicago Tribune
May 1–15, 1950	.06	.18	.00	.06
September 1–30, 1950	.03	.00	.00	.00
June 1–15, 1952	.00	.00	.00	.00
March 20–31, 1953	.25	.08	.00	.00
July 20–30, 1953	.00	.00	.00	.00
September 1–10, 1953	.00	.09	.00	.00
January 1–10, 1954	.00	.00	.09	.00
March 1–15, 1954	.16	.00	.16	.00
April 1–10, 1954	.82	.55	.18	.09
May 10–15, 1954	1.30	1.30	.83	.00
June 10–15, 1954	.33	.33	.00	.00
July 20–31, 1954	.55	.55	.55	.36
October 25–30, 1954	.17	.00	.00	.00
December 25–30, 1954	.17	.00	.00	.00
January 16–30, 1955	.00	.00	.00	.00
May 1–15, 1955	.55	.55	.18	.18
January 1–15, 1956	.06	.06	.00	.00

1954, the story was scarcely covered and was on the front pages still less. At that time the Geneva talks appeared to be stalled. Since they were no longer news stories and since there appeared to be little hope of reaching an agreement, the story was pushed off the front pages. More generally, the Indochina story appeared on the front pages of the *Times* and *Post* in at least half the days of four of the thirteen periods surveyed, in two periods in the *Chronicle*, and none in the *Tribune*.

Editorial Position

Editorial opinion in the four newspapers was categorized into three broad sets:
1. predominantly favorable to the position taken by the Administration, or positions taken by the pro-French government of Vietnam or of the French themselves when these positions were directly connected with American policy;
2. neutral toward United States or Allied policy in Indochina; usually these kinds of editorials prescribed an action to be taken by the Administration vis-à-vis Vietnam or both questioned and praised Administration policy; and
3. predominantly opposed to policies being pursued in Indochina

by the United States or its Allies, if these Allied actions were being taken with the approval of the United States.

Only the *Tribune* was overwhelmingly critical of Administration policy (Table 5). Of the remainder, the *Times* was most positively oriented toward Administration policy, and both the *Post* and the *Chronicle*, when their editorial writers expressed their opinions, were three times as likely to favor as to oppose this policy.

Table 5. Editorial Support of Administration Positions during Selected Periods

	New York Times	Washington Post	San Francisco Chronicle	Chicago Tribune
Favorable	43.7%	35.3%	50.0%	12.5%
Neutral	46.9%	53.1%	33.3%	12.5%
Unfavorable	9.4%	11.6%	16.7%	75.0%
Support Ratio*	4.7	3.0	3.0	.17

* Support Ratio = number of positive editorials divided by the number of negative editorials

A SURVEY OF PRESS COVERAGE, 1950–56

1950–52: Cursory Views on a Nonissue

Coverage during the first time period surveyed, 1950–52, was in general quite light. At this time, the government of the United States was making and reinforcing a major economic and political commitment. U.S. involvement with the war was illustrated by such events as the "Big Three" foreign ministers meeting in which the United States promised to give aid to Indochina; a visit to the United States by General de Lattre (commander of the forces in Indochina) to appeal for more help for the French; and a visit to the United States by Jean LeTourneau, Minister of Overseas France, and later Minister of the Associated States (of Indochina)—a visit after which the United States again agreed to step up aid to the French in Indochina.

During this period, the press did not treat the Indochina war as a central issue. The most avid reader of the *New York Times* could find some news of United States involvement there. For a less careful reader, Indochina would be brought to mind very rarely (Tables 2 and 4).

There were, however, differences among the four papers, despite the fairly high degree of acceptance of Administration action on the part of all except the *Chicago Tribune*. Although generalized initial reactions of the other three papers were that the granting of aid to the French in Indochina was something that had to be done, the

Times of May 6, 1950, was slightly critical of the Administration for being too hesitant in offering aid to France, while the *Post* of the same day was slightly critical of the Administration for having no firm policy. On the whole, however, the three papers accepted the notion expressed in the *Chronicle* of May 15, 1950, that, if the rebels won in Indochina, "the loss to Communism of the Malayan peninsula and Indonesia would be directly threatened," and that, as the *New York Times* added (May 6, 1950), "Indochina must be saved promptly." Nevertheless, the *Post* on May 6 injected a cautionary note questioning whether the Administration had a clear policy or knew what the facts were.

The *Tribune*, by way of contrast, was quite critical of the Administration. The feelings of the *Tribune* editors can be illustrated by the following editorial written on May 14, 1950, after the announcement of U.S. aid: "Mr. Acheson says we are to aid France because France is fighting in Indochina to free that country—from France. France is fighting to save that country from Communism. Was there ever a nobler purpose than to fight a costly war thousands of miles away from home, in order that colonials might be freed from your own rule, saved at the same time from Communism?" The *Tribune*, then, was skeptical of the whole operation in Indochina. While admitting that Ho Chi Minh's movement was Communist, the *Tribune* seemed equally hostile to the French, whom they perceived as a greedy colonialist power.

In the two time periods surveyed in 1951 and 1952, little coverage of the Indochina war was offered by either the *Chronicle* or *Tribune* (Table 2). Coverage by the *Post* was also light, although an editorial appeared on September 18, 1951, describing the importance of U.S. military and economic aid to the Indochinese states. In September, 1951, the Indochina problem was not an issue; U.S. action there had been basically accepted. By June, 1952, the military situation was itself on a downturn, and General de Lattre returned to France, critically ill.[4] However, little word of the reversal in the military fortunes of the French and their allies reached the reader of the American press. The *Times* (June 1 and 11) praised the French for giving independence, however belatedly, and seemed unaware of the extent of support Ho's forces were gaining with their nationalist appeals.

4   For a history of this period, see Robert Shaplen, *The Lost Revolution: The Story of Twenty Years of Neglected Opportunities in Vietnam and of America's Failure to Foster Democracy There* (New York: Harper and Row, 1965); Bernard B. Fall, *Street without Joy*, 4th ed. (London: Pall Mall Press, 1965).

By the end of 1952, before "Indochina" became a word frequently in the headlines, these elements of the press had adopted terms and definitions of the situation which clearly put the issues of the developing struggle in Indochina in the context of the worldwide Communist versus non-Communist battle. Indochina must be "saved" (from the Communists); "no free Indochina in a slave world"; the Viet-Minh were directed from Moscow, ready to do anything if "the Kremlin gives the order." The "domino theory" was not labeled as such, but the elements were present: "If (Indochina) falls to the Communist advance the whole of Southeast Asia will be in mortal peril."[5]

Hence already the terms of the future debate over U.S. policy were being hardened into usage by the press, even if the quantitative coverage was slim. The importance of Indochina to the United States and the necessity of trying to save it were the important aspects of the coverage.

From the coverage given by the press in this early stage of U.S. involvement, it seems clear that the press relied almost completely on Administration sources for information which was reported. Most of the attention that the Indochina story received was from State Department press releases and interviews with American and French officials. Almost none came from on-the-scene reports from American reporters, although occasionally reports on the military situation came through French sources from French reporters.

1953: Growing Concern

The three intervals surveyed in 1953 included periods covering the visit of French Premier Réné Mayer to the United States, the visit of General Mark Clark to Indochina (both March 20–31), the Senate debate over aid to Indochina as part of foreign aid bill (July 20–30), and a major policy address on Indochina by Secretary of State John Foster Dulles (September 1–10). Coverage in the *Times* increased above that of previous years, but coverage in the other papers increased only negligibly (Table 2).

The attention given by the press to the story carried further the points of view expressed earlier. The *Times*, the *Post*, and the *Chronicle* continued to express the "interlocking nature" of the struggle in the Far East, both in terms of the commonality of the struggles in Korea and Indochina and in terms of the emerging "domino

5 See, for example, *New York Times*, May 6, 1950, May 9, 1950, and June 11, 1952.

theory."[6] For example, the *Chronicle* editorialized on March 27 that
there is "an increasing awareness in the United States that France's
war in Indochina is vital to the entire free world in holding back a
Red tide that threatens to engulf all Southeast Asia, protecting Asia's
historical rice bowl, and maintaining the West's access to tin and
rubber." The *Post* (March 29) continued its secondary theme that
France should give more independence to the Indochinese, since
"the American people are against using American resources for the
purpose of aiding colonialism." During the first part of 1953, reports
in the press continued on the whole to express optimism about a
French military victory should more American aid be forthcoming.[7]

The first elements of doubt among government officials began to
creep in reports of the latter half of the year.[8] Although a *Times*
story on July 13 reported that Dulles was pleased with the nature
and prospects of the Navarre Plan, by September 3 it was relaying
Dulles's lack of optimism about the outcome of the Indochina struggle. When Dulles stated in a speech to the American Legion Convention in September that the outcome in Indochina affects "our
own vital interests," and that the Chinese Communists should realize
they cannot engage in a second aggressive action "without grave
consequences," and Undersecretary of State Walter Bedell Smith
noted that the struggle in Indochina has a "direct bearing on our
own security,"[9] these "conditional commitments" were accepted by
most groups with, as the *Post* commented on September 7, "hardly
a ripple." The *Chronicle* in fact editorialized on September 3 that
"such warnings might have prevented World Wars I and II."

At the other extreme was the *Tribune*, reflecting its consistent
policy of no intervention and no aid. When suggestions were made
that U.S. aid should go directly to Indochina, bypassing the French,
the *Tribune* commented on September 1 that "it is much more profitable for France to act as middleman in receiving American money
and disbursing it." The real question, said the *Tribune*, was which of
the two groups, France or Indochina, would get more American aid:
"There is something excruciatingly funny about a jurisdictional dispute between two pickpockets as to which is to work the juicy side
of the street." The *Tribune*'s opposition to U.S. involvement in Indo-

6 See *New York Times*, March 20, 27, 29, and 30, 1953.
7 This is implicit in many and explicit in most news stories in the first half of the
year. See, for example, *New York Times*, March 21 and 26, April 3, and July 10,
1953.
8 See, for example, *New York Times*, April 14, 1953, where Baldwin reports
increasing Viet-Minh offensive; April 23, 1953, with news of "worsening" situation; May 4, 1953, with "concern" expressed by congressional leaders.
9 *Chicago Tribune*, September 6, 1953; *New York Times*, September 3, 1953.

china (and indeed to any aid for the French effort there) was part of its generalized isolationist stance at this time. The degree of questioning of the policy on the part of the other papers was slight, and attention given to the policy was relatively little, except by the *Times*. The semantics of coverage relied heavily on domino-theory notions, with Indochina viewed as merely one target in a worldwide Communist campaign of aggression.

The coverage continued to rest almost completely upon official sources. Even the *Post*, for example, which had the highest proportion of nonhard news items, cited as its key sources for news in a typical week (March 24–29): "General Mark Clark said . . . ," "Premier Réné Mayer predicted . . . ," "President Eisenhower assured . . . ," "France and the United States warned . . . ," and "Premier Mayer says. . . ."[10] Two editorials that week dealt with reactions of *Post* editors to the developing situation. Thus the coverage consisted entirely of hard news stemming from Administration sources plus commentary upon that news by the editors of the *Post*; with few exceptions, such as Hanson Baldwin of the *Times*, very little independent reporting occurred.

January–March, 1954: An Emerging Crisis

For U.S. policy in Indochina, 1953 was a crucial but 1954 a crisis year. During the first three months of 1954, press discussion of U.S. military intervention was frequent. Except for the *Tribune*, adamantly opposed to U.S. military involvement in Indochina, none of the four papers raised a voice against the proposed intervention. Neither was any forthright in urging the Administration to take military action. Most columnists and editorialists seemed to agree with Joseph Alsop (*Post*, January 4) that the United States was going to be faced with "one of the ugliest choices of the postwar years . . . whether to take drastic measures to reinforce Indochina."

The frequency of coverage of the Indochina war increased in March, but did not reach its peak (Table 2). The news that was presented was a well-orchestrated coverage of Administration and congressional views of diplomatic and military progress. Of particular interest, however, were the remarks made by President Eisenhower at a news conference on March 10, at which he indicated that there would be no war without congressional consent.[11]

10 See *Washington Post*, March 24, 26, 27, 28, and 29, 1953.
11 The *Post* on March 12, 1954, expressed its disagreement with Eisenhower's contention that there could be no war without congressional consent, stating that this hinders the executive too much in crisis situations.

April-July, 1954: Decisions Reached

The four months preceding the final settlement at Geneva brought little evidence of new positions taken by the press. The importance of the story was emphasized by the prominent attention given it within the papers (Table 4). Stories of rumored intervention, Dulles's warnings to China of "major retaliation," congressional opposition to intervention, Allied dissension, and Dulles's attempts to achieve a pact among the Allies were all given front-page attention, except by the *Tribune*.

The *Times*, the *Post*, and the *Chronicle* continually called for firm action by the Allies. "It is only when the ranks of their enemies are tightly closed that Moscow and Peking are inclined to make procedural, let alone real, concessions," commented the *Times* on April 8 in calling for unity among the Western powers. The *Post* (April 10), too, called for unity among the Allies, who must have "a well thought out plan for Southeast Asia." The *Chronicle* on April 8 supported Eisenhower in his fight for "united action"; this "united action" would demonstrate to the Kremlin, the Chinese Communists, and the "local Reds" that a substantial military group opposed them.[12]

The *Tribune* never deviated from its opposition to intervention, united or otherwise. Its opinion of John Foster Dulles can most charitably be described as suspicious. Dulles was called "bellicose" on April 7 and accused of "wanting to go to war," his "reckless" diplomacy aimed merely at the "greater glory of the French empire." An editorial on May 12 called "Hankering for War" again accused Dulles of pushing the country toward war; if there were to be no war, the *Tribune* editorialized, credit would go to the Communists, for Dulles had put the initiative in their hands. America had no interests in Indochina, continued the *Tribune*; its editorialists could only hope that Congress would keep us out.

The views of various commentators can be ranked, with Joseph and

12   The necessity for this united action was buttressed by various arguments discussed previously. The *Times* (April 9, 1954) again reiterated its belief in the domino theory and the importance to the U.S. economy of the Southeast Asian nations; the *Post* (May 13 and 14, 1954) discarded the domino theory (after pointing out that the Administration itself was changing its assumptions midstream by indicating that all of Southeast Asia will not necessarily go Communist merely because parts of Indochina do). The *Post* called the domino theory "dubious and fatalistic" but indicated that the United States should draw a line to defend in Southeast Asia.

Stewart Alsop the most prointerventionist and Walter Lippmann the most uneasy about the developing Indochinese policy, although not specifically against it. Drew Pearson, Marquis Childs, and Roscoe Drummond appeared to be between the Alsops and Lippmann in their views. On June 11 in the *Post*, for example, the Alsops lamented the fact that the likelihood of U.S. intervention was becoming less and less. They blamed this on the British, commenting, "The British have always preferred a Far Eastern Munich to a Far Eastern war. . . ." Lippmann saw a military stalemate: the best hope of the French was to hold on to the main military strong points until a settlement was reached. The Western powers could not have victory, but then neither could the Communists (*Post*, April 8). Lippmann also pointed out the weaknesses of such pacts as NATO and ANZUS in trying to deal with revolutions from within, as opposed to aggression from without. In any Asian pact, therefore, the Asians must be wholly involved, he thought (*Post*, May 11, 13).

This phase of the Indochina question closed with the signing of the Geneva Agreements on July 21, 1954. After failing to win support from any of the Western Allies (most notably Britain) for an armed intervention in Indochina, and failing to win domestic support (probably both from Eisenhower and from important congressional leaders) for unilateral intervention, Dulles instructed Bedell Smith to agree that the United States would not obstruct the settlement reached at Geneva.[13]

The response to the Geneva settlements was mixed. The *Chronicle* and the Alsops saw it as a disaster. (The *Chronicle*'s editorial of July 22 on the agreements was even entitled "The Disaster at Geneva.") The *Tribune* and *Post* blamed past policy for the poor settlement, but the *Post* looked optimistically at the future of the independent nations protected by an Asian defense treaty, whereas the *Tribune* foresaw that with Dulles's plans for a SEATO treaty the United States would likely become entangled in another Asian adventure.[14] The *Times* grudgingly accepted the settlement; the editors were happy the problem had been transferred from the military to the

13   For full information on the agreement at Geneva, see Victor Bator, *Vietnam, a Diplomatic Tragedy: The Origins of the United States Involvement* (Dobbs Ferry, N.Y.: Oceana Publications, 1965); Bernard B. Fall, *Viet-nam Witness, 1953–66* (New York: Praeger, 1966); Jean Lacouture and Philippe Devillers, *La Fin d'une guerre: Indochine, 1954* (Paris: Editions du Seuil, 1960); Anthony Eden, *Full Circle: The Memoirs of Anthony Eden* (Boston: Houghton Mifflin, 1960).

14   For the reaction of the *Post*, see editorials of July 20, 22, and 23, 1954; for the comments of *Tribune* editors, see the editorial of July 23, 1954.

political sphere. The *Times* urged the Allies to unite to protect the rest of Asia and encouraged the forging of a Southeast Asian pact, as well as stepped up economic and technical aid to Indochina.[15]

In sum, then, except for the *Tribune*, the editors of these papers appeared to believe that U.S. policy had failed simply because alliances had not been firmly made beforehand, and because the Allies could not agree on united action. Since an alliance was about to come into being, there were great hopes that this would set a new course in protecting Asian nations from Communist domination. There was little evidence that other diagnoses of the situation were considered—that instead of a mere mechanical failure, for example, such setbacks in policy might have been due to fundamental misperceptions of the prospects for establishing democratic systems based on popular support without fundamental reforms, reforms that prospective pro-Western leaders might not be willing to make. Instead, the press anticipated the establishment in the immediate future of a third force, an alternative to Communist Ho and French-backed Bao Dai.

This last pre-Geneva period found a greater number of negative reports in the press about the Indochina situation. This negativism, however, directly reflected Administration disenchantment with the ability of the French to achieve a military victory in Indochina, rather than an increased ability on the part of the press to secure non-Administration information.

After Geneva

The coverage of the Indochina issue reached its peak in the March-July, 1954, period and then dropped sharply (Table 2). Only a week after the signing of the Geneva Accords, no newspaper mentioned Indochina. The major focus of later news coverage concerned the establishment, weakening, and finally recuperation of a strong South Vietnamese government headed by Ngo Dinh Diem.

After the Eisenhower letter of October 23, 1954, to Diem pledging U.S. support and economic assistance to be met by "a performance on the part of the Government of Vietnam in undertaking needed reforms,"[16] the *Times* commented that the suggested reforms

15   See *Times* editorials of July 20–23 and 25, 1954.
16   The heart of the letter read as follows: "The purpose of this offer is to assist the Government of Vietnam in developing and maintaining a strong viable state, capable of resisting attempted subversion or aggression through military means. . . . The Government of the United States expects this aid will be met by a performance on the part of the Government of Vietnam in undertaking needed reforms" (*New York Times*, October 25, 1954).

were vitally necessary in order to insure popular support for the South Vietnamese government when it participated in the 1956 elections. The *Times* on October 26 stressed the urgency and immediacy of the task facing the government of Vietnam: "Unless we, the Vietnamese, and the French can establish a working counterweight in all of Vietnam that is still free, we can expect that Vietnam will go behind the Curtain eighteen months hence with the ostensible sanction of popular election." On December 30, 1954, the *Times* rendered a somewhat negative verdict on the Diem regime: "The government of Premier Ngo Dinh Diem is riddled with feuds and incompetence and is woefully weak." A mere four weeks later, on January 29, it expressed a contrary view, that Premier Diem was "increasing in stature and influence as a nationalist leader who is serious about making peaceful, democratic, and thorough-going reforms in the Government of his country." He was characterized as a man of character, vigor, and determination; his enemies were thought (by the *Times*) to be those who did not want a strong, stable, and independent government.

The *Times*'s support of Diem wavered briefly during attempts by dissidents to overthrow his government in May, 1955, but the editors quickly returned to their position of support for Diem. On May 2 it editorialized that if Diem could not provide a Vietnamese government responsible to the Vietnamese people, then "his people should replace him with someone who can." Only thirteen days later the *Times* nonetheless asserted, "There is no alternative to a stable government under Premier Diem."

The editorial support for Diem by the *Post* and *Chronicle* was also quite high. Diem was most often labeled as a man of "high integrity," and those failings he had were usually labeled as "administrative ineptness."[17] The *Tribune* continued to be less than favorable to any aspect of U.S. involvement in Indochina, noting that General Lawton Collins, among others, was in Vietnam teaching Diem how to spend U.S. money. The *Tribune* complained on May 3 that these "gang fights" within the government of Vietnam were not fights between Communism and non-Communism.

By the end of May, 1955, U.S. support for Diem seemed to reach a point of no return. The area faded from public view for another five or seven years. But the administration was now firmly committed to Diem's government—by its agreements with France, by its support of Diem through a succession of crises, and by promises of aid

17 See *Washington Post* editorials of May 3 and 11, 1955; *San Francisco Chronicle* editorial of May 2, 1955.

based on the premise of a stable government. The government was supported in these policies by the same three papers that had gone along with Administration policy in Indochina in earlier months and years.

Coverage: Some Summary Remarks

The press has tremendous power to create issues. Newsmen pick the most important events from thousands of potentially newsworthy happenings each day.[18] Sustained coverage of an event by the press can insure that attention will be given to it by the public and by decision-makers not initially involved in the situation. Public officials can suddenly be forced by news revelations to give at least the appearance of attention to long-existing and long-ignored conditions.[19]

The Indochina issue at first was not given great attention by the press. U.S. policy was made and consolidated before the subject became a matter of daily news coverage. Thus we see that from 1950 to 1953, news coverage in the *Times* of U.S. involvement in Indochina amounted to only about one item every four days (Table 1), and most of these were inside-page stories. The story, until the last months of the period, was relatively noncontroversial. Basically the papers gave the same stories the same relative amount of coverage, although in total coverage the *Times* consistently led.

Reporters, by relying almost solely on Administration sources, laid a foundation for the way in which the situation was defined later in the more active 1954 debate. Support, then, for the Administration was forthcoming not only in editorials, but also in the rhetoric with which the war was discussed. That is to say, the press insured that the reading public would view the war as a struggle between Communism and the Free World, vital to the preservation of all of Southeast Asia and perhaps all of Asia; that Ho Chi Minh and the Viet-Minh were merely agents of Moscow and Peking whose primary means of gaining support was through terror and force (although occasional mention was made of their nationalist appeal); and that a gallant ally, France, was fighting alongside the United States to preserve liberty and justice in Asia. (The *Tribune* did not acknowledge

18   See Delmer Dunn, *Public Officials and the Press* (Reading, Mass.: Addison-Wesley, 1969), esp. Ch. 3; Bernard C. Cohen, *The Press and Foreign Policy* (Princeton: Princeton University Press, 1963), esp. Ch. 3.

19   For example, the impact on some public officials after the exposé of "poverty" in America, or "hunger" in America, is an illustration. These conditions obviously did not come into existence at the time they were brought to public attention; they existed long before.

this struggle to be vital to the United States; instead, it described the war in terms of a nation trying to escape French rule.)

Coverage in 1954 increased drastically over that of earlier years. There were in 1954, as noted in Table 1, an average of 2.5 stories per day, not distributed evenly over the year, but clustered in the months of March, April, May, and July. The importance of the Indochina story can be exaggerated, however. In the maximum period of coverage of the story, May 10–15, the *Times* printed only about 385 column inches; if that coverage had continued at the same rate over the month, about 2,000 inches would have been printed. This is a substantial amount, to be sure, but one-third less than the 3,312 inches that Cohen estimates the *Times* printed when the Japanese peace treaty was signed in September, 1952,[20] and less than one-tenth of the 4,081 inches of foreign news that the *Times* printed in one average week.[21]

In the debate over U.S. tactics in 1954, the assumptions of the administration continued to be accepted. The press helped fix in the mind of the public the assumptions that Indochina was an area vital to our interests, that it was under challenge in a clear case of Communist aggression that had to be stopped, and that, if the people of Indochina knew the facts, they would naturally support the West in any struggle against the Communists. The alternatives and suggestions for settling the Indochina question put forth by editors and columnists alike never challenged these assumptions. The kinds of questions discussed most often were entirely incremental: Should we give more aid, or should troops be sent? Should we tell France it must give more independence, or should we leave it up to them? Should we set up a formal Asian alliance, or can this be handled by the United Nations? These were important questions, but not directly relevant to the central question. The *Tribune*, which did challenge the Administration on the central questions, did so in such a generalized manner that it could have been directed at any foreign involvement, not just the Indochina crisis: the *Tribune* had its own standard program.

News stories also reinforced the preconceptions of the Administration, largely because most of the stories dealt with activities and comments of those involved in the decision-making—Dulles, Eisen-

20 Bernard C. Cohen, *The Political Process and Foreign Policy: The Making of the Japanese Peace Settlement* (Princeton: Princeton University Press, 1957), p. 115.
21 Cohen, *The Press and Foreign Policy*, p. 117.

hower, French officials, military officials, and so forth. There were, of course, criticisms of American policy reported but, again, these criticisms seemed to be the peripheral kinds of criticism noted above.

These basic assumptions were clung to throughout the whole period of our Indochina involvement. The settlement, unsatisfactory to U.S. policy-makers, did not occur because of our mistaken preconceptions of the problem, but, in this view, because our Allies could not be persuaded to go along with our schemes. Although the Administration was not immune to criticism, the criticism focused upon the means the Administration was employing to obtain a certain goal, not the goal itself. The press, as one element of a national opinion-making group, certainly did not contribute to the consideration of various alternative policies and their long-range implications, nor did it provide relevant information for consideration by those in policy-making positions.[22]

After the division of Vietnam at Geneva, there was no reevaluation of basic U.S. policy. The press, again except for the *Tribune*, enthusiastically supported the Dulles plan for a Southeast Asia Treaty Organization (SEATO). The feeling was expressed that a firming up of military commitments in advance was all that was needed to prevent a similar loss in the future. The press buttressed, not questioned, existing assumptions about the role of the Viet-Minh in the "worldwide Communist conspiracy," about the methods that that group used to gain support, and about the likelihood that a nationalist, non-Communist leader would emerge to win the support of the people and remain free of colonialist stigma. Most significantly, the story no longer was news. References to Indochina, except for one or two intervals mentioned above, were rare in the American press until the Kennedy era.

NEWSMEN AND THE INDOCHINA STORY

We have alluded frequently to the fact that newsmen relied heavily on official sources for their coverage of the Indochina story and hence, perhaps unwittingly, allowed the assumptions of the Administration to go without serious challenge. This is not to say that the entire coverage of the war consisted of passing on the Administration's press handouts. This, of course, was not the case. At the *Times*, for instance, some of the best reporters were filing Indochina stories: James Reston, Harold Callender, William White, Tillman Dardin, Elie Abel, and Hanson Baldwin, among others. And, as the

22 Ibid.

competent newsmen they are, in presenting each new development in Indochinese policy they frequently tried to examine the implications for future U.S. policy and for the outcome of the struggle itself. Some of them, for example Hanson Baldwin, preceded the Administration in noting that the war was going badly. Others were quick to point out dissension within the Administration as to what proper policy toward Indochina should be.

In the editorial pages, too, there was criticism of U.S. Indochina policy. As Table 5 indicates, the *Tribune* was consistently unfavorable to Administration policy, and the other three had a minority of items that were on the whole unfavorable. The impact of the negativism of the *Tribune*'s editorial pages was diminished by two factors. First, of the four papers surveyed, the *Tribune* usually had the least number of total items on Indochina and the smallest percentage of total items that were editorials. So, in relation to the other papers, the *Tribune* was speaking less frequently. Second, and more important, the *Tribune* was at this time so consistently against any form of U.S. involvement in foreign situations that its resistance to aid in Indochina was quite expected. It did not appear to be based on any specifics of the Indochina case, but only its own generalized predisposition against U.S. involvement in foreign adventures.

Some opposition was expressed on the part of the other three papers, not in terms of the kinds of fundamentals discussed above, but in terms of day-to-day types of policy decisions. Thus it is fair to say that press response mirrored Administration perceptions of the struggle. The question as to why this was so might logically be considered.

Some General Reasons for Type of Press Coverage

In the first place, in any normal foreign-policy reporting, official sources initiate some types of news. Reporters get the bulk of their news from State and Defense Department handouts, press briefings, informal meetings with State Department officials, and the like.[23] A reporter has to rely on these sources for basic information about what is going on. As Cohen reports, "The news agency men may grumble and call it propaganda, but they dutifully report as 'hard news' most of what the State Department News Officer offers them by way of official departmental statements at his noon briefings."[24]

Important stories can then be followed up with interviews of other

23 See Cohen, *The Press and Foreign Policy*; Dunn, *Public Officials and the Press*; Dan P. Nimmo, *Newsgathering in Washington: A Study in Political Communication* (New York: Atherton Press, 1964).
24 Cohen, *The Press and Foreign Policy*, p. 29.

relevant or congressional sources who may have contrary opinions, but the basic source is still the official one. In the case of the Indochina story, interviews with other Administration officials and most congressmen may have led to disputes over the efficacy of military or diplomatic policy, but scarcely to any serious challenge to basic assumptions underlying this policy.

Second, the pressure of day-to-day news coverage leaves little time for extensive background news about a current situation. If the story is "hot," newsmen are pressed to keep up with current developments; if the story is "cold," few are interested in background details. There were, in the present case, occasional attempts on the part of the *Times* or *Post* to provide the reader with more background on the story than just what had occurred in the previous week or month. Usually these "backgrounders" dealt with the recent history of Indochina under French rule, attempts by the "Communist-led" Viet-Minh to displace the colonial power, and the involvement of the United States in Indochina in an attempt to secure Asia from Soviet and Chinese Communist takeover. Such reports were more brief historical reviews than any serious consideration of most basic U.S. goals in Asia or probabilities of long-term success in Vietnam.

Third, any serious challenge to Administration assumptions about the war would most likely have had to be based on evidence gathered from sources completely extraneous to official ones; for example, information and new perspectives gathered from native Indochinese sources or perhaps from Frenchmen disillusioned with France's role in the war. These sources would be more likely to view U.S. involvement in a different light than official sources. For one thing, they could do so in terms of revealing or reaffirming information on the kind, extent, and bases of support held by the Viet-Minh, and perhaps the reasonable limits of success the United States could expect to have in Vietnam and Asia.[25] For another thing, even if someone within the Administration or congressional establishment had wished to challenge the Administration's views on Indochina, in the context of the domestic political situation of the early 1950s the ideological

25   For a brief description of the news sources of a foreign correspondent see ibid., pp. 94–97. For an account of news-gathering during a visit to Saigon during 1950, see C. L. Sulzberger, *A Long Row of Candles: Memoirs and Diaries* (New York: Macmillan, 1969), pp. 554–59. Sulzberger is hardly the average reporter, yet his account illustrates the kinds of sources on which foreign correspondents rely in a relatively unfamiliar situation like this: "French intelligence sources," "high French civil officials," "American chargé d'affaires," and, for Sulzberger, Bao Dai himself—in other words, sources that would tend to be not too antagonistic to existing policy. In fairness to Sulzberger, it must be noted that among *Times* reporters he was one of the most skeptical of U.S. policy.

implications of seeing the problem in a different manner than the Administration might be a formidable barrier. That is, there might have been a certain degree of risk in proclaiming Ho's nationalist appeal too loudly without immediate disclaimers of his status as a puppet of Moscow or Peking. The McCarthyism of 1950–56 created an internal political climate discouraging those who did not see Communism in the prescribed pattern. Even in 1966, over a decade later, those who spoke out against the Administration's rationale for Vietnam intervention faced imputations of disloyalty.

Fourth, and perhaps most important, in the case of Indochina the press, as well as the Administration, was faced with an extremely complex situation about which it had little first-hand information. Stated simply, there were issues of Communism vs. anti-Communism, colonialism vs. anti-colonialism, questions relating to the strategic and economic importance of the Indochinese states, concern over the degree to which the Viet-Minh was dominated by external (Russian and/or Chinese) forces, and questions about the relationship of this struggle to European defense and relations with our most powerful Allies. The Administration chose to put the Indochina situation in terms of a struggle between Communism and anti-Communism—a response that fit the struggle neatly into the generalized foreign policy "programs" of the postwar administrations. The postwar policies of the Cold War, "containing" Communist aggression, economic and military aid to nations under "threat from Communism," and the like were the guideposts of American foreign policy throughout the 1950s. Members of the press, too, adopted these definitions of the situation in the Indochina case. The reasons can partially be explained by examining briefly some basic postulates of organizational behavior, as they related to the behavior of the press.[26]

Some Organizational Explanations for the Behavior of the Press

Any organization has characteristics that shape and reinforce the attitudes of those who are part of it, and thereby influence the content of decisions made. Despite, or because of, the hierarchical structure of organizations that gives particular individuals key roles in decision-making, these decisions are made within an organizational context.[27] The totality of an objective situation is never perceived by

26 For a fuller discussion of organization theory as it applied to the series of Indochina decisions, see Welch, "Groups and Public Policy."
27 Some of the best expositions of organizational decision-making theory are Herbert Simon, *Administrative Behavior: A Study of Decision-Making Processes in Administrative Organization*, 2nd ed. (New York: Macmillan, 1957); James G.

any individual. Since reality is so complex, only a limited part of it can be observed and assimilated. Organizations in their division of labor and responsibility inherently specify a set of limits on a member's definition of reality.[28] Organizations thus provide an orderliness that may contribute to a thorough search for information and its orderly processing, or may depart radically from it. The perception of any individual organizational member must be a biased version of reality, not only because he shares the limitations of any human being, but because his role in the organization carries a built-in bias.

The further an individual is from the entity about which he is receiving information, the greater are the cumulative biases that enter into his perception of reality. Each person in the chain of information that connects him to the event will make judgments about what he has actually seen or been told, and draw certain conclusions. These selections from the total mass of information that serve to make judgments simpler and more consistent constitute "uncertainty absorption." This capacity to absorb uncertainty is not an isolated occurrence in an organizational structure, simply because each person in a subordinate level of authority wants to appear more certain of his information than he actually is. When it is possible, an individual will also want the information that he is relaying not to conflict with beliefs and notions previously and strongly held by those in higher levels of the organization. The conclusions drawn on a low level in an organization, as James March and Herbert Simon point out, become the reality of the next and successively higher stages of the organization.[29]

Members of the press are members of organizations subject to the kinds of limitations on rationality noted above. Those reporters pursuing the Indochina story may well have tended to interpret events in line with prior attitudes about the legitimate reasons for U.S. involvement, the goals that the United States was trying to accomplish, net gains achieved by other postwar policies, and so forth. Most of

---

March and Herbert A. Simon, *Organizations* (New York: John Wiley and Sons, 1958); Chester Irving Barnard, *The Functions of the Executive* (Cambridge: Harvard University Press, 1938, 1968); Anthony Downs, *Inside Bureaucracy* (Boston: Little, Brown, 1967); Herbert A. Simon, Donald W. Smithburg, and Victor A. Thompson, *Public Administration* (New York: Alfred A. Knopf, 1950); and with particular reference to foreign policy, Joseph de Rivera, *The Psychological Dimensions of Foreign Policy* (Columbus, Ohio: Charles E. Merrill, 1968), Ch. 2.

28   March and Simon, *Organizations*, pp. 150–61. In organizations, they suggest that simplification can occur by breaking down a task into several parts, each subgroup being given subgoals that are in reality means to the final end to be accomplished.

29   Ibid., pp. 155–65.

those writing about events in Indochina did not have direct contact with events there; other sources had to be relied upon and "uncertainty absorption" took place. Editors in Washington and New York, and even reporters in Asia, could discount signs suggesting that U.S. Indochinese policy was not working. Bleak news from the battlefield or the Saigon political scene would diminish in importance when mixed with news from other sources about increasing U.S. aid, greater participation by the Vietnamese in their army, or new talks between French and Indochinese governments leading to greater degrees of freedom.[30] Thus a good deal of latitude existed for interpretations placing Administration policy in its most favorable light, not because of deliberate distortion but simply because of the kind of biases inherent in an organizational setting.

Editors as well as newsmen responded to the situation in terms of preestablished programs of action. Editorial boards, too, have organizational memories prescribing patterns of response to situations. The *Post, Chronicle,* and *Times* all were middle-of-the-road to moderately liberal papers; each had previously favored Cold War policies of extending military and economic aid, and of repressing Communist aggression. The easiest solution, when faced with an editorial decision on the complex Indochina problem, would be to see it in this light—that is, as a clearcut case of American aid in the defense of a free, or almost free, people against Communist aggression. The Administration was making this kind of assertion about the situation: for the editors, faced with no direct knowledge to contradict these assertions, to go along with the Administration was perhaps the most rational thing to do. To discount any evidence that the situation was not under control was equally rational. That is, our program in Indochina was perhaps not optimal. There were annoying doubts concerning the lack of indigenous Vietnamese or Cambodian national movements or any evidence of political capabilities on the part of the Indochinese. But the program was proving satisfactory.

The *Chicago Tribune,* by way of contrast, perceived the Indochina crisis in line with its own preconceptions: fighting Communism is a worthy pursuit, but it is easier to fight internal Communism.

30 This provides an illustration of the March and Simon hypothesis: "The more complex the data that are perceived and the less adequate the organization's language, the closer to the source of the information will the uncertainty absorption take place, and the greater will be the amount of summarizing at each step of transmission" (ibid., p. 166); for a discussion as to how and to what degree newspaper policy is considered important by newsmen, see Warren Breed, "Social Control in the News Room," in *Mass Communications,* ed. Wilbur Schramm (Urbana: University of Illinois Press, 1960), pp. 178–94.

Sending American men and money overseas is not the proper way to combat this problem. The *Tribune,* moreover, seemed more interested in slinging mud at the Administration and the French than shedding any light on the complex situation in Indochina. In addition, the *Tribune* made no distinction between this case and any other case of proposed American aid.

The failure of the press to challenge Administration assumptions about the war is thus due to several factors. Some of these are inherent in the day-to-day demands of being a newsman or editor; others have deeper roots in more complex kinds of tendencies in organizational behavior. James Reston, in commenting upon the tendency of the press not to challenge policy until the costs of changing the policy are high, positions are hardened, and options are narrowed, observed, "What reporters have to do now is to move in much earlier in the development of policy. . . . Never before has there been such a need for aggressive reporting in the drafting process so there can be debate before it is too late."[31] This could enable the press to expose at an earlier date inconsistent and unwise aspects of policy as it conforms to existing goals and assumptions of U.S. policy. It would not necessarily, however, mean that the press would be any more likely to challenge the basic goals and assumptions themselves.

THE IMPACT ON ADMINISTRATION DECISION-MAKING

The foregoing analysis assumes that the press indeed has an impact on elite as well as public opinion, and that decision-makers as well as the public rely heavily on the press for information about events taking place. While it is certainly possible to overestimate the importance of the press, research that has examined this question has pointed to the considerable impact that the press has on elite opinion. For example, in his study of U.S. senators,[32] Donald Matthews points out, "A major source of the Senators' information on the outside world is the public press. They do not, unlike members of the executive, possess a far-flung information and intelligence network of their own." Yet a commentator on the relationship between the press and the foreign policy bureaucracy has also observed: "Although he is surrounded by official and unofficial private networks

31   Cohen, *The Press and Foreign Policy,* p. 79. The quotation comes originally from an article by Joe Kraft, "Washington's Most Powerful Reporter," *Esquire,* November, 1958, p. 126.
32   Donald Matthews, *U.S. Senators and Their World* (New York: Random House, 1960); see also Robert A. Dahl, *Congress and Foreign Policy* (New York: Harcourt Brace, 1950).

of communication designed to keep him informed, the policy maker in the State Department still turns to the press for basic factual information about the international political world he lives in—information from abroad as well as from his own political environment."[33] Even with regard to presidents themselves, James Reston notes that, although some presidents pay little attention to the press, others are extremely conscious of what news writers and the editorialists are saying.[34] For the mass public, the press is almost the sole source of foreign policy information, although the impact in terms of policy output is of course less when mass, rather than elite, opinion is being considered.

We cannot, of course, attribute to the press sole responsibility for either Administration policy in Indochina or the relatively recent rise of dissent toward that policy. Yet we have seen that the press *did* play a crucial role in developing and sustaining mass and elite public acceptance of the Administration's view of the Indochina situation. The press, by itself accepting basic Administration assumptions, enhanced the probability that others within the political system would also view the situation in the same light.[35]

33   Cohen, *The Press and Foreign Policy*, p. 209.
34   James Reston, *The Artillery of the Press: Its Influence on American Foreign Policy* (New York: Published for the Council on Foreign Relations by Harper and Row, 1967), pp. 67–68.
35   More recently, the press has played a mirror role: by publicizing "respectable establishment" dissent to Vietnamese policy, as well as "student and peace group" dissent, the press has made possible mass exposure to assumptions contrary to those of the Administration.

nine

Public Opinion and Foreign Affairs: The Mediating Influence of Educational Level

Alvin Richman

THE role of public opinion in the conduct of American foreign policy, at least as a limiting if not a permissive factor, is apparent today on such issues as the war in Vietnam, relations with Communist China, and the nature and level of American security commitments abroad. Among the factors explaining differences in public attitudes, the educational level of respondents has been found to be one of the most important. Level of education is, of course, associated with a number of other social background and personality characteristics, such as occupational status, income, and intellectual ability. But considerable research suggests that educational level is a core factor accounting for most of the differences among political opinions to be explained by the social background factors.[1]

This article examines some of the effects of educational level upon American attitudes on foreign affairs. Covering the period from 1942 to 1965, it studies trends and short-term changes in American public opinion as a whole, as well as in the opinions of three major subgroups: those with at least some college education, those with at least some high school education, and those with less than a high school education. The sources of data on which these time-series

---

1   Alfred O. Hero, *Americans in World Affairs* (Boston: World Peace Foundation, 1959), pp. 15, 21, 27–29; V. O. Key, Jr., *Public Opinion and American Democracy* (New York: Alfred A. Knopf, 1961), pp. 323–31, 336–43; John P. Robinson, *Public Information about World Affairs* (Ann Arbor: Survey Research Center, Institute for Social Research, University of Michigan, 1967), pp. 4–5; William N. Stephens and S. Stephen Long, "Education and Political Behavior," in *Political Science Annual, II*, ed. James A. Robinson (Indianapolis: Bobbs-Merrill, 1970), p. 5.

analyses of opinion change are based consist of nationwide surveys conducted by the American Institute of Public Opinion and the National Opinion Research Council.

SOME CHARACTERISTICS OF AMERICAN PUBLIC OPINION ON FOREIGN AFFAIRS

The literature regarding American public opinion on foreign affairs suggests a number of enduring traits. These hypotheses concern types of opinions held by the general public and its educational subgroups, as well as the nature of long- and short-term changes in their opinions. Summarized briefly here, these hypotheses form the framework for the analysis that follows. Of major interest are hypotheses about group differences and changes in the salience of foreign affairs, informational content, specific opinion levels (such as the level of favorableness toward the Soviet Union or the extent of war expectation), amount of opinion fluctuation, and the ambiguity of opinion.

Salience. American public opinion has been described as having a relatively low but increasing interest in foreign affairs. Alfred Hero remarks that of four criteria of foreign affairs participation—interest, information, rationality, and action—that of "interest" includes a greater number of persons than the others, but is still quite low: "Possibly as many as 15 percent of American adults display a significant degree of interest in world affairs [but] at least 25 percent . . . is not much interested in world affairs even in times of crisis."[2] There is a consistently positive relationship between interest and educational level; that is, the more educated groups have greater interest in foreign affairs than do those with less education.[3]

Information. American public opinion has been characterized as having a generally low informational content on foreign affairs issues (even lower than that on domestic issues) not directly related to the respondents' particular group interests. A strong positive relationship nevertheless exists between education and information levels. "Education," suggests Hero, "is even more closely connected with level and breadth of information about world affairs and understanding of the interplay of different aspects than it is with measures

2   Hero, *Americans in World Affairs*, pp. 6, 9.
3   Ibid., pp. 21–22; Gabriel A. Almond, *The American People and Foreign Policy* (New York: Praeger, 1960), p. 127; Paul A. Smith, "Opinions, Publics, and World Affairs in the United States," *The Western Political Quarterly* 14, no. 3 (September 1961): 700–705; and Stephens and Long, "Education and Political Behavior," p. 5.

of interest. The more specific the information, the higher the correlation with years of education completed."[4]

Direction of Opinions. Whether or not educational level affects the direction of opinion on foreign policy issues is a complicated and disputed question. The answer probably depends on the particular types of question and issue involved, as well as on the existing context of international relations. Whatever differences of opinion are observed among educational groups are probably much smaller than their differences in interest and information levels.[5] Differences in the content and direction of opinions are related to the complexity of the opinion structure (that is, the degree of differentiation, integration, and isolation), which in turn is related to education. In fact, several different attitudinal dimensions (such as involvement, militancy, dominance, and assurance) may underlie a single opinion. And usually the more education, the more dimensions involved. Moreover, some writers suggest that, because of their relatively simplified, ethnocentric, and antagonistic attitudes, the less educated tend to display more unfavorable opinions toward other countries, greater fear of war, and more readiness to resort to it as a means of policy.[6]

Opinion Fluctuation. American public opinion has been described as having a high affectational (as distinct from cognitive or evaluative) component and as being generally although decreasingly unstable. The better educated have a more complex opinion structure that, it is maintained, enhances their willingness to test reality and alter opinions under the impact of new events. This greater opinion flexibility or adaptability of the well educated should combine

4   Hero, *Americans in World Affairs*, p. 22. See also Almond, *The American People and Foreign Policy*, pp. 127, 129; John P. Robinson, "World Affairs Information and Mass Media Exposure," *Journalism Quarterly* 44, no. 1 (Spring 1967): 24–26, 30–31; Stephens and Long, "Education and Political Behavior," pp. 4–5; and Robert E. Lane and David O. Sears, *Public Opinion* (Englewood Cliffs, N.J.: Prentice-Hall, 1964), pp. 62–63. Acknowledging the generally positive relationship between information and education, Lane and Sears maintain further that "the difference between college and high school is greater than the difference between high school and grade school. Education is the most important of all factors in sorting out the informed from the ignorant."

5   Alfred Hero suggests that "the differences between educational groups are greatest for analytical, reality-testing behavior, somewhat less for information, still less for interest, and least of all for general feelings or attitudes on foreign issues" (Hero, *Americans in World Affairs*, pp. 22–24).

6   Michael J. Driver, *Effects of Education on American Public Opinion* (West Lafayette, Ind.: Prepared for the U.S. Arms Control and Disarmament Agency, Technical Report no. 43, December, 1968), pp. 2–8, 11–12; Smith, "Opinions, Publics, and World Affairs in the United States," pp. 703–5; and Hero, *Americans in World Affairs*, pp. 22–24.

with their greater interest and information (that is, sensitivity) to produce more responsiveness to the flow of international events. The simple opinion structures of the less educated by contrast tend to be more rigid and less susceptible to change except under extreme pressure, such as that produced by a grave international crisis. On such occasions, it is claimed, the less educated are more likely to react emotionally and uncertainly—that is, to overreact. As Gabriel Almond has observed, the response of the poorly educated to a crisis event is based on "mood," which changes (or can be manipulated) from one of indifference and withdrawal in normal circumstances to one of fervent intervention in the crisis situation.[7]

Ambiguity. The ambiguity of a response (vagueness, uncertainty, or lack of crystallization of an opinion, as indicated by the level of "no opinion," "don't know," or "undecided" responses on a survey) on a foreign policy issue varies according to the type of issue, the phrasing of the question, and the international context, as well as the educational level of the respondent. Public opinion surveys almost invariably find that ambiguity is inversely related to education. In addition to generating some verbal confidence to cope with survey questions, V. O. Key has suggested that education "probably equips people with sufficient familiarity with general ideas and probably also with a sufficient supply of value preferences to enable them to respond to issues put in rather general terms." The less the education, by way of contrast, "the more directly must an issue bear upon a person's immediate interest or experience to evoke an opinion."[8]

ANALYZING TREND DATA ON SOVIET-AMERICAN RELATIONS

The data forming the basis of this analysis consist of seventy-one different trend questions asked between 1942 and 1965 by the American Institute of Public Opinion (AIPO) and the National Opinion Research Center (NORC), focusing mainly upon the Soviet Union and related foreign affairs subjects. Educational breakdowns of the opinions of college, high school, and grade school subpopulations were obtained for forty-five of these trend questions (but not always

7   Almond, *The American People and Foreign Policy*, Chs. 3–5; Frank L. Klingberg, "The Historical Alternation of Moods in American Foreign Policy," *World Politics* 4, no. 2 (January 1952): 239–73; and Smith, "Opinions, Publics, and World Affairs in the United States," pp. 709–13.

8   Key, *Public Opinion and American Democracy*, pp. 335–36. See also Peter Hofstaetter, "The Actuality Measure in the Study of Public Opinion," *Journal of Applied Psychology* 37, no. 4 (August 1953): 281–87.

for all the data points along every opinion series). In order to obtain a relatively few aggregate indicators from the large number of opinion trends available, the poll data were categorized into five broad opinion variables:

1. Favorableness: degree of favorableness (or unfavorableness) of opinion toward the Soviet Union;
2. Attention: interest in or concern with international problems (or relations with the Soviet Union);
3. Information: degree of information on foreign affairs topics;
4. Expectation: long- or short-range general expectations of war or expectations of future Soviet-American relations; and
5. Respect: evaluation of Soviet capabilities or future prospects of success of the Soviet Union vis-à-vis the United States.

This chapter focuses primarily upon the "favorableness" and "expectation" variables.[9]

The assumption underlying this classification procedure is that a number of opinion series, although differing in their question wordings, still possessed sufficient common meaning along certain theoretically relevant dimensions to justify their combination for analytical purposes. The poll data categorizations (with asterisks indicating opinion series for which educational breakdowns are available) for "favorableness" and "expectation" are as follows:[10]

FAVORABLENESS
1. Cognitive component (that is, perception of Soviet hostility or friendliness)
   *a. Trust in Russian cooperation
   *b. Chance of Russia adopting a peaceful policy
   *c. Fixed alternative questions: Russia's foreign policy objectives are offensive or defensive in nature
   *d. Communists desire peace (or war); threat of Communism or likelihood of Communist attack
2. Affective component (that is, expression of own feelings of hostility or friendliness toward the Soviet Union)

9   The findings below concerning long-term changes in American public opinion and short-term opinion "variability" are based entirely on the "favorableness" and "expectation" variables. Findings on short-term opinion "responsiveness," however, consider all five opinion variables. For a more detailed examination of the data (including the precise wording of the questions used), the procedures, and findings on the variables not included in this report, see Alvin Richman, "The Changing American Image of the Soviet Union" (Ph.D. dissertation, University of Pennsylvania, 1968).

10   The wording of the opinion categories is intended to be similar, but not necessarily identical, to the actual survey questions employed. Many of the categories actually represent more than one opinion series.

   a. Feelings about Russia, the Russian people, and the Soviet government
   b. Feelings about Communism
3. Action orientation
   *a. Preventive war
   *b. Prevent Russian expansion: general (including Europe and Asia)
   c. Prevent Russian expansion (attack) against a specific area
   *d. Prevent Communist expansion via external attack, generally as well as against specific areas
   *e. Intervene to free Communist countries from Communist rule (that is, "liberation policy")
   *f. Break diplomatic relations with the Soviet Union
   *g. Cooperate with the Soviet Union, generally as well as in specific ways
   h. Negotiate with the Soviet Union
   *i. Fixed alternative questions: U.S. policy is too soft (should be firmer) or too hard (should be more willing to compromise) toward the USSR

EXPECTATION
1. Expectation of future Soviet-American relations
   a. Possibilities for the United States to reach a peaceful settlement of differences with the Soviet Union
   *b. Possibilities for continued peaceful coexistence vs. expectation of war with the Soviet Union sooner or later
2. Expectations of war (no direct reference to the Soviet Union)
   a. General (no time specified)
   *b. Long-range (25, 30, or 50 years into the future)
   *c. Medium-range (4, 5, 10, or 15 years)
   *d. Short-range (1, 2, or several years)

The major criteria guiding the selection of trend questions were: (1) all the question items on each opinion series (that is, trend line) must have been asked by the same survey organization, to control for differences in sampling procedures among the different polling organizations; (2) question items of slightly different wording were included in the same opinion series only if they neither altered the phrase order or essential meaning of the question nor introduced new, biased terms; and (3) each opinion series must contain at least four similarly or identically worded questionnaire items.

Each individual opinion series was fitted to a "least-squares" line, both to study different opinion trends and to control for the effects of the trend. Raw poll data results (such as the percentage of "yes" responses) were thereby converted into percentage deviations from trend for the month of their send-out date.[11] This procedure permits an examination of two types of changes in American public opinion: short-term fluctuations of different opinions about their respective trends, and long-term changes in the slopes or directions of the trend lines themselves.

Long-term Changes in American Public Opinion

This section discusses the findings for the general American public and three educational subgroups on such long-term opinion characteristics as the periodicities and slopes of opinion trends, levels of response over time on the "favorableness" and "expectation" opinion variables, and changes in the amount of "no opinion" or "don't know" responses (that is, ambiguity). The results in this section regarding long-term changes in opinion are based on the *average* of the slopes or response levels for the individual opinion series comprising the "favorableness" and "expectation" variables. The findings in the next section on short-term opinion fluctuations, however, will be based on deviations from the individual opinion trends themselves.

Periodicity and Slopes of Opinion Trends. On the opinion variables "favorableness" and "expectation" American public opinion as a whole was characterized by a definite and similar periodicity (that is, corresponding terminal dates) for the trend lines between 1942 and 1965. Thus, for these two opinion variables changes over time in the average slopes occurred more or less simultaneously. The four periods for both "favorableness" and "expectation" are approximately as follows: (1) 1942–August, 1945; (2) September, 1945–March, 1948; (3) March, 1948–November, 1950, and (4) December, 1950–1965.[12]

Since the variables "favorableness" and "expectation" possess definite periodicity, it is possible to obtain summary measures of their slopes for each of these periods of the study. This is accomplished by averaging the slopes of the trends (weighted by their num-

---

11 It was considered necessary to fit a trend line to each opinion series to control for any cumulative effects of events on public opinion. This then permits examination of the short-term fluctuations of opinion around their trend line, as well as the relationships between these opinion fluctuations and different types of events. It may also be useful to observe the characteristics of the secular trend itself and any long-term changes in these characteristics.

12 The fourth period is considerably longer than the others due to the absence of consistent trend characteristics and perhaps insufficient poll data to permit its further differentiation.

ber of points) contributing to each opinion variable for each of the several periods.

For the general American public the most marked long-term change for both "favorableness" and "expectation" was the steep negative trend from September, 1945, to March, 1948—with average decreases in "favorableness" and optimism ("expectation") of four-fifths and one-half of a percentage point per month, respectively. This unusually steep trend might be explained as the cumulative effect of a large series of American-Soviet conflict interactions between 1945 and 1948. The average slopes of the variables "favorableness" and "expectation" for the other periods of the study were comparatively level. However, the opinion series for "expectation," at least, suggest that the March, 1948–November, 1950, period itself is characterized by two shorter subperiods (divided around July, 1949) in which American public opinion at first showed increasing optimism regarding the future possibilities of war (average slope of +1.29), but later became increasingly pessimistic (average slope of −1.71).[13]

The most important individual international events coinciding with and presumably contributing to these long-term shifts in the direction of American public opinion were the end of World War II (August–September, 1945), the Communist coup in Czechoslovakia (February–March, 1948), the American advance to the Manchurian border during the Korean War (October–November, 1950), and the Communist counteroffensive (November–December, 1950). The Czech coup and the Chinese Communist entrance into the Korean War coincide with the low points of "favorableness" and optimism ("expectation") of the "Cold War" during the 1945–50 period.

Because of the intense conflict interactions between the two blocs during 1950, the halt in the steep negative trend of American opinion toward the Soviet Union in early 1948 and the relatively level character of the overall trend between 1948 and 1950 seem to require some additional explanation besides the dramatic occurrence of the Czech coup in February–March, 1948, that marked a low point in the Cold War. By early 1948 approximately 70 percent of

13 The similarity of the periodicities and average slopes for the trend lines of the opinion variables "favorableness" and "expectation" was not unexpected. A summary of published cross-tabular poll data presented in Richman, "The Changing American Image of the Soviet Union," revealed a definite relationship between these two variables. In the present study, moreover, "favorableness" and "expectation" display a very high rank-order agreement for the different periods with respect to their average level of "no opinion" response.

the American public viewed the Soviet Union unfavorably. It is reasonable to argue that the opinions of a large proportion of the remainder could not be affected under any circumstances.[14] Included in this remaining 30 percent were those whose views were particularly intense and rigidly pro-Soviet, those who were generally unaware of international events, and those who were aware, but characteristically did not wish to commit themselves to any definite opinion and who thus were inclined to select "no opinion" responses to many survey questions.[15]

The determination of periodicities for the three educational subgroups is somewhat more difficult than for the American public as a whole, since there are fewer opinion trends available for analyzing these subgroups. The trend data on "favorableness" and "expectation" do suggest, nevertheless, that the college-educated began to decline in "favorableness" and optimism regarding the Soviet Union somewhat later than the other educational groups at two different times—lagging approximately one month behind the other groups during August–September, 1945, and one month (behind high school) and two months (behind grade school) between June and August, 1949. Such delays by the college-educated might be interpreted as a hesitancy by this group to accept the negative attitudinal implications of the increased American-Soviet conflict occurring at these times. The three educational groups nonetheless appeared to agree on March, 1948, as a terminal point marking the halt to the sharp drop after World War II in U.S. friendliness toward the Soviet Union, and they also concurred on the months of October–November, 1950 (for "favorableness"), or December, 1950 (for "expectation"), as an additional terminal point during the Korean War.

As is evident in Table 1, all the groups, particularly the college-educated, exhibited a marked negative shift of opinion during the 1945–48 period. In fact, the college-educated group displayed the greatest long-term trend shifts of all of the groups between 1943 and 1950—moving in the most positive direction during 1943–45, the most negative direction during 1945–48, and continuing to show the largest long-term shifts between 1948 and 1950 (see especially

14 It is very likely that this "boundary phenomenon"—in which opinion changes along the extremes of the opinion spectrum are more difficult to produce than around the center—is characteristic of a large number of survey questions.

15 Another interpretation, supported by two of the opinion trends under "expectation," is that American public opinion became more positive during the first half of the 1948–50 period (i.e., around mid-1948 to mid-1949), but began to decline again around August, 1949, until reaching its low point of pessimism ("expectation") in December, 1950.

Table 1. Trends in Favorableness and Expectation, by Educational Group, 1943–65[a]

Opinion Variable and Educational Group	1943–45		1945–48		1948–49[a]		1948–50[a]		1949–50[a]		1950–65[b]	
	Average Slope	Total N	Average Slope	Total N	Average Slope	Total N	Average Slope	Total N	Average Slope	Total N	Average Slope	Total N
Favorableness[c]												
College	+0.43	7	−1.05	21			−0.09	25			+0.08	49
High school	+0.31	7	−0.79	21			−0.07	25			+0.14	49
Grade school	+0.01	7	−0.60	21			+0.06	25			+0.16	49
Expectation[c]												
College			−1.15	18	+1.72	10			−2.68	11	+0.45	54
High school			−1.05	18	+1.50	10			−1.94	11	+0.44	54
Grade school			−1.14	18	+1.14	10			−1.21	11	+0.29	54

[a] The boundaries of the periods are approximately as follows: August, 1943–August, 1945; September, 1945–March, 1948; March, 1948–July, 1949 (for *expectation* only); August, 1949–November, 1950 (for *expectation* only); March, 1948–November, 1950 (for *favorableness* only); and December, 1950–65.

[b] The "average slope" represents the average (net) slope of the trend lines for the opinion variable weighted by their respective number of points. The "total *N*" indicates the total number of points for the opinion variable.

[c] All values for *favorableness* and *expectation* are based on the positive dimension—that is, upward slopes denote increasing *favorableness* or optimism. Trend lines relating to "*Favorableness:* satisfaction with United States policy" were omitted from these tabulations.

the "expectation" trends). Somewhat surprisingly, the grade school group generally showed the smallest long-term oscillations over the several periods between 1942 and 1950.

Levels of "Favorableness" and "Expectation." The levels of "favorableness" and "expectation" (optimism), as indicated in Table 1, declined sharply for all three educational groups between 1943 and 1950, but this decline was particularly marked for the college educated. Utilizing the periodicities determined in the previous analyses, the three groups were found to produce fairly similar levels of "favorableness" for the 1943–45 and 1948–50 periods. Since the college group began its postwar decline somewhat later than the other groups, however, it had to fall more sharply to reach the same 1948–50 level. In fact, the decline in "favorableness" for the college-educated between 1945 and 1948 was approximately one and one-half percent per month, compared to roughly one percent and three-quarters of one percent declines per month, respectively, for the high school and grade school groups.

The most negative years for all groups appear to lie between 1948 and 1953. During this period an average of only about one-fifth of the Americans who volunteered an opinion said that they thought Russia could be trusted to cooperate with us. This contrasts with the World War II years in which roughly 60 percent of each educational group said they trusted Russia.

The levels of opinion concerning "expectation of war" also changed markedly. Whereas during the period October, 1945–December, 1946, between 18 percent (college) and 34 percent (grade school) of the respondents expected a future war, during the Korean War these figures rose to 75 percent and 68 percent, respectively. The college group here also appears to have been the most disillusioned with the postwar course of events, since well over half of this group shifted from an optimistic to pessimistic outlook within the space of six years after World War II.

Ambiguity of Opinion. As indicated in Table 2, the concept "ambiguity of opinion," as measured in this study, appears to represent an inverse measure of public hostility toward the Soviet Union for each of the educational groups. The first and third periods of the study (August, 1943–August, 1945, and March, 1948–November, 1950), established earlier by examining the terminal points of the opinion trends, contain the highest and lowest averages of "no opinion" responses, respectively, for both "favorableness" and "expectation" for each educational group. They also contain the most and least favorable American opinions of the Soviet Union. In fact, when

Table 2. Ambiguity in Opinion of the Soviet Union, by Educational Group, 1943–60[a]

Opinion Variable and Educational Group	1943–45 Average N.O. Response	No. Items[b]	1945–48 Average N.O. Response	No. Items[b]	1948–50 Average N.O. Response	No. Items[b]	1950–60 Average N.O. Response	No. Items[b]
Favorableness								
College	11.4	7	9.0	22	6.0	25	6.2	82
High school	17.7	7	11.0	22	8.0	25	8.5	82
Grade school	25.6	7	18.7	22	16.0	25	14.7	82
Expectation								
College			9.6	18	6.0	21	5.4	36
High school			10.9	18	7.5	21	8.6	36
Grade school			15.5	18	12.5	21	13.8	36
Average for *Favorableness* and *Expectation*[c]								
College	11.4	7	9.3	40	6.0	46	6.0	118
High school	17.7	7	11.0	40	7.8	46	8.5	118
Grade school	25.6	7	17.3	40	14.8	46	14.4	118

[a] The exact boundary dates of the periods for *favorableness* and *expectation* are similar to those given on Table 1, except that the two periods between 1948–50 for *expectation* have been collapsed here and the terminal date for the last period for both variables is 1960.
[b] This figure indicates the total number of questionnaire items on all the trend lines comprising each opinion variable. Only questions with dichotomous response categories (i.e., "yes"—"no"—"no opinion") were employed.
[c] These values represent the average of the *favorableness* and *expectation* "no opinion" response levels weighted according to their number of questionnaire items.

the first two periods are each divided into two intervals, the drop in the level of "no opinion" response between the periods 1943–44 and 1948–50 is continuous.[16] Thus it appears that many Americans who hesitated to commit themselves during World War II to the prevailing mood of friendship for the Soviet Union had less difficulty in adopting the prevailing hostile sentiment in the postwar periods (particularly between 1947 and 1950).

Comparing the three educational groups over all time periods and opinion variables reveals that the college-educated, as expected, consistently give the fewest "no opinion" responses, followed in order by the high school and grade school groups. Averaging the "no opinion" responses for the four periods between 1943 and 1960 (giving equal weight to each period), we find that for "favorableness" and "expectation" combined the three groups averaged 8.2, 11.5, and 18.2 percent, respectively, for college, high school, and grade school.

These findings suggest several empirical rules of thumb for estimating "no opinion" response levels in the future. First, "no opinion" levels for questions relating to "favorableness" and "expectation" are fairly similar for most periods and educational groups.[17] Second, "no opinion" responses to questions relating to both "favorableness" and "expectation" are influenced by the degree of hostility and tension in the international environment. Significant changes in the international climate of opinion may affect the level of "no opinion" response by as much as one hundred percent. Third, the level of "no opinion" response is related to education. Grade school respondents usually produce slightly more than twice as many "no opinion" responses as the college-educated group, and high school respondents yield on the average almost one and one-half times as many.

SHORT-TERM CHANGES IN AMERICAN PUBLIC OPINION

Two concepts relating to short-term changes of opinion are analyzed below: (1) general *variability* of opinion—that is, the general amount of fluctuation of opinion about trends, as indicated by the

16   Thus, for the American public as a whole the average "no opinion" responses for the four early subperiods (i.e., March, 1942–May, 1944, June, 1944–August, 1945, September, 1945–December, 1946, and January, 1947–February, 1948) and the March, 1948–November, 1950, period are 23.5, 16.0, 14.6, 11.2, and 9.8 percent, respectively, for the variables "favorableness" and "expectation" combined. The average "no opinion" response for these two variables rises to 12.8 percent during 1950–65.

17   In this study the differences in "no opinion" response levels obtained between the two opinion variables "favorableness" and "expectation" were meager compared to the effects of education and international tension level.

average of the standard errors of estimate (S) of the responses about individual trend lines relating to the variables "favorableness" and "expectation";[18] and (2) *responsiveness* of opinion to events—that is, the amount of opinion change coinciding with certain independently selected major events.

Variability of Opinion. The average standard errors of estimate for the trend lines relating to "favorableness" and "expectation" were inconsistent with respect to changes in S over time. Employing the periodization determined empirically for these two opinion variables in the previous section, the results for "favorableness" show that all three educational groups exhibited successively decreasing values of S between 1943 and 1950, after which the values increased. But for "expectation" the values of S display a generally opposite pattern, particularly those belonging to the college-educated group: S increases between 1945 and 1950 for all three groups, continues to increase during 1950–65 for the high school and grade school groups, but declines after 1950 for the college respondents. These results suggest that opinion "variability," as indicated here by the average size of the standard errors of estimate, might be an interacting function of the type of question employed and the period, as well as the personal and social characteristics of the respondents.

The three educational groups were compared with respect to their average values of S for "favorableness" and "expectation" combined over the entire 1943–65 period. Average S values of 5.08, 4.55, and 4.35 were obtained for the college, high school, and grade school groups, respectively.[19] These results suggest that education is positively associated with short-term opinion variability. Applying a test of the difference between two sample means, we found that none of the differences among these figures is significant at the 0.1 level (two-tailed test).[20] Nevertheless, the results were in the expected direction, if we assume a continuous event-opinion relationship and interpret the concept of opinion variability as being indicative of the general sensitivity and *responsiveness* of opinion to continuous changes in the international environment, rather than of an *instability* of opinion not associated with international events.

18 The standard error of estimate is similar in its conception to the standard deviation. It measures the divergence of the various data points of an opinion series from their *trend line* (i.e., regression line), just as the standard deviation measures the dispersion of the various values of a series around their single *mean*.

19 These figures represent the unweighted average values of S for the thirty-one opinion trends in our study relating to "favorableness" and "expectation."

20 The difference between the college and grade school means would have reached the 0.1 significance level for a one-tailed test.

Responsiveness of Opinion. With regard to short-term opinion fluctuations for the American public as a whole, twenty-one "major opinion fluctuations" from the trend (events being the dependent variable) and twenty independently "selected major events" (opinions being the dependent variable) were examined between 1943 and 1965.[21] Only two of the "major opinion fluctuations" exceed 20 percent. Thirteen of the fluctuations, almost two-thirds of the total, range between 10 and 20 percent, while the remaining six fall below 10 percent. Furthermore, examination of the opinion fluctuations from the trend coinciding with the twenty "selected major events" reveals that only nine of the sixty-three fluctuations obtained exceed 10 percent and only two exceed 20 percent.[22] In summary, short-term changes in opinion greater than 10 percent are found to be relatively infrequent, not likely to occur by chance, and therefore should be accorded considerable importance.

Examination of the opinion fluctuations of the three educational groups coinciding with the twenty "selected major events" reveals that the groups show fairly similar proportions of major opinion shifts. Of the fifty opinion fluctuations from the trend obtained for each educational group (employing all of the opinion series) the number exceeding 10 percent is eight for each of the educational groups. The number of opinion fluctuations exceeding 5 percent is nineteen for the college respondents, and twenty-one and seventeen, respectively, for the high school and grade school groups. Thus the groups seem quite similar in this respect. Moreover, when we employ the standard error of estimate (S) as our criterion of major

21   The criterion for determining a "major" opinion deviation from trend was based on the standard error of estimate (S) for each trend line. Deviations were classified as "major" if they were equal to or greater than 1.96 x S. (The use of the factor $+1.96$ sets the two-tailed 95 percent confidence level for each trend line under the assumption that the data are normally distributed about that line.) The twenty "major events" were selected by the writer from several chronologies independently of the poll data. Selection was based on the writer's own judgment regarding the outstanding and relative importance and/or salience of the events to the American public.

22   An opinion response was selected as "coinciding" with an event if the send-out date of the relevant survey occurred no more than thirty days *after* the event or not more than two days *before* it. Thus, by relating each of the twenty major events to each of our seventy-one opinion series in this manner, a total of sixty-three event-opinion "occurrences" were obtained.

No attempt is made to establish cause-and-effect relationships or to estimate the relative impact of the different individual events on the basis of the few event-opinion "occurrences" included here. An implication is that in a number of these cases the coinciding event or events contributed to the opinion fluctuation. However, the main feature of these sixty-three opinion fluctuations coinciding with twenty major events is that, taken as a whole, they are likely to be greater in size than any other comparable number of opinion fluctuations.

opinion deviations from the trend, the three educational groups produce almost equivalent numbers of significant opinion shifts.[23]

Among the international events for which coinciding opinion responses are available, those that seem to have produced considerable impact on public opinion were: the death of Stalin in March, 1953 (increased "favorableness" toward the Soviet Union among all educational groups, with shifts along one opinion series of between 14 and 17 percent from trend for the three groups); the purge of Khrushchev in October, 1964 (over 12 percent positive shift of general public opinion regarding future relations with Russia—no educational breakdowns available); the Gulf of Tonkin incident in August, 1964 (increases in satisfaction with U.S. policy in Vietnam of 21–22 percent for all educational groups and increases in attention to Vietnam of 18 percent for the high school and grade school groups and 8 percent for the college respondents); the Communist coup in Czechoslovakia in February, 1948 (negative shifts of about 8 percent in expectation of war for all educational groups); the North Korean invasion of South Korea (negative shifts of 15 percent for the college-educated and between 10 and 11 percent for the high school and grade school groups in expectation of war); and the signing of the Austrian State Treaty in May, 1955 (positive shifts of over 18 percent for the college educated and about 10 percent for the high school and grade school groups in "favorableness" toward the Soviet Union).

EDUCATIONAL LEVEL AND FOREIGN POLICY ATTITUDES

In the presentation of results the distinction has occasionally been drawn between opinion changes characterizing the American public as a whole and the comparison of opinion levels and change of the three educational subgroups. Among the more significant results concerning long-term opinion change, it was found that the general

23 For two-tailed tests at the 0.90 confidence level the number of significant opinion deviations from trend was eight for the college group, six for high school, and nine for grade school. At the two-tailed 0.80 confidence level the results were fourteen for the college group, fifteen for high school, and sixteen for the grade school respondents.

These numbers of significant opinion fluctuations for two-tailed tests are generally somewhat greater—but not very much greater—than those expected to occur by chance alone (i.e., five and ten opinion fluctuations expected at the 0.90 and 0.80 confidence levels, respectively). However, when one-tailed tests are used with appropriate hypotheses regarding the directions of expected opinion changes, the numbers of significant opinion deviations produced at the 0.90 and 0.95 confidence levels are still quite similar for the three educational groups, but in each case they are at least twice as many as the number expected to occur by chance.

American public was characterized by a definite periodicity on the opinion variables "favorableness" and "expectation" between 1943 and 1950, experiencing a particularly steep negative decline between September, 1945, and March, 1948. The concept "ambiguity," as indicated by the level of "no opinion" responses to questions relating to "favorableness" and "expectation," was shown to vary inversely with the international tension level. Regarding short-term changes in opinion for the general public, opinion fluctuations from the trend greater than 10 percent were found to be relatively infrequent, even when major events were known to have coincided with them.

These general findings on the nature of American public opinion changes apply to all educational groups. However, some group differences were found. For instance, concerning long-range opinion changes, the college-educated were somewhat slower to diminish their trust in the Soviet Union after World War II than were other groups. This may have been due to the greater ethnocentrism and suspiciousness toward other countries that is occasionally attributed to less educated persons (see page 234 and note 6). This initial hesitancy on the part of the college group to accept the negative implications of the intergovernmental relations of the immediate post–World War II period may partially explain the steep negative shift in direction of opinion which it subsequently displayed, since the levels of "favorableness" were fairly similar for all of the groups during the 1943–45 and 1948–50 periods.

In fact, except for the two or three years immediately following the end of World War II, differences among the educational groups along the "favorableness" and "expectation" dimensions were relatively small throughout the 1943–53 period. During September, 1945–December, 1946, the college-educated respondents were considerably more favorable to the Soviet Union than the other groups and much more optimistic about the future prospects for peace. The grade school group was the most negative in these respects. But after January, 1947, the figures began to converge so that after 1948, and at least until 1953, little difference among the groups in "favorableness" or "expectation" is apparent, although some inconsistencies do appear.

As expected, such differences among the educational groups in "direction" of opinion were considerably smaller than their differences in "ambiguity" of opinion (see page 234 and note 5). "Ambiguity" (indicated by the level of "no opinion" responses on a survey) was found to be closely and negatively related to educational level, as well as to the degree of international tension—a finding which conforms to most previous survey data (see page 235 and note 8).

Without doubt the most difficult part of our analysis to interpret concerns short-term changes in opinion among the educational groups. Gabriel Almond, as noted earlier, has remarked on the general instability of American public opinion, especially among the less educated. The better-educated sector of the public, it is held, is more attentive to the stream of international news and more ready to alter opinions under the impact of new events—that is, more "responsive" to international events. The less-educated sector, on the other hand, while generally indifferent to international affairs in normal circumstances, tends to overreact in times of crisis.

Our data reveal that college respondents exhibit greater "opinion variability" (though not significantly greater statistically) than the other groups. This is true both for long-term directional changes in opinion (that is, changes in the average slopes of opinion trends in Table 1) and short-term fluctuations of opinion (that is, average amount of oscillation around the individual trend lines, as measured by the standard errors of estimate). Does this greater amount of opinion variation mean that college respondents are more *unstable* in their opinions, or that they are *responsive* to the month-by-month vicissitudes in the flow of international events?[24] From the findings on levels of "attention" and "information," as well as studies on media usage, one may assume that the college group as a whole is relatively "sensitive" to monthly fluctuations within the international political environment. If one assumes further that the international context itself fluctuates considerably from month to month around a hypothetical trend of conflict and cooperation, for example, then a considerable amount of opinion variation about the trend could be indicative of responsiveness to international events.

However, the findings relating to "opinion responsiveness" suggest that, while all educational groups react sharply to major international events more frequently than expected by chance alone, there

24 Of course, we cannot entirely rule out the possibility that the results obtained here are primarily an artifact of the particular categorization and time-series procedures employed in this study. In particular, there is some arbitrariness involved in the decision to fit least-squares lines to all of the opinion series. This decision has a definite, but unknown, effect on the S values of the trends. Where no real trend exists, the construction of least-squares lines may minimize the actual amount of overall variation in opinion responses. But, where opinion series are basically characterized by a curvilinear trend, this procedure may exaggerate the actual amount of opinion variation.

is little difference between them in the number of significant changes of opinion response at times corresponding to the occurrence of major international events in the postwar era.[25]

Even though one group or another may sometimes react more strongly to a particular event, a problem remains of determining what is an "appropriate" level of opinion change to that event. What amount of opinion change is "responsive," and what amount is "*over*responsive"? For instance, does the fact that the college respondents displayed greater opinion shifts than the high school and grade school groups at the times of the North Korean invasion and the signing of the Austrian State Treaty (average of 16 percent vs. 10 percent) indicate that the college group as a whole is more "unstable" or more "responsive" with respect to these international events?

At the least, these findings emphasize the need for further specification and testing of the concept "mood instability." The latter term is not only excessively ambiguous; it also carries an unnecessary negative connotation. Two relatively specific and neutral terms have been introduced in this discussion: general opinion *variability* over time and *responsiveness* of opinion to specific events. Contrary to what we should expect from the "mood instability" hypothesis, it is the college-educated part of the sample—not the grade school group—that shows the greatest opinion variability over time. Furthermore, we have produced some evidence to suggest that the greater opinion variability of the college-educated does not result from their higher responsiveness to international events. Little difference in opinion responsiveness, in fact, was found among the three educational groups.

Actually, this is only one of several aspects of foreign policy opinion in which education seems to have little effect. Although it is important for many purposes to understand the differences in opinion levels and change among the educational groups, their similarities in this study are at least as impressive. All of the groups, for example, exhibit fairly similar periodicities and steep, if not quite parallel, directional changes in "favorableness" and "expectation" in cumulative response to events after World War II. All show sharp drops in "ambiguity" between the periods 1943–45 and 1948–50. And there is no evidence here to indicate that the three groups differ very much

25   This study is limited in the types of opinion effects it can examine to changes from one response category to another. Data are not available for analyzing other possible types of effects on opinions—for example, activation, reinforcement (i.e., certainty), or intensification (i.e., change along the same positive or negative dimension).

in the extent to which they react to major international events, using a monthly unit of analysis.

That there are some important similarities among the educational groups should not surprise us. Studies of the intermediary role of the mass media and interpersonal communications between events and opinion have demonstrated the widespread diffusion of news and opinion that often occurs following major national and international events. Perhaps if the data had permitted a shorter unit of time to be used in the analysis, a sharper differentiation might have been drawn among the educational groups, at least with regard to their immediate responsiveness to individual events. Within a week or two of major events, however, some degree of consensus or standardization of news and interpretations deriving from our mass media and opinion-makers can be expected to permeate American society.

ten

Events, Mass Opinion, and Elite Attitudes

Sophia Peterson

THE relationship between mass public opinion and foreign policy has been and continues to be a subject of disagreement among scholars. Walter Lippmann has argued that mass opinion has handicapped the American executive's conduct of foreign relations.[1] However, V. O. Key, Jr., suggested that such a view underestimates the capacity of leaders to influence and direct mass opinion that is general and not specific in its instructions.[2] William Buchanan and Hadley Cantril's extensive study of the attitudes of peoples of different nations toward each other concluded that the stereotypes people maintain toward other nations are not *causative* of political relations between nations but rather *symptomatic*.[3] Perhaps one reason for continuing disagreement rests, as Bernard C. Cohen recently wrote, in the fact that "the literature of public opinion and public policy in general, and of public opinion and foreign policy in particular, largely evades the question

1 Walter Lippmann, *Essays in the Public Philosophy* (New York: New American Library, 1956), pp. 19, 23.

2 V. O. Key, Jr., *Public Opinion and American Democracy* (New York: Alfred A. Knopf, 1961), pp. 552–53. See also Gabriel Almond: "Foreign policy still appears to be the area of policy least susceptible of being influenced by either the ordinary person or the opinion leaders" (*The American People and Foreign Policy* [New York: Praeger, 1960], p. xxiii). Also Milton Rosenberg: "Those who have some direct control over the shaping of policy do not take it as their primary obligation to simply interpret and execute the 'will of the people' " ("Attitude Change and Foreign Policy in the Cold War Era," in *Domestic Sources of Foreign Policy*, ed. James N. Rosenau [New York: The Free Press, 1967], p. 116).

3 William Buchanan and Hadley Cantril, *How Nations See Each Other: A Study in Public Opinion* (Urbana: University of Illinois Press, 1953), p. 57.

of the relationship between opinion and policy; it has simply not been the focal point of study."[4]

The focal point of this study is the relationship between mass opinion and one aspect of foreign policy, the public pronouncements of decision-makers. The aim has been to determine whether there is any congruence between mass opinion and official foreign policy attitudes over a ten-year period. If congruence were merely temporary, as for example during periods of crisis, this might be explained as an extraordinary and fleeting "closing of the ranks." If, however, congruence is the prevailing relationship during normal as well as crisis periods (which is the finding of this study), then we must seek more complex explanations, and additional research tasks arise to explore the means by which this congruence occurs—for example, the "two-step flow of communication" or James N. Rosenau's more discriminating "four-step flow."[5]

The relationship between public opinion in a democracy and the foreign policy process appears to be threefold: public opinion operates "as a *resource* in policy execution and as a *source* of policy innovation, [and] . . . as a *constraint* upon policy innovation." In its first role public opinion supports policy (a sustaining resource), thereby strengthening the position of the nation's leaders vis-à-vis other nations. But how does public opinion act as a source of policy?

> Can it, when strongly mobilized and effectively expressed, actually drive leaders to undertake changes that they would not otherwise have considered? . . . rarely can [campaigns to change foreign policy] . . . exert enough pressure, enough directed mass indignation, to force even the most democratic of governments into previously unconsidered or rejected paths of action. What they do sometimes accomplish is to change the image of public opinion held by persons capable of affecting policy decisions; indeed they may often alter the image of public opinion held by the public itself.

Finally, what of the role of public opinion as a constraint on the foreign policy process? Milton J. Rosenberg's view is that "while

4 Bernard C. Cohen, "The Relationship between Public Opinion and Foreign Policy Maker," in *Public Opinion and Historians,* ed. Melvin Small (Detroit: Wayne State University Press, 1970), p. 70.

5 Elihu Katz, "The Two-Step Flow of Communication: An Up-to-Date Report on a Hypothesis," *Public Opinion Quarterly* 21, no. 1 (Spring 1957): 61–78; and James N. Rosenau, *Public Opinion and Foreign Policy: An Operational Formulation* (New York: Random House, 1961), pp. 7–8.

public opinion operating as a constraint upon policy rarely stops innovations in their tracks, it may often transform them."[6] This transformation occurs because policy-makers' perceptions of public opinion lead them to make certain modifications in policy, a process of which the policy-maker himself may not be fully aware.[7] Therefore, the apparent growing scholarly consensus as to the relative lack of influence of public opinion in shaping foreign policy may be ill founded since, even if the public does not originate foreign policies, it may still restrict foreign policy modifications because of the perceptions that decision-makers have about the inflexibility and unpredictability of public opinion.[8]

The relationship between public opinion and the foreign policy process is complicated not only by the perceptions of policy-makers, but also by the effect of events. Karl Deutsch and Richard Merritt emphasize the stability of public attitudes in the face of world events unless a particular combination of factors operates together to bring about change:

> Almost nothing in the world seems to be able to shift the images of 40 per cent of the population in most countries, even within one or two decades. Combinations of events that shift the images and attitudes even of the remaining 50 or 60 per cent of the population are extremely rare, and these rare occasions require the combination and mutual reinforcement of cumulative events with spectacular events and substantial governmental efforts as well as the absence of sizable cross pressures.[9]

This stability of opinion is enhanced not only by various psychological processes favoring stability, but also by the relative ignorance of foreign affairs by 75 to 90 percent of the mass public.[10] Yet we cannot infer simply on the basis of evidence of public ignorance that

6   Milton J. Rosenberg, "Images in Relation to the Policy Process: American Public Opinion on Cold-War Issues," in *International Behavior: A Social-Psychological Analysis*, ed. Herbert C. Kelman (New York: Holt, Rinehart and Winston, 1965), pp. 279, 280, 285.

7   Key uses the image of public opinion as a "system of dikes which . . . fix a range of discretion within which government may act" (*Public Opinion and American Democracy*, p. 552).

8   Rosenberg, "Images in Relation to the Policy Process," pp. 329–30; Gerard Herberichs, "On Theories of Public Opinion and International Organization," *Public Opinion Quarterly* 30, no. 4 (Winter 1966–67): 625–26.

9   Karl W. Deutsch and Richard L. Merritt, "Effects of Events on National and International Images," in *International Behavior*, ed. Kelman, p. 183.

10   Rosenau, *Public Opinion and Foreign Policy*, p. 35.

mass acquiescence to any and all American policies would be automatic.[11]

This study examines first the empirical evidence on the relationship between governmental decision-makers and the population. The relationship will be explored by answering this question: Are mass opinion and decision-makers' attitudes congruent? Do they evaluate a salient foreign policy target similarly in terms of favorability? In particular, do they evaluate the Soviet Union similarly? The evidence suggests that the answer over a ten-year period from 1955 to 1964 is affirmative.

A further question then arises. If decision-makers and the public share similar evaluations of the USSR, is this congruence explained by another factor—the world of events? Perhaps the relationship between decision-makers and the public is not really evidence of interaction, but merely a coincidence as both react to events. The events selected for analysis are conflictual events initiated by the Soviet Union and the United States toward each other annually from 1955 to 1964, as reported in the mass media. Conflictual events are those most compatible with the "Cold War" set of attitudes that developed after World War II and are therefore the events least disturbing to preconceived views and least likely to engender cognitive dissonance.[12]

The evidence reveals that mass opinion regarding the Soviet Union is not at all correlated with conflictual events, either those initiated by the United States or by the Soviet Union. Decision-makers' attitudes are, however, weakly correlated with American conflict behavior directed toward the Soviet Union: a year characterized by a relatively high level of American conflict behavior directed toward the USSR is also a year of highly unfavorable official American attitudes regarding the USSR. Since the relationship between American mass opinion and decision-makers' attitudes is not explained by events, the likelihood of a genuine relationship is increased.

A final question is whether the evidence justifies any inferences about the *direction* of influence in this relationship. Only close examination of the data can answer this question even tentatively, so the analysis of this question will be deferred until the evidence is presented. But even the full presentation of data relating to mass

11 Rosenberg, "Attitude Change and Foreign Policy in the Cold War Era," pp. 149–50.

12 Deutsch and Merritt, "Effects of Events on National and International Images," pp. 133, 151–52.

opinion, elite attitudes, and events will leave many questions un-answered—such as, what is the role of opinion leaders, and by what means does the public pick up cues from officials, if in fact it does?

A FRAMEWORK FOR ANALYSIS

Little more than speculation has focused on the long-term congruence of mass opinion and official attitudes. Past research has dealt with mass evaluation of specific American foreign policies at a particular moment in time. The general, although not unanimous, conclusion is that the majority of the public, even of certain specialized publics such as students, tends to approve official U.S. policies. Many of the specific policies studied involved crises (such as the Bay of Pigs invasion or the Cuban missile crisis), however, and therefore such conclusions cannot be generalized to apply to all official pronouncements.[13] Past and present public controversy about such issues as the Vietnam war suggests that the assumption of unfailing public support of official positions must be qualified in instances where the cost of official policy in human and material resources is high.[14] The extent of public support of official policy that does exist is understandable, given the public's assumption that foreign policy is a subject for experts, especially for the president, and in view of the communication resources upon which the government may call to justify its policies, not to mention its ability to limit the information that does reach the public.[15]

13   William C. Rogers, Barbara Stuhler, and Donald Koenig, "A Comparison of Informed and General Public Opinion on U.S. Foreign Policy," *Public Opinion Quarterly* 31, no. 2 (Summer 1967): 248, 251–52; Mark Chesler and Richard Schmuck, "Student Reactions to the Cuban Crisis and Public Dissent," *Public Opinion Quarterly* 28, no. 3 (Fall 1964): 471.

14   See James N. Rosenau, "Foreign Policy as an Issue-Area," in *Domestic Sources of Foreign Policy*, ed. Rosenau, pp. 24–47. Gamson and Modigliani suggest that the "mainstream theory" which posits an "attachment to society and susceptibility to social influences" and thus public support of official policies is less likely to be accurate in the case of those with greater education and knowledge of foreign policy. (William A. Gamson and Andre Modigliani, "Knowledge and Foreign Policy Opinions: Some Models for Consideration," *Public Opinion Quarterly* 30, no. 2 [Summer 1966]: 197.)

15   Doris A. Graber, *Public Opinion, the President and Foreign Policy: Four Case Studies from the Formative Years* (New York: Holt, Rinehart and Winston, 1968), p. 340; Rosenau, *Public Opinion and Foreign Policy*, p. 61; Harwood L. Childs, *Public Opinion: Nature, Formation, and Role* (Princeton, N.J.: Van Nostrand, 1965), p. 292. Of course, decision-makers may not realize their capability to influence the public. It is Rosenberg's argument that American decision-makers underestimate their ability to cue mass opinion and therefore assume a more inflexible Cold War policy toward the USSR than is necessitated by the fixed "hard-line" attitudes of the public ("Images in Relation to the Policy Press," pp. 329–31).

Equally little research traces the relationship between mass opinion and events over an extended period of time. This is due partially to technical difficulties—variations in the questions used in opinion surveys, and in sampling methods, as well as a lack of polls taken as crucial events occurred.[16] It is thus not surprising that two recent time-series studies arrive at somewhat contrary conclusions. Scott and Withey conclude that, during 1945–55, public "satisfaction with the performance of the world organization followed closely the progress of world events in which the United Nations was involved."[17] Richman's tentative conclusion is that, during the period 1945–50, American attitudes of favorableness and attention toward the Soviet Union and expectation of war revealed no consistent relationship with Soviet-American conflictual and cooperative events, although there is a relationship between such attitudes and domestic Soviet events.[18] Other studies have explored the effect upon mass opinion of specific, dramatic events;[19] these studies, however, were not in all cases concerned with the same questions, making it difficult to draw general conclusions. The one possible exception is that certain dramatic events increase the proportion of people concerned with international affairs. But even this interest appears to be temporary; when the crisis subsides, so does the concern.

The American evaluation of the Soviet Union is the particular context within which this study is set. In the foreign policy world of Americans, Soviet-American relations are probably the most *salient* and are characterized primarily, though decreasingly, as *conflictual*. Three factors provide an annual index for 1955–64 of (1) the level of favorability of American foreign policy elite attitudes toward the Soviet Union, (2) mass opinion on the USSR, and (3) the level of conflict behavior between the United States and the Soviet Union.

---

16 William A. Scott and Stephen B. Withey, *The United States and the United Nations: The Public View, 1945–1955* (New York: Manhattan Publishing, 1958), pp. 42–43.

17 Ibid., p. 252.

18 Alvin Richman, "The Impact of International Events on American Public Opinion," (unpublished paper, Purdue University, 1969), pp. 20–22.

19 Chesler and Schmuck, "Student Reactions to the Cuban Crisis and Public Dissent"; Andrzej Sicinski, "Dallas and Warsaw: The Impact of a Major National Political Event on Public Opinion Abroad," *Public Opinion Quarterly* 33, no. 2 (Summer 1969): 190–96. (This study focused on the impact of President Kennedy's assassination.) Paul A. Smith, "Opinions, Publics, and World Affairs in the United States," *Western Political Quarterly* 14, no. 3 (September 1961): 698–714. (This study focused on the impact of the adoption of NATO [1949], the Greek-Turkish crisis [1947], the beginning of the Korean War [1950], and Chinese entry into that war later [1950].)

258   *Sophia Peterson*

Official American Attitudes toward the Soviet Union

The delineation of official American attitudes toward the USSR rests upon a content analysis of *The State Department Bulletin*. I selected randomly three articles per year—one from each third of the year—for the decade from 1955 to 1964. The unit of analysis comprised themes,[20] in particular, the theme of favorable, unfavorable, and neutral attitudes. These assertions of attitude (capsule statements) were translated into a separate index of favorability for each article using the Janis-Fadner coefficient of imbalance:

$$\frac{\text{Coefficient of}}{\text{Imbalance}} = \frac{f - u}{t} \text{ When } t = f + u + n$$

$u =$ unfavorable; $f =$ favorable; $n =$ neutral; $t =$ total.[21]

The coefficients of the three articles were averaged to produce an annual favorability index. Since I processed all the material myself, I used a standard formula for testing coder reliability at the beginning and again at the end of the study.[22] The reliability of the translations into capsule statements was 92 percent; reliability on the direction of attitude was 89 percent.

The Dulles-Eisenhower years revealed a seesaw trend of attitudes (Table 1). Crises such as the Hungarian Revolution and the Suez

Table 1. Favorableness toward the Soviet Union: Annual Indices of Elite Attitudes in *The Department of State Bulletin*, 1955–64

1955	−.28	1960	−.36
1956	−.50	1961	−.67
1957	−.33	1962	+.09
1958	−.54	1963	−.13
1959	−.06	1964	−.03

NOTE: A negative index represents a preponderance of unfavorable attitudes; a positive index represents a preponderance of favorable attitudes.

20   For a detailed description of the methodology used in the content analysis, see Sophia Peterson, "Conflict, Communication, and Mutual Threat in Soviet-American and Sino-Soviet Relationships" (Ph.D. dissertation, University of California, Los Angeles, 1969), pp. 135–55.
21   Harold D. Lasswell, Daniel Lerner, and Ithiel de Sola Pool, *The Comparative Study of Symbols: An Introduction*, Hoover Institute Studies, Series C: Symbols, no. 1 (Stanford: Stanford University Press, 1952), p. 44.
22   The formula is: $R = 2(C_1C_2)/(C_1+C_2)$. The number of capsule statements on which the first and last coding agreed is divided by the sum of all capsule statements determined on the first and on the last coding. The same reasoning was applied to testing reliability of judgments made as to the direction of attitude expressed. The number of judgments on which the first and last coding agreed is divided by the sum of all the judgments on the first and last coding (Robert C. North, Ole R. Holsti, M. George Zaninovich, and Dina A. Zinnes, *Content Analysis: A Handbook with Applications for the Study of International Crisis* [Evanston, Ill.: Northwestern University Press, 1963], p. 49).

Canal in 1956, the Berlin ultimatum and Middle East crises of 1958, and the U-2 incident in 1960 are reflected in increased unfavorability. But the low point of the entire ten-year period was 1961— the year when American and Soviet tanks faced each other across the Berlin wall and tensions rose with the Bay of Pigs invasion and the confrontation of the Vienna conference. The next three years, 1962–64, revealed the intent of the Kennedy administration to establish a less tense atmosphere in relations with the Soviet Union.[23]

The difference between the Dulles-Eisenhower and the Kennedy-Johnson periods is very clear. Three of the four years of highest favorability were in the Kennedy-Johnson administrations. The two best years for Dulles-Eisenhower were 1955 and 1959, years without crises in which important agreements or understandings were reached. The belief that the USSR initiated crises in 1956, 1958, and 1961 probably affected adversely the level of American favorability in these years.

One simple method of determining whether there was overall increase of favorable attitudes toward the end of the period is to determine the high, medium, and low periods of favorability. The years 1955–57 constitute the period of medium-level unfavorable attitudes (annual average $= - .37$), 1958–61 the period of most unfavorable attitudes (annual average $= - .41$), and 1962–64 that of least unfavorable attitudes (annual average $= - .02$).

American Public Opinion toward the Soviet Union

Many researchers have been concerned with the relationship between mass opinion and political relations between nations. Bruce M. Russett, for example, suggests that the degree to which conflict can be managed, military violence made unlikely, is related to the level of mutual identification among nations. Such "mutual identification" is measured by attitudes of "mutual sympathy and loyalties, 'we-feeling,' trust, mutual consideration, and willingness to treat the other's requests sympathetically"[24]—attitudes previously emphasized by the research of Deutsch and his associates.[25] Pruitt is similarly

23   The content analysis of American articles after the Cuban missile crisis verifies the impression of observers like Ross Stagner that "the Kennedy administration followed this crisis with conciliatory gestures, not with renewed belligerence" (Ross Stagner, "The Psychology of Human Conflict," in *The Nature of Human Conflict,* ed. Elton B. McNeil [Englewood Cliffs, N.J.: Prentice-Hall, 1965], p. 60). Though declining somewhat, favorability remained comparatively high during 1963–64.

24   Bruce M. Russett, *Community and Contention: Britain and America in the Twentieth Century* (Cambridge: M.I.T. Press, 1963), p. 27.

25   Karl W. Deutsch et al., *Political Community and the North Atlantic Area:*

concerned with the mutual images held by interacting nations and the role of these images in shaping international behavior. Pruitt focuses on three images in particular: threat perception, trust, and responsiveness.[26] The attitudes and images suggested as significant by these scholars provided guidance in the selection of the public opinion polls that served as the basis of this analysis.

The most serious drawback to trend analysis of American public opinion toward the Soviet Union is that surveys by the American Institute of Public Opinion, the National Opinion Research Council, and other polling agencies rarely utilize the same questions repeatedly over a long period of time. Given this fact, how was a consistent index of opinion to be developed? The first step was to select from the hundreds of surveys available those (seventy-seven in number) covering a total of twenty questions asked repeatedly at various intervals during the ten-year period. I selected at least one poll from each half of each year, so as to maximize the consistency over time.[27] The criterion for selection was whether or not the survey had questions on:

1. expectation of war or conflict;
2. estimation of the threat posed by the Soviet Union;
3. willingness to cooperate with the Soviet Union in such matters as trade and personal exchanges; and
4. the level of trust regarding the Soviet Union.

The polls were then divided into two separate groups. One listed the percentage of responses indicating unfavorable attitudes; the other listed the percentage of responses indicating favorable attitudes.

Favorable and unfavorable responses for all the surveys comprised the basis for indices of favorability and unfavorability. Least-squares estimates of the parameters used in the following model were obtained for each six-month period:[28]

$$Y_{IJ} = u + p_I + t_J + e_{IJ}$$

where Y_{IJ} is the percentage of favorable (unfavorable) responses

International Organization in the Light of Historical Experience (Princeton: Princeton University Press, 1957), p. 36.

26 Dean G. Pruitt, "Definition of the Situation as a Determinant of International Action," in *International Behavior*, ed. Kelman, pp. 392, 395.

27 Unfortunately, it was not possible to be certain that surveys taken before and after every key event were included, but some effort was made to meet this problem of variation within a year by selecting at least one poll from each half of each year.

28 Least-squares estimates of means were computed by Edwin C. Townsend, department of statistics, West Virginia University. The above equation represents the model for a two-way classification of data without interaction (in this case, the data were classified according to time period and according to poll—no interaction was assumed).

on poll *I* taken at time *J*; *u* is a constant for this time span (overall mean); p_I is the effect of the *I*th poll (this is a deviation from *u*); t_J is the effect of the *J*th time (time at which poll was taken in half-year intervals); and e_{IJ} is the random effect associated with the *I*th poll at time *J*.

This model makes allowance for variation in response to the same question from year to year and also allows for variation due to the fact that different questions were asked from year to year. The semi-annual indices for each year were averaged to arrive at an annual index of favorability and unfavorability for each year.

The next step was to subtract the unfavorable index from the favorable index for each year. The end product was an annual index of mass opinion. (If the index was negative, this meant the index of unfavorability was larger than the index of favorability for that year.) Two years, however, were not susceptible to this procedure: 1961 and 1964. For 1961 there was only a semi-annual index of favorability for the first half of the year, although both semi-annual indices of unfavorability were available. For 1964 there was only a semi-annual index of favorability available for the second half of the year, although both semi-annual indices of unfavorability were available. This fact required developing a procedure for estimating scores for these two years (Table 2).[29]

Table 2. Annual Indices of American Mass Opinion toward the Soviet Union, 1955–64

1955	.008	1960	.135
1956	.097	1961	−.049
1957	.015	1962	.115
1958	−.013	1963	.122
1959	.242	1964	.278

The seesaw trend of American public opinion is similar to that seen previously in American elite attitudes. The nadir of the ten-year period was 1961, the year of the Bay of Pigs, the Vienna confrontation of Kennedy and Khrushchev, and the Berlin wall. Public opinion was increasingly favorable during the next three years of the Kennedy-Johnson administrations.

American-Soviet Conflict Behavior

The last index presents a measure of conflictual events between the United States and the Soviet Union during 1955–64. The procedures

29 For details, see Peterson, "Conflict, Communication, and Mutual Threat," pp. 162–66.

used in this study and the categories and definitions of conflict behavior used to guide the collection of the data were adapted from the work of Rudolph J. Rummel.[30] The source of information was *Facts on File*.[31] I scanned the entire issue for each week searching for American-Soviet conflict behavior.

Basically, three types of conflict behavior were recorded: (1) warning or defensive acts and planned or unplanned violence; (2) negative behavior; and (3) written-oral communication. The criteria used to differentiate these three types of behavior were:

1. What does this type of behavior suggest about the probability of initiation of armed conflict?
2. What does this type of behavior suggest about the willingness of a nation to provoke the other nation into armed conflict?
3. Which type of behavior maximizes the possibility of an accidental precipitation of armed conflict?

The category of warning-defensive acts and planned-unplanned violence involved the manipulation of military forces, and in a few cases firepower was actually used. All the indexes (such as show of strength, maneuvers, strengthening forces, alert, discrete military action) suggest the distinct risk of conflict becoming violent either inadvertently or by plan. Negative behavior, while irksome and not contributive to friendly relations, and in some cases involving a discourteous ejection of a national from the other country or an active gesture of defiance of the wishes of the other country (canceling an official visit, discontinuing negotiations, boycott, military aid to the enemy), is one step removed from the actual manipulation of armed men and weapons, and thus less likely to precipitate immediate armed conflict. Finally, written-oral communication is still further removed from immediate risk, although threats and accusations can increase tensions, place the prestige of a nation in jeopardy, and thus eventually increase the disposition to use military force. In all there were twenty-one kinds of official behavior recorded (Table 3). Each occurrence of any one of the above categories of conflict was recorded separately on an index card with the following information:

30 For a complete description of methodology and definitions, see Rudolph J. Rummel, "Dimensions of Conflict Behavior within and between Nations," *General Systems: Yearbook of the Society for General Systems Research*, vol. 8 (Ann Arbor: Society for General Systems Research, 1963), pp. 1–50. Also, R. J. Rummel, "A Foreign Conflict Behavior Code Sheet," *World Politics* 18, no. 2 (January 1966): 283–96.

31 The reasons for relying solely on *Facts on File* are explained in Peterson, "Conflict, Communication, and Mutual Threat," pp. 170–71. See also Raymond Tanter, "Dimensions of Conflict Behavior within and between Nations, 1958–1960," *Journal of Conflict Resolution* 10, no. 1 (March 1966): 43.

Table 3A. Incidents of Conflict Behavior Initiated by USSR toward USA, 1955–64

Warning or Defense	1955 (1)	1956 (–)	1957 (–)	1958 (4)	1959 (2)	1960 (3)	1961 (2)	1962 (10)	1963 (–)	1964 (3)
Show of strength	–	–	–	1	2	–	1	8	–	–
Maneuvers	–	–	–	1	–	–	–	–	–	–
Strengthening forces	–	–	–	–	–	–	1	–	–	–
Alert	–	–	–	–	–	–	–	1	–	–
Discrete military action	1	–	–	2	–	3	–	1	–	3
Negative Behavior	**(6)**	**(1)**	**(6)**	**(7)**	**(3)**	**(15)**	**(4)**	**(15)**	**(6)**	**(5)**
Expel nationals	1	–	1	1	–	5	–	2	–	–
Cancel official visit	1	–	–	–	–	1	–	1	–	–
Limitation of movement of nationals	4	1	2	5	2	3	1	5	4	4
Expel lesser officials	–	–	3	1	1	3	–	–	1	–
Discontinue negotiations	–	–	–	–	–	2	–	–	–	–
Boycott	–	–	–	–	–	1	–	1	–	–
Military aid to enemy	–	–	–	–	–	–	2	3	1	1
Diplomatic rebuff	–	–	–	–	–	–	1	3	–	–
Embargo	–	–	–	–	–	–	–	–	–	–
Recall lesser officials	–	–	–	–	–	–	–	–	–	–
Written-Oral Communication	**(35)**	**(30)**	**(43)**	**(71)**	**(64)**	**(94)**	**(47)**	**(58)**	**(30)**	**(42)**
Accusation	24	13	28	31	18	29	18	20	10	8
Protest	1	6	2	9	5	10	9	6	5	5
Denunciation	8	9	12	23	31	41	15	25	9	26
Threat	1	2	1	7	9	13	5	5	4	3
Warning	1	–	–	1	–	1	–	2	2	–
Ultimatum	–	–	–	–	1	–	–	–	–	–

actor (nation initiating the conflict behavior), object (the nation toward whom the act was directed), date, and a description of the event. Intracoder reliability using Rummel's procedure was .86, roughly the equivalent of a product-moment correlation coefficient of .93.[32]

For each year a composite index was calculated by assigning weights to each occurrence of an event: a factor of three for warning-defense acts and planned-unplanned violence; two for events of

---

32 As has been suggested by Rummel, a coder's reliability improves with time. Therefore, I coded five years of data to develop consistency as to categories. Then these five years were recoded and the remaining five years coded. To check reliability, the conflict behavior initiated by the Soviet Union in 1958 was recoded after the rest of the coding was completed, to see to what extent the coder's judgment was consistent. Rummel's formula for coding reliability was adapted:
a = number of identical judgments at both coding times (measures agreement)
b = number of different judgments at both coding times (measures disagreement)
E (error) $= a/(a + b)$, or $E = 72/(72 + 12) = .86$, or roughly a correlation coefficient of .93
(Rummel, "A Foreign Conflict Behavior Code Sheet," pp. 295–96).

Table 3B. Incidents of Conflict Behavior Initiated by USA toward USSR, 1955–64

	1955	1956	1957	1958	1959	1960	1961	1962	1963	1964
Warning or Defense	(–)	(–)	(2)	(1)	(–)	(2)	(2)	(3)	(1)	(–)
Show of strength	–	–	1	–	–	1	–	2	–	–
Maneuvers	–	–	–	–	–	–	–	–	–	–
Strengthening forces	–	–	–	–	–	–	2	–	–	–
Alert	–	–	1	–	–	1	–	1	–	–
Discrete military action	–	–	–	1	–	–	–	–	1	–
Negative Behavior	(2)	(4)	(5)	(3)	(4)	(10)	(6)	(6)	(9)	(3)
Expel nationals	–	–	–	–	–	–	–	–	–	–
Cancel official visit	–	–	–	–	–	–	2	–	1	–
Limitation of movement of nationals	2	–	2	–	2	4	1	3	3	1
Expel lesser officials	–	1	3	1	–	2	–	1	2	1
Discontinue negotiations	–	–	–	–	–	1	1	–	–	–
Boycott	–	1	–	–	–	2	–	–	–	–
Military aid to enemy	–	–	–	–	1	–	–	–	–	–
Diplomatic rebuff	–	1	–	1	–	1	–	2	2	–
Embargo	–	1	–	1	1	–	1	–	1	–
Recall lesser officials	–	–	–	–	–	–	1	–	–	1
Written-Oral Communication	(23)	(27)	(23)	(52)	(55)	(75)	(52)	(38)	(18)	(19)
Accusation	4	4	7	24	19	32	15	12	5	5
Protest	5	7	3	6	10	7	11	12	6	6
Denunciation	14	15	10	21	26	32	21	13	6	5
Threat	–	1	3	1	–	3	5	1	–	3
Warning	–	–	–	–	–	1	–	–	1	–
Ultimatum	–	–	–	–	–	–	–	–	–	–

negative behavior; and one for each negative written or oral communication. Thus in 1958 (Table 3) the Soviet Union initiated four acts of warning or defense, planned or unplanned violence, plus seven instances of negative behavior and seventy-one negative communications:

4 events (warning-defense, planned-unplanned violence) x 3 =	12
7 events (negative behavior) x 2 =	14
71 events (written-oral communication) x 1 =	71
Composite index	97

The USSR's composite index for 1958 was therefore 97 (Table 4).

It is clear that, in the perception of world events held by *Facts on File*, the Soviet Union initiates a higher degree of conflict than does the United States, since for every year except two (1956, 1961) the USSR has a higher conflict index than does the United States. American conflict behavior steadily increased to the peak of 1960, after which it declined to the low point of 1964. The index of Soviet con-

Table 4. Annual Composite Indices of Conflict Behavior, 1955–64

USSR Behavior toward USA		USA Behavior toward USSR	
1955	50	1955	27
1956	32	1956	35
1957	56	1957	39
1958	97	1958	61
1959	76	1959	63
1960	133	1960	101
1961	61	1961	70
1962	118	1962	59
1963	42	1963	39
1964	61	1964	25

flict behavior is more erratic. A decline took place from 1955 to 1956, probably due to the fact that the Soviet Union's attention was directed toward its own intrabloc problems. Then conflict increased from 1956 to 1958, dropping sharply in 1959. The course of conflict was most erratic after 1959, never following the same direction for two years. Overall, 1955–57 was the lowest period of conflict (annual average for the USA = 34; for the USSR = 46); 1958–61 was the highest period of conflict (annual average for USA = 74; for USSR = 92); 1962–64 was the period of medium-level conflict (annual average for USA = 41; for USSR = 74).

THE CORRELATION OF FINDINGS

A year-by-year correlation of attitudes and events in 1955–64 (Table 5; see also Figure 1) reveals a strong positive relationship between American elite and mass attitudes. But, it was suggested earlier, conflictual events may have shaped both elite and mass attitudes. In fact, however, American mass opinion is *inversely* correlated with Soviet conflict behavior, suggesting that a year of comparatively high Soviet conflict behavior is paralleled by comparatively favorable American mass opinion—contrary to reasonable expectations and fairly strong evidence that the public is not aware of events. Mass

Table 5. Spearman Rank Correlation Coefficients

	American Elite	American Mass	Soviet Conflict
American Mass	.75[a]		
Soviet Conflict	−.12	−.33	
American Conflict	.38[b]	.04	.66[c]

[a] significant at the .01 level
[b] significant at the .13 level
[c] significant at the .05 level

Figure 1. Conflict Behavior, Elite Attitudes, and Mass Opinion

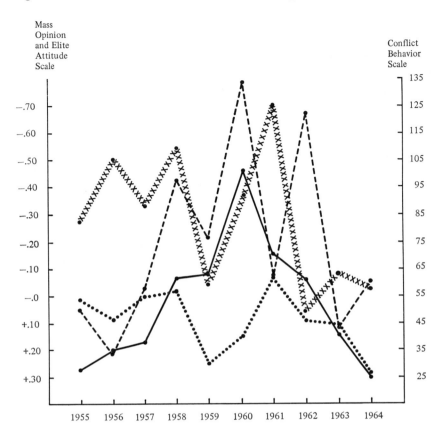

Right-hand values represent annual conflict behavior index.
Left-hand values represent annual mass opinion and elite attitudes indices (a negative
value signifies preponderance of unfavorable opinion over favorable opinion).
KEY: — — — Soviet-initiated conflict behavior
       ——— American-initiated conflict behavior
       • • • • American mass opinion
       × × × American elite attitudes

opinion is slightly but, in a statistical sense, insignificantly correlated
with American conflict behavior, which is at least the expected type
of relationship (that is, a year of comparatively favorable mass
opinion is paralleled by relatively little American conflict toward the
USSR).

Testing the relationship between mass opinion and events by
means of a time-lag, the results confirm the lack of influence of

events during one year upon mass opinion in the succeeding year: for Soviet conflict behavior in 1955–63 and American mass opinion in 1956–64, the Spearman rank correlation coefficient was +.07; for American conflict behavior in 1955–63 and mass opinion a year later, it was +.01. Whether testing the relationship by means of comparisons during simultaneous years or with a time lag of one year, American mass opinion seems aloof from the influence even of those conflictual events that would presumably confirm established patterns of thought.

Turning to the relationship between American elite attitudes and conflict behavior, Table 5 shows a slight *inverse* correlation, as far as Soviet conflict behavior is concerned, and a *positive* correlation with American conflict behavior (significant only at the .13 level). A year of comparatively favorable American elite attitudes toward the Soviet Union tends to be paralleled by relatively little American conflict initiated against the USSR. Time-lag correlations do not reveal any other significant relationships: for Soviet conflict behavior in 1955–63 and American elite opinion in 1956–64, the Spearman rank correlation coefficient was +.20; for American conflict behavior in 1955–63 and elite opinion a year later, it was −.07.

One final test was used to investigate whether the correlation between American mass and elite attitudes was really due to variation in American (or Soviet) conflict behavior. Holding American conflict behavior constant barely affected the correlation between American mass and elite attitudes: there was a Kendall rank correlation coefficient of +.56 between American mass and elite attitudes; using the Kendall partial rank correlation test and holding American conflict behavior constant, the correlation remained +.55. Holding Soviet conflict behavior constant for the ten-year period resulted in the same conclusion: there was a Kendall rank correlation coefficient of +.56 between American mass and elite attitudes; using the Kendall partial rank correlation test and holding Soviet conflict behavior constant the correlation remained +.55. Correlation between American mass and elite attitudes is evidently not due to variation in American or Soviet conflict behavior.

This finding raises more pointedly the question of whether mass opinion affects elite attitudes or vice versa. Time-lag correlations, while suggestive, are not conclusive: For elite attitudes in 1955–63 and mass opinion in 1956–64, the Spearman rank correlation coefficient was +.27; the other way around it was −.40. This suggests that, despite the fact that the relationship is not strong enough to be statistically significant, a year of comparatively favorable American elite attitudes regarding the USSR is followed by a year of comparatively favorable American mass opinion.

In sum, and beginning with the strongest datum (the positive correlation between mass opinion and foreign policy-making elite attitudes), the empirical evidence surveyed in this chapter confirms the oft-assumed relationship between them. Further, this relationship is not explained by the conflictual events between the United States and the Soviet Union. Over time, the public seems relatively unaffected by events, even those that tend to confirm established attitudes. Time-lag correlations, while inconclusive, suggest that influence is not exercised by mass opinion (1955–63) upon elite attitudes (1956–64); the time-lag correlation between elite attitudes (1955–63) and mass opinion (1956–64) is too low to be statistically significant, but at least it is positive ($r_s = +.27$).

The finding on the role of events throws some light on the strong positive relationship between elite and mass attitudes. Soviet and American conflict behavior tends to be reciprocal ($r_s = +.66$, significant at the .05 level). Elite attitudes are not necessarily congruent with behavior, to be sure. We may nonetheless hypothesize that, especially in a democracy where the decision-makers must reckon with the surveillance of the mass media and an attentive public (not to be confused with the mass public), there are pressures for some measure of attitudinal-behavioral consistency on the part of the policy elite. One piece of inconclusive evidence points in this direction: the weak positive correlation between American conflict behavior and American elite attitudes ($r_s = +.38$, significant at the .13 level).

The foregoing evidence suggests the following interaction model. What may occur is that Soviet and American decision-makers behave

Figure 2.

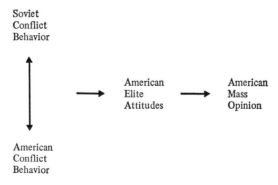

toward each other with a response in kind. When American foreign policy-makers publicly evaluate the Soviet Union, factors in addition to Soviet-American conflict behavior are operative. The mass public then adopts an evaluation of the Soviet Union very similar to that of the elite and is, apparently, unaffected by Soviet-American conflict behavior.

The findings of this study corroborate those of others which have found that the majority of the mass public and of specialized publics tend to confirm official governmental positions. The significance of this study is that it traces this congruence over a ten-year period instead of confining itself to single discrete policies, thereby suggesting that decision-makers can rely upon this support over time, during normal as well as crisis periods.

Beyond the question of congruence between mass opinion and decision-makers' attitudes lies the question of the means by which this congruence occurs. The data assembled for this study do not provide empirical evidence bearing on this problem; therefore, we can only speculate as to possibilities. Several studies have confirmed the operation of the "two-step flow of communication" by which mass media output is screened by citizen opinion leaders who then influence the less-attentive and less-informed public through word-of-mouth.[33] Rosenau suggests a more complex sequence: "News and interpretations of an event are first carried by, say, a newspaper; this is then read and adapted by opinion-makers, who assert (step 2) their opinions in speeches on the subject that are reported (step 3) by the press and thereupon picked up by 'opinion leaders' in the general public who in turn pass on (step 4) the opinions through word-of-mouth."[34] The key opinion-makers in foreign policy are, first and foremost, the president, and, secondarily, prominent foreign-policy officials. This study suggests that Rosenau's four-step flow of communication probably reflects reality more accurately than the simpler two-step flow of communication. Events occur and are reported and then adapted by "opinion-makers" (high-ranking government officials in particular) who then interpret events for the next echelon of "opinion leaders" among the citizenry.

One of the most serious stumbling blocks to research in this area has been the difficulty of determining exactly who these private "opinion leaders" are and what their impact upon mass opinion is. Even if agreement could be reached on who the opinion leaders are, determining whether they actually shape the opinions of the public

33   Katz, "The Two-Step Flow of Communication," pp. 61–78.
34   Rosenau, *Public Opinion and Foreign Policy*, pp. 7–8.

is a formidable research task, as William Rogers and Barney Uhlig suggested in their recent study:

> Do individuals who engage in such activities [lecturing, lending public support, etc.] shape the opinions of others? The ultimate answer can be had only by asking "the others." But opinion researchers have long since discovered that it is extremely difficult to discover the *effects* of influence and have usually been satisfied to examine *intent* or ability to influence opinion. Depth interviews of the people of Minnesota, or even of a single community, about who influences their opinion on foreign policy are not certain to be fruitful, but are certain to be expensive. . . . The thousands of dollars needed for such research is sadly lacking.[35]

This study is relevant to steps 1 and 2 of the Rosenau four-step flow of communication, in the sense that it measures the conflict-event output of the mass media, suggesting some modest congruence between such events and the public pronouncements of key decision-makers. The study is also relevant to step 4 by affirming the strong congruence between mass opinion and official attitudes. However, it was beyond the scope of this study to develop evidence relative to step 3—an area which obviously needs attention. Various hypotheses can be posed to account for the probable congruence between official opinion-makers and the private opinion-leaders who may act as the conveyor belts for interpersonal communication of official governmental positions. For example, mainstream theory suggests that "the politically educated are not better analysts of complex situations but are simply more aware of what official U.S. policy is. Being more integrated into their society, and more susceptible to the influence of its institutions, their opinions are more likely to fall within the narrow boundaries of open official discussion."[36] By focusing on step 3 of Rosenau's four-step model, further research may be able to account for the means by which congruence between official and mass attitudes occurs.

The policy implication of this study is that, while the American foreign policy elite often perceives public opinion as a constraint limiting their freedom of action, they are overestimating the rigidity of public opinion and underestimating their capacity to influence it: "If the policy elite did more openly pursue those conciliatory goals

---

35   William C. Rogers and Barney Uhlig, "Small Town and Rural Midwest Foreign Policy Opinion Makers," *International Studies Quarterly* 13, no 3 (September 1969): 310–11.

36   Gamson and Modigliani, "Knowledge and Foreign Policy Opinions," p. 188.

[regarding relations with the Soviet Union] that national humane interest may require, it would be likely to encounter more public acceptance than leaders often seem to expect."[37] At the same time, it should be emphasized that the evidence cannot support the position that no matter what attitude was expressed by decision-makers at a given moment, the public would emulate it. Nor can we assume that a spectacular event might not affect mass opinion at least temporarily —indeed, it may well do so. What the evidence *does* bear out is that, over an extended period of time, the foreign policy elite probably can influence the general evaluative orientation of the public toward a very salient target. The precise links in this suggested relationship, the role of mass media and of other nongovernmental opinion leaders, is yet another subject for investigation.

37 Rosenberg, "Attitude Change and Foreign Policy in the Cold War Era," p. 153.

eleven

Consistency in Foreign Policy Views

Robert Jervis

ATTEMPTS to apply balance and congruity theories of attitude organization and change[1] to decision-makers' perceptions of other states have often been misleading because of the failure to distinguish between attitudinal consistency that can be explained by a person's rational analysis (using this term in the broad sense of an intellectually defensible intellectual process) and consistency that cannot be so explained. Certain kinds of consistency are necessary in any attempt to understand phenomena. Neither in constructing scientific theories nor in developing images of other actors do facts "speak for themselves." All stages of the identification and analysis of bits of information are influenced by the person's beliefs. This fact alone imposes a certain consistency on the person's views.

Scholars have found a strong tendency for people's attitudinal structures to have a high degree of consistency or balance. A balanced structure is one in which "all relations among 'good elements' [that is, those that are positively valued] are positive (or null), all relations among 'bad elements' [that is, those that are negatively valued] are positive (or null), and all relations among good and bad elements are negative (or null)."[2] Thus we tend to believe that countries we

---

1 For the purposes of this discussion, these theories can be considered to be the same; the terms will be used interchangeably, since the differences are not relevant in this context. This essay is part of a larger study of misperception in international relations. I would like to thank Richard L. Merritt and Charles E. Osgood for comments on an earlier draft, and the Harvard Center for International Affairs for financial support.

2 Robert P. Abelson and Milton J. Rosenberg, "Symbolic Psycho-logic: A Model of Attitudinal Cognition," *Behavioral Science* 3, no. 1 (January 1958): 5.

like do things we like, support goals we favor, and oppose countries that we oppose. And we tend to think that countries that are our enemies make proposals that harm us, work against our interests and those of our friends, and aid our opponents. The reasoning by which this consistency is maintained, it is claimed, should be called "psycho-logic rather than logic" and "would mortify a logician."[3] While it is true that the elements of a balanced attitudinal structure do not follow from one another by the rules of logic, a logician would be mortified by the process only if the person who held the attitudes believed that they did so follow.[4] As Charles E. Osgood notes,

> It is important to point out that the inferences from psycho-logic are not necessarily invalid; they are simply illogical. [Nonlogical would be a better word, since it does not appear that Osgood is claiming that these inferences violate the rules of logic.] For example, if Khrushchev were to indicate that he favors a particular American presidential hopeful . . . many people would, psycho-logically, become suspicious of this candidate. Now, Khrushchev's support might be valid grounds for suspicion, but the inference is not logically necessary.[5]

This is true but uninteresting. Almost no significant inferences about other actors, and very few inferences in the social or even in the physical sciences, are strictly logical. The conclusions do not follow deductively from the premises, as in a syllogism. To answer empirical questions, such as the intentions and motives of other actors, one must employ less certain tools and inference processes. The question to ask of these ways of thinking is whether they yield perceptions that are as accurate as those that could be produced by other processes and whether, at a minimum, they are rational. By rational I mean those methods of thought that most people would not object to if they were conscious of them.

Irrational influences or processes of drawing inferences are those that most informed people would claim violate the legitimate and appropriate way of utilizing evidence. It could presumably be shown that such processes are less likely to lead to accurate perceptions

3 Ibid., emphasis omitted.

4 A related and more common intellectual error is for a person to think that evidence unambiguously supports his conclusion when in fact he sees the evidence as he does largely because of his preexisting views. I have discussed this phenomenon in "Minimizing Misperception," in *Forward from Failure: Towards New Norms for U.S. Foreign Policy*, ed. Thomas Franck and Edward Weisband, forthcoming.

5 Charles E. Osgood, "Cognitive Dynamics in the Conduct of Human Affairs," *Public Opinion Quarterly* 24, no. 2 (Summer 1960): 352.

than are rational methods of treating evidence, although I am not claiming that all people who rationally examine the same data would come to the same, correct conclusion. Rationality is thus a very loose constraint, implying the use of generally accepted rules of "scientific method" that cannot unambiguously specify a conclusion. It excludes only those ways of drawing inferences that are generally agreed to be unjustified.[6]

RATIONAL CONSISTENCY

Many of the applications of balance theory to opinions about foreign policy do not show this kind of irrationality. Cognitive consistency can often be explained by the actor's tested beliefs about the consistency operating in the world he is perceiving. Thus our cognitive structure is in balance when we think that two of our friends will like each other, or like similar things. But the expectation that this will be the case is not irrational, nor does it require a psychological explanation, if most people have found that their friends in fact *do* tend to like each other and share common values.[7]

In some cases consistency involves rationality because it not only accords with experience but invokes linkages that, if not strictly required by logic, are supported by logic as well as by an explicit

6   One problem with this conception is that it is not useful when people disagree about the rules for judging evidence and making decisions. Such a disagreement occurred between Premier Konoe and General Tojo in the fall of 1941: "At one of their meetings, Tojo told Konoe that at some point during a man's lifetime he might find it necessary to jump, with his eyes closed, from the veranda of [a temple located on one of the heights of Kyoto] into the ravine below. That was Tojo's way of saying that he and others in the army believed that there were occasions when success or failure depended on the risks one was prepared to take, and that, for Japan, such an occasion had now arrived. . . . It was a pronouncement in the tradition of the samurai, whose willingness to take up any challenge, regardless of the odds, was legendary. Konoe merely replied that the idea of jumping [into the ravine] might occur to an individual once or twice in his lifetime but that as the premier of Japan . . . he could not adopt such an approach to the Empire's problems" (Robert Butow, *Tojo and the Coming of the War* [Princeton: Princeton University Press, 1961], p. 267). For a similar definition, see Sidney Verba, "Assumptions of Rationality and Non-Rationality in Models of the International System," in *The International System*, ed. Klaus Knorr and Sidney Verba (Princeton: Princeton University Press, 1961), p. 94.

7   For a study showing that social units tend to be balanced, but that people perceive even more balance than exists, see Nathan Kogan and Renato Tagiuri, "Interpersonal Preferences and Cognitive Organization," *Journal of Abnormal and Social Psychology* 56, no. 1 (January 1958): 113–16. It is thus not unwise for a person to assume that his friends will like each other if he has no evidence to the contrary. The important question, and one for which there are few data or theories, is what kind and amount of evidence should and does lead the person to change his mind.

theory. Osgood argues that "if we like [Kennedy] and he happens to praise some diplomat from Afghanistan, we tend to feel favorably disposed toward this otherwise unknown individual. But let [Khrushchev] comment on this same diplomat's sound idea—a kind of association known as 'the kiss of death'—and we suddenly find ourselves distrusting the man." Similarly Osgood notes that consistency theory leads us to place a negative value upon any proposal made by a negatively valued actor (that is, an enemy). But these cases do not demonstrate the substitution of "emotional consistency for rational consistency."[8] For it is rational to believe that a person your enemy praises is likely to have interests opposed to yours. If a decision-maker thinks that the Russians are aggressive, then he will view their suggestions with suspicion—not only because he presumably will know of previous cases in which the Russians tried to deceive opponents, but because, almost by definition, the belief that the Soviets are adversaries implies that he should be skeptical of their proposals.[9] Similarly, the claim, "It is cognitively inconsistent for us to think of people we . . . distrust making conciliatory moves"[10] should be seen in light of the fact that the very meaning of the concept of "trust" implies that if one actor distrusts another he will think it unlikely that the other will help him.

Further doubts about the supposed irrationality of many of the foreign policy inferences produced by pressures toward cognitive consistency are raised by an examination of the meaning of affective judgments about other countries. William Scott's hypothesis is typical of those dealing with cognitive-affective consistency: "Favorable characteristics tend to be attributed to liked nations, and unfavorable characteristics to disliked nations."[11] But, for decision-makers at least, it is not clear that we can meaningfully talk of an affective dimension that is logically separate from cognitive judgments. The "liking" or "disliking" of another state is largely the product of a decision-maker's beliefs about the degree of conflict between that

8 Charles E. Osgood, *An Alternative to War or Surrender* (Urbana. University of Illinois Press, 1962), pp. 26–27.

9 Of course, if the basic views about Russia are wrong, then this suspicion will be unwarranted. Osgood and other spiral theorists base their position on the implicit belief that Russia is not aggressive. Although this makes their claims understandable, it does not make them valid. Osgood would probably agree that in the 1930s nations should have been much more critical of Germany's proposals for peace.

10 Osgood, "Cognitive Dynamics," p. 341.

11 William A. Scott, "Psychological and Social Correlates of International Images," in *International Behavior: A Social-Psychological Analysis*, ed. Herbert C. Kelman (New York: Holt, Rinehart and Winston, 1965), p. 100.

country and his own. American leaders "like" India more now than they did in the 1950s because they see India's new policies as more compatible with those of the United States.

To demonstrate the value of their approach, consistency theorists would have to show that liking a country leads decision-makers to come to unwarranted conclusions about extraneous aspects of the country and to maintain that attitude in the face of contradicting information (for example, if a decision-maker believed that only the citizens of Allied powers produced outstanding music and art). But most instances of affective-cognitive consistency in foreign policy-making can be explained by the actor's theories about correlations of national traits or by the fact that the "liking" of another state and views about its specific characteristics are linked through a third factor—the actor's beliefs about the other's interests, motives, and intentions.[12]

IRRATIONAL CONSISTENCY: AVOIDANCE OF VALUE TRADE-OFFS

A final type of consistency, not treated separately by psychologists, merits special attention because, unlike the kinds previously discussed, it cannot be explained by rational procedures for drawing inferences and making sense out of the world. These cases indeed merit the label "psycho-logic" with the implication that they are underpinned by psychological motives that inhibit accurate perception of the world and optimal decision-making. They involve instances in which a person's cognitive structure contains consistencies among elements that logic and the person's beliefs about the world cannot explain. There is a strong tendency for people who favor a policy to believe that it is supported by several logically in-

12   Milton J. Rosenberg, "Cognitive Structure and Attitudinal Affect," *Journal of Abnormal and Social Psychology* 53, no. 5 (May 1956): 367–72; Asahel D. Woodruff and Francis J. Di Vesta, "The Relationship between Values, Concepts, and Attitudes," *Educational and Psychological Measurement* 8, no. 4 (Winter 1948): 645–60; and Martin Fishbein, "A Consideration of Beliefs, and Their Role in Attitude Measurement," in *Readings in Attitude Theory and Measurement*, ed. Martin Fishbein (New York: John Wiley and Sons, 1967), pp. 257–66. For a related view, see Harry C. Triandis and Martin Fishbein, "Cognitive Interaction in Person Perception," *Journal of Abnormal and Social Psychology* 67, no. 5 (November 1963): 446–53. Another experiment has shown that a change in attitude toward an object followed from an experimentally produced change in the perceived instrumentality of that object for other values. See E. Carlson, "Attitude Changes through Modification of Attitude Structure," *Journal of Abnormal and Social Psychology* 52, no. 3 (March 1956): 256–61.

dependent reasons. When a person believes that a policy contributes to one value, he is also apt to believe that it contributes to other values, even though there is no reason why the world should be constructed in this neat and helpful a manner. When people's cognitions are organized in this pattern, choices are easier, since there is no need to consider value trade-offs. Nothing has to be sacrificed, since all considerations are seen as pointing to the same conclusion.[13]

People who think it important to stand firm in a dispute tend to believe that the adversary is bluffing, whereas those who place a lower value on the issue at stake tend to think that the other side will not retreat. And those people who dislike the goals of a protest movement tend to think that the movement's tactics are ineffective. Policies are acclaimed as accomplishing many goals and serving several important values, or they are criticized with multiple indictments.

Although no statistical evidence is available to show that this kind of consistency occurs more often than would be expected by chance, a number of examples can both illustrate the nature of this phenomenon and show the plausibility of the hypothesis. People who favored a nuclear test ban tended to believe that testing created a serious medical danger, would not lead to major weapons improvements, and was a source of international tension. Those who opposed the treaty tended to take the opposite position on all three issues. The health risks of testing are in no way connected with the military advantages, and a priori we should therefore not expect any correlation between people's views on these questions. Similarly, during the Chinese civil war those policy-makers who believed that economic and military aid would not increase the chances of a Nationalist victory also believed that Europe was the center of international politics and that a Communist government in China would have neither the intention nor the capability of menacing the United States. Those who favored aid thought that a victory for Chiang was both possible and very important.[14] An identical pattern is revealed by the debate in America over aiding the Allies before Pearl Harbor. Those who favored extensive aid believed that a German victory would endanger American national security and that

13 For a similar argument, see John Steinbruner, "The Mind and Milieu of Policymakers" (Ph.D. dissertation, Massachusetts Institute of Technology, 1968). Steinbruner has also conducted experiments that support this position.

14 Tang Tsou, *America's Failure in China, 1941–50* (Chicago: University of Chicago Press, 1963), p. 550.

Hitler could be defeated by American material aid alone. The isolationists tended to think that the United States could coexist with Germany and that a German victory over the Allies could not be prevented by American supplies and arms.

Later debates over policy in the Far East have shown the same consistency. General MacArthur believed that bombing China during the Korean War would be militarily effective and would not increase the risk of world war. Truman disagreed on both points. And, in the internal discussions that preceded knowledge of the Chinese intervention, MacArthur argued that minor concessions to China would do no good, that establishing a buffer zone in northern Korea would be seen in Asia as a defeat, that China would not intervene even if American troops went to the Yalu, and that, if China did, its troops could be destroyed by air power.[15] Today those who favor withdrawing from Vietnam even if this should mean that the country would fall under Communist domination tend to believe that the war cannot be won and also that the costs of defeat are relatively low. Those who think we can win tend to feel that the costs of losing are high (that is, that the "domino theory" applies).[16]

Arguments over more specific aspects of United States policy toward Vietnam reveal similar patterns. For example, in March, 1968, the advocates of an announced troop ceiling believed this policy would accomplish several ends: "To the South Vietnamese we wanted to say: this is it, dig in, do more yourselves. To the North Vietnamese the signal was a different one: we are leveling off for the long haul. Do not expect erosion of our public support to continue; our people now know this is no longer a bottomless pit."[17] Those on the other side of the debate did not believe that either audience would draw the desired inference from the message.

Two related phenomena are the tendency for actors to claim that they have found a dominant strategy—that is, one that is the best, no matter which of the contending interpretations of another state's intention is correct and no matter how the other responds—and the belief that the favored policy will maximize a country's national

15 Ibid., p. 584.
16 Although these two cognitive elements can be connected through general beliefs about the nature of guerrilla war (that is, one view holding that outcomes are determined mostly by indigenous social and political factors, with the other view arguing for the importance of external military power), this does not seem to be enough to explain the degree of consistency.
17 Phil G. Goulding, *Confirm or Deny: Informing the People on National Security* (New York: Harper and Row, 1970), p. 330.

interests and the chances of maintaining peace. Elsewhere I have argued that both the spiral and deterrence theories of the Cold War take these positions.[18] In many previous cases, too, both those advocating concessions and those calling for firmness have believed that their policies offered "an alternative to war or surrender." These claims were made, for example, in the debate within the United States on policy toward Japan before World War II, and in the debate between the United States and Britain on policy toward Spain and Portugal during the war. Neither side believed that their favored policy sacrificed a degree of one value to gain more of another one.

An especially striking case of this kind of consistency occurred in the debate within Finland over policy toward the Soviet demands preceding the Winter War of 1939–40. Those who believed that concessions would only lead to greater Russian demands also thought that the Soviets would back down in the face of Finnish firmness. And those who felt that concessions would not lead to a loss of major values believed that Russia would fight for what she had demanded. Similarly, at the end of the nineteenth century those British officials who believed that a Russian port on the Persian Gulf would be a major threat to British interests thought that a firm policy could deter Russia from moving strongly in this area. Those who believed that a Russian port would not change the political balance believed that Russia could not be stopped without either forcing her into a hostile diplomatic coalition or a war.[19] In these two cases, whatever logic connects the two elements would indicate that the belief that the other country would fight for its demands should be linked to the view that it has threatening long-run intentions, since it seems probable that it would be willing to pay the high costs of war only if it sought extensive gains.

American leaders' views on the important issue of the use of force in international relations have often contained the type of consistency that minimizes value conflict. A major theme of a study by Robert Osgood is that both "realists" and "idealists" refused to recognize the possible conflict between "ideals and self-interest in America's foreign relations." Although one group favored employing a high degree of military power and the other group opposed this, both

18   See my "The Security Dilemma, the Spiral Model, and Deterrence," mimeographed.
19   Max Jakobson, *The Diplomacy of the Winter War: An Account of the Russo-Finnish War, 1939–1940* (Cambridge: Harvard University Press, 1961), pp. 136–39; Briton Cooper Busch, *Britain and the Persian Gulf, 1894–1914* (Berkeley: University of California Press, 1967), pp. 121–29.

claimed that their policies served the values of American national interest and international well-being and morality. Osgood's conclusion about the effects of this complacent combination of beliefs is to the point:

> ... man's willingness to believe that moral contradictions either do not exist or else are easily reconcilable must certainly be one of the greatest sources of international sin. It is man's reluctance to face the inevitable moral dilemmas of social existence that robs him of his moral perspective and leads him into an easy identification of his own nation's self-interest with high moral purpose and the welfare of mankind. It is this common conceit that persuades men to view the inevitable moral compromises of international relations as good things in themselves rather than as unfortunate expedients designed to maximize ideal values in a society where partial morality is the best morality attainable. It is this moral corruption that encourages both egoists and idealists to satisfy their emotional predispositions by confusing what is with what ought to be, so that egoists persuade themselves that the unpleasant realities of national egoism are a positive good, and idealists are content merely to deprecate them as an unmitigated evil, which can be easily exorcized by virtuous men.[20]

Of course, this consistency does not automatically mean that some of the beliefs are wrong. The Finns who advocated making concessions to the Soviets, for example, seem to have been correct in both parts of their argument. But decision-makers who hold a position containing such mutually supportive beliefs should be suspicious of their own mental processes. This condition is psychologically comfortable, since it reduces conflict and makes decisions easier to reach because competing values do not have to be balanced against each other. The chances are thus considerable that at least part of the reason why a person holds some of these consistent beliefs is related to psychology rather than to the evidence.

Two possible arguments against the validity of this hypothesis should be mentioned. First, it could be claimed that actors consciously misrepresent their own views for political purposes. It is easier to persuade someone to follow a given policy by claiming that it maximizes a large number of values than by saying that it is on balance best but involves high costs. "Overselling" a policy may in-

20   Robert Endicott Osgood, *Ideals and Self-Interest in America's Foreign Relations: The Great Transformation of the Twentieth Century* (Chicago: University of Chicago Press, 1953), p. 22.

crease its chances of adoption,[21] and political leadership may require a minimization of costs and sacrifices. But if this kind of consistency were a conscious political strategy, one would expect to see this acknowledged in decision-makers' diaries and other private sources. Such admissions are rare.

Second, it could be that those actors whose policy preferences are supported by independent beliefs are most vocal. Those who are torn in their views would be apt to take a less vehement stand, and their positions would attract less attention. This view is consistent with most of the theory and data concerning cross-pressures. If this were true many of the active participants in a policy debate would hold a seemingly irrational consistency, but they would not constitute a larger percentage of the total number of concerned people than would be expected by chance. Although there is no firm evidence available, I do not think that enough people are rendered inactive by internally conflicting beliefs to validate this contention.

ASSIMILATION OF INFORMATION: THE BASIC DILEMMA

Many instances of cognitive consistency, especially those that are not irrational, can be seen as attempts to make sense out of the world and by perceiving specific characteristics and events in a way that is guided by logic and experience. That experience influences perception is well established by psychological theory and experiments. People tend to fit incoming information into preexisting images in such a way as to perceive what they expect to be there. They are more sensitive to evidence that confirms their images than to that contradicting it. Indeed, their views of the world and of other actors play a large part in determining what they notice in the first place. This means that actors' images tend to be resistant to discrepant information and to be maintained even in the face of mounting evidence that they are incorrect.

To many scholars, the interpretation of ambiguous evidence to make it consistent with positions already held seems pathological. They all too hastily see it as a blind and often affect-laden rejection of opposing views and a distortion of information that leads to inaccurate perceptions and inferior policies. The need to fit data into a wider framework of beliefs, however, even if doing so does not

21 Theodore J. Lowi, *The End of Liberalism: Ideology, Policy, and the Crisis of Public Authority* (New York: W. W. Norton, 1969); Stanley Hoffmann, *Gulliver's Troubles: Or, the Setting of American Foreign Policy* (New York: Published for the Council on Foreign Relations by McGraw-Hill, 1968).

seem to do justice to all the facts, is not, or at least is not only, a psychological drive. And it does not necessarily decrease the accuracy of perception. In a world in which not everything is clear and evidence is often contradictory, some degree of cognitive rigidity is "essential to the logic of inquiry."[22] One can be too open-minded, as well as too closed to new information. Karl Deutsch puts this point in a more general context:

> Autonomy . . . requires both intake from the present and recall from memory, and selfhood can be seen in just this continuous balancing of a limited present and a limited past. . . .
> No further self-determination is possible if either openness or memory is lost. . . . To the extent that [systems cease to be able to take in new information], they approach the behavior of a bullet or torpedo: their future action becomes almost completely determined by their past. On the other hand, a person without memory, an organization without values or policy . . . all these no longer steer, but drift: their behavior depends little on their past and almost wholly on their present. Driftwood and the bullet are thus each the epitome of another kind of loss of self-control.[23]

Ross Ashby makes a similar point: "Both extremes of delay may be fatal: too hurried a change from trial to trial may not allow time for 'success' to declare itself; and too prolonged a testing of a wrong trial may allow serious damage to occur. . . . This necessity for delay between one trial and the next . . . is an essential part of the ultrastable system's method of adaptation."[24]

COGNITIVE DISTORTION?

People preserve their images of other actors, in the face of what seems in retrospect to have been clear evidence to the contrary, by ignoring data that do not fit, twisting them so that they confirm (or at least do not contradict) their beliefs, or denying the validity of the data (for example, by saying that the source is unreliable or mis-

22   I have borrowed this phrase from Abraham Kaplan, who uses it in a different but related context in *The Conduct of Inquiry: Methodology for Behavioral Science* (San Francisco: Chandler, 1964), p. 86.

23   Karl Deutsch, *Nationalism and Social Communication: An Inquiry into the Foundations of Nationality* (Cambridge: M.I.T. Press, 1953), pp. 167–68. Also see Karl W. Deutsch, *The Nerves of Government: Models of Political Communication and Control* (New York: The Free Press, 1963), pp. 98–109, 200–256.

24   William Ross Ashby, *Design for a Brain: The Origin of Adaptive Behavior* (New York: John Wiley and Sons, 1952), p. 132.

taken).[25] In many cases, discrepant information simply is not noticed. For example, intelligence analysts, not expecting the Soviets to bring offensive missiles into Cuba, did not think about the possible interpretations and significance of the fact that Soviet ships with wide hatches were riding high in the water.

When actors do not spontaneously perceive evidence as conforming to their images, they may go through mental gymnastics that to contemporary opponents and later scholars seem indefensible. Thus the common view of Neville Chamberlain is of a man who was so sure of the accuracy of his image of Germany and confident of the correctness of his policy that he twisted almost all aggressive German behavior to fit the theory that Germany merely wanted to revise the inequities of the Treaty of Versailles. Cases of outright refusal to believe the report of evidence that completely undermines a belief are also common. An extreme case occurred on the morning of June 22, 1941, when, in response to the message from a Soviet front line unit, "We are being fired on. What shall we do?" the headquarters replied, "You must be insane. And why is your signal not in code?" Similarly, when Secretary of the Navy Knox was told of the Japanese attack on Pearl Harbor, he said, "My God, this can't be true. This [message] must mean the Philippines."[26]

In explaining the causes and consequences of these image-maintaining influences we should not stop at a discussion of psychological pressures or conclude that they are distortions that decrease the accuracy of perceptions. To go further, we should examine the nature of the distortion of information in the context of perceptions of other actors, ask if people whose views were wrong treated evidence differently from those who were right, and, most important, look at the necessary interaction between facts and theories.

In some cases images are preserved by processes that deserve to

---

25 These resistances will be reinforced if people tend to expose themselves selectively to information that supports their beliefs. Until recently it seemed well established that such a tendency existed, but a reanalysis of the evidence casts doubt on the hypothesis. See Jonathan L. Freedman and David O. Sears, "Selective Exposure," in *Advances in Experimental Social Psychology*, ed. Leonard Berkowitz (New York: Academic Press, 1965), pp. 57–97; and David O. Sears and Jonathan L. Freedman, "Selective Exposure to Information: A Critical Review," *Public Opinion Quarterly* 31, no. 2 (Summer 1967): 194–213. For a critique of these articles, see Charles Atkin, "Reassessing Two Alternative Explanations of De Facto Selective Exposure," summarized in *Public Opinion Quarterly* 34, no. 3 (Fall 1970): 464–65.

26 Quoted in John Erickson, *The Soviet High Command: A Military-Political History, 1918–1941* (London: Macmillan, 1962), p. 587; and in Harry Howe Ransom, *Central Intelligence and National Security* (Cambridge: Harvard University Press, 1958), p. 54.

be labeled "cognitive distortion," with the implication that evidence is being treated illegitimately. First, and most obviously, a person could violate the rules of logic or the agreed-upon methods for drawing inferences in a field. We discussed this above in the context of consistency and balance theories. Second, there is distortion if a person cannot correctly place incoming information on a continuum according to the degree to which it agrees with his position. Research indicates that views close to those of the actor tend to be assimilated to his while those beyond his "latitude of acceptance" tend to be contrasted with his and seen as farther away.[27] It is nonetheless hard to tell what the individuals mean when they report that a specified communication is a certain distance from their positions. They may explicitly believe that, once a view differs from theirs to a certain degree, it is so wrong that it can be considered similar to a wide range of other incorrect positions. Third, we may be able to detect distortion if a person does not come to grips with the information that could indicate that his views are incorrect. For example, someone might refuse to discuss an issue and the arguments on the other side.[28] Or an actor may be totally unable to refute large amounts of evidence indicating that he is wrong. Or he may not seek information that could settle the argument. Thus, although the cornerstone of General Hurley's policy in China was his belief that the Communists were weak and would therefore have no choice but to accept Chiang's offers, "his rejection of the Communist claims was not based on a careful evaluation of the actual strength of the Chinese Communists. Insofar as one can ascertain from published materials, Hurley made no systematic efforts to seek the information necessary to arrive at the best possible estimate."[29] Similarly, British policy in the months following the nationalization of the Suez canal was posited on the belief that the Egyptians could not run the canal on their own, especially because almost all of the pilots who guided the ships through the canal were European and would quit. They never, however, sought the information readily available on whether it really took extensive training to produce competent pilots. It did not, as any ship's captain could have told them (and did tell the Norwegians,

27 Carolyn W. Sherif, Muzafer Sherif, and Roger E. Nebergall, *Attitude and Attitude Change: The Social Judgment-Involvement Approach* (Philadelphia: Saunders, 1965).
28 For an example, see Krishna Menon's attitude toward nuclear weapons as reported by Michael Brecher, *India and World Politics: Krishna Menon's View of the World* (New York: Praeger, 1968), pp. 228, 332. But there may have been political calculations behind this attitude. See the review of this book by Dina Zinnes in *The American Political Science Review* 63, no. 4 (December 1969): 1341.
29 Tsou, *America's Failure in China*, p. 194.

who made inquiries), and Nasser had no trouble keeping the canal open, thus undermining England's plans.[30]

But in other cases in which some information is ignored or seemingly stretched to fit a prevailing view, outright condemnation is not appropriate. And statesmen's handling of evidence about other actor's intentions rarely fits one of these three categories. The evidence is usually compatible with more than one interpretation. There are cases of visual perception where this is also true. Different stimuli can produce exactly the same pattern on an observer's retina. Thus, for an observer looking with only one eye, the same pattern would be produced by a sphere the size of a golf ball quite close to the observer, a baseball-sized sphere further away, and a basketball-sized sphere still more distant. There is no way for the observer to determine which of these stimuli he is faced with. Statesmen are often placed in analogous situations. There is a right answer to the question of the intentions of the state they are facing, but there is no way to determine this answer objectively from the available data. Not only is the evidence inherently ambiguous, but the actors have to filter out the "noise" of irrelevant information and cope with attempted deception. In these circumstances, no matter how long, carefully, and "objectively" the evidence is analyzed, people can differ in their interpretations—and there are no general rules to indicate who is correct.

For this reason it is hard to find general differences between the way information was handled by those who were later shown to have been right and those who were wrong. Indeed, if we consider only the evidence available to the decision-makers at the time policies were set, the inaccurate perception is often supported by at least as much evidence as the correct one. Roberta Wohlstetter's studies of the failure of American officials to detect the cues that preceded the attack on Pearl Harbor and the Cuban missile crisis[31] could surely be replicated in a perverse way. We could look at cases in which an event did not take place, and, acting as though it had occurred, find a large number of clues indicating the event's probable occurrence that the officials had ignored or explained away.

Scholars have often been too unsympathetic with people whom history has proved wrong, arguing that only a person unreasonably wedded to his views could have warded off the correct information.

30 Terence Robertson, *Crisis: The Inside Story of the Suez Conspiracy* (New York: Atheneum, 1965), pp. 94–95, 109.
31 Roberta Wohlstetter, *Pearl Harbor: Warning and Decision* (Stanford: Stanford University Press, 1962); Roberta Wohlstetter, "Cuba and Pearl Harbor: Hindsight and Foresight," *Foreign Affairs* 43, no. 4 (July 1965): 691–707.

But in most cases it is not at all apparent that those who were right were any more open to new information and showed a greater willingness to modify their images. Vansittart, the British permanent under-secretary in the Foreign Office who has earned a reputation for courage and foresight by his opposition to appeasement, perceptively noted all indication of German aggressiveness. But he was convinced that Hitler was aggressive after the latter had been in office only a few months[32] and did not open-mindedly view each Nazi action to see if the explanations provided by the appeasers accounted for the data better than his own beliefs. Instead, like Chamberlain, he fitted each bit of ambiguous information into his own hypotheses. Similarly, Robert Coulondre, the French ambassador to Berlin in 1939, was one of the few diplomats to appreciate the Nazi threat. Partly because of his earlier service in the USSR, "he was painfully sensitive to the threat of a Berlin-Moscow agreement. He noted with foreboding that Hitler had not attacked Russia in his *Reichstag* address of April 28. . . . So it went all spring and summer, the ambassador relaying each new evidence of an impending diplomatic revolution and adding to his admonitions his pleas for decisive counteraction."[33] He and Vansittart were correct, but it is difficult to detect differences between the methods of noting and interpreting evidence they employed and those used by the appeasers. The members of both groups perceived incoming information within the framework of their preexisting images.[34] Only to the extent that the fear of war influenced the appeasers' perceptions of Hitler's intentions did the appeasers' views have an element of psycho-logic that was not present in their opponents' position.

32   Ian Colvin, *Vansittart in Office: An Historical Survey of the Origins of the Second World War Based on the Papers of Sir Robert Vansittart, Permanent Under-Secretary of State for Foreign Affairs, 1930–38* (London: Victor Golancz, 1965), p. 23; and Martin Gilbert and Richard Gott, *The Appeasers* (London: Weidenfield and Nicolson, 1963), p. 34.

33   Franklin Ford and Carl Schorske, "The Voice in the Wilderness: Robert Coulondre," in *The Diplomats, 1919–1939*, ed. Gordon A. Craig and Felix Gilbert (Princeton: Princeton University Press, 1953), pp. 573–74.

34   In an earlier article ("Hypothesis on Misperception," *World Politics* 20, no. 3 [April 1968]: 460–61) I applied this argument to Churchill. While it is difficult to show that he did modify his beliefs more quickly than Chamberlain, one bit of evidence does point in this direction. In the 1920s he argued strongly for appeasing Germany, relaxing the economic clauses of the Treaty of Versailles, and treating her as a member in good standing of the family of nations. This is especially impressive in light of the fact that before World War I Churchill had been quite suspicious of Germany's intentions. For a critical view of the way Churchill handled information and made decisions, see Robert Rhodes James, *Churchill: A Study in Failure, 1905–1939* (New York: World Publishing, 1970).

THE INTERDEPENDENCE OF FACTS AND THEORIES

Dilemmas of drawing inferences are not unique to policy-making. Scientists must also develop hypotheses and theories out of ambiguous data and interpret facts in light of those hypotheses and theories. And philosophers of science have made clear that the fitting of information into preexisting images is not only ubiquitous but necessary for an understanding of any phenomenon. Thomas Kuhn shows that in any scientific field there is an accepted body of concepts and a basic theory that set the framework for research. They constitute the "paradigms" that are only challenged and changed during "scientific revolutions." The bulk of science consists of problem-solving within the paradigm, or "normal science." "Normal science does not aim at novelties of fact or theory and, when successful, finds none."[35] The paradigm indicates what "makes sense" and what phenomena are both important and in need of further research. It similarly marks out areas to be ignored, either because they can shed no light on problems defined as interesting or because the theory indicates that there is nothing there. And instruments built on these assumptions may not detect the presence of unexpected phenomena.

Most important for our purposes, the paradigm leads scientists to reject flatly evidence that is fundamentally out of line with the expectations that it generates. An experiment that produces such evidence generally will be ignored by the scientist. If he writes it up and submits it to a journal, the editors will reject it. Even if it is printed and there are no obvious flaws in his method or argument, most of his colleagues will not pay any attention to it.[36] Thus scientists maintain cognitive consistency and retain their images and beliefs in the face of discrepant information. Sometimes this practice means that major discoveries will be missed and the paradigm will continue to be accepted when it is no longer appropriate. Thus one reason why Germany did not develop the atom bomb in World War II was that Otto Hahn, a leading physicist, did not correctly interpret one of his experiments. Prevailing theory indicated that the bombardment of a uranium nucleus should yield a heavier element. When Hahn found lighter elements he admitted to being "extremely reluctant to

35 Thomas S. Kuhn, *The Structure of Scientific Revolutions* (Chicago: University of Chicago Press, 1962), p. 52.
36 For an example, see the discussion in Michael Polanyi, "Commentary," in *Scientific Change: Historical Studies in the Intellectual, Social, and Technical Conditions for Scientific Discovery and Technical Invention, from Antiquity to the Present*, ed. A. C. Crombie (New York: Basic Books, 1963), p. 376.

announce as a new discovery a result that did not conform to existing ideas." He could not accept an associate's claim that the only explanation could be fission, because "this conclusion violated all previous experience in the field of physics."[37]

Although in any given instance the rejection of discrepant information may lead to incorrect conclusions, it is a necessary part of theory-building. Scientific investigations could not be carried out if men were too open-minded. A physicist makes this point in terms strikingly similar to Karl Deutsch's discussion of the bullet and driftwood epitomizing opposite kinds of the loss of autonomy: "It is clear that if one is too attached to one's preconceived model, one will miss all radical discoveries. It is amazing to what degree one may fail to register mentally an observation which does not fit the initial image. . . . On the other hand, if one is too open-minded and pursues every hitherto unknown phenomenon, one is almost certain to lose oneself in trivia."[38] Pure empiricism is impossible: facts do not speak for themselves. It is not wise—indeed, it is not possible—to follow Thomas Huxley's injunction to "sit down before fact as a mere child, be prepared to give up every preconceived notion, follow humbly wherever nature leads, or you will learn nothing."[39] Theories guide the questions that are asked, the instruments that are designed, the data that are collected, and the inferences that are drawn. "Every step of the [scientific] procedure—from the initial identification of 'phenomena' requiring explanation to the final decision that our explanation is satisfactory—is governed and directed by the fundamental conceptions of the theory." As a result "theories are built on facts, while at the same time giving significance to them and even determining what are 'facts' for us at all."[40]

The crucial role of theory and the concomitant (and seemingly obtuse) closed-mindedness are necessary because the world is not so neatly constructed that all the evidence unambiguously supports the correct theory. A theory and its attendant hypotheses will never explain all the data—"There is no such thing as research without

37   Quoted in William Gilman, "The Road to the Bomb," *New York Times Book Review*, January 8, 1967, p. 38.

38   Martin Deutsch, "Evidence and Inference in Social Research," in *Evidence and Inference: The Hayden Colloquium on Scientific Concept and Method*, ed. Daniel Lerner (Glencoe, Ill.: The Free Press, 1969), p. 102.

39   Quoted in W. I. B. Beveridge, *The Art of Scientific Investigation*, 3rd ed. (London: Heinemann, 1957), p. 50.

40   Stephen Toulmin, *Foresight and Understanding: An Inquiry into the Aims of Science* (New York: Harper and Row, 1961), pp. 57, 95. For an appreciation of this dual role of theory in the perception of other actors, see Raymond A. Bauer, "Problems of Perception and the Relations between the United States and the Soviet Union," *Journal of Conflict Resolution* 5, no. 3 (September 1961): 223–29.

counter-instances." And it is almost impossible to find one bit of crucial evidence that will clearly show which theory is correct— "Only in fairy tales do Cinderellas have a unique size in footwear, and thieves clap their hands to their heads on hearing the shout that the thief's hat is burning."[41]

Thus the rejection or "distortion" of evidence that contradicts the paradigm is not automatically unscientific. Paradigms and theories gain acceptance by their ability economically to explain a wide variety of phenomena. They are supported by a large body of evidence, have shown their utility over a period of time, and have indicated fruitful lines of research. Furthermore, "experience has shown that, in almost all cases, the reiterated efforts . . . [of scientists] do at last succeed in producing within the paradigm a solution to even the most stubborn problems." Sometimes the scientist will discover that a simple amendment to his theory accounts for the discrepant data. In still other cases the original experiments may be shown to be faulty. On occasion "the objections raised by a contradiction to a theory may eventually be met not by abandoning it but rather by carrying it one step further. Any exception to a rule may thus conceivably involve, not its refutation, but its elucidation and hence the confirmation of its deeper meaning."[42] In light of this it would be unwise and even irrational for the scientist to drop or significantly modify his paradigm in the light of a small amount of discrepant information. Instead he must follow the implications of the weight of the evidence. This will necessarily involve ignoring or twisting bits of evidence that seem to contradict the theory he thinks is correct.

The necessary role of theory in the interpretation of data means that a person who holds an unusual theory will believe that proponents of the established view are ignoring crucial evidence and devising unnecessarily complex and ad hoc explanations to try to save the theory. This treatment of evidence will seem obstinate and misguided. And it may be. But it is not automatically unscientific. As Kuhn puts it:

> Lifelong resistance, particularly from those whose productive careers have committed them to an older tradition of normal science [that is, science within the accepted paradigm], is not a violation of scien-

41 Kuhn, *The Structure of Scientific Revolutions*, p. 79; Kaplan, *The Conduct of Inquiry*, p. 152.
42 Thomas Kuhn, "The Function of Dogma in Scientific Research," in *Scientific Change*, ed. Crombie, p. 363; Michael Polanyi, *Science, Faith, and Society* (Chicago: University of Chicago Press, 1964), p. 31.

tific standards but an index to the nature of scientific research itself. The source of resistance is the assurance that the older paradigm will ultimately solve all its problems, that nature can be shoved into the box the paradigm provides. Inevitably, at times of revolution, that assurance seems stubborn and pig-headed as indeed it sometimes becomes. But it is also something more. That same assurance is what makes normal science or puzzle-solving science possible.[43]

As Kuhn notes in his study of the Copernican revolution:

> What to Copernicus was stretching and patching was to them a natural process of adaptation and extension, much like the process which at an earlier date had been employed to incorporate the motion of the sun into a two-sphere universe designed initially for the earth and stars. Copernicus' predecessors had little doubt that the system would ultimately be made to work.[44]

Thus basic disputes in historical analysis are rarely settled by an appeal to one or two documents. Referring to a disagreement between Gerhard Ritter and Fritz Fischer over the interpretation of one of the memoranda of Bethmann-Hollweg, the pre–World War I German chancellor, a scholar points out:

> If one reads the report in question dispassionately, it can, it seems to me, to be taken *either* way, and one's interpretation is not conditioned by the document itself, or even entirely by the circumstances in which it was drafted, but rather by one's view of Bethmann's character and policies as a whole. A historian's view of a man's aims and motives is formed to a large extent by the documents, but it necessarily also influences the way he reads them; and it is unrealistic to expect Professor Fischer, who, on his reading of the evidence, has formed one opinion of Bethmann's political personality, to agree with Professor Ritter, who, from the same evidence, has come to a radically different conclusion. Each, when interpreting a particular document, is looking for support for a view already formed through reading many other pieces of evidence.[45]

This analysis casts a different light on the instances in which decision-makers ignored or assimilated discrepant information. Such a pro-

43   Kuhn, *The Structure of Scientific Revolutions*, pp. 150–51. For a related discussion, see Norman W. Storer, *The Social System of Science* (New York: Holt, Rinehart and Winston, 1966), pp. 116–22.
44   Thomas S. Kuhn, *The Copernican Revolution: Planetary Astronomy in the Development of Western Thought* (New York: Vintage Books, 1959), p. 76.
45   James Joll, "The Nineteen Fourteen Debate Continues," *Past and Present*, no. 34 (July 1966): 105.

cedure will perpetuate inaccurate images and maintain unsatisfactory policies, but it is necessary if decision-makers are to act at all. In exploring why the United States was taken by surprise at Pearl Harbor, Roberta Wohlstetter points out that "for every signal that came into the information net in 1941 there were usually several plausible alternative explanations, and it is not surprising that our observers and analysts were inclined to select the explanation that fitted the popular hypotheses."[46] As long as the hypotheses were "popular" because they were consistent with theories that successfully accounted for a great deal of data, this is not only not surprising but not unwise. Crucial observations are so difficult and facts so ambiguous that "the route from theory or law to measurement can almost never be travelled backwards."[47] A theory is necessary if any pattern is to be seen in the bewildering and contradictory mass of evidence. Thus in discussing the inability of Ambassador Hurley to comprehend the situation in China, Tang Tsou points out:

> One could have understood the complexity of Soviet policy toward China only if one had perceived that this complexity arose out of the necessity for constantly balancing national against ideological interests, immediate against long-range considerations, temporary expedience against fundamental hostility, tactical objectives against strategic aims, the apparent strength of the Nationalists against the potentiality of the Communists, and finally, Soviet capabilities against the uncertainty about America's intention to intervene. Hurley's naïveté and optimism prevented him from even beginning to tackle this complex problem.[48]

Observers who lack a theoretical framework will, like Deutsch's driftwood, be strongly influenced by the most recent bits of data they receive or the latest short-run trend that emerges. Thus American observers of China in the 1940s who had little experience in foreign policy analysis and few deeply held beliefs about Chinese politics exhibited a marked instability of opinion.[49] If this kind of incoherence is to be avoided, decision-makers and scientists must ignore or twist much data.

46 Wohlstetter, *Pearl Harbor*, p. 393.
47 Thomas Kuhn, "The Function of Measurement in Modern Physical Science," in *Quantification: A History of the Meaning of Measurement in the Natural and Social Sciences*, ed. Harry Woolf (Indianapolis: Bobbs-Merrill, 1961), pp. 44–45.
48 Tsou, *America's Failure in China*, p. 340.
49 Ibid., pp. 228–29.

part III

Influencing Foreign Cultures

twelve

International Transfer
of the Ombudsman

Larry B. Hill

THE increasingly prevalent phenomenon of political institutional transfer is best understood as a communications process. This chapter, dealing with the international transfer of the originally Swedish office of ombudsman, identifies and focuses attention upon the following elements of the communications net.[1] A *source* institution actively or passively sends messages encoded by a *transmitter*. The signal thus created passes through a *channel*; it is decoded by the *receiver*, whose message is institutionalized as the *response*. This model's primary departure from Lasswell's useful early formulation ("Who / says what / in which channel / to whom / with what effect?")[2] is that it bifurcates his "who" and conceptually distinguishes source from transmitter. Furthermore, the proposed model may be differentiated from the usual unilinear model of information theory in which, as Warren Weaver has stated, "the *information source* selects a desired *message* out of a set of possible messages."[3] The present formulation considers the source to be the *origin* of the communication but not necessarily its *initiator*. That role is usually fulfilled by a discrete agent of transmission.

1   For an amplification of the model outlined here, see Larry B. Hill, "The Inter-Systemic Transfer of Political Institutions: A Communications Strategy for the Analysis of Political Change" (unpublished paper delivered at the sixty-sixth annual meeting of the American Political Science Association, Los Angeles, September 8–12, 1970).

2   Harold D. Lasswell, "The Structure and Function of Communication in Society," *The Communication of Ideas*, ed. Lyman Bryson (New York: Harper and Brothers, 1948), p. 37.

3   Claude E. Shannon and Warren Weaver, *The Mathematical Theory of Communication* (Urbana: University of Illinois Press, 1949), p. 98.

SOURCE: THE OMBUDSMAN AS SWEDISH INNOVATION

The term "ombudsman" in modern Swedish refers to any agent, such as a lawyer, who represents a personal interest. Of concern here is the parliamentary commissioner for justice (*Riksdagens Justitie-ombudsman*, or JO). Originally, the JO's primary duty was to focus a watchful eye on the courts and administrative agencies and to prosecute any infractions of the law, but since its formal inception in 1809 the ombudsman has undergone considerable institutional evolution.

First, the early ombudsmen devoted most of their energy to patrolling the activities of the court system, including judges, prosecutors, and police. Though the prisons were inspected, little attention was paid to the administrative system for two reasons: first, the bureaucracy at that time was not very extensive, and the citizen's contacts with it were not numerous; second, the JOs themselves were usually former judges.[4] The increased size and scope of the state's administrative structure have forced the JO to devote most of his energies to supervising it, particularly since a parliamentary order in 1904. Cases involving the judicial system remain the largest single category of the ombudsman's complaints, to be sure, but those involving various administrative agencies are now much more numerous in toto.[5] This gradual reorientation has been intensified due to the recent growth of the welfare state agencies.[6]

The second major modification in the nature of the institution was that the ombudsman came to prosecute officials less and to admonish them more often. Until a 1915 decision by parliament this practice had no legal basis. Its use thereafter has nonetheless given the ombudsman an element of prior control over the actions of public officials which can extend even to the determination of how much compensation a guilty officer should pay the victim.[7] Since Swedish

4   See Alfred Bexelius, "The Ombudsman for Civil Affairs," in *The Ombudsman: Citizen's Defender*, ed. Donald C. Rowat (London: Allen & Unwin, 1965), p. 36; and Stig Jägerskiöld, "The Swedish Ombudsman," *University of Pennsylvania Law Review* 109, no. 8 (June 1961): 1095.

5   Walter Gellhorn, *Ombudsmen and Others: Citizens' Protectors in Nine Countries* (Cambridge: Harvard University Press, 1966), p. 209.

6   Steven D. Anderman criticizes the ombudsman's reaction to this growth in "The Swedish Justitieombudsman," *American Journal of Comparative Law* 11 (Spring 1962): 236–37.

7   Responding to criticisms, Alfred Bexelius maintains that he has performed a valuable function in moving toward uniformity. See "The Swedish Institution of the Justitieombudsman," *International Review of Administrative Sciences* 27, no. 3 (1961): 252–54.

law does not allow the civil servant to force the ombudsman to take him to court so that he might be vindicated, he usually has no choice but to accept a reprimand, and this deterrent function has nearly replaced the JO's prosecuting role. Between 1960 and 1964 only twenty-seven prosecutions were initiated, but 1,220 informal but effective reprimands were given out.[8] The JO's ability to make informal criticisms greatly increases the scope of his office, since he can influence administration without finding an infraction so flagrant that he could prove its illegality.

A third change is that the JO's primary job is now to act as a citizens' complaint bureau. The idea was prevalent even in 1809 that he should also defend the citizens from bureaucratic dictation through periodic inspections of courts, prisons, the church, and other institutions. Large numbers of complaints from private individuals did not pour into the ombudsman's office until the twentieth century. In fact, only seventy complaints per year were made by citizens until 1900, whereas the five-year period 1960–64 saw an average of 1,078 such complaints.[9] Fully 86 percent of his cases now reach him through citizens' complaints. This shift in his clientele makes it less likely that he will become a creature of the bureaucracy than if his dealings were primarily with governmental institutions. Additional transformations, of a structural-legal sort, occurred in 1915 when a separate office of *Militieombudsman* was created for military complaints, in 1957 when the JO was authorized to investigate local administrations, and in 1968 when the civil and military ombudsmen were merged and three officers of equal status, all called JO, were appointed.

Before evaluating the ombudsman's potential transferability, it is necessary to examine the institution's relationship with particular elements of the Swedish political milieu. The ombudsman was established as Parliament's rival to the already venerable king's chancellor of justice or JK—over whom he gained predominance. To avoid duplication of effort, the two officials have worked out an informal communication system and division of labor:[10] the chancellor of justice emphasizes questions raised by government departments themselves, while the JO usually deals with individual complaints against administrators; the chancellor of justice prosecutes minor officials, leaving the more important ones to the ombudsman. The JO also

8 Gellhorn, *Ombudsmen and Others*, p. 206.
9 Computed from data ibid., Table 12, p. 208. Following tradition, the JO continues the attempt to inspect every government agency each ten years.
10 Sten Rudholm, then the CJ, discusses this division in "The Chancellor of Justice," *The Ombudsman*, ed. Rowat, pp. 17–22.

represents the ultimate hope in the Swedish hierarchy of administrative appeals.

Adding to the ombudsman's position is the fact that Swedish ministers are unable to control completely the actual operation of their departments which, since the seventeenth century, have been under a system of semi-autonomous boards. Those boards employ thousands of civil servants, whereas the ministries' administrative staffs range from only six to 130.[11] The ombudsman can thus investigate their administrations without forcing the government to defend their administrative actions against hostile questions in parliament.[12] Also, ministers were placed outside his jurisdiction.

An additional factor increasing the independent position of the administration is the civil servants' privileged position. Administrators have traditionally considered their protected status an unimpeachable property right.[13] The growth of the modern administrative state and its demands for a flexible bureaucracy, however, have necessitated certain modifications in its historic independence. Tenure is no longer absolute and officials can be forced to accept an "obligatory transfer" clause in their contract.[14] But, even so, two-thirds of today's civil servants cannot be fired by higher administrative officials without, in most cases, a court order.[15]

The historic independence of the boards makes possible a genuine internal administrative review of a protested decision. Nils Herlitz, noting that in many countries the usual difficulty of such appeals is the predisposition to support the original decision, argues that in Sweden "there is little administrative bias of this sort, because . . . to a much greater extent than in other countries a superior is not held generally accountable for the acts of his subordinates. An appellant has good reason to believe that in moving his case from one authority to the other he will receive the same fresh consideration he would get if he sought a judicial remedy."[16] Such appeals have continued to be an important part of Sweden's machinery. Since the ombudsman's investigation of a particular civil servant is not neces-

11   See Pierre Vinde, *The Swedish Civil Service: An Introduction* (Stockholm: Finansdepartementet, 1967), Appendix.

12   Poul Meyer, "The Development of Public Administration in the Scandinavian Countries Since 1945," *International Review of Administrative Sciences* 26, no. 2 (1960): 136.

13   Stig Jägerskiöld, "Swedish State Officials and Their Position under Public Law and Labour Law," *Scandinavian Studies in Law* 4 (1960): 106.

14   Jägerskiöld, "The Swedish Ombudsman," pp. 110–20.

15   Anderman, "The Swedish Justitieombudsman," p. 227.

16   Nils Herlitz, "Legal Remedies in Nordic Administrative Law," *American Journal of Comparative Law* 15 (Winter 1966–67): 693.

sarily a potential threat to the entire agency, the agencies, as corporate bodies, have been less sensitive to his operations than in a hierarchically organized system.

Although Swedish civil servants are not impotent ciphers at the disposal of a minister, the onus of legal responsibility is placed upon their every action. In addition to the usual charges, such as dishonesty and flagrant neglect, even their discretionary decisions can be reviewed. The accused civil servant might be prosecuted by the chancellor of justice in an ordinary court or, depending upon the circumstances, in special administrative tribunals from which he could ultimately appeal to the "King in Council." In 1909, after Parliament's ombudsman had been in operation for a century, the Supreme Administrative Court—modeled after but even more powerful than France's *Conseil d'État*—was established to rationalize the system of tribunals.

Other unusual features of the Swedish milieu must be mentioned. Parliamentary decrees in 1766 established the associated principles of disclosure of government documents (with exceptions to protect individuals or national security) and freedom of the press.[17] This fact facilitates the access of private citizens to information needed to substantiate their claims. Then, too, Sweden has an electoral system of proportional representation. Citizens are unlikely to have personal contact with a Riksdag member, for a single constituency might elect a score or more of representatives on the basis of their party label. Thus members of Parliament need not feel that the ombudsman is competing with them for their constituents' favors, and hence they may be less inclined to interfere with his activities.

The peculiar administrative environment in which the ombudsman exists raises a question about the extent to which his operations rest upon its very presence. If many or all of the supportive institutions were missing in a country possibly interested in creating the office, would a successful transfer be possible? Such concerns partially explain why such an otherwise attractive institution—in terms of its apparent success, low cost, ease of explainability, structural simplicity, and nonpervasiveness—was not transferred earlier than it was in fact. In addition, the Swedish language is not widely known outside of Scandinavia, and Swedish incumbents did not undertake purposive signal transmission activities. The annual reports laden with statistics and short case notes having high human-interest value were not translated, nor did ombudsmen make proselytizing foreign

17 Hilding Eek, "Protection of News Sources by the Constitution," *Scandinavian Studies in Law* 5 (1961): 12–13.

tours or write articles for magazines in foreign countries. Even the present incumbent, Alfred Bexelius, who has participated in all of these activities, has usually done so in response to requests rather than voluntarily.

TRANSMITTERS AND CHANNELS: OMBUDSPOLITICS

Although the messages emanating from the Swedish ombudsman were weak, they resulted in international transfers to Finland (1919), Denmark (1954), New Zealand (1962), Norway (1963), and Britain (1967).[18]

Finland. Less is known about the process of transferring the ombudsman to Finland than about the others.[19] A new radically republican constitution, promulgated two years after Finland's break with Russia in 1917, included such innovations as universal suffrage and the establishment of the (unicameral) parliament's control over the government. One of the measures taken to insure the latter was the establishment of a parliamentary ombudsman. The idea actually had deep historical roots. Several private proposals based upon the Swedish pattern were made in the Diet in the latter half of the nineteenth century. The Russian czar, however, who opposed increasing the legislature's powers, rejected the plans.[20] The Diet's 1919 adoption of an ombudsman reflected a Finnish distrust of executive power over the citizens; the selection of this particular method of control illustrated the framers' awareness of the success of the Swedish ar-

18   A specialized military ombudsman, which is not discussed here, was appointed for West Germany in 1957. Guyana and Tanzania have adopted ombudsman-like institutions, and the Canadian provinces of Quebec, Alberta, and New Brunswick as well as the American states of Hawaii and Nebraska now have ombudsmen. Gellhorn (*Ombudsmen and Others*) describes each of the new ombudsmen under discussion here except the British one. See also Mikael Hidén, "Finland's Defenders of the Law," *Annals of the American Academy of Political and Social Science* 377 (May 1968): 31–41; Henry J. Abraham, "The Danish Ombudsman," ibid., pp. 55–62; Larry B. Hill, "The New Zealand Ombudsman's Authority System," *Political Science* 20, no. 3 (September 1968): 40–51; Ingunn N. Means, "The Norwegian Ombudsman," *Western Political Quarterly* 21, no. 4 (December 1968): 624–50. For Britain, see Geoffrey Marshall, "The British Parliamentary Commissioner for Administration," *Annals of the American Academy of Political and Social Science* 377 (May 1968): 86–96.

19   No comparative investigation of the transfers of the ombudsmen has been undertaken, and only the British and New Zealand transfers have been studied in depth. See my "The Transference of the Institution of Ombudsman, with Special Reference to Britain" (M.A. thesis, Tulane University, 1966), "The International Transfer of Political Institutions: A Behavioral Analysis of the New Zealand Ombudsman" (Ph.D. dissertation, Tulane University, 1970), Chs. 1–5.

20   See Hidén, "Finland's Defenders of the Law," p. 32, and Paavo Kastari, "Finland's Guardians of the Law: The Chancellor of Justice and the Ombudsman," *The Ombudsman*, ed. Rowat, p. 61.

rangement. No record of any effort or agitation by any individual or organized group for or against the adoption of the ombudsman, however, has been found.

Denmark. The steady growth of administrative machinery to meet the requirements of new welfare legislation caused concern among many Danes who feared that the traditional methods of controlling the administration were inadequate. Increasing the incidence and scope of bureaucratic contacts with the citizens produced greater friction between them. A parliamentary committee established in 1946 to revise the constitution considered the possibility of introducing an administrative court system. In 1949, while the committee was still deliberating, Stephan Hurwitz, a highly respected professor of criminology at the University of Copenhagen, publicly argued that the Danish dislike for administrative courts made that option undesirable. Instead, he suggested consideration of the Swedish concept of an ombudsman.

The idea was not at all welcome in some quarters, particularly since the drafting of the new constitution was already well under way. Considerable opposition to Hurwitz's proposal was voiced, not only by some constitutional lawyers but especially by the Civil Servants' Trade Unions that commanded widespread support from the Social Democratic Party. Their fear was that the ombudsman would become an all-encompassing supervisor of their every action. Some senior civil servants and politicians in office shied at the notion of subjecting the inner workings of government to detailed scrutiny. A few members of parliament thought that such a system would be detrimental to the position of the minor civil servant and that it might cause him to be overly cautious and rigid in his care to follow strictly the regulations. Such a loss of initiative and imagination, it was argued, might create as many evils as it corrected.[21]

The parliamentary committee carefully evaluated the applicability of the Swedish ombudsman to the Danish context. One of the major arguments against it was that the ombudsman would interfere with ministerial responsibility. Apparently, however, the Finnish experience with the ombudsman—in a context that included ministerial responsibility and hence was relevant to the Danish situation—was not seriously considered. The fact that the committee, most of whom had ministerial experience, pragmatically rejected this argu-

21 See Stephan Hurwitz, "Control of the Administration in Denmark," *Journal of the International Commission of Jurists* 1 (Spring–Summer 1958): 231. This account is partially based upon the author's personal interview with Hurwitz in London in November, 1966.

ment and recommended the ombudsman was an important factor leading to its adoption in Denmark, but pressure from the civil servants succeeded in modifying some of the original provisions.[22] Section 55 of the new constitution enabled Parliament to establish two ombudsmen; but the Ombudsman Act, passed in 1954, provided for a single officer.

The controversy about the merits of the proposal did not end with the passage of the new Danish constitution but continued for the next two years while parliament sought its first ombudsman. Various candidates were proposed, mostly by the center and right-wing parties, but not until 1955 was a candidate found who commanded general support—Hurwitz, himself a nonpartisan figure. He was elected without opposition (but with the abstention of Communist deputies).

New Zealand. Whereas indigenous transmitters created the ombudsman signals in the Finnish and Danish cases, international transmitters served this function in both New Zealand and Britain. The foremost transmitter was Stephan Hurwitz, who was also a new ombudsman source. Between 1956 and 1961 Hurwitz disseminated at least nine articles about his office through internationally circulated English-language publications. Several New Zealanders who later became advocates first heard about the ombudsman through them. The New Zealand Labour party's attorney general, H. G. R. Mason, and the deputy secretary for justice, J. L. Robson, were directly exposed to the idea of the ombudsman through a supranational agency of transmission, a United Nations seminar on law and public administration. Working papers for the seminar (held at Kandy, Ceylon, in May, 1959) had been prepared by Professor C. J. Hamson, a leading British academic lawyer, and by Hurwitz.[23] Upon returning to New Zealand, Robson gave his copy of the Hurwitz paper to the editor of *Political Science*, a journal published at the Victoria University in Wellington. Its reprinting in the September, 1960, issue attained wide currency in New Zealand intellectual circles and popularized the name "ombudsman."

The report of the first British Broadcasting Corporation interview with Hurwitz, printed in the British *Listener* of July 16, 1959, also attracted some New Zealand attention. Thus far, however, aware-

---

22   I. M. Pedersen, "Denmark's Ombudsman," *The Ombudsman*, ed. Rowat, p. 77.
23   The papers and the discussion are printed in United Nations, *1959 Seminar on Judicial and Other Remedies against the Illegal Exercise or Abuse of Administrative Authority* (ST/TAO/HR/4), Peradeniya (Kandy), Ceylon, May 4–15, 1959. Both papers were discussed by the conference in their authors' absence.

ness of the ombudsman had only penetrated a small segment of the political elite. *Time*'s condensation of the *Listener* article in its July 27, 1959, issue increased public awareness, since it was the first ombudsman piece to be circulated in New Zealand on a mass scale. Focusing upon the increasing frustrations of citizens exposed to bureaucratic tyranny, the article lamented the inadequacies of the existing parliamentary remedies and reported that many British citizens were looking "longingly" at Scandinavia's answer to this problem, the ombudsman. As a result of these exogenously transmitted signals, in 1959 the newly formed Constitutional Society began to lobby the leaders of both political parties for the ombudsman. The Labour government rejected the proposal, saying only that an ombudsman was not needed because of the comprehensive nature of existing methods of citizen protection. The National party, however, some of whose leaders had already developed an interest in the ombudsman, decided that the institution might make a good issue for the forthcoming election. For several reasons, not the least of which was the fact that it might mollify the Constitutional Society and others on its right flank for their failure to obtain more far-reaching programs, the National party wrote an ombudsman plank into its election platform.

The 1960 election campaign was generally a dull one. Nor did the ombudsman plank turn out to be an issue that aroused partisan passions. Following National's victory, the justice department under J. L. Robson, who had come to favor the ombudsman concept strongly, was charged to draft a bill based upon the Danish act. It was scrutinized on a clause-by-clause basis, and deviations from the Danish model occurred only when the department perceived the necessity of allowing for differences between New Zealand and Denmark on particular details. After exhaustive debate the cabinet decided to alter the draft in two important ways: to exempt ministers from the ombudsman's jurisdiction, and to retain the crown's prerogative to claim privilege in the release of documents. Attorney General R. J. Hanan, the minister in charge of the bill, introduced it in parliament on August 29, 1961. After a first reading, the bill was allowed to lapse for the parliamentary session. Not only did other more important measures consume Parliament's calendar, but the government felt chastened by critical responses to weaknesses of its bill. The only direct opposition to the ombudsman concept came from the Public Service Association. Some initially intemperate editorials in its *Journal* notwithstanding, the association soon recognized that an ombudsman would be established and directed its energies toward insuring that he would not become an inquisitor or anti–civil servant creature.

After further intense governmental debate, the bill was reintroduced in the new session on June 14, 1962, with crown privilege against the ombudsman effectively removed but with the exemption of ministers retained. A major theme of the government's parliamentary strategy was to align itself directly with the Scandinavian source.[24] Indeed, Hanan was anxious to prove that his official, whatever he might be called, would be a real Danish ombudsman, rather than "an anaemic and ineffective version of the model." Despite some obviously necessary modifications to fit local conditions, "the provisions of the Bill are similar in scope, and in some respects this Bill goes further than its Danish prototype." The opposition did not strongly object to the bill except to contend that the government was not following the Danish model closely enough. The most important partisan clash was over the name, ombudsman. It is an important index to the level of intensity of the debate that, after that issue was won, on a rare free vote, Labour did not force a major division on the final bill.

Norway. Although the ombudsman for civil affairs in Norway assumed his duties on January 1, 1963, exactly three months after his New Zealand counterpart, there was no important feedback in which one influenced the other. As in the other countries, the question of the ombudsman's transfer to Norway was not an important political issue, nor did it involve intense partisan clashes. Instead, in 1958 the Expert Commission on Administrative Procedure, appointed by the king to review the adequacy of administrative controls, recommended its establishment. Following this report's acceptance by the cabinet in January, 1960, and some parliamentary modifications, the bill was passed on June 22, 1962. The commission was directly influenced by the Swedish and Danish examples, and occasionally the Finnish case was mentioned.[25] The commission report and accompanying draft bill circulated widely among many groups, both in and out of government, such as local government

24 New Zealand *Parliamentary Debates* 330 (June 14, 1962): 118–20; ibid. (July 25, 1962): 1118–21.

25 This account is largely drawn from Audvar Os, "The Ombudsman for Civil Affairs," *The Ombudsman*, pp. 95–110. Surprisingly, Os does not mention that Norway's military ombudsman was used as a precedent for the ombudsman for civil affairs. Long before the committee's report, the chairman of the Storting's judiciary committee, Lars Ramndal, introduced a private member's bill in 1953, which was not passed. See James A. Storing, "The Norwegian Ombudsman for Civil Affairs: The First Three Years 1963–66," *Western Political Quarterly* 21, no. 2 (June 1968): 303.

organizations, police chiefs, professional associations, and the Chamber of Commerce. The replies received were usually positive though, as in the case of the ministry of Commerce, they often lacked enthusiasm; even the civil servants' unions did not fight the measure as those in Denmark had. Audvar Os, one of the chief architects of the Norwegian ombudsman, attributes this to the commission's foresight in determinedly depicting the ombudsman as an impartial arbiter between citizen and civil servant rather than as a people's watchdog against the administrator. Hence, not only did the ombudsman have potent allies (such as the National Association of Commerce and Industry and the Bar Association), but also his most likely natural enemies were mollified and no others appeared.

The bill introduced by the government nonetheless attempted to preclude the ombudsman's jurisdiction over administrative discretion. During the public debate over this change (extended because of an intervening parliamentary election), Hurwitz, in his role of international ombudsman transmitter, contributed to a Norwegian law journal an article discussing his experience with discretionary decisions. The government also received heavy criticism in the press and parliament.[26] When the bill was reconsidered in the Storting's committee, its members paid serious attention to the Danish ombudsman's apparent success in reviewing administrative discretion without becoming either a super-administrator or a political meddler. Accordingly, a compromise was reached which gave the ombudsman limited jurisdiction over discretionary decisions. He could investigate and comment if the decision was "clearly unreasonable." However, overriding the commission's recommendation, he was not given access to departments' internal memoranda. Parliament's passage of the completed bill was unanimous.

Great Britain. The first ombudsman signals were transmitted to Britain by Professor David Mitrany, using the *Manchester Guardian* of August 6 and 7, 1957, as his channel. Mitrany, an internationally respected scholar, described the Swedish office, discussed Britain's need for the office, and indicated how it might fit into the British context. After these acquaintance signals, support for the ombudsman began to grow. Justice (the British section of the International Commission of Jurists), which was the single most important group in bringing the ombudsman to Britain, set up a committee in 1957 to secure that end. A first major activity was to bring Hurwitz to England in November, 1958, to lecture in London, Bristol, Oxford, Nottingham, and Manchester. However, the lectures were neither

26 Means, "The Norwegian Ombudsman," p. 628.

well attended nor extensively reported by the mass media. Public attention was nonetheless captured by two articles by L. J. Blom-Cooper, a Justice member, in *The Observer* on May 31 and June 7, 1959. Blom-Cooper, who had visited both Sweden's and Denmark's ombudsmen, described their success and argued that Denmark's was more appropriate for Britain than was Sweden's.

In early 1960 Justice obtained foundation financing for a study to be chaired by Lord Shawcross on the feasibility of the ombudsman. The high prestige of Justice and of this committee is illustrated by the Conservative prime minister's announcement that he would reserve comment on the ombudsman controversy until the Justice report was published. In the interim Hurwitz returned to England amidst much greater publicity than on his first trip. He was interviewed on the B.B.C. by H. W. R. Wade and J. A. G. Griffith,[27] whose questions were generally designed to popularize the ombudsman idea, to establish the fact of its success in Denmark, and to discuss how it could be adapted to meet England's needs. Hurwitz showed himself to be familiar with relevant English developments and suggested possible adaptation to England's large population: either the cases could be functionally divided (that is, one for housing, another for the health service, and so forth), or regional ombudsmen could be appointed.

The most important single event of the ombudsman campaign was the publication of the Whyatt Report in October, 1961.[28] The committee had received extensive cooperation from the government, such as would have been given to an official group. The Treasury coordinated the collection of data that the permanent secretaries of the Ministries of Agriculture, Education and Health, the Home Office, the Board of Trade, and the Post Office submitted in the form of memoranda and statistics. Sweden's and Denmark's ombudsmen gave them advice. The Norwegian plan was discussed, but Finland's ombudsman did not seem relevant and, most surprisingly, the New Zealand ombudsman campaign was not known in time to be mentioned (although the first New Zealand bill was included as an appendix).

Justice's concept of an ombudsman (or parliamentary commissioner) was considerably weaker than the Scandinavian counter-

27   It was this interview which was printed in *The Listener* and which sparked New Zealand interest and inspired the *Time* article cited above. Griffith, professor of English law at London University, was editor of *Public Law*. Through 1965 that journal printed sixteen articles and editorials on the ombudsman.
28   Justice [Sir John Whyatt, Director of Research], *The Citizen and the Administration: The Redress of Grievances—A Report* (London: Stevens, 1961).

parts. He was not allowed to investigate discretionary decisions, but only matters of "maladministration." Other important modifications were motivated by a desire to fit into the doctrine of ministerial responsibility and to coexist with the traditional role of members of parliament. As a consequence, the Justice ombudsman was directed to notify and, in effect, to obtain the prior approval of the appropriate minister before beginning an investigation. Second, complaints would be filtered through members of parliament, who would thus not suffer a loss of prestige as grievance men in their own right. Following the Conservatives' rejection of the Whyatt Report, Justice's role in convincing Labour to endorse the ombudsman and then in helping to draft the bill was crucial.

The Society for Individual Freedom, a small group dedicated to libertarian principles, promoted the adoption of the ombudsman, if somewhat ambivalently. Its journal, *Freedom First*, presented warm signals about the ombudsman. One member even wrote an ombudsman book.[29] But another of its leading members, Donald McI. Johnson, M.P., although encouraging discussion of the ombudsman through his questions in Parliament, feared the impact of this Scandinavian on the traditional role of the M.P. Some reform, he felt, was needed, and the ombudsman was an ideal focal point for discussion.[30]

The Conservative government rejected the Whyatt Report, saying that the ombudsman would contravene the doctrine of ministerial responsibility and unduly delay administration, and claiming that present measures for the redress of grievances were adequate. It was clear that the existence of ministerial responsibility in Denmark was unknown to the Conservatives.[31] Nevertheless, the Conservative party did not campaign against the ombudsman in the 1964 election. In fact, the ombudsman was a quite unimportant electoral issue.[32] In

29 Thomas E. Utley, *Occasion for Ombudsman* (London: Christopher Johnson, 1961). At the later stages of the campaign the Society presented news about the New Zealand ombudsman. See Mrs. Leslie Hardern, Editorial, *Freedom First* (Summer 1964): 2–4.
30 Great Britain *Parliamentary Debates* (House of Commons), 5th ser., 640 (1960–61): 1695.
31 Great Britain *Parliamentary Debates* (House of Lords), 5th ser., 236 (December 7, 1961): 204–9.
32 David E. Butler and Anthony King only mention in one sentence that there was a useful television discussion on the ombudsman (*The British General Election of 1964* [London: Macmillan, 1965], p. 162). Stephan Hurwitz, who was a panel member on it, recommended a series of under-and-over ombudsmen for Britain. The Conservative, Lord Mancroft, felt Labour's plans would kill "the existing Ombudsman" and conflict with ministerial responsibility. See *The Guardian*, September 22, 1964.

opposition, Conservatives remained skeptical but did not make the ombudsman an issue in the 1966 election.

Official Labour spokesmen were not at first enthusiastic about the ombudsman,[33] but the proposal was congenial with the ideas of some Labour intellectuals, such as R. S. H. Crossman, who had complained about the "new despotism" of the bureaucracy. Also, no powerful enemies of the ombudsman in the press or elsewhere had appeared.[34] Conservative rejection of the Whyatt Report provided a fortuitous political opportunity and may account for Labour's solid backing of the office in its 1964 electoral program. Even so, the new Labour government did not place a very high priority on the ombudsman, and its White Paper was not published until October 1, 1965. In its essential features, that document and the following bill, published in February, 1966, hardly differed from the cautious Whyatt proposals. The government's actions in amending its own bill at the reporting stage to specify that the ombudsman could not question the merits of discretionary decisions also seemed to indicate opposition from civil service quarters. The appointment of Sir Edmund Compton, the comptroller and auditor-general, as the parliamentary commissioner for administration was an adroit move designed to provide a linkage between this radical foreign institution and the highly respected British one.

Patterns of Signal Transmission. This examination of the ombudsman transmitters and their activities in sending signals through the channels has highlighted three characteristics of the processes. First, ombudspolitics has interested only a comparatively narrow group of high-status advocates, including supreme court justices, law professors, lawyers, political scientists, editors, reporters, parliamentary deputies, government officials, and other ombudsmen. Through their high status, these innovators had direct access to the political decision-making centers in each country. In cases in which minority groups or less politically prominent citizens proposed an ombudsman, success would be less likely. An interesting recent development is that incumbent ombudsmen, particularly Hurwitz and Sir Guy Powles, have become international ombudsman transmitters.

Second, the institution has not tended to make enemies. Civil servants in Denmark, New Zealand, and Britain were suspicious of the new office, but they did not throw the full weight of their organiza-

33   See, for example, Great Britain *Parliamentary Debates* (House of Commons), 5th ser., 640 (1960–61): 1714.

34   Indeed, the press served as a most important channel for the ombudsman campaign. Such media as *The Times, The Economist, The Observer, The New Statesman, The Spectator,* and *The Guardian* editorially endorsed the ombudsman.

tions against it. The mass media have almost uniformly endorsed the ombudsman and were instrumental in New Zealand in obtaining a stronger bill. Those who did oppose the ombudsman were not in conflict with the goals of the institution; they simply believed that no changes were needed, or they preferred another solution. Most opponents gave ombudsman advocates a major part of the argument by agreeing that some improvements were necessary in the individual grievance procedures.

This dearth of dedicated opponents illustrates a third characteristic of ombudspolitics: its low level of intensity. In Finland and Denmark the institution was adopted as a part of a new constitution; the politics operated almost exclusively at a very high level among the leaders of the constitutional committees. A similar pattern of high-level activity took place in Norway, where the report of the Expert Commission on Administrative Procedure was so important. There was nevertheless some broader participation when the bill was modified. Only in New Zealand and Britain did the ombudsman really become a public issue; yet in comparison with other problems, such as whether or not New Zealand should play rugby with South Africa or Britain's controversy over joining the Common Market, it could hardly be considered major.

RECEIVER: THE OMBUDSMAN'S
NEW STRUCTURAL CONTEXTS

In every case the signals beamed by ombudsman transmitters encountered pre-existing institutions that substantially controlled the activities of its administrators. In Finland, Denmark, and Norway written constitutions spelled out the proper activities of the state and the citizens' rights; New Zealand and Britain maintained systems of ordinary laws and deeply ingrained tacit understandings about individual rights not to be found in any single document. Ombudsman receivers in all five countries delegated spheres of power to local authorities, but all were unitary states (although Finland was organized into provinces for administrative purposes) in which most governmental activities were carried out by the respective national governments. As a result, citizens' complaints against the government were likely to involve national institutions.

Unlike the other four administrative structures, Finland had a chancellor of justice patterned after but stronger and more independent than the Swedish model for over a century before adopting an ombudsman. The attorney general or the procurator, as he was called before the 1917 revolution, could even call to account the czarist-appointed governor general. The new constitution of 1919 made the chancellor of justice an officer of the executive branch but retained much of his independent and powerful status. His general directive to insure the proper administration of the law included the instruction to attend the meetings of the Council of State, the official decision-making body of the Finnish government, to check on the legality of its actions.[35] He could do no more than report to Parliament what he saw as illegal activities, but his opinion carried great authority within the Council of State. The chancellor of justice even supervised the agenda for Council meetings, and ministers sought advance clearance from him to include certain items.

Norway was the only one of the five new receivers that had a military ombudsman prior to the establishment of a similar civilian institution, perhaps because Norwegian soldiers who escaped to Sweden during the German occupation were first exposed to the office and became interested in it while in Sweden.[36] The Norwegian military ombudsman became the head of a seven-man ombudsman board whose other members were only part-time and held seats in Parliament. This arrangement supplemented and capped, but did not replace, the existing system of representative committees of the soldiers, which had enjoyed only limited success. Generally the Norwegian military ombudsman was assigned duties that were similar to those of his Swedish counterpart, such as receiving complaints, making inspections, and advising the military commanders.[37]

All five new receivers had an administrative system in which ministers were held responsible by Parliament for the actions of their civil servants to a greater extent than in Sweden. Only Finland adopted the Swedish practice of allowing private citizens access to official documents. Civil servants in Finland, like those in Sweden, were strictly accountable for their administrative decisions: private citizens with a grievance could bring an administrator to court and receive damages. Though considerably more powerful than their Swedish counterparts, Finnish ministers were less independent of administrative boards and Parliament than British ministers;[38] in

35   Donald C. Rowat discussed this feature of the CJ's authority in "Finland's Defenders of the Law: The Chancellor of Justice and the Parliamentary Ombudsman," *Canadian Public Administration* 4, no. 3 (September 1961): 319.

36   Stanley V. Anderson, "The Scandinavian Ombudsman," *American Scandinavian Review* 12, no. 4 (December 1964): 404.

37   Arthur Ruud, then the Norwegian MO, described his office in "The Military Ombudsman and His Board," *The Ombudsman*, ed. Rowat, pp. 111–18.

38   See Herlitz, "Legal Remedies in Nordic Administrative Law," p. 689.

some fields a separation between ministries and independent boards existed on the Swedish pattern. Access to Danish ministers was comparatively simple, for the tradition existed that they meet with citizens with an appeal or complaint, without appointment, every Thursday morning.[39] New Zealand, again following the British model, held its ministers strictly accountable for the administrative departments. However, the constitutional fiction that they were responsible for every action of every civil servant was not perpetuated.[40] In Norway even most "independent" agencies were ultimately responsible to a minister.[41] The proportional representation[42] of parliaments in Finland, Denmark, and Norway may have made it more difficult for the citizen to identify with a parliamentary deputy and to use him as a channel for complaints, perhaps enhancing the ombudsman's appeal.[43] Deputies in all five countries, however, could ask ministers embarrassing questions forwarded by their constituents in accordance with the principle of ministerial responsibility.

Finally, legal traditions also differed among the five countries. Britain's and New Zealand's common-law arrangement contrasted with that of the Finns who, following the Swedish lead, relied strictly upon statutory law that set for the courts specific standards of legality.[44] Though the Danish and Norwegian systems used written statutes and precedents, their most outstanding feature was a tradition

39   Noted by Pedersen, "Denmark's Ombudsman," p. 75.
40   See R. J. Polaschek, *Government Administration in New Zealand* (Wellington: New Zealand Institute of Public Administration 1958), pp. 211–24.
41   See James A. Storing for an account of the development of ministerial responsibilities in Norway, *Norwegian Democracy* (Boston: Houghton Mifflin, 1963), pp. 53–54, 102.
42   For discussions of the various systems of proportional representation, see Jan-Magnus Jansson, "Some Remarks on Parliamentary Procedure in Finland," *Democracy in Finland*, ed. Kansantaloudellinen Yhdistys (Helsinki: Finnish Political Science Association, 1960), pp. 52–53; Kenneth E. Miller, "The Danish Electoral System," *Parliamentary Affairs* 18, no. 1 (Winter 1964–65): 71–82; Storing, *Norwegian Democracy*, pp. 67–69.
43   Robert N. Kelson discusses the difficulties New Zealand legislators experience in representing the interests of their constituents before government ministers in *The Private Member of Parliament and the Formation of Public Policy: A New Zealand Case Study* (Toronto: University of Toronto Press, 1964), pp. 120–26. John E. Kersell, *Parliamentary Supervision of Delegated Legislation: The United Kingdom, Australia, New Zealand and Canada* (London: Stevens, 1960), pp. 126–37, thoroughly describes and evaluates the M.P.'s role in acting as a citizen's grievance agent. The British legislator is likely to enjoy closer relations with his constituents than is his New Zealand counterpart, but his relationship to the minister to whom he will carry the complaint will probably be a considerably more formal one (pp. 140–41).
44   Finnish officials can be easily prosecuted for failure to follow their written instructions and rules of procedure. See Kastari, "Finland's Guardians of the Law," p. 69.

of customary law.[45] Like Sweden, Finland also had an administrative court system, at the apex of which was a Supreme Administrative Court even more powerful than that of Sweden.[46] Neither Denmark, New Zealand, Britain, nor Norway had an administrative court system. Special administrative agencies, such as licensing and insurance boards, nonetheless exercised quasi-judicial functions in all the countries. Sometimes appeals were allowed from these bodies; sometimes they were not. Thus all of the ombudsman's five new receivers had previously institutionalized a number of protections for the citizen. The ombudsman was interpreted as being compatible with these institutions. This factor helps account for the peculiar characteristics of ombudspolitics discussed in the previous section, and for the receivers' relative success in institutionalizing patterns that were reasonably similar to the Swedish source.

RESPONSE: THE INSTITUTIONALIZATION OF THE OMBUDSMAN

To judge the relative success of the attempted transfers it is necessary to compare the fidelity of the responses with the original source.[47] In all cases Parliament is the agency of recruitment. The ombudsman is elected in Sweden by a vote of a parliamentary committee—on which the government has a majority—but in the adapted versions by a general parliamentary vote. Although the

45   "Some Cardinal Points in the Dano-Norwegian Conception of Law," *Danish and Norwegian Law: A General Survey*, ed. Danish Committee on Comparative Law (Copenhagen: G. E. C. Gad, 1963), pp. 15–41.

46   A minister was protected in that only the legal basis for his decisions could be questioned by the court, whereas the administrative courts also had jurisdiction over the discretionary activities of administrative employees. See V. Merikoski, "Legality in Administrative Law—Some Trends in Evolution and Practical Experiences," *Scandinavian Studies in Law* 4 (1960): 133, 138–49.

47   Unless otherwise noted, all references in this section are to the acts or constitutional provisions. For Sweden and Finland, see Amos J. Peaslee, *Constitutions of Nations: The First Compilation in the English Language of the Texts of the Constitutions of the Various Nations of the World, Together with Summaries, Annotations, Bibliographies, and Comparative Tables*, 2nd ed. (The Hague: Martinus Nijhoff, 1956), vol. 3, pp. 318–19, and vol. 1, pp. 763–64; "The Regulations for the Solicitor General of Parliament" are reprinted in *The Parliamentary Ombudsman of Finland* (n.p.: The Finnish Embassy, n.d.). "The Danish Act and Directives" are reprinted as Appendices A and B in Stephan Hurwitz, *The Ombudsman: Denmark's Parliamentary Commissioner for Civil and Military Administration* (Copenhagen: Det Danske Selskab, 1962). The New Zealand act and amendments are reprinted in Hill, "The International Transfer of Political Institutions," pp. 865–88. "The Norwegian Act and Instructions" are translated by Audvar Os and are printed in *The Ombudsman*, ed. Rowat, pp. 322–27. The British act is printed in Donald C. Rowat, ed., *The Ombudsman: Citizen's Defender*, 2nd ed. (Toronto: University of Toronto Press, 1968), pp. 343–56.

government in each case proposes a candidate, the other parties are consulted; approval is usually unanimous. Only in Finland have partisan political clashes occurred over the selection. The Finnish ombudsman is irremovable during his four-year term of office; but those of Denmark, New Zealand, and Norway have terms coinciding with the terms of the parliaments that elected them.[48] The British parliamentary commissioner has no definite term. Legal qualifications are demanded for all the Scandinavian ombudsmen, but not for their Anglo-Saxon colleagues. Ombudsmen universally are prohibited from being members of Parliament or from holding other jobs or offices. Their staff size is regulated by Parliament in Scandinavia, but by the prime minister in New Zealand and the treasury in Britain. The size of the Swedish ombudsman's bureaucracy is fifteen, whereas the newer offices range from three in New Zealand to sixty in Britain. The Swedish and Finnish ombudsmen have deputies; in case of the ombudsman's incapacity in Denmark, Parliament can elect a substitute; in Norway, New Zealand, and Britain a member of the ombudsman's staff can temporarily exercise his powers.

The ombudsman is competent to investigate decisions that appear to be illegal or mistaken. He may even investigate, within certain limits, discretionary decisions. The Finnish regulations do not mention discretionary decisions: the ombudsman has jurisdiction where an official has been guilty of "dishonesty, partiality or gross negligence, has infringed upon the legal rights of a private citizen, or acted *ultra vires*." Given Finland's legalistic tradition and system of tightly drafted law borrowed from Sweden, however, actions that in other countries would be matters of administrative discretion are in Finland judged to be *ultra vires*.[49] The Danish directives give the ombudsman jurisdiction over "arbitrary or unreasonable actions." The Norwegians modified this authority to comprise only those decisions that are "unlawful or clearly unreasonable." The New Zealand expression of his authority contains very sweeping language including situations that appear to be unreasonable, unjust, oppressive, discriminatory, or even "wrong." Britain, however, much more closely circumscribed her parliamentary commissioner's authority. He is explicitly forbidden "to question the merits of a decision taken

48 A two-thirds vote of the Storting is necessary to dismiss the Norwegian ombudsman. Only simple majorities are required elsewhere.

49 Donald C. Rowat has noted that though the Swedish ombudsman has no specific right to consider discretionary decisions, he can usually intervene in a case by broadly construing the meaning of illegality. See "The Parliamentary Ombudsman: Should the Scandinavian Scheme Be Transplanted?" *International Review of Administrative Sciences* 28, no. 4 (1962): 400.

without maladministration by a government department or other authority in the exercise of a discretion vested in that department or authority." It is difficult to determine how substantively important this limitation is, for the government did not necessarily intend to preclude his *investigation* of decisions made under discretionary authority; maladministration might have been involved. However, he is not allowed to question the merits of the decision.[50]

Only the Swedish and Finnish ombudsmen have jurisdiction over the judicial system; for the other four the courts are specifically placed off limits because of fears of undermining the doctrine of judicial independence (Table 1). Following the Swedish lead, Nor-

Table 1. The Ombudsman's Comparative Jurisdictions

Areas in Which the Ombudsman May Have Jurisdiction	Sweden	Finland	Denmark	New Zealand	Norway	Britain
Judicial system	Yes	Yes	No	No	No	No
Ministers	No	Yes	Yes	No	No	Yes
Administrative agencies	Yes	Yes	Yes	Yes	Yes	Yes
Prisons and mental institutions	Yes	Yes	Yes	Yes	Yes	Yes
Armed forces	Yes*	Yes	Yes	No	Yes*	No
Local government	Yes	Yes	Partially	Partially	Partially	No

* Norway has a separate Military Ombudsman.

way and New Zealand exclude cabinet ministers from the ombudsman's jurisdiction, although in New Zealand the advice of civil servants to ministers can be considered. The Finnish ombudsman, who has even prosecuted ministers, demands a report from individual ministers on the actions they have taken on measures Parliament has recommended to them. These reports are included in his report to Parliament.[51] However, it is always assumed that policy decisions can be distinguished from those areas in which the ombudsman properly exercises jurisdiction.[52] Like Finland, Norway and Britain have included ministers. Prisons are invariably included, and it is specified in the acts or regulations of the Danish, New Zealand, and Norwegian ombudsmen that any individual in a prison or mental institution may communicate directly with the ombudsman via a sealed letter. A substantial limitation over the British ombudsman's scope of investigation of the administration is that he is precluded from dealing with civil service personnel cases. Complaints from the

50 See Marshall, "The British Parliamentary Commissioner for Administration," pp. 93–94.
51 See Kastari, "Finland's Guardians of the Law," pp. 72–73.
52 The Scandinavian ombudsmen's jurisdictions cover almost the entire administrations, but the two Anglo-Saxons have a schedule limiting their jurisdictions.

armed forces are included in the ombudsmen's jurisdictions, except in New Zealand and Britain. Although Norway has a separate military ombudsman, the civil official also has a legal right to investigate military complaints.)

Sweden's action in extending the ombudsman's jurisdiction to include certain local authorities in 1957 influenced Denmark's behavior. Denmark's ombudsman was originally excluded from considering local questions, but a 1962 amendment gave him powers to investigate local authorities in cases in which there already existed an appeal to the central government. Finland has had such jurisdiction from the beginning. Local hospital and education boards were placed under the New Zealand ombudsman's purview in 1969. Norway has not yet extended its ombudsman's jurisdiction to include local authorities, but it is expected that it will. Cases of overlapping central and local authority and cases of deprivation of liberty have always been included. The Finnish ombudsman is instructed to inspect state agencies, while those of Sweden, Denmark, and New Zealand are only permitted to examine them. The Norwegian ombudsman is not given this general warrant, but he may inspect government offices only in the investigation of a complaint. Section 8 of the act creating the office, however, which states that "the Ombudsman shall keep himself informed about conditions in the administrative branches covered by his jurisdiction," would seem to make such inspections legally possible. The matter of inspections is not raised in the British act. Citizens' complaints to the ombudsmen must usually be written and signed, but this is not demanded in Finland. An important limitation of the British version is that complainants do not approach him directly. Instead, they must ask a member of Parliament to pass their letter on to him. In fact, members do usually agree to forward them, and they can be sent to any M.P. The Danish ombudsman can order that citizens be given free legal aid. And everywhere except in Sweden and Finland existing appeals and remedies must be exhausted before appealing to the ombudsman, although the ombudsman may usually take up such a case at his option. Again except for Finland and Sweden, the ombudsman may at his discretion refuse to take up a grievance that is more than a year old. New Zealand and Norway, intending to reduce frivolous complaints, have specifically authorized their ombudsman to reject cases in which the complainant does not have a sufficient personal interest. Only the New Zealand ombudsman charges a fee (of two dollars) for his services.

In conducting his investigation the ombudsman normally works informally by contacting the accused official or department, explaining the complaint, and getting a reaction.[53] Ombudsmen are granted access to the necessary documents and files—except that national security information can be kept secret, and Norway has apparently exempted departmental working papers and memoranda from the ombudsman's province.[54] Information can also be obtained through the subpoena of witnesses to testify in a judicial or semijudicial proceeding. Though the Swedish and Finnish ombudsmen must operate within the publicity of documents rule, they and the other ombudsmen are normally committed to secrecy about the official investigations.

Once his investigation is completed, the ombudsman who discovers an error or a fault has varying courses of action open to him, excepting the power to change any administrative decision. Often the question can be resolved through the ombudsman's advice to the concerned department about how to modify its procedure, or through a fuller explanation of the decision to the complainant. This informal adjustment procedure in which the ombudsman acts as an arbiter between the civil servant and the citizen is the essence of the modernized Swedish version. The ombudsman is always empowered to state his opinion; it is through such informal means that he exercises considerable influence, especially in administrative procedure. If this is not possible, however, the ombudsman employs various degrees of coercion: the Swedish and Finnish ombudsmen can themselves prosecute government officials, while in Denmark the ombudsman can order prosecution or disciplinary proceedings to be started.[55] The three newest ombudsmen can only recommend such measures. A final potent weapon is the ombudsman's ability to publicize cases through special or regular reports. All must file with the parliamentary committees to which they are responsible detailed annual reports that include statistical accounts of their work and provide details of some of the more important cases. In addition to this, ombudsmen may report to Parliament any poorly drafted laws

53   The Danish ombudsman must interview the accused agent unless it would be "absolutely incompatible with the investigation of the case." A Danish civil servant may demand that the ombudsman cease his investigation of him and that a disciplinary proceeding be initiated. Both the New Zealand and the British statutes specify that the permanent head of the department be notified before the investigation begins.

54   Storing, "The Norwegian Ombudsman for Civil Affairs," p. 309, does not believe that this limitation is consequential.

55   Abraham, "The Danish Ombudsman," p. 59, has noted that, out of 1,106 complaints in 1966, criticism or recommendations were made in only thirty-six cases.

that contain inconsistencies or loopholes that have shown up in the course of their investigations.

This investigation of the communications responses to the attempt to transfer the Swedish ombudsman has thus indicated successful communication in each case. The ombudsman is not an invariable institution. There is not in any case complete correspondence between response and source. The distortions, however, have been relatively minor and have evidently not precluded the success of the new ombudsmen.

thirteen

Madison Avenue Imperialism

Herbert I. Schiller

MANY currents feed the international flow of communications. Tourists, governmental agents and officials, student travelers, trade (exports and imports), international games and sports, religious organizations, and cultural exchanges are only some of the well-recognized contributing elements to international communications. While each element does not necessarily match the next in volume, force, or impact, in theory at least there is supposed to be no dominant, thrusting component that overshadows the rest. There is, it is claimed, a diffusion of influence, with culture, entertainment, travel, and commerce nicely balancing each other in an international equilibrium that offers advantage to all participants. We hear, therefore, "Trade is good," "Cultural exchanges create understanding," and "Travel is broadening." All this folk wisdom contributes ultimately to the almost mystical and revered concept of the "free flow of information." The free flow of information, until recently at any rate, has been regarded as the ultimate good for which all sensible nations should strive.[1]

Actually, this view of beneficial and pluralistic international communications is about as realistic as the economists' model of free competition and the self-adjusting market economy. Not surprisingly, both systems are disrupted by the same force. Domestically,

---

1 A UNESCO meeting in Canada in June, 1969, recognized for the first time some of the problems associated with the free flow of information. *UNESCO Meeting of Experts on Mass Communication and Society: Report of the Meeting*, Montreal, June 21–30, 1969 (COM/MD/8; Paris: UNESCO, August 29, 1969).

the giant corporation, as Galbraith and others have effectively demonstrated,[2] makes a shambles of the notion of a free market of
countless uninfluential producers and consumers. Internationally,
the multinational corporation, the intercontinental extension of the
domestic behemoth, now dominates similarly the global economy
and has become the chief organizer and manufacturer of the international flow of communications.

The internationally active corporation is not an altogether new
phenomenon, but its extensive involvement in overseas communications is relatively recent. Since the end of World War II, both the
volume and the character of international economic activity have
changed considerably. Perhaps $85 billion of direct private overseas
investment is owned and controlled by a few hundred United States–
based companies, the so-called multinational corporations. The
massive build-up of private U.S. investment abroad requires no
elaboration here. Though American-controlled raw materials and
extractive industries have maintained and even extended their holdings around the world, the largest part of the postwar American
investment flow abroad has been into manufacturing and service
industries in already-developed regions and countries (Western Europe, Canada, Australia). The changing nature of this investment
has affected directly and consequentially both the apparatus and
content of international communications. A trade publication comments thus on this shift of activity of private United States investment overseas: "For the international advertiser and marketeer, [for
instance,] this means expanded horizons. The shift in investment
means a greater concentration by international business on the production of goods and services and a more rapid development of consumer markets. *Hence, a growing emphasis on the advertising and
marketing of those goods and services is to be expected*"[3] (italics
mine).

U.S. raw materials and heavy goods producer interests overseas
in the pre–World War II days availed themselves of some communications talent to provide their local activities with favorable imagery,
but such expenditures were marginal, at most. Today the situation
is entirely reversed. Now the mass media, wherever U.S. manufacturing companies operate, have been summoned to promote the

2   John Kenneth Galbraith, *The New Industrial State* (Boston: Houghton Mifflin, 1967).

3   Editorial, *International Advertiser* 10, no. 1 (1969): 25. An editorial comment reviewing an address by Alexander Trowbridge, president of the American
Management Association and former Secretary of Commerce.

global expansion of American consumer goods sales and services.

The international community is being inundated by a stream of commercial messages that derive from the marketing requirements of (mostly) American multinational companies. The structure of national communications systems and the programming that they offer are being transformed according to the specifications of international marketeers.

Advertising requires total access to the mass media. It is through the multimillion circulation magazines, the car and kitchen radio, and the home television screen that the marketing message comes across incessantly and effectively. Advertising cannot tolerate, if it wishes to be successful, mass communication channels that exclude its commercials and its commercially oriented "recreational" programming. Therefore, it strives untiringly to penetrate each available communications outlet that has a sizable audience. Advertising's appetite is insatiable, and nothing less than the total domination of every medium is always its objective. Once subordinated, the medium, whatever its original attributes, becomes an instrument of the commercial culture.

Accordingly, one measure of a nation's loss of control of its own mass media (apart from the obvious loss through foreign ownership) is the degree of penetration of *foreign* advertising agencies in the national marketing mechanics. Such a penetration signals also fundamental changes in the country's cultural ecology. It indicates a changed communications structure that increasingly transmits and reinforces an attitudinal condition thoroughly compatible with the requirements of the multinational corporate goods producers that are financing the new system.

The emerging pattern reveals a mixture of economics and electronics that is enormously powerful.

Sophisticated communications methodologies—those that have proved themselves the most effective in regimenting and securing the attachment of the domestic population—are being applied internationally at an accelerating tempo. The culture of commerce (or, more precisely, of corporate power) is radiating from its American base in a dazzling display. To sell its goods and products and itself, U.S. business overseas employs the familiar services of advertising, public relations, opinion surveys, and market research. And to carry the carefully synthesized messages of these bought services, it enlists or subverts the mass media of the many national states in which it operates.

THE AMERICAN ADVERTISING AGENCY AS
AN INTERNATIONAL MESSAGE-MAKER

Though advertising has become the indispensable adjutant of the business system, in its own organizational structure it is not different in many ways from the corporations whose interests it promotes and represents. Advertising agencies illustrate the same concentrated pattern of development as the rest of American enterprise. In 1968, less than 10 percent of the firms in the industry received almost three-quarters of the domestic business (billings).[4] International billings are much more heavily concentrated.

The major U.S. advertising agencies, much like the manufacturing companies they service, possess resources and obtain revenues that put them far ahead of most of their international competitors. Of the world's ten largest agencies in 1969, only one was not an American firm, and in the top twenty-five international agencies, twenty-three were American companies.[5]

The rich domestic consumer market in the United States was the original stimulus for the growth of these word and image factories. It hastened their initial development. Now they are grazing in pastures far from home. The stupendous growth of American direct-owned business overseas has brought with it, of necessity, the marketeers. American factories worth more than $20 billion are manufacturing their products in Western Europe. Another $20 billion worth of U.S. plant is in Canada. Latin America, Africa, and the Middle East, though mainly still serving as raw material depots of Western enterprise, have some U.S. manufacturing capacity, too. The ad men follow their manufacturing clients wherever the potential markets lead, generally where the capital investment is set down. In 1968 American advertising agencies operating outside the United States had billings exceeding $1.5 billion, a large part of which (though by no means all) was accounted for by the advertising programs of U.S. companies overseas. In 1970 advertising expen-

---

4   James V. O'Gara, "$8.9 Billion Billed by 600 Agencies in Record 1968; JWT Boosts Lead," *Advertising Age*, February 24, 1969, p. 1.

5   "Profile of Agencies around World: Billings, Incomes, New Accounts, Media Used, Total Employees," *Advertising Age*, March 23, 1970, pp. 35–103. And the big U.S. agencies get most of the business. J. Walter Thompson; McCann-Erickson; Ted Bates; Young & Rubicam; Ogilvy and Mather; Norman, Craig & Kummel; Leo Burnett; Foote, Cone and Belding; Compton; and Kenyon and Eckhardt are the elite ten American agencies in the world marketing swim.

ditures abroad by American companies were expected to reach
$5 billion.[6]

WHO'S WHERE AROUND THE WORLD?

No part of the globe (except, and perhaps only temporarily,[7] the
socialist-organized sector) avoids the penetration of the internationally active American advertising agency. A special international
edition in 1967 of *Printers' Ink*[8] entitled "Who's Where around the
World" listed forty-five U.S. agencies with hundreds of overseas
affiliates. Consider, for example, the far-flung activities of the largest agency in the world, J. Walter Thompson. In 1969, JWT had
$740 million in billings, of which $292 million (a sizable 39 percent) originated in twenty-eight countries outside the United States.
JWT worldwide has 700 accounts and employs 8,000 people in
forty-two offices, in some instances several in one country. It operates in Argentina, Austria, Australia, Belgium, Brazil, Canada,
Ceylon, Chile, France, Denmark, Britain, India, Italy, Switzerland,
Spain, Japan, Mexico, Holland, Pakistan, Peru, the Philippines,
Puerto Rico, South Africa (with five offices throughout the country
and billings of $10,000,000), Uruguay, and Venezuela. JWT is the
largest advertising agency in seven countries *outside* the United
States.[9]

Young and Rubicam, the second largest American agency in 1969,
had $523 million in billings of which $152 million (over 29 percent)
came from the international market. Y&R International now has
eighteen offices with 1,446 employees in seventeen countries. As an
indication of the pace of ongoing international penetration, six Y&R
overseas offices were opened within the four-year period January,
1965, to January, 1969.

McCann-Erickson in 1969 secured $511 million in billings, of
which $258 million (more than 50 percent) were derived from its
international branches. McCann-Erickson has sixty-nine offices in

6 "U.S. Ad Spending Abroad Expected to Rise Sharply," *Broadcasting*, September 1, 1969, p. 53.
7 Edward N. Ney, president of Young and Rubicam International, said his
agency had been "holding exploratory discussions in Moscow 'as are other major
U.S. agencies.' " "Y & R Rides High on TV's Star," *Broadcasting*, January 20, 1969,
p. 55.
8 "Who's Where around the World," *Printers' Ink*, June 9, 1967, pp. 21–30.
(Now titled *Marketing/Communications*.)
9 Ralph Leezenbaum, "JWT: Mystical Melding of the Swinging and the Staid,"
Marketing/Communications, March, 1970, pp. 22–30.

forty-six countries as well as in Hong Kong and Okinawa. It has a particularly heavy concentration in Latin America, maintaining offices in Brazil (nine branches), Chile (three branches), Colombia (two branches), Costa Rica, Ecuador, El Salvador, Guatemala, Jamaica, Mexico, Nicaragua, Panama, Peru, Puerto Rico, Trinidad, Uruguay, and Venezuela.

The expansion of U.S. advertising agencies is accelerating, increasingly bringing foreign competition under the American umbrella. In fact, as of 1970, only two of the top twenty-five American agencies still did not possess overseas offices. By contrast, the Leo Burnett Company, fifth-ranked agency in the United States in 1969, announced the acquisition of the two largest advertising subsidiaries of the London Press Exchange: LPE Ltd., one of England's largest agencies, and LPE International, Ltd., a combination of nineteen agencies in Europe, Latin America, Africa, and Asia. "It is a natural alliance," said Philip H. Schaff, Jr., chairman of Burnett; "Leo Burnett is strong in the United States and Canada and very weak outside. London Press Exchange is strong outside but very weak here."[10]

In addition, Lennen and Newell, seventeenth-largest agency in the United States, announced in 1969 the establishment of an international network embracing foreign agencies in joint ventures in thirty overseas offices, enabling it "to cover an area responsible for 85 per cent of the business of the free world."[11] Sullivan, Stauffer, Colwell and Bayles announced its intention to buy a big slice of Lintas, the huge Unilever house agency. The deal hoisted "this conglomerate into ninth place among the world's top agencies," with total annual billings in 1969 around $300 million. Needham, Harper & Steers exchanges stock with Havas Conseil, France's largest agency (with 54 percent ownership by the French government); together with a British affiliate, S. H. Benson Ltd., they maintained offices in eleven European countries, Canada, the Pacific, and the United States.[12] America's eleventh-ranked agency, Dancer-Fitzgerald-Sample, "joined the crowd and moved into the international field" in early 1970.[13] Gray Advertising's 1968 annual report rhapsodized

10   Philip H. Dougherty, "Advertising Agency Plans Giant Merger," *New York Times*, May 12, 1970, p. 69.

11   Philip H. Dougherty, "Advertising: Lennen and Newell Active Afar," *New York Times*, June 10, 1969, p. 73.

12   "The Agency Pot: Bubbling Again," *Television Age*, July 14, 1969, pp. 22–23.

13   Philip H. Dougherty, "Advertising: Dancer Joins the Foreign Set," *New York Times*, March 2, 1970, p. 52.

about "co-ordinated globalization" among the twelve countries and eighteen cities served by its "global network." And each month brings new investment mergers.

The internationalization of the American advertising business is an integral part of the expansion of U.S. industry abroad. It is the latter's voracious marketing requirements that elicit and support the agencies' worldwide activities. The client list of American advertising agencies operating internationally is a roster of *Fortune*'s directory of the largest 500 U.S. nonfinancial corporations, supplemented by a heavy representation of major European companies.

In Canada, for instance, the main revenues of commercial radio-television broadcasting come mostly from the giant American companies operating across the border. In 1969, the top ten broadcasting advertisers were: General Motors of Canada, Ltd., Proctor and Gamble of Canada, Ltd., Canadian Breweries, General Foods, Ltd., Imperial Tobacco of Canada, Colgate-Palmolive, Ltd., Ford Motor Company of Canada, Lever Bros., Ltd., Government of Canada, and Bristol-Myers of Canada.[14] Ninth-ranked U.S. advertising agency Ogilvy and Mather, with one-third of its income earned outside the United States and with thirty offices in fourteen countries, notes in its 1969 annual report that it serves seventeen clients in three or more countries.

J. Walter Thompson, successful in penetrating five continents for its billings, has practically taken over the informational activities of the Nixon administration as well. One trade magazine, inquiring whether the "White House [was a] Branch of J. Walter Thomson?"[15] observed that five former employees of the agency were now working on the White House staff, including H. R. Haldeman, chief of staff to the President, and Ron Zeigler, presidential news secretary. Internationally, JWT notes in its 1969 annual report, "we have been retained by the British Government to aid in the introduction of the new monetary system [and] in India we are engaged in a campaign designed to spread information about planned parenthood to the people."

The omnipresent advertising message, jarring or insinuatingly effective, now constitutes a major current in the flow of international communications. The mass media lend themselves as the ideal instruments of transmission—especially television, which captures the viewer in his own, allegedly secure, living room. The media, if they

14   "Radio-TV Budgets Rise in Canada," *Broadcasting*, May 11, 1970, p. 56.
15   "White House Branch of J. Walter Thompson?" *Broadcasting*, February 24, 1969, p. 36.

were not commercial to begin with (as they were in the United States), end up eventually as business auxiliaries, particularly in the less-developed countries. The lure of advertising revenues is too tempting. Furthermore, the business system cannot permit as influential a "sales tool" as radio-television to function noncommercially, free to reject the transmission of its consumer messages.

In the developed countries, long-standing national sovereignty, powerful domestic business interests (some of which resist foreign penetration), and sometimes a tradition of concern for cultural integrity combine to resist the advertising invasion but generally serve only to slow it down. Actually, in the high-income nations, a considerable domestic business structure functions as a preparatory internal agent for international commercialism.

It is no surprise, therefore, to discover that American advertising agencies have made deep inroads in most of the already industrialized states. In Great Britain, for example, "The situation now is that of the top twenty London advertising agencies, only seven are totally British. All the rest are American owned, or, in a few cases, have strong American links. In the top ten, the U.S. dominance is even greater, with only two of the ten retaining total independence."[16] In West Germany, France, Italy, and even Japan, American advertising agencies now account for the bulk of nationally placed advertising.[17] On the other side of the world there is the same loss of national control of the image-making apparatus. A report from *Advertising and Newspaper News* notes, "Overseas agencies gain whole or partial control of 15 of 24 largest Australian ad agencies and Australians berate themselves for lack of self-faith."[18]

In many of the less-developed states, the control of internal communications by foreign (generally American) business interests is often overwhelming. *Le Monde* reports, for example, that in Peru "more than 80 per cent of the advertising carried by Peruvian newspapers, radio and television is channelled through big American advertising firms, such as J. Walter Thomson [*sic*], McKann Erickson [*sic*], Grant Advertising and Katts Acciones, Inc."[19] Venezuela is even more monopolized by American agencies; a similar pattern, varying in degree, applies in Rhodesia, Kenya, Nigeria, India, Ma-

16   *The Financial Times*, November 17, 1969.
17   "Profile of Agencies around World."
18   Robert P. Knight and John D. Stevens, eds., "Articles on Mass Communications in U.S. and Foreign Journals, a Selected Annotated Bibliography," *Journalism Quarterly* 47, no. 1 (Spring 1970): 198–99.
19   Marcel Niedergang, "Double-Edged Reform for Peruvian Press," *Le Monde* (English language weekly edition), April 1, 1970, p. 3.

326 *Herbert Schiller*

laysia, Pakistan, Thailand, and many other low-income nations.[20]

Advertising and the mass media that it eventually traduces are, therefore, the leading agents in the business of culture, and the culture of business. Other services, such as public relations, marketing research, and opinion surveying, all of which are utilized to make the marketing effort more effective, feed further the stream of international commercial communications.

PUBLIC RELATIONS AS AN INTERNATIONAL INFORMATION SOURCE

Public relations, a practice of American business since the early years of the twentieth century, also has become an international phenomenon following the migration of American capital overseas. Compared with the growth of international advertising, PR is still a rather modest but steadily expanding activity. Whereas advertising commonly aims to sell the corporation's output, PR's goal more specifically is to sell the company itself—as a useful, productive, and beneficial entity to the society in which it is located. As American capital floods into a country and wrests control of key industries, this is no mean task. Here is the problem as seen by the executive vice-president of Hill & Knowlton, Inc., the most important American company engaged in international public relations:

> Let us review the situation confronting the American corporation today in Western Europe [Mr. William A. Durbin suggests]: For a time following World War II, American companies found European countries eager for dollar investment—and the markets seemed almost limitless. In the past decade or so, American business responded with a tremendous increase in direct U.S. investments in Western Europe. In 1965 the total approached $14 billion, compared with $1.7 billion in 1950 [closer to $20 billion in 1969].
>
> In recent years the climate has changed: the "welcome" sign has been replaced with one reading "Yankee Go Home!" A recent survey by Opinion Research Corporation disclosed considerable pressure to restrict the growth of U.S. firms in four Common Market Countries. Fifty-six percent of the *businessmen* [italics mine] in Germany believe their government should discourage U.S. investment. For Italy the figure was 44 percent, France 40 percent, and the Netherlands, 31 percent.
>
> . . . Under these circumstances, American corporations face difficult problems. They cannot merely withdraw—they must work

20 "Profile of Agencies around World."

harder than ever—and much of their attention must be given to the public relations aspects of their international operations.[21]

Or, put otherwise, it is the task of U.S. corporate-supported public relations to overcome widespread resistance to American penetrations of the national economy wherever they may be occurring.

The manipulation of symbols to achieve this objective is applied skillfully, generally unobtrusively, and intensively by the professional image-makers. As noted in one business bulletin, "Worldwide PR is, quite simply, the art of using ideas and information through all available means of communications, to create a favorable climate of opinion for products, services, and the corporation itself."[22]

When PR has its way, the flow of communications becomes a stream of unidentifiable (by source) promotional messages for the sponsoring company or complex or even the entire business system itself. Years ago, an American business periodical observed:

> As expert communicator, PR plays a unique and quite startling role in the whole flow of communications between the business community and the public. This role is often glossed over, but the simple fact is that much of the current news coverage of business by the American press, radio, and TV is subsidized by company PR efforts. . . . one hundred thousand public relations practitioners serve as a tremendous source of communications manpower. Without them, only a handful of newspapers and radio or TV stations would have the staff or resources to cover business activities. . . .[23]

Emphasizing the fanciful means that are required to promote modern business, a later study concluded:

> The relative significance of public relations cannot be gauged by estimating total expenditures for this work. We have no such estimates, and the figure would probably be small in comparison with advertising proper. The most telling test of the significance would be to determine the portion of the contents of our newspapers [and television and radio programming] that has originated from public-relations offices. This portion is probably quite remarkable.[24]

21   William A. Durbin, "International Public Relations," in *Current Thoughts in Public Relations: A Collection of Speeches and Articles*, eds. Malcolm M. Johnson, Thomas A. Kindre, and Will H. Yolen (New York: M. W. Lads, 1968), pp. 120–21.
22   *International Public Relations*, Gallatin International Business Aids, June, 1967.
23   "Public Relations Today," *Business Week*, July 2, 1960, p. 42.
24   Fritz Machlup, *The Production and Distribution of Knowledge in the United States* (Princeton: Princeton University Press, 1962), p. 271.

In this curiously inverted state of affairs, the public is supposed to benefit from the privately prepared press releases that are fed into the mass media, because the latter would be unable, if left to its own resources, to produce enough of such material. Now the international community is receiving these communications benefits as well. *Business Week*, a decade ago, estimated that "among the top three hundred companies in the country, three out of four have full-fledged PR departments, a broad jump from the one out of fifty reported in 1936. New corporation PR departments are starting at the rate of one hundred a year."[25] The top 300 companies, it may be recalled, are the major exporters of capital and are the main owners of overseas plants and facilities. In a survey undertaken by Opinion Research Corporation in January, 1968, the 500 largest industrial corporations listed in the *Fortune* directory were asked to fill out questionnaires about their foreign public relations programs. Only 153 replies were received and, of these, forty-three reported no overseas PR activities. The survey therefore represents a self-selected response of 110 major U.S. companies engaged in foreign public relations. The basic findings with respect to these firms were:

> . . . The number of companies engaging in international public relations activities has increased markedly in recent years.
> . . . These companies are carrying out public relations programs on every continent and in every major country.
> . . . The programs are usually handled by staff members based in the overseas countries.
> . . . Only one-third of the respondents use either a public relations firm or advertising agency to implement their overseas public relations programs.
> . . . The principal activities are press releases, product publicity, and exhibits and special events.

Other activities include community relations, employee relations, and government regulations. *Public Relations Quarterly* sums up the study in these words: "Not only are more companies entering the overseas public relations field, they also seem to be more active."[26] Though most of the major U.S. corporations active internationally use their own staff for public relations work (General Motors has a several hundred–man PR corps spread around the world),[27] some

25   "Public Relations Today," *Business Week*, July 2, 1960, p. 41.
26   Hugh C. Hoffman and Robert C. Worcester, "The International Scene: A Review of Current Practices," *Public Relations Quarterly* 13, no. 1 (Spring 1968): 12, 17.
27   "Public Relations Today," p. 42.

rely on the efforts of companies organized entirely for that purpose. Accordingly, U.S. public relations firms, much like their ad agency rivals, have organized subsidiaries and affiliate relationships abroad.[28]

Recapitulating, the overarching aim of international PR is to make U.S. corporate penetration palatable or at least tolerable to the host areas overseas. In the Latin American countries, Anaconda, Braden, Braniff, Chrysler, Du Pont, Esso, Ford, General Motors, W. R. Grace, Kaiser, and Pan American Airways "are all too conscious of the tremendous importance of keeping a regular flow of communications with local publics as a means to gain their acceptance, understanding and esteem."[29]

National and local mass media systems are infiltrated by business messages not necessarily identified by their sources of origin. Hill and Knowlton even prepared a guidebook to familiarize less knowledgeable PR men with the techniques of overseas promotion, and concern with the local media has the highest priority.[30]

With the advent of space communications, the opportunity to achieve a worldwide audience for promotional ends has not been ignored. In June, 1969, for example, the space satellite system was used to herald the opening of an iron ore complex in Australia, owned and operated by an American multinational corporation in association with other business companies. "Co-ordinated planning, American techniques and Intelsat make Australian mine opening a world event," reported the *Public Relations Journal*.[31]

It may seem superfluous to add that the ultimate goal of all this communications activity is control of resources and markets that will produce profits. Sometimes this simple but consuming aim is overlooked. It is useful, therefore, to reflect on some PR wisdom from a man who was a partner with Ivy Lee, the cosmetician for John D. Rockefeller. T. J. Ross, in a talk in 1961, observed:

> A public relations man is not worth his salt if he succumbs to "pie-in-the-sky" thinking divorced from the realities of his business. And he will not stay long on the management team if he does. In his zeal to place his corporation in the most favorable public light,

28 For a compilation made a few years ago (and probably not comprehensive even at that time) of American PR firms in the international arena, see *International Public Relations*, Gallatin International Business Aids, June, 1967.

29 Harry Muller, "Latin America: How U.S. Corporate Prestige Stacks Up," *Public Relations Journal* 22, no. 6 (June 1966): 20.

30 Hill and Knowlton International, *Handbook on International Public Relations*, 2 vols. (New York: Praeger, 1968).

31 Arthur Reef, "The Satellite Beams Its First PR Program," *Public Relations Journal* 25, no. 11 (November 1969): 17.

he must not forget that a business is first and foremost a profit-making enterprise, not an eleemosynary institution. In the relationships he seeks to create between the corporation and its publics he may be soft-hearted, but he must not be soft-headed.[32]

THE OPINION-TAKERS AND THE MARKETING RESEARCHERS

Two other media-related services supplement the information-generation business that engages so much of the attention and resources of American companies active in international markets: the opinion survey organizations and the market research companies.

Opinion polls are considered generally as part of the contemporary political infrastructure of parliamentary-electoral societies. In fact, by volume and character of the work, market-economic undertakings account for a substantial part of the poll-takers' overall business. The distinction between survey and market research is often extremely thin, and the techniques of uncovering political attitudes and desires may serve to give orientation to economic activities and policies. For example, the Opinion Research Corporation recently announced the establishment of a new company, Market and Opinion Research International, Ltd. (MORI), with headquarters in London. This is a joint venture with NOP Market Research, Ltd., London. MORI, the new outfit, is expected to provide facilities for research in North America, the United Kingdom, and Europe.[33]

The Gallup Organization, Inc., the best-known U.S. opinion surveying company, identifies itself as providing "marketing and attitude research." Gallup International, which includes its autonomous overseas associates in a loose network of affiliate relationships, "covers 36 countries or regions throughout the world. It undertakes surveys on a world-wide or European scale in the fields of marketing research and of public opinion and behavioral sciences, to be conducted on a contract and client basis."[34]

A. C. Nielsen Co., the major market research company in the United States, engages in surveys as a matter of course and operates in twenty different countries on four continents. It supplies some of its research services to eighty-six international organizations with

32   T. J. Ross, "Some Observations on Public Relations Progress," in *Perspectives in Public Relations*, ed. Raymond Simon (Norman: University of Oklahoma Press, 1966), p. 20.
33   Joseph T. Klapper, ed., "News and Notes," *Public Opinion Quarterly* 33, no. 2 (Summer 1969): 284.
34   Gallup Organization, Inc., "International Opinion Trends" (Princeton, N.J.: Gallup Organization, Inc., n.d.).

parent companies located in eight different countries. Its television audience research services have been established directly in Canada and Japan and through joint ventures in Ireland and West Germany. This rating service, which creates frenzy among commercial TV broadcasters scrambling to achieve high viewing ratios, is described by Arthur C. Nielsen, founder of the company, thus: "Since this type of research exerts a significant and favorable effect on the efficiency of one of the most important methods of moving goods from producer to consumer [television] . . . it is lowering the cost of distribution and creating increased profits for manufacturers and greater values for consumers."[35]

The view of television as essentially a "method of moving goods from producer to consumer" explains, of course, the pathetic condition of television in the United States. The "increased efficiency" that the medium provides for the marketing function can be balanced against the human dysfunction imposed on its audience.

Other firms also have worldwide surveying operations. International Research Associates, Inc. (INRA), conducts market and opinion research in the United States, Latin America, Europe, Africa and the Middle East, Southeast Asia, and the Far East. The company has a network of associated research organizations operating in more than forty countries and principalities around the world.[36] Gallup International, financed by whomever will foot the bill, conducts periodic omnibus surveys in Argentina (bimonthly); Australia (bimonthly); Austria (quarterly); Belgium (weekly); Chile (bimonthly); Great Britain (weekly); Greece (biweekly); India (quarterly); Italy (quarterly); the Netherlands (weekly); Norway (monthly); Philippines (annually); Sweden (monthly); Switzerland (quarterly); Union of South Africa (bimonthly, when the "European" adult population is sampled); Uruguay (bimonthly); Vietnam (quarterly); and West Germany (monthly).

The opinion survey, whether conducted under national or foreign auspices (incidentally, no easy matter to ascertain), is ostensibly "designed to obtain information, not to create it."[37] In fact, however, it often *creates* not only information but also the *attitudes* that it is

35 Arthur C. Nielsen, Sr., *Greater Prosperity through Marketing Research: The First 40 Years of the A. C. Nielsen Company* (New York: Newcomen Society in North America, 1964), p. 34.

36 Ernest S. Bradford, comp., *Bradford's Directory of Marketing Research Agencies and Management Consultants in the United States and the World, 1965–1966* (Fairfax, Va.: Bradford's Directory of Marketing Research Agencies, 1965–66), p. 44.

37 V. Lewis Bassie, "Question That Survey," *Illinois Business Review* 10, no. 11 (November 1953): 2.

supposed only to poll. The problem lies not with faulty sampling or poor interviewing; even the questions can be phrased with complete objectivity. Deficiencies in these matters can and do appear but, with increasingly sophisticated polling techniques available, technical errors are likely to be minimal among well-established organizations.

A less-acknowledged consequence of opinion surveying, however, is what might be termed its *legitimization effect*. This means that once political, social, or economic questions are put in a fixed perspective and called to the attention of the respondent, a validation of certain ideas or even of a frame of reference may occur. Consumer preference studies, for instance, inquire about choices between one product or another, not whether either or both of the products should have been produced in the first place. Political inquires ask individuals to choose between candidates, thereby validating the electoral process rather than questioning its mechanics.

In short, in most instances, and not necessarily with a deliberate intent to influence, the question-answer format creates for the respondent (and the viewer, listener, or reader of the poll's published results) a pattern within which to view reality. This is set according to the structure of the inquiry. The conditions of the response are set by the poll-taker in the way he already views the relationships he wishes to uncover. The respondent is forced into that mold once he accepts the role of participant in the survey.

A case in point as an illustration: a Roper poll, conducted and paid for by the National Association of Broadcasters (the commercial broadcasters), asked its respondents, "Do you agree or disagree that having commercials on TV is a fair price to pay for being able to watch it?"[38] Roper reports, no doubt to the great satisfaction of the NAB, that "people agreed, eight to one, with the concept that having commercials is a 'fair price to pay.'" Yet what has been learned from this question and the overwhelming affirmative response it obtained? Alternatives of having television *without* commercials were not offered to the respondents. A commercial structure of relationships was assumed by the question formulated by Roper, and those answering, by the very fact of responding, had to accept the underlying set of assumptions. In effect, the prevailing institutional pattern of commercial television was sanctioned in the very process of poll-taking.

It is important also to know who is taking the survey, who is

38 Burns W. Roper, *A Ten-Year View of Public Attitudes toward Television and Other Mass Media, 1959–1968* (New York: Television Information Office, 1969), pp. 22–23.

financing it, and who is receiving the information that it produces. Unfortunately, this information is not always readily available. Consider this account of the polling techniques of the U.S. Information Agency overseas:[39]

> The backbone of the research program [of the USIA] is the public-opinion poll, conducted in every area accessible to communications researchers. . . . One thing the polls have in common is that they are not openly conducted on behalf of the U.S. Government. A typical procedure is to hire outside firms, generally located in the countries to be surveyed, to conduct research. People who are interviewed know only that a private polling organization is asking them questions. It is felt that knowledge of the government's connection would compromise survey results, so this rule has been strictly observed.

Moreover, polls conducted under obscure sponsorship may provide information to those with limited social responsibility, thereby increasing their potential for further manipulation of local populations.

In any event, opinion surveys conducted for American corporations or governmental information agencies present a twofold threat to the societies in which they are undertaken. The polls are structured commercially, and, when published as national sentiment, they cannot fail to aggravate the marketeering influence in the country by still further legitimizing existing inclinations to consumerism. Of more moment, perhaps, they probe surreptitiously for national opinions that may determine or increase the scope of U.S. official or private information-makers' future policy in that country.

It should also be clear that in many advanced, industrial market societies local market research and polling occur alongside of and sometimes without competition from American-supported operations in the same territory. To the extent that they do exist independently,[40] they provide for their domestic sponsors the same methodology of control and manipulation that these activities offer their American

39   Edith Marie Bjorklund, "Research and Evaluation Programs of the U.S. Information Agency and the Overseas Information Center Libraries," *Library Quarterly* 38, no. 4 (October 1968): 414. The USIA has not limited its clandestine dealing to opinion poll–taking. Secret USIA subsidies were made to Hearst-Metro-Tone News, owned half by Metro-Goldwyn-Mayer and half by Hearst Publications. The movie newsreels of this company were distributed overseas and included specially inserted USIA clips in the programs. The subsidies kept this newsreel company solvent long after their competitors had disappeared. (*Variety*, May 7, 1969.)

40   It is not always simple to determine the independence of the poll-taker/surveyor. BMRB (British Market Research Bureau), for example, is the subsidiary of J. Walter Thompson. (J. Walter Thompson, *Annual Report, 1969*, p. 4.)

counterparts. Though this discussion is concerned primarily with the promotion of American business ideology overseas through advertising, PR, polls, and market research, the imposition of a value structure riddled with commercialism is made easier to the extent that it finds societies already prepared and enmeshed in these practices.

U.S. BUSINESS CONSULTANTS AND BROKERAGE OFFICES OVERSEAS

In this far from exhaustive overview of business-generated information flows emanating from American enterprises abroad, a brief account of private U.S. management-consulting firms and American brokerage offices outside the continental boundaries is relevant and instructive.

According to a recent survey by *Fortune*, the European market for American business advice is lush and still ballooning. "Over seventy U.S. consulting organizations have stepped into Europe's ripe climate . . . [and] the real invasion has only just begun."[41] *Fortune* lists McKinsey and Co., Booz, Allen & Hamilton, A. T. Kearney, Arthur D. Little, and Leasco as the currently most active firms, noting that they went into Europe initially to serve American multinational companies that were setting up plants or acquiring subsidiaries there. Now they are attracting many European businesses and organizations as their clients. McKinsey, for example, secured the unprecedented responsibility for studying the administration of the Bank of England, "the first time in its two hundred and seventy-four years that the Old Lady of Threadneedle Street had opened her arms to a foreigner."

What is the significance of this highly specialized business communications flow? Since it is entirely confidential, no one knows with certainty. *Fortune* describes McKinsey's activity as having "an aura of mystery: the work is often hard to define in advance, and even harder to appraise in retrospect." *Science*'s European reporter, D. S. Greenberg, concurs: "What McKinsey tells its clients and what, if anything, they do about it is difficult to discern."[42] Yet the general thrust of the advice, he believes, moves in a familiar direction. Greenberg quotes one U.S. consultant addressing a European marketing conference:

41 Robert C. Albrook, "Europe's Lush Market for Advice—American Preferred," *Fortune*, July, 1969, pp. 128, 131.
42 D. S. Greenberg, "Consulting: U.S. Firms Thrive on Jobs for European Clients," *Science*, November 29, 1968, p. 986.

The traditional thrift of Europeans . . . has been replaced by an eagerness to spend and a willingness to go into debt. There is a growing dissatisfaction with the old and the established, and an intense desire to improve, experiment, to try new products and services—to demonstrate affluence. Europeans have even recently come to believe in planned obsolescence. . . . Consider the impact of television. Both the commercials and the programs themselves flood the consumer with new products and a vision of a better living standard. . . .

Greenberg concludes: "the efficiency of American industry is not unrelated to the social irresponsibility with which much of it has been permitted to operate, and, whatever it is that the consultants are whispering into the ears of their European clients, it is to be hoped that there is someone else around to point out that making more, cheaper and faster, is not the whole answer to making life better."[43] Given the rising flow of information generated by U.S. business abroad, countervailing voices are less and less likely to find outlets in their own media.

One additional flow of business data can be identified. The internationalization of capital and the magnetism of the American securities market (which, until the present bear market at least, provided liquidity to easily unnerved and affluent foreign investors) have occasioned the spread of brokerage offices, investment advisers, and mutual funds abroad. In a recent report a Bache & Company employee attributes this trend to direct wire connections and computerized information systems. "We can give the investors a faster and more complete story on the market or an individual company than anyone else. An investor in Amsterdam can get information on a U.S. stock faster than he can on a stock listed on the local exchange."[44]

Accordingly, share quotations now move across oceans by cable or satellite[45] and U.S. stock exchange firms have overseas offices in scores of exotic locations: Kuwait and Saudi Arabia (each has an American branch office); Nassau in the Bahamas (one); Belgium (thirteen); Austria (one); Brazil (two); Canada (thirteen); England (twenty-five); France (twenty-five); West Germany (seven); Greece (two); Holland (eleven); Hong Kong (six); Italy (six);

---

43   Ibid., p. 987.
44   Clem Morgello, "The Stock Market's Foreign Market," *Newsweek*, January 27, 1969, p. 82.
45   In Israel the *Jerusalem Post* carries on its front page the daily Dow-Jones performance of the U.S. stock exchange.

Japan (two); Lebanon (five); Liechtenstein (one); Monaco (three); Panama (two); the Philippines (two); Puerto Rico (three); Spain (four); Switzerland (twenty-five); Uruguay (two); Venezuela (four); and the Virgin Islands (one).[46]

AMERICAN BUSINESS AND THE WORLD MARKET

The economic power of American corporate capitalism has long been manifest. Its postwar global expansion has made it an international system that affects, and is affected by, national decision-making in scores of countries on all continents. Its economic impact, if not thoroughly documented, is at least generally recognized and includes raw material flows and explorations, balance-of-payments conflicts, dividend and profit repatriation pressures, migrations of human talent ("the brain drain"), currency and gold speculation, and shifting shares of world markets. Political consequences, too, of the international operations of American companies are beginning to be appreciated. Instabilities or at least tensions in local political structures are sometimes analyzed with respect to inflows of American capital.

Only the cultural-information sphere has gone almost unacknowledged in the appraisal of America's global influence. Yet today the control of men and of societies requires, before anything else, the manipulation of words and images. Whatever the degree of raw power that can be brought to bear on a people, it is unavailing in the long run (that may not be so very long in arriving) if it cannot make its objectives seem, if not attractive, at least benign to those it seeks to control. The methods and the messages of communications, therefore, are the most significant and indispensable instruments of modern power-wielders. The attitudinal state of a population helps to determine its political behavior. And beliefs and opinions are remarkably vulnerable to the sort of modern mass communications that the American system of power uses with fantastic dexterity.

Commercially produced entertainment and recreation are the chief channels that convey internationally the values and life-styles of U.S. corporate capitalism, but the information generated directly by the sizable American business community overseas also is imposing and far-reaching in its effects. It is difficult to overstate the impact of the promotional and "research" activities of the large corporations on peoples subjected to them. Moreover, since the agent of influence is

46   *New York Stock Exchange Directory, 1969* (New York: Commerce Clearing House, 1969), pp. 697–98.

often unrecognized as such, the more powerful though less measurable it is likely to be.

The great American stream of business-financed and commercially saturated communications pouring through the mass media are aimed at protecting the physical operations of American enterprises abroad, as well as at fostering values and attitudes of privatism and consumerism which are the ultimate supports of the business system. Few are the regions removed from this wave of commercialism. The culture of American business is enveloping everything in its path as it appeals to individualistic instincts while it reinforces its messages with the imagery of technological gadgetry and consumer delights.

It derives strength also from its utilization of two of the currently strongest human desires: the yearning of people everywhere for an end to bloody conflict and warfare, with some condition of universality in their place, and the equally powerful popular impulse to freedom. Accordingly, the rhetoric of corporate communications, disseminated one way or another through the mass media, makes much of internationalism and freedom of the special sort that maximizes private benefits.[47] Identifying human freedom with property ownership and classifying the worldwide activities of business corporations as an inspiring model of internationalism provide the chief ideological underpinnings of today's business-originated messages. For instance, the advice of Tom Sutton, executive vice-president-international of J. Walter Thompson, the world's largest advertising agency, on this subject is forthright: "I believe it is the job of international organizations such as [the] International Advertising Association and the International Chamber of Commerce to preach the gospel of freedom and to see that the best systems of control and restraint—in areas where they [*sic*] may have to be some—are exported for adoption elsewhere, and not the worst."[48]

On the internationalist theme, Robert Sarnoff, chairman of the board and president of RCA, the electronics super-corporation, invokes the image of a boundary-free world, accessible to everyone but especially to the undertakings of the few hundred multinational corporations. In a call for a "global common market of communications," Sarnoff enthusiastically recommends reducing national responsibility in communications so that it can be considered a "global resource." Such a development, he claims,

47 I have written of this in *Mass Communications and American Empire* (New York: Augustus M. Kelley, 1969), esp. Ch. 1, "Electronics and Economics Serving an American Century."

48 Tom Sutton, "A Profits' Prophet," *International Advertiser* 10, no. 2 (1969): 6.

would foster an increasing worldwide flow of information that would bring benefits as tangible as the increasing trade among the countries of Western Europe. The distribution of knowledge by such a system would provide greater stimulus to growth than any conceivable program of economic aid.

For the public of all countries, it would provide entertainment, cultural and informational programming from abroad as a routine rather than a rarity.

Furthermore, Sarnoff adds:[49]

As data transmission becomes less and less expensive, we will see greater use of computerized controls and even long-distance time-sharing to strengthen the multinational firm as a vehicle for the transfer of technology. The increases in production and productivity, resulting from the global surge of business information, could parallel the economic advances made in the common market over the past 20 years.

All this would occur apparently in the absence of genuine international structures of control and alongside diminished national authority. Beneficiaries in this context could only be the giant, transnational corporations.

Economic output, technological mastery, and military power have been the traditional strengths of the American corporate economy. Now, increasing reliance is being placed on communications control. The heavy informational flow produced and supported by American companies overseas makes a powerful contribution to the domestic maintenance and global extension of the business system and its values.

49   Robert Sarnoff, "Toward a Global Common Market of Communications," address before the American Chamber of Commerce in France and the American Club of Paris, France, February 12, 1970, p. 15.

fourteen

Nuclear Desalting in the Middle East

Paul D. Wolfowitz

IN recent years the U.S. foreign aid program has come under strong criticism from individuals and groups that formerly supported it, on the grounds that it is too interventionist. Bilateral aid, it is charged, involves the United States in determinations it lacks the competence to make, is demeaning to the recipient countries over whom control is thus exercised, and is ultimately self-defeating because short-run political considerations are too often allowed to jeopardize long-term objectives of economic development. An additional criticism, and perhaps the reason for much of the current opposition, is that bilateral aid brings with it unwanted political and military commitments by involving the United States too closely with established foreign governments. The solution proposed by such men as Senator J. William Fulbright is greater use of multilateral channels for aid.[1]

The present paper considers some of the potential consequences of interventionist foreign aid when the intervention is guided by neither political nor economic objectives, but by technological ones. Since President Eisenhower's famous "Atoms for Peace" address at the United Nations in 1953, the United States has actively encouraged the development of peaceful nuclear technology throughout the world. This encouragement, to which the United States is now further committed by Article V of the Nuclear Non-Proliferation Treaty, has included both the dissemination of technical information and the provision of technical and financial assistance in the construction of commercial nuclear power reactors. The great benefits predicted to

1 J. William Fulbright, *The Arrogance of Power* (New York: Random House, 1966), p. 223.

come from the peaceful atom have been promised to developed and developing nations alike. Indeed, it has often been suggested that nuclear power can play a particularly important role in closing the gap between rich and poor nations.

Two decades of development of peaceful nuclear technology have nonetheless indicated that nuclear energy can compete successfully with fossil fuels only in very large power plants. However, few developing countries have a demand for electricity great enough to absorb the output of a large plant efficiently. There has thus been little immediate prospect for peaceful nuclear development in these countries on the basis solely of electric power production. By combining power production with sea water distillation, however, it appears possible even in less industrialized countries to utilize nuclear power reactors that are large enough to take advantage of the critical economies of scale that characterize nuclear technology. This fact links naturally the Atoms for Peace program and the more recent Water for Peace proposal that President Johnson heralded as providing the only commodity that "can give future generations a chance to escape wholesale misery and wholesale starvation."[2]

From its inception, among the most obvious candidates for the Water for Peace program have been countries of the Middle East, a region where the scarcity of both water and peace strikes even the most casual observer. The most detailed proposal to date for a foreign nuclear desalting plant has been an American-Israeli project to build a nuclear plant on Israel's Mediterranean coast for the joint production of water and electric power. In June, 1964, President Johnson and Israeli Premier Eshkol agreed to set up a commission to explore the prospects for desalting. Kaiser Engineers completed a detailed feasibility study in 1966 for a plant with a capacity of 100 million gallons per day.[3] Negotiations between the United States and Israel on financing arrangements were in progress when war broke out in 1967. Since that time the project has been held in abeyance. Shortly after the announcement of the Israeli study, the United Arab Republic expressed its interest in the use of nuclear desalting to provide supplemental water for agriculture. In the late fall of 1964 a team of American experts visited the UAR to examine its proposed Borg

2   Lyndon Baines Johnson, speech to the First International Symposium on Water Desalination, Washington, D.C., October 6, 1965.
3   Kaiser Engineers, *Engineering Feasibility and Economic Study for Dual-Purpose Electric Power-Water Desalting Plant for Israel* (Oakland, Calif.: Prepared for U.S.-Israeli Joint Board by Kaiser Engineers in association with Catalytic Construction Company, Philadelphia, Report no. 66-1-RE, January, 1966). Referred to hereafter as *Kaiser Report*.

El-Arab project.[4] The UAR government requested preliminary bids from manufacturers at the end of 1964 and the following spring announced that it had tentatively chosen Westinghouse as the contractor.[5]

The June war of 1967 pushed both proposals into the background. While not abandoning its interest in water, the American government became more openly preoccupied with the task of securing peace in the region. It was at this point that a proposal came from former Atomic Energy Commission (AEC) Chairman Lewis Strauss, with the endorsement of former President Eisenhower. It suggested that massive investment in nuclear desalting could not only bring tremendous economic benefits but could make a major contribution to peace as well. The Strauss plan, envisioning three large nuclear desalting plants to provide water for arid areas of Egypt, Jordan, and Israel, was larger by an order of magnitude than the earlier Israeli plant proposed by the Kaiser Engineers, itself an order of magnitude larger than any desalting plant in existence. The objectives of the Strauss plan were also more ambitious than those of the earlier proposals. Whereas the earlier projects aimed primarily at promoting economic development, Strauss suggested that his plan could provide the "new and dramatic element . . . required to establish a climate in which peace can begin to be negotiated."[6] It was hoped that massive American aid for desalting would provide an inducement to negotiation and cooperation between Israel and her Arab neighbors, that it would provide a means for the satisfactory resettlement of the Palestinian refugees, and that it would promote economic development and thereby peace.

Our concern in this paper is not so much these intended objectives of nuclear desalting proposals for the Middle East, but rather some unintended, and usually unexamined, consequences of developing peaceful nuclear technology in a region marked by war and conflict. The last of the objectives just mentioned, the promotion of peace through economic development, has been characterized by Leonard

4   U.S. Desalting Team (Melvin E. Mattson, Office of Saline Water; Jack O. Roberts, U.S. Atomic Energy Commission; Lawrence R. Swarner, Bureau of Reclamation), *Preliminary Report on Proposed Borg El-Arab (Sidi Kreir) Project in the United Arab Republic*, May, 1965, revised October, 1965.

5   Michel d'Orival, *Water Desalting and Nuclear Energy* (Munich: Karl Thiemig Verlag, 1967), p. 178.

6   The full text of the Strauss memorandum, and the most complete discussion thereof, can be found in U.S. Congress, Senate Committee on Foreign Relations, *Construction of Nuclear Desalting Plants in the Middle East, Hearings*, before a subcommittee of the Committee on Foreign Relations, Senate, 90th Cong., 1st sess., 1967, pp. 60–62.

Binder as "an attractive idea, drawn from the mythology of the idea of perpetual progress. . . . But even if we should accept for a moment this mythology of benign progress, how could we be sure that development would bring benevolent peacefulness before it would bring the material capacity to fight and win a war?"[7] This reservation applies with particular force to proposals for promoting peaceful nuclear technology. The overlap between the peaceful atom and the military atom is considerable, and the introduction of nuclear technology on the scale proposed could materially increase the likelihood of nuclear weapons being introduced into the Middle East. It is perhaps not surprising that the *Kaiser Report*, focusing on the engineering and economics of a desalting plant in Israel, should have ignored this problem.[8] It is nonetheless curious that the problem received so little attention from Admiral Strauss, whose major interest was in bringing peace to the area. The explanation lies in Admiral Strauss's suggestion that the operation of the plants would be made the responsibility of the International Atomic Energy Agency. The IAEA, he added, "would also have jurisdiction and control of reprocessing of fuel elements to insure that all nuclear material was accounted for." Presumably the potentially destructive nuclear materials produced as a byproduct in the peaceful reactors could thus be controlled, and the benefits of the desalting plants could be enjoyed without risk.

This brings us to a central question. Is it possible to control the applications of a new and potentially dangerous technology while encouraging its development in foreign countries?[9] To a certain extent, as will become clear in the discussion that follows, the question of control is a technological one and hence properly the subject of a technical analysis. But, as will also become clear, the possibility of control depends as much or more on political considerations. The

7 Leonard Binder, *The Middle East Crisis: Background and Issues* (Chicago: University of Chicago Center for Policy Study, 1967), p. 26.

8 The *Kaiser Report* went so far as to recommend the construction of a large nuclear reactor in Israel only eleven miles from the then Egyptian-held Gaza Strip, without so much as a mention of the possibility of hostile military action.

9 The desirability of keeping countries of the Middle East from acquiring nuclear weapons is simply assumed here, since detailed discussion of this assumption would go beyond the scope of the present paper. However, even those who are optimistic about the consequences of an increase in the number of nuclear powers usually make an exception regarding the Middle East. Occasionally it is suggested that the possession of nuclear weapons by Israel alone could have stabilizing consequences. (See for example George H. Quester, "Israel and the Non-Proliferation Treaty," *Bulletin of the Atomic Scientists* 25, no. 6 [June 1969]: 7–9.) Such suggestions, however, generally neglect the difficulties for Israel of developing a secure retaliatory force, and minimize the adverse consequences of reactions by outside powers.

technological and political factors are interwoven to a high degree. Analyses focusing on one but not the other inevitably go astray, producing results that are less than helpful.

THE PROBLEM OF CONTROLLING
PEACEFUL NUCLEAR TECHNOLOGY

The imposition of safeguards, as envisioned in the Strauss proposal, in the Nuclear Non-Proliferation Treaty, and in all U.S. programs for peaceful nuclear assistance, reflects concern with the fact that all large reactors produce large quantities of plutonium, the essential material required for the production of crude nuclear bombs of the type dropped on Nagasaki.[10] A medium-sized reactor of the type proposed for Israel in the 1966 study would produce about ninety kilograms of plutonium annually, enough to produce between ten and twenty weapons per year. Safeguards are intended to insure that this material is not used for weapons production.

The progress in nuclear technology which has been achieved in many countries of the world in the last two decades, and the widespread U.S. dissemination of formerly classified technical information that encouraged this progress, have made it impossible to talk about "atomic secrecy" as a means of controlling the applications of nuclear technology. Control of nuclear proliferation now depends on making the construction of nuclear weapons as costly as possible for the country involved and as visible as possible to the outside world. Increasing the visibility of a decision to produce nuclear weapons is in fact a way of increasing the cost, both directly in terms of world public opinion (particularly if the country involved has undertaken treaty obligations) and indirectly in terms of the risks that may be incurred if the production of nuclear weapons is discovered before it has been completed. Increasing the visibility of a decision to build also means increasing the time during which sanctions and other pressures can be brought to bear to prevent the nuclear force from actually coming into being.

The possession of large peaceful power reactors can reduce both the visibility and the cost of a decision to build rudimentary plutonium bombs of the Nagasaki type. Let us first examine the matter of costs.

10 The other material that can be used in making atomic bombs, and which is required for more advanced fusion bombs and low-yield fission weapons, is uranium enriched in the isotope U-235. The enrichment process is so complex and so expensive that, for the present, it can be ruled out as a route to nuclear weapons for any country of the Middle East.

Once a country possesses reactor-produced plutonium, two major hurdles remain on the way to producing weapons. First, it must separate the plutonium from other materials, particularly uranium, contained in the spent fuel elements of the reactor. Second, it must construct the bomb mechanism itself, a problem largely of electronic and chemical engineering. The costs of both of these latter processes are much smaller than the cost of the earlier stage of reactor construction. Beaton and Maddox estimate the investment cost alone of the reactor for a small plutonium production program to be three to four times the cost of a corresponding plant for the chemical separation of the plutonium.[11] This probably understates the difference between plutonium production costs and plutonium separation costs. Thus the construction of peaceful nuclear power reactors could help the recipient country complete what is by far the most costly stage of a nuclear weapons program.

Perhaps even more important, the possession of reactors would greatly reduce what we have called the visibility of a decision to produce nuclear weapons. Since the construction of the actual device is a project that could apparently be largely completed before any fissile material actually becomes available, only the problem of plutonium separation would stand between the decision to obtain nuclear weapons and its realization. Not only is there then only one step, and therefore less time, required for the production of weapons, but the process at that point is probably less conspicuous than the construction of a reactor.

Israel may in fact already have surmounted many of the hurdles mentioned above. A small reactor at Dimona, built with substantial French assistance and apparently with no bilateral controls, is capable of producing annually four to six kilograms of plutonium (or enough for one bomb). American scientists have apparently "visited" Dimona on a regular basis, a procedure that is obviously far less thorough than official inspection but that may be sufficient for determining the uses to which a small reactor (like the Dimona facility) is being put.[12]

Considerable ambiguity still surrounds the status of the Israeli nuclear program. But whether or not Israel already has plutonium,

11   Leonard Beaton and John Maddox, *The Spread of Nuclear Weapons* (New York: Praeger, for the Institute of Strategic Studies, London, 1962), pp. 19, 22.
12   Even a recent report that Israel may already have nuclear weapons suggests that the plutonium used was obtained directly from France, not produced at Dimona; see Hedrick Smith, "U.S. Assumes the Israelis have A-Bomb or Its Parts," *New York Times*, July 18, 1970, p. 8.

the problem of controlling the application of non-military power reactors must be carefully considered. First, it would be difficult and probably dangerous to build nuclear desalting plants for Israel while refusing similar aid to Arab nations. Second, no matter what the present Israeli capability, we must be wary of the consequences of adding to it.

Controlling Clandestine Diversion

The "safeguards" referred to in discussions of nuclear technology have clear limitations. The use of this term should not call up visions of padlocked plutonium stores under twenty-four-hour guard. Safeguards do not provide physical control over the diversion of plutonium from peaceful to military uses. Their function is simply to provide early warning if any diversion does take place, so that sanctions and adverse world reactions may come to bear in time to prevent the production of nuclear weapons.

Even with respect to this somewhat limited function, there are a number of reasons, both technical and political, for questioning the effectiveness of safeguards, at least in the circumstances of the Middle East. Not the least of these is the lack of sufficient inspectors and an adequate budget for the IAEA. Although it would cost very little if reactors in the Middle East were subject to particularly thorough inspection, this discriminatory treatment would raise some sensitive political issues.[13] But this is only one of the minor problems in making safeguards effective.

American officials have stated that the IAEA "now has in operation an effective safeguards system that is suitable for application to a wide variety of peaceful nuclear activities."[14] This evidently does not mean that they believe inspection can be expected to detect all possible diversions of potential weapons material, no matter how small. AEC Chairman Glenn T. Seaborg himself has cautioned that "safeguards are not foolproof, nor should we develop a complacency that they are all we need to prevent or detect nuclear weapons pro-

13 The political sensitivity of this issue will be even greater where countries have signed the Nuclear Non-Proliferation Treaty. It is particularly significant to note that in the course of discussion of the draft treaty in the Eighteen-Nation Disarmament Conference, it was the representative of the United Arab Republic who called specifically for a nondiscriminatory "compulsory and uniform" application of safeguards under the treaty. Cited in Mason Willrich, "The Treaty on Non-Proliferation of Nuclear Weapons: Nuclear Technology Confronts World Politics," *Yale Law Journal* 77, no. 8 (July 1968): 1485, n. 89.

14 Glenn T. Seaborg, "The International Atom—A New Appraisal," the Rosenfield Lecture delivered at Grinnell College, Grinnell, Iowa, January 30, 1969.

grams being carried on secretly in violation of treaty commitments."[15] Apparently, as William Hoehn pointed out, "current safeguards methods lack the necessary discrimination to determine, in the absence of direct evidence, that small diversions from power reactors have occurred."[16]

The problems of inspection are particularly acute for chemical reprocessing plants, in which plutonium is extracted from the spent nuclear fuel. The recovery of plutonium from the spent fuel is desirable for economic reasons, even if there is no intention to build bombs. If and as nuclear power grows in the Middle East, the possibility of peaceful plutonium separation facilities will grow with it.[17] Although it is extremely doubtful that independent separation facilities would be economically justified even for the very large plants of the Strauss plan, it should be remembered that India built her own separation plant at a very early stage in her nuclear power development.[18] A report prepared for the AEC by the Battelle Institute concludes that "if there is not continuous inspection, the plant operator could easily divert 2 to 5 per cent of the throughput without being detected," while continuous inspection "would unquestionably be too expensive" and would "create intolerable interference problems with plant personnel."[19]

Technical obstacles to effective inspection are only one of the means a country might exploit if it were seriously intent on covert diversion. Human and political obstacles to the inspection process are perhaps more important. These begin with the nontrivial problem of securing international agreement to the details of inspection arrangements. H. D. Smyth, U.S. representative to the IAEA, acknowledged that "we may have to be satisfied with a system of . . . international safeguards that is perhaps 95 to 96 per cent effective in detecting diversion and is accepted by 98 per cent or 90 per cent of the members," because that would be much more useful than a system which is 99.44 per cent effective and accepted by only 10

15   Ibid., p. 7.
16   William E. Hoehn, "Clandestine Diversion of Nuclear Source Materials in a Power Reactor," in *Proceedings*, Symposium on Safeguards Research and Development, Lemont, Illinois, June 26, 1967 (Lemont, Ill.: Argonne National Laboratory, WASH-1076, June, 1967), p. 86.
17   Quester, in the article cited above, writes that as "newer and larger reactors . . . come into use . . . a plutonium separation plant may . . . become advisable. . . . Still further along, an investment in an enrichment plant for uranium might become advisable."
18   Beaton and Maddox, *The Spread of Nuclear Weapons*, pp. 141–42.
19   D. P. Granquist and R. A. Schneider, *Application of Safeguards to Nuclear Fuel Processing Plants* (Richland, Wash.: Pacific Northwest Laboratory, BNWL–301, September, 1966), p. 4.

or 20 percent of the member nations.[20] This level of effectiveness may be adequate in most parts of the world, but not in the special circumstances of the Middle East.

Inspection also requires a considerable degree of cooperation between the inspector and the plant personnel. This need arises in part because determination of the amount of plutonium that should be in the reactor depends on rather detailed information on the plant operation, and this requires access to plant records. When the IAEA made a much-publicized first inspection of Japan's first commercial power reactor at Tokai-Mura, the inspectors encountered not only technical difficulties of the sort already mentioned. They also discovered that all the plant records are in Japanese. The inspectors were warned by the staff of the Japan Atomic Power Company that "they should not expect many English speaking senior staff members to accompany them each time, when inspections become routine and take several days." They said that they "have to consider the station operation first and senior engineers are likely to be very much occupied with that job."[21]

The dependence of the inspector on the cooperation, and even the good will, of the plant staff, plus an ordinary human desire to get along with one's colleagues, combine to make it unlikely that inspection will be a real adversary proceeding, in which every suspicious operation is subjected to exhaustive and hence costly and time-consuming investigation. Far more probable would be a relationship like that developed by IAEA inspector Carlos Buchler during four years of inspecting Japanese nuclear facilities:

> As we learned to work with our Japanese colleagues the atmosphere in which our activities took place became more relaxed. . . . One difficulty which I have always found particularly hard to overcome is the natural feeling on the part of the facility operator that he is, in the eyes of the inspector, not 'trustworthy.' . . . Although it is possible to attempt to dispel this attitude by way of reasoning, it is my considered view that the only effective method of overcoming it is through patient and prolonged cooperation between facility personnel and safeguards' staff.[22]

Some inspectors will be less amiable than this, but it will not relieve them of the need for cooperation from the plant staff, or of the need

20 H. D. Smyth, "Background of International Safeguards," in *Proceedings, Symposium on Safeguards Research and Development*, p. 16.
21 "A Learning Process at Tokai-Mura," *Nuclear Industry* 15, no. 7 (July 1968): 29.
22 Letter to the Editor, *Atoms in Japan* 12, no. 5 (May 1968): 10–11.

for approval by the country being inspected, that has the right to reject individual inspectors.

The critical question is how much material a country could hope to divert from a reactor without risking early detection. Answers to this question are necessarily uncertain. Even if one knew the precise limits that unavoidable measurement uncertainties place on detection techniques, it would still be impossible to know what loopholes remain for an ingenious thief to exploit. The indications are that undetected diversions could not be very large. Hoehn mentions a 5 percent diversion rate as a probable upper limit.[23] Nevertheless, even as little as 5 percent diversion from the moderate-sized desalting plant proposed for Israel would provide enough plutonium for one bomb each year. The same rate of diversion from the larger plants of the Strauss plan would of course accumulate plutonium at an even greater rate. Although such a rate of plutonium production would be insignificant in comparison to the potential military requirements of countries like West Germany and Japan, even a single crude nuclear bomb in the Middle East could have significant, and disastrous, consequences. In the context of the Middle East strategic quantities of fissionable materials may be very small, too small to be detected with great certainty by safeguards inspection and procedures.[24]

The Problem of Overt Diversion

Safeguards, at their best, do no more than give warning of attempts to divert nuclear materials to military purposes. Therefore, their effectiveness depends ultimately on the pressures that can be exerted on a country violating a peaceful uses agreement. This means that safeguards are of no help in dealing with a problem that, in the words of one observer, "like an hereditary defect in the family line, is mentioned only in a whisper, if discussed at all"[25]—the open diversion of plutonium from peaceful nuclear facilities.

Rather than risk being detected in the diversion of small quantities of fissile material, a country might decide to renounce its agreements openly and thereby gain access to the entire output of the facility.

23 Hoehn, "Clandestine Diversion of Nuclear Source Materials in a Power Reactor," pp. 141–42.

24 Evidence of plutonium diversion would probably be highly circumstantial. When international agreements are violated, it is not infrequent for even the offended party to use whatever ambiguity the agreement or the evidence of the violation allows in order to preserve the appearance of amicable international relations. The possibility that a safeguard alarm could be genuinely in error would make governments more reluctant to take serious action on such a basis.

25 Hoehn, "Clandestine Diversion of Nuclear Source Materials in a Power Reactor," p. 85.

This course of action would also enable the offending nation to operate the facility in the manner most compatible with military needs. The possibility of preventing such an action depends not on safeguards at all, but on the belief that strong sanctions would be invoked against violators.

The most directly effective sanction, and the one least painful to apply, would be to close down the plutonium-producing facility by peaceful means. The reactors that the United States supplies abroad use enriched uranium as fuel. Discussions of safeguards assume that the United States would immediately stop fuel shipments if the agreements under which the reactors are supplied were violated. Unfortunately, for several reasons this control is not nearly as effective as it appears, and it will become less effective with the passage of time.

1. A reactor of the type proposed for the Israeli desalting plant is refueled only once a year, with one-third of the fuel replaced each time. The unloaded fuel batch thus contains approximately a full year's output of plutonium. With the use of the new fuel shipment the reactor could be run for a least another year. Plainly, there is no capability for shutting down the reactor instantaneously, and the interim production of plutonium could be enough for forty or more bombs.

2. There is no reason to assume that a desalting plant would be run with an enriched uranium reactor, unless specific restrictions to this effect are imposed by the United States. Natural uranium reactors might be used instead, precisely to be less dependent on the United States for fuel. This may have been the motivation behind Argentina's recent decision to purchase a natural uranium reactor from West Germany.[26] When Egypt engaged consultants in 1963 to study the possibility of building a nuclear power plant, it requested that it be "preferably one using natural uranium."[27] The fuel for such a reactor could be obtained much more easily, as the sources of natural uranium are numerous and much more difficult to control.

3. The near-monopoly position which the United States now enjoys as a supplier of enriched uranium may not continue indefinitely. Besides the possibility of changes in policy by the present producing nations—Britain, China, France, and the Soviet Union—there are already strong indications that a num-

26 *Nucleonics Week* 9, no. 18 (May 2, 1968), p. 3.
27 "Egypt to Build 150–MWE Nuclear Power Plant," *Nucleonics* 21, no. 6 (June 1963): 31.

ber of West European countries (among them the Netherlands and West Germany), as well as Japan, are planning to develop their own facilities for enriching uranium. This development is likely to be accelerated if breakthroughs are achieved in certain new enrichment technologies on which active research is under way abroad.[28]

4. In an apparent attempt to discourage the development of foreign enrichment facilities, the United States has announced a new policy under which it will agree to "preposition" enriched uranium fuel as much as five years in advance of actual needs, thus enabling foreign users to obtain a considerable degree of independence from the United States.[29] It might, of course, be possible to deny this option at least to countries in the Middle East. But, again, this would constitute politically sensitive discrimination, which will become even more difficult if the Nuclear Non-Proliferation Treaty goes into effect.

It is therefore probable that only direct military action by the United States could stop the operation of a Middle East desalting plant in time to frustrate an attempt at overt diversion. Such a course might prove advisable, all things considered, but its undesirable consequences are obvious. The United States would almost certainly try less direct forms of pressure to induce the offending nation to reverse its course. The sanctions available may, however, be much too weak to influence a decision of this importance, especially in the case of the Arab states. Even in the case of Israel, where strong pressures could be applied, their success is not certain and reliance on them imposes costs in terms of other policy objectives.

Long-Range Effects of Peaceful Nuclear Technology

The military impact of peaceful nuclear technology goes beyond the production of weapons material by peaceful reactors. As Seaborg has noted, "A country which increases its capabilities to develop and exploit the peaceful uses of nuclear energy by training people or by building up its scientific and industrial capacity, inescapably increases its potential ability to develop and manufacture nuclear weapons.[30]

The contribution of power reactors, even large ones, to the growth of this double-edged technological capability may be less important

28   See, for example, "Nuclear Enrichment: Gut Question, What Will Private Ownership Cost the Customer?" *Nuclear Industry* 15, nos. 11–12 (November–December 1968): 23–28; and "Alternate Enrichment Methods," ibid., pp. 69–72.

29   "AEC Offers Enrichment Customers Five-Year Inventory Option," ibid., p. 76.

30   Seaborg, "The International Atom," p. 2.

than that of smaller programs of aid for nuclear education and research. Nevertheless, they would provide experience and employment for personnel who could eventually be useful in a weapons program. Moreover, as the civilian nuclear power industry grows, the problem of control grows with it, particularly if a point is reached at which plutonium reprocessing plants can be justified.

Consideration of the long-term effects of nuclear technology is especially important in weighing the desirability of building the first large plant or plants in the Middle East, because construction of these first plants is likely to strengthen pressures for more. Excessive importance is already attached by many developing countries to the prestige derived from the possession of nuclear technology. Construction of a few nuclear plants could weaken arguments against the construction of others. In view of the phenomenal fossil fuel resources of the Middle East there are probably few locations where the use of nuclear energy would be economically justified. Nevertheless, the mere existence of such facilities could be taken as a demonstration of their economic feasibility. Since decisions on power investment are usually made by governments or government corporations, considerations of prestige may override considerations of economics. Attempts to limit the growth of peaceful nuclear technology are therefore most likely to be effective before there has been any substantial development, when indigenous pressures for nuclear development are likely to be weakest.

Support of Peaceful Technology as a Means of Control

Seaborg and others have argued that, however weak the control that the United States exercises over nuclear developments in which it participates, it is preferable to the independent and therefore unregulated development of peaceful nuclear technology.[31] This argument has a good deal of validity. For example, the policy of prepositioning shipments of enriched uranium fuel as far as five years in advance weakens American control over enriched fueled reactors. Over a longer term, however, it may delay the development of foreign enrichment facilities that would weaken American control even more.

The difficulty with this line of reasoning is that it is much too general. We have seen a number of times that determination of an appropriate policy depends critically on specific circumstances, and that the circumstances of the Middle East are different in essential respects from those of Western Europe. In the present context, two

31 Ibid., p. 6.

important differences must be noted. First, the controls the United States retains over reactors built with its assistance are of much greater value in Europe than in the Middle East. Not only are treaty obligations likely to have greater importance, but also safeguard mechanisms will be more effective when strategically significant quantities of nuclear materials are large, as in Europe, than when they are very small, as in the Middle East. The second and critical difference is that early development of nuclear technology in Europe is a certainty, even if the United States witholds its assistance, whereas the development of peaceful nuclear technology in the Middle East without American assistance still seems rather distant.

The critical question is not whether science and technology can be kept under lock and key, but whether they can be delayed instead of encouraged. The answer depends not only on the technological capabilities of the countries in question but also on the incentives for technological development. Clearly the contrast between the situations of Europe and Japan on the one hand, and the Middle East on the other, with respect to the availability of fossil fuels, bears significantly on the incentives for nuclear power. As we have seen earlier, desalting appears to offer the most attractive economic prospects for large-scale nuclear technology of any of the possible peaceful applications in the Middle East. We will examine these prospects in a moment.

Aid for nuclear desalting has further been suggested as a means of inducing countries—in particular Israel—to sign the Nuclear Non-Proliferation Treaty, and thereby securing some control over possible military developments of nuclear technology, such as the Dimona reactor.[32] But except for the possible military value of developing peaceful nuclear technology, the importance of desalting aid as an incentive for signature is, again, a function of its economic value. It must be compared with other kinds of economic inducements. Noneconomic inducements may be necessary to obtain Israel's signature, but in view of the objectives of the Nuclear Non-Proliferation Treaty, the chief noneconomic benefit to be derived from nuclear assistance is an exceedingly strange inducement to offer.

32 The importance of an Israeli signature of the Nuclear Non-Proliferation Treaty consists primarily in the symbolic value attributable to a formal renunciation of nuclear weapons. There is a danger that the treaty would prevent only actual deployment, while leaving Israel free to complete most of the prior steps in weapons development: adherence to the treaty would facilitate the construction of large nuclear reactors, and might even legitimate the open development of facilities such as "peaceful" plutonium separation plants, making possible a rapid movement from peaceful to military technology if the escape clause of Article X is eventually invoked. The same considerations apply with little modification to the case of Egypt.

Economics of Desalting

The economics of nuclear desalting are critical, not only for determining the direct value of the proposed projects, but also for judging the probable growth of peaceful nuclear technology in the absence of U.S. assistance. In addition, economic benefits determine the value of such projects as inducements to secure adherence to the Nuclear Non-Proliferation Treaty. Here we can only summarize some of the more important economic considerations.[33]

The investment involved in proposed desalting projects is large by the standard of other development projects in the region. The investment in the Israeli plant proposed by the Kaiser engineers would be at least $200 million. The plan proposed by Admiral Strauss would entail investment of more than $1 billion—probably more than the cost of the Aswan High Dam, which is intended to provide ten times as much water. The hint that the water to be provided by nuclear desalting will be very expensive, by current standards, is one of the key points which must be considered in evaluating the project.

The report of the Kaiser engineers cites figures for water costs as low as 28.6 cents per thousand gallons. Admiral Strauss uses a figure of 22 cents per thousand gallons. Both estimates greatly understate the probable cost of water, for the following reasons.

1) Both estimates are based on costs for reactors and other equipment that correspond to prices quoted in 1965, before any significant commercial sales of nuclear reactors had been made and when, for a number of reasons, reactor prices were artificially low. Since that time costs of reactors and desalting equipment have increased at a rate far exceeding that of the general inflation. The 22-cent figure cited by Admiral Strauss appears to stem from estimates prepared for a giant nuclear power and desalting project that the Metropolitan Water District of Southern California planned. That project was abandoned in 1968 after *estimated* capital costs had increased from $444 million to $765 million.[34]

2) Because of the tremendous investment involved, the costs of desalting depend on the percentage of time the plant stands idle.

33   Details of the arguments summarized here are to be found in William E. Hoehn, *The Economics of Nuclear Reactors for Power and Desalting* (Santa Monica, Calif.: RAND Corporation, RM-5227, November, 1967), particularly Ch. X, and in a RAND Research Memorandum by this writer now in preparation, *Middle East Nuclear Desalting: Economic and Political Considerations*.

34   *Nucleonics Week* 9, no. 21 (May 23, 1968): 2. It should be noted that the latter figure was still only an estimate and did not represent any actual construction experience.

About one month each year is needed to refuel the reactor. Planned and unplanned maintenance can increase idle time further, particularly since radiation hazards pose great difficulties in the maintenance of nuclear facilities. The *Kaiser Report*, assuming that the plant runs properly practically all of the time it is not shut down for refueling, uses an average plant availability of 85 percent. Nuclear plants to date have encountered repeated operational difficulties, limiting availability to about 70 percent at best. Although performance should improve with experience, the 85 percent figure used by the Kaiser engineers is an optimistic upper limit. It is very unlikely to be sustained, particularly in view of the added difficulties entailed in water desalting and in foreign operations.

3) The estimates cited give only the cost of water *at the plant*. This excludes the considerable costs, and water losses, entailed in storage and conveyance. Considerable storage capacity, for example, is necessitated by the seasonal character of agricultural water consumption. Conveyance will be important, particularly for very large plants.

4) The most important single factor in determining water costs is the interest rate, since the projects are extremely capital intensive. The Kaiser engineers estimate costs of 28.6, 43.4, and 67.0 cents per thousand gallons, corresponding to interest rates of 1.6, 4.6, and 8.4 percent, respectively. My own estimates, taking conservative account of the implications of the three points above, indicate water costs of about 45 cents per thousand gallons at the 1.6 percent interest rate and $1.00 per thousand at 8.4 percent. The question of the appropriate rate to apply is thus a complex one. The Israeli government uses a rate of 8 percent as a criterion for evaluating development projects, and there is considerable evidence to suggest that the marginal return to capital in Israel is, in fact, even higher. It seems a reasonable assumption, in view of the scarcity of capital in Egypt, that the opportunity cost of capital there is higher still.

The opportunity cost of capital is a measure of the probable return to capital if invested elsewhere in the economy. This is the appropriate measure of the cost of nuclear desalting as an alternative to other forms of aid. By this standard, a reasonable estimate of the real cost of desalted sea water, after delivery, would be in the neighborhood of $1.00 per thousand gallons.

The Value of Desalted Water

At $1.00 per thousand gallons desalted water still costs only a fraction of a cent per pound. But the Middle East needs water for agricultural use, not direct human consumption. Agriculture consumes enormous quantities of water, on the order of thousands of tons per acre. Even costs of 5 cents per thousand gallons (about $16 per acre-foot) are considered high for agricultural water in the United States. It is impossible, however, to estimate the value of water in the Middle East simply on the basis of American experience.

One Israeli economist has estimated that at present the value of agricultural output attributable to a thousand gallons of water in that country is between 11 and 19 cents.[35] The upper estimate represents output measured in producer prices; the lower estimate corresponds to market prices. The difference is the subsidy paid to producers by the government, so the relevant figure for our purposes is the market price of 11 cents.

The case of each of the Arab countries is different from either Israel or the United States, although reliable estimates are lacking. My own calculations based on official Egyptian output statistics indicate that the *total value* of output from water used in Egypt today is in the neighborhood of 5–10 cents per thousand gallons. This includes the contributions of all factors: labor, land, and capital, as well as water. It is difficult to say what portion of output should be attributed to these other factors, but 5 cents per thousand gallons appears to represent an *upper limit* for the value of water in Egyptian agriculture.

Given the apparent disparities between these figures and the cost estimates discussed in the preceding section, it is hardly surprising that Israel, for one, has shown little interest in using its own resources to develop nuclear desalting. At one time, before the 1967 war, some Israeli officials felt that with very favorable financial terms from the United States aid for desalting would be better than no American aid at all, but it seemed to be taken for granted that an equivalent amount of aid, with no strings attached, would not be spent in this manner.

The Prospects for Controlling Nuclear Development

It was seen earlier that no absolute guarantees exist to assure that assistance given for the development of peaceful nuclear technology will not be used to further military nuclear development. At any given point in time, varying degrees of control can be exercised over peaceful nuclear facilities, depending on the costs the United States

35   Ezra Sadan, "An Estimation of Returns to Irrigation Water in Israel with Reference to Seawater Desalting Proposals" (Berkeley: Giannini Foundation Research Report no. 305, November, 1969), p. 35.

is willing to incur. These include direct and indirect economic costs, such as salaries of inspectors, production losses during inspections, and the added costs, if any, of technological developments adapted for control purposes (such as the use of enriched uranium fuel). In addition, and perhaps more important, the exercise of control has political costs, such as the discriminatory treatment of different countries, the loss of bargaining power on other issues, or the allegation of violations on the basis of perhaps ambiguous evidence. It is obvious that these costs must be reckoned as part of the price of promoting peaceful nuclear technology; what is perhaps less obvious is that they also virtually guarantee that the degree of control exercised will be less than the technically possible maximum.

In considering policies for the long run, more attention might be given to the possibility of encouraging the development of competitive technologies, such as non-nuclear methods of desalting. There is nothing mysterious about the role of the atom in desalting sea water. Its function is simply to provide a heat source, a function that can also be performed by fossil fuels such as oil and natural gas found in abundance in many parts of the Middle East. Israel is a partial exception to this statement, and this helps to explain the conclusion of the Kaiser engineers that nuclear energy is preferable to fossil fuels for desalting in Israel. But two other factors further bias the results in favor of the nuclear alternative. First, the use of unreasonably low interest rates favors the more capital-intensive nuclear process. Second, the use of a fixed ratio between water and power production affects the comparison between nuclear and fossil fuels. For technical reasons, the lowest water costs for a fossil plant occur at lower water-power ratios than for a nuclear plant.[36] The water-power ratio used in the *Kaiser Report* tends to favor nuclear energy in comparison with fossil fuels. Elimination of these biases might alter the comparison between the two energy sources.

In any case, in view of the difficulties that attend the use of nuclear energy, the United States might consider subsidizing fossil fuel desalting if necessary to make it more competitive. Over the longer run, attention could be given to research on desalting processes which are more efficient users of fossil, rather than nuclear, fuels. Unfortunately, whatever biases currently exist in the American research effort are probably in the opposite direction.

36   See Wolfgang Fichtner, "Energy as a Factor of Planning in the Field of Sea Water Desalination," in *Proceedings*, First International Symposium on Water Desalination, Washington, D.C., 1965 (Washington: U.S. Department of the Interior, Office of Saline Water, 1967), p. 445.

The Underlying Fallacies

From the analysis of the costs and benefits of nuclear desalting in the Middle East presented in the preceding sections, it is difficult to understand why there should be any support at all for such projects in the United States. Four main explanations suggest themselves.

First, the key points of disagreement between critics and proponents center on the economic evaluation of the projects. The proponents for the most part are technologists who tend to pay more attention to technical feasibility, which is already well established, than to the more critical question of economic feasibility. Technology and economics cannot be neatly separated, but it may be noted that of the four factors discussed earlier as responsible for downward biases in estimates of desalting costs, only one, the assumption regarding plant performance, might be called primarily a question of engineering. The most critical single factor, the interest rate, is not a matter of technology at all. The evaluation of benefits is even more clearly a matter of economics. Moreover, the agricultural technology that is involved is not necessarily within the expertise of the AEC or the Oak Ridge National Laboratory. Some engineers, such as the Kaiser team, entirely ignore the need for economic evaluation of benefits and talk simply in terms of rigidly defined water "requirements" that are assumed not to depend significantly on costs.

Second, even with a positive view of the economics of desalting, one must still face the question of whether the economic advantages are sufficient to outweigh the nuclear proliferation hazards. Technologists tend to see the problem in terms of the technical possibility of controlling proliferation, not in terms of the vital question of the economic and political feasibility of imposing adequate controls. Technical sophistication is often accompanied by apparent naïveté regarding the political mechanisms, such as treaties, on which control is assumed to rest. Finally, the possibility of slowing technological development, rather than merely controlling its applications, is rarely considered seriously by technologists, who often regard the attempt to postpone technological progress as comparable to King Canute attempting to hold back the tides.

A third basis of support for nuclear desalting in the Middle East, despite its apparent limitations, is the belief that the situation there is so desperate and so fraught with danger that nothing that might contribute to peace should be rejected just because the costs are too high. Nevertheless, it is absurd to ignore relative costs and benefits. If the United States is prepared to provide $1 billion aid for an area where capital is scarce, better uses than nuclear desalting can be found. What may explain the choice of desalting is the attractiveness of a single large, visible project to American experts who are more familiar with the technological tools than with the specific needs of the Middle East. The proper way to use $1 billion might be in fifty different projects of $20 million each, but such a program lacks dramatic appeal and would certainly be more difficult to design.

A fourth major factor behind support for nuclear desalting is the commitment of various groups and individuals to the promotion of nuclear power for its own sake. The reasons for this commitment vary. Sometimes it may be the result of nothing more than the same kind of self-promotion that appears often in professional groups and bureaucratic organizations, that tend to see their own work as being more important and more deserving of public support than any other. This does not, however, explain support for nuclear development from disinterested members of the scientific community, from U.S. senators, or from the public at large. At the risk of oversimplifying a complex phenomenon, this often uncritical support seems to derive from a deeply ingrained faith in scientific progress and from the accompanying belief that the discovery of nuclear energy, which adds so much to man's power, must be capable of bringing virtually incalculable benefits. This commitment to nuclear energy is responsible in part for the bias against fossil fuels in current desalting proposals for the Middle East.

Technocracy and Common Sense

Must one conclude from the case we have examined that American promotion of particular technologies in foreign countries is bound to be misguided, and that it is therefore better to leave the determination of specific applications of aid to the judgment of the recipient nations? One of the difficulties with intervention is that it is based on the judgments of individuals and agencies that are removed from the actual countries affected. They are likely to be more familiar with tools, such as nuclear technology, than with the problems to which these tools must be applied. Similarly, the notions of the public interest that guide such intervention are often merely reflections of the private interests of the individuals or bureaucratic agencies involved. But transferring decisions from the U.S. government to foreign governments does not eliminate the influence of selfish interests of bureaucrats and bureaucracies. For example, it has been suggested by one Israeli[37] that much of the intangible benefit attrib-

37   Sadan, "An Estimation of Returns," p. 40.

uted to water in that country merely reflects the interests of officials who would have to contend with irate pressure groups if the present water allocation were made more efficient.

Even assuming that governments make decisions in accordance with their national interests, there is still the problem that national interests may conflict. Since the donor nation derives much of its benefit from the visibility of the project, rather than from ultimate economic effects, it may tend to take inadequate account of the usefulness of its aid for economic development. The recipient country, as the ultimate consumer, presumably has a greater interest in hardheaded examination of the economic benefits. This is one argument in favor of nonintervention, at least from the standpoint of economic development.

Economic criteria, however, cannot be the sole determinant of public policy. In the domestic area, increases in individual welfare cannot be equated with increases in social welfare unless, at a minimum, allowance is made for the secondary effects of the economic behavior of individuals. The major secondary effect in the case of nuclear desalting is the potential application of peaceful technology to the production of nuclear weapons. The United States and the recipients of nuclear assistance clearly assign different values to this external effect. Without the exercise of control by the United States, the results might be disastrous for world peace as well as for American interests. In the circumstances it might even be desirable for the United States to intervene by subsidizing non-nuclear desalting technologies, to discourage nuclear development as much as possible.

The fact is, however, that American intervention so far seems to have been contrary to its own interests. This raises serious questions about the possibility of effective intervention in the future. The causes of this failure cannot be attributed, however, to the bilateral character of American aid. In fact, some of the problems in controlling the applications of nuclear technology in the Middle East arise because of what may have been premature multilateralization of American nuclear assistance. Under IAEA control procedures, for example, it may be impossible to make the inspection of facilities in the Middle East more rigorous than in Japan, although circumstances justify such discrimination. The creation of the IAEA has intangible benefits in other areas, but part of the price of those benefits has been reduced control over peaceful nuclear technology in the Middle East.

Much of the blame for mistakes in American policy to date lies in the technical character of many of the questions that has led to a domination of policy-making by technologists, and hence to inadequate allowance for broader policy considerations. This difficulty is probably inherent in any commitment to a particular form of technological development. The lessons of the case of nuclear desalting may thus be applicable to other cases of technology transfer. Technology establishes some limits within which national aims are pursued. But within these limits there is usually more than one purpose that a new technology can serve. The applications of a transferred technology are determined ultimately by the political and economic motivations of recipient states. Their perceptions of desirable consequences may conflict sharply with those of the transferring nation. In such cases the transfer of technology cannot be viewed as a purely mechanical communication of knowledge from one culture to another. It becomes a matter of choice, a fundamentally political problem. Although the technological dimension cannot be ignored, it must be treated as subordinate to the political.[38]

38   The author wishes to acknowledge research support received as a National Science Foundation graduate fellow at the University of Chicago and as a consultant to the Ford Foundation-RAND Middle East project. He is especially indebted to Albert Wohlstetter of the University of Chicago and to William Hoehn and Victor Gilinsky of RAND for invaluable guidance and suggestions.

fifteen

Germans and American Denazification

Anna J. Merritt

TOWARD the end of World War II representatives of Great Britain, the Soviet Union, and the United States met—as other high-level representatives had met only a generation earlier—to find a way to keep Europe's problem child, Germany, from ever again leading the world into war. Emotions ran high, not only because of the painful awareness of the catastrophic failure in 1919 to accomplish this same goal, but also because this time there was the added dimension of Nazism with its ideology of racism and world conquest. While there was disagreement among the wartime allies as well as within the various allied nations about the course of action to be taken, there was no doubt among them that the Nazis would have to be punished and that the whole of German society would have to be reevaluated and reeducated. So vast an undertaking had never before been attempted in modern history. The result was a wide range of specific programs including the Nuremberg war crimes trials, the destruction of Nazi institutions, school reforms, the drawing of new state boundaries, reorganization of political parties and local governments, and the distribution of millions of *Fragebogen*, or questionnaires, designed to ascertain the activities of every German during the National Socialist era.

This chapter analyzes the impact on the German population of one of these programs—the denazification program—as an example of government policy aimed at changing the content of a foreign culture. The data stem from reports based upon surveys taken by the U.S. Military Government in the American zone of occupation between 1945 and 1949.[1] In addition to the poll data, I shall also note briefly a number of pertinent political statements and newspaper comments.[2]

PLANNING THE DENAZIFICATION PROGRAM

The question of what to do about Nazism and the various National Socialist institutions was debated long before the war was actually over. The first official action related to the subject came in early 1944 with the establishment of the Anglo-American Country Unit of Supreme Headquarters.[3] Its primary function was planning nonmilitary aspects of the prospective occupation. Out of these efforts came the *Public Safety Manual*, drawn up by the Public Safety Section of the Country Unit, and the *Handbook for Military Government in Germany*. The former, the first edition of which appeared in September, 1944, called for the removal from public life or responsible positions of all Nazis who had joined the National Socialist party before 1933, all high-level civil servants, high-level officials in economic organizations, and all high-level military personnel. It was also the Country Unit that suggested the distribution of *Fragebogen* to all Germans by Special Branch of Military Government; the Country Intelligence Corps was to be in charge of making arrests. At about the same time the Country Unit itself issued the more general *Handbook*, subsequently turned down by President Roosevelt but nonetheless used unofficially by Military Government personnel for a number of years. The section of this *Handbook* dealing with the National Socialist party was brief, calling only for the liquidation of the party and leaving the handling of lesser Nazis to future discussion.

Simultaneously, at the Quebec Conference of September, 1944, one of the better-known and still controversial plans for the future

1   For a more detailed discussion of the original 75 surveys and the resulting 194 reports, see the introduction to Anna J. Merritt and Richard L. Merritt, eds., *Public Opinion in Occupied Germany: The OMGUS Surveys, 1945–1949* (Urbana: University of Illinois Press, 1970), pp. 3–65.

2   For an understanding of the total situation, one would clearly have to look at public opinion data in the United States as well. Except for a few passing remarks, I shall not, however, go into this aspect of the denazification program, for I feel that it is somewhat beyond the scope of this paper. For some general insights into the American situation, see William E. Griffith, "The Denazification Program in the United States Zone of Germany" (Ph.D. dissertation, Harvard University, 1950), pp. 455–78.

3   In the fall of 1944 this binational unit was broken up and the American section renamed U.S. Group, Control Council for Germany. When the occupation began, further changes were made; ultimately in the fall of 1945 the Office of Military Government for Germany, or OMGUS, was established.

of Germany emerged into the public limelight from the higher levels of government, where it had been debated for some time: Secretary of the Treasury Henry Morgenthau's plan for the disarmament, breakup, deindustrialization, and virtual pastoralization of Germany, a plan that can only be termed as one of revenge. Although the extent to which Roosevelt favored this plan is still not known, it is a fact that many people both here and in Germany thought that it would form at least the basis of American policy. Those who approved felt that, even though it might be hard on the German people, it was the only way to insure against future militarism in Germany. Those who opposed the plan pointed to the importance of German industry for the future of not only this one nation but for all of Europe. And it should not be forgotten that, even at this stage, there were those more concerned with the threat of Communism than with the recurrence of German military adventurism.[4]

The report issued after the Yalta Conference of February 3–11, 1945, seemed to confirm Roosevelt's intention to include some aspects of the Morgenthau proposal in the final occupation program. No one, however, was certain precisely how the Allies meant to implement their announced intent

> to destroy German militarism and Nazism and to ensure that Germany will never again be able to disturb the peace of the world. We are determined to . . . wipe out the Nazi Party, Nazi laws, organizations and institutions, remove all Nazi and militarist influences from public office and from the cultural and economic life of the German people. . . . It is not our purpose to destroy the people of Germany, but only when Nazism and militarism have been extirpated will there be hope for a decent life for Germans, and a place for them in the comity of nations.[5]

During this entire period, starting in early 1944, the Joint Chiefs of Staff were engaged in writing a directive that they hoped would serve all four Allied zones of occupation. Here, too, the hard-liners com-

4 For a lengthy discussion of Morgenthau's influence on President Roosevelt and the controversy surrounding it, see Harold Zink, *The United States in Germany, 1945–1955* (Princeton, N.J.: Van Nostrand, 1957), pp. 153–56, as well as Griffith, "The Denazification Program in the United States Zone of Germany," pp. 20–32. It is known that FDR's attitudes toward the Germans were fairly harsh, but one can only guess what the President would actually have done concerning a denazification policy if he had lived; for one of his own comments on the situation, see John M. Blum, *From the Morgenthau Diaries: Years of War, 1941–1945* (Boston: Houghton Mifflin, 1967), pp. 348–49.

5 Quoted in Hajo Holborn, *American Military Government, Its Organization and Policies* (Washington: Infantry Journal Press, 1947), pp. 154–55.

peted with the advocates of a soft line. The sixth and final draft, dated April 26, 1945, came to be known as Joint Chiefs of Staff (JCS) 1067.[6] It was clearly a compromise among the opposing viewpoints. As such, it did not go far enough for the proponents of Morgenthau's plan but brought sighs of relief from those who feared the consequences of that plan. On the whole, however, and in retrospect it strikes one as being more negative than positive, more concerned with eliminating certain things than with creating something new and presumably better. The approach taken on denazification, dealt with in a fairly long section of this document, is characterized by the following sentence:

> All members of the Nazi party who have been more than nominal participants in its activities, all active supporters of Nazism or militarism and all other persons hostile to Allied purposes will be removed and excluded from public office and from positions of importance in quasi-public and private enterprises. . . .[7]

JCS 1067 was an American product. Two months after its completion in April, 1945, and some time before it was made public, a new American president had to try to sell the ideas embodied in this document to his fellow allies. Germany had by this time been divided into zones of occupation, and the Allied Control Council had been established in Berlin. The big question was whether this Council would have a uniform policy for the occupation. Furthermore, would JCS 1067 serve as a guideline for this policy? The Potsdam agreement of July and August, 1945, shows that President Harry S. Truman was fairly successful in selling his product:

> Nazi leaders, influential Nazi supporters, and high officials of Nazi organizations and institutions and any other persons dangerous to the occupation or its objectives shall be arrested and interned.
> All members of the Nazi Party who have been more than nominal participants in its activities and all other persons hostile to Allied purposes shall be removed from public and semi-public office, and from positions of responsibility in important private undertakings.[8]

6 For an excellent account of the background of JCS 1067, see Paul Y. Hammond, "Directives for the Occupation of Germany: The Washington Controversy," in *American Civil-Military Decisions: A Book of Case Studies*, ed. Harold Stein (Birmingham: University of Alabama Press, 1963), pp. 311–464.

7 Carl J. Friedrich and Associates, *American Experiences in Military Government in World War II* (New York: Rinehart and Company, 1948), p. 42. For the full text of JCS 1067, see Holborn, *American Military Government*, pp. 157–72.

8 Cited in Zink, *The United States in Germany*, pp. 165–66. For the full text,

Although the Potsdam agreement was binding for all four zones, it was still vague enough that its practical implementation varied greatly from one area to another.[9]

IMPLEMENTING DENAZIFICATION PLANS

In the United States zone, or AMZON, the Military Government issued a clarifying denazification directive on July 7, 1945. One of its more significant contributions was establishing that all high-level civil servants who had joined the party before May 1, 1937, were to be removed from office. In addition, harking back to the *Public Safety Manual* and the *Handbook for Military Government*, it contained a list 136 items long, entitled "Mandatory Removal and Exclusion Categories."

It was during this period that a new figure appeared on the scene, perhaps the single most powerful figure in the drama of denazification: General Lucius D. Clay, deputy and later military governor of the American zone. In fact, denazification seems to have been one of the general's major concerns. Almost immediately he became aware of the complexities involved in the undertaking. In his account of his four years in Germany, Clay quotes part of his first report to General Eisenhower, at that time military governor of Germany, concerning the problems facing the Military Government officer:

> His mission is to find capable public officials. . . . at the same time, he must seek out and remove the Nazis. All too often, it seems that the only men with the qualifications . . . are the career civil servants

---

see Holborn, *American Military Government*, pp. 195–205; cf. also Herbert Feis, *Between War and Peace: The Potsdam Conference* (Princeton: Princeton University Press, 1960).

9 Which of the occupying powers carried out the most stringent policy is a moot question. There can be little doubt, however, that since the Soviet Union aimed at a totally new society, the end result in its zone showed the most sweeping changes. Although the exact procedures are not known, it is a fact that many high-level Nazis fled to the West, many were imprisoned or given low-level jobs in other fields, and quite a few simply became loyal Communists. Many top positions were therefore filled with inexperienced people in the early postwar period. This is unquestionably one—although only one—reason why it took the Soviet zone somewhat longer to get on its feet; by the same token it does not have West Germany's problem with ex-Nazis in high places. For further comments on denazification in the other zones, see Friedrich, *American Experiences in Military Government*, pp. 254–55, and Zink, *The United States in Germany*, pp. 165–67, as well as Raymond Ebsworth, *Restoring Democracy in Germany: The British Contribution* (London: Stevens & Son, 1960) and F. Roy Willis, *The French in Germany, 1945–1949* (Stanford: Stanford University Press, 1962). For some public opinion data on the subject, see OMGUS Survey Report no. 7, May 11, 1946, reported in Merritt and Merritt, *Public Opinion in Occupied Germany*, pp. 79–80.

> . . . a great proportion of whom were more than nominal partici-
> pants (by our definition) in the activities of the Nazi Party.[10]

Finding trustworthy men to help identify the active Nazis was no mean task, especially when one considers how many anti-Nazis had fled, had died in concentration camps, or were in such poor physical or psychological shape as to be incapable of helping. The military forces had interned the highest-ranking and most obvious Nazi leaders as they swept north and east through Germany in the spring of 1945. Following this preliminary action, Military Government took the next step and required all Germans who were applying for or were already in high-level positions to fill out *Fragebogen*, containing some 150 questions. By the end of 1945 the public safety officers had looked at over 1,650,000 such *Fragebogen*; in more than 300,000 of these cases it was decided that the person in question should be permitted to work only as a common laborer.[11]

In addition to the practical problems facing those charged with carrying out the denazification program in its early months, Clay also faced the larger ethical problem of balancing any denazification measures against very real and tremendous economic pressures, the alleviation of which required manpower.[12] Since the directives were rather vague, the various Military Government officials could do more or less what they deemed appropriate, with the result that denazification was anything but uniform throughout the zone. Matters were brought to a head in August with the famous "Patton incident" in which General George Patton is reported to have stated during a press conference that he did not see what all the fuss concerning denazification was about; to him the members of the National Socialist party were pretty much like the members of the Republican or Democratic parties back home.[13]

Clearly, existing agreements and directives were not providing sufficient guidelines to fulfill the spirit of either Yalta or Potsdam. Additional clarifications were necessary.[14] Law No. 8, issued by the Military Government on September 6, 1945, and the Allied Control Council Directive No. 24 of January 12, 1946 (signed by all four of the Allied powers), expanded the categories of persons to be af-

10   General Lucius D. Clay, *Decision in Germany* (Garden City, N.Y.: Doubleday, 1950), p. 67.
11   Ibid., p. 69.
12   For Clay's views and experiences in this sphere, see ibid., pp. 16–19.
13   For a lengthy account of this international cause célèbre, see Griffith, "The Denazification Program in the United States Zone of Germany," pp. 73–93.
14   A lucid description of the situation is contained in Clay, *Decision in Germany*, pp. 67–68.

fected by the denazification program. The former barred businessmen from their positions if they had been members of the Nazi party; it also provided for German judges in the appeals courts. The latter reaffirmed the ideas worked out at Potsdam and automatically classified many high-ranking officials from the National Socialist era as offenders.

By early 1946, then, the denazification program was in full swing in the American zone of Germany. But the going was not entirely smooth. Not only was there still dissension between the hard-liners and the soft; not only were there myriad vaguely worded and seemingly conflicting directives, laws, pronouncements, and announcements from various official sources. In the fall of 1945 anti-denazification rumblings also began to be heard from the German people. By early 1946 the public opinion controversy on this subject was also in full swing.

GERMAN PUBLIC OPINION ON DENAZIFICATION

In order to obtain continuous and systematic information on what the broad mass of Germans thought about specific issues and felt about a variety of problems, the U.S. Army set about to sample popular opinions almost before the shooting war was over. When it became apparent that a formal structure was needed for this purpose, the Intelligence Branch of the Office of the Director of Information Control, Office of Military Government for Germany (United States), established in October, 1945, its Opinion Survey Section, with Frederick W. Williams as its head.

The first opinion poll it conducted on the subject of denazification consisted of interviews with nine mayors and twenty-four political leaders in seventeen AMZON cities and towns. Without exception, all thirty-three of these men supported the principle of denazification. In fact, although a number of the mayors complained that dismissals had caused inefficiency in the administration of their cities, none suggested that known and genuine Nazis be retained to maintain governmental efficiency. Several respondents mentioned injustices in the program and quite a few expressed the fear that undemocratic procedures would, and in some cases already had, caused disillusionment in democracy. Law No. 8 was uniformly hailed as a great step forward, both because it permitted differentiation between activists and those who had been forced to join the party and because it called for some German participation.

As for the future, most of the mayors were concerned over the possible long-range political effects of denazification. Would those who had been dismissed become radicalized? Would they turn against their society either by joining the Communists, starting a new right-wing party, or retreating completely from political life?[15]

The opinions revealed in this poll of political leaders were also reflected in a number of other written and spoken statements made at the time. Newspapers, especially their editorial pages, frequently commented on the need for denazification and the positive aspects of Law No. 8.[16] At the same time, however, newspapers, magazines, and other printed sources carried pleas by a wide variety of personalities for still greater differentiation as well as warnings about the future repercussions of the program as it was being carried out.[17] Since these points also become a major issue in the OMGUS surveys, I shall defer comments on them until the end of this inquiry.

SHARED RESPONSIBILITY FOR DENAZIFICATION

Opposition to the course taken by the Military Government in its denazification program, together with a growing feeling among U.S. officials that they could not possibly complete the task by themselves within any reasonable amount of time,[18] led General Clay and his associates to press for a German denazification law and a German

15   For further discussion of these interviews, cf. OMGUS, *Weekly Information Bulletin*, no. 19, December 1, 1945, pp. 30–35, and John G. Korman, *U.S. Denazification Policy in Germany, 1945–1950* (Historical Division, Office of the Executive Secretary, Office of the United States High Commission for Germany, 1952), pp. 56–62.

16   For an especially trenchant comment that appeared in a German newspaper, cf. OMGUS, *Weekly Information Bulletin*, no. 16, November 10, 1945, p. 23. Since newspapers during this period were extensively controlled by the occupation forces, it is difficult to use their editorials as a measure of public opinion; in fact, the Germans themselves placed little stock in the newspapers, although this seemed to be the result of a general disillusionment in mass media, an after-effect of the Nazi years (see OMGUS Survey Report no. 58, May 1, 1947, reported in Merritt and Merritt, *Public Opinion in Occupied Germany*, pp. 158–59).

17   A very strong plea for thoroughness mixed with compassion and reason was made in late 1945 and early 1946 by a long-time opponent of National Socialism, Ernst Müller-Meiningen, Jr., in *Die Parteigenossen* (München: Verlag Kurt Desch, 1946). A number of biographies and memoirs from this period also emphasize these points, e.g., Lewis J. Edinger, *Kurt Schumacher: A Study in Personality and Political Behavior* (Stanford: Stanford University Press, 1965), esp. pp. 90–91; also Theodor Heuss, *Aufzeichnungen, 1945–1947* (Tübingen: Rainer Wunderlich Verlag, Hermann Leins, 1966), as well as Carlo Schmid, *Der Weg des deutschen Volkes nach 1945* (Berlin: Haude & Spenersche Verlagsbuchhandlung, 1967).

18   By November 10, 1945, Military Government had received 920,073 *Fragebogen*, representing only slightly more than 6 percent of the total AMZON population; of these, 642,955 (or 70 percent) had been processed, and the remaining 277,118 were still to be done (cited in OMGUS, *Weekly Information Bulletin*, no. 18, November 24, 1945, p. 17).

denazification program—with U.S. supervision.[19] The task of drawing up such a law was given to the state ministers of justice in late 1945. After much discussion within the newly elected Council of the States (*Länderrat*) and between Military Government officials and the Germans, the Law for Liberation from National Socialism and Militarism was finally passed on March 5, 1946.[20] The law established five classes of Germans: Class I, major offenders; Class II, offenders (activists, militarists, profiteers); Class III, lesser offenders; Class IV, followers; Class V, exonerated persons. And, once again, *Fragebogen* or, as they were frequently called to distinguish them from the questionnaires used in the first phase of denazification, *Meldebogen* were used in determining the classifications; all persons over eighteen were required to fill one out. The machinery for this immense task consisted of 545 tribunals (*Spruchkammer*) and appeals courts employing over 22,000 persons.

It was this law that prompted the first large-scale survey in AMZON by the Intelligence Branch of OMGUS, reported on March 15, 1946 (#7).[21] Knowledge concerning the new denazification law was astonishingly low. To be sure, 59 percent had heard that there was a new law but less than half of these (28 percent of the full sample) could describe with any accuracy at all the changes it brought. A somewhat larger percentage (36%) could pick one of four sentences that best described the new program. Interestingly enough, 51 percent were unable to choose any among the four statements.

Lack of knowledge, however, did not preclude an opinion on the subject. In answer to the question, "In general, are you satisfied or dissatisfied with the manner in which denazification is being conducted?" 57 percent expressed satisfaction, 30 percent were dissatisfied, and 13 percent had no opinion. The new law halted a downward trend in the number of those satisfied. Whereas in early December, 1945, in response to the same question, 50 percent had

19 Clay, *Decision in Germany*, pp. 69 70.
20 For a comprehensive discussion of the controversy between OMGUS and German leaders surrounding the writing of this law, especially regarding the very basic differences in the legal systems of the two nations, as well as the problem of presumptive guilt that formed the basis of the American denazification policy, see Friedrich, *American Experiences in Military Government*, pp. 263–75; Griffith, "The Denazification Program in the United States Zone of Germany," pp. 347–55; and John Gimbel, *The American Occupation of Germany: Politics and the Military, 1945–1949* (Stanford: Stanford University Press, 1968), pp. 103–6.
21 The numbers in parentheses here and subsequently refer to the OMGUS Information Control Division Reports; for further details, see Merritt and Merritt, *Public Opinion in Occupied Germany*.

been satisfied, 41 percent dissatisfied, and 9 percent had had no opinion, by the end of the same month the percentage of those satisfied had dropped four points, those dissatisfied had risen two, and those with no opinion had also gone up two percentage points.

What exactly they were dissatisfied about, however, is not quite clear. Bearing in mind the relatively low percentage of persons having some knowledge of the denazification program, as well as the 57 percent figure for those satisfied with that program, it is interesting to note the responses to a question in which each person was asked to pick the one statement out of four most closely approximating the policy he favored. A plurality (39%) chose the statement describing the existing situation. But almost the same number (35%) said that they liked the situation described in two other statements in which the Military Government carried the major responsibility; this, as we know from our earlier discussion, was the situation before March 5, 1946.

Another indication of a relative lack of concern with the precise nature of the denazification program is shown by a cross-tabulation between knowledge and satisfaction: of those who had heard about the new law (59%), just over half (52%) were generally satisfied with it, but a solid majority (64%) of those who had not even heard about it also expressed satisfaction with it.

Obviously a good many people were far more concerned about matters other than denazification. Nonetheless, 30 percent of those questioned were concerned enough to be able to offer some concrete suggestions for improving the program. The one point made more frequently than any other—and the one that comes up over and over throughout all subsequent surveys—is that "small (nominal) Nazis should be treated less harshly, and great care should be used in deciding who are the activists."

THE MASS PUBLIC AND LEADERSHIP GROUPS

The March 15, 1946, survey report was the first of seven dealing in part or exclusively with various aspects of the denazification program. The data in it give one an idea of some of the problems and questions raised in the German people's minds by that program. Reports of subsequent surveys examine them in greater detail, suggest trends and changes as new laws and directives were handed down, or world events altered perspectives, and ultimately permit an evaluation of the entire denazification procedure.

One survey question not asked in March, 1946, but crucial to an understanding of the full denazification picture concerned attitudes toward the principle underlying the program. Was the idea of denazifying German society accepted as necessary and good? Unfortunately, such a question was asked only once (January, 1949), so that there is no possibility of comparison over time. The fact that it came when the program was virtually finished is on the one hand good, since those interested and capable of forming an opinion would certainly have done so by then. On the other hand, it presents a definite drawback in that the hardships imposed and the sometimes adverse publicity due to scandals may have colored the respondents' basic predisposition. In any event it might be well to remember that all thirty-three political leaders interviewed in late 1945, as discussed earlier, were basically in favor of denazification.

In early 1949 a clear majority (66%) of the AMZON population thought it was "a good idea to hold to account—through denazification—such people as furthered National Socialism in any way." Even in the case of former members of the Nazi party 56 percent felt this way; for those with a former party member in the family the figure was slightly higher (59%). The breakdowns according to education and socioeconomic level reveal one highly significant fact: whereas persons with eleven years or less of schooling and from lower-middle or lower socioeconomic status were more favorably disposed toward the principle of denazification than unfavorably disposed, the situation was reversed for the better educated and those with higher socioeconomic status. In both of these categories the percentage of those who felt denazification was a bad idea was higher: almost half (49%) of the respondents with twelve or more years of education said it was bad while 47 percent thought it was good; but well over half (55%) of those of upper-middle and upper socioeconomic status felt it was bad and only 42 percent termed it good. These two groups, from which the German elites are undoubtedly drawn (although each respondent clearly is not necessarily a member of the elite), turn out to be among the more interesting groups in this study, as later discussion will bear out.

Among all those opposing the very idea of denazification, the most frequently heard argument (almost half of the 24 percent in AMZON) was that the Nazi party members had been idealists, that only criminals ought to be punished. The second (but far less frequently heard) counterargument centered around the feeling that political freedom is the basis for democracy: "Many people today are members of parties—they also wouldn't like it if they were later punished for that, after all, we have freedom of thought and conviction" (#182). This critical attitude, while itself not very prevalent in Germany, was reflected otherwise in a rather widespread apathy toward things political. Numerous studies in recent years have shown that the Germans do go to the polls in large numbers, but not out of conviction so much as out of a sense of duty.[22]

The implications of a low level of involvement in the political life of a country for a viable democracy is a large and crucial question, but it is one that cannot be dealt with here. For the purpose of this study, however, there is fortunately one survey that relates the problems of denazification and basic democratic principles rather nicely; it seems worth discussing here, at least briefly (#93).

During the war a group of specially selected German prisoners of war was sent to Fort Getty in the United States for training in democracy and American values. At the end of the war they were returned to Germany with a certificate showing that they had completed the course; no other special provisions were made for them. In the spring of 1947 each of them was sent a lengthy questionnaire; seventy-eight responded. The men under discussion here were not typical Germans. Their original selection was based on political outlook, intelligence, and good education. By the time of the survey a high percentage (73%) of them filled white-collar jobs or held some professional status. They were more willing to participate in local affairs and to join political parties than was the general public. Their responses to all the questions—ranging from purely political to highly personal—reflected a great deal of differentiation and critical judgment.

Asked what they considered to be the most urgent problems facing the German people, only about one-fourth (23%) of the sample included Nazism; far greater importance was attached to matters of everyday living such as the increase in production (73%) and the stabilization of the food supply (60%). Given the very real physical problems facing the people immediately after the war, this set of priorities is actually not terribly surprising.

While Nazism was not ranked as a major problem by many, there was one nonphysical problem that was ranked as such by at least

22   Cf. Gabriel A. Almond and Sidney Verba, *The Civic Culture: Political Attitudes and Democracy in Five Nations* (Princeton: Princeton University Press, 1963), pp. 428–29; Ralf Dahrendorf, *Society and Democracy in Germany* (Garden City, N.Y.: Doubleday, 1968), esp. Ch. 5; and Merritt and Merritt, *Public Opinion in Occupied Germany*, pp. 43–50.

half the respondents: the reeducation of the German people. In this light it is interesting to note the responses to the question, "What impressed you most strongly on your return to Germany?" The two most frequently mentioned items were "corruption, red-tape" (44%) and the "remains of Nazism and militarism, people did not learn from the past" (42%).

For those in Military Government and the State Department concerned with the reeducation and reevaluation of German society, these statistics must have been somewhat unsettling. And the fact that three out of ten felt that the denazification program was an outright hindrance to the democratization of Germany must have been unnerving. As one respondent put it, "The fact that denazification is frequently carried out in an unjust way makes it impossible to educate Germans in a democratic sense." Other arguments were that the whole program rested on ex post facto law, and hence was legally inadmissible, and also that the really guilty Nazis were not being tried.

Again, it must be stressed that the Fort Getty group was not typical of the AMZON population. Whether their opinions are worth more because they are politically knowledgeable and active, or whether in studying a democracy one must bear the total population in mind regardless of how one thinks policies are arrived at, cannot be discussed here. One facet of the question is relevant, however. If democracy presupposes a knowledgeable public, what, for instance, was the level of knowledge in Germany concerning the denazification program?

THE CHANGING CONTEXT OF DENAZIFICATION

The fact that denazification was the subject of a great many newspaper editorials, radio discussions, and even books has been mentioned earlier. In late 1946 three events took place that put the program squarely in the limelight for some time. The first came in August when the American military governor granted an amnesty from all denazification proceedings to persons born after January 1, 1919. The second important event was General Clay's speech before the fourteenth meeting of the *Länderrat* in Stuttgart on November 5, 1946, in which he expressed dissatisfaction with the progress being made by the German denazification tribunals.[23] Finally, on Christmas

---

23 For a discussion of the possible political considerations behind these remarks, see Gimbel, *The American Occupation of Germany*, pp. 106–10.

day of that year a second amnesty was announced affecting some 800,000 persons; it absolved all those with incomes of less than RM 3,600 and taxable property valued below RM 20,000 during the Nazi era, since they had evidently not profited by their party memberships; it also included the disabled.

In December, 1946, and January and February, 1947, three separate surveys were conducted in AMZON and Berlin dealing with denazification in general and Clay's Stuttgart speech in particular (#55). Despite the publicity attendant upon the program, only a bare majority (56%) of the people polled were able to pick the one correct statement out of four describing the existing situation. (It may be recalled that, shortly after publication of the Law for Liberation from National Socialism and Militarism, only 36 percent could pick the correct statement.) Again, as in the case of attitudes toward the principle underlying denazification, former party members tended to be more knowledgeable (73%) than those with just a former member in the family (57%) or no affiliation whatever (53%). The same was true of persons with higher levels of education (78 percent of those with twelve years or more of education) and with upper socioeconomic status (75 percent from the upper and upper-middle level) than their counterparts. Able-bodied men chose the correct statement more often (68%) than those unable to work (54%), and both were more knowledgeable than women who were able to work (49%).

Answers to questions dealing with knowledge of Clay's speech reveal much the same results. With less than half (47%) of the AMZON population aware of the speech, it is again the former NSDAP members (79%) and the better educated and financially well-off rather than their counterparts who were in the knowledgeable category. Comparisons of those aware of both the denazification program and Clay's speech show that only 32 percent of the population were informed on both matters and that 29 percent knew nothing about either one. Going one step further, 73 percent of those with twelve years or more of school were in the former group, as were 64 percent of those from upper-middle or upper socioeconomic status, 62 percent of those who were former NSDAP members, and 51 percent of the able-bodied men in the sample. In contrast, only 25 percent of those with seven years of schooling or less fit into this highly aware group, 18 percent of those with very low socioeconomic status, and 28 percent of those who were neither former party members nor had such a relative.

KNOWLEDGE, SATISFACTION, AND THE
CHANGING CONTEXT OF DENAZIFICATION

As the earlier discussion of the first survey pointed out, knowledge
or lack thereof did not necessarily have much bearing on attitudes
toward denazification. The Opinion Survey Unit of OMGUS ran
several surveys between 1946 and 1949 asking people what they
thought of the actual procedures followed, as opposed to their opinion
concerning the underlying principle. Throughout the period under
consideration, the percentage of the total AMZON population ex-
pressing satisfaction with the way denazification was being carried
out went steadily downhill except for one brief period: immediately
following the announcement of the new Law for Liberation from
National Socialism and Militarism in March, 1946.

Placed in the historical context of the period, this downward trend
permits a number of possible explanations for the ultimate outcome
of the denazification program, as well as for the German situation
in general. The first poll was conducted shortly after the promulga-
tion of Law No. 8, requiring all persons who managed or owned
a private business to pass the *Fragebogen* test. In November, 1945,
50 percent of the AMZON population expressed satisfaction with
the denazification procedures, 41 percent expressed dissatisfaction,
and 9 percent had no opinion. Hardly one month later these percentages had changed to 46 percent, 43 percent, and 11 percent,
respectively. It was shortly thereafter that the Allied Control Council
Directive No. 24 and the new law placing control of the proceedings
in German hands were announced; the poll reflecting the attitudes
toward these changes shows satisfaction rising abruptly to 57 percent,
opposition dropping equally dramatically to 30 percent, but the
"don't knows" still rising, this time to 13 percent. This exultant feeling
of satisfaction with the way denazification was now being run was
short-lived. Just nine months later, despite the two large amnesties,
the percentage of those satisfied had dropped far below the original
level (to 34 percent), those opposed had gone higher than ever (to
45 percent), and the "don't knows" had also continued to rise (to
21 percent).

During this period the quarrel between the United States and the
Soviet Union became increasingly apparent.[24] By mid–1948 the

24   A detailed account of the controversy between the two occupying powers
concerning the denazification program is contained in Griffith, "The Denazification
Program in the United States Zone of Germany," pp. 446–54.

Cold War was regarded as an international fact of life. Churchill had delivered his famous "Iron Curtain" speech in Fulton, Missouri, on March 5, 1946; the Truman Doctrine speech came one year and one week later; the Marshall Plan received its first public announcement on June 5, 1947, and just one year later, following the currency reform for the three western zones of occupation, Berlin, Germany, and the United States were confronted with the apparently insoluble dilemma of the Berlin blockade. The Cold War clearly forced western Germany to choose whether or not to place its fate in the hands of the Americans. By the same token it forced the United States to reevaluate its relationship with its former enemy. American public opinion turned increasingly away from a retributive attitude. If Germany was to be an ally, should not the German people be treated as a trustworthy and capable population? Could the denazification policy, already bogged down administratively and a source of controversy from the very outset, be squared with this new attitude? The Germans were certainly not unaware of this dilemma. Public opinion surveys on the denazification procedures suggest that the Germans definitely thought the program was wrong as it was being conducted: in September, 1947, only 32 percent expressed satisfaction with it; by January, 1949, this percentage had dropped as low as 17 percent with 65 percent opposed; interestingly, the "don't knows" showed a decrease (to 18 percent), suggesting growing certainty as to the program's worth.

What forms did this opposition, as reflected in the OMGUS surveys, take?[25] As noted earlier, of the 30 percent in March, 1946, who had suggestions concerning the way denazification should be handled, 10 percent mentioned that small Nazis should be treated less harshly than activists and greater care should be taken in determining who was an activist. The Fort Getty group, it will be remembered, had similar criticisms. Adverse comments offered by respondents in the survey dealing with Clay's Stuttgart speech were broken down in the report according to whether they thought it too harsh or too easy: once again, fully three-quarters of those who thought it too harsh felt it was too harsh on the little people, while another 10 percent mentioned inconsistencies in the judgments. Among those who were neither satisfied nor dissatisfied, 45 percent felt it was too harsh on little people, and 42 percent mentioned the problem of incon-

25 For a detailed and extremely illuminating discussion of the opposition to denazification procedures on the part of such groups as the clergy and university professors, as well as individuals like the liberal editor of *Frankfurter Hefte*, Eugen Kogon, and Deputy Minister of Political Liberation in Hesse Karl Heinrich Knappstein, see ibid., pp. 390–407.

sistencies in judgments. Turning to the knowledgeable group discussed in the same report, it is worth noting that once again those able to pick the one correct statement out of four describing the existing situation were also more likely to express dissatisfaction with that situation: among those satisfied, only 57 percent knew what the program was all about but, among those who were dissatisfied because they thought the program too harsh, fully 67 percent had a good idea of what that program was; of those who felt it was too easy, 62 percent were in the knowledgeable category.

By early 1949, when the denazification program was all but completed, there was no single group in Germany in which a greater percentage thought that it had been well carried out than thought it had *not* been well carried out. Here too, men (71% vs. 18%), those with twelve years of education or more (85% vs. 12%), earning DM 750 or more per month (83% vs. 11%), with higher socioeconomic status (90% vs. 7%), and former NSDAP members (78% vs. 17%) were more likely to oppose the denazification proceedings than were their counterparts. Even at this late date, most of the criticism centered around the feeling that the minor party members were punished too severely in comparison with the major ones (37% out of a total of 65% opposed); in addition, rather frequent mention (12%) was made of the belief that "they did not judge objectively; accusers, judges, and witnesses could be bribed" (#182).[26]

FORMER NAZIS AND DENAZIFICATION

In addition to the salience for this study of the well-educated and upper socioeconomic groups, the foregoing paragraphs point to yet another group that should be given some attention: former NSDAP members. Obviously, they were the ones most directly affected by the denazification program. In September, 1947, two concurrent surveys were conducted by OMGUS. One dealt with a random sample of 300 persons from among those Germans who had been party members and whose *Meldebogen* had been kept on file because of the individual's high level of activity in the party. The other survey dealt

26 How widespread corruption actually was is not known; in so large an operation there was bound to be some and, as is usual in such a situation, a number of particularly juicy stories made front page headlines. For a listing and discussion of some of these, cf. John H. Herz, "The Fiasco of Denazification in Germany," *Political Science Quarterly* 63, no. 4 (December 1948): 569–94, esp. 581–89; also HICOG Surveys, report no. 8, series no. 2, March 17, 1950, "Reactions toward the Württemberg-Baden Denazification Affair."

with 3,000 randomly selected Germans among whom 359 volunteered the information that they had been affected by denazification in some way or had been *Parteigenosse,* or party members (hereinafter referred to as "claimed PG's"). To put the three groups into sharper focus: 5 percent of the *Meldebogen* group had been classified as major offenders (the highest category), while none of the "claimed PG's" had been given this ranking. By the same token, 15 percent of the "claimed PG's" and none of the *Meldebogen* group had been exonerated. In contrast, however, these two groups resembled each other remarkably closely with regard to background, while differing strongly with the unaffected group; thus, for example, 40 percent of the *Meldebogen* group and 41 percent of the "claimed PG's" had had nine years of education or more, while the figure for the unaffected group was only 16 percent (#80).

The attitude toward denazification on the part of these three groups reinforces what we have discovered so far: greater differentiation of opinion comes with awareness. Far more of those who were not affected by denazification expressed satisfaction (34%) or no opinion (15%) than was true of the "claimed PG's"; of the latter group only 15 percent expressed satisfaction, 15 percent felt the proceedings were too harsh, 2 percent thought them too mild, 61 percent had other reservations (mostly concerning the contention that little people were treated too harshly, important ones too mildly), and only 4 percent had no opinion. It should also be noted that, when the *Meldebogen* group was asked whether it thought denazification was justified, 60 percent replied in the affirmative.

Concern over the effects of denazification took specific forms, in addition to the somewhat nebulous idea that all the little PG's were being punished while the big ones were getting off scot-free.[27] Asked "In which realm do you think denazification has had the more important impact—in the economic or the political?" a majority of both the *Meldebogen* group (56%) and the "claimed PG's" (54%)

27   According to OMGUS Survey Report no. 80, November 26, 1947, p. 6, a report in September, 1947, from the American Military Government stated that 82 percent of the cases dealt with "heavily incriminated" persons. Another point, made earlier with regard to the original argument concerning the form denazification ought to take, and that ought to be borne in mind here, is the fact that for those who felt that denazification was less important than getting the wheels of production rolling again, there may well have been occasion to let an important person or former Nazi leader through relatively easily. As Harold Zink, *The United States in Germany,* p. 164, points out, "The very fact that the net was so widely spread made it possible for certain shrewd and wily Nazi 'big boys' to get through the mesh." Even Clay, *Decision in Germany,* p. 261, expressed doubts about whether it was possible to accomplish what the United States had set out to do.

indicated the former; in contrast, the unaffected respondents split fairly evenly, with 31 percent saying economic, 30 percent political, and 39 percent having no opinion. When questioned about which of seven points they thought were the result of denazification, respondents from all three groups mentioned the lack of expert officials most frequently; next most frequent mention was made of the lack of experts in business, and third came the feeling that former party members found themselves in economic need.[28]

Precisely what the effect of denazification on the economic sphere was, will never be known. A survey conducted in September, 1946 (#38), concerning job status revealed that the probability that a former party member had received at least some university training was twice as great as for those who had not been party members. Given Germany's traditional social and educational structure,[29] it might be expected that a preponderance of these well-educated former party members would fill high-level business and government positions. The data do indeed bear this out: while 28 percent of the former party members held such positions, only 12 percent of those who had not been party members did so. This does not, however, mean that there were no changes in jobs among persons in these positions. As a survey conducted in the latter part of October, 1946 (#38), revealed, only 53 percent of those classified as professional during the war were still in jobs fitting this classification; for officials the figure was even lower, only 40 percent. In contrast, 77 percent of the independent businessmen were still in their chosen fields, and for farmers the figure was as high as 86 percent. The changes in job status were undoubtedly as much due to the inevitable upheaval caused by war, especially a lost war, as to other causes, including denazification.[30] Yet it seems reasonable to assume that, with so many party members in the groups in which the greatest switches were made, there was more than a coincidental relationship.[31]

28   It must be noted, however, that the unaffected mentioned this less than half as often (23%) as did the other two groups (50% and 49%); in fact, those unaffected put "Active National Socialists are removed from responsible positions and replaced by people who are truly democratic" in third place.

29   See Ralf Dahrendorf, *Society and Democracy in Germany*.

30   For a discussion of some of these other causes, as well as a brief description of personnel changes in sixty companies and firms, see Gimbel, *The American Occupation of Germany*, pp. 171–72.

31   A survey conducted in 1953 by the Operations Research Office of Johns Hopkins University under the direction of John D. Montgomery seems to confirm this assertion: "A total of 8% stated that they had personally 'been disadvantaged' because of denazification, and an additional 15% stated that members of their families had. Many more of the university graduates had felt its effects (23%) than those with grammar school (6%) or high school (10%) education" (from an un-

DENAZIFICATION AND RESTORATION

During the spring and summer of 1948 American involvement in the denazification program was brought to a rapid conclusion.[32] The Germans completed what was left in the *Meldebogen* files,[33] then went on to search out, bring to trial, and punish numerous others. (Every year since then there have been several individual and group trials going on in various parts of Germany.) Just recently debate was also begun once again on whether or not to suspend the statute of limitations on crimes committed during the Nazi era.

Several questions remain to be answered. Regarding this particular study, it is of course necessary first to question whether or not the OMGUS survey data are of any use in evaluating American denazification policy. There is little doubt that the survey reports played some role in the decision-making process pertaining to this policy. As Frederick W. Williams, head of the Opinion Surveys Branch, has written, "General Clay was a faithful reader of our reports. On a couple of occasions he quoted detailed data to me from the reports. I concluded that he not only read and remembered but he thought about meaning and implications."[34] But there is also little doubt that for the policy-makers they were only one among several German sources of information, along with the newspapers and respected leaders from various walks of life. In addition there were pressures from within the United States and OMGUS itself. The enormity of the task, as originally planned, might have discouraged the most zealous denazifier once he had become involved in its practical application; but, even after it had been pared down somewhat, there was continued bickering over the purpose of a denazification program and its effect on a future Germany. These problems led to a weariness with the entire operation. The Cold War and the growing perception of the need for German friendship may well have

published manuscript by John D. Montgomery, who kindly sent me portions of it). See Montgomery's *Forced to Be Free: The Artificial Revolution in Germany and Japan* (Chicago: University of Chicago Press, 1957).

32   Denazification had been officially ended in the Soviet zone of occupation in February of that year.

33   The final figures, as cited in Clay, *Decision in Germany*, p. 260, show that a total of 13,000,000 *Fragebogen* were submitted; of these 3,000,000 were chargeable, but amnesties reduced the figure to 930,000. The final results were: 1,549 major offenders; 21,000 offenders; 104,000 lesser offenders; 475,000 followers. The punishments meted out were: 9,000 prison terms; 30,000 special labor; 22,000 ineligible for public office; 122,000 restricted in employment; 25,000 had their property entirely or partly confiscated; 500,000 received fines.

34   Personal correspondence, April 2, 1969.

been the deciding factor in ending the program. German public opinion, then, while not decisive in itself, doubtless served to confirm the extent and trend of feeling making it possible to change policy when and in the manner that it was.

More interesting perhaps, is the question of what the poll data tell us about popular attitudes toward denazification. First, and most important, they suggest that a majority of the population always favored the principle underlying the program. Unfavorable attitudes were directed at the practical application of that program. Indeed, many aspects of the denazification procedure did leave something to be desired. By the same token, it is understandable that the rather different approaches taken from one area to another aroused a certain amount of suspicion and anxiety.

Another possible explanation for growing disenchantment with the denazification program is far more complex. Just as a direct question in the United States on blacks or Jews frequently elicits responses suitable to the American ideal of equality, so too a question in Germany concerning anti-Semitism prompts lip-service to the democratic ideal; these may or may not correspond to the person's true feelings. Carrying this idea one step further, just as most white Americans were shocked recently at the suggestion that their attiudes might be termed racist, so too it was difficult for the bulk of the German population to accept the notion of collective guilt implicit in the denazification program. The Germans were willing to see "the Nazis"—as long as this term referred to high officials or remained nebulous—punished. But, as soon as it became evident that denazification was a wide net ready to catch all manner of fish, they became uneasy. The obvious and well-publicized shortcomings of the program provided a relatively simple solution to this psychological dilemma. Dissatisfaction with denazification rested on injustices and inconsistencies in the program, but certainly the idea behind the program was very good. To make matters worse, as far as the future of the program was concerned, the trend toward increasing disenchantment with denazification was most marked among potential leadership groups and ex-Nazis.[35] On the plus side is the fact, borne out by the survey data, that strong minorities not only favored the idea of denazification but were also satisfied with the program as it was conducted during its entire and varied existence. Thus one can only conclude that the American denazification program, despite its many

35 It should be stressed that, although these two groups exhibit a great many similarities, the poll data do not provide any proof that they were identical.

and serious drawbacks, was not an unmitigated disaster in the public view.

The final and most crucial question to be answered by this study is, what are the implications of these data for a policy such as the denazification program? Obviously, there was no point at which opposition to denazification was sufficiently great to warrant cancellation of the program; as discussed above, other considerations led to this. Clearly, however, it did not garner the support needed from among the various leadership groups. If world and American domestic conditions had been different, perhaps a consistent and persistent implementation of even the existing program might have succeeded over a long period of time. But this was not to be. Alternatively, and taking a cue from the respondents themselves, perhaps revising the priorities would have been a good idea. Even better would have been a clear idea at the very outset on the part of American policy-makers about what National Socialism was, what role it played in the fabric of German society, and precisely which Germans were to be punished. Since the first two points are still subject to debate today, one can hardly fault those in charge twenty-five years ago for not having had the answers. As for the third point, given the large number of people involved in National Socialism and the numerous theories and objectives circulating among Americans on this subject, it is perhaps utopian to expect clearcut policies. In view of these considerations, as well as the retrospective information available through the survey data, the wisest course might well have been to concentrate first and thoroughly on those who profited most visibly from the Nazi regime. Such an approach, together with the democratization program in the schools and reorganization of local governments and national political parties, might have prevented much of the confusion and ill will generated in the immediate postwar period.

It is true that many of the same people would have been dissatisfied with this selective approach, but non- and anti-Nazi members of various leadership groups, as well as the bulk of the population, would have been more likely to give it the sort of support so sadly lacking in the program as it was in fact conducted. The failure to do so undercut the credibility of the program by making it appear as though the high and mighty could slip through the net; the little man, once again, became the scapegoat. In fact, with the growing intensity of the Cold War, the need for German support meant the end of denazification. By 1948 those who had laid low, or whose cases had been postponed because of the enormous number of *Melde-*

bogen on file, were able to regain their former positions. This, in turn, helped discredit the entire preceding program.[36] It also made it easier to enact subsequent legislation that undid many of the actual accomplishments of the program.

The failure of the American denazification program did not mean a reascension to power of hard-core Nazis. National Socialism as a movement was and is dead. Its leaders, who had lost the war and brought disaster to Germany, were discredited. What the failure did mean, however, was that those who had accepted, facilitated, or profited from the Nazi regime had suffered only a temporary setback. Those who rose to positions of political and economic power in the Bonn government were by and large the traditional, national conservatives of the Wilhelmine Reich and the Weimar republic. Denazification, then, rather than bringing about a thorough reevaluation and the construction of something new, merely contributed to the restoration of the old.

36   This is also borne out by the data in a survey conducted in November, 1953, by the West German public opinion polling agency, Institut für Demoskopie. The survey showed that 12 percent of the West German population thought denazification had had defects, but they were in general satisfied; 23 percent said it was necessary but badly carried out; 26 percent felt it had been unnecessary and badly carried out; and 14 percent termed it chicanery. See Elisabeth Noelle and Erich Peter Neumann, eds., *The Germans: Public Opinion Polls, 1947–1966* (Allensbach and Bonn: Verlag für Demoskopie, 1967), p. 219.

part IV

Government to Government

sixteen

Old Boys, Alumni, and Consensus at ECLA Meetings

John R. Mathiason

SEVERE problems of lack of economic scale, lack of industrialization, and trade dependence on large industrialized countries have provoked a growing number of attempts to form regional economic associations. The importance of communication in the formation of these associations has been frequently noted.[1] Most empirical research on communication and regional integration has been in the area of aggregate national data analysis, such as rates of transaction

1 The main exponents of this have been Karl Deutsch, *Political Community at the International Level* (Garden City, N.Y.: Doubleday, 1954); Karl Deutsch et al., *Political Community and the North Atlantic Area: International Organization in the Light of Historical Experience* (Princeton: Princeton University Press, 1957); Bruce M. Russett, *Community and Contention: Britain and America in the Twentieth Century* (Cambridge: M.I.T. Press, 1963); Amitai Etzioni, *Political Unification: A Comparative Study of Leaders and Forces* (New York: Holt, Rinehart and Winston, 1965); Ernst B. Haas, *The Uniting of Europe* (Stanford: Stanford University Press, 1958); Ernst B. Haas, "International Integration: The European and the Universal Case," *International Organization* 15, no. 3 (Summer 1961): 366–92; Ernst B. Haas, *Beyond the Nation State* (Stanford: Stanford University Press, 1964); Ernst B. Haas, "The Uniting of Europe and the Uniting of Latin America," *Journal of Common Market Studies* 5, no. 4 (June 1967): 315–43; Phillipe C. Schmitter and Ernst B. Haas, *Mexico and Latin American Integration* (Berkeley: University of California, Institute of International Studies, Research Series, no. 5, 1964); Ernst B. Haas and Phillipe C. Schmitter, "Economics and Differential Patterns of Political Integration: Projections about Unity in Latin America," *International Organization* 18, no. 4 (Autumn 1964): 705–37; Ernst B. Haas and Phillipe C. Schmitter, *The Politics of Economics in Latin American Regionalism* (Denver: University of Denver, Monograph Series in World Affairs, 1965); Mario Barrera and Ernst B. Haas, "The Operationalization of Some Variables Related to Regional Integration," *International Organization* 23, no. 1 (Winter 1969): 150–60. John P. Mitchell, "Cross-Cutting Memberships, Integration, and the International System," *Journal of Conflict Resolution* 19, no. 1 (March, 1970): 49–55, makes a case for the importance of interpersonal communication through a review of the above.

flows, economic indicators, and the like.[2] There has also been some research on interpersonal communication, mostly case studies of integrative institutions and their political processes, especially dealing with Western Europe.[3]

Very little empirical research has been done, however, on the influence of interpersonal communication in the decision to establish a regional economic association. In part this is not unusual since, with the exception of the European Economic Community (EEC), COMECON in Eastern Europe, and the Central American Common Market, there have been almost no such regional associations successfully formed. Moreover, in a sense, analysis of the question involves problems of empirical historical social research, since data are generally unavailable. There nevertheless exists some evidence that interpersonal communication played an important role in the process of founding the Common Market—the creation of an expert class of "Eurocrats" or such multinational pressure groups as Jean Monnet's "Action Committee."[4] Such evidence suggests that interpersonal communication could have a role in the multinational decision-making implied in the formation of regional economic associations.

ECLA AND LATIN AMERICAN INTEGRATION

The United Nations Economic Commission for Latin America (ECLA) has been the fountainhead of thinking on Latin American integration since its inception in 1948. ECLA was established with a mandate to encourage attempts at continent-wide economic cooperation and to collect information for this end. But under the leadership of its secretary-general, Dr. Raul Prebisch, ECLA actively promoted developmental doctrine among its member states, especially economic integration doctrine after the advent of the European Common Market.

2   This is true of both Deutsch and the Haas group cited above.
3   Cf. Leon M. Lindberg, *The Political Dynamics of European Economic Integration* (Stanford: Stanford University Press, 1963). There is some evidence that the European Economic Community utilizes a finely honed web of interpersonal communication in formulating and selling its economic policies to member states. See Leon M. Lindberg, "Decision-Making and Integration in the European Community," *International Organization* 19, no. 1 (Winter 1965): 56–80, and Lawrence Scheinman, "Some Preliminary Notes on Bureaucratic Relationships in the European Economic Community," *International Organization* 20, no. 4 (Autumn 1966): 750–73.
4   Cf. Scheinman, "Some Preliminary Notes," and Walter Yondorf, "Monnet and the Action Committee: The Formative Period of the European Communities," *International Organization* 19, no. 4 (Autumn 1965): 885–912.

ECLA's role in promoting doctrine stemmed from its virtual monopoly for many years over continent-wide planning and economic expertise.[5] ECLA was the only organization that carried out economic and social studies of the entire continent, and as such was the only agency which could claim to have, via its detailed studies, "the big picture." Moreover, the ECLA secretariat could recruit the best economists of the member countries to staff its studies. These men frequently advanced in later years to key positions in their national governments. The result of these factors has tended to give ECLA a high credibility as a source of information on the Latin American economy and to give credence to the doctrines advocated by ECLA. The importance of ECLA in Latin American regional integration was noted by Schmitter and Haas:

> It would be difficult to overestimate the influence of ECLA both on Latin American economic thought in general and on the regional market scheme in particular. From its first meeting in 1948, ECLA evinced a vague interest in a "Latin American customs union." This interest lay dormant—with the exception of the creation of a Committee of Economic Cooperation for Central America in 1951—until 1956 when the newly formed Trade Committee was specifically instructed to consider the formation of a regional market. Starting cautiously and advancing on several fronts, ECLA's *expertos* developed a comprehensive theoretical statement supporting the desirability of regional integration.[6]

As a formal entity under the United Nations, ECLA is governed by accords reached by general meetings of the Commission, a body made up of the various member states.[7] The discussions and resolutions of these meetings authorize and direct the activities of the ECLA secretariat and make recommendations of policy to the member states, especially in the areas of data collection and in the continent's position in worldwide meetings. In principle, the Commission meetings set ECLA's policy, but in practice the discussions tend to center around the various reports presented to the

5 See Raymond F. Mikesell, "The Movement toward Regional Trading Groups in Latin America," in *Latin American Issues*, ed. Albert O. Hirschman (New York: Twentieth Century Fund, 1961), pp. 125–51; Gustavo Lagos, "The Political Role of Regional Economic Associations in Latin America," *Journal of Common Market Studies* 6, no. 4 (June 1968): 291–309; Robert W. Gregg, "The UN Regional Economic Commission and Integration in the Undeveloped Regions," *International Organization* 20, no. 2 (Spring 1966): 208–32.

6 See Schmitter and Haas, *Mexico and Latin American Integration*.

7 The current members are those listed in Table 1 plus Barbados and Guyana, admitted at the 1967 meeting.

Commission by ECLA's professional secretariat. The secretariat thus programs, or at least attempts to program, the Commission's discussion and its consequent formal resolutions. Moreover, an integral part of each meeting comprises the secretary-general's annual report that, especially under Prebisch but even under his two successors, José Antonio Mayobre and Carlos Quintana, in reality is a lecture detailing the prevailing ECLA doctrine. Commission meetings are therefore as much an educational experience for the various delegates as they are policy-making meetings of Latin American countries. Although there are frequently disagreements among member states about policy, the resolutions passed tend to be by unanimous vote and represent the maximum consensus obtainable by the secretariat at a given meeting.[8]

The importance of the experts (or *técnicos*), both national and inter-American, in regional integration in Latin America emerges clearly in studies of such attempts at economic integration as the Latin American Free Trade Area (LAFTA) and the Central American Common Market.[9] But beyond noting that the *técnicos* are important, such studies rarely describe empirically who the *técnicos* are and what effect, if any, they have on promoting integration.

It seems reasonable to assume that the national *técnicos*, at least, would most likely appear as members of their national delegations to commission meetings of the ECLA. Indeed, an examination of the delegates to the thirteen meetings of ECLA since 1948 indicates that delegates either are members of the national diplomatic corps (such as ambassadors to the countries hosting the meetings) or persons whose positions indicate that they could be *técnicos* (such as heads of central banks, national planning agencies, and finance

8   Until recently, dissenting votes, if any, have not been reported in official minutes of ECLA meetings. Under the rules of procedure of the commission, each member nation has one vote and voting is by secret ballot. Beginning with the twelfth session of the Commission in 1967, however, negative votes and abstentions on resolutions have been reported. The dissenters and abstainers have almost without exception been the non–Latin American members (Canada, France, Netherlands, United Kingdom, and United States) and Cuba. There has apparently been unanimity among the Latin American countries on resolutions (although Brazil abstained once in the twelfth session and once in the thirteenth).

9   Cf. Mikesell, "The Movement toward Regional Trading Groups"; Haas and Schmitter, "Economics and Differential Patterns of Political Integration"; Schmitter and Haas, *Mexico and Latin American Integration*; Gustavo Magariños, "Integration Instruments and LAFTA Achievements," in *Latin American Economic Integration*, ed. Miguel S. Wionczek (New York: Praeger, 1966), pp. 124–37; Miguel S. Wionczek, "A History of the Montevideo Treaty," in *Latin American Economic Integration*, pp. 67–104; and Victor L. Urquidi, *Free Trade and Economic Integration in Latin America* (Berkeley: University of California Press, 1962), to name a few.

ministers). Thus José Antonio Mayobre of Venezuela, secretary-general of ECLA after Prebisch, was a member of the Venezuelan delegation prior to his assumption of the secretary-generalship, as well as after leaving that post. Placido Garcia Reynoso of Mexico, Sergio Molina of Chile, and José Garrido Torres of Brazil were frequently members of their national delegations.[10]

The research reported in this chapter, exploratory in nature, seeks to determine what role, if any, prior associations of delegates to the ECLA meetings since 1949 may have had on the substantive output, or consensus, of those meetings. It is a systematic examination of the annual reports submitted by ECLA to its parent body, the United Nations Economic and Social Council. These reports contain, among other things, rosters of all delegations to all official ECLA meetings, the minutes of those meetings, and copies of all resolutions passed by the commission. The rosters of delegations enable us to chart interpersonal communication on the basis of which individuals attended more than one meeting. A content analysis of the resolutions gives us some notion of the nature of "consensus" reached by the meetings.[11]

The limitations of the study are apparent from the data sources used. We are not measuring interpersonal communication directly. The best we can say is that the individuals who appeared at more than one meeting, whom we label "alumni" and "old boys," *could* have communicated with each other at these meetings. This is not at all certain, since the number of delegates in the relevant meetings ranged from 64 to 195. As an individual went to meeting after meeting, however, the likelihood that he would have recognized familiar individuals and engaged in communication with them over the normal ten-day period of the meeting increased, especially since most of the work of the meetings is done in smaller committees.

A further limiting factor is that the delegates to the ECLA meetings may not be the illusive *técnicos* at all. It could be that the *técnicos* are really the anonymous members of the ECLA secretariat, or technicians in national ministries who themselves do not attend ECLA

10 Ernst Haas, in personal correspondence, points out that there is no accepted definition of *técnico*. In his project, economists who were trained in ECLA courses and went on to become either regional officials or national officials and politicians were considered as *técnicos*. If so, our data provide only an indirect test of the *técnico* hypothesis, depending on the degree to which they appear in national delegations.

11 The inventory of delegations and the coding scheme for the content analysis of ECLA resolutions were done by Robert Simpson and Catherine Abbee, together with the author; the actual content analysis of the resolutions was done by María Christina Mathiason, Robert Simpson, Don LaCombe, and the author.

meetings, or even individuals who meet in other types of meetings of a more technical or academic character, like the Inter-American Planning Association or the meetings of continent-wide product associations mentioned by Haas and Schmitter.[12] This is to an extent an academic question since, like most United Nations agencies, the ECLA secretariat does its work anonymously, and rosters of national ministries, or of other types of meetings, were impossible to come by short of field work in Latin America. In any case, the role of ECLA in pushing integration and the positions held by most delegates suggest that there are as good reasons to believe that the *técnicos* attended these meetings as there are to believe that they are to be found elsewhere.

A last limiting factor is our dependent variable: the formal resolutions as an indicator of consensus in a meeting. It may be argued that the resolutions do not fully mirror the consensus or dissent of the meetings. Indeed, the most important effects of the meetings might come later, in national policies toward integration, or in slowly changing cognitions of delegates as a result of interactions. But it seems certain that the resolutions represent what could be called the minimum agreement reached by the delegates, if not all of it.

Given these limitations, what the study attempted to determine concretely was the relationship between the relative number of individuals in a given meeting of the Commission who had been to prior meetings and the consensus about Latin American integration reflected in the formal resolutions at that meeting for the twelve Commission meetings held between 1949 and 1969.[13]

"OLD BOYS" AND "ALUMNI" AT ECLA MEETINGS

At any given meeting, a delegate is either a first-timer, "alumnus," or "old boy."[14] An "old boy," a term characterizing the British "inner establishment" made up of alumni of prestigious secondary schools, is any individual who attended two or more meetings of ECLA prior

12　Haas and Schmitter, "Economics and Differential Patterns of Political Integration."

13　ECLA meetings are actually of three kinds, but those other than Commission meetings ("committee of the whole" and "extraordinary meetings") almost always deal with internal procedural matters rather than substance and were dropped from the analysis, as was the inaugural Commission meeting in 1948, for that reason.

14　A delegate was defined as any individual included in the roster of personnel officially attending Commission meetings as part of a member state's representation. In practice, one individual is designated as the official "representative," while others are "alternate representatives" or "advisers."

to the one in question. These individuals represent the real veterans of ECLA meetings, the individuals most likely to know other repeaters at the meeting. An ECLA "alumnus" is any individual who attended one ECLA meeting prior to the meeting in question. Categorization of delegates was accomplished by comparing the rosters of each meeting with those preceding it to determine who had attended prior meetings.[15]

There are sound theoretic reasons for believing that large numbers of "old boys" or "alumni" would aid in the development of consensus at a given meeting. Studies of communication behavior have frequently found that shared experience facilitates communication.[16] That is, individuals are likely to be cooriented to objects in a situation because of extended experience in similar situations. Thus delegates to an ECLA meeting who have attended prior meetings have presumably "learned the ropes" about ECLA and absorbed ECLA doctrine. Their prior experience should facilitate discussion and agreement in working committees, since they do not have to concern themselves with structuring the conference environment itself. In fact, with communication in the meetings thus facilitated, we might expect more substantive output in favor of pro-integration resolutions.

But, it could be argued, delegates represent governments rather than themselves and in their resolutions may merely reflect policies of their governments. Observers have noted that only infrequently do personalities enter into serious negotiations. If so, we might expect no relationship between having large numbers of "old boys" and "alumni" among national delegations on the one hand and, on the other, the outcomes of the conferences.

An examination by country of the total number of delegates to the various ECLA meetings indicates that an average of about 18 percent of national delegates attend more than one meeting (Table 1).

15   The actual procedure was to examine delegations to all thirty ECLA meetings (see n. 13 above) country by country. From this, individuals who had attended more than one meeting over the twenty-year period were isolated and punched on cards by name with meetings attended also coded. Then, for each meeting, sorts were made on a counter-sorter to find those "repeaters" who had attended a given meeting. These individuals were then examined by sorting to previous meetings to determine if, for the present meeting, they could be classified as either "old boys" or "alumni." Although "old boys" or "alumni" status could be based on meetings of the committee of the whole or extraordinary meetings as well as Commission meetings, we discovered that the "old boy" or "alumni" status was almost always based on one type of meeting. It should also be noted that an "old boy" is also an "alumnus" by definition.

16   E.g., Theodore M. Newcomb, "An Approach to the Study of Communicative Acts," *Psychological Review* 60, no. 6 (November 1953): 393–404.

Members of the ECLA from outside Latin America (Canada,
France, Netherlands, United Kingdom, and United States) have
relatively more repeaters. This reflects the fact that these countries
tend to send, out of their large foreign ministries, delegates who are
specialists in Latin American organization to defend their countries'
interests. These individuals are political representatives rather than
técnicos. It is also clear from the table that smaller nations in Latin

Table 1. Delegation Composition 1948–69, by Country

Country	Total Number of Delegates	Number of Delegates Attending More Than One Meeting	Percentage of Delegates Repeating
*Argentina	121	16	13%
*Bolivia	88	11	13
*Brazil	125	23	18
**Canada	19	5	26
*Chile	112	32	29
*Colombia	111	6	5
Costa Rica	29	5	17
*Cuba	78	15	19
Dominican Republic	23	4	17
Ecuador	47	8	17
El Salvador	34	7	21
France	72	18	25
Haiti	21	3	14
Honduras	38	7	18
**Jamaica	9	0	0
*Mexico	102	16	16
Netherlands	53	21	40
Nicaragua	25	5	20
*Panama	79	9	11
Paraguay	30	3	10
*Peru	88	8	9
**Trinidad	9	3	33
United Kingdom	66	15	23
United States	97	28	29
*Uruguay	58	11	19
*Venezuela	85	17	20
Total	1,619	296	18.3%

* Has been host country for one or more Commission meetings.
** Membership in ECLA has been recent.

America sent fewer delegates (presumably a function of cost), although the proportions of repeaters are consistent with Latin America as a whole.

The presence of "old boys" and "alumni" at specific meetings is
highly variable from meeting to meeting (Table 2). At the ninth
session of the Commission in 1961, 33 percent of delegates were

"alumni," whereas at the sixth session in 1955 less than one delegate in ten was an "alumnus." The pattern of "old boys" differs somewhat as well, from a maximum of 15 percent in 1957 (mostly accounted for by "old boys" from non–Latin American countries) to a minimum of 4.6 percent in 1955 and 1959.

If the common experience theory has any validity, more consensus would be expected in those meetings, like 1961 and 1951, where the

Table 2. "Old Boy" and "Alumni" Presence at Commission Meetings

Commission meeting and year	All Delegates			Latin American Delegates		
	Total number	Percentage "alumni"	Percentage "old boys"	Total number	Percentage "alumni"	Percentage "old boys"
1 (1948)	64	——	——	51	——	——
2 (1949)	72	15.3%	——	57	14.0%	——
3 (1950)	70	25.8	10.1%	55	21.8	9.1%
4 (1951)	74	25.6	8.2	54	27.8	11.2
5 (1953)	146	19.2	4.7	121	17.4	4.1
6 (1955)	195	8.7	4.6	166	7.2	4.2
7 (1957)	147	15.0	15.0	129	13.2	3.8
8 (1959)	175	16.0	4.6	145	13.7	4.2
9 (1961)	147	32.7	12.3	114	29.0	11.4
10 (1963)	143	17.4	6.9	101	14.9	4.0
11 (1965)	157	21.6	10.8	120	21.7	9.2
12 (1967)	135	22.2	11.1	104	20.2	8.7
13 (1969)	152	21.1	10.5	125	16.1	8.8
(Average)	(129)	(18.5%)	(7.6%)	(103)	(16.7%)	(6.1%)

proportion of "old boys" and "alumni" among delegates was higher than in other meetings, especially those of 1955 and 1957.

CONSENSUS IN ECLA MEETINGS

The measure of minimal agreement or consensus is an analysis of the resolutions passed by Commission meetings coded on two dimensions: substantive content and communication behavior.[17] By

17 Because of the complex nature of both the resolutions and the codes, each resolution was coded twice to obtain a reasonable reliability. One coder coded all resolutions and several others coded various segments. The principal coder was María Christina Mathiason, who was chosen because she is not a native speaker of English and would be less concerned with detecting nuances in phraseology ("reading things into data"). The coding checks were made by Simpson, LaCombe, and the author. Whenever discrepancies between coders were found, we returned to the text of the resolution and determined who was correct. In half of the first codes there were discrepancies, and of these, half were resolved in favor of the principal coder, giving us a .75 reliability on the principal coder's work. All codes, however, were agreed upon before processing.

ECLA's formal numbering procedure there have been 295 resolutions passed since 1948, most of them at Commission meetings. We discovered, however, that these resolutions did not provide an adequate unit for analysis. First, the length and comprehensiveness of resolutions were extremely variable. Some resolutions would be on a specific subject (such as provisions for a Latin American census), while others would deal with a broad subject area (such as Latin American trade). Second, the preambles in the resolutions were complexes of "whereases," "notings that," and "mindful of" clauses, frequently establishing precedents for action on the basis of conference documents, Economic and Social Council resolutions, and the like. To make our unit of analysis as manageable as possible, we decided to ignore the preambles in resolutions and code only the enacting clauses of the resolution (usually keyed by the words "decides" or "resolves"), on the assumption that any material from the preamble that was important would be repeated in the enacting clauses of varying lengths. To deal with the problem of enacting clauses, we decided to treat each separate statement in an enacting clause as a separate resolution. In practice, when there was more than one enacting statement, it was usually numbered in the text of the general resolution. By this procedure 812 "resolutions" of commission meetings from 1949 to 1959 were coded on our two dimensions.

The substantive content of resolutions was coded into four categories, based on the predominant concern of the resolution: direct integration, indirect integration, national development, and other. "Direct integration" resolutions were any whose content indicated that Latin American countries are, or should be, working together as a group for a common purpose with common procedures. The resolution's content indicated that the system level being discussed was "Latin America as a unit." These made up 14.2 percent of the total.

"Indirect integration" resolutions were those whose content indicated that Latin American countries are, or should be, acting as individual countries but either for a common purpose or in a way that would further future integration. Basically this category mostly concerned Latin American countries in their relations with the industrialized countries. Here the system level is between the individual country and Latin America treated as a coalition.[18] These made up 28.9 percent of the total.

"National development" resolutions called for Latin American

18   E.g., "Latin America countries should establish a common market."

countries to act as individual countries on purely internal problems. Here the system level is the nation-state. These made up 14.5 percent of the total.

"Other" resolutions were all those remaining, mostly dealing with such internal mechanics of ECLA as instructions or authorizations to the secretariat as well as a few ceremonial or "bread and butter" resolutions. These made up 42.4 percent of the total.

There was great variability in the substantive content of resolutions passed over time (Table 3). Pro-integration resolutions tended to increase steadily (with the exception of 1961) until 1965, after which they decreased drastically. This seems generally to follow

Table 3. Substantive Content of ECLA Resolutions by Commission Meeting

Substantive Category (percentages)

Commission meeting and year	Direct integration	Indirect integration	Direct and indirect integration	National development	Other	Total number of resolutions
2 (1949)	3.0%	37.9%	40.9%	39.4%	19.7%	66
3 (1950)	6.7	53.3	60.0	11.1	28.9	45
4 (1951)	2.3	23.5	25.8	12.1	62.1	132
5 (1953)	14.1	26.9	41.0	17.9	41.0	78
6 (1955)	18.2	31.2	49.4	10.4	40.3	77
7 (1957)	18.5	24.6	43.1	6.2	50.8	65
8 (1959)	19.1	34.0	53.1	14.9	31.9	47
9 (1961)	8.2	29.8	38.0	16.5	45.4	97
10 (1963)	25.6	19.2	44.8	14.1	41.0	78
11 (1965)	46.7	13.3	60.0	2.2	37.8	45
12 (1967)	16.3	44.2	60.5	4.7	34.9	43
13 (1969)	10.3	25.6	35.9	23.1	41.0	39
(Average)	(14.2%)	(28.9%)	(43.1%)	(14.5%)	(42.4%)	(68)

Latin American attempts at actual integration: these countries sought to emulate the emerging Common Market between 1955 and 1965, by which time repeated failures to achieve subregional integration and the increasingly evident stagnation of the LAFTA led individual countries to reconsider the whole idea.

The gross subject matter of resolutions may, of course, mask the level of consensus achieved. Consequently, a second dimension was coded under the assumption that certain communication behaviors implied in the resolutions were stronger than others. Only resolutions in the first three substantive categories were so coded. It was postulated that there are five fundamental types of communication acts: to state or order a desired behavior, state information, seek information, reiterate past communications, or engage in meaningless ritualistic or expressive communication. Similarly, the purpose of communication can either be to define a situation (any specific organization of objects at a specific time or in a specific context) or to define a procedure (a behavioral rule for organizing communicative acts that defines the order in which such acts should occur; for example, if X, then Y and Z). Combining these, we postulated an order of communications behavior from strongest to weakest, with eight coding categories. A resolution:

1. "States behavior" if it specifies that some preexisting procedure is to be followed in a specific instance—for example, "Latin American countries should establish the LAFTA by March 1960";

2. "States information to define a procedure" if it specifies a new procedure and its content without ordering it to be followed in a specific instance—for example, "Latin American countries should not accept external financing that jeopardizes their national sovereignty";

3. "States information to define a situation" if it specifies the attribute for a given situation or gives what was agreed to be "reality"—for example, "a common market is the only solution for Latin America's economic ills";

4. "Seeks information to define a procedure" if it requests someone to attempt to define a procedure or seek information to that end—for example, "a committee will be formed to find ways to standardize customs nomenclature";

5. "Seeks information to define a situation" if it requests someone to gather information for further consideration in defining a situation—for example, "there should be a study of balance of payments in Latin America";

6. "Reiterates past communication about procedures"—for example, "the secretariat will *continue* to publish yearly reports";

7. "Reiterates a past definition of the situation"—for example, "we reaffirm that the fundamental problem in Latin America is an unfavorable balance of trade"; or

8. Is "expressive behavior" if it contains only formalities like expression of gratitude and so forth—for example, "ECLA thanks the government of Bolivia for offering to hold the next Commission meeting in La Paz."

Over time the emphasis in the meetings' communicative behavior tended to fluctuate (Table 4).

The presence of "old boys" and "alumni" at ECLA meetings was, if anything, negatively related to pro-integration resolutions (Table

Table 4. Communication Behavior in ECLA Substantive Resolutions by Commission Meetings

Commission meeting and year	Communication Behavior Categories (*percentages*)								Total resolutions
	1 States behavior	2 States procedure	3 States definitions	4 Seeks information for procedure	5 Seeks information for definition	6 Reiterates procedure	7 Reiterates definition	8 Expressive behavior	
2 (1949)	17.0%	26.4%	26.4%	13.2%	15.1%	—%	—%	1.9%	53
3 (1950)	9.4	15.6	21.9	15.6	18.8	12.5		6.3	32
4 (1951)	30.0	14.0	4.0	12.0	20.0	12.0	6.0	2.0	50
5 (1953)	23.9	23.9	8.9	15.2	15.2	8.7	4.3		46
6 (1955)	32.6	15.2	19.6	8.9	4.3	15.2	2.2	2.2	46
7 (1957)	21.9	9.4	9.4	25.0	21.9	9.4	3.1		32
8 (1959)	21.9	25.0		18.8	15.6	15.6		3.1	32
9 (1961)	18.9	15.1	5.7	26.4	20.8	5.7	3.8	3.8	53
10 (1963)	8.9	15.2	4.3	32.6	19.6	10.9	2.2	6.5	46
11 (1965)	14.3	28.6	3.6	14.3	21.4	7.1	10.7		28
12 (1967)	10.7	35.7		28.6	17.9	7.1			28
13 (1969)	—	56.5	4.3	17.4	4.3	13.0	4.3		23
(Average)	(17.5%)	(23.4%)	(9.0%)	(19.0%)	(16.2%)	(9.8%)	(3.1%)	(2.2%)	(39)

5).[19] When "alumni" and "old boys" make their weight felt, there is more emphasis on procedural resolutions dealing with the internal workings of ECLA rather than with exhorting Latin American countries to integrate. Concealed in the correlations may be an implicit effect, in fact, of reducing incentives for making substantive

Table 5. Relationships between "Old Boys," "Alumni," and Substantive Resolutions*

| | Proportions of Resolutions | | | |
	Direct integration	Indirect integration	National development	Procedural
All "alumni"	−.13	−.21	−.06	.41
All "old boys"	.21	−.13	−.66	.50
Latin American "alumni"	−.19	.00	−.17	.36
Latin American "old boys" N = 12	−.02	−.02	−.47	.48

* Product-moment correlation coefficient and significance levels, with a two-tailed test of significance; underlined values are significant at the $p < .10$ level.

resolutions. Figure 1 indicates that on the two occasions when Latin American "old boys" and "alumni" made up sizable proportions of the total Latin American delegates in 1951 and 1961, direct integration resolutions were at their lowest relative point. Furthermore, when Latin American "old boys" and "alumni" were at their lowest relative levels (1955, 1957, 1959, and 1963), direct integration resolutions were at their relatively highest levels.

At least four possible explanations of this phenomenon exist. First, in those years Latin American countries may purposely have avoided sending "old hands" to the ECLA meetings in order to stimulate the Commission to action. This does not make a great deal of sense, however, since the secretariat has consistently pushed for an activist role for the Commission on integration. Another explanation is that, due to extraneous factors, fewer "old hands" showed up at meetings and the infusion of new blood pushed ECLA discussion away from

19 Interpersonal communication measures and the consensus measures were examined both by comparing time-series graphs and by correlations of the proportions of "old boys" and "alumni" in meetings with the proportions of different categories in the resolution codes.

It may be statistically dubious to correlate with a product-moment coefficient what are essentially percentages expressed with a one-place decimal number (e.g., 10.5). But given that the actual raw scores depended on the number of delegates and number of resolutions that varied from meeting to meeting, and because the main variable is the proportion of each type of delegate or resolution, it seemed more reasonable to convert all of the scores in the study to a common base.

Figure 1. Relationship between Proportions of Latin American "Old Boys,"
"Alumni," and Direct Integration Resolutions over Time

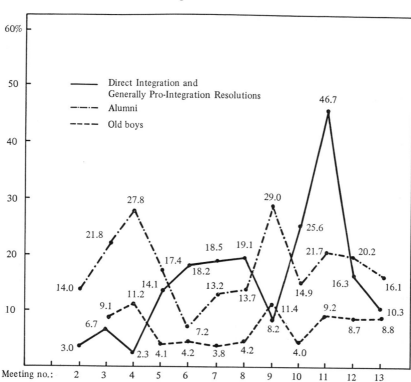

the familiar, if trivial, internal mechanics of the organization itself
into a more advocatory context. Or, third, it may have been that the
first-time delegates were more easily swayed by the secretariat than
the more or less inoculated veterans of ECLA's biennial ten-day
marathon meetings. Either of these is plausible and merits further
investigation.

A final explanation is that the data may show nothing at all about
interpersonal communication or meeting dynamics. Rather, they
reflect a growing continent-wide consensus about integration developed outside ECLA from 1953 to 1965, primed by the European
Common Market and reinforced by LAFTA. This may well be. The
general upward trend of pro-integration resolutions observable from
1953 to 1965, however, is interrupted in 1961, the year of greatest
"old boy" and "alumni" participation. There seems to be no salient

event in 1961 that could explain ECLA's temporary abandonment of integration as a subject area.[20]

Since we did not code nonsubstantive resolutions on the dimension of communication behavior, and since the major effect of "old boys" and "alumni" is in terms of a dichotomy of substantive and nonsubstantive resolutions, the relevance of this dimension as a variable is considerably reduced. Some differences nonetheless emerge to strengthen the finding that relatively large numbers of "alumni" in presence impedes pro-integration activity. First, there is a consistent (if not always very significant) negative relationship between stating behavior or stating definitions of situations in resolutions and having relatively few "alumni" present (Table 6).

Table 6. Relationships between "Old Boys" and "Alumni" and Communication Behavior in Substantive Resolutions*

| | | *Proportions of Resolutions* | | |
	Stating behavior	Stating definition of situation	Seeking information to define procedure	Seeking information to define situation
All "alumni"	−.16	−.54	.33	.42
All "old boys"	−.29	−.44	.46	.38
Latin American "alumni"	−.10	−.32	.14	.58
Latin American "old boys" N = 12	−.18	−.45	.06	.22

* Product-moment correlation coefficients and significance levels, with a two-tailed test of significance; underlined values are significant at the $p < .10$ level.

Second, there is a general positive relationship between having relatively many "alumni" on hand and passing substantive resolutions that seek information. Both exhortation and advocacy as well as information-gathering are mandated functions of ECLA but, when "alumni" are strongly present, there is a tendency to emphasize the more passive of the two. This raises an awkward question: if "alumni" represent the *técnicos*, do the *técnicos* actually impede integration by emphasizing "more research" instead of "more action"?

From an examination of the content of ECLA resolutions in relationship to interpersonal communication, it would seem that there are indications that the "alumni" and "old boys" act to brake ECLA's attempts to promote integration by becoming concerned with

20 Additionally, the measures of "old boy" and "alumni" concentration in meetings are rather crude and may only be sensitive in correlations at their extreme values. This is especially true of the "old boy" concentrations, where the maximum variance from the mean is only 5 percent.

ECLA's own internal matters (who shall do what research, and so forth). This impression is strengthened when levels of "alumni" and "old boy" participation in meetings are correlated with the volume of output of meetings measured by the number of resolutions passed at a meeting (Table 7). The more "alumni" at a meeting,

Table 7. Relationships between "Old Boys" and "Alumni" and Volume of Resolutions Passed*

	Number of Resolutions Passed
All "alumni"	.71
All "old boys"	.28
Latin American "alumni"	.56
Latin American "old boys"	.42
$N = 12$	

* Product-moment correlation coefficients and significance levels, with a two-tailed test of significance; underlined values are significant at the $p < .10$ level.

relatively speaking, the more resolutions passed by the meeting. Thus in 1951 and 1961, the years with highest levels of "alumni," the meetings adopted 132 and 97 resolutions, respectively.

This fact places the "alumni" effect into a more meaningful context. Groups work best when there is some familiarity among group members and common knowledge of the subject matter. There may also be some desire to avoid potential conflict situations, and consequently to deal with those aspects of problems that are not likely to be contested. Turning inward to ECLA, whose tasks are not subject at least to national conflicts and whose organization is familiar to delegates, would seem to be a logical step. "Old boys" and "alumni" in large numbers at a meeting whose major work is done in a committee setting may well be caught up in considering nonconflictful items that are familiar to most. And, uninterrupted by naïve questions like "Why are we resolving to make more studies instead of encouraging a common market?" they may forget the previous trends of ECLA resolutions or even forget their instructions (if such are given to national delegations) in the dynamic of the friendly meeting. In such circumstances it would be relatively easy for a ten-day meeting to turn out great numbers of amicably reached but innocuous resolutions. If this interpretation has merit, the term "alumni" has a certain symbolic meaning. ECLA meetings with many veterans of prior meetings indeed tend to be like reunions of college alumni where old friends gather to discuss items of mutual interest but of trivial importance.

The communication dynamics of international conferences (or large-scale decision-making bodies generally) is a new and almost nonexistent field of study in international communications. Our study indicates that it is a worthy one, and the interpersonal communication component cannot be ignored. It calls into question the notion that such conferences are devoid of individual personal variables and that, in fact, genuine progress at such conferences can be impeded by having delegates who are old friends.

seventeen

The National Boundary in Politics and Economics

Hans O. Schmitt

POLITICAL integration and disintegration are questions of redrawing boundaries on the map. We are not concerned in this paper with exactly where a boundary gets drawn, but with why a boundary is to be drawn at all, and between whom. The political boundary has been defined as "a line of contact of territorial power structures."[1] Specific boundaries at any given time are "the political geographic expression of the existing balance of forces at that period."[2] The power structures we are concerned with are modern nation-states.

Three types of boundaries can be distinguished: those of the nation, the state, and the economy. Their exact coincidence defines the modern nation-state in the abstract. Each boundary, however, is affected by its own set of principles, as well as by interactions among them. Boundaries rarely coincide in fact, therefore, but any substantial deviation will produce conflicts whose resolutions determine whether a particular nation-state will remain viable or not. Much work has already been done by Karl Deutsch and his associates on communications systems as the basis for national integration.[3] The work done by Ernst Haas and his students on the integration of state

1 Stephen B. Jones, "Boundary Concepts in the Setting of Place and Time," *Annals of the Association of American Geographers* 49, no. 3 (September 1959): 253.
2 Nicholas J. Spykman and Abbie A. Rollins, "Geographic Objectives in Foreign Policy, I," *American Political Science Review* 33, no. 3 (June 1939): 391.
3 Karl W. Deutsch, *Nationalism and Social Communication: An Inquiry into the Foundations of Nationality,* (Cambridge: Technology Press of the Massachusetts Institute of Technology; New York: John Wiley and Sons, 1953), and subsequent works.

structures through bureaucratic practice is also far advanced.[4] This paper focuses attention primarily on the economic aspect, where theorizing has remained relatively backward.

The key to the analysis is that political activity is not identified with any one of the three spheres just listed. Instead, politicization is thought to be possible—and indeed necessary, for boundary formation—within all three. Politicization is defined as a process by which the basic allocative decisions in a society are called in question. This can occur equally well on the basis of nationality, bureaucratic power, or economic interest.

The paper falls into three parts. In the first section the need for theory on political integration in the national, state, and economic contexts is reviewed. The second section proposes a paradigm on political integration for the economic sphere. An analysis of its relation to parallel paradigms for state and nation is postponed. Instead, a final section explores the credibility of the economic construct alone, with reference to contemporary European experience in an Atlantic setting.

CURRENT THEORY

Analytically we distinguish three spheres of social activity in which integration or disintegration can take place. The *nation* is a culturally homogenous group that is politically active as such. Culture involves common traditions, aspirations, and symbols for communicating them. Two problems arise in theorizing about it.[5] First, the process by which an ethnic group that does not amount to a nationality becomes an ethnically based nationality, active in politics, needs to be better understood. Second, nationalities are not stable phenomena. They shift about on the map, some appearing and others disappearing in ways that need to be more precisely explained than they are.

The *state* is "the residual authority par excellence in the world today."[6] It is represented by a set of institutions and by their personnel, on whom a population calls to meet new and unexpected needs, whose satisfaction cannot be ensured by other more functionally

4   Ernst B. Haas, *The Uniting of Europe: Political, Social, and Economic Forces, 1950–57* (Stanford: Stanford University Press, 1958), and subsequent works.

5   Benjamin Akzin, *States and Nations* (Garden City, N.Y.: Doubleday, 1966), pp. 41–42. In the present essay "nation" and "nationality" are used interchangeably.

6   Karl W. Deutsch, "Communications Theory and Political Integration," in *The Integration of Political Communities*, eds. Philip E. Jacob and James V. Toscano (Philadelphia and New York: J. B. Lippincott, 1964), p. 73.

specific agencies. Loyalty most easily attaches to this locus of ultimate recourse. What needs to be explained are the factors that affect the capabilities of a state, more particularly of its bureaucracy, to meet demand loads placed upon it by constituents. A second query concerns the conditions under which expanding loads result in integration with other state structures, or in disintegration of particular structures into component parts.

The *economy* is usually identified with the market, a set of customs by which goods and services are produced and distributed. The market is bounded by its currency. Within a currency area actors operate as individuals in competition with each other. Toward other currency areas they act collectively as well, by changes in the exchange rate, or in other ways that affect the terms of exchange among business communities rather than among businessmen. The fundamental problem is to determine whether the limits of a currency area are imposed on the market, or whether economic factors themselves can account for them. If the latter, then it becomes useful to trace its interaction with other boundaries in shaping the modern nation-state.

The Nation

Deutsch concentrates on the factors that determine national cohesion. The question he poses is "why people insist at certain times upon having a sovereign state of their own which occupies a sharply bounded area of the world."[7] His method is characterized as, in a sense, "market research for regional or interregional government."[8] His basic premise appears to be that "political integration cannot occur until after a process of social assimilation creates a homogenous transnational population."[9] Since his tests fail to indicate that a homogeneous people has yet evolved across the continent of Europe, he remains pessimistic about the political future of the European Community.[10]

7 Deutsch, *Nationalism and Social Communication*, p. 46.
8 Ibid., p. 56.
9 William E. Fisher, "An Analysis of the Deutsch Sociocausal Paradigm of Political Integration," *International Organization*, 23, no. 2 (Spring 1969): 254. "Homogeneous" may be too strong a term; what is basically required is "complementarity of communications habits." (See Deutsch, *Nationalism and Social Communication*, p. 96.)
10 In Karl W. Deutsch, "Integration and Arms Control in the European Political Environment: A Summary Report," *American Political Science Review* 60, no. 2 (June 1966): 354–65. See also Karl W. Deutsch, Lewis J. Edinger, Roy C. Macridis, and Richard L. Merritt, *France, Germany, and the Western Alliance: A Study of Elite Attitudes on European Integration and World Politics* (New York: Charles Scribner's Sons, 1967).

The boundaries of the nation do not necessarily coincide with those of the state or of para-statal supranational institutions. A dual relation between them could more plausibly be postulated. The state requires a degree of compliance and popular support to function, and it will have neither if it is perceived as unresponsive to national expectations.[11] The state, however, is in turn a factor in the formation of nations. "It is the capabilities and performances of government," writes Deutsch, "that provide the key to integration and cohesion in societies."[12] The relationship between state and nation is likely therefore to be reciprocal. At any one time they may fail to overlap precisely. In a hypothetical equilibrium they will coincide, as each adjusts to the other.

Economic factors similarly affect the evolution of nationality, although the economy appears to be a more ephemeral concept here than is the state. Social communication, the essence of nationality for Deutsch, includes a wide range of transactions that are normally considered to be economic. The communications centers, around which nations are thought likely to crystallize, are identified not only in terms of governmental structures with superior capabilities of response, but also as concentrations of capital and technology and as centers of trade, credit, and currency.[13] Economic transactions may well provide the motivation for the bulk of the communications flows from which the sense of nationality is presumed to derive.

The correspondence between transactions flows and nationality is again unlikely to be exact. To be sure, the growth of community and a sense of obligation to it is improbable without active social intercommunication. But transactions as such are a doubtful indicator for their existence or their bounds.[14] The nature of the transaction needs to be taken into account. The relation between state and nation has already been sketched as reciprocal, not unidirectional. That between economic transactions and the nation can fruitfully be considered the same. What is still lacking, in that case, is a theory for the growth of nationality itself—one that can account for its boundaries differing from those of the economy and the state at once.[15]

11   Deutsch, "Communications Theory and Political Integration," p. 60.
12   Karl W. Deutsch, "The Price of Integration," in *The Integration of Political Communities*, ed. Jacob and Toscano, p. 143.
13   Deutsch, *Nationalism and Social Communication*, pp. 33, 143.
14   Philip E. Jacob and Henry Teune, "The Integrative Process: Guidelines for Analysis of the Bases for Political Community," in *The Integration of Political Communities*, ed. Jacob and Toscano, p. 4.
15   The most promising approach to take is probably through a study of political socialization. On the pitfalls, see my "Decolonization and Development in Burma," *Journal of Development Studies* 4, no. 1 (October 1967): 97–108.

The State

Ernst Haas focuses attention on "political institutions capable of translating ideologies into law."[16] Integration is thought of as "the process whereby political actors in several distinct national settings are persuaded to shift their loyalties, expectations and political activities toward a new center, whose institutions possess or demand jurisdiction over the pre-existing nation states."[17] The emphasis is on the role of "bureaucratic practice, organizational ideology, and the creative interventions of administrative and political elites."[18] Note that the new center here is not conceived as geographic or economic; it is an administrative arrangement whose particular location is irrelevant.

An integrative process is set afoot when cooperation between states for specific welfare-oriented benefits is seen to be possible, even where political cooperation is not.[19] Assuming interlocking relations between various policy tools and targets, however, the attainment of even partial goals will seem to require delegation to cooperative institutions of progressively more controversial responsibilities.[20] As long as the participating actors make the kind of decisions that will continue to safeguard their collective economic welfare, the process is likely to become cumulative. It will in the end require a redefinition of aims in explicitly political terms.[21]

A logic of political integration in the strictly bureaucratic sphere is thus clearly spelled out. Its relationship to similar processes in the economy or the nation is less defined. National integration is explicitly ruled out as a necessary condition. It is instead assumed that "identity and loyalties will gradually follow interests and expectations in clustering around and supporting institutions associated with policy integration."[22] The economy enters in as providing the original, welfare-oriented material for institutional cooperation, but it is left

16 Haas, *The Uniting of Europe*, p. 7.
17 Ibid., p. 16.
18 Philippe C. Schmitter, "Three Neo-functional Hypotheses about International Integration," *International Organization* 24, no. 1 (Winter 1969): 164.
19 Samuel A. Bleicher, "UN vs. IBRD: A Dilemma of Functionalism," *International Organization* 25, no. 1 (Winter 1970): 42.
20 Schmitter, "Three Neo-functional Hypotheses about International Integration," p. 166.
21 Ernst B. Haas and Philippe C. Schmitter, "Economics and Differential Patterns of Political Integration: Projections about Unity in Latin America," *International Organization* 18, no. 4 (Autumn 1964): 707.
22 Joseph S. Nye, "Comparative Regional Integration: Concept and Measurement," *International Organization* 22, no. 4 (Autumn 1968): 871.

behind as administrative requirements alone generate the demands that drive the process on from there.

A progression from economy to state to nation, with little if any feedback, permits a considerable degree of optimism concerning the prospects of the European community. Speculation continues, how-ever, on the extent to which institutional capabilities can still be im-paired by lack of popular loyalty and support.[23] It is also not clear that welfare concerns alone will provide a sufficient basis for insti-tutional centralization. To achieve purely welfare aims, an inter-government approach appears to be sufficient without a progressive strengthening of central institutions.[24] How far bureaucratic momen-tum on its own can carry, therefore, remains an outstanding question.

The Economy

Theorizing on economic boundaries is less developed than theorizing on the state or nation. To be sure, various degrees of economic in-tegration have been identified, such as free trade areas, customs unions, common markets, economic unions, and full integration, depending on the elimination of internal tariffs, the establishment of external tariffs, the freeing of factor movements, currency unification, or political amalgamation.[25] These alternatives are analyzed mainly in terms of their differential effects on economic efficiency and wel-fare, narrowly conceived. It is recognized that some of the alternatives would presuppose "profound political changes" to be realistic pos-sibilities.[26] However, no need has been felt to formulate a logic of politicization within the economic sphere itself.

The lack of a theory of economic boundaries creates the impression that economic processes are unbounded. Inasmuch as economic forces are not seen to create boundaries, they are assumed to dissolve them. It is on this basis that Gottfried Haberler speaks of "worldwide integration through freer trade" as having been frustrated only by arbitrary political intervention.[27] His views have not gone unchal-lenged. Both Gunnar Myrdal and Albert Hirschman argue that trade

23   This is particularly relevant for the transition from "low" to "high" politics. See Stanley Hoffmann, "The Fate of the Nation State," *Daedalus* 95 (Summer 1966): 882.

24   Lawrence B. Krause, *European Economic Integration and the United States* (Washington: The Brookings Institution, 1968), p. 24.

25   Bela A. Balassa, *The Theory of Economic Integration* (Homewood, Ill.: Richard D. Irwin, 1961), p. 2.

26   Robert A. Mundell, *International Economics* (New York: Macmillan, 1968), p. 182.

27   Gottfried Haberler, "Integration and Growth of the World Economy in Historical Perspective," *American Economic Review* 54, no. 2 (March 1964): 1–22.

liberalization, by exacerbating regional inequalities, is an essentially disruptive force that requires deliberate political intervention to overcome.[28] Neither view perceives economic forces as drawing territorial boundaries on their own.

The role of economic concentration in the integrative process is as uncertain in political theory as it is in economics. Haas holds that, at least among the poor, "the more homogeneous the countries are in economic power the greater the chance of union."[29] Deutsch by contrast argues that integration presupposes concentrations of population, capital, and technology, association with which carries promise of economic reward.[30] Even among the rich, Haas would maintain that such "core areas" are perceived as a threat by their neighbors who may, however, seek political integration in part to restrain their power.[31] To resolve the issue, a more searching analysis of the interaction between core area and hinterland is clearly required.

The salient characteristic of a core area is that it draws factors of production from its environs. It therefore tends to undermine the classical distinction between national and international markets in terms of a mobility of factors of production within, but not across, national boundaries.[32] The same distinction appears once more in modern literature with the notion of an optimum currency area. A depressed area will want to promote exports and employment through depreciation of its own currency, except to the extent that its factors of production are drawn out instead. A currency area should, therefore, reach as far as factor mobility does.[33] Observation shows it does not always do so. That is where the matter rests. Still, it may serve as a starting point for the argument to be developed here.

A FRESH PARADIGM

To fill the gap in political theory, a paradigm must be formulated specifying how boundaries can be drawn by economic forces alone.

28 Gunnar Myrdal, *Economic Theory and Underdeveloped Regions* (London: G. Duckworth, 1957), p. 63; Albert O. Hirschman, *The Strategy of Economic Development* (New Haven: Yale University Press, 1958), p. 187.

29 Mario Barrera and Ernst B. Haas, "The Operationalization of Some Variables Related to Regional Integration: A Research Note," *International Organization* 24, no. 1 (Winter 1969): 195.

30 Karl W. Deutsch et al., *Political Community and the North Atlantic Area: International Organization in the Light of Historical Experience* (Princeton, N.J.: Princeton University Press, 1957), p. 141.

31 Ernst B. Haas, "The Challenge of Regionalism," *International Organization* 12, no. 4 (Autumn 1958): 444–58.

32 Harry G. Johnson, *Comparative Cost and Commercial Policy Theory for a Developing World Economy* (Stockholm: Almqvist & Wiksell, 1968), p. 10.

33 Mundell, *International Economics*, pp. 179ff.

Three basic concepts will be used for this purpose. *Direct investment*, first, refers to an expansion of assets abroad in enterprises effectively controlled by industries at home. It is distinguished from indirect or portfolio investment, which represents a contribution of resources to firms abroad for purposes of participating in their income, not their control. The distinction, as with many like concepts in social science, is difficult to draw precisely in practice. As a rule of thumb, the U.S. Department of Commerce considers a firm abroad to be U.S.-controlled, if the American share in its ownership comes to no less than 10 percent.[34]

The second fundamental concept is that of a *monetary union*. The usual definition of money identifies it as a generally accepted means of payment. It is not the only means of payment. In barter, first, a delivery of goods can cancel a debt incurred by the receipt of other goods. Second, a bill of exchange is an order to pay that a creditor draws on his debtor and which he may pass to his own creditor in settlement of debt. Third, money is similarly a claim that debtor passes to creditor, but this time a claim not on any one other individual, but on the business community collectively. By accepting the implied joint liability, a collection of merchants becomes a business community. Money is very likely, therefore, a social as much as an economic phenomenon.

Labor migration is the third fundamental component to be considered. Labor in this context includes all types of human resource inputs that derive a contractual income from participation in the productive process. As in the case of capital flows, some differentiation will be required—in this case, between wage labor and managerial or salaried labor. Roughly, the distinction is between those drawing an hourly wage and those receiving an annual salary, but the line, again, should not be drawn too sharply. Labor and capital flows together help to shift the limits of a monetary system and, by interacting with the determinants of other types of frontier, the boundaries of the nation-state as well.

Direct Investment

In concentrated industries, each firm sees an advantage in developing a position in each important or potentially important market. Even though its operations may not be immediately profitable in all, the potential payoff from expenditure on applied research and product

---

34 U.S. Department of Commerce, *Survey of Current Business* (October 1968), p. 21.

development will be larger, when the combined market to which it can be applied is larger.[35] To protect their individual stakes, firms may attempt to integrate all stages of production in one enterprise. This allows better coordination of new investments required by technological advances at various stages of production, and it enlarges the financial "ante one needs to amass in order to join the game."[36]

Where markets are separated, direct investment will be necessary to insure regular access to all. An investing company must first have an advantage over actual or potential competitors in the host country, however. Otherwise local entrepreneurs will be better situated to compete. The typical advantage turns on the exclusive possession by the investor of a more advanced technology in marketing, product design, or production methods, as well as management skills and access to finance. If these advantages are clustered in a particular country, then direct investment outflows are likely to exceed inflows. On balance, therefore, an entire business community will be expanding its domain relative to rival business communities elsewhere.

While marginal markets contribute to making innovative investment potentially profitable, technologically progressive firms tend to cluster in the largest ones. Agglomerative tendencies reflect two main factors. "The development of commercial production of a new product requires close contact not only with the customers but more important with the suppliers of machinery, components and so forth, in order to deal with unexpected problems encountered in the process of moving from the planning to the production stage."[37] While successful firms are therefore likely to extend their operations into several markets, they are likely to retain a primary identification with the major industrial centers that produced them.

Portfolio investments are likely to move in the opposite direction from direct investment; they will tend to flow from the industrial periphery to the center. For as long as capital movements are reasonably unrestrained, savers are likely to place their funds with the most successful enterprises whose prospects are favorable and whose payoff is high. Such enterprises are mainly clustered at the center. Persistent resource losses will further narrow the resource base of independent business communities at the periphery, however. At some point they may find it futile to retain a separate identity. That development will be reflected in their currency arrangements.

35   Johnson, *Comparative Cost and Commercial Policy Theory*, p. 20.
36   Charles P. Kindleberger, *American Business Abroad: Six Lectures on Direct Investment* (New Haven and London: Yale University Press, 1969), p. 186.
37   Johnson, *Comparative Cost and Commercial Policy Theory*, pp. 33–34.

A Common Currency

The economic function of money is well known.[38] Specialization in production makes it impossible for the employer to pay his workers in the commodity they helped to produce. Instead, he will pay them with undifferentiated claims against the business community as a whole. Its political significance lies in the fact that a disciplined surrender of command over its own resource base is required of each participating region, if the monetary authority's currency issues are to have unchallenged purchasing power in all. Thus a set of economic relations becomes politicized as soon as it begins to affect the currency arrangements in force over any particular territory, or alters established relationships among competing currency areas.

The existence of more than one currency in the world implies variable exchange rates. A particular rate of exchange depends on the balance not only between exports and imports on current account, but also between inflows and outflows of investment funds. Whether an exchange rate can be judged as an equilibrium rate depends, therefore, on whether the particular pattern of capital flows associated with it is also acceptable. Each such pattern implies a different set of prospects for the business communities involved, and is therefore unlikely to be acquiesced in by all. Rather than accept an adverse "equilibrium," each community will instead attempt to widen its room for maneuver by maintaining a current surplus in its balance of payments.

A surplus on current account indicates that, at the given exchange rate, a particular country's industries are on the whole more efficient than those of its competitors. Hence, as long as the exchange rate holds, the country in question is likely to attract portfolio investment rather than lose it, augmenting the foreign exchange available for direct investment abroad, and perhaps for other more directly political expenditures as well. The largest industrial countries have typically minimized exchange-rate variations, preferring instead to compete in terms of the pace of their technical progress. Exchange-rate instability has characterized the competitive fringes of the world economy instead.[39]

38   This section is drawn largely from my "Integration and Conflict in the World Economy," *Journal of Common Market Studies* 8, no. 1 (September 1969): 1–18.
39   Robert Triffin, *Our International Monetary System: Yesterday, Today and Tomorrow* (New York: Random House, 1968), p. 6.

For any given rate of increase in wages, technical progress allows the center to enjoy an additional degree of freedom in international competition which countries at the periphery do not share to the same extent. As long as the weaker country is not able to accelerate its rate of technical progress to match that of the center and is not willing to slow down economic activity to adjust wages and prices, its rate of exchange will have to be on a chronic slide. To protect and expand its industries and jobs, it must break any currency link with the metropolis in favor of repeated devaluations. A currency union will seem attractive only when citizens of the periphery expect to do better individually within it than they can collectively outside.

Labor Migration

With freedom of capital movements, the business community at the periphery is likely to find itself progressively displaced by foreign enterprise. To the extent that foreign firms become the major employers of the local population, local government ceases to represent more than the interests of labor in its own society, without the balancing influence of managerial representation. The political system will no longer perform the function of interest aggregation.[40] As labor relations become international relations, the potential for conflict is enhanced, until arrangements can be worked out to represent local labor along with foreign management in a single new polity. The viability of such a polity will depend on the mobility of labor.

The demand for labor is affected by the movement of both direct and indirect investment. The flow of direct investment from the center tends to carry along its own technical and managerial personnel. Where the host country's technology is notably backward, it is unlikely to have a ready supply of technically qualified personnel to offer. Where the local supply of human resources is ample, the lead in technology required for direct investment is also likely to be small, and local enterprise is therefore likely to be strong enough to stave it off. In the intermediate case, where some local recruitment for skills is possible, it is apt to be transferred abroad to maintain balance in the company's staffing policies.

A flow of portfolio savings to the metropolis will, meanwhile, tend to starve local enterprises for funds, and hence reduce employment opportunities offered by them at any particular wage. Direct

40 Gabriel A. Almond and James S. Coleman, *The Politics of the Developing Areas* (Princeton: Princeton University Press, 1960), pp. 28–45.

investment is unlikely to make up more than part of the loss. As long as enterprises continue to cluster, the center's attraction for portfolio savings is likely to exceed the periphery's for direct investment. Once direct investment has helped to break down boundaries, furthermore, its superiority over exports diminishes, and investments already made may be liquidated. The demand for labor, as for capital, tends therefore to concentrate at the center. On economic principles alone labor should move, if its wages are to be equalized.

Where labor mobility is barred, however, a conflict potential remains. It may, as in a colonial situation, be suppressed by making local government responsive to metropolitan enterprise without integration. But the progressive proletarianization of the local population is unlikely to make this a stable solution. At some point the metropolitan authorities are likely to find "the costs of trying to give political order and shape to the disarrayed transitional societies" to have become prohibitive for them.[41] Foreign enterprise will then withdraw, taking back such capital as it can within more limited national boundaries.

CURRENT TRENDS

It is clearly possible to spell out a paradigm on economic integration to set alongside those by Haas and Deutsch on state and national integration. The next step should be to trace out the possible interactions among the three, by which at last political boundaries are drawn. This cannot be done unilaterally. It requires a cooperative effort. Meanwhile it may be useful to examine shifts in specifically economic boundaries currently in progress. Nationality still seems confined to its traditional boundaries even in Europe; institutional integration seems to transcend these boundaries, at least in the Europe of the Six. Economic integration reaches further still, with the United States at the center and Europe resisting. Two key phenomena provide the major evidence.

The first phenomenon is the *multinational firm*. What is referred to under this title is a cluster of companies incorporated in two or more national jurisdictions but "joined together by ties of common ownership and responsive to a common management strategy."[42] National companies become multinational through direct investment. They may, it is sometimes claimed, develop further into inter-

41   Lucian W. Pye, *Politics, Personality, and Nation Building: Burma's Search for Identity* (New Haven: Yale University Press, 1962), p. 13.
42   Raymond Vernon, "Economic Sovereignty at Bay," *Foreign Affairs* 47, no. 1 (October 1968): 114.

national corporations.[43] Such corporations will have cut their ties to any particular country to take a global view of resource allocation. When the corporation comes into its own, so to speak, "national boundaries no longer play a critical role in defining economic horizons."[44] Some four out of five multinational corporations are meanwhile headed by American parents.[45]

A second phenomenon of importance to economic integration is the *Euro-dollar*. By taking deposits and making loans in dollars, European banks have taken the lead in developing an efficient international market for short-term funds; bonds floated in Europe by major enterprises and governments are also frequently denominated in dollars. West German marks and Swiss francs are used for similar purposes, but together they account for only about 15 percent of total foreign currency claims and liabilities reported by European banks in 1968.[46] American corporations in Europe, and their banks, have become major participants in the market both as suppliers and as users of funds.

Multinational Firms

The attention that international corporations have received in recent years is closely related to a sharp acceleration of American investment in Europe over the last decade. By the end of 1967, the value of American private long-term assets in Western Europe was reported as $22.6 billion; that of European assets in the United States was $20.2 billion, or about the same. The composition of these assets, however, shows a striking difference. About $17.9 billion of U.S. holdings in Europe, but only $7.0 billion of European holdings in the United States, were classed as direct investments.[47] The remainder was on portfolio account. This pattern suggests an integration process at work with the United States at the core.

Though direct investment is not a recent practice on the part of American (or for that matter European) firms, the large-scale penetration of Europe by American companies is. Plant and equipment expenditures by U.S. subsidiaries have risen rapidly as a proportion of gross domestic fixed-capital formation. By 1965 they approached 5 percent in the European Community and had reached 10 percent

43 Kindleberger, *American Business Abroad*, p. 184.
44 George W. Ball, "Cosmocorp: The Importance of Being Stateless," *Columbia Journal of World Business* 2, no. 6 (November–December 1967): 26.
45 Vernon, "Economic Sovereignty at Bay," p. 116.
46 Bank for International Settlements, *Thirty-ninth Annual Report* (Basle: Bank for International Settlements, 1969), p. 143.
47 U.S. Department of Commerce, *Survey of Current Business* (October 1968).

in the United Kingdom.[48] By the logic of direct investment, they were concentrated in industries leading in technical progress. If this trend were to continue into the future, both the means for and the profitability of European investment in research and development would cumulatively shrink with their markets.

The European response to the challenge has been to develop through mergers "firms with sufficient technological and financial means to compete on equal terms."[49] With few exceptions, however, the merger movement has thus far been restricted to firms within individual countries. For the European Community this limitation raises the threat of reviving "domestic economic forces that would inevitably side with national interest rather than with common economic and industrial policies."[50] The commission has therefore proposed a European company statute to be adopted alongside national statutes, which would grant enterprises incorporated under it equal treatment in all member countries of the community.

The purpose of such a statute would be to denationalize certain enterprises. If a "European" company were to enlarge its share of the market, it would perhaps not be "associated with any particular national flag."[51] The concern in the European community appears to be focused on West Germany. American firms already look upon West Germany as the favored location for their subsidiaries. At the end of 1967, the value of U.S. direct investment in Germany amounted to $3.5 billion, compared to less than $2.0 billion in France.[52] An initial location in Germany appears to convey a competitive advantage to a firm that companies elsewhere in the community seem hard put to match.

Euro-Dollars

American corporations have accounted for up to one-half of dollar bond issues in Europe in recent years; American banks absorbed about one-third of the Euro-dollar market's short-term funds.[53] Thus

48 John H. Dunning, "Technology, U.S. Investment and European Economic Growth," in *The International Corporation: A Symposium*, ed. Charles P. Kindleberger (Cambridge: M.I.T. Press, 1970), p. 145.

49 Commission of the European Economic Community, *Tenth General Report on the Activities of the Community* (Brussels: n.p., 1967), p. 35.

50 Guido Colonna di Paliano, "Why Europe Needs Continental-scale Firms," *European Community* 116 (September 1968): 3.

51 Ibid.; Ball, "Cosmocorp," recommends the same but on a "cosmic" scale.

52 U.S. Department of Commerce, *Survey of Current Business* (October 1968).

53 Bank for International Settlements, *Thirty-ninth Annual Report*, p. 46, and Julien-Pierre Koszul, "American Banks in Europe," in *The International Corporation*, ed. Kindleberger, p. 280.

the use of the dollar has spread beyond the transactions specifically of American firms. The same technological leadership that gives American firms a competitive edge makes their currency an attractive asset for others to use. The dollar offers reasonably constant purchasing power over a larger and more diversified national product than any other currency can command. Its use remains precarious, however, as long as its backing continues to be narrowly based on gold.

The appeal of the dollar was enhanced, therefore, by placing alongside gold as an ultimate reserve asset "special drawing rights" in the International Monetary Fund, increases in which can be voted by the United States with other members of the Fund.[54] The next step would be to regulate the conditions under which exchange-rate changes can occur. The U.S. proposal is to allow small but automatic changes in official exchange rates against the dollar, whenever market rates persistently press against agreed limits of permissible variation around par. The European Community countries insisted on collective veto power in activating drawing rights; negotiations on the "crawling peg" are still under way.

A crawling peg may tend to make the dollar progressively cheaper as American deficits continue to place ample supplies of dollars on the world market. As European currencies become correspondingly more expensive, so will their exports, aggravating any competitive disadvantage European enterprises may already feel subject to. It would help the European bargaining position if they could threaten competitive depreciation of a unified European currency against the dollar. The member countries of the European Community have in fact recently agreed on the need to fix a timetable for currency unification and the pooling of reserves.[55]

Within the European Community the West German mark is currently the strongest currency, based on the competitive strength of the German economy.[56] There is some concern in the rest of the Community, and in Britain, about its role in a unified currency area. Freedom to vary exchange rates may remain useful to counteract adverse trends in competitive positions. "To make up for the fact that their trade unionists are not as logical as the German trade unionists are," other member countries would have to protect their balance of payments by deflation if exchange-rate changes no longer

54 See Fred Hirsch, "SDRs and the Working of the Gold Exchange Standard," *International Monetary Fund Staff Papers* 18, no. 2 (July 1971): 221–53.
55 *Kredietbank Weekly Bulletin*, April 17, 1970, p. 164.
56 For a fuller discussion, see my "Capital Markets and the Unification of Europe," *World Politics* 20, no. 2 (January 1968): 228–44.

offer an option, thus "constantly starving their manufacturing investment."[57]

Labor Markets

But the point in economic integration is, precisely, to substitute factor mobility for exchange-rate variation. Within the Atlantic context capital flows have been the leading integrative force. There has in consequence been some flow of managerial personnel to Europe. A substantial outflow of wage labor to America, however, has not occurred and is not likely to materialize on any scale. Within some of the multinational companies efforts have been made "to train up a truly international staff, who will be ruled less and less by considerations of national interest and national psychology, and increasingly by their care for their company's well-being."[58] This does not extend to the wage-earning categories.

Within the European subsystem the situation is reversed. The treaty establishing the European Community calls for the free movement of workers among member countries by the end of the transition period.[59] Two regulations have since sought to give substance to this provision.[60] Work permits are now automatically renewable for any employment after one year; equal treatment in pay and discharge is required; priority in hiring for nationals is now permissible only in specific manpower surplus areas; and preference for Community workers as opposed to outsiders is to be given within a two-week notification period. Partly in consequence, migration within the Community increased from 170,000 in 1958 to 320,000 in 1965.[61]

The dominant factor flows within the Community have therefore been of wage labor from south to north. Capital flows have normally been of the right kind and in the right direction, but have thus far been barred from reaching a size able to affect the ownership of industry or the flow of managerial personnel to any significant extent. The effect of labor mobility on wages and profits has been slowed down (1) by periodic upward revaluations of the West German

57   Norman Macrae, "The Phoenix Is Short-sighted," *The Economist* (London), May 16, 1970, p. 26.
58   Caroline M. Miles, "The International Corporation," *International Affairs* 45, no. 2 (April 1969): 263.
59   Article 48 of the Treaty of Rome.
60   Helen S. Feldstein, "A Study of Transaction and Political Integration: Transnational Labour Flow within the European Economic Community," *Journal of Common Market Studies* 6, no. 1 (September 1967): 27.
61   Kenneth A. Dahlberg, "The EEC Commission and the Politics of the Free Movement of Labour," *Journal of Common Market Studies* 6, no. 4 (June 1968): 310–33.

mark to reduce the competitive advantage of German industry; and (2) by liberal access for workers from outside the Community altogether. From 1958 to 1965, these increased from 80,000 to 630,000, or from 35 to 64 percent of the total transnational labor force.[62]

The dilemma for a European economic strategy appears to lie in a choice between American dominance without complete integration and complete integration around a German core. The German core is not an overwhelmingly strong one, and in the absence of a reaction to an American challenge, it would probably not be strong enough to precipitate integration at all. Its relative weakness may, however, be its chief attraction now. There is more opportunity to exercise countervailing power within a European than within an Atlantic union. A European union would, furthermore, offer genuine integration through labor mobility; an Atlantic solution would for lack of it remain unstable.

NATIONAL BOUNDARIES IN POLITICS AND ECONOMICS

An attempt has been made to begin filling in a rather large gap in theorizing about national boundaries. The boundaries of the modern nation-state reflect the interaction of three separately bounded phenomena: the nation, the state, and the economy. Political theorists have been mainly concerned with state and nation. Economic theorists have given scant attention to the political dimensions of economic processes. They have typically avoided wandering "too far from economic territory into the morass of politics."[63]

A possible logic of boundary formation within the economic sphere itself has been sketched out. Its components are capital flows, currency unification, and labor migration. Each follows strictly economic incentives. Hence the political consequences that they induce need not be the product of conscious design. The invisible hand here, too, may lead actors to produce "a result that was no part of their intention."[64] To suggest that direct investment tends to shift boundaries, therefore, is not to claim that there is "a plot by the U.S. to dominate the world."[65]

The key turn in the argument is to see that trade relations alter the identity of the trading nations. In this, the argument breaks with

62 Ibid.
63 Kindleberger, *American Business Abroad*, p. 88.
64 Adam Smith, *An Inquiry into the Nature and Causes of the Wealth of Nations* (New York: Modern Library, 1937), p. 423.
65 Kindleberger, *American Business Abroad*, p. 38.

the conventional theory of international trade that postulates the boundaries of its trading units to be given and unchanging. As a result, economic transactions are recognized as far indeed from "non-conflictual." On the contrary, they are best analyzed not in terms of any harmony of interest, but of conflict and conflict resolution.

The propositions advanced apply to the process of boundary formation within the economic sphere alone. Even if they were all correct as stated, the theory of national boundaries would be far from complete. Apart from further work on state and nation separately, the greatest gap remains in tracing out the interactions between state, national, and economic boundaries in shaping the modern nation-state as a single, coherent unit of social action and experience.[66]

66   A previous draft was commented upon by Harry G. Gelber, Ernst B. Haas, Anthony Lanyi, and Richard L. Merritt whose critical contributions are gratefully acknowledged. Responsibility of course remains with the author.

eighteen

Political Aspects
of Exchange-Rate Systems

Anthony Lanyi

FOR the last few years the liveliest and most significant debate in international economics has been over the question of how to reform the methods by which exchange rates between national currencies are determined, maintained, and changed. The set of these methods is what economists call an "exchange-rate system." The present system is commonly known as "the adjustable peg," meaning that exchange rates are fixed, or *pegged*, by the monetary authorities, with changes occurring from time to time. In practice, the changes have been infrequent, at least for the major industrial countries; in a few important cases, they have been fairly large (10–15%), followed by difficult periods of adjustment for the economies concerned and preceded by periods of "crises" for the entire international monetary system, during which it has occasionally appeared uncertain whether the monetary authorities would be able to maintain the system of pegged rates in the face of huge international capital movements. The backers of reform seek a system which will generate less difficult adjustments for the economy of the country whose currency is being revalued, as well as fewer and less dangerous crises. The favorite reform of academic economists is the "crawling peg," a system under which changes in parity would be frequent (as often as once a month) but at the same time limited to a small annual magnitude (e.g., 2%).

The analysis of the relative merits of alternative exchange-rate systems is complicated by the presence of both economic and political factors. Characteristically, economists have studied the *economic* problems with thoroughness and rigor but have incorporated *political* aspects into the analysis in an ad hoc and unsystematic manner;[1] political scientists have generally ignored this question entirely. It turns out, however, that the validity of predictions about the performance of a reformed exchange-rate system depends crucially on the validity of the assumptions made about the behavior of national governments. In this paper I will try to show how game theory provides a unified framework for considering both political and economic aspects and defining their interplay. The first section presents the economic background to the analysis. In the second section, I discuss the political and economic aspects of the present exchange-rate system in a game-theoretic framework. The third section of the paper will apply the previous analysis to the comparison of the adjustable- and crawling-peg systems, and the final section will discuss the relationship of these results to the question of international integration.

I have focused the analysis and examples presented in this paper on the monetary relations of the industrial nations. It should not be forgotten that the model displayed here is only a model. It is not intended as a literal description of explicit negotiation; it leaves out, of course, the various special relationships (both economic and political) that exist within subgroups of the major trading nations, and that necessarily temper the process of reaching agreement on international monetary matters. Nor should my emphasis on the major trading nations lead the reader to forget that the question of exchange-rate flexibility is of great importance to the developing countries. I have chosen to focus on relations among the major trading countries primarily because this topic presents the interesting problem of perceived international interdependence.[2]

1   I have tried to organize a more systematic analysis in *The Case for Floating Exchange Rates Reconsidered*, Essays in International Finance, no. 72 (Princeton: International Finance Section, Princeton University, 1969). Original and interesting insights are provided by Stephen N. Marris in *The Bürgenstock Communiqué: A Critical Examination of the Case for Limited Flexibility of Exchange Rates*, Essays in International Finance, no. 80 (Princeton: International Finance Section, Princeton University, 1970) and "Decision-Making on Exchange Rates," in *Approaches to Greater Flexibility of Exchange Rates: The Bürgenstock Papers*, ed. George N. Halm (Princeton: Princeton University Press, 1970), pp. 77–88. Since finishing this paper, I have discovered that the notion of international monetary policy as a "game" was discussed by L. Officer and T. Willett in "The Interaction of Adjustment and Gold-Conversion Policies in a Reserve-Currency System," *Western Economic Journal* 8, no. 1 (March 1970): 47–60.

2   In general, no single less-developed country is so important in world trade that its government need worry about the repercussions of its policies on the countries with which it trades.

THE POLICY ALTERNATIVES

Under a system of *freely floating exchange rates*, the exchange rates between national currencies would be determined by supply and demand in the foreign exchange market. Under any other system, in which the monetary authorities fix the permissible band of variation of the exchange rate around some fixed rate, or *parity*, the authorities must possess international reserves of foreign exchange in order to support the officially determined rate. In fact, the extent of change in the level of these reserves, or in the magnitude of direct official claims against them, provides us with the simplest and most workable definition of a deficit or surplus in the international payments of a country: if reserves have fallen (or liabilities have risen), this indicates a *deficit*; an increase in reserves (or decrease in liabilities) indicates a *surplus*.[3]

The use of a country's reserves, or the incurring of official indebtedness to foreign monetary authorities to buy up the excess supply of its currency on the foreign-exchange market, is referred to as financing a deficit. This has two undesirable aspects: (1) the lower reserves are, the less is the extent to which the deficit country (*D*-Country) will be able to finance deficits in the future,[4] and (2) the greater the external indebtedness (on which the payment of interest is usually required), the greater the extent to which future national income has been promised away to foreigners. By the same token, the surplus country (*S*-Country) finds itself accumulating reserves and—in the case of intergovernmental loans—claims on foreign governments. If the latter claims are interest-bearing, the chief cost involved is the difference between the income on the intergovernmental debt and the return on the best alternative investments available to the surplus country's government. In addition, *undesired* accumulations of gold and foreign currency or other noninterest-bearing foreign assets by the monetary authority of the surplus country represent an unrequited transfer of goods or assets from the surplus to the deficit country; that is, the excess foreign exchange

3 Many alternative definitions of deficit or surplus are used by governments or have been proposed by academic economists. An excellent discussion of alternative definitions can be found in U.S. Review Committee for Balance of Payments Statistics, *The Balance of Payments Statistics of the United States: A Review and Appraisal; Report to the Bureau of the Budget* (Washington: U.S. Government Printing Office, 1965), Ch. 9.

4 The alternative to financing future deficits is either changing exchange rates or resorting to measures to inhibit trade or deflate domestic income.

results from purchases of *S*-Country exports and assets that are not matched by *S*-Country purchases of foreign goods and assets.

Since both *D*- and *S*-Countries suffer direct costs as a result of the imbalance in international payments, there is an interest on both sides in *eliminating* (as distinct from merely *financing*) the imbalance.[5] Note, however, that the burden of additional external debt for *D*-Country is greater than *S*-Country's net cost of investing in *D*-Country debt; and, furthermore, that although a fall of reserves threatens *D*-Country with a future situation in which no financing of the deficit will be possible (and painful elimination of the deficit will be the only available policy), no such threat exists to *S*-Country. We have arrived, therefore, at a fundamental premise of the argument that follows: *The pressures on a D-Country to eliminate an international payments imbalance are greater, and generally far greater, than the pressures on an S-Country.*

There are several types of policies for eliminating payments imbalances:

(1) *Policies to change the level of aggregate demand.* Demand-reducing policies will tend to reduce an external deficit by reducing the demand for imports; conversely, demand-increasing policies can be used to reduce a surplus. Demand-reducing policies are exemplified by raising taxes, reducing government spending, and restricting credit; demand-increasing policies include lowering taxes, increasing government spending, and expanding credit.

(2) *Changing exchange rates.* A *devaluation* will improve the trade balance by raising the relative prices of foreign to domestic goods; an *upward revaluation* reduces the trade balance by lowering the relative prices of foreign goods.

(3) *Changing interest rates.* Raising interest rates increases the net inflow (or reduces the net outflow) of capital, thereby improving the balance of payments; lowering interest rates, by analogous reasoning, leads to a worsening of the balance of payments.

(4) *Selectively restricting international trade and payments.* An imbalance can be eliminated either by taxes and prohibitions

5   The distinction between financing and eliminating a deficit is crucial for the analysis of balance-of-payments policy. Certain types of policy, such as raising interest rates to attract private capital from abroad, cannot be easily classified. A useful, if arguable, discussion of this distinction can be found in Fritz Machlup, "Real Adjustment, Compensatory Corrections and Financing of Imbalances in International Payments," in *Trade, Growth and the Balance of Payments: Essays in Honor of Gottfried Haberler*, eds. Richard E. Caves, Harry G. Johnson, and Peter B. Kenen (Chicago: Rand-McNally, 1965), pp. 185–213.

on imports and capital outflows (in the case of a deficit) or by reducing such taxes and prohibitions (in the case of a surplus).

Any of these policies can, of course, be employed in tandem as well as separately.

A fifth alternative policy is that nothing at all be done to eliminate the payments imbalance, so that the latter is merely financed. As long as D-Country has sufficient reserves, its deficit could theoretically be financed without the acquiescence of S-Countries. But, as a practical matter, all monetary authorities cooperate in day-to-day interventions in the foreign exchange market, so that the authorities of S-Countries will (in general) be purchasing the currencies of D-Countries, requiring afterwards from the latter a payment of foreign exchange or gold in lieu of undesired stocks of D-Country currencies. Once, however, a D-Country has exhausted its reserves—as apparently occurred in November, 1967, in the United Kingdom—the S-Country may no longer help support the price of D-Country currency. It can simply refuse to purchase the latter on the foreign-exchange market,[6] and if it also refuses to loan foreign exchange to the D-Country, the latter will be forced to accept a depreciation of its currency on the foreign-exchange market. Although this development could also be seen as the *S-Country* being forced to revalue *its* currency upward, this is, in fact, not a correct interpretation, since the parity of S-Country's currency vis-à-vis only D-Country's currency has changed, whereas the parity vis-à-vis all other currencies has remained unchanged. The surplus country thus has, on such occasions, a sixth alternative policy: refusal either to finance *or* to eliminate an imbalance. This policy will eventually force the deficit country to eliminate its deficit.

Policies aimed at eliminating imbalance are costly or beneficial to the government undertaking them, depending on the state of the domestic economy. It is useful here to distinguish between dilemma and nondilemma cases.

A *dilemma case* is one in which the aggregate-demand policies called for by the domestic situation are the opposite of those required to eliminate the external imbalance. For instance, the government of an S-Country with inflation may wish to use demand-reducing policies to combat the inflation, but this will only increase the balance-of-payments surplus; conversely, the government of a D-Country with unemployment will naturally resort to demand-increasing policies,

6 Such a policy may be invoked even if the D-Country still has international reserves—for instance, when the D-Country is expected to devalue its currency.

but this will only exacerbate the external deficit. The way out of these dilemmas is to employ so-called "expenditure-switching" policies: for the *S*-Country with inflation, an upward revaluation (or a reduction in trade restrictions) will tend both to reduce aggregate demand and eliminate the external surplus, while, in the second case, a devaluation (or increase in trade restrictions) will tend to eliminate the deficit and raise aggregate demand.[7]

A *nondilemma case* is one in which the aggregate-demand policies serve both to combat domestic economic ills and to eliminate an external imbalance. For instance, the government of an *S*-Country with unemployment could fight both surplus and unemployment by demand-increasing measures, whereas, conversely, for a *D*-Country with inflation, demand-reducing policies serve both internal and external purposes.[8]

To avoid a multiplication of cases and examples in the analysis that follows, we will assume that the *S*-Country and *D*-Country maintain "full employment," meaning more accurately the politically desirable compromise between the incompatible goals of zero price inflation and the elimination of all but purely "frictional" unemployment. This assumption leaves us with the essence of the problem: how to correct the international payments imbalance without affecting domestic economic goals. In fact, for both types of country, the solution here involves the simultaneous use of at least *two* of the policies we have mentioned, and this is very difficult to accomplish because of the different lengths of lags in the effects of different policies. For instance, if *D*-Country simply devalued, this would create inflationary pressures. To offset the latter, it would be necessary to employ demand-reducing policies. But, since such policies take considerable time to eliminate inflation once it has got started, the only way to devalue without inflation is to precede the devaluation by some months with demand-reducing policies. The economic and political costs of creating unemployment in such circumstances need hardly be spelled out. Nor is it difficult to see the political hazards of revaluation when there are no strong inflationary pres-

7 The changes in aggregate demand just mentioned occur because a change in relative prices of domestic and foreign goods changes the aggregate demand for domestic goods—e.g., if a country devalues, there is a rise in both foreign demand for its exports and in home demand for import-competing goods. (If restrictions are raised, only the second of these effects occurs.)

8 Note that in these cases expenditure-switching policy *alone* is insufficient: for the *S*-Country, an upward revaluation will worsen unemployment, while, for the *D*-Country, a devaluation will exacerbate the inflation.

sures at home. Moreover, an exchange-rate adjustment ordinarily entails changes in relative prices and a consequent reallocation of resources among industries and sectors of the economy; in fact, adjustment without such reallocation will generally not achieve the desired effects. But any such reallocation of resources entails dislocations and temporary unemployment of labor and capital resources; injured groups will put pressure on the government, and it will, temporarily, be more difficult to maintain the desired rate of employment without higher-than-average inflationary pressures. For all these reasons, then, we come to our second fundamental premise: *Countries are extremely reluctant to undertake exchange-rate changes in the presence of "full employment" at home.* Governments are acutely aware of what some economists call the *burden of adjustment*, and the *distribution* of that burden among surplus and deficit countries becomes the crucial issue of international monetary affairs.

The analysis in the next section is based on several other premises regarding the relative costs of alternative policies (the assumption of maintaining full employment being made in all cases):

(1) Changing the exchange rate is less attractive to both S- and D-Countries than changing interest rates, changing restrictions, or financing; of the three latter policies, financing is regarded as the least costly.

(2) The cost of an imbalance-eliminating policy is always reduced if other countries simultaneously undertake policies accomplishing the same objectives; the cost is *most* reduced if other countries reduce exchange rates in the required direction (because the other policies are reversible and in practice are often reversed).

(3) In the cases of raising restrictions and raising interest rates, there is the danger of what Richard Cooper has called international policy competition.[9] This process is initiated by a deficit country raising restrictions or interest rates; other deficit countries, or surplus countries fearing an imminent deficit, follow suit to protect their own balance-of-payments positions, and the vicious upward spiral continues until brought to a halt by international agreement. The events of the 1930s well exemplify such competition with regard to

9 See Richard N. Cooper, *The Economics of Interdependence: Economic Policy in the Atlantic Community* (New York: Published for the Council of Foreign Relations by McGraw-Hill Book Company, 1968), Ch. 6.

trade and exchange restrictions. The events of the 1960s show some tendency toward competition with respect to interest rates. No government desires a general increase in restrictiveness; all have supported the impressive progress made toward trade liberalization since World War II under the aegis of the General Agreement on Tariffs and Trade. Similarly, a general upward rise in interest rates is disliked because of its dampening effects on world investment and growth. The long-run effects of a deficit country's raising restrictions or interest rates are less feared if surplus countries simultaneously lower restrictions and interest rates, since in such cases no clear upward trend is established.

(4) The most costly policy of all is devaluation in a crisis situation. *S*-Country governments also prefer deficit countries to devalue *without* first being confronted with a crisis situation.

(5) The best alternative for either *S*-Country or *D*-Country is when the other type of country does all the adjusting, preferably through permanent exchange-rate changes, since changes in interest rates or restrictions are considered more transitory.

(6) A deficit country will prefer raising restrictions to raising interest rates because of the former's less damaging effect on the domestic economy. If full employment is to be maintained, a rise in interest rates must be accompanied by fiscal expansion, always a tricky feat to engineer; furthermore, while restrictions affect only some sectors of the economy, interest rates have a widespread impact. For analogous reasons, surplus countries will prefer lowering restrictions to lowering interest rates. Procedures for negotiating tariff reductions under the GATT, however, greatly inhibit the willingness of *S*-Countries to lower tariffs on a nonreciprocal basis, whereas "temporary" surcharges for balance-of-payments reasons may be used by deficit countries; for this reason, the range of international transactions affected by an increase in restrictions in a *D*-Country is likely to be larger than the range affected by a reduction in restrictions in an *S*-Country.

Having now discussed the basic features of balance-of-payments policy and the premises of the argument that follows, we can proceed to our analysis of the adjustment process under the adjustable and crawling pegs.

A GAME-THEORETIC ANALYSIS OF ADJUSTMENT
UNDER THE ADJUSTABLE PEG

Many years ago economists referred to the conventions of international monetary policy under the gold standard as "the rules of the game." In this section of the paper, I will try to suggest ways in which strategic considerations might be integrated with conventional economic analysis by regarding the makers of international monetary policy as participants in an international game.

In line with our previous discussion of policy alternatives, we shall assume that both deficit countries and surplus countries are maintaining full employment, so that what we are really interested in is what might be called the full-employment deficit (or surplus).[10] The *players* of the game are *D*-Countries on one side and *S*-Countries on the other. We shall assume that there are a small number of major countries on each side. The *strategies* of the two sides are the alternative policies. The *pay-off matrix* shows the costs of each combination of policies to each side: the left-hand number in each cell shows the cost to *D*-Countries; the right-hand number, the cost to *S*-Countries (Table 1).

Before presenting an analysis of this game, it is necessary to clarify some problems that arise in defining a payoff matrix in this case. First, the costs of policy surely must include political as well as economic considerations, but, if this is so, no cardinal number can be attached to these costs. (What is the dollar cost of losing the next election?) For this reason, *ordinal* numbers are given in Table 1 representing the ranking of alternative situations by each side (de-

Table 1. A Hypothetical Payoff Matrix for Exchange-Rate Policies

| | | | *Surplus Countries* | | |
Deficit Countries	Refusal to finance	Financing	Upward revaluation	Reducing interest rates	Reducing restrictions
Financing	X	(4, 4)	(1, 19)	(3, 18)	(2, 17)
Devaluation	(19, 11)	(16, 1)	(11, 14)	(13, 8)	(12, 5)
Increasing interest rates	(18, 12)	(15, 2)	(5, 15)	(7, 9)	(6, 6)
Increasing restrictions	(17, 13)	(14, 3)	(8, 16)	(10, 10)	(9, 7)

10 This concept is analogous to the full-employment budgetary deficit (or surplus) used as a tool of analysis by students of fiscal policy.

rived from the premises advanced earlier). Second, we must consider the question of whether countries take the short or long view in evaluating costs: for example, should the cost of trade restrictions include the long-term results of possible international policy competition? Since there is more than one deficit country, and each D-Country must reckon with the effect of retaliatory (defensive) reactions of other D-Countries to policies designed to improve the first D-Country's balance of payments, this evaluation must somehow enter into the cost estimate of each policy.

A third difficulty in defining the payoff matrix arises from the fact that the cost of a policy depends not only on the type of policy involved but also on the magnitude of the action taken. A 3 percent increase in interest rates involves far greater political costs, and greater economic dislocation as well, than an increase of 1 percent; a devaluation of 10 percent involves far greater costs of reallocating domestic resources than a devaluation of 1 percent. Thus the rankings contained in the payoff matrix are meaningless without some specification of the magnitudes of the policies involved. The definition we use is that (1) in the case where only one country acts to eliminate its imbalance, the policy action is of a magnitude sufficient to eliminate the imbalance within a specific period of time, say two years, and (2) in the case where both countries (or groups of countries) act to eliminate an imbalance, each takes measures sufficient to eliminate *half* of its own imbalance. This definition seems workable enough to avoid invalidating the analysis being made (although it should be mentioned that it covers up some rather nasty problems of interdependence among countries belonging to the same type, that is, either S- or D-Countries).

Finally, the policies considered here are not mutually exclusive alternatives; they may be (and usually are) undertaken in many possible combinations. Presenting them as distinct alternatives is only a means of simplifying the analysis to focus on some essential properties of the system. Note, too, that the costs of the three imbalance-eliminating policies include the costs of supplementary policies undertaken to maintain the desired rate of employment. It should also be understood that the extra policy available to surplus countries, "refusal to finance," is ordinarily available only in cases where the reserves of a deficit country have been exhausted. Otherwise, it must be ignored in the analysis that follows.

The reader conversant with game theory will notice that the game shown in Table 1 has a saddle point, namely, the cell in which the Financing column and Financing row intersect; for convenience, we shall call this cell "the financing solution." In the absence of explicit agreement, coupled with credible promises, each group of countries will choose the financing strategy as the only one assuring a cost no greater than 4. This conclusion would hold with quite different pay-off matrices: for example, suppose a cooperative interest-rate policy yields a payoff of (3,3), better for both sides than the financing solution (4,4). It would still be true that, without close cooperation, the financing strategy would be chosen by both *S*- and *D*-Countries (because of the costliness of undertaking such a policy *if* the other side is passive).[11]

With the imminence of a crisis, the make-up of the payoff matrix will be altered. If the reserves of a major deficit country are nearing exhaustion, the cost of financing to both *D*- and *S*-Countries will increase. As mentioned previously, a *D*-Country would rather de-value in a noncrisis than in a crisis situation, and an *S*-Country as well would rather avoid a crisis. Thus, as a crisis nears, the cost of the financing solution to the deficit country will approach the cost of policies undertaken during a crisis, and the optimum strategy will be one of the bottom three rows, starting in all probability with increased restrictions and interest rates and ending, possibly, in devaluation.

It is remarkable how often a change in parity occurs only when a crisis is either imminent or present. This phenomenon is inexplicable in terms of economic rationality. Less elaborate explanations than mine, based on some of the same considerations as those mentioned here, have been given, but seem to me weakened by their failure to take into account the motives, expectations, and actions of all countries concerned. Such explanations, advanced usually by econ-omists rather than by political scientists, generally end up con-demning the *irrationality* of political authorities and their failure to recognize economic necessity. My explanation assumes rationality, yet it produces the possibility of a nonoptimal solution. While econ-omists tend to regard such a solution as evidence for the "imperfec-tions" of, or unwarranted governmental intervention in, the market, political scientists will recognize this result as similar to that in a number of other areas, such as defense and arms-control policy.

At the same time, the financing solution is not the only combina-

11   It is a basic tenet of the theory of non-zero-sum games that a noncoopera-tive solution may well be inferior for *both* players to *some* cooperative solution. See, for instance, John C. Harsanyi, "Game Theory and the Analysis of Inter-national Conflict," in *International Politics and Foreign Policy: A Reader in Re-search and Theory*, rev. ed., ed. James N. Rosenau (New York: The Free Press, 1969), pp. 370–79.

tion of noncrisis policies that we find in fact occurring. Unilateral or bilateral changes in interest rates or restrictions are fairly frequent occurrences. If the payoff matrix presented here is a moderately realistic assessment of national preferences, how can we explain a divergence from the equilibrium solution? The answer lies in a combination of the ever-impending threat of crisis and the existence of well-established channels of communication and cooperation among the players. The financing solution is a good one for both players in the short run, but it cannot be maintained indefinitely in the face of a continuing deficit and limited amounts of international liquidity. An examination of the matrix shows that there are several cells that are better for *both* players than any cell in Column 1 (representing the crisis situation). *Without* cooperation, however, the surplus country has no reason whatsoever to choose a strategy other than financing or refusal to finance; this is so despite the many times academic economists have berated the surplus countries for not assuming their "fair share" of the burden of adjustment. With cooperation, the bottom three cells of the last two columns are superior to any crisis solution for *both* players. But, in practice, only the four most southeasterly solutions are likely to prevail, for reasons that will be made clear in the following discussion.

The *number of players* on each side of the adjustment game has importance for the latter's outcome and for the strategies that are employed. If there are many players on each side, and none of dominant importance, no single surplus country will have any reason to take upon itself responsibility for preventing a crisis. As a result, we would expect an unbridled and successful attempt of surplus countries to shift the burden of adjustment onto the deficit countries, producing either a deflationary bias in the world economy (if *D*-Countries are unwilling to change exchange rates), or international policy competition, or (if *D*-Countries devalue without hesitation while maintaining full employment) a bias toward inflation. (This bias occurs because a devaluation, by raising import prices, stimulates cost-push tendencies.) This situation is analogous to that of pure competition in price theory.

The situation analogous to oligopoly is one where there are relatively few major countries on each side of the game; this is the case we have described in this section. Each country must take upon itself a certain degree of responsibility for preventing a crisis. In particular, surplus countries will be willing to take steps to avert a crisis, even more so when the major deficit country is the one whose currency is the world's chief *reserve currency* (currency making up other countries' foreign exchange reserves) and *vehicle currency* (currency used as the means of payment in international commercial transactions). In terms of the payoff matrix, the surplus countries in this case may always evaluate the cost of refusal to finance as higher than that of upward revaluation or of any other imbalance-eliminating policy. Up to now, this has been the response of surplus countries to the chronic payments deficit of the United States.

In a situation in which single currencies are important enough to affect the entire system by their rise or decline, crises are more dangerous than in the case of pure competition. At the same time, cooperation to avoid crises becomes more manageable than in the many-small-countries case. Whether or not this game of the few produces a healthier world economy than the game of the many depends crucially, then, on the extent and nature of cooperation.

There are, in principle, a number of different ways in which co-operative solutions might be reached, including (1) leaving the outcome to market processes (for instance, allowing the exchange rate to float); (2) leaving decisions to an autonomous international organization; (3) agreeing to a set of rules binding for all participating nations; and (4) ad hoc negotiations among national governments.

Economic liberals prefer exchange-rate flexibility as a means of reaching a solution. A powerful nation will prefer international negotiations as a method of cooperation—or, possibly, an autonomous international organization, provided the powerful nation has assured itself a strong influence within the organization. A weak nation will prefer a set of rules—or an autonomous international organization, provided there are sufficient checks on the influence of the powerful nations within it. In deciding which mode of cooperation is preferred, a government will be torn between the *safeguards* the system provides against disruptive actions by other governments in the future and the *freedom for future action* for one's own government that it allows. On the first count, a set of binding rules is optimal; on the second count, international negotiations will be preferred; on both counts, a dim view will be taken of reliance on the price system for eliminating imbalances in international payments. The lack of adequate sanctions against nations that either bypass rules, interfere in the market, or ignore an international organization leaves international negotiations as the major form of international cooperation on balance-of-payments matters, at least as far as the major trading nations are concerned.

The effectiveness of negotiations as a means of international cooperation on monetary matters is conditioned by a rather complex set of considerations. The negotiating process itself presents a confused picture even for the participants. All governments, both those of developed and less-developed countries, must subject their policies to consultation with the International Monetary Fund. In addition, regular discussions on economic problems of joint interest to the industrial countries occur not only on the ministerial (or subministerial) level under the aegis of the Organization for Economic Cooperation and Development and within smaller groups of national governments, but also within the "Basle Club" of central bankers. The latter, with their (generally) longer terms in office, relatively homogeneous viewpoints, independence from partisan politics, and shared mystique of being members of the international banking fraternity, tend more to see eye-to-eye than ministers who must defend the national interest in public and who are more likely to be affected by international animosities in noneconomic spheres. Moreover, the decision-making process within each country may result in no clear locus of responsibility in international monetary affairs,[12] and this in turn limits the abilities of countries to make either binding commitments or credible threats, not to speak of constructive proposals. There has been much talk of trying to "harmonize" the economic policies of major countries to prevent major imbalances from occurring. Yet the extent to which such harmonization is possible is limited not only by the inherent conflicts of interest (as shown by the widely differing cost evaluations by S- and D-Countries in most cells of the payoff matrix, Table 1) but also by the constraints on the extent to which governments can bind themselves to carry out specific policies. These constraints occur for several reasons: national governments may have inadequate control over the tools of economic policy; they may be subject to the veto power of national legislatures (which have not participated in the international negotiations); and their plans may be upset by unforeseen events such as strikes, changes of governments, or large shifts in public opinion.

Difficulties of communication among national governments con-

12   Richard N. Gardner, *Sterling-Dollar Diplomacy: The Origins and the Prospects of Our International Economic Order,* new ed. (New York: McGraw-Hill, 1969), relates how the State and Treasury Departments vied with each other during World War II for control of international monetary policy within the U.S. government. Since the wartime victory of the Treasury, under the leadership of Harry Dexter White, the Council of Economic Advisers and the Federal Reserve Bank have occasionally shared the Treasury's leadership.

stitute another serious obstacle to effective cooperation. For one thing, the cost to a country of any particular set of adjustment policies is bound to be greater in the eyes of that country's government than in the eyes of other governments. Thus it is virtually impossible to agree even in principle on what constitutes an "equal" or "equitable" distribution of costs. Moreover, with the adjustable peg, a full consideration of alternatives is hindered by the reluctance of officials to raise the topic of devaluation in discussions with each other. *S*-Country officials do not want to establish a precedent of international pressure being placed on a country's exchange-rate policy, and *D*-Country officials fear that candid discussion of the problem with representatives of foreign governments will produce "leaks" with disastrous impact on the foreign exchange market.[13]

Even if none of these difficulties existed, negotiations on international monetary problems would not be easy. Conflicts of interest over the distribution of the costs of eliminating (or financing) payments imbalances are serious, particularly in cases where it is impossible to distribute costs in such a way that *all* countries avoid serious divergences from domestic economic goals.[14] In any case, the solution is likely to be less than equitable, owing to the tendency of powerful countries to use their power to their own advantage. In this context power is determined not only by the familiar factors of population, gross national product, and military strength, but also by a country's balance-of-payments position and its supply of international reserves. A country with a large surplus in its balance of payments and plentiful reserves, and therefore an actual or potential creditor to deficit countries, may be able to exert an influence in international monetary affairs out of proportion with its national power measured in conventional terms. This being the case, there is the well-known tendency to solve adjustment problems by placing relatively light burdens on surplus countries and heavy ones on deficit countries. The one deficit country able to avoid a heavy burden has been the United States, for reasons mentioned earlier in this chapter.

Despite the difficulties just cited, a considerable degree of international monetary cooperation has occurred in the postwar period. The game-theoretic analysis above explains this to a large extent,

---

13 This imperfection of communication channels under the adjustable peg has been pointed out in Marris, *The Bürgenstock Communiqué*, pp. 16–17.

14 These cases will occur, for instance, when exchange rates have been permitted to remain seriously out of line for an extended period.

but there are two other factors that ought to be mentioned: the desire to avoid a major change in the present system, and what Keynes has called "the gradual encroachment of ideas."

A *change* in the present exchange-rate system, or, more generally, the present system of international trade and payments, could occur in several ways: through a serious reversal of the postwar trend toward removing restrictions to international trade and capital movements, wholesale resort to more frequent changes in exchange rates, the creation of currency blocs among major trading countries, or permitting exchange rates to be determined solely by private market forces. The greater the desire to avoid change in a system of trade and payments, the greater will be the willingness of national governments to find a mutually satisfactory solution whenever an adjustment problem arises. One of the greatest strengths of the present system is its acceptability relative to alternative ones. If statesmen and financiers were indifferent between maintaining the adjustable peg and permitting it to lapse into a system with greater exchange-rate flexibility, then it is unlikely that the present system would have survived as long as it has. As a result of the desire to preserve the present system, vast means for intergovernmental financing of payments imbalances have been created, thereby permitting both deficit and surplus countries to avoid intolerable burdens of adjustment and the United States to avoid a devaluation of the dollar that would be tolerable neither to the American government nor to the governments of other major countries. By way of contrast, the greater the appeal of an alternative system of arranging trade and payments, the less compelling will be the need for finding ad hoc solutions to difficulties arising in the present system. Sooner or later, crises will arise that result in changes in the system itself.[15]

It is, therefore, of great importance how those in positions of responsibility evaluate possible reforms of the system. This will affect not only (to use a tautology) their acceptance of the reform per se, but also their behavior within the existing system while reforms are under discussion. Academic economists are often impatient with the reluctance of government officials and private bankers to accept reform proposals, sometimes ignoring the logic of preferring to untried utopias a system whose shortcomings, although undeniably present, are at least known and can be combatted with fairly successful methods developed through trial and error. A "gradual encroachment of ideas" has nonetheless occurred in the past several years, in part

15 For instance, the crisis of February–March, 1968, resulted in a change in the role of gold in the international monetary system.

because of the severe difficulties the system has experienced during that period, and in part because of the efforts of a few senior academic economists, notably Fritz Machlup of Princeton, to arrange discussions between leading international economists from the universities and those from business and government. As a result, the notion of reforming the system in the direction of greater exchange-rate flexibility is no longer completely unacceptable to most members of the international financial community, as it was only a few years ago.

By way of summary, two factors determine the politics of the international monetary system: the underlying strategic situation, illustrated by the payoff matrix described earlier, and the ability of the participants in the system to reach a *cooperative*, as opposed to an *equilibrium noncooperative*, solution. In examining the workings of the present system, we have seen how the underlying payoff matrix produces a tendency to avoid elimination of payments imbalances by means of financing and to postpone changes in parity until a crisis occurs. This tendency has to some extent been tempered by international cooperation in the postwar period, although it should also be pointed out that a great deal of that cooperation has done no more than to effect arrangements whereby imbalances are financed and not eliminated. These intergovernmental solutions to the so-called "liquidity problem" are in fact testimony not so much to the effectiveness of international cooperation as to the tacit agreement that the financing solution is the best possible in the absence of the kind of cooperation that would be necessary to *eliminate* imbalances. Growing recognition of the difficulties standing in the way of such cooperation has led to an increasing desire for some kind of reform of the exchange-rate mechanism. Whether the "crawling-peg" proposal would, if effected, improve matters, is the next topic on our agenda.

COMPARING ALTERNATIVE EXCHANGE-RATE SYSTEMS

When considering the relative advantages of alternatives to the present system, the analytic framework developed in the previous section permits us to distinguish between two types of questions that are frequently confused in discussions of this problem: first, whether the ranking of policy combinations shown in the payoff matrix is affected, and second, whether the mode of international cooperation is in any way changed.

Here I shall focus solely on a comparison of the present system with the "crawling peg" (or "gliding parity," as it is sometimes called). According to this scheme, governments would be authorized, without consulting the International Monetary Fund, to change the official parity by as much as 2 percent a year and (in the most widely discussed version of this proposal) as often as once a month. Considerable controversy exists over the extent to which individual governments could or should be compelled to change, or restrained from changing, the exchange parity of their nation's currency. The alternatives range from a compulsory formula (based on an average of past changes in reserves or market exchange rates) to total discretion for the individual governments. The weight of academic opinion seems to lean toward a compromise formula called "presumptive rules," the political implications and indeed meaningfulness of which are not altogether clear, except that such rules would give an additional arguing point to countries urging exchange-rate changes on others.[16]

How would such a reform affect our payoff matrix? First we must make clear the nature of our comparison: since the proposal specifies a maximum size to any annual change in the exchange rate, we must compare a devaluation of some size (say, 10 percent) with a policy of changing the exchange rate by 2 percent per year over a period of five years. The question, then, is whether *gradual* change of the exchange rate is less costly, either from an economic or political standpoint, than sporadic change. There are several reasons for thinking that it is.

The greatest apparent advantage of a series of frequent small changes in parity over a large occasional change lies in the greater invisibility of the accompanying policy measures required to maintain full employment (or prevent inflation). As Marris has pointed out, for a 10 to 15 percent change in parity in an economy like that of the United Kingdom or Germany, "the required policy change is likely to be larger than the largest ordinary conjunctural demand-management package; and the impact on income distribution equivalent to that of a major tax reform."[17] Not only will small frequent changes in the exchange rates be removed from the headlines (or at least provide headlines of smaller type than at present), but the accompanying policy changes will become less visible as well. Therefore, politicians will attach a smaller subjective cost to parity changes than is the case at present. So, at least, runs the argument. Whether

16 See Richard N. Cooper, "Sliding Parities: A Proposal for Presumptive Rules," in *Approaches to Greater Flexibility of Exchange Rates*, ed. Halm, pp. 251–60.

17 Marris, *The Bürgenstock Communiqué*, p. 15.

it is a correct argument might better be judged by political scientists than economists. One important question is whether *trends* affect the decisions of the electorate less than *large discrete changes*. For the short run, the answer seems obvious; for the longer run, however, the opposite may be the case, particularly if the last large discrete change is considered to have settled matters once and for all, while small frequent changes are considered to presage continued changes in the future.

In addition, it has been argued that smaller, more frequent changes reduce the total amount of parity change necessary to eliminate an imbalance. The reasons for this are rather technical, and discussion of them would be beyond the scope of this paper.[18] If the assertion is correct, then this is another reason why parity change would be relatively more attractive to the authorities under limited flexibility than under the present system.

Whether this change in the payoff matrix is sufficient to produce a different noncooperative solution depends on whether in any given year a small devaluation or revaluation is considered more or less costly than the alternative degree of necessary financing. If it is considered less costly by both *S*- and *D*-Countries, in the *absence* of parity changes by the other side, then the financing solution will be replaced as the noncooperative equilibrium by the cell at which the devaluation row intersects the upward-revaluation column. If only *S*-Countries and not *D*-Countries prefer changing the exchange rate to financing, then the new equilibrium cell will be defined by the financing row and the upward-revaluation column. If, alternatively, *D*-Countries and not *S*-Countries prefer exchange-rate changes, then equilibrium will occur at the financing column–devaluation row cell. The last two possibilities are of particular interest to economists who are concerned with whether the present system, and the proposed alternatives, contain a systematic bias toward devaluation or reval-

18   The argument is correct only if one or both of the following are true: (a) the longer-standing a given misallocation of resources resulting from under- or overvalued exchange rates, the greater the change in exchange rates necessary to remove it, and (b) the *larger* such a misallocation of resources, the greater *proportionally* the change in exchange rates necessary to remove it. If either of these statements is true, then the gliding parity, by reducing both the size and longevity of undervaluations or overvaluations of exchange rates, will also reduce the cumulative size of necessary changes in parities over time. The only argument I have seen for this position is in ibid., pp. 8–9. The argument seems to be based on the assumption that the cost of the decision-making process resulting in the reallocation either grows with the longevity of the misallocation or grows more than proportionally with the size of the misallocation.

uation. A bias toward devaluation (accompanied by full employment) tends to be inflationary in its impact, and for this reason a bias toward revaluation might be preferred.

What the cooperative solution to the crawling-peg system would be depends not only on the considerations just discussed, but also on the way such a system would affect the structure and techniques of international cooperation itself. On this point we have little to go on besides Marris's observation that the smaller impact of the changes involved and their (presumed) smaller impact on public opinion would make exchange-rate changes a less unmentionable topic in international councils, and that increased communication among national representatives on this subject would result in increased cooperation.[19] Against this it might be argued that the greater frequency of possible changes in the exchange rate may lead to more frequent occasion of international conflict, particularly if governments are tempted to use the now more flexible parity as an instrument for regulating aggregate demand rather than the balance of payments. Once changes in the exchange rate become considered a matter of "fine tuning," which is how changes in interest rates are usually regarded under the present system, it will also become more arguable than it is now which countries ought to change their rates, in what direction, and by how much. It is easier to harmonize domestic and foreign views of a country's economic problems when exchange rates are obviously out of line than when the indications are smaller and more tentative. If those domestic interests with a stake in the level of exchange parity are convinced that the latter is changed only when absolutely necessary, they will put less pressure on the government than when the matter seems more debatable. Thus, while Marris's assumption that increased communication will result seems a sound one, the conclusion that increased cooperation will result is less clear.[20]

In summary, there are some grounds to suppose that the payoff

19 *Ibid.*, pp. 16–18.
20 The point I wish to make here is related to Thomas Schelling's interesting observation that the common perception of a conspicuously prominent solution may significantly influence the outcome of a bargaining situation, particularly when communication is limited. A simple solution, not necessarily the best possible compromise, will be hit upon simply in order to avoid the bargaining difficulties inherent in the admission of additional criteria. Changing the exchange-rate system to one in which an infinity of solutions is possible complicates the process of reaching agreements among national economic authorities on the proper configuration of exchange rates, interest rates, and fiscal policies for any given period. See Thomas C. Schelling, *The Strategy of Conflict* (Cambridge: Harvard University Press, 1960), Ch. 3.

matrix under a crawling-peg system would increase the likelihood of reaching an equilibrium noncooperative solution that results in the elimination, and not merely in the financing, of payments imbalances. This argument in favor of the crawling peg is quite independent of whether or not international cooperation on monetary matters is made easier by the new system.

EXCHANGE-RATE SYSTEMS AND
INTERNATIONAL INTEGRATION

Exchange-rate systems affect a major common concern of political scientists and economists: international integration. To an economist, integration has at least two quite different meanings: integration of the political decision-making process, meaning anything from cooperation in areas of common interest to the creation of common political institutions, and integration of markets, meaning (in economists' jargon) high price elasticities of demand and supply between similar goods or assets of different national origin.[21] Political scientists are interested primarily in the first kind of integration because of its implications for the reduction of international conflict; economists are interested in the second because of its effect on the efficient international allocation of goods and resources.

The choice of alternative exchange-rate systems has implications for both types of integration.[22] Opponents of greater exchange-rate flexibility argue that more frequent changes and greater variations in parity would increase the riskiness, complexity, and cost of international business activities, thereby discouraging and reducing the scale of the latter. Proponents of greater exchange-rate flexibility reply that solving the adjustment problem by changes in parity will enable the authorities to avoid restrictive measures (import quotas, exchange controls, and the like) whose discouraging effect on international commerce is far greater than frequent, moderate, and controlled changes in exchange rates would be. Although this debate could be settled in part by examining a number of testable proposi tions regarding the response of financial and goods markets to restrictive measures and exchange-rate changes, a good deal also hinges on the way in which a given exchange-rate system is employed by governments. The presentation of ideal methods of economic policy-

21 Put more simply, this means that both buyers and sellers have a high degree of responsiveness to price changes abroad.

22 See the various papers in *Approaches to Greater Flexibility of Exchange Rates*, ed. Halm; also Lanyi, *The Case for Floating Exchange Rates Reconsidered.*

making notwithstanding, economists have advanced little in trying to predict how governments will generally behave. To include such considerations in the comparison of alternative exchange-rate systems has been the major purpose of this paper.

As for political integration, the effects of alternative exchange-rate systems are not clear, although some assume them to be of considerable significance. The ancient prejudice of economists has always been that fixed exchange rates are "internationalist"—a kind of substitute for a common world currency—whereas flexible exchange rates are "nationalist": a system of fixed exchange rates forces upon governments an adjustment process that requires the "harmonization" of the several national economic policies, while flexible exchange rates enable each government to go its own way without regard to policies in other countries. The inability to harmonize policies leads inevitably to changes in parity or to measures (such as increased trade and exchange restrictions) which themselves hinder economic integration. This has been the sobering experience of the European Economic Community (EEC) in the last several years, and a few observers have even begun to wonder whether limited exchange-rate flexibility among EEC members might not assist rather than hinder further political integration:

> With a large-change-or-not-at-all system too much is at stake; like it or not, national sovereignty rears its ugly head. But under rules that encouraged small and more frequent changes, it would be much easier to insist on proper consultation within the Community, and more likely that effective pressure could be brought to bear to insure that the exchange rate policies followed were consistent with the interests of the Community as a whole. . . . What is wanted is a set of rules that exerts continuous pressure on member countries to make progress along the road to monetary integration, without demanding the impossible in terms of current economic and political realities. The proposals for a "crawling peg" now under consideration seem to meet these requirements rather well.[23]

The considerations cited by Marris may also apply to a broader context than that of the EEC. But, as mentioned in the previous section, there is some doubt as to whether the additional degree of indeterminacy lent to international discussions by the possibility of frequent exchange-rate changes would indeed facilitate agreement and co-

23   Stephen N. Marris, "Comments on the Papers by Messrs. Mosconi and Kasper: Red Herrings, Carts, and Horses," in *Approaches to Greater Flexibility of Exchange Rates*, ed. Halm, pp. 392–93, 398.

operation. More than ever, the exchange rate will assume a leading role as an instrument of national economic policy, and it seems counter to the ordinary behavior of the national state that such an instrument, once in hand, be yielded either to a regularized procedure of international negotiation or to an international organization of some sort. In view of these competing considerations, it is not clear how a change in the exchange-rate system would affect the internationalization of decision-making in the area of economic policy.

Finally, on the normative side, it is by no means clear from the point of view of economic welfare that integration is always a good thing. This is certainly not a new insight for students of colonialism or imperialism; it is generally believed that substantive national independence is a necessary (although certainly not a sufficient) condition for the continued economic development of an initially backward country. What may be less understood is that neither political nor economic integration among developed countries is *necessarily* conducive to increased *economic* welfare (although there may be political or cultural considerations that override economic ones). For instance, a monetary (or "currency") union between two countries or regions implies a common price level and a common rate of inflation. If, however, the two countries or regions maintain separate labor markets and separate institutions for settling wage disputes, the region with the greater tendency for rising wages will soon suffer from severe unemployment. Similar results occur when productivity is growing more rapidly (relative to changes in wage rates) in one region than in another; we have experienced this in the United States with our depressed regions. In such cases, where a currency union is used as an attempt to paper over interregional differences in institutions and the quality of human resources, the region that suffers unemployment may be better off without union with its more successful neighbor—*if* it is large enough to sustain an independent currency.[24] What is "integration" to a dominant region may be "dependence" or "imperialism" to the others.

"Integration," then, cannot be a goal in itself. We need to specify what types of integration we want, how much of each, and between

24 The first important contributions to the problem of "optimum currency areas" were R. A. Mundell, "A Theory of Optimum Currency Areas," *American Economic Review* 51, no. 4 (September 1961): 657–65, and Ronald I. McKinnon, "Optimum Currency Areas," *American Economic Review* 53, no. 4 (September 1963): 717–25. See also Lanyi, *The Case for Floating Exchange Rates Reconsidered*, pp. 18–21, and Thomas D. Willett and Edward Tower, "The Concept of Optimum Currency Areas and the Choice between Fixed and Flexible Exchange Rates," in *Approaches to Greater Flexibility of Exchange Rates*, ed. Halm, pp. 407–15.

which regions. Until we have studied the normative aspects of integration more carefully, we cannot set up either economic or political integration as the objective of reforms of the exchange-rate system. For the time being, it is more practicable to choose as our criterion the extent to which the system enables participating countries to achieve their economic goals. This criterion is itself complex enough, since it involves assigning weights to specific economic objectives (such as full employment, price stability, and growth) that may not be mutually compatible, as well as giving weights to the performance of different countries. If this is what the governments of the West aim for, they cannot end up very far from the degree and type of integration they really desire.[25]

25   The author gratefully acknowledges the helpful comments contributed by Harry G. Gelber, Hans O. Schmitt, and Richard L. Merritt. Remaining errors in analysis and judgment are his own responsibility.

CONTRIBUTORS

FREDERICK C. BARGHOORN, professor of political science at Yale University, served with the State Department and was press attaché at the American embassy in Moscow from 1942 to 1947. Among his numerous books and articles on Soviet affairs are *The Soviet Image of the United States* (1950), *The Soviet Cultural Offensive* (1960), *Soviet Foreign Propaganda* (1964), and *Politics in the USSR* (1966).

DAVIS B. BOBROW is professor of political science and public affairs and director of the Center of International Studies, University of Minnesota. Before that he was special assistant for the behavioral and social sciences in the Office of the Director of Defense Research and Engineering, U.S. Department of Defense, and Acting Director, Behavioral Science, Advanced Research Projects Agency. In addition to numerous journal articles, he has edited and co-authored *Components of Defense Policy* (1965), *Computers and the Policy-Making Community* (1968), and *Weapons System Decisions* (1969).

LARRY B. HILL, assistant professor of political science at the University of Oklahoma, has concentrated his research on the role of the ombudsman in political systems. He received a Fulbright scholarship at Victoria University in Wellington, New Zealand, and has since published several articles and finished a monograph on this topic; his dissertation won the American Political Science Association's Public Administration Award in 1971. He is also the author of the forthcoming *Comparative Political Systems*.

ROBERT JERVIS is Research Fellow at the Center for International Affairs and assistant professor of government, Harvard University. In addition to several articles on image formation and change, particularly among foreign policy decision-makers, he recently published *The Logic of Images in International Relations* (1970).

RITA KELLY is presently Senior Research Scientist at the American Institutes for Research, Inc., Kensington, Maryland. Her research has focused on ideology and its impact on political behavior, on which she has published (with Frederic J. Fleron, Jr.) "Personality, Behavior, and Communist Ideology" (*Soviet Studies,* January 1970) and "Motivation, Methodology, and Communist Ideology" (in *The Behavioral Revolution and Communist Studies,* 1971), as well as a forthcoming work on American civil strife. She is also co-author of "Ideology: Its Meaning and Measurement," *Journal of Comparative Political Studies* (July 1972).

HERBERT C. KELMAN is Richard Clarke Cabot Professor of Social Ethics in the department of social relations at Harvard University. He has served as president of the Society for the Psychological Study of Social Issues (1964–65) and the Division of Personality and Social Psychology, American Psychological Association (1970–71); he received the AAAS Sociopsychological Award in 1956. Among his many writings, those of particular interest for students of international communication are *International Behavior* (editor, 1965), *A Time to Speak: On Human Values and Social Research* (1968), and, with Raphael Ezekiel, *Cross-National Encounters* (1970).

ANTHONY LANYI, currently an economist working in Washington, D.C., was assistant professor of economics at Princeton University when he wrote the chapter in this volume. He previously taught at the University of California, Berkeley, where he received his doctorate. He is the author of *The Case for Floating Exchange Rates Reconsidered* (Princeton Essays in International Finance, 1969).

JOHN R. MATHIASON, who was assistant professor of communications at the University of Washington when he prepared the chapter in this volume, has since moved to the United Nations (the views of which those expressed in the article do not necessarily reflect) where he is Associate Social Affairs Officer in the Regional and Community Development Section. He has concentrated his research on agrarian reform and urban poverty, particularly in Latin America.

ANNA J. MERRITT is a free-lance editor and translator, with special emphasis on German politics. She has co-authored (with Richard L. Merritt) *Public Opinion in Occupied Germany: The OMGUS Surveys, 1945–1949* (1970) and *West Germany Enters the Seventies* (1971), and is currently completing *Public Opinion in Semisovereign Germany: The HICOG Surveys, 1949–1955.*

RICHARD L. MERRITT is professor of political science and research professor in communications at the University of Illinois. His research focuses on international communication and quantitative research in comparative politics. Among his books are *Symbols of American Community, 1735–1775* (1966), *Comparing Nations* (coeditor with Stein Rokkan, 1966), and *Systematic Approaches to Comparative Politics* (1970).

ELLEN MICKIEWICZ, associate professor of political science at Michigan State University, has concentrated her attention on Soviet and East European politics. She is the author of *Soviet Political Schools* (1967), "The Modernization of Party Propaganda in the USSR" (*Slavic Review*, June 1971), and *Handbook of Soviet Social Science Data* (1972).

SOPHIA PETERSON is assistant professor of political science at West Virginia University. She has also taught at Miami University. She is the author of the forthcoming *Conflict, Communication and Mutual Threat in Soviet-American and Sino-Soviet Relationships* and of *The Nuclear Test-Ban Treaty and Its Effect on International Tension* (1967).

EDWARD A. RAYMOND, presently assistant professor of political science at the University of Connecticut, Stamford, was for three decades a U.S. government specialist on Soviet affairs, on which he has written some forty-five periodical articles and sixteen government monographs, including *U.S. Army Psychological Warfare Handbook on the U.S.S.R.* (1951). He has also taught at the University of Maryland, George Washington University, and William and Mary College.

ALVIN RICHMAN wrote the article in this volume while he was assistant professor of political science at Purdue University. Since 1971 he has been project director in the Research Service of the U.S. Information Agency. He has published several articles on public opinion and foreign affairs, including "The Nation-State and Internationalism" (*Journal of International Affairs*, 1958) and, with Harry R. Targ, "The Impact of Instruction and External Events on Student Orientations and Opinion Consistency Concerning the Vietnam War" (*Sociology of Education*, Spring 1970).

HERBERT I. SCHILLER is professor of communications and coordinator of the communications program, Third College, University of California, San Diego. He has taught at Pratt Institute, CCNY, and the University of Illinois. He was editor of the *Quarterly Review of Economics and Busi-*

ness and is the author of *Mass Communications and American Empire* (1969) and the forthcoming *Mind Management* (1972), as well as co-editor of *Superstate* (1970).

HANS O. SCHMITT, currently an economist working in Washington, D.C., was formerly associate professor of economics at the University of Wisconsin, Madison, and Senior Economist with the International Bank for Reconstruction and Development in Washington, D.C. Among his works relevant to readers of this volume are "Political Conditions for International Currency Reform" (*International Organization*, Summer 1964), "Capital Markets and the Unification of Europe" (*World Politics*, January 1968), and "Integration and Conflict in the World Economy" (*Journal of Common Market Studies*, September 1969).

LORAND B. SZALAY, Senior Research Scientist at the American Institutes for Research, Inc., Kensington, Maryland, has taught international communications and social psychology at American University and George Washington University. He has written widely on verbal associations in the analysis of subjective culture, including "Attitude Research for Intercultural Communications" (*Journal of Communication*, 1970) and "Research Requirements Posed by Tasks of Intercultural Communication" (*Psychological Research in National Defense Today*, 1967). He is also co-author of "Ideology: Its Meaning and Measurement," *Journal of Comparative Political Studies* (July 1972).

SUSAN WELCH is assistant professor of political science and Fellow of Centennial College, University of Nebraska, Lincoln. She is the co-author (with Cal Clark) of "Western European Trade: Untangling the Interpretations" (*Journal of Conflict Resolution*, forthcoming in 1972).

PAUL D. WOLFOWITZ is assistant professor of political science at Yale University. Formerly with the RAND Corporation in Santa Monica, California, he is the author of the forthcoming monograph, *Middle East Nuclear Desalting: Economic and Political Considerations*.

INDEX

Abbee, Catherine, 391n
Abelson, Robert P., 272n
Abraham, Henry J., 300n, 316n
Acheson, Dean, 115
Acuff, F. Gene, 87n
Adjustment of foreign students:
 U-curve, 77–79
Adler, Kenneth P., 44n
Advertising: as international
 communicator, 27, 321–38
Africa: workshop on border disputes
 in, 172–75
Aich, Prodosh, 73n, 77n, 80n, 81n
Akzin, Benjamin, 406n
Albrook, Robert C., 334n
Alexander, Franz, 193n
Alker, Hayward R., Jr., 26n, 93n,
 167n
Allen, Donald E., 87n
Almond, Gabriel A., 44n, 233n,
 234n, 235, 249, 252n, 372n, 415n
Alsop, Joseph: on Indochina, 211,
 217–19
Alsop, Stewart: on Indochina, 211,
 218–19
Amar, Andrew R., 138n, 139n, 143n
Anderman, Steven D., 296n, 298n
Anderson, Stanley V., 310n
Angell, Robert C., 66, 79n
Arnheim, Rudolf, 43n

Aronson, Elliot, 35n
Ashby, William Ross, 282
Associative Group Analysis (AGA),
 29, 97–119; technique, 97–101
Atkin, Charles, 283n
Ayangira, N., 139n

Balassa, Bela A., 410n
Baldwin, Hanson, 211, 216n, 217,
 224–25
Ball, George W., 417n, 418n
Barghoorn, Frederick C., 29, 38n,
 131, 137, 447
Barnard, Chester I., 34n, 228n
Barrera, Mario, 387n, 411n
Bass, Elizabeth, 132n
Bass, Robert, 132n
Bassie, V. Lewis, 331n
Bator, Victor, 219n
Bauer, Raymond A., 288n
Beals, Ralph L., 72n, 75n, 79n
Beaton, Leonard, 344, 346n
Becker, Tamar, 78n
Benedict, Ruth, 16, 34n
Bennett, John W., 75n
Benton, William, 96n
Berelson, Bernard, 38n, 42n, 44n
Berger, Joseph, 48n
Berkowitz, Leonard, 283n
Bernstein, Marver H., 107n

Bertalanffy, Ludwig von, 31n, 54n
Bethmann-Hollweg, Theobald von: and World War I, 290–91
Beveridge, W. I. B., 288n
Bexelius, Alfred, 296n, 300
Bhatnager, J. K., 81n
Binder, Leonard, 341–42
Bjorklund, Edith Marie, 333n
Blackmer, Donald L. M., 114n
Bleicher, Samuel A., 409n
Bliss, Chester I., 167n
Blom-Cooper, J. L., 306
Blum, John M., 363n
Blumenstock, Dorothy, 37n
Bobrow, Davis B., x, 4, 7, 18, 32n, 40n, 44n, 51n, 447
Boundaries: economic and political, 21–22, 405–22
Bradford, Ernest S., 331n
"Brain drain," 84–87
Brandstrom, Elsa, 133n
Brecher, Michael, 284n
Breed, Warren, 229n
Brent, Jack E., 99n, 100n
Bressler, Marvin, 75n
Brody, Richard A., 46n
Brokerage firms: and international business interests, 334–36
Bronfenbrenner, Urie, 167n
Bryson, Lyman, 4n, 295n
Brzezinski, Zbigniew K., 132n
Buchanan, William, 39n, 115n, 117n, 252
Buchler, Carlos, 347
Buck, Tom, 130
Bunyan, James, 134n
Burmeister, Alfred, 130n
Burnor, Duane R., 72n, 75n
Burton, John W., 54, 168–72, 175–204
Busch, Briton Cooper, 279n
Butler, David E., 307n
Butow, Robert, 274n
Byrnes, Robert F., 141n

Cantril, Hadley, 35n, 38n, 39n, 45n, 115n, 117n, 167n, 252
Carey, James W., x, 32n
Carlson, E., 276n
Carr, Edward H., 123n
Carr, Robert K., 107n

Carroll, John B., 34n
Cartwright, Dorwin, 50n, 60n
Caves, Richard E., 426n
Centre for the Analysis of Conflict (London), 168–72, 175–204
Chapin, Emerson, 86n
Charlesworth, James C., 18n
Chase, P. E., 54n
Chee, Ch'angboh, 112n
Chen, Kwailing, 167n
Cherry, Colin, 7, 56n
Chesler, Mark, 256n, 257n
Chicago Tribune: coverage of Indochina conflict, 207–31
Childs, Harwood L., 256n
Childs, Marquis: on Indochina, 219
China: consistency of views and civil war in, 277, 284, 291
Christ, June R., 75n
Clark, R. Inslee, Jr., 89n
Clay, General Lucius D.: and German denazification, 365–66, 369n, 373–74, 376, 378n, 380
Clews, John C., 38n
Coelho, George V., 75n, 77n, 95n
Cognitive balance paradigm, 18–20, 48–52, 272–91
Cohen, Bernard C., 222n, 223, 224n, 225, 230n, 231n, 252, 253n
Coleman, James S., 415n
Colvin, Ian, 286n
Comintern schools, 122–30
Communication: definition, 4–5, 7, 56–57; process, 4–5, and transfer of institutions, 295; political, 10–11; international, 12–13; models, 18, 46–55; between elites and mass publics, 36–40
Communicators: international political, 13–17; governmental actors as, 14–15, 20–25; nongovernmental actors as, 15–16, 25–28; cultures as, 16–17, 28–32
Conflict behavior: U.S.-USSR, 257–71; indicators of, 261–65
Conflict resolution: problem-solving workshop in, 30, 168–204
Conquest, Robert, 130n
Consistency: cognitive balance, 18–20, 48–52, 272–91; rational, 274–76; irrational, 276–81

Cook, Stuart W., 75n, 97, 98n, 117
Cooper, Richard N., 429, 440n
Core area: and integration, 411; Germany as for Europe, 421
Cormack, Margaret L., 96
Corporations: international, 319–38, 416–18
Craig, Gordon A., 286n
Crombie, A. C., 287n
Crossman, R. S. H., 308
Cultures: as communicators, 16–17, 28–32
Culture shock: in foreign students, 78
Currency: exchange-rate systems, 22, 423–46; and economic boundaries, 414–15
Cybernetic paradigm, 52–55
Cyprus: problem-solving workshop and, 170–72, 175–204
Czechoslovakia: 1948 coup and American public opinion, 239, 247

Dahl, Robert A., 230n
Dahlberg, Kenneth, 420n, 421n
Dahrendorf, Ralf, 372n, 379n
Dallin, David J., 133n
Das, Man Singh, 87n
Daugherty, William E., 39n
Davidsen, Oluf M., 75n, 77n
Davidson, Alexander B., 75n
Davis, James A., 68n
Davis, James M., 72n, 75n
Davison, W. Phillips, 44n
Dawson, John L., 80n, 97n
Decision-makers: and public opinion, 253–71
Decision-making, 17–20; theory of personal, 48–52
Dedijer, Stevan, 85, 87
Deese, James, 99n
De Grazia, Sebastian, 38n
Denazification, 24–25, 361–83
Denmark: ombudsman in, 301–2, 308, 309, 311–16
De Reuck, Anthony, 181–82
De Rivera, Joseph, 228n
Desai, Ram, 139n, 140n
Desalting: nuclear, in Middle East, 24, 339–60
Deutsch, Karl W., ix, 7–8, 18, 26n, 31n, 43n, 54, 93n, 254, 255n, 259,

282, 288, 291, 387n, 388n, 405, 406n, 407, 408, 411, 416
Deutsch, Martin, 288n
Deutsch, Steven E., 81n, 98n
Deutscher, Isaac, 132n
Deviller, Philippe, 219n
DeVos, Ton, ix, 32n
Diem, Ngo Dinh, 220–22
Di Paliano, Guido Colonna, 418n
Di Vesta, Francis J., 276n
Doob, Leonard W., 38n, 168–70, 172–204
D'Orival, Michel, 341n
Dougherty, Philip H., 323n
Dowling, Leo R., 76n, 81n
Downs, Anthony, 228
Draper, Theodore, 125
Driver, Michael J., 234n
Drummond, Roscoe: on Indochina, 219
Du Bois, Cora, 75n
Dulles, John Foster: and Indochina conflict, 207–31
Dunn, Delmer, 222n, 225n
Dunning, John H., 418n
Dupeux, Genevieve, 77n, 80n
Durbin, William, 326–27

Ebsworth, Raymond, 365n
ECLA, 21, 387–404
Economic integration, 405–22
Economics: and electronics in modern world, 320; of desalination, 353–55
Economy, 410–11
Eden, Anthony, 219n
Edinger, Lewis J., 368n, 407n
Education and foreign affairs, 19, 232–51
Eek, Hilding, 299n
Einsfedel, Heinrich von, 136n
Eisenhower, Dwight D.: and Indochina conflict, 207–31
Electronics and economics in modern world, 320
Elites: communication with mass publics, 36–40; American, view of USSR, 258–59
Emerson, Gloria, 87n
Engineering: and international political communication, 18, 33–61

Erickson, John, 283n
Ethiopia: border dispute with Kenya and Somalia, 168–70, 172–204
Etzioni, Amitai, 387n
Eudin, Xenia Joukoff, 129n
Euro-dollar: and economic integration, 417–20
Exchange-of-scholars programs: U.S.-USSR, 29–30, 146–67
Exchange-rate systems, 22, 423–46

Fagan, Richard R., 49n
Fall, Bernard B., 214n, 219n
Feis, Herbert, 365n
Feldman, Sheldon, 99n
Feldstein, Helen S., 420n
Ferguson, Charles K., 185n
Fermeda Workshop, 168–70, 172–204
Fichtner, Wolfgang, 356n
Finland: Soviet policy and consistency of views in, 279; ombudsman in, 300–301, 309–16
Finlay, David J., 49n
Fishbein, Martin, 276n
Fischer, Fritz, 290
Fischer, Ruth, 124n
Fisher, Roger, 41n
Fisher, William E., 407n
Flack, Michael J., 96
Foltz, William J., 172
Ford, Franklin, 286n
Foreign affairs: press and, 18–19, 207–31; public opinion and, 19–20, 232–51, 272–91
Foreign students, 23, 29–30, 65–94, 95–119, 120–45; in the Soviet Union, 23, 120–45; Korean in America, 29, 86–87, 97–119; impact of foreign visit, 67–77, 83–84, 95–119; characteristics of, 68; and nonstudent foreign travelers, 69–70; major fields of study, 69–71; motivation of, 70–75; countries of origin, 71, 88; and achievement orientation, 72, 74; U-curve of adjustment, 77–79; changed perspectives during stay, 77–84, 95–119; and the "brain drain," 84–87; from India, 86; structural changes in flows of, 87–94; Japanese, 90–

92; and racial discrimination in Soviet Union, 138–39; recruitment of for study in Soviet Union, 140–43
Franck, Thomas, 273n
Frank, Howard, 60n
Fraser, Stewart, 89n
Free, Lloyd A., 35n
Freedman, Jonathan L., 283n
French, Thomas M., 193n
Frey, Frederick W., 90n
Friedrich, Carl J., 364n, 365n, 369n
Frisch, Ivan T., 60n
Fröhlich, Dieter, 84n
Fulbright, J. William, 339

Galbraith, John Kenneth, 319
Galtung, Ingrid Eide, 77n, 80n, 81n
Game theory: and international exchange rates, 431–39
Gamson, William A., 256n, 270n
Gardner, Richard N., 436n
Garner, Wendell R., 57n
Gaudet, Hazel, 44n, 45n
Gelber, Harry G., ix, 422n, 446n
Gellhorn, Walter, 296n, 297n, 300n
George, Alexander, 39n
Germany: denazification in, 24–25, 361–83; POWs in USSR, 133–36; consistency of views and Chamberlain's policy on, 283, 286; and Vansittart, 286
Gilbert, Felix, 286n
Gilbert, Martin, 286n
Gilinsky, Victor, 360n
Gilman, William, 288n
Gimbel, John, 369n, 373n, 379n
Gitlow, Benjamin, 124n, 125n, 126n
Goldsen, R. K., 98n
Gott, Richard, 286n
Goulding, Phil G., 278n
Graber, Doris A., 256n
Granquist, D. P., 346n
Great Britain: ombudsman in, 305–15
Greenberg, D. S., 334–35
Gregg, Robert W., 389n
Griffith, J. A. G., 306
Griffith, William E., 362n, 366n, 369n, 375n, 376n
Gruber, Helmut, 122n

Guetzkow, Harold, 41n
Gulf of Tonkin: and American public opinion, 247
Gullahorn, Jeanne E., 72n, 107n, 108
Gullahorn, John T., 72n, 107n, 108

Haas, Ernst B., 387n, 388n, 389, 390n, 391n, 392, 405, 406n, 409, 411, 416, 422
Haberler, Gottfried, 410, 426n
Halm, George N., 424n, 440n, 443n, 444n, 445n
Hammond, Paul Y., 364n
Hamson, C. J., 302
Hanan, R. J., 303–4
Hanson, Russell G., 72n, 75n
Harary, Frank, 50n, 60n
Harbison, Frederick, 88n
Hardern, Mrs. Leslie, 307n
Harrisson, Tom, 38n
Harsanyi, John C., 433n
Hartenstein, Wolfgang, 77n
Hartley, Eugene L., 44n
Havel, Joan, 75n
Heider, Fritz, 18, 48–50
Henderson, Gregory, 87n, 110n
Herberichs, Gerard, 254n
Herlitz, Nils, 298n, 310n
Hero, Alfred O., 42n, 232n, 233, 234n
Herz, John H., 377n
Herzog, Elizabeth A., 38n
Herzog, Herta, 43n, 45n
Heuss, Theodor, 368n
Hidén, Mikael, 300n
Higher Komsomol school: in Soviet Union, 131–32
Higher Party school: in Soviet Union, 130–31
Hill, Larry B., 24, 295n, 300n, 312n, 447
Hiniker, Paul, 49n
Hirsch, Fred, 419n
Hirschman, Albert O., 389n, 410, 411n
Hladun, John, 125n, 126n, 128n, 130n
Hodgson, John H., 128n
Hoehn, William E., 346, 348, 353n, 360n
Hoe-yong, Lee, 112n

Hoffman, Hugh C., 328n
Hoffmann, Max von, 134n
Hoffmann, Stanley, 281n, 410n
Hofstaetter, Peter, 235n
Holborn, Hajo, 363n, 364n, 365n
Holst, Johan Jörgen, 40n
Holsti, K. J., 21n
Holsti, Ole R., 46n, 47n, 49n, 57n, 258n
Holt, Robert T., 37n
Hong, Sung-Chick, 115n
Hopmann, P. Terrence, 49n
Hopsen, A. L., 98n
Horowitz, Irving Louis, 28n
Hovland, C. I., 44n
Hughes, Barry B., 49n
Hughes, Helen MacGill, 44n
Humphrey, Norman D., 72n, 75n, 79n
Hungarian revolution: and official American attitudes, 258
Hurwitz, Stephan, 301–2, 305–6, 307n, 308, 312n
Hyman, Herbert H., 44n

Indian foreign students, 86
Indochina: American press and, 18–19, 207–31; newspaper editorials on, 212–13
Informal communication networks, 21, 387–404
Influence: theory of interpersonal, 48–52
Information: transactions as, 7–8; *vs.* transfer of meaning, 57–58
Inkeles, Alex, 35n, 37n
Institute of International Education, 69n, 70n, 71n, 88n, 93n, 96n, 120, 137n
Integration: through international transactions, 6; Latin American, 21, 387–404; political and economic, 21–22, 405–22; and exchange-rate systems, 443–46
Interaction: social, American and Korean attitudes toward, 107–15
International communication, 12–13; development of, 33–46; types of flows, 17
International relations and systems, 55–56

Investment: direct and indirect, 412–13, 415–16
Irrational consistency, 276–81
Isard, Walter, 31n, 47n, 53n
Israel: and nuclear desalting, 339–60

Jacob, Philip E., 406n, 408n
Jacobson, Max, 279n
Jägerskiöld, Stig, 296n, 298n
James, Robert Rhodes, 286n
Janis, Irving L., 44n
Janowitz, Morris, 39n, 42n
Jansson, Jan-Magnus, 311n
Japanese foreign students, 90–92
Jervis, Robert, 19–20, 273n, 279n, 286n, 447–48
Johnson, Donald McI., 307
Johnson, Harry G., 411n, 413n, 426n
Johnson, Lyndon B.: and desalting project in Israel, 340
Johnson, Malcolm M., 327n
Joll, James, 290n
Jones, Stephen B., 405n

Kaiser Engineers, 340–43, 353–57
Kalnins, Bruno, 131n
Kaplan, Abraham, 6n, 8–9, 282n
Kaplan, Morton A., 41n
Kastari, Paavo, 300n, 311n, 314n
Katz, Elihu, 44n, 253n, 269n
Kautsky, John H., 110n
Kelley, E. Ann, 167n
Kelly, Rita M., 29, 81n, 448
Kelman, Herbert C., 18n, 29n, 30, 39n, 41n, 44n, 169n, 193n, 254n, 260n, 275n, 448
Kelson, Robert N., 311n
Kenen, Peter B., 426n
Kennedy, Malcolm D., 129n
Kenya: border dispute with Ethiopia and Somalia, 168–70, 172–204
Kersell, John E., 311n
Key, V. O., Jr., 232n, 235, 252, 254n
Khrushchev: purge of and American public opinion, 247
Kim, C. I., 112n
Kim, T'ae-gil, 110
Kindleberger, Charles P., 413n, 417n, 418n, 421n
Kindre, Thomas A., 327n

King, Anthony, 307n
King, Henry H., 75n
Klapper, Joseph T., 44n, 330n
Klensin, John C., 46n
Klineberg, Otto, 77n
Klingberg, Frank L., 235n
Klingman, David, 167n
Knight, Robert P., 325n
Knorr, Klaus, 274n
Koenig, Donald, 256n
Kogan, Nathan, 274n
Komsomol schools in USSR, 131–32
Korean foreign students, 29, 86–87, 97–119
Korean War: and American public opinion, 239, 240, 242, 247, 250, 278
Korman, John G., 368n
Kornfelder, Joseph Zack, 125n
Koszul, Julien-Pierre, 418n
Kramer, John Francis, 46n
Krause, Lawrence B., 410n
Kris, Ernst, 37n
Krivitsky, Walter G., 134
Kuhn, Thomas S., 287, 289–90, 291n

Labor migration, 412, 415–16
LaCombe, Don, 391n, 395n
Lacouture, Jean, 129n, 219n
Laffal, Julius, 99n
Lagerstrom, Richard P., 53n
Lagos, Gustavo, 389n
Lambert, Richard D., 75n
Lane, Robert E., 234n
Lang, Gladys Engel, 45n
Lang, Kurt, 45n
Language and values, 5
Lanyi, Anthony, 22, 422n, 424n, 443n, 445n, 448
Laqueur, Walter, 123n, 128n
Lasky, Victor, 141n
Lasswell, Harold D., v, x, 4, 6n, 8–9, 11, 32n, 34n, 35n, 37n, 38n, 39n, 43n, 93n, 258n, 295
Latin American economic integration, 387–404
Lazarsfeld, Paul F., 42n, 43n, 44n
League of German Officers, 135–36
Leezenbaum, Ralph, 322n
Leites, Nathan, 38n, 39n, 43n
Leonhard, Wolfgang, 130n

Lerner, Daniel, 35n, 38n, 43n, 258n, 288n
Levinson, Daniel J., 35n
Lewin, Kurt, 44n
Liepelt, Klaus, 77n
Lindberg, Leon M., 388n
Lindzey, Gardner, 35n
Lippitt, Ronald, 75n, 84n
Lippmann, Walter, 37n, 252; on Indochina, 211, 219
Long, S. Stephen, 232n, 233n, 234n
Lowenthal, Leo, 43n
Lowi, Theodore J., 281n
Lumumba University (Moscow), 139–40, 142, 143
Lysgaard, Sverre, 75n, 77n
Lysne, Dale, 99n

McCarry, Charles, 138n, 142
McClelland, Charles A., 57n
Maccoby, Eleanor E., 44n
Machlup, Fritz, 327n, 426n, 439
McKinnon, Ronald I., 445n
McKnight, Robert K., 75n
Maclean, Fitzroy, 135n
McNeil, Elton B., 259n
Macrae, Norman, 420n
Macridis, Roy C., 407n
Maddox, John, 344, 346n
Madge, Charles, 38n
Magariños, Gustavo, 390n
Majak, R. Roger, 18n
Maletzke, Gerhard, 66n
Management consultants: and international business interests, 334–36
March, James G., 228, 229n
Marketing research and international business interests, 330–34
Marris, Stephen N., 424n, 437n, 440, 441n, 442, 444
Marshall, Geoffrey, 300n, 314n
Mason, H. G. R., 302
Mason, Paul, 167n
Mass media research, 41–46
Mathiason, John R., 21, 26, 391n, 395n, 448
Mathiason, María Christina, 391n, 395n
Matthews, Donald, 230
Mattson, Melvin E., 341n
Mayo, Elton, 34n

Mead, George Herbert, 34n
Mead, Margaret, 35n
Meaning: systems for transferring, 57–61
Means, Ingunn N., 300n, 305n
Media technology: changes in, 41–46
Mediated stimulus-response paradigm, 46–48
Meier, Richard L., 54n
Merikoski, V., 312n
Merritt, Anna J., x, 24–25, 362n, 365n, 368n, 369n, 372n, 448–49
Merritt, Richard L., 29, 31n, 66n, 76n, 167n, 254, 255n, 272n, 362n, 365n, 368n, 369n, 372n, 407n, 422n, 446n, 449
Methvin, Eugene, 126n, 127n
Meyer, Frank S., 126
Meyer, Poul, 298n
Mickiewicz, Ellen, 29, 449
Middle East: nuclear desalting in, 24, 339–60
Migration: labor and economic boundaries, 412, 415–16
Mikesell, Raymond F., 389n, 390n
Miles, Caroline M., 420n
Miller, Kenneth E., 311n
Millikan, Max F., 114n
Milstein, Jeffrey, 53n
Mishler, Anita, 39n
Mitchell, John P., 387n
Mitchell, William Charles, 53n
Mitrany, David, 305
Models of communication, 18, 46–55
Modelski, George A., 137n
Modigliani, Andre, 256n, 270n
Mohraz, Jane E., 83n
Monetary union, 412, 414–15
Montgomery, John D., ix, 379n, 380n
Moody, Peter, 167n
Moon, Won T., 95n
Moore, Wilbert E., 114n
Morgello, Clem, 335n
Morgenthau plan for Germany, 362–64
Morris, Charles W., 4n, 34n
Morris, Richard T., 75n, 77n, 98n
Müller-Meiningen, Ernst, Jr., 368n
Muller, Harry, 329n
Multinational corporations, 318–38; and economic integration, 416–18

Mundell, Robert A., 410n, 411n, 445n
Muromcew, Cyril, 40n
Murphy, Walter F., 107n
Myers, Charles A., 88n
Myrdal, Gunnar, 410, 411n

Nagle, John D., 46n
National Committee "Free Germany," 135–36
N'Diaye, Jean-Pierre, 77n
Nebergall, Roger E., 284n
Neumann, Erich Peter, 383n
Newcomb, Theodore M., 18, 44n, 48–51, 393n
New York Times: coverage of Indochina conflict, 207–31
New Zealand: ombudsman in, 302–4, 308–9, 311–15
Ney, Edward N., 322
Nicolson, Harold, 36n
Niedergang, Marcel, 325n
Nielsen, Arthur C., 331
Nikolaevski, Boris I., 133n
Nimmo, Dan P., 225n
Noble, C. E., 100n
Noelle, Elisabeth, 383n
Nollau, Guenther, 122n, 125n, 128n
Norman, Robert Z., 60n
North, Robert C., 46, 128n, 129n, 258n
Norway: ombudsman in, 304–5, 309–16
Novogorodseva, K. T., 133n
Nowell, William O., 128n
Nuclear desalting: in Middle East, 24, 339–60
Nye, Joseph S., 409n

Occupation of Germany, 24–25, 361–83
O'Donnell, Hazel, 167n
Officer, L., 424n
O'Gara, James V., 321n
Ombudsman: international transfer of, 24, 295–317
OMGUS surveys in U.S.-occupied Germany, 361–83
Os, Audvar, 304n, 305, 312n
Osgood, Charles E., ix, 4n, 32n, 49n, 99n, 272n, 273, 275

Osgood, Cornelius, 111n
Osgood, Robert Endicott, 279–80

Pace, C. Robert, 69n
Paradigms: in international communication, 18, 46–55; and normal *vs.* revolutionary science, 287–91; of integration, 411–16
Parenti, Michael, 29n
Passin, Herbert, 75n
Patterson, Leonard, 126n, 127
Pearl Harbor: consistency of views and attack on, 285, 291
Pearson, Drew: on Indochina, 211, 219
Peaslee, Amos J., 312n
Pedersen, I. M., 302n, 311n
Peterson, Sophia, 19, 258n, 261n, 262n, 449
Pfeffer, K. H., 77n, 84n
Polanyi, Michael, 287n, 289n
Polaschek, R. J., 311n
Political communication, 10–11
Pool, Ithiel de Sola, x, 4, 7, 29n, 39n, 43n, 46n, 258
Possony, Stephen, 122n, 125
Power: as value, 9–12
Powles, Sir Guy, 308
Press: American and Indochina, 18–19, 207–31
Price, Derek J. de Solla, 84n, 90, 91n, 92
Prisoners of war: Soviet education of, 123, 133–36
Problem-solving workshops, 30, 168–204
Propaganda: rising interest in study of, 37–38
Pruitt, Dean G., 41n, 259–60
Psycho-logic, 272–73
Public opinion: and foreign affairs, 19, 232–51; and German denazification, 361–83; polls and international business interests, 330–34
Public relations: influence on international relations, 27, 326–30
Puchala, Donald J., 26n
Puttkamer, Jesco von, 136n
Pye, Lucian, 43n, 90, 416n

Quester, George H., 342n, 346n

Racial discrimination: and foreign students, 80; in Soviet Union, 138–39
Ramndal, Lars, 304n
Ransom, Harry Howe, 283n
Rapoport, Anatol, 31n, 54n
Rational consistency, 274–76
Rauch, Georg von, 134n
Raymond, Edward A., 23, 449
Reef, Arthur, 329n
Reston, James: comments on Indochina problem, 224, 230, 231
Richman, Alvin, 19, 236n, 239n, 257n, 449
Riegel, O. W., 83n, 96
Ritter, Gerhard, 290
Roberts, Jack O., 341n
Robertson, Terence, 285n
Robinson, James A., 17n, 18n, 232n
Robinson, John P., 232n, 234n
Robson, J. L., 302–3
Rogers, William C., 256n, 270
Rokkan, Stein, 76n
Rollins, Abbie A., 405n
Rollio, Howard R., 99n
Roper, Burns W., 332n
Rosen, Seymour M., 139n, 140n
Rosenau, James N., 18n, 252n, 253, 256n, 269n, 270, 433n
Rosenberg, Milton J., 252n, 253, 254n, 255n, 256n, 271n, 272n, 273n, 276n
Rosenberg, Morris, 42n
Ross, T. J., 329–30
Rowat, Donald C., 296n, 300n, 302n, 310n, 312n, 313n
Rudholm, Sten, 297n
Rummel, Rudolph J., 31n, 262–63
Russett, Bruce M., 93n, 167n, 259, 387n
Ruud, Arthur, 310n

Sadan, Ezra, 355n, 358n
San Francisco Chronicle: coverage of Indochina conflict, 207–31
Sapir, Edward, 5, 6, 7
Sarnoff, Robert, 337–38
Savage, I. Richard, 26n
Schade, Burkhard, 84n
Schaff, Philip H., Jr., 323
Schaffer, Robert H., 76n, 81n

Scheinman, Lawrence, 388n
Schelling, Thomas C., 40n, 442n
Scheurig, Bodo von, 135n
Schild, Erling O., 108
Schiller, Herbert I., 26n, 27, 337n, 449–50
Schmid, Carlo, 368n
Schmitt, Hans O., 21–22, 408n, 414n, 419n, 446n, 450n
Schmitter, Philippe C., 387n, 389, 390n, 392, 409n
Schmuck, Richard, 256n, 257n
Schneider, R. A., 346n
Schorske, Carl, 286n
Schramm, Wilbur, 42n, 229n
Scott, Franklin D., 75n, 84n
Scott, William A., 44n, 257n, 275
Seaborg, Glenn T. (chairman of AEC): and desalting project in Middle East, 345, 350, 351
Sears, David O., 234n, 283n
Selby, Henry A., 81n
Seligman, Edwin R., 5n
Selltiz, Claire, 75n, 76, 77n, 78, 79n, 81n, 82, 83n, 84n, 97, 98n, 117
Seong-hi, Yim, 112n
Seton-Watson, Hugh, 134n
Sewell, William H., 75n, 77n
Shannon, Claude E., 56n, 295n
Shaplen, Robert, 214n
Sheatsley, Paul B., 44n
Sheffield, F. D., 44n
Sherif, Carolyn W., 284n
Sherif, Muzafer, 284n
Shils, Edward, 110
Shizume, Eri Yagi, 90, 91n, 92
Sibley, John, 167n
Sicinski, Andrzej, 257n
Sigmund, Paul E., 114n
Sills, David L., 4n
Simon, Herbert, 227n, 228, 229n
Simon, Raymond, 330n
Simpson, Robert, 391n, 395n
Singer, J. David, 26n, 36n, 46n, 47n, 57n
Singer, Marshall R., 90n
Singh, Amar Kumar, 77n, 78n
Small, Melvin, 253n
Smith, Adam, 421n
Smith, Hedrick, 344n
Smith, M. Brewster, 44n

Smith, Paul A., 233n, 234n, 235n, 257n
Smithburg, Donald W., 228n
Smyth, H. D., 346–47
Snyder, Richard C., 17n, 41n
Somalia: border dispute with Ethiopia and Kenya, 168–70, 172–204
Spartacus revolt in Berlin, 134
Speier, Hans, 35n, 37n
Spiller, Robert E., 116
Spykman, Nicholas J., 405n
Stagner, Ross, 259n
Stalin: death of, and American public opinion, 247
Stanton, Frank, 42n, 43n
Star, Shirley A., 44n
Stasova, E. D., 133n
State, 409–10
Statistisches Bundesamt, 70n, 71n
Stein, Harold, 364n
Steinbruner, John, 277n
Stephens, William N., 232n, 233n, 234n
Stevens, John D., 325n
Stevens, Robert B., 172
Storer, Norman W., 290n
Storing, James A., 304n, 311n, 316n
Stouffer, Samuel A., 42n, 44n
Strauss, Lewis (chairman of AEC): and desalting project in Middle East, 341–42, 346, 353
Students, foreign. *See* Foreign students
Stuhler, Barbara, 256n
Suchman, E. A., 98n
Suci, George J., 4n
Suez Canal: consistency of views and British policy on, 284–85; crisis of 1956 and official American attitudes, 258–59
Sulzberger, C. L.: on Indochina, 226n
Sutton, Tom, 337
Swarner, Lawrence R., 341n
Sweden: ombudsman in, 295–317
Systems: for transferring meaning, 57–61; international relations and, 55–56; social, American and Korean attitudes toward, 101–7
Szalai, Alexander, 76n

Szalay, Lorand B., 29, 81n, 99n, 100n, 450

Tagiuri, Renato, 274n
Tajfel, Henri, 80n, 97n
Tannenbaum, Percy H., 4n
Tanter, Raymond, 262n
Taylor, Charles L., 167n
T-groups: conflict resolution, 170, 173–75, 184–85, 194n
Technology: changes in, and social science, 41–46; and foreign aid, 24, 339–60
Teune, Henry, 408n
Thomas, Carol, 167n
Thomas, Stewart, 167n
Thompson, Kenneth W., 95n, 97
Thompson, Victor A., 228n
Time-budget studies: foreign students, 76–77
Tjioe, Loan Eng, 77n
Toscano, James V., 406n, 408n
Toulmin, Stephen, 288n
Tower, Edward, 445n
Townsend, Edwin C., 260n
Trade transactions, 7–8
Trade-union schools in USSR, 132–33
Transactions: secondary effects of, 5–6; trade, 7–8
Triandis, Harry C., 276n
Triffin, Robert, 414n
Trowbridge, Alexander, 319n
Trushchenko, N. V., 131
Tsou, Tang, 277n, 278n, 284n, 291
Tuchman, Barbara, 26
Tuomimen, Arvo, 124n, 125n, 128n

U-curve of adjustment to foreign culture, 77–79
Uhlig, Barney, 270
UNESCO, 88n, 137n, 141n, 142n, 318n
UNITAR: conference on conflict resolution, 173, 182n; role in Fermeda Workshop, 176
United Nations Economic Commission for Latin America (ECLA), 21, 387–404
United Nations Statistical Office, 88n

United States: American and Korean attitudes toward, 115–17; conflict behavior with USSR, 257–71; measure of conflict events with USSR, 261–69; and international corporations, 319–38

Union of Soviet Socialist Republics: educational exchange in, 23, 120–45; American views of exchange program, 29–30, 146–67; opinions of American visitors to, 146–67; American public opinion and, 235–51, 255, 257, 259–61, 265–71; American elite opinion on, 255, 257–59, 265–71; conflict behavior with United States, 261–69

Urquidi, Victor L., 390n

Useem, John, 75n, 84, 86

Useem, Ruth Hill, 75n, 84, 86

Utley, Thomas E., 307n

Value configurative approach, 5–6, 8–10

Values: Lasswellian, 8–10; power as, 9–12

Van de Velde, Robert W., 37n

Verba, Sidney, 274n, 372n

Vernon, Raymond, 416n, 417n

Veroff, Joseph, 97n

Vietnam: American press views of, 207–31; U.S. policy and American public opinion, 247; and consistency of attitudes, 278

Vinde, Pierre, 298n

Voevodsky, John, 52n, 53n

Wade, H. W. R., 306

Walton, Richard E., 169n, 172n, 173, 196–97

Waples, Douglas, 42n

Washington Post: coverage of Indochina conflict, 207–31

"Water for Peace" program in Middle East, 340

Watson, Jeanne, 75n, 84n

Weaver, Warren, 56n, 295n

Wedge, Bryant, ix, 40n, 96n, 101

Weisband, Edward, 273n

Welch, Susan, 18, 209n, 227n, 450

Westin, Alan F., 96

Whaley, Barton, 38n, 40n

Wheeler, W. Reginald, 75n

Wheeler-Bennett, John W., 133

White, Ralph K., 49n, 101

Whorf, Benjamin L., 34n

Whyatt, Sir John, 306–8

Wickes, Thomas E., 184n

Wiener, Norbert, 18, 52n

Willer, David, 54n

Willett, Thomas D., 424n, 445n

Williams, Frederick W., 367, 380

Williams, R. M., 98n

Willis, F. Roy, 365n

Willrich, Mason, 345n

Wilson, James A., 85

Windle, Charles, 99n

Wionczek, Miguel S., 390n

Wirth, Louis, 43n

Withey, Stephen B., 44n, 257n

Wohlstetter, Albert, 360n

Wohlstetter, Roberta, 40n, 285, 291

Wolfenstein, Martha, 43n

Wolfowitz, Paul D., 24, 353n, 360n, 450

Wolpert, Julian, 47n, 53n

Won, George Y. M., 98n

Woodruff, Asahel D., 276n

Woods, Clyde M., 81n

Woolf, Harry, 291n

Worcester, Robert C., 328n

Wrigley, Charles F., 167n

Yhdistys, Kansantaloudellinen, 311n

Yolen, Will H., 327n

Yondorf, Walter, 388n

Ypsilon, 135n

Yu, Frederick T. C., 37n

Zaninovich, M. George, 258n

Zink, Harold, 363n, 364n, 365n, 378n

Zinnes, Dina A., 47n, 258n, 284n

Zipf, George Kingsley, 31

BETHANY
COLLEGE
LIBRARY

DISCARD